Spaghetti Westerns—
the Good, the Bad and the Violent

Spaghetti Westerns—
the Good, the Bad
and the Violent

A Comprehensive, Illustrated
Filmography of 558 Eurowesterns
and Their Personnel, 1961–1977

by

Thomas Weisser

Foreword by CRAIG LEDBETTER
Foreword by TOM BETTS
Comments by WILLIAM CONNOLLY

McFarland & Company, Inc., Publishers
Jefferson, North Carolina, and London

The present work is a reprint of the library bound edition of Spaghetti Westerns—the Good, the Bad and the Violent: A Comprehensive, Illustrated Filmography of 558 Eurowesterns and Their Personnel, 1961–1977, *first published in 1992 by McFarland.*

LIBRARY OF CONGRESS CATALOGUING-IN-PUBLICATION DATA

Weisser, Thomas, 1947–
  Spaghetti westerns—the good, the bad and the violent : a comprehensive, illustrated filmography of 558 Eurowesterns and their personnel, 1961–1977 / by Thomas Weisser.
    p.   cm.
  Includes bibliographical references and index.

  ISBN 0-7864-2442-7 (softcover : 50# alkaline paper)

  1. Western films—Europe—Catalogs. I. Title.
PN1995.9.W4W32   2005
016.79143'6278—dc20   92-50002

British Library cataloguing data are available

On the cover: *The Good, the Bad and the Ugly,* 1966 (Photofest)

Manufactured in the United States of America

McFarland & Company, Inc., Publishers
  Box 611, Jefferson, North Carolina 28640
  www.mcfarlandpub.com

This book is dedicated to my children,
Jeff and Jessica

*   *   *

I wish to thank
Craig Ledbetter and Tom Betts
for their help, without which
this book could not have been written.

*   *   *

I also wish to thank the following people
for their help and contribution to the cause:
Bill Connolly, Dave Todarello, Tim Paxton, Bill George,
Louis Paul, Eric Hoffman, Alain Petit, Ally Lammaj,
Jorge Patiño and Rick Martinez.

Contents

Foreword
(Craig Ledbetter)

The term «Spaghetti Western» brings an instant sneer to any "serious" critic. In the United States, except for a few token acknowledgments to the films of Sergio Leone, no one has written an overview of this most curious film phenomenon. Over 600 European Westerns were made from the early 1960s to the late 1970s, yet very few pages of text have explored the plots of these films or detailed the contributions made by the many excellent professionals in front of and behind the cameras. Now, thanks to exhaustive research and hours of viewing by Thomas Weisser, you're holding just such a book at last.

As early as 1961, the Italians were producing imitations of standard U.S.-styled Westerns. These films featured such stars as Richard Basehart, Rod Cameron, Gordon Scott, and Edmund Purdom, among others, and until 1964 these movies were basically "B" Westerns filmed on foreign soil.

Then in mid-decade, Sergio Leone (along with star Clint Eastwood, composer Ennio Morricone, and cinematographer Massimo Dallamano) created what quickly became known as the «Spaghetti Western.» With three films, A Fistful of Dollars, For a Few Dollars More, and The Good, the Bad, and the Ugly, the staples of this genre were created and put into motion, including: the no-name bounty hunter who cared for nothing except money, the search for a fortune in gold, and the settling of accounts for a betrayal in attaining said fortune. All of these soon-to-become clichés had their origins in the Leone trilogy. There were a group of directors who took Leone's work and expanded it into many other areas. The other Sergios, Corbucci and Sollima, used the Spaghetti Western to address political concerns often found in the many Third World countries that, ironically, formed the traditional audience for these films.

As you read this volume, you will also discover that certain Spaghetti Western characters were so popular that an entire series of films based on their exploits was produced. Django, Sartana, Ringo, and Sabata are just a few of the more prolific ones. The "Django" series is a perfect example of how fractured and perverse the Spaghetti Western universe could become. Sergio Corbucci's Django featured Franco Nero as the laconic, grizzled, world-weary gunfighter whose main motivation was revenge. Alberto De Martino's *Django Shoots First* would feature Glenn Saxon as a more traditional Western hero tracking down his father's killer. True perversity reigns in Giulio Questi's *Django Kill*, a hallucinogenic gorefest starring Tomás Milian. Here, Django is a wronged Mexican peon who must fend for himself against homosexual cowboys, talking parrots and an entire town of greed-infected citizens.

The American actors who headed overseas to become Euro-sensations include a list of has-beens and never-weres. After you see them in several Spaghetti Westerns, however, you realize that actors like Craig Hill, Brad Harris, and Robert Woods deserve their place in the spotlight as much as their better known counterparts like Stewart Granger, Charles Bronson, and Jack Palance who, no doubt, felt as though they were slumming, at best.

After several years of successfully ripping off all the characteristics of the Leone universe, the Spaghetti Western began to look for other modes of expression. The comedic Trinity series (featuring Terence Hill and Bud Spencer) became so popular that this slapstick parody of Spaghetti Western conventions became a genre unto itself. Providence, Carambola, and Invincible were just some of the characters used to ape the more well-known Trinity boys. By this time in the seventies, final nails were being hammered into the coffin of the Spaghetti Western. The emerging Kung Fu genre was even stirred into the pot (without a doubt, one of the more bizarre cross-fertilizations of genres ever) if for no other reason than to try and lengthen the Spaghetti's already exhausted stay. Then, when Sartana and Django or Sabata and Halleluja began teaming together (much like in the forties when Universal Studios teamed up Frankenstein, the Wolfman, and Dracula near the end of their run) you knew it was only a matter of time before it all collapsed.

Before the end came, however, such jewels as Lucio Fulci's *Four Gunmen of the Apocalypse* and Enzo G. Castellari's hauntingly poetic *Keoma* managed to appear. By the early eighties, the Spaghetti Western had disappeared. Now, some ten years later, Thomas Weisser has performed a marvelous service for a heretofore little appreciated period of filmmaking that featured a depth and imagination every bit as important and interesting as its U.S. counterpart. As videotape exposes more people to the wonder and intensity of these films, their appreciation for this project can only grow.

June 17, 1991
Mr. Ledbetter is editor of E.T.C. Magazine

Foreword
(Tom Betts)

Spaghetti Westerns are remarkable. Watching them, the viewer is immediately captured by the sharp contrast between a European-made Western and an American-made Western.

For starters, Spaghetti Westerns deal primarily with the Mexican border region of the American Southwest. A viewer hears the wind blowing across the hot desert sands. He can feel the heat rising from these same sands, and he is captured by the barren landscape sprawling before him.

The Europeans focused on this part of the American West mostly because of convenience. Usually, the plains of Spain were used for the exterior photography, and this region closely resembles the border area of the United States. Furthermore, the towns are never neatly-erected buildings with fresh coats of paint. Instead, they are crudely constructed, developed from whatever materials could be found close by; or they are "Mexican" adobe and stucco villages.

The Spaghetti directors then created the characters to match this rugged landscape. These are rough men; men who, like the landscape, didn't give an inch. Only the fittest survived in this hell. You can see it in the faces of the Spanish extras, hired to play villagers or bandidos. Their faces are weathered, dried from the sun, often missing teeth or an eye. These are faces that have withstood the test of the land and have survived. It's obvious that these people could only be controlled by raw, brutal strength. And each could be defeated only by a man who was equally strong, but who used his brains to tip the scales in his favor.

This is not a world of black and white. This is a world of black and gray. No more would we see the evil villain destroy an innocent rancher and his family, or control an entire town under his tyrannical rule, only to be beaten in a fistfight. Or receive a flesh wound and be sent to trial for his deeds. The villain in a Spaghetti Western is made to suffer the same type of penalty that he inflicted upon others, but from an avenging angel who could be just as evil.

This angel usually had a meaningless name (Sabata, Sartana, Ringo,

Holy Ghost, Django) or no name at all. The avenging angel wasn't trying to right the villain's wrongs, or save the townspeople, or even rescue the heroine. He was out to make a profit for himself; therefore, he received his reward, not with a kiss or a handshake, but usually with a saddlebag full of dollars or a strongbox brimming with treasure. The Spaghetti Western is the epitome of the ME generation watching a ME hero.

The Spaghetti hero also had the best wardrobe in all of filmdom. He was usually dressed in style, wearing anything from cavalry outfits, frock coats, dusters, and ponchos to gambling outfits and flat-brimmed hats. Weapons were also his specialty. He used sawed-off shotguns, Buntline Specials, four-barreled guns, shooting banjos (and other converted musical instruments), plus the run of the mill Colt .45's and Winchester rifles. A weapon in his hand made him almost invincible. Even if he were captured, you knew he would somehow escape and turn the tables on his enemy. James Bond in the Wild West.

I've purposely saved the best ingredient for last: the music. When you ask fans of the genre what initially caught their attention, the majority will say the "musical score." I think too much has been made of the fact that "use of sounds" sets Ennio Morricone and the other Italian composers apart from their American contemporaries. Yes, they did use bells, whips, spurs, etc., but these were not predominant, only background props used as percussion instruments to help set a mood. Even without these props the Italian composers are heads above American composers. For instance, let someone who has never seen a Spaghetti Western hear the soundtrack to *Once Upon a Time in the West* or *The Great Silence* or *Seven Dollars on the Red*, then ask for an opinion. Almost inevitably, the response will be "beautiful!" If you tell the novice listener that this is music from a Western, he won't believe you. Tell him that the music is from a Spaghetti Western and he'll stare at you in disbelief.

Many times, I've watched poor Spaghetti Westerns just to hear the soundtrack. It is the most captivating music ever written for film. Today, the film world recognizes Ennio Morricone as "the Maestro," a title he truly deserves. I am proud to say his career began in the world of the Spaghettis.

I've mentioned the main ingredients of these films: the landscape, the supporting players, the main characters, the wardrobe and weapons, the music. But what does Hollywood owe the Spaghetti Western? It owes a debt for creating new actors such as Clint Eastwood, Franco Nero, Terence Hill, Bud Spencer, William Berger, Gianni Garko, Giuliano Gemma, Anthony Steffen, George Hilton, Klaus Kinski, Peter Lee Lawrence, George Martin, Tomás Milian, Fernando Sancho, Frank Wolff, Robert Woods, Pierre Brice, Horst Frank, and Gian Maria Volonte. Perhaps some of these names are not familiar to you, others are household celebrities, but all owe their popularity to the Spaghetti Western.

Other actors such as Lee Van Cleef, Guy Madison, Woody Strode, Lex Barker, Mark Damon, Richard Harrison, Brad Harris, Mickey Hargitay, Dan Vadis, John Ireland, Gordon Mitchell, Jack Palance, Wayde Preston, and Eli Wallach used the Spaghetti Western to keep their careers alive after their popularity faltered in America. Or they used it as a springboard to launch a successful comeback. Most of these actors continued their careers after the Spaghetti Western craze died in the late 1970s. Hollywood also owes a debt of gratitude to the directors of the Spaghetti Westerns. They showed the industry how to get the most from the actors, recognizing their worth and value to the overall productions.

I want to thank Thomas Weisser for letting me help with this project. It's not very often one gets to work on a dream project, but this was one of those moments. This book is an outstanding contribution to a genre long ignored by the American film market. Long live the Spaghetti Western!

July 3, 1991
Mr. Betts is editor of Westerns All-Italiana

I. The Films

Introduction

All entries in the Film portion of the book are listed in alphabetical order according to the "most popular" English language title. They are cross-referenced from lesser known retitlings, video titles, and various other alternate titles including foreign language titles. For reference purposes, the original production title is also included, and further identified with an abbreviation (Ital — Italian; Fr — French, Sp — Spanish, Ger — West German; Brit — British; Czech — Czechoslovakia; Rus — Russia).

Immediately following the main title (and date) are the alternate titles.

All production crew information (particularly the directorial reference) is based on the "official credit listing" as highlighted in the opening sequence of the motion picture. Pseudonyms, commonplace in these Euro productions, are identified in the text. Initially, Anglicized names were used by performers and directors to avoid the stigma of a "Western" filmed on foreign soil. These names were used to disguise European productions in an attempt to gain wider distribution and, ultimately, greater acceptance in the international marketplace. Because of this widespread use of pseudonyms, there are still some true identities this author has been unable to uncover.

Producer credits for many films tend to be politically nationalized and, as such, are not very reliable, especially when culled from English language prints.

The "releasing" dates are generally taken from the year of production, rather than the film's release, except in some circumstances as explained by the corresponding text.

3

The Films, A–Z
(with cross-references)

Abre Tu Fosa, Amigo ... Llega Sabata see **Dig Your Grave, Friend ... Sabata's Coming**

Account Rendered see **Big Gundown**

Ace High (1967)

Revenge at El Paso; Four Gunmen of Ave Maria; I Quattro dell'Ave Maria Ital. *Director:* Giuseppe Colizzi; *Script:* Giuseppe Colizzi/Bino Cicogna; *Camera:* Marcello Masciocchi; *Music:* Carlo Rustichelli; *Producer:* Bino Cicogna, Crono/Finanzia San Marco (Italy/Spain). *Cast:* Eli Wallach, Terence Hill, Bud Spencer, Brock Peters, Kevin McCarthy, Tiffany Hoyueld, Rick Boyd, Livio Lorenzon.

Fundamentally, Eli Wallach replays the same character he popularized in Sergio Leone's *The Good, the Bad, and the Ugly*, with a different name. And ancestry. Rather than being a Mexican named Tuco, he's Cacopulos from Greece.

As this film opens, Cacopulos is in jail (about to be executed) when a banker buys his freedom and then hires him to find two con-men, Cat Stevens (Terence Hill) and Hutch (Bud Spencer). These bandits had swindled him out of a large amount of money and the banker wants it back. But, instead Cacopulos kills him and rides off to find Cat and Hutch on his own. And he does. After stealing their money, Cacopulos flees to Fair City where he loses the loot in a crooked gambling hall, run by a man named Drake (Kevin Mc-Carthy). About that time, Cat and Hutch finally catch up with Cacopulos, and the three of them, along with a former-slave-turned-professional-acrobat (Brock Peters), plot to rob Drake's swindling casino.

The story is an uneven, rambling "heist" tale that oddly loses momentum during the climactic gambling house sting. Too much emphasis on circus-style acrobatics (a motif director Colizzi incorporates again in *Boot Hill*) makes the proceedings unnecessarily campy. The film is an obvious attempt to capitalize on the notoriety of Wallach's "the Ugly" role from Leone's film, but instead it's Terence Hill (doing his best Clint Eastwood imitation) who steals the show. The music is provided by Carlo Rustichelli (alias Carl Rustic), best known for his striking score to Mario Bava's *Blood and Black Lace*; Marcello Masiocchi handles the camera work in gritty brown and green hues.

ELI WALLACH
S 4 DE L'AVE MARIA
HILL · BROCK PETERS · KEVIN McCARTHY · BUD SPENCER
Realiza por GIUSEPPE COLIZZI

From left: Terence Hill, Eli Wallach and Brock Peters in *Ace High* (1967).

Acquasanta Joe see *Holy Water Joe*

Ad Uno ad Uno Spietatamente see *One Against One . . . No Mercy*

Adios Cjamango (1969)

Twenty Thousand Dollars for Every Corpse; 20.000 Dolares por un Cadaver Sp. *Director:* Harry Freeman; *Script:* J. M. Zabalza; *Camera:* Leopoldo Villaseñor; *Music:* Gianni Marchetti/Ana Satrova; *Producer:* Procensa Film (Italy/Spain). *Cast:* Mike Rivers, Dianik Zurakowska, José Truchado, Luis Induñi, Franco Fantasia, Miguel de la Riva.

An obscure, virtually unknown, loosely related sequel to Edward Muller's *Cjamango* (1967), this time with Mike Rivers in the title role, originally played by Sean Todd (aka Ivan Rassimov). He's a bounty hunter who decides to assist a young widow (Dianik Zurakowska) in her range war with a rich land baron, an evil tyrant (José Truchado) secretly assembling an underground army of outlaws and banditos. The director hiding behind the Anglo pseudonym is José Maria Zabalza.

A poster for *Adios Gringo* (1965).

Adios Gringo (1965)

Adios Gringo Ital. *Director:* George Finley; *Script:* Giorgio Stegani/José Jerez/ Michele Villerot; *Camera:* Francisco Sempere; *Music:* Benedetto Ghiglia; *Producer:* Bruno Turchetto, Dorica/Trebol/Corona (Italy/Spain/France). *Cast:* Giuliano Gemma, Evelyn Stewart, Ted Carter, Peter Cross, Max Dean, Roberto Camardiel, Frank Braña, Jesus Puente, Jean Martin.

Brent Landers (Giuliano Gemma) is tricked into buying stolen cattle. When the rightful owner confronts him, gunplay is unavoidable. Now with a murder rap on his head, he goes on the lam to find the real cattle-thieving culprit. Soon Brent meets, and becomes involved with, Lucy (Evelyn Stewart), a girl recently raped by three men, one of whom is the sought after double-crossing rustler, Tex Slaughter (Jesus Puente). Another of the rapists is the son of a rich land baron named Ranchester (Peter Cross). The story then "switches gears" as the wealthy Ranchester tries to silence Brent and Lucy to keep his son (Max Dean) from being implicated in the rape.

There's a lot of action in this Continental coproduction, stylishly directed and cowritten by Giorgio Stegani (using the pseudonym George Finley). The film was a huge success in Italy, rated the fourth biggest grossing motion picture of 1965 (Sergio Leone's *For a Few Dollars More* was number one). Although she made many Westerns (see Performers filmography), Evelyn Stewart (alias for Ida Galli) is best known for her roles in Italian thrillers, especially Sergio Martino's *Tail of the Scorpion* and Umberto Lenzi's *Il Coltello di Ghiaccio*.

Adios Hombre (1966)

Seven Pistols for a Massacre; Adios Hombre Ital. *Director:* Mario Caiano; *Script:* Eduardo M. Brochero/Mario Caiano; *Camera:* Julio Ortas/Sergio Martino; *Music:* Francesco de Masi; *Producer:* United Pictures/Copercines (Italy/Spain). *Cast:* Craig Hill, Eduardo Fajardo, Piero Lulli, Giulia Rubini, Nello Pazzafini, Eleanora Vargas, Spartaco Conversi, Roberto Camardiel, Jacques Herlin.

Another sleazy (but wonderfully) psychotic performance from master villain Eduardo (*Django*) Fajardo (see Performers filmography for a complete listing of his 25+ Westerns) in this story about a gang of outlaws who forcibly take over a bordertown saloon, using it as a hideout while they wait for a bank's gold shipment to arrive. They kill the sheriff and many other innocent citizens, generally tormenting and brutalizing everyone until finally a falsely accused escaped convict, Will Flarity (Craig Hill), gets angry and thwarts their plans. The story may sound familiar. A slight variation was used two years later by R. W. Creese for his American-made exploitation Western, *The Scavengers*.

Like Clint Eastwood, Ty Hardin, and Edd Byrnes, genre actor Craig Hill began his career in a long-running U.S. television series, *Whirly Birds* (1954–57), featured in over 110 episodes as helicopter adventurer P. T. Moore. He migrated to Europe in the mid–60s. His first Spaghetti Western was called *Hands of a Gunman* (1965) directed by prolific Rafael Romero Marchent. Besides making 15 Westerns, Craig Hill went on to star in many European productions, including Antonio Bido's excellent thriller, *Solamente Nero (Only Black)* (1980), José Luis Merino's espionage war picture *When Heroes Die* (1978), and *Esmeralda Bay* (1987), a sexy adventure story from legendary filmmaker Jess Franco.

Yul Brynner in his only Spaghetti Western—*Adios Sabata* (1970).

Adios, Sabata (1970)

Indio Black; Sabata 2; Bounty Hunters; Indio Black, Sai Che Ti Dico... Sei un Gran Figlio di... Ital. *Director:* Frank Kramer; *Script:* Renato Izzo/Gianfranco Parolini; *Camera:* Sandro Mancori; *Music:* Bruno Nicolai; *Producer:* Alberto Grimaldi, P.E.A. Cine (Italy). *Cast:* Yul Brynner, Dean Reed, Pedro Sanchez, Susan Scott, Franco Fantasia, Joseph Persuad, Andea Scotti, Sal Borgese, Gerard Herter, Rick Boyd.

　　　　Initially, he was "Indio Black." But after the international success of

Sabata, director Frank Kramer (Gianfranco Parolini) authorized Indio's name be changed, in the dubbing, to Sabata. Thus, a sequel was born.

Yul Brynner, in his only Spaghetti Western (dressed in all black, including an embarrassing pair of bell-bottom pants with fringe), leads an expedition to steal the gold reserve from sadistic Austrian commandant Skimmel (Gerard Herter) working for Emperor (called General in the movie) Maximillian in Mexico. Sabata's sidekick, petty thief Ballantine, is played by Dean Reed, the early 60s U.S. pop singer who (in protest of the Vietnam War) defected to Russia in 1969. He continued a European acting career in other Westerns, *Twenty Paces to Death* and *The Winchester Does Not Forgive,* plus "giallo" (the Italian term for "thrillers") exploitation films like Harald Phillipp's *Death Knocks Twice* with Fabio Testi and Anita Ekberg. In a 1985 *Entertainment Tonight* Interview, he boasted of "acting in 18 movies and making 13 record albums for the Communist Bloc Nations," but expressed a desire to return to the United States, saying "I fear of growing old in a country that's not mine." Six months later, Dean Reed was found dead "under mysterious circumstances" in a lake on his East German estate.

Actress Susan Scott's real name is Nieves Navarro, and that's how she is credited in *A Pistol for Ringo.* She went on to appear in a couple of Joe D'Amato (aká Aristide Massaccesi) sex-'n'-horror films, *Voodoo Baby* and *Trap Them and Kill Them* (alternate title: *Emanuelle & the Last Cannibals [Emanuelle e gli Ultimi Cannibali]).* Sal Borgese, a widely used character actor, is best known for his starring role in the Italian-made comedy/adventure *Three Supermen* films (see *Three Supermen of the West*). He also shared top billing with Peter Martell in the slapstick Western *Patience Has a Limit, We Don't.* The director of photography is Sandro Mancori, initially from the Sergio Garrone stable; Bruno Nicolai aptly handles the musical score. Also see *Sartana,* generally considered director Frank Kramer's most accomplished Western.

Adios, Texas see *Texas, Adios*

Adventures in the West see *Seven Hours of Gunfire*

Agguato sul Grande Fiume see *Pirates of the Mississippi*

Ah Si? E Io lo Dico a Zzzzorro! see *Who's Afraid of Zorro*

Al di là della Legge see *Beyond the Law*

Alive or Preferably Dead (1969)

Sundance and the Kid; Vivi... o Preferibilmente Morti Ital. *Director:* Duccio Tessari; *Script:* Duccio Tessari/Giorgio Salvioni; *Camera:* Manuel Rojas; *Music:* Gianni Ferrio; *Producer:* Hesperia/Ultra Film (Spain/Italy). *Cast:* Giuliano Gemma, Nino Benvenuti, Sydne Rome, Julio Peña, Antonio Casas, Cris Huerta, Georges Rigaud.

This film is, perhaps, the best of director Duccio Tessari's Western com-

GIULIANO GEMMA ··· NINO BENVENUTI

MORT OU VIF...

... de préférence mort

EASTMANCOLOR   REGIE DE DUCCIO TESSARI

DOOD OF LEVEND... *liefst dood*

This page and next: movie posters for *Alive or Preferably Dead* (1969) and *All Out* (1968).

edies, but not as impressive as his serious films (*Pistol for Ringo, Return of Ringo*, nor even *Zorro*). It's a fluffy cotton-candy story about two estranged brothers, city slicker Monty (Giuliano Gemma) and country bumpkin Ted (former professional boxer from the 60s, Nino Benvenuti) who will inherit their dead uncle's fortune if they can live together for six months. Of course the

whole thing gets very complicated when they both fall for the same girl (played by Sandusky, Ohio's, Sydne Rome, star of Roman Polanski's *What*). The believable camaraderie between Gemma and Benvenuti helps make it all work. Plus, there's an enjoyable score from ex–medical student Gianni Ferrio, who quit his schooling to become a musical composer.

In the United States, a West Coast–based company (Monteray) released the home video of this film under the title *Sundance and the Kid,* inexplicably cutting 25 minutes and changing all the credits to bogus Anglo pseudonyms.

All'Ombra di una Colt see *In a Colt's Shadow*

All Out (1968)

Go for Broke; Tutto per Tutto Ital; *One for All* Brit. *Director:* Umberto Lenzi; *Script:* Nino Stresa/Eduardo Brochero; *Camera:* Alejandro Ulloa; *Music:* Marcello Giombini; *Producer:* P.E.A./Estella (Italy/Spain). *Cast:* John Ireland, Mark Damon, Raf Baldassarre, Fernando Sancho, Monica Randall, Spartaco Conversi, Armando Calvo, Eduardo Fajardo, Miguel del Castillo, José Torres, Tito Garcia, Joaquin Parra.

John Ireland is the bounty hunter and Mark Damon (the star of Roger Corman's *Fall of the House of Usher*) is the misunderstood outlaw with a price on his head. There are other strange characters with names like the Owl and Copper Face. Everybody is looking for a hidden treasure of gold ingots. So, what else is new? A considerably less than impressive musical score from Marcello Giombini (*Garringo, Sabata, For a Few Dollars Less,* etc.) doesn't help the already tedious story.

Director Umberto Lenzi has done virtually every type of film from comedy *(Cicciambomba)* to horror *(City of the Walking Dead),* from action *(Free Hand for a Tough Cop)* to sleaze *(Dirty Pictures),* but he is best remembered by the cultists for the first Italian cannibal movie, *Man from Deep River,* and the highly controversial "sequels" *Make Them Die Slowly* (alternate title: *Cannibal Ferrox*) and *Eaten Alive by Cannibals* (alternate title: *Doomed to Die*). He made one other Western, *Pistol for a Hundred Coffins* (also in 1968), before abandoning the genre.

In the late 1970s, Mark Damon moved from acting (see Performers filmography) to production when he became the head of PSO Films.

All'Ovest di Sacramento see *Judge Roy Bean*

All the Brothers of the West Support Their Father see *Miss Dynamite*

All'Ultimo Sangue see *Bury Them Deep*

Alla Conquista dell'Arkansas see *Massacre at Marble City*

Alla Larga Amigos . . . Oggi Ho il Grilletto Facile see *With Friends, Nothing Is Easy*

Allegri Becchini Arriva Trinità see *They Called Him Trinity*

Alleluja e Sartana Figli di . . . Figli di Dio see *Halleluja and Sartana Strike Again*

Alleluja & Sartana Are Sons . . . Sons of God see *Halleluja & Sartana Strike Again*

Amico Mio, Frega Tu . . . Che Frego Io! see *Anything for a Friend*

Amico, Stammi Lontano Alemno un Palmo see *Ben and Charlie*

Amigo, Stay Away see *Ben and Charlie*

Los Amigos see *Deaf Smith and Johnny Ears*

Ammazzali Tutti e Torna Solo see *Kill Them All and Come Back Alone*

Among Vultures (1964)

Frontier Hellcat; Là Dove Scende il Sole Ital; *Unter Geiern* Ger. *Director:* Alfred Vohrer; *Script:* Eberhard Keindorff/Johanna Sibelius; *Camera:* Karl Löb; *Music:* Martin Böttcher; *Producer:* Preden Philipson, Rialto/Atlantis Film (West Germany/Italy/France/Yugoslavia). *Cast:* Stewart Granger, Pierre Brice, Elke Sommer, Renato Baldini, Walter Barnes, Götz George, Mario Girotti, Sieghardt Rupp.

Here is the first of the Stewart Granger *Winnetou* films, a series that ran in tandem with the Lex Barker *Winnetou* films. An explanation for the uninitiated: Winnetou is a young Apache chief (always played by Pierre Brice, star of 1960's *Mill of the Stone Women*). His blood brother and his freedom-fighting partner is "Old Shatterhand" (when portrayed by Lex Barker), "Old Surehand" (when played by Stewart Granger), and to confuse things even more, "Old Firehand" (once, when Rod Cameron stepped in). All the movies are loosely based on the novels of European pulp writer, Karl May.

This particular German production has a "saga" quality about it, mostly concentrating on the plight of the settlers as they cross the Rockies, but specifically on that of Lisa (Elke Sommer) who is kidnapped by a bandit (Götz George) disguised as an Indian. Eventually everyone is helped by Winnetou and his Apache tribe.

For other Stewart Granger entries see *Rampage at Apache Wells* and *Flaming Frontier*. For Lex Barker "Winnetou" films see *Treasure of Silver Lake, Half-Breed, Apache's Last Battle, Winnetou the Warrior* (also *Apache Gold*), *Winnetou: Last of the Renegades, Winnetou and Shatterhand in Valley of Death, Winnetou: The Desperado Trail* and a non–Winnetou film (but with Pierre Brice), *Place Called Glory City*. The Rod Cameron effort is *Winnetou: Thunder at the Border*.

Incidentally, this is Terence Hill's first Eurowestern (listed as Mario Girotti, his real name). In 1970, when he found international success with the *Trinity* series, critics called him "an overnight sensation." In reality, his first role came 20 years earlier when he costarred in Dino Risi's 1951 crime movie, *Vacanze col Gangster (Gangster Vacation)*. After that, he was featured in numerous films (at least 18 and many students of the genre think much higher), working for a variety of directors including Mario Bava and Giorgio Simonelli, before making *Among Vultures*.

In addition to Winnetou films, the production company, Rialto Film, and director Alfred Vohrer (plus his cameraman and musical composer) also were extensively involved in many Edgar Wallace adaptations during the 60s and 70s. Vohrer is generally recognized as Germany's most innovative thriller director, and as such, he's treated to resolute admiration similar to the respect most American film buffs harbor for Alfred Hitchcock.

Amore, Piombo, e Furore see *China 9, Liberty 37*

Anche nel West, C'era una Volta Dio see *Between God, the Devil and a Winchester*

Anche per Django Hanno un Prezzo see *Even Django Has His Price*

Ancora Dollari per i MacGregor see *More Dollars for the MacGregors*

And God Said to Cain (1969)

E Dio Disse a Caino . . . Ital. *Director:* Anthony Dawson; *Script:* Antonio Margheriti/Giovanni Addessi; *Camera:* Luciano Trasatti/Riccardo Pallottini; *Music:* Carlo Savina; *Producer:* Giovanni Addessi, D.C. 7 (Italy). *Cast:* Klaus Kinski, Peter Carsten, Cella Michelangeli, Lee Burton, Antonio Cantafora, Giulaina Raffaelli, Alan Collins, Lucio De Santis.

A lesser Anthony Dawson (Antonio Margheriti) film. Especially irksome because the final 20 minutes look as though they were filmed at the bottom of a coal mine—on a moonless night. This is remarkably uncharacteristic of Margheriti's work. As a prolific horror/thriller director, he has effectively demonstrated (many times) his ability to shoot "highly visual" night scenes, an attribute which makes viewing this movie all the more frustrating. Director "Dawson" has made some good Spaghetti Westerns; this isn't one of them. Watch *Stranger and the Gunfighter* or *Vengeance* instead. Even Klaus Kinski (playing a welcome full-length role) can't save this film. The same story was better told in Tonino Cervi/Dario Argento's *Today It's Me . . . Tomorrow You.*

It's the implausible tale of Gary Hamilton (Kinski), imprisoned for a robbery and murder that he didn't commit. Somehow, because of a presidential pardon, he is freed. But freedom means only one thing: revenge. Specifically, revenge against the true perpetrator, a wealthy land baron named Acombar.

Actor Alan Collins (aka Luciano Pignozzi) is a familiar face in the films of "Anthony Dawson"; they have worked together at least 15 times since Margheriti's first motion picture, *Assignment Outer Space* (1960). And, Lee Burton, another recognizable Spaghetti Western "feature" player, is actually Guido Lollobrigida (the cousin of famous Italian actress, sexy Gina Lollobrigida).

. . . And His Name Was Holy Ghost see *He Was Called the Holy Ghost*

And the Crows Will Dig Your Grave (1971)

I Corvi Ti Scaveranno la Fossa Ital. *Director:* John Wood; *Script:* Juan Bosch/Roberto Gianviti; *Camera:* Giancarlo Ferrando; *Music:* Bruno Nicolai; *Producer:* P.E.A. Oliveira Films (Italy/Spain). *Cast:* Craig Hill, Fernando Sancho, Boschero, Dominique, Maria Pia Conte, Frank Braña, Indio Gonzales, Raf Baldassare, Ivano Staccioli, Angel Aranda.

One of the great Spaghetti Western titles, but it's only a so-so Italian-Spanish coproduction directed by Ignacio Iquino (using the pseudonym John

Wood) and cowritten by "Juan Bosch" (Iquino's Latino alias; "bosque" is Spanish for "wood").

The Wells Fargo Bank enlists the aid of notorious bounty hunters to put a stop to an outlaw gang (headed by Raf Baldassare) terrorizing their gold shipments. One of the deputized bounty killers, Jess Sullivan (Craig Hill), visits a rural prison where a former member of the gang, Don Parker (Angel Aranda) is incarcerated. Laredo buys Parker's freedom with hopes that he will lead him to the secret hideout. An episodic cat-and-mouse game ensues (very similar to the exploits in *The Big Gundown*) before the climactic battle.

This film features two of Spain's best known character actors, Fernando Sancho and Frank Braña (see Performers filmography). Heavy-set Sancho appeared in many kinds of movies (*Night of Hate, King of Kings, 55 Days at Peking, Lawrence of Arabia, Invisible Dead*, etc.) until his death in 1990, but is best recognized for his Spaghetti Western roles, usually typecasting him as a Mexican bandido in a wide sombrero, wearing two bandoleers across his chest. Frank Braña, instantly recognizable by his snow-white hair, tends to play "authority figures" (e.g., the police detective in Juan Piquer Simón's *Pieces*).

And Then a Time of Killing see *Time and Place for Killing*

And They Smelled the Strange, Exciting, Dangerous Scent of Dollars (1973)

Sentivano . . . Uno Strano Eccitante Pericoloso Puzzo di Dollari Ital. *Director:* Italo Alfaro; *Script:* Piero Regnoli; *Camera:* Sandro Mancori; *Music:* Bruno Zambrini/Gianni Meccia; *Producer:* Enzo Boetani/Giuseppe Collura, Starkiss-Falcon Films (Italy). *Cast:* Robert Malcolm, Piero Vida, Rosalba Neri, Luigi Meccia, Salvatore Puntillo, Peter Landers, Spartaco Conversi.

The charming outlaw Bronco Kid (Robert Malcolm) teams up with bounty hunter Charity Jenkins (Piero Vida) against Al Costello, owner of Costello Financial, Ltd., who is planning (with the help of a Mexican bandit named Ramírez) to rob a million dollar payroll convoy. The best thing about this film is the surreal title. And, the brief, but appreciated, Rosalba Neri performance.

Scriptwriter Piero Regnoli is secretly the director (hiding behind the "Italo Alfaro" pseudonym). During the 60s, he made a variety of Italian black-and-white vampire pics, including the cult film *Playgirls and the Vampire* (1960). Ever since his first job as film critic for the Vatican newspaper, writing has remained Regnoli's "bread and butter." Over the years, he has penned countless scripts ranging from Riccardo Freda's *I Vampiri* (1956) to Lucio Fulci's controversial zombie-nun movie, *Demonia* (1988).

Anda Muchacho Spara! see *Dead Men Ride*

An Angel with a Gun Is a Devil see *Colt in the Hand of the Devil* (1967)

Animal Called Man (1973)

Animale Chiamato Uomo Ital. *Director:* Roberto Mauri; *Script:* Roberto Mauri; *Camera:* Luigi Ciccarese; *Music:* Carlo Savina; *Producer:* Virginia Cinematografica (Italy). *Cast:* Vassili Karis, Lillian Bray, Craig Hill, Gilberto Galimbi, Amero Capanna, Carla Mancini, Paolo Magalo.

This is a *"Trinity*-wanna-be" written and directed by Roberto Mauri, an eccentric filmmaker responsible for a bizarre collection of cheaply made erratic Westerns (see Directors filmography) and some outlandish nongenre entries (i.e., *Madaleine* and *King of Kong Island* using his "Robert Morris" alias).

A rogue, but charming, bandit Bill Masson (Vassili Karis, aka Wassilli Karamensinis) gets involved in a sharpshooting contest with a coveted first prize of $500 *plus* a night with sexy dancehall singer Yvette (Lillian Bray). Embarrassingly, Bill outshoots the traditional winner, a local gunman (and town boss) Mark Forester (Amero Capanna), who is obviously angry over the results. While in Yvette's bed collecting the second part of his prize, sharpshooting Bill discovers that his whore is actually a doctor (!) from Paris.

"Men in the West are so prejudiced," she complains. "I came out here with high hopes and look at what I've become." Meanwhile, evil Forester plots to eliminate Masson but when all his schemes backfire, he resorts to a fullscale war. The end result is a new town boss, obviously Bill. And a new town doctor. Certainly, a doctor with a "heart-of-gold" and a very unique bedside manner.

Animale Chiamato Uomo see *Animal Called Man*

Another Man, Another Chance see *Another Man, Another Woman*

Another Man, Another Woman (1977)

Another Man, Another Chance; Un Autre Homme, une Autre Chance Fr. *Director:* Claude Lelouch; *Script:* Claude Lelouch; *Camera:* Jacques LeFrançois/ Stanley Cortez; *Music:* Francis Lai; *Producer:* Alexandre Mouchkine/Georges Dancigers, United Aritist (France). *Cast:* James Caan, Geneviève Bujold, Francie Huster, Jennifer Warren, Susan Tyrell, Walter Barnes.

A sequel in style and (sort of) in title to *A Man and a Woman* (1966), Claude Lelouch's Academy Award winning "romance" film about a young widow and widower who fall in love. It was short on story, but high on breathtakingly beautiful photography and tearjerking sentimentality. Here is more of the same, with the setting changed from contemporary France to the American West. This time Geneviève Bujold is the widow Jeanne Leroy, who leaves France and journeys across the Atlantic Ocean to make a new home in America (New Mexico), where she meets a veterinarian widower, David Williams (James Caan).

Like the original, the charisma of the film lies in Lelouch's exquisite co-camerawork (under a peculiar pseudonym, Jacques LeFrançois) which gives the West an abstract utopian appearance, effectively contrasting against the violence of the revenge-related subplot. The other cameraman on this project is veteran U.S. cinematographer Stanley Cortez, who started as a "big shot" in the 30s and 40s, but ended up filming mostly schlock science fiction in the 50s and 60s.

Any Gun Can Play see *Go Kill and Come Back*

Anything for a Friend (1973)

Amico Mio, Frega Tu ... Che Frego Io! Ital. *Director:* Miles Deem; *Script:* Demofilo Fidani/Mila Vitelli/Filippo Perrored; *Camera:* Claudio Morabito; *Music:* Lallo Gori; *Producer:* Tarquina Internazionale (Italy). *Cast:* Gordon

Mitchell, Red Carter, Simone Blondell, Dennys Colt, Bud Randall, Carla Mancini, Sleepy Warren, Angela Portaluri, Rick Boyd.

The scriptwriters should be arrested. They are professional con-men, taking money for air. But, in this case, that's S.O.P., Standard Operating Procedure. After all, it's a Miles Deem (Demofilo Fidani) movie. . .

Under various pseudonyms (Dick Spitfire, Lucky Dickerson, Sean O'Neal, Diego Spataro, Dennis Ford, Alessandro Santini and, the most notorious, Miles Deem), Demofilo Fidani has directed 13 terrible, but highly entertaining, Spaghetti Westerns.

This one tells the story of Jonas Dickerson (Red Carter, actually, Lionel Stander) and Mark Tabor (Bud Randall), two smalltime hustling bandits who discover gold in Dead Man's Gulch, just outside of Denver. Meanwhile, town boss Muller (Gordon Mitchell) appoints himself mayor and takes over the saloon, turning it into a crooked casino. When he attempts to cheat Jonas and Mark in a fixed poker game, they turn the tables (literally) and expose him.

All the familiar Demofilo Fidani touches are here, plus there's a sheriff with hemorrhoids, a palsy-afflicted prospector named Tripper (get it?), and a definitive answer to the burning question: "Why do people wash their feet?" Of course it's bad. That's why it's so good.

L'Apache Bianco see *White Apache*

Apache Gold see *Winnetou the Warrior*

Apache Woman (1976)

Una Donna Chiamata Apache Ital. *Director:* George McRoots; *Script:* Giorgio Maruizzo/Antonio Raccioppi; *Camera:* Serge Rubin; *Music:* Budy-Maglione; *Producer:* Zenith Cinematografica (Italy). *Cast:* Al Cliver, Yara Kewa, Corrado Olmi, Fran Marie Boyer, Rick Boyd, Roque Oppedisano.

More sensuously sleazy than Spaghetti Westerns tend to get, starring exploitation magnet Al Cliver aka Pier Luigi Conti (*Alcove, Endgame, Mandingo Hunter*, etc.). He's Tommy, a naive calvary soldier (a character similar to Peter Strauss' "Jonas" in 1970's *Soldier Blue*) who falls in love with the Apache Woman (Yara Kewa). It is cowritten by Giorgio Maruizzo (alias director George McRoots) and filmmaker Antonio Raccioppi (responsible for *Erotic Congressman*, starring Femi Benussi).

When a beautiful Indian squaw is kidnapped by an unscrupulous guntrafficker named Honest Jeremy (Corrado Olmi), she is rescued by tenderfoot Tommy. Eventually, Honest Jeremy and his "partners" track the lovers down. The result is a decidedly disturbing jolt of excessive brutality, an inordinate amount of violence mixed with a strong dose of 70s softcore sexuality.

Apache's Last Battle (1964)

Old Shatterhand; Battaglia di Fort Apache Ital. *Director:* Hugo Fregonese; *Script:* Ladislas Fodor; *Camera:* Siegfried Hold; *Music:* Martin Bottcher; *Producer:* Arthur Brauner, Avala/Criterion/Serena (West Germany/Yugoslavia/France/Italy). *Cast:* Lex Barker, Guy Madison, Pierre Brice, Daliah Lavi, Rick Battaglia, Ralf Wolter, Kitty Mattern, Bill Ramsey.

This is one of the early German-produced (with Yugoslavian, French, and Italian partners) *Winnetou* films, the third in a series to *Treasure of Silver Lake* and *Winnetou the Warrior* (or, *Apache Gold*). And the only one to be filmed in 70 mm Superpanorama, for which producer Brauner demanded more outdoors photography highlighting the picturesque Yugoslav mountain range, which doubled for the American Rockies.

Old Shatterhand (Lex Barker) has left the railroad "to live off the land." He and his blood brother, Apache chief Winnetous (Pierre Brice), are harassed by a war-hungry, glory-grabbing Cavalry officer (Guy Madison) who is trying to stir up trouble between the "savage" Comanches and "noble" Apaches.

For the other Lex Barker "Winnetou" films see *Treasure of Silver Lake* and *Winnetou the Warrior* (both mentioned above), plus *Half-Breed, Last of the Renegades, Winnetou and Shatterhand in the Valley of Death,* and *Winnetou: Desperado Trail.* Without Brice, Barker made two related adventure/westerns, *Pyramid of the Sun God* and *Treasure of the Aztecs.* Meanwhile, beautiful co-star, Daviah Lavi, is best known for her performance in Mario Bava's *What?* (or *Whip and the Body*) (1963).

Apocalypse Joe (1970)

Man Called Apocalypse Joe; Man Called Joe Clifford; L'Uomo Chiamato Apocalisse Joe Ital. *Director:* Leopoldo Savona; *Script:* Brochero/Savona; *Camera:* Franco Villa; *Music:* Bruno Nicolai; *Producer:* Transeuropa/Copercines (Italy/Spain). *Cast:* Anthony Steffen, Eduardo Fajardo, Mary Paz Pondal, Stelio Candeli, Fernando Cerulli, Fernando Bilbao.

A good, action-oriented Spaghetti Western written and directed by Leopoldo Savona (who also made the tough and wanton *Killer Kid*). It tells the story of a traveling Shakespearean actor in the west, secretly a vigilante gunman, Apocalypse Joe (beardless Anthony Steffen) who learns that he has inherited a rich gold mine in the city of Landberry. When he arrives to take ownership, he finds that another man (posing as his uncle) has already taken possession and, with an outlaw gang, is terrorizing the city.

Costar Eduardo Fajardo is his usual oily, sleazy self as the "dignified" phony uncle/villain (see *Django* for Fajardo's best known role; check the Performers filmography for a complete listing). The solid musical score is composed by Bruno Nicolai; the director of photography is Franco Villa, who besides lensing many Westerns (see Cinematographers filmography), has also shot cult thrillers (Giuseppe Vari's *Who Killed the Prosecutor and Why*) and war pictures (Al Bradly's *Kill Rommel*).

Stelio Candeli, who looks like a blond mutation of Klaus Kinski and Peter Lorre, made his mark two years later by playing the hunchback brother of Ewa *(Candy)* Aulin in Joe D'Amato's classic *Death Smiles on a Murderer* (1973).

Arizona (1970)

Arizona Lets Fly and Kills Everybody; Arizona Colt Returns; If You Gotta Shoot Someone . . . Bang! Bang!; Arizona Colt Si Scatena . . . E Li Fece Fuori Tutti Ital. *Director:* Sergio Martino; *Script:* M. Massimo Tarantini/Ernesto Gastaldi; *Camera:* Miguel F. Mila; *Music:* Bruno Nicolai; *Producer:* Vittorio Galiano, Devon Film/CC Astro (Italy/Spain). *Cast:* Anthony Steffen, Rosalba Neri, Aldo Sambrell, Roberto Camardiel, José Manuel Martin, Raf Baldassare, Luis Barboo.

Although you wouldn't guess it from the alternative titles nor the embarrassingly campy theme song, this is actually a serious revenge Western with Anthony Steffen delivering one of his better performances as Arizona Colt. Arizona and Double Whiskey (Roberto Camardiel) are retired bounty hunters, living off the land at a rural horse ranch. An arch enemy, Keene (Aldo Sambrell), is released from prison. Still holding a grudge against the capturing bounty hunter, Keene concocts a damning accusation (of horse thievery) against Arizona, producing false evidence that convicts him to the gallows. But the hanging is faked. It's a trick to make everybody think that the famous gunman is dead, thus allowing him to live peacefully with his woman, Sheena (Rosalba Neri).

Believing Arizona has been executed, Keene raids the ranch stealing five boxes of gold, and killing Double Whiskey and Sheena. Arizona is enraged. He tracks down Keene and his outlaw gang, gruesomely killing everyone.

Cult thriller/horror filmmaker Sergio Martino (*Torso, Next Victim, Slave of the Cannibal God*, etc.) has an eye for atmosphere and tension. He demonstrates his talent effectively in this film (and to a greater degree, in another Western *A Man Called Blade*). The scriptwriter, Michele Massimo Tarantini, worked with Martino on many of his sex farces (i.e., *Dishonor with Honor, Sexy Relations, Sex with a Smile*) before he, too, began directing scorchers with Gloria Guida *(The License)* and Edwige Fenech *(The Policewoman)*.

There is an unsolved mystery regarding the perplexing Bruno Nicolai soundtrack for this film. Not only doesn't it match the action on the screen but, astonishingly, the same musical tracks (including the theme song) are also used again in Ignacio Iquino's *My Horse, My Gun, Your Widow* (1972) and then once more in Anthony Ascott's film *A Man Called Invincible* (1973). How come?

Arizona Bill see *Road to Fort Alamo*

Arizona Colt (1965)

Man from Nowhere; Il Pistolero di Arizona Ital. *Director:* Michele Lupo; *Script:* Luciano Martino/Ernesto Gastaldi/Michele Lupo; *Camera:* Guglielmo Mancori; *Music:* Francesco De Masi; *Producer:* Elio Scardamaglia, Leone/ Orphee Film (Italy/France). *Cast:* Giuliano Gemma, Fernando Sancho, Corinne Marchand, Nello Pazzafini, Andrea Bosić, Roberto Camardiel, Mirko Ellis, Rosalba Neri, José Manuel Martin.

The popular screen star Giuliano Gemma is notorious gunfighter Arizona Colt, unjustly jailed after a frame-up. Hoping to enlist Colt in his gang, a Mexican bandit named Torrez Gordon (Fernando Sancho) raids the prison, releasing the desperado. But Arizona Colt refuses to join Torrez and instead he goes to Blackstone City to warn the townspeople about the pending outlaw attack. As always, Rosalba Neri (this time in a very early role) is a welcome delight.

The motion picture is a serious, angry Western unlike director Michele Lupo's other genre entries, *Ben and Charlie, Buddy Goes West* or *For a Fist in the Eye* with Franco and Ciccio. He later became one of Italy's leading exploitation filmmakers, responsible for movies like *Seven Times Seven* (with Lionel Stander), and *Love Me, Baby, Love Me* (starring Anna Moffo). He retired from moviemaking in the mid–80s after inheriting a chain of successful department stores. Michele Lupo died from a heart attack in 1989.

Interestingly, in 1966, producer Elio Scardamaglia (using a "Michael Hamilton" alias) tried his hand at directing with a horror flick, *The Murder Clinic* starring Western regular William Berger as a skin-grafting psycho.

Arizona Colt Returns see *Arizona*

Arizona Colt Si Scatena ... E Li Fece Fuori Tutti see *Arizona*

Arizona Kid (1974)

I Fratelli di Arizona Ital. *Director:* Luciano Carlos; *Script:* Lino Brocks/ Luciano B. Carlos; *Camera:* Felipe Saodalan; *Music:* Restie Umali; *Producer:* Cirio H. Santiago (Philippines/Italy). *Cast:* Mamie Van Doren, Gordon Mitchell, Chaquito, Mariela Branger, Bernard Bonnin, Pilar Velazquez.

Produced by Cirio H. Santiago, a Filipino exploitation director (*Demon in Paradise, Caged Fury, Vampire Hookers, Women in Cages*, etc.), this is certainly the only Manila/Roma Western co-production in history.

Starring the Southeast Asian comedian, Chaquito, in a story of mistaken identity, it is difficult to understand who this film was designed to entertain. Exactly who is the targeted audience — Euro, Anglo, or Filipino? Throughout the movie, Chaquito jabbers away in his native tongue (more irritating than funny) while everybody else is speaking English. The plot has to do with the citizens of Sierra Vista believing that Chaquito is the renowned "good guy" named Arizona Kid, and they convince him to protect their town against Coyote (Gordon Mitchell) and his gang of bandidos.

Sex queen from the 1950s, Mamie Van Doren, plays Chaquito's sometimes girlfriend. The "blonde bombshell with torpedo breasts" also starred in a much better German-made Spaghetti Western, *Sheriff Was a Lady* (1965).

Arizona Lets Fly and Kills Everybody see *Arizona*

Arizona on Earth see *God in Heaven ... Arizona on Earth*

Armed and Dangerous: Time and Heroes of Bret Harte (1977)

Wooruzhyon i Ochen Opasen Rus. *Director:* Vladimir Vainstok; *Script:* Vladimir Vladimirov/Pavel Finn; *Camera:* Konstantin Ryzhov; *Music:* Lev Durov; *Producer:* Vladimir Vainstok (Soviet Union). *Cast:* Donatas Banionis, Ludmilla Senchina, Leonid Bronevoy, Vsevolod Abdulov, Sergei Martinson.

Here's a maverick production from the Soviet Union, by their most celebrated action director, Vladimir Vainstok, who also made successful movies from the writings of Jules Verne and Robert Louis Stevenson. This one is loosely based on the books of American "Wild West" author Bret Harte, or (more particularly) on his personal, and highly fictionalized, life story as serialized in various pulp publications at the turn of the century.

Vsevolod Abdulov is Bret Harte, who joins with a miner (Donatas Banionis) and a dance-hall singer (Soviet pop star, Ludmilla Senchina) to help the oppressed farmers fight against a land baron (Sergei Martinson) when oil is discovered.

The movie is a lengthy (over two hours) adventure-oriented, rambling production similar to the stylized "epics" of American filmmaker Cecil B. DeMille.

Arriba Trinity! see **They Called Him Trinity**

Arrière-Train Sifflera Trois Fois see **Gunfight at O Q Corral**

Arriva! Il Crow see **On the Third Day Arrived the Crow**

Arriva Durango, Pago o Muori see **Durango Is Coming, Pay or Die**

Arriva Sabata see **Sabata the Killer**

Arrivano Django e Sartana . . . È la Fine see **Django and Sartana Are Coming . . . It's the End**

The Artist Is a Gunfighter see **Prey of Vultures**

As Man to Man see **Death Rides a Horse**

L'Assault du Fort Texan see **Charge of the Seventh Cavalry**

Assault on Fort Texan see **Charge of the Seventh Cavalry**

L'Attaque de Fort Adams see **Buffalo Bill, Hero of the Far West**

Attento Gringo, È Tornato Sabata see **Watch Out Gringo! Sabata Will Return**

Au Nom du Père, du Fils et du Colt see **In the Name of the Father, the Son and the Colt**

Un Autre Homme, une Autre Chance see **Another Man, Another Woman**

Avec Django . . . Ça Va Saigner see **Machine Gun Killers**

Avenger see **Texas, Adios**

Avengers of the Ave Maria see **Fighters from Ave Maria**

Une Aventure de Billy le Kid see **A Girl Is a Gun**

Les Aventures Galantes de Zorro see **Red Hot Zorro**

Awkward Hands (1968)

When Satan Grips the Colt; Clumsy Hands Brit; Quando Satana Impugna la Colt Ital; Manos Torpes Sp. Director: Rafael Romero Marchent; Script: Joaquin Romero Marchent/Santiago Monicada; Camera: Miguel Mila; Music: Anton Garcia Abril; Producer: Ricardo Sanz, Ricardo/Uni (Spain/Italy). Cast: Peter Lee Lawrence, Alberto de Mendoza, Pilar Velazquez, Aldo Sambrell, Vidal Molina, Luis Induñi, Frank Braña, Antonio Casas.

A nonviolent ranch hand, Kitt (Peter Lee Lawrence) is shot and left to die in the desert, punishment because he dared to marry the daughter of the wealthy Mexican rancher, El Pantera (Aldo Sambrell). A bounty hunter known as "the Whip" (Alberto de Mendoza) saves him and nurses him back to health. While Kitt is recuperating, an Old Chinese Master of "the Arts" teaches him that there are three kinds of men in the world: 1) killers; 2) those who are killed; and 3) those who run away. (Obviously, an unimaginative variation of the famous Clint Eastwood philosophical quip in *The Good, the Bad, and the Ugly*: "There are two kinds of men . . . men with loaded pistols, and men who dig. You dig.") At any rate, Kitt is so moved by the words of the wise Asian that he returns to collect his revenge and rescue his wife from a life of forced prostitution. However, the final showdown (after every other bad guy has been killed off) finds Kitt facing the double-crossing Whip.

Lensed in dark earth tones by cinematographer Miguel Mila, the entire production looks bleak and gritty. There's lots of mud and squalor, a cornerstone of the Spaghetti Western. Marchent's deft direction borderlines on raw, and his extreme close-ups give the film an additional claustrophobic intensity. The script was cowritten by Rafael's filmmaking brother, Joaquin Romero Marchent (sometimes, Hernandez) and Santiago Monicada, a popular Spanish pulp writer. Musical composer Anton Garcia Abril who also did the soundtrack for *Texas, Adios* and other Westerns (see Music Composers filmography), later wrote the music for Hammer's "cave-man" movies, including *When Dinosaurs Ruled the Earth* (1970).

Bad Kids of the West (1967)

Kid, Terror of the West; Western Kid; Kid il Monello del West Ital. *Director:* Tony Good; *Script:* Mario Amendola/Bruno Corbucci; *Camera:* Silvio Fraschetti; *Music:* Enrico Simonetti; *Producer:* Roberto Amoroso. *Cast:* Andrea Balestri, Mirko Ellis, Ray O'Connor, Flavio Colombaioni, Franco Ressel, Carlo Carlini, Maurizio Fiori.

Scriptwriter Mario Amendola, with help (?) from directors Bruno Corbucci and Tonino Ricci, has made an incredibly bad Spaghetti Western here. This one is so terrible, so off-the-wall, that these three filmmakers have hidden behind the innocuous pseudonym, Tony Good.

It's the story of two desperate killers "with a price on their heads" who decide to take refuge in a deserted ghost town. But surprise—it's not a ghost town at all. This town is totally populated by children. Children who dress, talk and act like adults. Well, they dress, talk and act like a pedophile's impression of children dressing, talking and acting like adults. Actually, the girls all look like saloon-dancing whores; the boys desperately try to be Clint Eastwood.

The movie is filled with moronic, tasteless gags: when the killers demand beer ("But we don't have any," the kids whine; "You'd better find us some," the killers threaten; "All we have is warm beer," the kids answer), the boys go behind the bar and urinate into a pitcher. Funny. Right?

It's sort of the *Bugsy Malone* motif gone haywire.

Bad Man's River (1971)

E Continuavano a Fregarsi il Milione di Dollari Ital; *El Hombre del Río Malo* Sp; *Les Quatre Mercénaires d'El Paso* Fr. *Director:* Eugenio Martin; *Script:*

Philip Yordan; *Camera:* Alejandro Ulloa; *Music:* Waldo De Los Rios; *Producer:* Bernard Gordon (Italy/France/Spain). *Cast:* Lee Van Cleef, James Mason, Gina Lollobrigida, Eduardo Fajardo, Gianni Garko, José M. Martin, Simon Andrev, Aldo Sambrell, Daniel Martin, Diana Lorys, Barta Barri.

The Italian title translates to *And They Go on Losing a Million Dollars.* Besides referring to the lame plot, it must also apply to the unfortunate production company. Certainly, they dropped a bundle on this turkey.

Here's an impressive cast in a silly movie about on-again/off-again marriages, a riverboat along the Texas-Mexican border (huh?) and the Mexican revolution. Bank robber Bomba (Lee Van Cleef) falls in love with Alice (Gina Lollobrigida) who marries him, and then has him committed to an insane asylum, after which she steals all his money. But Bomba escapes, reorganizes his gang and goes after Alice.

By now, she has married riverboat captain Mondero (James Mason in an unusually embarrassing role), and they convince the outlaw (and first husband, Bomba) to join them in their secret mission to destroy a Mexican federal arsenal and secure a million dollars at the same time. Eventually, the plan works. But Alice double-crosses both Bomba and Mondero. The film ends with her stealing all the money and escaping with her father.

Some controversy surrounds the career of the scriptwriter, American Philip Yordan. Initially, he was known for his neurotic, but critically acclaimed, American Westerns of the 50s (i.e., *Johnny Guitar*) but then word leaked that Yordan was merely acting as a "front" for Hollywood blacklisted writers. A decade later, starting with the release of this film, his name began popping up again, connected predominantly with Z-grade horror films (i.e., *The Nightmare Never Stops, Cataclysm, Night Train to Terror*).

Badlands Drifters see *Challenge of the Mackennas*

Badmen of the West see *Magnificent Brutes of the West*

La Balada de Johnny Ringo see *Who Killed Johnny R.?*

Ballad of a Bounty Hunter see *I Do Not Forgive ... I Kill!*

Ballad of a Gunman (1967)

Ringo, Pray to Your God and Die; Ballata per un Pistolero Ital. *Director:* Alfio Caltabiano; *Script:* Alfio Caltabiano/Ernst Von Theumer; *Camera:* Guglielmo Mancori; *Music:* Marcello Giombini; *Producer:* Giano/Prodi Cinematografica (Italy/West Germany). *Cast:* Anthony Ghidra, Angelo Infanti, Anthony Freeman, Al Northon, Dan May, Monica Teuber.

This one tells the story of two gunmen, Blackie and Hud (Anthony Ghidra and Angelo Infanti), who are (independently) chasing the same outlaw, a Mexican bandido named El Bedoja (played by the director Alfio Caltabiano, under the alias Al Northon).

Blackie is a professional bounty hunter and his quest is motivated strictly by the large ransom offered; the other man's pursuit is "revenge inspired" since the outlaw had killed his father, falsified evidence, and "pinned the rap on him," causing Hud to spend the last 15 years in prison.

Anthony Ghidra in *Ballad of a Gunman* (1967)

Sort of a poor man's *For a Few Dollars More,* but the whole thing takes too long to get started. There is, however, a good Marcello Giombini score during the wait. From Alfio Caltabiano, director of the "Amen" series. Cowritten by Ernst Von Theumer, who (despite persistent rumors) is not director Mel Welles.

Ballad of Death Valley (U.S. title) see **Return of Ringo**

Ballad of Death Valley (Euro title) see **Sartana in the Valley of Death**

Ballad of Django see *Fistful of Death*

Ballata per un Pistolero see *Ballad of a Gunman*

Banda J & S, Cronaca Criminale del Far West see *Bandera Bandits*

Bandera Bandits (1973)

Sonny and Jed; Far West Story Brit; *Banda J & S, Cronaca Criminale del Far West* Ital. *Director:* Sergio Corbucci; *Script:* Sergio Corbucci/Mario Amendola/ Sabat Ciuffini/Adriano Bolzoni; *Camera:* Luis Cuadrado; *Music:* Ennio Morricone; *Producer:* Orfeo/Loyola/Terra (Italy/Spain/West Germany). *Cast:* Tomás Milian, Susan George, Telly Savalas, Eduardo Fajardo, Rossana Vanny, Franco Giacobini, Herbert Fux; Werner Pochath.

Sergio Corbucci takes the "Bonnie and Clyde" myth and pushes it back a few years, into a Western motif. It's a lighthearted film that teams escaped bandit Jed (Tomás Milian) with free-spirited, wanna-be-an-outlaw ragamuffin-of-a-girl Sonny (Susan George). Telly Savalas is the determined lawman, Franciscus, who interrupts their fun. Unfortunately, this is not one of Sergio Corbucci's better efforts. Much of the problem lies in the brutish, overtly cruel relationship between Sonny and Jed which, of course, is the very crux of the film. It is difficult to understand why Sonny fancies him in the first place. Her acquiescence to his coarse behavior gives her a "wacko" mystique, reducing her charm, and making her unattractive to the audience in general.

Most likely, this wasn't the effect intended by filmmaker Corbucci. But he's showing signs of ennui with the Western motif. His next film, *The White, the Yellow, and the Black* would be his last. However, on the plus side, there's yet another memorable soundtrack from Italian wizard Ennio Morricone.

Bandidos (1967)

Crepa Tu ... Che Vivo Io Ital. *Director:* Max Dillman; *Script:* Romano Migliorini/Giambattista Mussetto/Juan Cobos; *Camera:* Emilio Foriscot; *Music:* Egisto Macchi; *Producer:* Solly Bianco, Epic/Hesperia (Italy/Spain). *Cast:* Terry Jenkins, Enrico Maria Salerno, Luigi Pistilli, Chris Huerta, Marco Guglielmi, Venantino Venantini, Antonio Pica, Maria Martin.

A gunman, Richard Martin (Enrico Maria Salerno), is accosted by outlaw Billy Kane (Marco Guglielmi) who "spares his life" but destroys his hands (a theme used again in 1972's *Fasthand Is Still My Name*). Some years pass and Richard is now running a traveling circus/Wild West show, He gives shelter to a mysterious, escaped convict, Ricky Shot (Terry Jenkins), to whom he teaches the "tricks of the gun." The two friends eventually hunt down Billy Kane, and even though Richard is killed in the process, revenge has come full circle.

The opening credit sequence is outstanding, coupled with a rousing macho score from Egisto Macchi. Director Massimo Dallamano (alias Max Dillman) was Sergio Leone's chief cameraman for *Fistful of Dollars* and *For a Few Dollars More* (using the pseudonym Jack Dalmas). While he made many Italian sleaze-and-thriller movies (i.e., *What Have You Done to Solange, Secret of Dorian Gray, Night Child,* and *What Have They Done to Our Daughters?*), this good-looking film remains his only Spaghetti Western. Unfortunately.

I Bandoleros della Dodicesima Ora see *Desperado*

Bang Bang Kid (1968)

Il Bang Bang Kid Ital. *Director:* Luciano Lelli; *Script:* José Luis Bayonas; *Camera:* Antonio Macasoli; *Music:* Nico Fidenco; *Producer:* Sidney Pink (Italy/Spain/U.S.). *Cast:* Tom Bosley, Guy Madison, Riccardo Garrone, Sandra Milo, José Caffarel, Dianik Zurakowska.

There's a gunfighting robot (predating *West World* by five years) plus Guy Madison as Bear Bullock, the evil power-hungry town boss, who actually lives in a castle (apparently the same one used in the previous year's "serious" Western *Death Walks in Laredo*) overlooking the oppressed mining community.

This continental coproduction is harmless fun, also starring Tom Bosley (of television's "Happy Days" and "Murder She Wrote" fame) and Riccardo Garrone, the brother of famed filmmaker Sergio Garrone (alias Willy S. Regan). Directed by Stanley Praeger (using a fake Italo moniker Luciano Lelli), best known for helming the mid–60s cult TV series "Car 54, Where Are You?" Composer Nico Fidenco gave numerous *Emmanuelle* soundtracks to the world.

Il Bang Bang Kid see *Bang Bang Kid*

Bara per lo Sceriffo see *Coffin for the Sheriff*

Bastard, Go and Kill (1971)

Bastardo, Vamos a Matar Sp. *Director:* Gino Mangini; *Script:* Sergio Garrone/Luigi Mangini; *Camera:* Aristide Massaccesi; *Music:* Carl Rustic; *Producer:* Elektra Film (Italy). *Cast:* George Eastman, Scilla Gabel, Furio Meniconi, Lincoln Tate, Vincenzo Norvese, Tómas Rudy, Renzo Moneta, José M. Martin.

George Eastman is blinded by fury and bent on revenge when a band of renegade Union soldiers destroy his homestead and murder his family. Carl Rustic's (Carlo Rustichelli's) soundtrack is reminiscent of his *Minute to Pray, Second to Die* score.

This is Gino (Luigi) Mangini's only Euro Western, but he was strongly aided by the superb camera work of Aristide Massaccesi (Joe D'Amato) and the no-nonsense Sergio Garrone script. There has been unconfirmed speculation that Garrone clandestinely handled the directorial chores.

Bastardo, Vamos a Matar see *Bastard, Go and Kill*

Bataille de San Sebastian see *Guns for San Sebastian*

Battaglia di Fort Apache see *Apache's Last Battle*

Beast (1970)

Rough Justice; The Bell; La Belva Ital. *Director:* Mario Costa; *Script:* Franco Calabrese/Mario Costa; *Camera:* Luciano Trasatti; *Music:* Stelvio Cipriani; *Pro-*

ducer: West Devon (Italy). *Cast:* Klaus Kinski, Steven Tedd, Gabriella Giorgelli, Luisa Rivelli, Lee Burton, Gianni Pallavicino.

Klaus Kinski is a sex crazed outlaw, Machete, who rapes and ravages his way across the west. And also wears one of the goofiest hats ever seen in a Western.

This film was much anticipated and long awaited but (unfortunately) it is a major disappointment from one of the genre pioneers, Mario Costa (director of *Buffalo Bill, Hero of the Far West* in 1964).

Behind the Mask of Zorro (1965)

Oath of Zorro; Il Giuramento di Zorro Ital. *Director:* Ricardo Blasco; *Script:* Ricardo Blasco/Mario Amendola; *Camera:* Julio Ortas; *Music:* Pagan Ramirez Angel; *Producer:* Hispames/Prodimex Films (Italy/Spain). *Cast:* Tony Russell, Jesus Puente, José Alfonso, Roberto Paoletti, Rosita Yaraza, Naria Seoane.

A sequel of sorts to director Blasco's earlier *Three Swords of Zorro* (1963) finds Patricio (Tony Russell) traveling to the governor's estate in Mexican California, where he will become the new butler. It is an undercover assignment from the emperor because, secretly, Patricio is the notorious freedom fighter "El Zorro" (the Fox). His real job is to protect the count and the governor from a revolutionary bandit named Don Esteban (José Alfonso). Typical, over all.

The Bell see Beast

Belle Starr Story (1968)

Il Mio Corpo per un Poker Ital. *Director:* Nathan Wich; *Script:* Nathan Wich; *Camera:* Alessandro D'Eva; *Music:* Charles Dumont; *Producer:* Gianni Varsi. *Cast::* Elsa Martinelli, Robert Woods, George Eastman, Francesca Righini, Dan Harrison, Bruno Corazzari, Vladmer Nedar.

It's the famed Italian artsy director, Lina Wertmuller, hiding behind the male pseudonym, Nathan Wich. She is best remembered for the critically acclaimed *Swept Away, Seven Beauties* and *Seduction of Mimi* (but don't forget the slumming-for-a-buck days when she co-authored *When Women Had Tails* and *When Women Lost Their Tails;* Festa Campanile directed).

The story is nothing new; another retelling of the notorious female outlaw's exploits in the west. However, Elsa Martinelli is a very beautiful Belle Starr. Robert Woods and George Eastman are the two men in her (love) life, who introduce Belle to "the wonderful world of crime."

At the film's finale, Eastman shouts to Martinelli: "Hey, Belle Starr! Your story isn't over yet. I'll see you at the next poker game!" Promises. Promises.

Il Bello, il Brutto, e il Cretino see Handsome, the Ugly and the Stupid

La Belva see The Bell

Ben and Charlie (1970)

Amigo, Stay Away; Humpty Dumpty Gang; Amico, Stammi Lontano Alemno un Palmo Ital. *Director:* Michele Lupo; *Script:* Luigi Montefiore/Sergio Donati;

méfie-toi Ben, Charlie veut ta peau...

kijk uit Ben, Charlie wil je vel!

GIULIANO GEMMA dans MÉFIE-TOI BEN, CHARLIE VEUT TA PEAU in (BEN AND CHARLIE) met GEORGE EASTMAN et avec la participation de MARISA MELL (BEN AND CHARLIE) · VITTORIO GONGIA · GIACOMO ROSSI STUART · en de deelneming van · REGIE MICHELE LUPO · PROD. JUPITER GENERALE CINEMATOGRAFICA S.p.A. · Technicolor-Techniscope · Distrib. 20th Century-Fox

Camera: Aristide Massaccesi; *Music:* Gianni Ferrio; *Producer:* Jupiter Generale Cinematografica (Italy). *Cast:* Giuliano Gemma, George Eastman, Vittorio Congia, Giacomo Rossi Stuart, Marisa Mell.

Here's another one of those fluffy "Buddy" pictures, cut from the same mold as the hit *Trinity* series. This time Ben Bellow and Charlie Logan (Giuliano Gemma and George Eastman) are amigos. Their wanderings have brought them to Desert City where they are mistaken for dangerous criminals. Enjoying the attention and notoriety, they encourage the scam until an unscrupulous sheriff falsifies evidence (to protect himelf) and puts them in prison. They manage to escape from jail and expose the sheriff, but in the end (after they lose all their ill-gotten money and fame), Ben and Charlie are content in knowing "that they are rich in friendship." It almost makes your teeth hurt. Too sweet.

The script is written by the (customarily) "left wing" politically motivated Sergio Donati (author of *The Big Gundown*) and by costar George Eastman (using his real name, Luigi Montefiore). Aristide (Joe D'Amato) Massaccesi's cinematography is one of the film's major strong points. The other is actress Marisa Mell, the highly recognizable beauty of many Italian thrillers including Mario Bava's *Danger: Diabolik* (1968) and Lucio Fulci's *One on Top of the Other* (1972).

Director Michele Lupo, veteran filmmaker of numerous "sword and sandal" movies (*Goliath and the Sins of Babylon, Colossus of the Arena, Vengeance of Spartacus,* etc.), made four Spaghetti Westerns (see Directors filmography) plus a variety of exploitation films (*Love Me, Baby, Love Me; Fearless,* etc.). In the mid–80s he inherited a chain of profitable department stores and retired from the motion picture business. Michele Lupo died unexpectedly from a heart attack in 1989.

Between God, the Devil and a Winchester (1968)

God Was in the West, too, at One Time; Anche nel West, C'era una Volta Dio Ital. *Director:* Dario Silvestri; *Script:* Marino Girolami/Martin Remis/Tito Carpi; *Camera:* Pablo Ripoll/Alberto Fusi; *Music:* Carlo Savina; *Producer:* Circus Film/R.M. Film (Italy/Spain). *Cast:* Gilbert Roland, Richard Harrison, Ennio Girolami, Folco Lulli, Raf Baldassare, Roberto Camardiel, Luis Barboo.

There's a band of outlaws led by Bob Ford (Folco Lulli) plus a priest disguised as gunfighter Pat Jordan (Richard Harrison), both independently on the trail of a treasure stolen from a church in Texas. Both try to convince scout Chasquido to help them in the search. With all the emphasis on "the treasure map" and its purloined existence, the plot is reminiscent of Robert Louis Stevenson's adventure tale, *Treasure Island,* set against a Western motif.

Actually directed by veteran Marino Girolami (rather than the erroneously credited industry production manager "Dario Silvestri"), this film features Marino's son Ennio Girolami as one of the villains. Marino has another son, Enzo, who is the popular genre director Enzo G. Castellari (see *Go Kill and Come Back, Keoma, Sting of the West,* etc.).

Opposite: **Movie poster from *Ben and Charlie.***

Beyond the Frontiers of Hate see *Four Came to Kill Sartana*

Beyond the Law (1968)

Bloodsilver; Good Die First; Al di là della Legge Ital. *Director:* Giorgio Stegani; *Script:* Warren Kiefer/Fernando Di Leo/Stegani; *Camera:* Enzo Serafin; *Music:* Riz Ortolani; *Producer:* Alfonso Sansone, Sancrosiap/Roxy Film (Italy/West Germany). *Cast:* Lee Van Cleef, Antonio Sabàto, Gordon Mitchell, Lionel Stander, Bud Spencer, Graziella Granata, Herbert Fux, Carlo Gaddi.

A good cast in a disconcerting film. "Disconcerting" because it is very discomforting and (initially) annoying to see Lee Van Cleef portray such a wishy-washy character. But that's the very focus of the film, and as such, perhaps a compliment to Van Cleef's (critically disregarded) acting ability.

Here is the story, cowritten by future action/horror director Fernando Di Leo (i.e., *Slaughter Hotel, Mr. Scarface, Vacation for a Massacre*) about a weak con man Cudilip (Van Cleef) who, during the length of the film, moves from outside the law to a position of authority within society. Giorgio Stegani (using his George Findley alias) made two other Eurowesterns, *Adios Gringo* and *Gentleman Killer.*

On the lighter side, this movie features a rare opportunity to see Bud Spencer without his beard (and wearing a suit) as the mine manager, Cooper. Character actor Herbert Fux (obviously a ribald pseudonym) is a familiar face in Euro exploitation films; he played a graverobber in Mel Welles' *Lady Frankenstein* and was the tongue-yanking torturer in the German sickie, *Mark of the Devil.*

Il Bianco, il Giallo, il Nero see *White, Yellow and the Black*

The Big and the Bad see *It Can Be Done . . . Amigo*

Big Gundown (1966)

Account Rendered; La Resa dei Conti Ital. *Director:* Sergio Sollima; *Script:* Sergio Donati/Sergio Sollima/Franco Solinas; *Camera:* Carlo Carlini; *Music:* Ennio Morricone; *Producer:* Alberto Grimaldi/Tullio Demichelli (Italy/Spain). *Cast:* Lee Van Cleef, Tomás Milian, Fernando Sancho, Neives Navarro, Roberto Camardiel, Tom Felleghy, Walter Barnes, Gerard Herter, Maria Granada.

This is one of the best non–Leone Westerns, and certainly Lee Van Cleef's most memorable role. He plays Texas lawman Jonathan Corbett, who accepts the job of tracking down Cuchillo (Tomás Milian), a Mexican bandit accused of raping and murdering a little girl.

The search is long and hard. And it eventually takes Corbett into Mexico, where he reunites with his employer, the senator (Walter Barnes), and his henchmen. These men turn the pursuit into a cold-blooded "sport hunt" complete with dogs and high-powered weapons, but Corbett begins to realize the

Opposite: Movie poster from *Beyond the Law.*

truth. He has been duped by these dangerous men. Cuchillo is actually innocent; framed. And Corbett decides to help him.

The "hunt in the cane field" is among the greatest ten minutes ever put on film, comparable to the "Ecstasy of Gold" sequence in *The Good, the Bad, and the Ugly* and the "Only at the Point of Death" scene in *Once Upon a Time in the West*. It's director Sergio Sollima's most remarkable achievement. Plus there's an amazing musical score composed by Ennio Morricone, conducted by Bruno Nicolai. Sergio Sollima also directed a sequel called *Run Man, Run* starring Tomás Milian, but not Lee Van Cleef.

Big Gundown 2 see *Run Man, Run*

Big Ripoff (1967)

The Dirty Outlaws; El Desperado; King of the West Brit; *Massacre et le Sang* Fr; *El Desperado* Sp. *Director:* Franco Rossetti; *Script:* Franco Rossetti with Ugo Guerra and Vincenzo Cerami; *Camera:* Angelo Filippini; *Music:* Gianni Ferrio; *Producer:* Daiano Film/Leone Film (Spain/Italy). *Cast:* Chip Gorman, Rosemarie Dexter, Aldo Berti, Franco Giornelli, Dana Ghia, Giovanni Petrucci, Piero Lulli, John Janos Bartha.

It's one double cross after another in this needlessly confusing tale about a secret cache of gold coins, squabbling outlaws in a cholera-infested vacated town, Confederate troops escorting a paymaster through the west, and a bandit (Chip Gorman, aka Andrea Giordana) who can't decide which he loves most: gold or his girl (a very beautiful Rosemarie Dexter). Without giving too much away, only his girlfriend is alive when the final credits roll.

Written and directed by popular genre scriptwriter, Franco Rossetti (see Scriptwriters filmography for a complete listing of film writing credits). Chief cameraman is Angelo Filippini; Gianni Ferrio, talented composer of *Blood for a Silver Dollar* and *Fort Yuma Gold*, provides the musical score.

Big Showdown (1972)

Storm Rider; The Grand Duel; Hell's Fighters Brit; *Il Grande Duello* Ital. *Director:* Giancarlo Santi; *Script:* Ernesto Gastaldi; *Camera:* Mario Vulpiani; *Music:* Sergio Bardotti; *Producer:* Corona/Nouvelle de Ciné/Terra (Italy/France). *Cast:* Lee Van Cleef, Horst Frank, Peter O'Brien, Marc Mazza, Jess Hahn, Klaus Grumberg.

The story is an intricate and engaging whodunit (very atypical for a Spaghetti Western) involving a lawman, Clayton (Lee Van Cleef), as he protects Newland (Horst Frank), a wrongly accused murderer, from bounty hunters and vigilantes, while he tries to figure out who really committed the crime.

Good direction from Giancarlo Santi, the initial director for *Duck You Sucker* before costars Rod Steiger and James Coburn demanded Sergio Leone's personal attention. This film features another stirring score from *Django* composer Luis Enriquez Bacalov, using an unusual pseudonym, "Sergio Bardotti."

Storm Rider (the American video title) is an edited version and as such, it is missing a few minutes of nudity and violence.

Movie poster of Lee Van Cleef in *Big Gundown* (1966).

Big Silence see *Great Silence*

Bill il Taciturno . . . *Django Uccide* see *Django Kills Softly*

Movie poster from *Big Ripoff* (1967).

Billy the Kid (1962)

Furia de la Ley Ital. *Director:* Leon Klimovsky; *Script:* Bob Sirens/Angel Del Castillo; *Camera:* Manuel Hernandez Sanjuan; *Music:* Daniel White; *Producer:* Carthago (Spain). *Cast:* George Martin, Jack Taylor, Juny Brunell, Tomás-Blanco, Alberto Dalbes, Luis Induni, Esther Grant.

Here's a seldom seen rarity from Spanish filmmaker Leon Klimovsky, who later made a name for himself by directing stylish, atmospheric horror films, often starring cult actor Paul Naschy. But apparently, poor distribution has sent this Billy the Kid feature to the cinematic boneyard.

Movie poster from *Big Showdown* (1966) featuring Lee Van Cleef.

The cast is impressive, marking genre debuts for George Martin, Jack Taylor, and Luis Induni.

Black Eagle of Santa Fe (1964)

Gringos Do Not Forgive; Die schwärzen Ädler von Santa Fe Ger; *I Gringo non Perdonano* Ital. *Director:* Ernst Hofbauer; *Script:* Jack Lewis; *Camera:* Hans Jura; *Music:* Gert Wilden; *Producer:* Gunter Raguse, Constantin/Rapid/Metheus (Germany/Italy/France). *Cast:* Brad Harris, Horst Frank, Tony Kendall, Joachim Hansen, Werner Peters, Helga Sommerfeld, Thomas Moore, Serge Marquand.

This German-scripted, "good Indian" plot (similar to the Karl May "Winnetou" stories) benefits from a competent cast. The film is very significant because it was one of the first Eurowesterns to receive major international distribution. Nonetheless, the bulk of its popularity remained along the Rhine.

Cliff McPherson (Brad Harris) is a secret government agent sent to Santa Fe from Washington. His mission is to find out why "peaceful" Indians have suddenly turned hostile. He discovers that a land-grabbing rancher named Morton (Werner Peters) is disguising his men as Army soldiers and instructing them to kill the Comanches. Obviously, these "unprovoked" raids have instigated Indian retaliation. McPherson and journalist Blade Carpenter expose the deception to Chief Black Eagle (Tony Kendall, aka Luciano Stella) who leads the Indians in attack against Morton and his gang.

Filmmaker Hofbauer is better known for his sex farces and action-oriented comedies (i.e., *Three Super Guys* with Robert Widmark). He was also the original director of the "humorously" redubbed *A Spy's Bold Sexual Adventures*.

In addition to the credits listed above, future genre filmmaker Alberto Cardone (alias Paul Martin) is the assistant director for this project.

Black Jack (1968)

Blackjack Ital. *Director:* Gianfranco Baldanello; *Script:* Luigi Ambrosini/ Augusto Finocchi/Gianfranco Baldanello/Mario Maffei; *Camera:* Mario Fioretti; *Music:* Lallo Gori; *Producer:* Mercedes/Ronbi International (Italy). *Cast:* Robert Woods, Lucienne Bridou, Rik Battaglia, Larry Dolgin, Federico Chentres, Mimmo Palmara, Fredy Unger, Sascia Krusciarska.

An odd Eurowestern entry because everybody is "a bad guy." Black Jack (Robert Woods) and his gang rob the bank at Tucson City. When it comes time to divide the loot, the other bandits complain over the size of Jack's share. So he steals it all. In the end, Black Jack is betrayed by an Indian friend (Mimmo Palmara). And, along with his sister and her husband, Jack is murdered.

However, this amoral tale lacks the conviction found in Gianfranco Baldanello's (aka Frank G. Carroll's) better films, *This Man Can't Die* and *Thirty Winchesters for El Diablo*.

Black Killer (1971)

Black Killer Ital. *Director:* Lucky Moore; *Script:* Luigi Angelo/Charlie Foster; *Camera:* Franco Villa; *Music:* Daniele Patucchi; *Producer:* Tegica Cinematografic (Italy/West Germany). *Cast:* Klaus Kinski, Fred Robsahm, Antonio Cantafora, Marina Mulligan, Paul Craine, Tiziana Dini, Claudio Trionfi.

Here's a textbook example of the Spaghetti Western genre, incorporating the "revenge for a slaughtered family" theme with the "evil town boss" motif. There's even a pair of mysterious gunfighting "strangers," and (as a special bonus) there's a nasty gang of seven Mexican brothers discordantly named "O'Hara," plus, Klaus Kinski in a prominent full-length role.

Nobody wants to be sheriff in Tombstone. Twenty-six of them have died over the past two years. And the last sheriff didn't make it beyond the first 24 hours. It's all because of the O'Hara Brothers, seven wild Mexican killers (Miquel, Paco, Chico, Brian, Billy, Ramon, and the leader, Pedro) who, along with corrupted Judge Wilson (Claudio Trionfi), control the city.

Movie poster from *Black Jack* (1968).

When rancher Peter Collins is killed and his beautiful Indian wife Sarah (Tiziana Dini) is gang-raped by the lunatic O'Hara bunch, a bent-on-revenge bounty-hunting brother, Bud Collins (Fred Robsahm), pins on the "tin star" and accepts his "license to kill." He's aided by a mysterious, dressed-in-black stranger (Klaus Kinski), who turns out to be a sharpshooting frontier lawyer named James Webb. Together, with help from vindictive Sarah, they take on (and kill off) the entire O'Hara gang.

While Bud and Sarah are completing the job (Sarah blinds Chico with the old dynamite-on-an-arrow trick, and Bud shoots him dead), James Webb eliminates the land-grabbing "respectable" Judge Wilson with an effective gun-hidden-inside-a-law-book gag.

Just for the record, there's also a haughty saloon hostess named Consuela (Marina Mulligan). She serves no purpose in the overall action. But she does get naked a lot. This gives the film the dubious distinction of being one of a limited handful (also see *Apache Woman, Man Called Amen,* and *Three Musketeers of the West*) that contain female frontal nudity.

It's directed by Carlo Croccolo (calling himself Lucky Moore) and cowritten by Croccolo (under a different pseudonym, Charlie Foster). Using his real name, he also appears in a brief cameo role as a government agent. Carlo Croccolo made another, less impressive, Western called *Gunmen of One Hundred Crosses* (1971) with Tony Kendall, plus, an earlier genre flick *Sheriff Was a Lady* (1965), lots of fun, with Mamie Van Doren.

Black Tigress (1967)

Lola Colt Ital. *Director:* Siro Marcellini; *Script:* Luigi Angelo/Lamberto Antonelli/Mario Bianchi; *Camera:* Giuseppe La Torre; *Music:* Ubaldo Continiello; *Producer:* Cines Europa (Italy). *Cast:* Peter Martell, Lola Falana, German Cobos, Franco Balducci, Tom Felleghy, Andrea Scotti, Erna Schurer.

A prostitute (songstress Lola Falana) is clandestinely interested in more than the obvious, as she "pumps" her clients for information regarding a missing treasure. But don't expect a lot of sex. It all takes place off camera. Don't expect much violence either.

Blackjack see *Black Jack*

Blake's Marauders see *Payment in Blood*

Blazing Guns see *His Name Was Holy Ghost*

Blindman (1971)

Blindman Ital. *Director:* Ferdinando Baldi; *Script:* Vincenzo Cerami/Tony Anthony; *Camera:* Riccardo Pallottini; *Music:* Stelvio Cipriani; *Producer:* Tony Anthony/Saul Wimmer (Italy). *Cast:* Tony Anthony, Ringo Starr, Lloyd Battista, David Dreyer, Lucretia Love, Isabella Savona, Magda Konopka, Ken Wood, Raf Baldassare.

Obviously inspired by the Japanese blind Samurai films, this movie features Tony Anthony's best acting (something he's not really known for) as the sightless gunfighter. Former Beatle Ringo Starr, the film's weakest element, is around for awhile but then (mercifully) dies off early.

It is truly an enjoyable picture, as Blindman is trying to recover his stolen merchandise, a wagonload of 50 (count them, 50) beautiful women that he was escorting to "a house of ill repute." But they were stolen by a vicious group of Mexican bandidos led by Domingo (Lloyd Battista) and Candy (Ringo Starr).

There's good, fast-paced direction from one of the genre's best filmmakers, Ferdinando Baldi (*Hate Your Neighbor, Forgotten Pistolero, Texas, Adios,* etc.), with principal camera work by Riccardo Pallottini and music from talented

Movie poster from *Blindman* (1971), featuring Tony Anthony and former Beatle Ringo Starr.

Stelvio Cipriani. Character actor Magda Konopka went on to play the title role in the European hit *Satanik!* (1967), adapted from the Italian comic book series. Amazingly, even though *Blindman* was a big-grossing, worldwide success, there is no sequel.

Blood and Guns (1968)

Long Live the Revolution; Tepepa . . . Viva la Revolución Sp. *Director:* Giulio Petroni; *Script:* G. Petroni/Franco Solinas/Ivan Della Mea; *Camera:* Francisco Marin; *Music:* Ennio Morricone; *Producer:* Lafredo Cuomo and Nicolo Pomilia, Filmamerica S.I.A.P. (Italy/Spain). *Cast:* Tomás Milian, Orson Welles, John Steiner, Luciano Casamonica, Angel Ortiz, José Torres, George Wang, Giancarlo Badessi, Paco Sanz.

Not a Western in the strictest sense, but there are many of the genre characteristics at work in this story of greed and treachery among three men in the aftermath of the Mexican Revolution. Tomás Milian is especially noteworthy as Tepepa, a revolutionary with a conscience. From the director of the classic *Death Rides a Horse*.

Blood at Sundown (1967)

Stop the Slayings; Why Kill Again?; Blue Summer Brit.; *Perché Uccidi Ancora?* Ital. *Director:* José Antonio De La Loma/Edward Muller; *Script:* Glen Vincent Davis; *Camera:* Hans Burmann; *Music:* Felice Di Stefano; *Producer:* Promo/Action Films (Spain/Italy). *Cast:* Anthony Steffen, Evelyn Stewart, Aldo Berti, Pepe Calvo, Hugo Blanco, José Torres, Franco Pesce.

Now, this is confusing. Here's a Spanish production directed by José Antonio De La Loma and Edward Muller (Edoardo Mulargia). The title is *Blood at Sundown* starring Anthony Steffen. Two years later, a competing Italian company, retitled and rereleased a film (originally *One Thousand Dollars on the Black*) calling it *Blood at Sundown* (see below); it also stars Anthony Steffen.

This one is the story of Steve McDougall (Steffen), who deserts the Army so he can find the men who crippled him. It turns out that Lopez (Pepe Calvo), his girlfriend's land-grabbing father, is the culprit. Steve's blood vengeance causes a major feud between the two families.

Written by genre filmmaker Glenn Vincent Davis, alias Vincenzo Musolino.

Blood at Sundown (reissued title) (1969)

One Thousand Dollars on the Black (original title) (1967); *Mille Dollari sul Nero* Ital.; *Sartana: Sangue e la Penna* Ital. *Director:* Albert Cardiff; *Script:* Ernesto Gastaldi/Vittorio Salerno/Giorgio Stegani; *Camera:* Gino Santini; *Music:* Michele Lacerenza; *Producer:* Marlon Sirko, Metheus Film/Lisa Film (Italy/West Germany). *Cast:* Anthony Steffen, Gianni Garko, Erika Blanc, Franco Fantasia, Sieghardt Rupp, Angelica Ott, Daniella Igliozzi.

Depending on the print, director Albert Cardone uses either the alias Albert Cardiff or his real name. This was originally released in 1967, preceding the popular John (Gianni) Garko *Sartana* series; however, in this one, Garko happens to play an evil villain named "Sartana." So, the film was rereleased in 1969 and promoted as a new *Sartana* movie under the title *Blood at Sundown* (or the translated Italian banner, *Sartana: Blood at Sundown*).

The story is a Cain and Abel tale of two brothers (Steffen and Garko), one good and one bad. The good one, Johnny (Anthony Steffen) was mistakenly imprisoned for a murder actually committed by his brother. When finally released from prison, he returns home to find that Sartana has taken over the town, ruling by fear and brutality. Plus, Sartana is married to Steffen's girl. Enough is enough — no more Mr. Nice Guy. Johnny rallies the townspeople to rise up against his brother.

Blood Calls to Blood (1968)

Sangue Chiama Sangue Ital. *Director:* Lewis King; *Script:* Fulvio Pazziloro; *Camera:* Tino Santoni; *Music:* Frank Mason; *Producer:* Zalo Film (Italy). *Cast:* Fernando Sancho, Stephen Forsyte, German Cobos, Lea Nanni, Antonella Judica, Marisa Salinas, Lea Nanni, Frank Farrel.

A despicable bandit, Rodriguez (Fernando Sancho), steals a diamond from the Madonna statue in a monastery, killing all the friars including a young novice named Louis. Louis' brother, Angel (Stephen Forsyte), is a notorious outlaw gunman who vows revenge in this Italian/Spanish coproduction directed by Luigi Capuano, under the Anglo pseudonym Lewis King (also see his other Western entry, *The Magnificent Texan*).

A good soundtrack from Francesco De Masi (using the "Frank Mason" alias), similar to his *Vendetta at Dawn* score.

Blood for a Silver Dollar (1965)

One Silver Dollar; Un Dollaro Bucato Ital. *Director:* Calvin J. Padget; *Script:* Giorgio Ferroni/George Finley; *Camera:* Tony Dry; *Music:* Gianni Ferrio; *Producer:* P.E.A. (Italy/France). *Cast:* Montgomery Wood, Evelyn Stewart, Peter Cross, Andrew Scott, Max Dean, Nello Pazzafini, Frank Farrel, John Mac-Douglas, Pedro Sanchez.

Cowritten by director Calvin J. Padget (pseudonym for Giorgio Ferroni) and his friend, filmmaker George Finley (alias Giorgio Stegani), responsible for three Spaghetti Westerns *(Adios Gringo, Beyond the Law,* and *Gentleman Killer),* this Italian-French coproduction is one of Padget's best, partially due to a convincing performance from Giuliano Gemma (under the alias Montgomery Wood).

Like many other Giuliano Gemma films, this one also opens with him being released from a Union prison camp at the end of the Civil War. He is an ex–Confederate officer named Gary O'Hara, and his first goal is to return home to his wife Judy (Evelyn Stewart) in West Virginia. His second goal, as he informs her, is to "start a brand new life in the West." The plan: he'll go to Yellowstone and secure a job; after that, he'll send money so she can take a stagecoach and join him there.

In Yellowstone, a banker-brute, McCory (John McDouglas), is the town boss. Supposedly, a former reb named Blackie is trying to take over. McCory hires Gary O'Hara to "convince" Blackie to leave town. It turns out to be a planned double cross; Blackie and O'Hara are to be killed.

The gravedigger discovers that O'Hara is still alive, barely. Secretly, he's nursed back to health. Meanwhile, O'Hara's wife arrives in Yellowstone. Con-

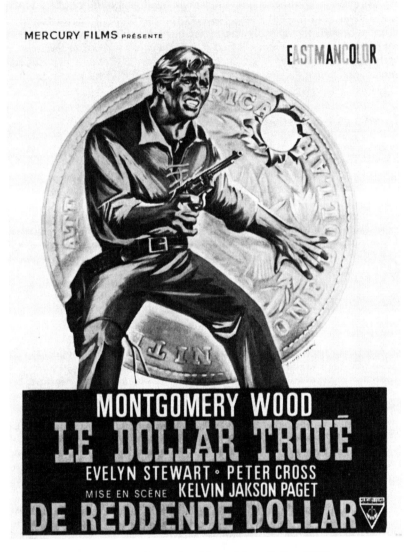

Movie poster from *Blood for a Silver Dollar* (1965).

vinced that her husband is dead, she becomes "involved" with McCory which gives O'Hara one more reason for the inevitable vengeance finale.

The excellent animated title sequence is drawn by Adelchi, punctuated by Gianni Ferrio's memorable theme. Chief cameraman is Tony Dry (pseudonym for Tony Secchi) who also directed the Western *Caliber .38.*

Blood Money see **Stranger and the Gunfighter**

Blood River (1974)

Dieci Bianchi Uccisi da un Piccolo Indiano Ital. *Director:* Gianfranco Baldenello; *Music:* Piero Umiliani. *Cast:* Fabio Testi, John Ireland, Rosalba Neri,
Julie Newmar, Daniel Martin.

Here's a very obscure Spaghetti Western with an impressive cast and competent director. Apparently, since it came so late in the cycle, the production
company had little faith in the movie's ability to compete at the box office. It
received limited distribution and almost no promotion.

This is not to be confused with an earlier film, Enzo G. Castellari's *Go Kill
and Come Back* (1967), which was released in England and South America as
Blood River.

Blood River see *Go Kill and Come Back* and *God Forgives . . . I Don't*

Bloodsilver see *Beyond the Law*

Blu Gang Vissero per Sempre Felici e Ammazzati see *Brothers Blue*

Blue Summer see *Blood at Sundown* (1967)

Boldest Job in the West (1969)

El Más Fabuloso Golpe del Far West. Director: José Antonio De La Loma;
Script: José Antonio De La Loma; *Camera:* Hans Burmann; *Music:* Gianni Mar-
chetti/Stelvio Cipriani; *Producer:* José Carcasona, Promo/Action/Les Films
(Spain/Italy/France). *Cast:* Mark Edwards, Fernando Sancho, Carmen Sevilla,
Yvan Verella, Charlie Bravo, Piero Lulli, Frank Braña.

A combined Italian-Spanish-French production by lackluster director José
Antonio De La Loma *(Blood at Sundown)* starring former Peplum player Mark
Edwards. He and Fernando Sancho are Michigan and El Reyes, leaders of a
bandit gang, who plan a "bloodless" bank robbery. But it goes horrendously
wrong. Not only is there a resulting massacre in the streets of Sun Valley, but
one of their men escapes with all the loot.

Unfortunately, the direction is so inadequately deadpan that it is impossible to tell if this is supposed to be a parody or not. Nonetheless, it doesn't work
as a comedy, barely as action.

It is, however, fun to see sinister Charlie Bravo in an early role. He would
later star in Bruno Mattei's *Scalps* (1987) and the nongenre Claudio Fragasso
film, *Monster Dog* (1986).

Boot Hill (1969)

La Collina degli Stivali Ital. *Director:* Giuseppe Colizzi; *Script:* Giuseppe Co-
lizzi; *Camera:* Marcello Masciocchi; *Music:* Carlo Rustichelli; *Producer:* Crono/
Finanzia San Marco (Italy/Spain). *Cast:* Terence Hill, Bud Spencer, Lionel
Stander, Woody Strode, Alberto Dell'Acqua, Victor Buono, Eduardo Ciannelli.

An exgunfighter, Thomas (Woody Strode), now works with a traveling circus as a trapeze artist (again, an example of director Colizzi's preoccupation
with acrobatics, a mania which taints both this film and *Ace High*). Terence Hill
is the befriended gunman, Cat Stevens, hounded by some nasty badmen, including the genre's most (unintentionally) nonthreatening villain, Victor Buono.

Terence Hill, Bud Spencer, Lionel Stander and Woody Strode appeared in *Boot Hill* (1969).

This is Colizzi's last Western. He suffered a heart attack and died in 1979.

Born to Kill (1967)

Nato per Uccidere Ital. *Director:* Tony Mulligan; *Script:* Tony Mulligan; *Camera:* Oberdan Troiani; *Music:* Felice Di Stefano; *Producer:* Franco Ortenzi (Italy). *Cast:* Gordon Mitchell, Femi Benussi, Aldo Berti, Tom Felleghy, Giovanni Lenci, Ettore Manni, Aldo Cannistanni.

It's difficult to imagine, but Gordon Mitchell is wearing a "white" hat in this Spaghetti Western. After years of playing the heavy, he finally gets to be a good guy (well, sort of). At any rate, he's the hero even though his manners and rough treatment of female costar Femi Benussi leave much to be desired.

The story is a rambling, brooding tale about a silent stranger named Gordon (Gordon Mitchell, aka Charles Pendleton) who is both fast and accurate with a pistol. The townspeople of Tree Crossing, including the beautiful prostitute Lauri Waldman (Femi Benussi), spend the entire film trying to convince him to help protect the city against the aggressive land baron, Dodge (Aldo Berti). Eventually, Gordon agrees and he kills the bad guy in a showdown.

The director and scriptwriter, Tony Mulligan, is actually Antonio Mollica. This is his only Western. The incredible Femi Benussi also stars in eight more genre pics (see Performers filmography for other titles), plus numerous Italian sex and action films.

Bounty Hunter in Trinity (1972)

Un Bounty Killer a Trinità Ital. *Director:* Oskar Faradine; *Script:* Scandariato Massaccesi; *Camera:* Aristide Massaccesi; *Music:* Vasil Kojucharov; *Producer:*

Avis Films (Italy). *Cast:* Jeff Cameron, Paul McCren, Pat Miner, Attilio Dottesio, Carla Mancini, Antonio Cantafora.

The townspeople of Trinity decide to hire a notorious bounty hunter named Alan Boyd (Jeff Cameron) to protect them (and eliminate) a fierce band of Mexican outlaws who are terrorizing the community. Alan accepts the assignment and visits Trinity "undercover." After his investigation, he exposes the owner of the saloon as the secret leader of the bandidos. A lively gunfight ensues, but of course, Alan emerges unscathed. The conclusion finds the bounty hunter collecting his "reward" money from the local bank, when an excited man from yet another town offers him an equally huge sum to liberate their city. And so it goes...

As always, the excellent photography from Aristide (Joe D'Amato) Massaccesi makes this an enjoyable film. The director, Oskar Faradine, is thought to be Massaccesi "twice-removed," hiding behind yet another pseudonym of "Oscar Santaniello," a name he later employed as a "producer" moniker for many films, including *Grim Reaper*, also called *Anthropophagus* (1980). Most likely, the scriptwriter (Scandariato Massaccesi) is secretly Aristide, too. If the research is correct, then this film would be Massaccesi's directorial debut, rather than the generally accepted *Death Smiles on a Murderer* (1973).

Bounty Hunters see Adios, Sabata

Bounty Killer see Ugly Ones

Un Bounty Killer a Trinità see Bounty Hunter in Trinity

Brandy see Ride and Kill

Bravo Django see Few Dollars for Django

Brennende Zelte in den schwarzen Bergen see Trail of the Falcon

Brother Outlaw (1971)

Rimase Uno Solo e Fu la Morte per Tutti Ital. *Director:* Edward G. Muller; *Script:* Alessandro Chiro/Edoardo Mulargia; *Camera:* Antonio Modica; *Music:* Gianfranco and Felice De Stefano; *Producer:* Tritone Filmindustria (Italy). *Cast:* Tony Kendall, James Rogers, Celso Faria, Sophia Kammar, Dean Stratford, Sergio Sagrotti, Mimma Maggio.

Dakota Thompson (Tony Kendall) is convicted on a bogus robbery charge, but his brother Slim (James Rogers) helps him escape from jail. The two men spend the rest of the film tracking down the real thieves, an outlaw gang led by notorious gunfighter Alvarez (Celso Faria) and the brain behind the schemes, Donovan (Dean Stratford). When the smoke clears, only Dakota remains alive.

Although he's made eight competent Spaghetti Westerns, director and cowriter Edward G. Muller (pseudonym for Edoardo Mulargia) is better known for his "women in an Amazon prison" movies, *Hotel Paradise* (oddly retitled in the U.S. as *Hell Fire on Ice*) and *Escape from Hell*.

Brothers Blue (1973)

Blu Gang Vissero per Sempre Felici e Ammazzati Ital. *Director:* Marc Meyer; *Script:* Augusto Caminito; *Camera:* Vittorio Storaro; *Music:* Tony Renis; *Producer:* B.R.C. (Italy/France). *Cast:* Jack Palance, Antonio Falsi, Guido Mannari, Tina Aumont, Maurizio Bonuglia, Lee Burton.

In a film obviously influenced by the on the lam pace of *Butch Cassidy and the Sundance Kid*, this is the story of the ill-fated Blue Gang as they are doggedly pursued by an unrelenting bounty hunter named Helliman (Jack Palance).

Marc Meyer is actually a pseudonym for director Luigi Bazzoni (see *Man: His Pride and His Vengeance*), who also uses the alias "Alex Burkes" (for *Long Ride from Hell*). His cinematographer, Vittorio Storaro, later won awards and critical acclaim for the remarkable camera work in Francis Ford Coppola's *Godfather* series. Scriptwriter Augusto Caminito went on to direct Klaus Kinski in the sequel to *Nosferatu* called *Nosferatu in Venice* (1988), plus he produced Kinski's controversially erotic *Paganini* (1989).

Bruciatelo Vivo see **Land Raiders**

Brute and the Beast see **Massacre Time**

Buckaroo see **Winchester Does Not Forgive**

Un Buco in Fronte see **Hole in the Forehead**

Buddy Goes West (1981)

Occhio alla Penna Ital. *Director:* Michele Lupo; *Script:* Sergio Donati; *Camera:* Franco Di Giacomo; *Music:* Ennio Morricone; *Producer:* Horst Wendlandt, Rialto Films (Italy). *Cast:* Bud Spencer, Amidou, Joe Bugner, Piero Trombetta, Carlo Reali, Sara Franchetti.

A lightweight (not a good description of Spencer's bulk) but entertaining Western comedy from director Michele Lupo (*Arizona Colt* also called *Man from Nowhere*) aided by a melodic Ennio Morricone score.

The meandering, episodic adventures of the "big" man and his dim-lit Indian sidekick do nothing for Bud Spencer's desire to escape the stereotypical image of the likeable brute.

Buffalo Bill, Hero of the Far West (1964)

Buffalo Bill, l'Eroe del Far West Ital.; *L'Attaque de Fort Adams*, Ital. *Director:* John W. Fordson; *Script:* Nino Stresa/Luciano Martino; *Camera:* Jack Dalmas; *Music:* Carlo Rustichelli; *Producer:* Solly Bianco, Filmes/Gloria/Corona (Italy/West Germany/French). *Cast:* Gordon Scott, Mario Brega, Jan Hendriks, Catherine Ribeiro, Piero Lulli, Mirko Ellis, Hans von Borsody, Roldano Lupi.

One of the original Eurowestern classics, released within days of Sergio Leone's *Fistful of Dollars* and Sergio Corbucci's *Minnesota Clay*. Former Peplum star, Gordon Scott, portrays the American hero in an oddly surreal, fictionalized account. None of the "fraud" elements suggested by Robert Altman in his Paul Newman vehicle, *Buffalo Bill and the Indians*, are even insinuated in this impractical, mythological homage.

Buffalo Bill, l'Eroe del Far West see **Buffalo Bill, Hero of the Far West**

In this one, Buffalo Bill is sent by President Grant into Sioux country to stop the young, rebellious Yellow Hand (Mirko Ellis) from buying stolen guns through trafficker Donaldson (Mario Brega, who looks like Bud Spencer possessed by the devil). His mission is further complicated by Indian-hating Colonel Peterson (Rolando Lupi), commander of Fort Adams. Director John W. Fordson, actually a pseudonym for Mario Costa, later made the less successful, Kinski as a cowboy sex killer *Beast* (also called *Rough Justice*), 1970. The cinematographer is future sleaze and action filmmaker Massimo Dallamano (who shot the Sergio Leone epics *Fistful of Dollars* and *For a Few Dollars More* using a "Jack Dalmas" moniker; plus, he directed a remarkable Spaghetti Western, *Bandidos,* under the "Max Dillman" alias). The story was written by veteran moviemaker Luciano Martino (interestingly, the father of future cult director Sergio Martino). Gordon Scott returned to the screen, wearing a cowboy hat, in Albert Band's *The Tramplers.*

Bullet for a Stranger see They Call Him Cemetery

Bullet for Sandoval (1969)

Vengeance Is Mine; Those Desperate Men Who Smell of Dirt and Death; Quei Disperati Che Puzzano di Sudore e di Morte Ital.; *Desperate Men.* Brit. *Director:* Julio Buchs; *Script:* José Mallorqui/Federico De Urrutia; *Camera:* Francisco Sempere; *Music:* Gianni Ferrio; *Producer:* Elio Scardamaglia/Ugo Guerra, Leone Film/Daiano/Atlantida (Italy/Spain). *Cast:* Ernest Borgnine, George Hilton, Annabella Incontrera, Alberto De Mendoza, Leo Anchóriz, Gustavo Rojo, Manuel Miranda, José Manuel Martin, Antonio Pica.

An Italian-Spanish coproduction combining the frequently used vengeance theme with the "Romeo and Juliet" motif, the result is an entertaining (but indulgent) film directed by Julio Buchs (alias Julio Garcia) who also made *The Man Who Killed Billy the Kid* and *Django Does Not Forgive.*

British-bred thespian George Hilton is a confederate deserter turned outlaw John Warner, bent on avenging his family's death. They had died of the plague while he was off fighting in the Civil War. Their rich neighbor and landlord Don Pedro Sandoval (Ernest Borgnine) had done nothing to help them, thus making him (at least in Warner's eyes) responsible for their deaths. The whole thing is further complicated by the fact that the outlaw is secretly "carrying on" with Sandoval's daughter Rosa (a talented, beautiful actress with a wonderful name, Annabella Incontrera).

Bullet for the General (1966)

Quien Sabe? Ital. *Director:* Damiano Damiani; *Script:* Salvatore Laurani/Franco Solinas; *Camera:* Antonio Secchi; *Music:* Luis Enrique Bacalov; *Producer:* Bianco Manini, M.C.M. (Italy). *Cast:* Gian Maria Volonté, Lou Castel, Klaus Kinski, Martine Beswick, Andrea Checchi, Spartaco Conversi, Joaquin Parra, Aldo Sambrell.

Here is Gian Maria Volonté *(For a Few Dollars More* and *Face to Face)* in one of his finest roles as the renegade Mexican Revolutionary general, El Chuncho. Lou Castel plays "blonde gringo" Bill, who joins the marauding guerrillas after they attack and annihilate a train. Bill's true interests are unclear but, seemingly, he is a bandit and wants to join with El Chuncho for personal greed-oriented reasons. As the general eventually discovers, that's not quite the truth. Bill is actually a hired mercenary for the Mexican government, and at the film's conclusion, he thinks that he has convinced El Chuncho to betray the revolution and return with him to society. However, in a surprise ending, the general (while singing the liberation anthem) kills Bill.

An amazingly good film, with a singularly impressive Luis Enrique Bacalov musical score, perhaps his best. Cameraman Antonio Secchi (director of *Caliber .38*) also photographed many Spaghetti Westerns under his pseudonym, Tony Dry.

Klaus Kinski turns in another typically brief, but effective, performance as El Santo, the general's bloodthirsty assistant. Well-rounded Martine Beswick went on to play the lead cavegirl in Hammer's *Prehistoric Women* (1967), then, "Sister Hyde" in *Dr. Jekyll and Sister Hyde* (1971) and, later, "the Queen of Death" in Oliver Stone's first film, *Seizure* (1974).

Ten years later, Director Damiano Damiani returned to the Eurowestern genre with *The Genius*, or *Trinity Is Back Again*. He is best known for *Confessions of a Police Captain* (1970) and *The Empty Canvas* (1964), plus an overlooked, but excellent, horror film, *The Witch* (1966), *The Devil Is a Woman* (1975), *Goodbye and Amen* (1978) and (strangely) *Amityville Horror 2: The Possession* (1982).

Bullet from God see *God's Gun*

Bullets and the Flesh (1965)

Il Piombo e il Carne Ital.; *I Sentieri dell'Odio* Ital. *Director:* Fred Wilson; *Script:* Marino Girolami/Gino De Santis; *Camera:* Mario Fioretti; *Music:* Carlo Savina; *Producer:* Hercules Film/Orphée/Arturo Gonzales (Italy/France/Spain). *Cast:* Rod Cameron, Patricia Viterbo, Thomas Moore, Dan Harrison, Manolo Zarzo, Marie Versini, Alfredo Mayo, Enzo Girolami, Julio Peña.

Once again, it is the "Romeo and Juliet" theme transposed to the old West. A white girl, Mabel (Patricia Viterbo), is in love with a Cherokee brave (Dan Harrison). None of the parents approve; however, her father, Masters (Rod Cameron), is especially indignant over the affair because it reminds him of his wife's suicide resulting from a rendezvous with an Indian, years before.

A subplot finds the devious bigot, Masters, setting fire to the trees on his land and blaming the Indians so he can get lumber rights to their Holy Forest. It is a last ditch effort to fulfill his "wooden track" commitment to the railroad.

This early Spaghetti Western from veteran director Mariono Girolami (using the Fred Wilson alias) is influenced more by "Hollywood" than the budding Euro counterparts. But it is still entertaining. The "Enzo Girolami" in the cast is one of Marino's two sons (his other show biz son is actor Ennio). Enzo later became popular cult filmmaker Enzo G. Castellari.

Bullets Don't Argue (1964)

Las Pistolas no Discuten Sp; *Le Pistole non Discutono* Ital. *Director:* Mike Perkins; *Script:* Frank Foster; *Camera:* Julio Ortas; *Music:* Ennio Morricone; *Producer:* Atlantis Film/Rialto Films/S.N.C. (Italy/West Germany/Spain). *Cast:*

Rod Cameron, Horst Frank, Angel Aranda, Vivi Bach, Ludwig Duran, Dick Palmer, Hans Nielsen, José M. Martin.

Workhorse director Mario Caiano (using the Mike Perkins moniker) has made an engaging Spaghetti Western here, telling the story of a sheriff (Rod Cameron) who goes into Mexico in pursuit of two bandido brothers, Ike and Logan Clanton (Horst Frank and Angel Aranda).

The Clanton boys had robbed the bank while Sheriff Johnston was getting married. Angry because of the inconvenience, Johnston wastes no time finding the outlaws. His big problem comes next when he tries to take them and the $30,000 back to the United States. Unfortunately, a gang of mercenaries (with their own ideas about who should get the money) had also followed them into the desert. There's lots of action plus a slam-bang ending.

Buon Funerale Amigos . . . Paga Sartana see *Have a Good Funeral, My Friend . . . Sartana Will Pay*

Il Buono, il Brutto, il Cattivo see *The Good, the Bad, and the Ugly*

Bury Them Deep (1968)

To the Last Drop of Blood; All'Ultimo Sangue Ital. *Director:* John Byrd; *Script:* Enzo Dell'Aquila/Paolo Moffa; *Camera:* Franco Villa/Aristide Massaccesi; *Music:* Nico Fidenco/Willy Brezza; *Producer:* Oscar Santianello, Ambrosiana Film (Italy). *Cast:* Craig Hill, Ettore Manni, Ken Wood, José Greci, Francesco Santoveti, Luciano Doria.

The title *(Bury Them Deep)* has no relation to the plot of the film; instead it is meant to set a mood, specifically the violent macho tone singular to the Spaghetti Westerns (similar to other interchangeable titles, *Today It's Me . . . Tomorrow You, Find a Place to Die, Heads You Die . . . Tails I Kill You, Hole in the Forehead,* etc.). Enzo Dell'Aquila, who directed *Time and Place for Killing* under the "Vincent Eagle" pseudonym, cowrote this story with director Paolo Moffa (using the "John Byrd" alias), interestingly aided by the "borrowing" of the sets from *For a Few Dollars More,* particularly the fortress-like bank and the scrubbed white adobe village (also highlighted in *Days of Hate*).

A bandit, Johnny Gunn (Ken Wood), has robbed the payroll gold from an army convoy. Bounty hunter Clive Norton (Craig Hill) is hired to find the outlaw and the booty. He enlists the aid of Gunn's imprisoned brother Chaleco Hunter (Ettore Manni); he abducts Chaleco during his execution ceremony and convinces him to help in the pursuit. Later, a Mexican outlaw Kordero (Francesco Santovetti) joins them as well. He, of course, has ulterior motives and eventually betrays the two heroes by switching sides at an inopportune moment and teams up with Gunn. The finale features a four-way showdown. Norton and Chaleco emerge victorious.

Ken Wood (alias Giovanni Cianfriglia), who also starred in Enzo G. Castellari's *Keoma* and Frank Kramer's *Sabata* (see Performers filmography for complete listing), began his career as a stand-in for Steve Reeves in various peplums and later played the title role in Nick Nostro's *Super Argo* films *(Super Argo* and *Super Argo vs. Diabolicus).*

Calibre .38 (1971)

Panhandle Calibre .38; Padella Calibro .38; Poëlla Calibro .38; E alla Fine lo Chiamavano Jerusalem l'Implacabile Ital. *Director:* Toni Secchi; *Script:* Mario Amendola/Tony Dry/Massimo Franciosa; *Camera:* Giorgio Regis; *Music:* Franco Micalizzi; *Producer:* Montagna/Franciosa Films (Italy). *Cast:* Scott Holden, Alberto Dell'Acqua, Keenan Wynn, Mimmo Palmara, Ray O'Connor, Carla Mancini, Ted Carter, Philippe Leroy.

Here's another variation on the "big trouble with the town boss" theme, as Jerusalem Wade (Scott Holden, son of actor William Holden), a benevolent gunfighter (and sometimes bounty hunter), tries to help his sister in a struggle against a wealthy land baron, Kile Richards (Keenan Wynn, son of popular 40s comedian, Ed Wynn).

The film is (mostly) significant as a curiosity item, chiefly because it's the only genre outing directed by popular cinematographer Toni Secchi (aka Tony Dry), responsible for lensing many of the better Spaghetti Westerns, including Calvin Jackson Padget's *Wanted* and Carlo Lizzani's *The Hills Run Red.*

California (1976)

Lo Chiamavano California Ital. *Director:* Michele Lupo; *Script:* Franco Bucceri/Roberto Leoni; *Camera:* Alejandro Ulloa; *Music:* Gianni Ferrio; *Producer:* Manolo Bolognini, Cinematografica/José Frade (Italy Spain). *Cast:* Giuliano Gemma, William Berger, Malisa Longo, Raimund Harmstorf, Chris Avram, Paola Bosè, Dana Ghia, Alfio Caltabiano, Robert Hundar, Miguel Bosè, Tom Felleghy, Franco Ressel, Diana Lorys.

Grittily photographed in a continuous blend of earth tones, browns with dark greens and burgundy reds, this film is a long and rambling tale about a displaced Southern soldier, California (Giuliano Gemma). It is directed by one of the genre's best filmmakers, Michele Lupo (see Directors filmography), who died unexpectedly from a heart attack in 1989.

The Civil War is over. And, after being released from a Union prison (in a segment reminiscent of Gemma's 1965 *Blood for a Silver Dollar*), California is aimlessly traveling through Missouri, looking for some purpose to his war-torn life. He finds the hanged body of a former comrade (executed for stealing a horse in enthusiastic zeal to get home and see his parents and sister, Helen) so, California decides to complete the journey for him. He takes the soldier's belongings to his family's ranch where he meets Helen (Malisa Longo). It's love at first sight. California agrees to stay on and help with the chores around the farm.

Before long, the peaceful ranchers are visited by a gang of outlaws, with a band of bounty hunters close behind. There's a massive, bloody gunfight. California is wounded, Helen kidnapped, and everybody else is murdered by the sadistic bounty killer Rupp Whittaker (Raimund Harmstorf). A journalist named Nelson (Chris Avram) accompanies California as he goes after Rupp and his band of mercenaries. Eventually, Helen is rescued and all the bad guys are destroyed.

After establishing himself in a long and impressive list of Spaghetti Westerns (see Performers filmography), William Berger continued his career into the 90s. His most significant later films include Marcello Avalone's *Maya*

(1988), and *Control* (1987) directed by Giuliano Montaldo. Actress Malisa Longo starred in most of the Al Bradly interchangeable science fiction *War of the Planets* films, plus a collection of Eurociné war 'n' torture sleaze fests (i.e., *S. S. Fraulein Devil, Hell Train, She Wolf of Spilberg*). Alfio Caltabiano is best known as a director (for *Man Called Amen, Ballad of a Gunman* and *They Still Call Me Amen*).

Camino de Fuerte Alamo see *Road to Fort Alamo*

Camino de Sur see *Seen Guns from Texas*

Campa Carogna . . . la Taglia Cresce see *Those Dirty Dogs!*

Canada Salvaje see *Canadian Wilderness*

Canadian Wilderness (1969)

Rebeldes en Canada; Rebels in Canada; Revolt in Canada; Canada Salvaje Sp. *Director:* Armando De Ossorio; *Script:* Armando De Ossorio; *Camera:* Pablo Ripoll; *Music:* Carlo Savina; *Producer:* Coperfilm/Produzioni Eurpee (Spain/Italy). *Cast:* George Martin, Diana Lorys, Luis Marin, Santiago Rivero, Pamela Tudor, Franco Fantasia, Raf Baldassare, Francisco Nieto, Giovanni Petti, Mirko Ellis.

A plodding adventure-oriented Western dealing with the problems of settlers in the rugged Canadian wilderness. These hearty pioneers encounter hostile Indians, plus every conceivable type of natural disaster. The whole thing is very reminiscent of "White Fang" movies, but without the dog.

Popular composer Daniel White is responsible for the theme, *Los Arboles Blancos (The White Trees)*, which sounds like something that should be played during a ride in Disney World while a bevy of stuffed animals dance arm in arm.

O' Cangaceiro see *Viva Cangaceiro*

Captain Apache (1971)

Captain Apache Brit. *Director:* Alexander Singer; *Script:* Philip Yordan/Stuart E. Whitman/Milton Sperling; *Camera:* John Cabrera; *Music:* Dolores Claman/Pepe Nieto; *Producer:* Milton Sperling/Philip Yordan, Scotia International (England/Spain). *Cast:* Lee Van Cleef, Carroll Baker, Stuart Whitman, Elisa Montes, Charlie Bravo, Percy Herbert, Tony Vogel.

This is a British-Spanish Western directed by Alexander Singer, best known for his movies made for U.S. TV *(Return of Marcus Welby, Hunters of the Reef* and *Time Travelers).* He is annoyingly "out of his element" here. Plus a wretched miscasting job finds Lee Van Cleef looking especially naked without his mustache *and* wearing an embarrassingly goofy Indian wig.

He's supposed to be the vindictive Captain Apache, hired to track down the Indian Commissioner's killer. Stuart Whitman (in another over-the-top scenery-chewing role) wants to assassinate President Grant. Carroll Baker is the white woman who (biblically) knows them both.

Carroll Baker, forever known as "Baby Doll" (due to the controversial 1956 Tennessee Williams/Elia Kazan film), also made quite a few Giallos (Italian thrillers) for director Umberto Lenzi throughout the late 60s and 70s (i.e., *Paranoia, So Sweet . . . So Perverse, Orgasmo,* and *Detras del Silencio*), plus one for Eugenio Martino *(Death at the Deep End of the Swimming Pool).*

Actor Charlie Bravo was featured in a goodly number of Spaghetti Westerns (see Performers filmography), but his starring role didn't come until *Scalps* in 1987. Incidentally, wearing a grizzled hat and carrying a rifle (as if he just walked off the set of a Western), he played a part in the Italian-made Alice Cooper horror pic *Monster Dog* (1986).

In a particularly embarrassing moment, Lee Van Cleef sings (!) the opening theme song to this film, with amazingly inept lyrics like: "They tail me/ trail me/ try to nail me there/ but they haven't got a prayer." Believe it, or not.

Carambola (1974)

Carambola Ital. *Director:* Ferdinando Baldi; *Script:* Mino Roli/Nico Ducci/Ferdinando Baldi; *Camera:* Aiace Parolini; *Music:* Franco Bixio/Vince Tempera; *Producer:* Armando Todaro, Elos Flms (Italy). *Cast:* Paul Smith, Michael Coby, Horst Frank, William Bogart, Pino Ferrara, Franco Fantasia, Pedro Sanchez.

An unabashed and total ripoff of the "Trinity" series, featuring "Terence Hill/Bud Spencer" lookalike clones: Michael Coby (Antonio Cantafora) and Paul Smith (best known for his "Bluto" in the movie version of *Popeye*). However, the emphasis is on more action (Ferdinando Baldi's influence) and less humor, plus the film has an impressive supporting cast. Both of these elements contribute positively to an (otherwise) bleak motion picture experience.

Two con-men, Coby and Lynn Butch (Coby and Smith), become wary (or maybe, weary) partners when they escape from prison together. While "laying low" in Desert City, they find themselves sucked into a gun trafficking scheme headed by the shifty town boss, Howard (William Bogart). The highlight of the film is an unexpected (and unrelated) kung fu fight (big man Lynn against a martial arts school) photographed in weird, distorting mirrors.

Most of the "Trinity gags" are bewilderingly pilfered and recycled including the famous "gun-slap/gun-slap/gun-slap." There are also Indians that actually greet with "How," plus a remarkably decadent Coby-in-drag sequence. The music is a wacky combination of an insipid theme, *(Hello) You Can Fly* sung by the Dream Bags (!?!), and Bixio/Tempera's Spanish-influenced compositions very reminiscent of the 60s pop hit *Come a Little Bit Closer.*

Besides his many Spaghetti Westerns (see Directors filmography), Ferdinando Baldi directed *David and Goliath* with Orson Welles, *Killers' Company, The Sicilian Connection* starring Ben Gazzara and Malisa Longo, *Tenzan, Warbus,* plus the "Indiana Jones" ripoff *Treasure of the Four Crowns* with Tony Anthony. He continues to be an active Italian filmmaker, usually working under the pseudonym "Ted Kaplan."

Carambola's Filosofo . . . Tutti in Buca see *Carambola's Philosophy*

Carambola's Philosophy: In the Right Pocket (1974/5)

Carambola Filosofo . . . Tutti in Buca Ital. *Director:* Ferdinando Baldi; *Script:* Ferdinando Baldi/Nico Ducci/Mino Roli; *Camera:* Aiace Parolini; *Music:* Franco

Bixio/Vince Tempera; *Producer:* Armando Todaro, Elos Films (Italy). *Cast:* Paul Smith, Michael Coby, Clauco Ontario, Gabriela Andreini, Giovanni Pazzafini, Piero Lulli.

There is some evidence that the two "Carambola" films were shot back to back, or possibly at the same time (most notably, there are similar credits plus an identical soundtrack). Also, the plot is an extension of the first film, but without town boss Howard (William Bogart).

Coby and Lynn Butch (Michael Coby and Paul Smith) are two *Trinity*-esque con-men (Terence Hill and Bud Spencer clones) who make a living by exploiting their unique attributes. Lynn, a bear of a man, wagers on "physical bets" (like personal tugs-of-war and boxing matches), while Coby cleans up as a skilled pool shark (thus, the title).

The film is a lightweight Western spoof of *The Hustler* with an inordinate amount of time spent inside a saloon pool hall. The "amazing" pool table tricks are disappointingly achieved through the magic of stop-action animation. It's not impressive.

The lightweight Terence Hill/Bud Spencer clone team of "Coby and Smith" didn't stop with the two *Carambola* films. They also continued the paltry impersonations into the action/adventures genre with a rip-off of the Hill and Spencer jungle paradise films (i.e., Sergio Corbucci's *Whoever Finds a Friend . . . Finds a Treasure,* Italo Zingarelli's *I'm for the Hippopotamus*) called *Diamond Peddler* (1977), directed by Anthony Ascott. Plus, a sequel called *Kid's Stuff* (1978).

La Carga de la Policia Montada see *Cavalry Charge*

La Carica del 7 Cavalleggeri see *Charge of the Seventh Cavalry*

Carogne Si Nasce see *If One Is Born a Swine*

Cavalco e Uccidi see *Ride and Kill*

Cavalry Charge (1964)

La Carga de la Policia Montada Sp. *Director:* Ramon Torrado; *Script:* Ramon Torrado; *Camera:* Ricardo Torres; *Music:* Daniel J. White; *Producer:* CC Trebol Films (Spain). *Cast:* Alan Scott, Frank Latimore, Diana Lorys, Maria Silva, Alfonso Rojas, Juan Cortes, Barta Barry.

Little is known about this esoteric Spanish production. Apparently, poor distribution relegated it to a limited regional run without much success. Director Ramon Torrado fared much better with *Shoot to Kill* the previous year.

Composer Daniel White is best known for scoring dozens of Jess Franco films. He even played a supporting role in Franco's *La Fille de Dracula*.

C'è Sartana, Vendi la Pistola e Comprati la Bara see *I Am Sartana . . . Trade Your Guns for a Coffin*

Cemetery Without Crosses (1968)

The Rope and the Colt; Cimitero Senza Croci Ital.; Une Corde, un Colt Fr. Director: Robert Hossein; Script: Dario Argento/Robert Hossein/Claude DeSailly; Camera: Henri Persin; Music: André Hossein; Producer: Fono Foma/Coisias du Monoe Film (Italy/France). Cast: Michèle Mercier, Robert Hossein, Lee Burton, Daniel Vargas, Anne-Marie Balin, Ivano Staccioli, Sergio Leone, Serge Marquand, Pierre Collet.

Italian cult filmmaker Dario Argento contributed cowriting skills to an otherwise French dominated production, helmed mostly by Robert Hossein (with musical assistance from his brother, André). Robert Hossein (the star, the director and the cowriter for this film) is best known for his role in Warrior's Rest (1963) as the psychopathic drifter who drives Brigitte Bardot insane, plus his performance in Claude Lelouch's ambitious (but tediously slow) art film Bolero (1982). He also received critical acclaim for directing the controversial I Killed Rasputin (1967) with Geraldine Chaplin.

This film is a rather cautious variation on the vengeance-for-a-slaughtered-family theme as a gunfighter (Hossein) takes revenge against a wealthy land baron (Serge Marquand) who killed his best friend and married his former love (Michèle Mercier). Of special historical note, famed Western director Sergio Leone is featured in a cameo part as the hotel desk clerk.

Michèle Mercier went on to star in a series of Angelique sex farces, German-produced comedies usually featuring male leads like Glenn Saxson and Jeff Hunter.

American pop artist Scott Walker sings this film's opening theme song, Rope and the Colt, which became a surprise smash hit in England.

100.000 Dollari per Lassiter see Dollars for a Fast Gun

100.000 Dollari per Ringo see $100,000 for Ringo

5000 Dollari sull'Asso see $5000 on One Ace

C'era una Volta il West see Once Upon a Time in the West

C'era una Volta questo Pazzo Pazzo West see Once Upon a Time in the Wild, Wild West

Chakmull, l'Uomo della Vendetta see Chuck Moll

Challenge of Pancho Villa see Pancho Villa

Challenge of the Mackennas (1969)

Badlands Drifters; Sfida dei MacKenna Ital. Director: Leon Klimovsky; Script: José L. Navarro; Camera: Francisco Sanches Muñoz; Music: Francesco De Masi; Producer: Filmar Cinematografica (Italy/Spain). Cast: Robert Woods, John Ireland, Annabella Incontrera, Vidal Molina, Roberto Camardiel, Ken Wood, Daniela Giordano.

John Ireland's character (Jones) sums up the plot to this film when he says:

"I don't want to run anymore. I've got the feeling this is where I've been running to." Basically, it's the story of a drifter who gets caught in a range war between two powerful ranchers.

Filmed under the working title *A Dollar and a Grave*, this is one of Leon Klimovsky's better movies about power, revenge and greed. The prolific director has done everything from horror *(Vengeance of the Zombies* and *Night of the Werewolf)* to Westerns (also see *Reverend Colt, Rattler Kid,* and *Few Dollars for Django,* to name a few). Unfortunately, his static type of "zoom and pan" filmmaking usually offers limited entertainment value, but this time he's subsidized by an exceptional cast.

Chapaqua see Gold of the Heroes

Charge of the Seventh Cavalry (1964)

Assault on Fort Texan; Hornon of Fort Worth; La Carica del 7 Cavalleggeri Ital.; **L'Assault du Fort Texan,** Fr. *Director:* Herbert Martin; *Script:* Eduardo M. Brochero/Eduardo Manzanos; *Camera:* Eloy Mella; *Music:* Gianni Ferrio; *Producer:* Emo Bistolfi, Fenix Film (Italy/Spain/France). *Cast:* Edmund Purdom, Paul Piaget, Priscilla Steele, Aurora Julia, Isarco Ravaioli, Miguel Del Castillo, Eduardo Fajardo, Tomás Blanco.

Here is another Spaghetti Western with a cockeyed view of American history. It's 1863. The Civil War is in full action, but Arkansas and Texas have requested permission to step out of the conflict (!?!). This has, obviously, put Confederate General Lee in a compromising position. He sends a regiment of soldiers off to Mexico to request reinforcements from the South's ally, Emperor Maximilian. But the unit is stopped at Wichita Pass by the Northern Seventh Cavalry. It looks hopeless for the South, until Sugar (Edmund Purdom) gets help from an Indian girl, Amanda (Aurora Julia), who convinces her tribe to counterattack the Union army.

This film is directed by Alberto De Martino (under his "Herbert Martin" alias). In addition to his Westerns (see Directors filmography), De Martino has amassed a remarkable amount of nongenre favorites, including *Medusa vs. the Son of Hercules* (1962), *The Blancheville Monster* (1960), *Man with the Icy Eyes* (1970), *Strange Shadows in an Empty Room* (1976), *Holocaust 2000* (1978), and *Miami Horror* (1985).

Charley One-Eye (1972)

Director: Don Chaffey; *Script:* Keith Leonard/Don Chaffey; *Camera:* Don Chaffey; *Music:* John Cameron; *Producer:* James Swann, Paramount (England/Spain). *Cast:* Richard Roundtree, Roy Thinnes, Nigel Davenport, Jill Pearson, Aldo Sambrell, Luis Aller.

Another British attempt to cash in on the Spaghetti Western craze (also see *Hannie Caulder, Town Called Hell, Hunting Party, Captain Apache* and *Shalako),* but director Don Chaffey's limited knowledge of the Western genre is sadly showing. Best remembered for his fantasy flicks *(Jason and the Argonauts* and *One Million Years B.C.)* plus Disney family features *(Pete's Dragon* and *The Magic of Lassie),* Chaffey (with cowriter Keith Leonard) tries to make an allegorical "adult" Western, however the tiresome "brotherhood and unity" theme is so incredibly naive that the movie (despite all its gruff posturing) seems very juvenile.

Two misfits (Richard Roundtree as a black deserter from the Union army; Roy Thinnes, doing his cockeyed best but it's not convincing at all, as a crippled Indian) meet in the desert. They create a home inside an abandoned church, but lose everything when a bounty hunter (Nigel Davenport) shows up.

Che C'Entriamo Noi con la Rivoluzione? see *What Am I Doing in the Middle of the Revolution?*

Chetan, Indian Boy (1972)

Tschetan der Indianer Junge Ger. *Director:* Mark Bohm; *Script:* Mark Bohm; *Camera:* Michael Ballhaus; *Music:* Peer Raben; *Producer:* Produktion 1 Im Filmverlag (Germany). *Cast:* Marquard Bohm, Deschingis Bowakow, Willy Schultes, Horst Schram.

A quiet movie. A sentimental story of two outsiders, an elderly rancher and an orphaned Indian boy. It focuses mainly on the bittersweet relationship between the two, and how Chetan (Deschingis Bowakow) copes with life when the old man (director Marquard "Mark" Bohm) eventually dies. Don't expect a lot of action.

Cinematographer Michael Ballhaus later moved to America where he found himself much in demand, working constantly for Martin Scorsese and many others.

Chiedi Perdono a Dio ... Non a Me see *May God Forgive You ... But I Won't*

China 9, Liberty 37 (1978)

Clayton and Catherine Brit.; *Love, Bullets and Frenzy; Amore, Piombo e Furore* Ital. *Director:* Monte Hellman; *Script:* Jerry Harvey/Douglas Venturelli; *Camera:* Giuseppe Rotunno; *Music:* Pino Donaggio; *Producer:* Gianni Bozzacchi/Valerio De Paolis (Italy/Spain/U.S.). *Cast:* Fabio Testi, Warren Oates, Jenny Agutter, Sam Peckinpah, Luis Prendes, Gianrico Tondivelli, Charlie Bravo, Helga Line.

Some railroad men save a notorious gunfighter named Shaw (Fabio Testi) from the gallows because they need him to do "some dirty work." They want him to kill a farmer, Sebanek (Warren Oates). Seemingly, his land is in the railroad's way and the farmer won't sell.

Shaw goes to the ranch, but he doesn't kill Sebanek. Instead he befriends him. A bit later, he cuckolds the farmer when he makes love to Catherine (Jenny Agutter), Sebanek's wife (secretly a gunfighter groupie). The rail barons find out that Shaw failed and they send out more men, this time to kill him.

Eventually Shaw and farmer Sebanek team together to defeat the railroad men (accompanied by newspaper reporter Wilber Olsen, played by American *Wild Bunch* director, Sam Peckinpah). After the gunfight, Shaw leaves. The farmer gives his wife the option to chase after the gunman, but she decides to stay with her husband. Together they torch the farm as a symbolic gesture of starting a new life together (similar to the ending of *Chino*).

Record jacket of the soundtrack from *China 9, Liberty 7* (1978).

This Italian-Spanish-U.S. coproduction is directed by U.S. filmmaker Monte Hellman, best known for the anti-establishment movie *Two-Lane Blacktop* and a "gangsters meet the monster" flick, *Beast from Haunted Cave*. After this film, he didn't make another one for ten years, when he released *Iguana.* Costar Jenny Agutter is the beauty from *American Werewolf in London* and *Logans Run* (remember the nude scene in the lake?).

The haunting music is composed by Pino Donaggio who also did the score for Brian DePalma's *Dressed to Kill* and *Body Double*. Of special note, the soundtrack album (see photo) lists (an otherwise unknown) Antonio Brandt as director, not Monte Hellman. Curious.

Incidentally, the odd title comes from a mile-marker sitting at a crossroad adjacent to Sebanek's farm, pointing "China 9 miles" (to the right) and "Liberty 37" (to the left).

Chino (1973)

The Valdez Horses; Valdez, il Mezzosangue Ital. *Director:* John Sturges; *Script:* Dino Maiuri/Massimo De Rita/Clair Huffaker; *Camera:* Armando Nannuzzi;

Music: Guido and Maurizio de Angelis; *Producer:* Duilio Coletti, Coral Film (Italy/Spain/France). *Cast:* Charles Bronson, Jill Ireland, Marcel Bozzuffi, Vincent Van Patten, Fausto Tozzi, Ettore Manni, Diana Lorys, Melissa Chimenti.

Here's a Spaghetti Western from American director John Sturges (*Magnificent Seven, Bad Day at Black Rock, The Great Escape, Gunfight at the OK Corral, Hour of the Gun,* etc.), his only movie produced and financed by European motion picture companies. Shot entirely in Spain, this film remains curiously anticlimactic (for both Sturges and Charles Bronson). Rather than portraying a vengeance-seeking vigilante, Bronson plays a sensitive man who wants nothing more than to be left alone. Very unusual, especially since he had just found such tremendous success with his macho role in *The Mechanic* (1972).

A halfbreed horse rancher named Chino (Charles Bronson) clashes with a prejudiced land baron, Maral (Marcel Bozzuffi), when he falls in love with the bigot's sister, Louise (Jill Ireland). Obviously, Maral doesn't like the idea of the interracial romance very much, so he has Chino beaten and tortured. When Chino returns to his ranch, he destroys everything, burning it to the ground (primarily to keep Maral from taking it) and rides off into the sunset.

Interestingly, German and Dutch prints of this film list producer Duilio Coletti as the director. It's a curious error which has led to considerable (and apparently unfounded) speculation regarding John Sturges' actual involvement.

"Bad guy" actor Marcel Buzzuffi made numerous crime films for Max Dillman (alias Massimo Dallamano) throughout the 70s. And scriptwriter Dino Maiuri (with American filmmaker Henry Levin) wrote and codirected the 1966 Mike Connors spy film, *Kiss the Girls and Make Them Die.*

Christmas Kid (1966)

Joe Navidad Sp.; *Lo Sceriffo Senza Stella* Ital. *Director:* Sidney Pink; *Script:* James Henaghan Rodrigo Rivero; *Camera:* Manuel Hernandez Sanjuan; *Music:* F. Garcia Morcillo; *Producer:* Sidney Pink (Spain/Italy). *Cast:* Jeffrey Hunter, Louis Hayward, Gustavo Rojo, Perla Cristal, Luis Prendes, Reginald Gilliam, Jack Taylor.

Displaced U.S. filmmaker Sidney Pink directs this good (don't judge a movie by the title) Italian-Spanish production (also see his *The Tall Women* and *Finger on the Trigger*).

Valuable copper is discovered in Jasper, Arizona, transforming the city (seemingly overnight) from a sleepy community into a bustling boom town, filled with corruption and greed, prostitution and gambling. The Christmas Kid (so named because his mother died on Christmas Eve while giving birth) is played by Jeffrey Hunter. Upon arriving in Jasper, the Kid is hired as a gunman for the new (and dishonest) town boss (Louis Hayward). But when his girlfriend, Lisa (Perla Cristal), is killed, the Kid switches sides and, acting as sheriff, tries to bring an end to the widespread lawlessness.

Chief cameraman is Manuel Hernandez Sanjaun, working from a script penned by Jim Henaghan and Rodrigo Rivero. Actress Perla Cristal is best known for her starring role in Jess Franco's *Awful Dr. Orloff.*

Jeffrey Hunter became popular (or perhaps, infamous) for playing the role of Jesus Christ in the Nicholas Ray film, *King of Kings* (1961). American critics were so unkind to his performance that he left the United States for "greener pastures" in Europe, primarily making films in Italy and Germany. He starred in three Spaghetti Westerns (see Performers filmography) plus a variety of other exploitation features including José M. Elorrieta's *Witch Without a Broom* (1967), but he never recovered from the nasty notices. Jeffrey began drinking heavily, and eventually died in 1969, after falling down the stairs in his home.

Chrysanthemums for a Bunch of Swine (1968)

Crisantemi per un Branco di Carogne Ital. *Director:* Sergio Pastore; *Script:* Sergio Pastore/Dino Santoni/John Manera; *Camera:* Dino Santoni; *Music:* Piero Umiliani; *Producer:* Società Cine Artisti Alleati (Italy). *Cast:* Edmund Purdom, John Manera, Marilena Possenti, Ivano Davoli, Livio Lorenzon, Joseph Logan.

Malo (John Manera) and his outlaw gang invade a small city where a wedding is taking place. They raid the church and kidnap the bride Sharon (Marilena Possenti), taking her to an abandoned monastery where she is rescued by a mysterious sharp-shooting monk (Edmund Purdom).

An oddity with music by prolific Piero Umiliani, based on a script by the cameraman, Dino Santoni. This film is director Pastore's only Western; his cult reputation is based on bloody thriller-type crime movies (like *Crimes of the Black Cat* with Anthony Steffen).

Chuck Moll (1970)

Unholy Four; Chakmull, l'Uomo della Vendetta Ital. *Director:* E. B. Clucher; *Script:* Franco Rossetti; *Camera:* Mario Montuori; *Music:* Riz Ortolani; *Producer:* Manolo Bolognini, B.R.C./Atlas (Italy). *Cast:* Leonard Mann, Woody Strode, Peter Martell, Helmut Schneider, Dino Strano, Evelyn Stewart, Luigi Montefiore, Andrew Ray.

Written by prolific scenarist Franco Rossetti (also director of the *Big Rip-off*), this is a good action Western with Leonard Mann in the stoic (yet, sullen) role of Chuck Moll. He's a man suffering from amnesia, a rather universal motion picture theme, also employed in the Spaghetti Westerns *A Man Called Noon* and *Twice a Judas*.

The plot, specifically, has to do with a man (Helmut Schneider) posing as Chuck's father, attempting to trick him into killing an arch enemy, who happens to be Chuck's real father. This uncommon (but welcome) serious film from E. B. Clucher (pseudonym for former cinematograther Enzo Barboni) plays better than it sounds. After the tremendous international success of his *Trinity* series, the director concentrated on mostly comedy/action movies, usually starring Terence Hill and Bud Spencer.

Incidentally, George Eastman gives a marvelous supporting performance under his real name, Luigi Montefiore. It's also interesting to note that actor Woody Strode went from appearing in John Ford Westerns (i.e., *The Man Who Shot Liberty Valance* and *Two Rode Together*) to the Spaghettis (see Performers filmography).

Ci Ridiamo, Vero Provvidenza? see *Here We Are Again, Eh Providence?*

Movie poster from *Chuck Moll* (1970).

Ciccio Forgives, I Don't (1968)

Ciccio Perdona . . . Io No! Ital. *Director:* Frank Reed; *Script:* Amedeo Sollazzo/
Marcello Ciorciolini; *Camera:* Alessandro D'Eva; *Music:* Roberto Pregadio/
Mario Capuano; *Producer:* P.E.A. (Italy). *Cast:* Franco Franchi, Ciccio Ingrassia,
Fernando Sancho, Adriano Micantoni, Mario Maranzana, Gia Sandri.

"Franco and Ciccio" are an Italian comedy team, similar to America's Abbott and Costello. Their emphasis is on broad "lowest common denominator" humor and they are responsible for over 150 movies (23 made in 1965–66 alone). Most of their films are silly slapstick parodies that capitalize on other popular movies or fads (*The Handsome, the Ugly, and the Stupid; Two Sons of Trinity; Two R-R-Ringos from Texas;* etc.).

In the case of this film, the title (but not the plot) is stolen from the movie *God Forgives, I Don't.* Director Frank Reed (pseudonym for Marcello Ciorciolini) tells the goofy story of two insurance salesmen (Franco and Ciccio) trying to sell accident coverage to outlaws (particularly to El Pantera played by Fernando Sancho).

Ciccio Perdona . . . Io No! see *Ciccio Forgives, I Don't*

Cimitero Senza Croci see *Cemetery Without Crosses*

I Cinque della Vendetta see *Five Giants from Texas*

Cinque Dollari per Ringo see *Five Dollars for Ringo*

Cipolla Colt (1975)

Spaghetti Western; Cry Onion; Cipolla Colt Ital. *Director:* Enzo G. Castellari; *Script:* Sergio Donati/Luciano Vincenzoni; *Camera:* Alejandro Ulloa; *Music:* Guido and Maurizio De Angelis; *Producer:* Filmes Cinematografica (Italy/Germany). *Cast:* Franco Nero, Martin Balsam, Sterling Hayden, Dick Butkus, Leo Anchoriz, Romano Puppo, Emma Cohen.

It is difficult to imagine a worse movie. Even the Franco and Ciccio films aren't as offensively inept (at least you know what to expect from them and can brace yourself).

This stupid, slapstick drivel about an onion farmer, Stark (Franco Nero), who owns the last independent acre in a city controlled by a land-grabbing oil kingpin with a faulty mechanical hand, Lamb (Martin Balsam), is especially abominable because of the bewildering waste of talented actors.

Enzo G. Castellari (director of the classic *Keoma*) should have known better. To quote Clint Eastwood's line in *The Good, the Bad, and the Ugly:* "I've never seen so many men wasted so badly."

Cisco (1966)

El Cisco Ital. *Director:* Sergio Bergonzelli; *Script:* Paolo Lombardo/Aldo Greci/ Sergio Bergonzelli; *Camera:* Aldo Greci; *Music:* Bruno Nicolai; *Producer:* Filmepoca (Italy). *Cast:* William Berger, George Wang, Antonella Murgia, Tom Felleghy, Nino Vingelli, Cristina Gajoni, Lucye Bomez.

Here's a film written and directed by Sergio Bergonzelli with the help of his "right hand," cameraman Aldo Greci. In an attempt to attract a wider "Anglo" audience, some American prints are titled *The Cisco Kid* (to capitalize on the popular early 1950s television series). In reality, there is no relationship between the two stories.

All hell breaks loose when the sheriff of Calabasas leaves town on official

George Wang (right) in a scene from *Cisco* (1966).

business. His deputy (Tom Felleghy), in cahoots with a Mexican gang, plots to rob the local bank. But Cisco (William Berger) beats them to it. He hides the money, and (because he now has a price on his head) Cisco pays a doctor to declare that he is, in fact, dead. But the plan fails when the deputy and a bandit (Nino Vingelli), anxious to collect the bounty, dig open Cisco's grave and find nothing. Then Cisco must come out of hiding, face the two in a showdown, and reveal the truth: that he was working with the sheriff and he stole the money to keep it out of the bandit's hands. The End.

An okay Bruno Nicolai score, but that's about all.

Una Ciudad Llamada Bastardo see *Town Called Hell*

Cjamango (1967)

Cjamango Ital. *Director:* Edward G. Muller; *Script:* Glen Vincent Davis; *Camera:* Vitaliano Natalucci; *Music:* Felice Di Stefano; *Producer:* Cio Film (Italy). *Cast:* Sean Todd, Mickey Hargitay, Hélène Chanel, Livio Lorenzon, Pedro Sanchez, Piero Lulli, Rick Boyd, Gilsua Fioraranti.

One of eight Eurowesterns directed by exploitation sleaze-meister Edward G. Muller (alias for Edoardo Mulargia), whose nongenre films include *Escape from Hell*, *Hotel Paradise* and *Tropic of Cancer*. This one is based on a screenplay written by Vincenzo Musolino (using the Glen Vincent Davis alias), with camera work by Vitaliano Natalucci, and music from Felice Di Stefano.

A bandit named El Tigre (Livio Lorenzon) has stolen a gold treasure from Cjamango (Sean Todd, aka Ivan Rassimov). With the help of Don Pablo (Mickey Hargitay), the gold is recovered. But sadistic El Tigre captures Cjamango's girlfriend, Perla (Hélène Chanel), and her young brother Manuel (Gilsua Fioraranti). The bandit ties little Manuel to a keg of dynamite and threatens to "explode the child" unless the gold is returned. Now, that's vicious.

Cjamango gives up his fortune to save the boy, but then Don Pablo and the Mexican peasants attack. During the raging battle, Don Pablo shows "his true colors" by stealing the gold and escaping to the desert. Everyone chases him, which leads to another bloody gun war. Only Cjamango and El Tigre are left alive, but Cjamango has lost his weapon. Just as El Tigre is about to kill him, Perla unexpectedly jumps the bandit and she is fatally wounded. Cjamango retaliates with a new vengeance, killing El Tigre.

Pretty actress Hélène Chanel began her career in sword 'n' sandal movies; her best role was in Riccardo Freda's *Maciste in Hell*. Ex–Mr. Universe, Mickey Hargitay, who plays Cjamango's friend and ally, appeared in other Spaghetti Westerns (see Performers filmography) but he will always be remembered for his over-the-top performance in Massimo Pupillo's *Blood Pit of Horror*, and for being married to Jayne Mansfield. A sequel (without Sean Todd and not directed by Muller) is called *Adios Cjamango* and was also known as *Twenty Thousand Dollars for Every Corpse*.

Clayton and Catherine see *China 9, Liberty 37*

Clint il Solitario see *Clint the Stranger*

Clint the Loner see *Clint the Stranger*

Clint the Nevada Stranger see *Clint the Stranger*

Clint the Stranger (1968)

Clint the Nevada Stranger; Clint the Loner; Clint il Solitario Ital. *Director:* Alfonso Balcazar; *Script:* José Antonio De La Loma/Helmut Harum/Alfonso Balcazar; *Camera:* Victor Monreal; *Music:* Nora Orlandi; *Producer:* Balcazar of Barcelona (Italy/Spain/West Germany). *Cast:* George Martin, Marianne Koch, Francisco J. Huetos, Fernando Sancho, Walter Barnes, Xan Das Bolas, Paolo Gozlino, Beni Deus.

Although he acted in self defense, rancher Clint Harrison (George Martin) is imprisoned for killing two henchmen (sent by greedy land baron Walter Shannon, played by Walter Barnes) who were tormenting his family. Years later, he returns from jail to find that his wife, Julie (Marianne Koch), and the rest of his family have mysteriously disappeared.

The film is a series of episodic encounters, most notably with the Shannon clan, as Clint searches for his missing family. There is a sequel, *Return of Clint the Stranger*, starring and directed by George Martin.

Filmmaker Alfonso Balcazar has made ten Spaghetti Westerns (see Directors filmography) plus a variety of action/adventures flicks, including *Night of the Scorpions* with Teresa Gimpera and *Night of Hate* starring Tomás Milian and Fernando Sancho.

Cloud of Dust . . . Cry of Death . . . Sartana Is Coming! see *Light the Fuse . . . Sartana Is Coming*

Clumsy Hands see *Awkward Hands*

Coffin for the Sheriff (1965)

Una Bara per lo Sceriffo Ital.; *Lone and Angry Man. Director:* William Hawkins; *Script:* James Reed/David Moreno; *Camera:* Julio Ortas; *Music:* Francesco De Masi; *Producer:* Titan Films (Italy/Spain). *Cast:* Anthony Steffen, Eduardo Fajardo, Jorge Rigaud, Armando Calvo, Arthur Kent, Luciana Gilli, Miguel Del Castillo, Tomás Torres.

Director Mario Caiano (this time using his "William Hawkins" alias) seems fascinated with the "sheriff against town boss" theme, especially if the sheriff is debilitated (i.e., town drunk becomes lawman in *Ride and Kill* [also *Sheriff Brandy*]) or indolent *(Train for Durango)* or fatefully preoccupied (i.e., bridegroom sheriff in *Bullets Don't Argue).*

This time, it's a sheriff with a checkered past (Anthony Steffen) against the always ("I'm a respectable businessman") oily Eduardo Fajardo. Initially, the scared townspeople side with Russell (Fajardo) but eventually they come to the aid of the sheriff.

Scriptwriter James Reed is actually Guido Malatesta, who directed nongenre films *Goliath Against the Giants, 087 Mission Apocalypse, Formula 1,* and *The Fire Monsters Against the Sons of Hercules.*

Coffin Full of Dollars see *Showdown for a Badman*

La Collera del Vento see *Trinity Sees Red*

La Collina Degli Stivali see *Boots Hill*

Colorado Charlie (1965)

Colorado Charlie Ital. *Director:* Robert Johnson; *Script:* Nino Stresa; *Camera:* Marcello Midei; *Music:* Gioacchino Angelo; *Producer:* P.E.A. (Italy/Spain). *Cast:* Jack Berthier, Charlie Lawrence, Barbara Hudson, Erika Blanc, Luis Chavarro, Andrew Ray, Paul Solvay.

Sheriff Bill Danders (Jack Berthier) retires from his lawman position, passing the duties on to his deputy, Jimmy (Andrew Ray). When notorious outlaw Colorado Charlie (Paul Solvay) and his gang attack the town and kill Jimmy, Bill feels responsible. Despite intense protests from his wife (Barbara Hudson), Bill Danders returns to the sheriff's job. He hunts down Colorado Charlie and shoots him dead in a showdown.

Besides his impressive output (quantity, not quality) of Spaghetti Westerns

Movie poster from *Colorado Charlie* (1965).

(see Directors filmography), director Roberto Mauri (using his "Robert Johnson" pseudonym) also made other cult films, including an atmospheric horror flick called *Slaughter of the Vampires* (1962).

Paul Solvay, the actor who plays the villainous Colorado Charlie, is genre filmmaker Paolo Solvay (aka Luigi Batzella), responsible for *Even Django Has His Price* and *Paid in Blood*.

Colt, Cinque Dollari, una Carogna see *Colt 45, Five Dollars, and a Bandit*

Colt è la Mia Legge see *Colt Is the Law*

Colt e Wincester Jack see *Roy Colt and Winchester Jack*

La Colt Era il Suo Dio see *God Is My Colt .45*

Colt 45, Five Dollars, and a Bandit (1967)

Colt, Cinque Dollari, una Carogna Ital. *Seven Guns for Seven Bandits. Director:* Richard Chardon; *Music:* Rudolph J. Cooper. *Cast:* William Cliff.

Very little information is available regarding this film. An admat has survived from an Italian newspaper, but apparently poor distribution kept the movie from circulating beyond limited Continental venues.

Una Colt in Mano del Diavolo see *Colt in the Hand of the Devil (1972)*

Una Colt in Pugno del Diavolo see *Colt in the Hand of the Devil (1967)*

A scene from *Colt in the Hand of the Devil* (1967) with Bob Henry (left) and Gerardo Rossi.

Colt in the Hand of the Devil (1967)

Devil Was an Angel; An Angel with a Gun Is a Devil; Una Colt in Pugno del Diavolo Ital. *Director:* Sergio Bergonzelli; *Script:* Sergio Bergonzelli; *Camera:* Aldo Greci; *Music:* Gianfranco Reverberi; *Producer:* Filmepoca (Italy). *Cast:* Bob Henry, Marisa Solinas, George Wang, Gerardo Rossi, Lucretia Love, Luciano Benetti.

The title more correctly translates to "Colt in the *Fist* of the Devil," an obvious attempt to capitalize on the popularity of *Fistful of Dollars*. But, unfortunately, the story is an outlandish journey into the preposterous.

A caravan of settlers is missing somewhere in the Mojave desert. A military fort in California sends reconnaissance officer Pat Scotty (Bob Henry) to investigate. He stumbles upon (and is captured by) a band of Mexican outlaws who have seized a sulphur mine (?) and have enslaved hundreds of people (including the settlers) to work it.

The bandit leader, Muñez (Gerardo Rossi), is so dynamic that Scotty takes an immediate liking to him, in spite of his tyrannical practices. When the Cavalry arrives, Scotty convinces Muñez to surrender, and then intercedes on his behalf. Amazingly, the result is amnesty. The two men become partners and ride off together.

Director Sergio Bergonzelli dabbled with Spaghetti Westerns in the mid–60s (*Last Gun* with Cameron Mitchell is considered his best) before abandoning the genre for the budding sex/exploitation/horror market where he eventually made his fortune with films like *Folds of the Flesh*, *Young Bride*, *Student Rebel*, etc.). In 1988, he directed *Blood Delirium*, a horror flick that received good critical notices and did very well at the European box office.

Colt in the Hand of the Devil (1972)

Una Colt in Mano del Diavolo Ital. *Director:* Frank G. Carrol; *Script:* Gianfranco Baldanello/Alfonso Brescia; *Camera:* Marcel Mascot; *Music:* Piero Piccioni; *Producer:* Mercedes/Givar Film (Italy). *Cast:* Robert Woods, William Berger, José Torres, George Wang, Mila Stanić, Harry Baird.

Not to be confused with Sergio Bergonzelli's identically titled film from 1967, this obscure collaboration between cult directors Frank G. Carrol (pseudonym for Gianfranco Baldanello) and Al Bradly (Alfonso Brescia's alias) is an obvious "right vs. wrong" Spaghetti Western, similar in style to their *Thirty Winchesters for El Diablo*.

Robert Woods is Texas Ranger Wilton hunting down the notorious Butch Brown outlaw gang (led by William Berger, in a particularly nasty mood). There's also a mildly interesting romantic subplot involving Wilton and a widow settler named Lisa (Mila Stanic). But overall, it's very familiar.

Colt Is the Law (1965)

My Colt Is the Law; Colt è la Mia Legge Ital. *Director:* Al Bradly; *Script:* Al Bradly/Peter White/Ramon C. Turner; *Camera:* Eloy Mella; *Music:* Carlos Castellananos Gomez; *Producer:* U.C.I. Cine 3/Procensa (Italy/Spain). *Cast:* Anthony Clark, Lucy Gilly, Miguel de la Riva, Peter White, Aldo Cecconi, Michael Martin, Jim Clay, Grant Laramy.

The characters in an Al Bradly film are either on the "good" or the "bad" side of the fence. The line is definitively drawn, and there is no room for a gray area. Usually, this results in lots of action, but not much substance. No exception here.

Undercover lawmen Steve and Clinton (Anthony Clark and Michael Martin) infiltrate the tiny explosive city of San Felipe in an attempt to unravel the mysterious disappearance of the railroad construction funds. There's no mystery in this film, just lots of gunfire.

Colt pour Trois Salopards see *Hannie Caulder*

Comanche Blanco see *White Comanche*

Comin' at Ya (1981)

Director: Ferdinando Baldi; *Script:* Tony Pettito/Lloyd Battista/Gene Quintana; *Camera:* Fernando Arribas; *Music:* Carlo Savina; *Producer:* Tony Anthony (Italy). *Cast:* Tony Anthony, Victoria Abril, Gene Quintana, Ricardo Palacios, Lewis Gordon.

In a movie designed for its 3-D effects, Tony Anthony plays a bumbling, reluctant bandit named Hart; Victoria Abril is his girlfriend (and accomplice) Anne. They decide to give up lawlessness (at one point a bank president says: "Those two are the worst bank robbers I've ever seen!") and get married. But during the ceremony (in a segment reminiscent of one from *Chrysanthemums*

Tony Anthony and crew members prepare to shoot a scene with the new 3-D camera used in filming Filmways Pictures' Western, *Comin' at Ya!* (1981).

for a Bunch of Swine), a band of renegade psychos (led by Gene Quintana, who also wrote the script) break into the church and kidnap Anne. The resulting sequences are similar to Tony Anthony's *Blindman* (also directed by Ferdinando Baldi), as Hart conducts a search for his stolen wife.

The unique 3-D camera work is the responsibility of Baldi's cinematographer, Fernando Arribas, usually found in the Jorge Grau camp where he lensed *The Female Butcher* (also called *Legend of Blood Castle*). Ricardo Palacios starred in Jess Franco's "Fu Manchu" film, *Kiss and Kill* (1968) and in Alice Cooper's Italian-made horror film, *Monster Dog* (1988).

In the late 80s, Tony Anthony moved to an executive position in the movie business, producing the controversial *Wild Orchid* starring Mickey Rourke; meanwhile, costar Victoria Abril hit big time with Pedro Aldomavar's *Tie Me Up, Tie Me Down* (1990).

Compañeros (1970)

Vamos a Matar, Compañeros! Director: Sergio Corbucci; *Script:* Dino Maiuri/Massimo De Rita/Fritz Ebert/Sergio Corbucci; *Camera:* Alejandro

A scene from *Compañeros* (1970).

Ulloa; *Music:* Ennio Morricone; *Producer:* Tonio Morelli, Tritone/Atlantida/ Terra (Italy/Spain/West Germany). *Cast:* Franco Nero, Tomás Milian, Jack Palance, Karin Schubert, Fernando Rey, José Bodalo, Eduardo Fajardo, Victor Israel, Iris Berben, Simon Arriaga, Francisco Bodaló.

A companion piece to director Corbucci's *Mercenary*, this film is also one of his "political" Westerns disguised as an adventure/comedy. The rousing Ennio Morricone score, excellent characterization with a worthy cast, and bittersweet story backdropped against the Mexican Revolution make this an extraordinary film experience.

The "Swede" (Franco Nero) arrives in "Mexican occupied" San Bernardino where he befriends a young revolutionary, Chato (Tomás Milian). Together they attempt to rescue a popular political prisoner, Professor Xantos (Fernando Rey), but the Swede's real motivation is the contents of a safe inside the fortress.

This story of greed and avarice is one of Sergio Corbucci's best, filled with private satirical excesses like, for example, the villain Jack (Jack Palance) feeding "America," his pet hawk, chunks of flesh from slaughtered Mexican peasants; photographed by Corbucci's right hand, Alejandro Ulloa. The next year, costar Fernando Rey finally received the international fame he "long deserved" when he starred opposite Gene Hackman as the elegant master criminal in William Friedkin's award-winning *French Connection* (1971).

Director Corbucci turned his talents to other types of film after this production, but returned to the genre in 1973 with *Bandera Bandits* (also called *Sonny and Jed*) starring Tomás Milian and Susan George.

Con Lui Cavalca la Morte see *Death Rides Alone*

Con Men see *Sting of the West*

Condenados a Vivir see *Cut-Throats Nine*

Conquerors of Arkansas see *Massacre at Marble City*

Continuavano a Chiamarlo Trinità see *Trinity Is Still My Name*

Une Corde, un Colt see *Cemetery Without Crosses*

Corri, Uomo, Corri see *Run Man, Run*

I Corvi Ti Scaveranno la Fossa see *And the Crows Will Dig Your Grave*

Cosi Sia see *Man Called Amen*

Cost of Dying (1968)

Taste of Death; Quanto Costa Morire Ital. *Director:* Sergio Merolle; *Script:* Biagio Proietti; *Camera:* Benito Frattari; *Music:* Francesco De Masi; *Producer:* Cine Azimut/Les Corona (Italy/France). *Cast:* Andrea Giordana, John Ireland, Raymond Pellegrin, Betsy Bell, Bruno Corazzari, Giovanni Petrucci.

This Italian-French coproduction deals with matters of oppression and power through force, as "on the lam" cattle thieves take refuge in (and then take over) a Colorado mountain town. Retired sheriff Bill Ramson (John Ireland) finally decides to do something about the hostile subjugation. He and his stepson Tony (Giovanni Petrucci) wage war on Skaif (Andrea Giordana) and the outlaws. When Tony is killed, the townspeople finally take up arms against the intruders.

The final showdown is particularly unique in the shrouded snow-covered silence of the Rockies (captured on film by capable chief cameraman Benito Frattari) instead of the dry and barren desert backdrop usually found in a Spaghetti Western.

Also, there's a good musical score from Francesco De Masi.

Cowards Don't Pray (1968)

Taste of Vengeance; I Vigliacchi non Pregano Ital. *Director:* Marlon Sirko; *Script:* Eduardo Brochero/Ernesto Gastaldi/Oscar Chianetta/Marlon Sirko; *Camera:* Gino Santini; *Music:* Manuel Parada; *Producer:* Marlon Sirko, Metheus/ Copercines Film (Italy/Spain). *Cast:* John Garko, Sean Todd, Elisa Montes, Jerry Wilson, José Jaspe, Alan Collins, Maria Mizar, Luis Barboo, Manuel Galiana, Luis Induni, Miguel Del Castillo, Frank Braña, Julio Peña.

Here's an interesting film with more depth and character development than the genre usually tends to offer. It's also quite black in tone, in many ways a very ugly movie. Mario Siciliano (using his Marlon Sirko moniker, customarily reserved for his "Producer" credits) directs this film humorlessly, making it an oddity since his other Westerns are the lame comedies *Halleluja and Sartana Strike Again* and *Trinity and Sartana Are Coming.* The attitude of this film is more similar to Siciliano's action/exploitation hard-boiled films *Malocchio* (also called *The Evil Eye*), (1975), *Seven Red Berets* (1978) and *Skin 'Em Alive* (1980).

The Civil War is over and Brian (John Garko) returns home to find that his ranch has been destroyed and his wife killed by a group of vigilantes. He meets Daniel (Sean Todd, aka Ivan Rassomov) who is on the gang's trail because they had kidnapped his brother. The two men join forces. After destroying the marauders and rescuing Robert (Jerry Wilson), the three men decide to start a new life together.

But Brian was affected by all the bloodshed, and he is now possessed with violence. He begins to take on "pistolero" jobs and eventually he becomes a notorious outlaw. Daniel, Robert and cousin Julie (Elisa Montes) leave him. They move to the city, where Daniel eventually becomes the sheriff. He dreads the day (everybody, including the audience, knows it's coming) when he must face his old friend in a showdown. That day comes when Brian (with his gang) arrives in town for a bank robbery. He is surprised to find "Sheriff" Daniel in charge, but it doesn't stop him. In fact, Brian (quite insane now) kills both Robert and Julie, forcing Daniel to draw on him. The outcome is obvious.

Coyote (1964)

Judgment of Coyote; Giustizia del Coyote Ital. *Director:* Joaquin L. Romero Marchent; *Script:* Joaquin Romero Hernandez/Jesus Navarro; *Camera:* Rafael Pacheco; *Music:* Odon Alonso; *Producer:* Centauro Films (Spain/Italy). *Cast:* Abel Salazar, Gloria Marin, Manuel Monroy, Miguel Palenzuela, Billy Hayden.

Abel Salazar produced and starred in a number of 60s black and white Mexican horror films, his most famous being *The Brainiac* for which he played the lead role (of the conspicuous baron with the long tongue). In this film, he's a notorious gunman turned freedom fighter, Coyote (sort of a poor man's Zorro). Gloria Marin plays his girlfriend, Mara, who "stands by her man."

Here is one of the first entries from Joaquin Romero Marchent (aka Joaquin Romero Hernandez), brother of filmmaker Rafael Romero Marchent. After this project, he directed the popular Richard Harrison genre Western, *Gunfight at High Noon* (1964), but he made his mark with the very violent *Cut-Throats Nine* in 1973.

Crazy Westerners see *Rita of the West*

Crepa Tu . . . Che Vivo Io see *Bandidos*

Crisantemi per un Branco di Carogne see *Chrysanthemums for a Bunch of Swine*

I Crudeli see *Hellbenders*

The Cruel Ones see *Hellbenders*

Movie poster from *Cowards Don't Pray* (1968).

Cry for Revenge (1968)

Quien Grita Venganza Sp.; *I Morti non si Contano* Ital. *Director:* Rafael Romero Marchent; *Script:* Marco Leto/Vittorio Salerno/Rafael Romero Marchent; *Camera:* Franco Delli Colli; *Music:* Riz Ortolani; *Producer:* Tritone/21-Producciones (Italy/Spain). *Cast:* Mark Damon, Anthony Steffen, Raf Baldassarre,

Maria Martin, Luis Induñi, Piero Lulli, Luis Barboo, Dianik Zurakowska, José Marco.

There is some confusion regarding the title of this film. Apparently, the Italian "working title" was *I Morti Non Si Contano (Dead Are Countless)* but the Spanish production company changed it to *Quien Grita Venganza (He Who Cries Vengeance* and also the English title, *Cry for Revenge)* upon its release. However, some prints are still circulating with the bogus title. To confuse matters even more, the following year (1969) director Marchent made another film (also with Anthony Steffen) under the same *I Morti Non Si Contano* banner, which the Spanish production company promptly changed to *Garringo* (see *The Dead Are Countless*).

Starring actor turned production executive Mark Damon (in the early 1980s he was the head of the now-defunct PSO Films) and brooding Anthony Steffen. They are two bounty hunters, Johnny and Fred, who agree to help the widow Reed (Maria Martin) avenge her husband's death at the hands of a vicious, but elusive, outlaw gang.

Cry of Death see *If One Is Born a Swine . . . Kill Him*

Cry Onion see *Cipolla Colt*

Cuatreros see *Shoot to Kill*

Los Cuatro de Fort Apache see *Those Dirty Dogs!*

Cut-Throats Nine (1973)

Condenados a Vivir Sp. *Director:* Joaquin Romero Marchent; *Script:* Joaquin R. Hernandez/Santiago Monicada; *Camera:* Luis Cuadrado; *Music:* Carmelo Bernaola; *Producer:* Films Triunfo Madrid (Spain/Italy). *Cast:* Robert Hundar, Emma Cohen, Manuel Tejada, Alberto Dalbes, Antonio Itanzo, Carlos R. Marchent, Ricardo Diaz.

Generally considered to be the most graphically violent Spaghetti Western, this film lives up to its reputation. There are countless stabbings, bloody gunfights and "onscreen" dismemberments, plus a bounteous dose of brutality, including a very disturbing rape. It's all punctuated against an unsettling backdrop of perpetual snow and bitter cold, symbolically adding to the overall bleakness.

A Union Army sergeant (Robert Hundar) with his daughter (Emma Cohen) are escorting a chain gang of hardened criminals over the Rocky Mountains to Fort Utah when their wagon is destroyed in an icy accident. Everyone is forced to continue the journey on foot. And very quickly it becomes "survival of the fittest."

Cowritten by director Marchent (using his pseudonym Juan Romero Hernandez), the film was highly successful because it appealed to a larger exploitation audience base, seizing support from "horror" and "action" fans in addition to the Western buffs. Free "terror masks" (designed to "hide your eyes when the violence became *too* much) were given to theater patrons as a promotional gimmick.

Da Uomo a Uomo see *Death Rides a Horse*

Dai Nemici Mi Guardo Io see *Three Silver Dollars*

Dallas (1972)

Il Mio Nome è Scopone e Faccio Sempre Cappotto Ital. *Director:* Juan Bosch; *Script:* Steve MacCohy/Roberto Gianviti; *Camera:* Giancarlo Ferrando; *Music:* Marcello Giombini; *Producer:* Astro Cinematograficia (Spain/Italy). *Cast:* Anthony Steffen, Frank Braña, Angel Aranda, Karin Heske, Luis Induñi, Ralph Birks.

A muddled cowboy drama about "misunderstood" outlaw Jake (Anthony Steffen) who tries to hang up his guns and settle down in Dallas. Obviously, he finds trouble instead. Things get especially hot when bounty hunter Johnny Black (prolific character actor Frank Braña) wanders into town.

The film was cowritten and directed by Ignacio Iquino (using his alias Juan Bosch/John Wood as well as his screenwriting "Steve McCohy" pseudonym), and lensed by his usual cinematographer of choice, Giancarlo Ferrando. Incidentally, Ferrando has also shot most of Sergio Martino's nongenre films, including *Torso* (also called *Bodies Bear Traces of Carnal Violence*) (1973), *The Great Alligator* (1979), and *Slave of the Cannibal God* (also called *Mountain of the Cannibal God*) (1978).

Costar Angel Aranda, featured in many Spaghetti Westerns, initially got his break when Mario Bava cast him for *Planet of the Vampires* (1965). Composer Marcello Giombini was the force behind the demented music for all the Al Bradly "War in Space" films, including the crazed theme song, *We Are Not Alone in Space (There Are Boulders)*.

Damned Hot Day of Fire see *Machine Gun Killers*

Damned Pistols of Dallas (1964)

Three Dollars of Lead; Le Maledette Pistole di Dallas, Ital.; *Tre Dollari di Piombo* Ital. *Director:* Joseph Trader; *Script:* Luigi Emanuelle; *Camera:* Edmondo Atfronti; *Music:* Gioacchino Angelo; *Producer:* Hesperia/Claudia (Spain/Italy/France). *Cast:* Fred Bier, Evi Marandi, Olivier Mathot, Rob Messenger, Angel Alvarez, Luis Induñi, Dina De Saint.

An early (mostly) Spanish coproduction directed by José Maria Zabalza (using the "Joseph Trader" pseudonym; "Pino Mercanti" for Italian prints) telling the story of the vulnerable Dallas townspeople under siege from the advancing Mexican army. The sheriff (Fred Bier) organizing the citizens and teaches them to defend their city, as everybody waits anxiously for the cavalry to arrive.

Oliver Mathot became a regular in many of the Jess Franco films of the 70s, particularly *Sadist of Notre Dame, Das Frauenhaus* and *Two Female Spies with Flowered Panties*.

Dans la Poussière du Soleil see *Dust in the Sun*

Day After Tomorrow see *One After Another*

National General Pictures Presents

LEE VAN CLEEF

"DAY OF ANGER"

[M] Technicolor® Techniscope® ℗

Ad photo for *Day of Anger* (1967) starring Lee Van Cleef.

Day of Anger (1967)

Days of Wrath; I Giorni dell'Ira Ital. *Director:* Tonino Valerii; *Script:* Ernesto Gastaldi/Tonino Valerii; *Camera:* Enzo Serafin; *Music:* Riz Ortolani; *Producer:* Alfonso Sansone, Sancrosiap/Corona (Italy/West Germany). *Cast:* Lee Van Cleef, Giuliano Gemma, Walter Rilla, Crista Linder, Piero Lulli, Yvonne Sanson, Andrea Bosić, Ennio Balbo.

This German-Italian coproduction is written and directed by one of the genre's master filmmakers, Tonino Valerii, who made five Spaghetti Westerns. Of those, three are considered classics: *Price of Power, My Name Is Nobody* and this film.

Here's another example of the "student/teacher" theme (similar, in fact, to Van Cleef's *Death Rides a Horse* from the same year). Frank Talby (Lee Van Cleef) is a seasoned gunfighter who teaches a mistreated orphan, Scott Mary (Giuliano Gemma), the tricks of the trade. As anticipated, the finale finds them facing each other in a showdown. Proficient director Valerii would satirize this scene (five years later) in his *My Name Is Nobody* with Terence Hill and Henry Fonda.

Be aware of severe edits in the American video release of *Day of Anger*, haphazardly reducing the running time from 109 minutes to a butchered 78 minutes. Almost one-third of the film is missing. It's inexcusable.

Day of Judgment see *Drummer of Vengeance*

Days of Violence (1967)

I Giorni della Violenza Ital. *Director:* Al Bradly; *Script:* Gian Luigi Buzzi/Mario Amendola/Paolo Lombardo/Antonio Boccacci; *Camera:* Fausto Rossi; *Music:* Bruno Nicolai; *Producer:* Concord Films (Italy). *Cast:* Peter Lee Lawrence, Rosalba Neri, Beba Loncar, Luigi Vanucchi, Nello Pazzafini, Andrea Bosić, Lucio Rosato, Harold Bradly.

One of five Euro Westerns directed by fecund cut 'n'dry filmmaker Al Bradly (pseudonym for Alfonso Brescia), with his chief cameraman, Fausto Rossi. But, fundamentally, it's just another variation on the "revenge for a slaughtered family" theme.

The setting is a farm in Missouri during the Civil War. John and Clem (Peter Lee Lawrence and Lucio Rosato) are brothers. When the Union soldiers destroy the ranch and kill Clem, John retaliates by joining an outlaw gang called the Southern Rebels, led by a soldier named Butch (Luigi Vanucchi). However, the leader is more interested in robbing stagecoaches than fighting the Northern enemy. During a holdup, violence erupts and John is forced to kill a passenger. At that moment he becomes a "wanted man." Even after the war, he is still haunted by his past. Finally, urged by his girlfriend (Rosalba Neri), John exposes Butch as a true scoundrel and outdraws him in a showdown.

Thank God for the participation of Rosalba Neri, otherwise this would have been unbearable.

Days of Wrath see *Day of Anger*

Dead Aim see *Lucky Johnny: Born in America*

Dead Are Countless (1969)

Garringo; I Morti Non Si Contano Ital. *Director:* Rafael Romero Marchent; *Script:* Joaquin Romero Marchent/Vittorio Salerno; *Camera:* Aldo Ricci; *Music:* Marcello Giombini; *Producer:* Berto Solino, Tritone/21-Producciones (Italy/Spain). *Cast:* Anthony Steffen, Peter Lee Lawrence, Solvi Stubing, José Bodaló, Luis Barboo, Raf Baldassare, Frank Braña, Luis Martin, Luis Induñi, Barta Barry, Alfonso Rojas.

An oddity, of sorts. Director Rafael Romero Marchent has constructed a "serial killer" motif set against a Western backdrop, a welcome variation to the standard Spaghetti Western plot lines. Cowritten by his brother (filmmaker Joaquin Romero Marchent) and busy scriptwriter Vittorio Salerno (who later wrote and directed two Italian thrillers, *Libido* and *Notturno con Grida*), this film remains Rafael Romero Marchent's best Western.

As a child, Johnny was forced to watch his father's execution at the hands of some Union officers. Years have now passed, and Johnny's brain is so twisted that every time he sees an Army officer, he is blinded by hate. Johnny (Peter Lee Lawrence) is the terror of the West, stalking and killing every officer that he mets. Finally Lieutenant Garringo (Anthony Steffen) is ordered to "bring the madman in, dead or alive." After finding time to fall in love with Julie (Solvi Stubing) and also thwart a gold robbery, Garringo concludes his mission. He brings killer Johnny in. Dead.

There is some confusion regarding the title of this film. In the Spanish market, it's called *Garringo*. The English title is a direct translation from the Italian *I Morti Non Si Contano (The Dead Are Countless)*. This is where it becomes perplexing: Anthony Steffen (and Mark Damon) made a film with director Marchent the previous year (1968) under the working title of *I Morti Non Si Contano* (apparently the brainchild of Vittorio Salerno, who wrote both movies) but the Spanish production company changed it to *Quien Grita Venganza* (English title: *Cry for Revenge*) upon its release. However, some prints are still circulating with the original bogus title.

Dead for a Dollar (1968)

Trusting Is Good . . . Shooting Is Better; Fidarsi è Bene, Sparare è Meglio Ital.; *T'Ammazzo, Raccomandati a Dio* Ital. *Director:* Osvaldo Civirani; *Script:* Tito Carpi/Luciano Gregoretti/Osvaldo Civirani; *Camera:* Osvaldo Civirani; *Music:* Angelo Francesco Lavagnino; *Producer:* Denver Films (Italy). *Cast:* George Hilton, John Ireland, Dick Palmer, Gordon Mitchell, Piero Vida, Monica Pardo.

A broader (and supposedly) humorous version of *Go Kill and Come Back* (also called *Any Gun Can Play*), without any of the engaging attributes of the original. Three outlaws (George Hilton, John Ireland, Piero Vida) steal $200,000 from a bank. They trick and double-cross each other until, finally, a prostitute (Monica Pardo) finds the loot and scams them all.

Poor characterization and a ridiculously illogical plot make this film a tedious, predictable bore. And there's only one person to blame. Osvaldo Civirani. He was the cowriter, the chief cameraman, and the director. Too bad. It had a good cast.

Dead Men Ride (1970)

Anda Muchacho Spara! Ital. *Director:* Aldo Florio; *Script:* Aldo Florio/Bruno Di Geronimo/E. M. Brochero; *Camera:* Emilio Foriscot; *Music:* Bruno Nicolai; *Producer:* Alfredo Nicolai, Italian/Transeuropa (Italy/Spain). *Cast:* Fabio Testi, Eduardo Fajardo, Massimo Serato, Alan Collins, Daniel Martin, Charo Lopez, José Calvo, Ben Carra, Romano Puppo.

Although the title suggsts otherwise, this is not a Horror Western. The men are "dead" in the figurative sense.

Roy Greenford (Fabio Testi) escapes from a sado-prison. He is befriended (and nurtured back to health) by an old Mexican peasant, Pedro (José Calvo) and some oppressed farmers. A thinner (but still slimy) Eduardo Fajardo is the rich town boss, Redfield, waging war against the peons for control of their land. The mysterious ex-con becomes an avenging guardian angel fighting for the poor Mexican farmers.

This is a better film than director Florio's previous *Five Giants from Texas*, perhaps due to Emilio Foriscot's exquisite camerawork. Foriscot also lensed many nongenre giallos, including the best Sergio Martino thrillers, *Blade of the Ripper* and *Tail of the Scorpion*.

And it seems that Bruno Nicolai learned well from his mentor, Ennio Morricone; the musical soundtrack is amazingly similar to Morricone's *Big Gundown* score. Years before, there was close collaboration between Nicolai and Morricone, usually with Bruno conducting Ennio's compositions (initially, many fans thought they were the same person). Then, in late 1968, the two musicians had a "tremendous disagreement" (neither will say about what) and they have worked together sparingly since, on *Compañeros* (in 1970) and *Moses* (in 1976).

Dead or Alive see *Minute to Pray, a Second to Die*

Deadlock (1970)

Deadlock Ital. *Director:* Roland Klick; *Script:* Roland Klick; *Camera:* Robert Van Ackerman; *Music:* Can; *Producer:* Roland Klick (Italy/Germany/Israel). *Cast:* Mario Adorf, Anthony Dawson, Marquard Bohm, Mascha Elm-Rabben, Sigurd Fitzek, Betty Segal.

Perhaps this Italian-German-Israeli coproduction does not qualify as a "Western" since it takes place in a "contemporary" setting, but the theme, characterization, music, and style so resemble a Spaghetti Western that inclusion here seems appropriate. In fact, the German director/writer Roland Klick *(Little Vampires)* announced that his purpose in making this film was to "breathe new life into the exhausted cliches of the Italo-American Western." Whether or not he achieved his goal has been fiercely argued by critics for many years, but (despite the brief inclusion of an old truck) the film looks like and can be enjoyed as a true genre "Western."

The Kid (Marquard Bohm) and Sunshine (Anthony Dawson) rob a bank in Santa Cruz and escape with $700,000. They agree to meet in Sierra, a desert ghost town, to divide the money. Then things go wrong. They are surprised by the police; Kid is wounded, but he manages to get away (with the suitcase of loot) by sneaking onto a passing baggage train. Then, half dead, he jumps off the train near Sierra.

Charles Dumm, a rugged vagrant (played with sadistic glee by Mario Adorf), discovers the injured Kid and the precious suitcase. Just as he is about to abscond with the cash, he finds himself looking down the barrel of Kid's gun. The bandit forces Charles to help him, specifically to take him to the "safety" of his home, a dilapidated shack in the desert. But while the Kid is asleep, Charles steals the suitcase and buries it somewhere in the sandy wilderness.

The story escalates into a cruel and greedy bloodbath, especially after the arrival of Sunshine and entanglement with Charles Dumm's only neighbors, an aging nymphomaniac (Betty Segal) and her beautiful deaf daughter, Jessi (Mascha Elm-Rabben).

The stark soundtrack is composed by a German experimental rock band, "Can." Robert Van Ackerman is responsible for the gritty photography shot entirely on location in Israel, near the war-torn Jordanian border.

Deadly Trackers (1972)

Long Cavalcade of Vengeance; La Lunga Cavalcata della Vendetta Ital. *Director:* Amerigo Anton; *Script:* Tanio Boccia; *Camera:* Romolo Gearroni; *Music:* Carlo Esposito; *Producer:* R.K. Cinematografica (Italy). *Cast:* Richard Harrison, Anita Ekberg, Rik Battaglia, George Wang, Men Fury, Dada Gallotti, Omero Gargano, Lorenzo Piani.

Not to be confused with 1973's *Deadly Trackers,* an American production starring Richard Harris, this is a Spaghetti Western starring Richard Harrison. It is a familiar story about a wagon train of settlers who hire a cavalier guide, James Luke (Harrison), to escort them through the wilds of Wyoming. Obviously, he falls in love with Anita Ekberg.

Director Amerigo Anton is a pseudonym for Tanio Boccia who also wrote the screenplay. Amazingly, this movie is one of six Westerns that Richard Harrison made in 1971 alone. The others were *His Name Was King, Holy Water Joe, Sheriff of Rickspring, Shoot Joe,* and *Shoot Again,* and *With Friends, Nothing Is Easy* (also called *Los Fabulosos de Trinita*).

Deaf Smith and Johnny Ears (1972)

Los Amigos Ital. *Director:* Paolo Cavara; *Script:* Oscar Saul/Harry Essex/Paolo Cavara; *Camera:* Tonino Delli Colli; *Music:* Daniele Patucchi; *Producer:* Joseph Janni/Luciano Perugia, Idea (Italy), *Cast:* Franco Nero, Anthony Quinn, Pamela Tiffin, Ira Furstenberg, Adolfo Lastretti, Franco Graziosi, Tom Felleghy, Renato Romano.

Paolo Cavara is one of the filmmakers responsible for creating a subgenre of Italian movies called "schockumentaries" with the release of his *Mondo Cane* in 1963.

Ten years later, he directed this highly visual story of two friends, Johnny Ears (Franco Nero) and a deaf mute appropriately named Erastus "Deaf" Smith (Anthony Quinn). They are assisting Sam Houston in his quest to fulfill a statehood dream for the Republic of Texas. It is their job to squash any "outside agitators" that might have traitorous ideas, and to pay especially close attention to the notorious German-puppet rebel-rouser, Mexican General Morton (Franco Graziosi).

Pamela Tiffin is Johnny's permanent prostitute, Susie. And, as such, she looks good but is mostly insignificant in the (onscreen) action.

Three of the main actors (Nero, Tiffin and Furstenberg) went on to make a thriller, *The Fifth Chord,* the same year. Cameraman Tonino Delli Colli became the director of photography for Sergio Leone's gangster epic *Once Upon a Time in America,* plus he lensed many Italian action films throughout the 80s. And the cowriter's name, Harry Essex, may sound familiar. He wrote the 50s hit, *Creature from the Black Lagoon.*

Death at Owell Rock (1967)

No Killing Without Dollars; La Morte Non Conta i Dollari Ital. *Director:* George Lincoln; *Script:* Luigi Masini/Riccardo Freda; *Camera:* Gabor Pogany; *Music:* Nora Orlandi/Robbe Poitevin; *Producer:* Cinecidi (Italy). *Cast:* Mark Damon, Stephen Forsyte, Luciana Gilli, Pamela Tudor, Giovanni Pazzafini, Pedro Sanchez, Spartaco Conversi.

This is the only Spaghetti Western directed by popular veteran filmmaker Riccardo Freda (using a "George Lincoln" pseudonym); he is best known for his atmospheric thrillers *(I Vampiri, Double Face, Horrible Dr. Hitchcock, Iguana with the Tongue of Fire),* spy films *(FX 18 Superspy* and *Mexican Slay Ride)* and peplums *(Maciste in Hell* and *Giants of Thessaly).*

Although the movie looks great, the story is yet another variation of the "vengeance for a slaughtered family" theme as a gunfighter named Lawrence (Mark Damon) arrives in Owell Rock to find out who killed his father. The witnesses are afraid to talk. They've all been threatened by town boss Harry Boyd (Stephen Forsyte). Eventually, Doc Lester (Giovanni Passafini) befriends Lawrence and together they confront and conquer the evil Boyd.

Mark Damon made many Spaghetti Westerns, including the very odd *Let Them Rest* (see Performers filmography for complete listing), but he is best remembered for his roles in Roger Corman's *Fall of the House of Usher* and Mario Bava's *Black Sabbath*. Cinematographer Gabor Pogany also lensed Freda's *Unconscious* (also called *Fear*).

Death Is Sweet from the Soldier of God (1972)

Django . . . Adios!; Seminò la Morte . . . Lo Chiamavano il Castigo di Dio Ital. *Director:* Robert Johnson; *Script:* Roberto Mauri/Roberto Montero; *Camera:* Mario Mancini; *Music:* Vassili Koiucharov; *Producer:* Aurelio Serafinelli, Virginia Film (Italy). *Cast:* Brad Harris, José Torres, Paolo Magalo, Zara Cilli, Vassili Karis, Roberto Messina, Franco Pasquetto.

One of two films that director Roberto Mauri (using his "Robert Johnson" alias) made with Brad Harris (also see *Wanted Sabata*), this is a compliant meshing of the *Spirito Santo* films with Sergio Garrone's *Django the Bastard* (1969).

Perhaps, secretly, Roberto Mauri envies the dubious notoriety of Miles Deem (Demofilo Fidani). Both directors seem to be sparring for the same "favorite hack" title. (However, it's really no contest; Miles Deem is the undisputed champion.) Even though Mauri is a master of banal and trite films mostly dependent on already established characterizations (i.e., *Sartana in the Valley of Death* and his blatant "Trinity" ripoff, *Animal Called Man*), his movies tend to be adequately shot and are generally entertaining in their aberration.

Evidently with this production, Mauri was "testing the waters" to see if the audience wanted more *Spirito Santo*–esque Westerns. Initially created by director Anthony Ascott and developed by actor Gianni Garko in two films, *His Name Was the Holy Ghost* (1970) and *Forewarned, Half-Killed . . . The Word of the Holy Spirit* (1971), the series was abandoned when the filmmaker decided to concentrate on horror and action pics (*Rat Man, Exterminators of the Year 3000, What Are Those Strange Drops of Blood Doing on the Body of Jennifer?*, etc.) and less on Westerns (only the marginal *Dick Luft in Sacramento* was produced by Ascott after 1972).

In this film, Brad Harris plays a mysterious stranger (is he a ghost? an angel? or just a bounty hunter?) who takes on the responsibility of judge and executioner. He's an avenging vigilante on the trail of a bad guy outlaw (Paolo Magalo), and he occasionally stops to help God-fearing folks along the way.

Roberto Mauri found conflicting reactions to the film, and so he changed the title to *Django . . . Adios!* for the international marketplace. Apparently, he didn't like rugged Brad Harris in the lead, so he decided to continue the *Spirito Santo* motif with Vassili Karis (aka Wassilli Karamesinis). No longer hiding behind the "Soldier of God" euphemism, Mauri directed two unofficial "Holy Ghost" sequels, *He Was Called the Holy Ghost* (1972) and *Gunman and the Holy Ghost* (1973).

Death Knows No Time (1968)

Tierra Brava; E Intorno a Lui Fu Morte Ital. *Director:* Leon Klimovsky; *Script:* Miguel Cusso/Leon Klimovsky/Odoardo Fiory; *Camera:* Emilio Foriscot; *Music:* Carlo Savina; *Producer:* Nike Cinematografica/Estela (Spain/Italy). *Cast:* William Bogart, Pedro Sanchez, Wayde Preston, Agnes Spaak, Miguel Del Castillo, Eduardo Fajardo, Andrea Bosić, Sydney Chaplin.

An aimless mess dealing with a no-named bounty hunter (William Bogart) who is looking for the notorious Cactus Kid. He never finds him. Instead, he decides to settle in a Texas border town overrun by Mexican bandits, and eventually, after taming the city, he becomes Sheriff "Johnny Silver."

It's just more zoom-and-pan nonsense from director Leon Klimovsky. Simply, irritatingly ponderous.

Death on High Mountain (1969)

La Morte sull'Alta Collina Ital. *Director:* Fred Ringoold; *Script:* Vincenzo G. Palli/José Mallo Figuerola; *Camera:* Julio Ortas; *Music:* Luis Enrique Bacalov; *Producer:* Bruno Turchetto, Spagnola/Copercines (Italy/Spain). *Cast:* Peter Lee Lawrence, Luis Dávila, Tano Cimarosa, Agnes Spaak, Antonio Gradoli, Nello Pazzafini, Jesus Guzman, Frank Braña.

One of two Spaghetti Westerns directed by popular peplum filmmaker Fernando Cerchio, this time using the pseudonym Fred Ringoold (also see *Mutiny at Fort Sharp*). It's an erratic entry, vacillating between a somber nihilistic tale and moments of inane slapstick.

A dimwitted Mexican revolutionary bandit, General Valiente (Jesus Guzman), is secretly in cahoots with town boss Braddock (Antonio Gradoli). They plan a major robbery. While everybody is in church (celebrating a wedding), the outlaw gang breaks into the local bank and steals the loot. But, two innocent bystanders, young Lorring Vanderbuilt (Peter Lee Lawrence) and a stranger named Mark Harrison (Louis Dawson, aka Luis Dávila), suddenly find themselves in the middle of the robbery and they "open fire." A massive gunfight eliminates most of the Mexican gang, but a few members (including General Valiente) escape. Lorring and Mark chase after them, recovering the stolen money. The two men decide to keep it, a decision that results in an abundance of silly segments involving chicanery, squabbling and preposterous double-crossing. Eventually Mark identifies himself as a federal marshal and he exposes the evil town boss, Braddock, plus another "secret" partner, a U.S. cavalry officer named McClain. Meanwhile, General Valiente, with his trusted (but equally stupid) assistant, flee to safety in Mexico.

Baby-faced actor Peter Lee Lawrence is the unlikely star of many Spaghetti Westerns (see Performers filmography), but he also appeared in a variety of nongenre films including a thriller with Erika Blanc called *Death on the Edge of a Razor Blade*, and the jungle girl opus, *Gungala and the Treasure of the Emerald Cave*, starring Kitty Swan. In 1973, after weeks of depression, Peter Lee Lawrence killed himself.

Death Played the Flute (1972)

Lo Ammazzo Come un Cane ... Ma Lui Rideva Ancora Ital. *Director:* Elo Panaccio; *Screenplay:* Elo Panaccio/Craig Marina; *Camera:* Jaime Deu Casas;

Lobby card from *Death Rides a Horse* (1967).

Music: Daniele Patucchi; *Producer:* Cineproduzioni Daunia (Italy/Spain). *Cast:* Michael Forrest, Steven Tedd, Aldo Berti, Chet Davis, Anthony Freeman, Suzanne Levi, Clara Hope.

When Sergio Leone had Charles Bronson play the harmonica in *Once Upon a Time in the West* (1968), the flood gates swung open for other cloned gunfighting "musicians," ranging from the sublime *(Requiem for a Gunfighter)* to the ridiculous *(Kill or Die)*. In this one, Michael Forrest is Ryan, the flute-intensive bounty hunter. The producers wisely avoided potentially dangerous titles like *They Called Me Flute*.

Death Rides a Horse (1967)

As Man to Man; Da Uomo a Uomo Ital. *Director:* Giulio Petroni; *Script:* Luciano Vincenzoni; *Camera:* Carlo Carlini; *Music:* Ennio Morricone; *Producer:* Alfonso Sansone/Enrico Chroscicki (Italy). *Cast:* Lee Van Cleef, John Phillip Law, Anthony Dawson, José Torres, Mario Brega, William Bogart, Luigi Pistilli, Carla Cassola, Bruno Corazzari.

In a story similar to *Days of Anger* (which also starred Lee Van Cleef), Bill (John Phillip Law) lives only to avenge the massacre of his family. He meets a gunfighter Ryan (Van Cleef) who teaches him the "art of the pistol." But after they eliminate the evil killers, the student and the teacher (in typical Spaghetti fashion) must face each other in a showdown.

Lensed in claustrophobic closeup style (by Carlo Carlini), one stormy night a group of bandits break into an isolated farm house. They murder the husband, rape and murder the wife. The only survivor is a terrified child who, 15 years later, has become a brooding bent-on-revenge man. He befriends a bounty killer and together they stalk the outlaws, eliminating them one by one until it becomes obvious that the bounty hunter also used to be a member of the gang. And as such, was also involved in the slaughter of Bill's parents.

This film is John Phillip Law's only genre Western. He is best known for his "angel" role in Roger Vadim's futuristic fantasy, *Barbarella* (1968) with Jane Fonda.

The lead bad guy, Manina, is played by Anthony Dawson (contrary to rumor, *not* the Italian director Antonio Margheriti, aka Anthony Dawson). This Dawson is a British actor who initially became popular when he tried to strangle Grace Kelly with a telephone cord in Alfred Hitchcock's *Dial M for Murder* (1954). He is also a standout in Roland Klick's contemporary Western *Deadlock* (1970).

The surprisingly effective direction from Giulio Petroni (one of his five Spaghetti Westerns, and certainly his best) is punctuated with an outstanding Ennio Morricone score, giving this film a "bigger than life quality" bordering on horrific. Especially memorable is the opening rape/murder sequence. Assistant director Giancarlo Santi went on to "helm the ship" as a promising genre filmmaker with *The Big Showdown* (1969), and he worked as Sergio Leone's right hand for *Duck You Sucker* (1971).

Death Rides Alone (1968)

Con Lui Cavalca la Morte. Director: Joseph Warren; *Script:* Augusto Caminito/ Fernando Di Leo; *Camera:* Amerigo Gengarelli; *Music:* Lallo Gorri; *Producer:* Tigielle 33 (Italy/Spain). *Cast:* Mike Marshall, Robert Hundar, Peter Martell, Giorgio Gargiulo, Carlo Gaddi.

Another "vengeance for a slaughtered family" theme, with Mike Marshall playing Bobby, the self-taught gunfighter looking for the outlaws who killed his mother and sister. It's directed with style (but not much imagination) by Joseph Warren, pseudonym for Giuseppe Vari.

Actor Peter Martell had a busy year in 1968. In addition to this film, he also did two Rafael Romero Marchent Westerns *(Two Crosses at Danger Pass* and *Ringo the Lone Rider)*, plus Paolo Bianchi's *God Made Them . . . I Kill Them,* Gian Baldanello's *Man with the Golden Winchester,* and Albert Cardiff's *Long Day of the Massacre.* Interestingly, none of Martell's 1968 movies, including this one, are very good.

By 1968, many of the genre directors had settled into a stabilized period of "just crankin' 'em out." They introduced very few new ideas. Most of the films continued to rely on "what was already working" (i.e., more variations on the vengeance motif or the "big trouble with the town boss" theme). However, this creative stagnation had no immediate bearing on the continued popularity of the Spaghetti Western. European studios churned them out at an amazingly vigorous rate. And 1968 became the number one "most prolific year," seeing the release of 75 Spaghettis (that's the equivalent to a new Western opening theatrically almost every four days!).

Death Sentence (1967)

Sentenza di Morte Ital. *Director:* Mario Lanfranchi; *Script:* Mario Lanfranchi; *Camera:* Toni Secchi; *Music:* Gianni Ferrio; *Producer:* B. L. Vision (Italy). *Cast:* Robin Clarke, Richard Conte, Tomás Milian, Enrico Maria Salerno, Adolfo Celi.

This is a "pure" revenge film. There are no insignificant details nor subplots to get in the way; not even a girlfriend to provide "love interest." Mario Lanfranchi has written and directed (lensed by Toni Secchi, alias Tony Dry) a "lean and mean" story about a young gunman named Cash (Robin Clarke) who avenges his brother's death by tracking down and killing the four men responsible. Of course, it's a familiar theme but Lanfranchi's deft pacing and unique vision gives it a renewed life.

Richard Conte does well in his only genre outing, best known for his "film noir" roles of the 1940s and 50s (i.e., *New York Confidential, Under the Gun, Thieves' Highway, Cry of the City, Whirlpool*). Tomás Milian, who always enjoys "disguise" roles (see his "hunchbacked villain" in *Banda del Gobbo* for a good example) is especially delightful as an evil epileptic albino gunman. Accomplished character actor Enrico Maria Salerno (see Performers filmography) also starred in Dario Argento's *Bird with the Crystal Plumage, From the Police with Thanks,* and Aldo Lado's *Night Train Murders.* Plus, he directed Florinda Bolkan in *Dear Parents* (1972).

Death Walks in Laredo (1966)

Three Golden Boys; Tre Pistole Contro Cesare Ital.; *Tre Ragazzi d'Oro* Ital. *Director:* Enzo Peri; *Script:* Carmine Bologna/Dean Craig/Enzo Peri; *Camera:* Otello Martelli; *Music:* Marcello Giombini; *Producer:* Carmine Bologna, De Laurentiis/Casbah (Italy/Spain). *Cast:* Thomas Hunter, James Shigeta, Nadir Moretti, Femi Benussi, Delia Boccardo, Umberto D'orsi, Enrico Maria Salerno, Gianna Serra.

Bizarre. Three men (of different backgrounds and nationalities) each receive a notice of inheritance and a map to a gold mine. When the three run into each other, they are instant enemies until they discover the truth: the three men are, in fact, related. They are half brothers, sons of the late Mr. Langdon and three different mothers. Then, their bond is immediate.

But the gold mine is not so easily accessible. It is in Laredo, and Laredo is under the complete and utter power of dictator Giulio Cesare Fuller (Enrico Maria Salerno), an eccentric megalomaniac who controls the entire territory from his castle perched on a hilltop above the city. Fuller believes that he is the rightful descendant of Julius Caesar and, as such, he wears tunics and robes of royalty, soaks in steam baths surrounded by beautiful slaves, and executes his enemies in the "coliseum." The gold mine is his, and he will never give it up. Instead, he sends a hit squad of gorgeous (but deadly) female assassins to eliminate the three brothers.

But the "Three Golden Boys" have secret powers of their own. Whitey (Thomas Hunter) is a sure-shot gunman, Lester (James Shigeta) is an accomplished acrobat/martial arts master, and Étienne (Nadir Moretti) is a doctor of magic. Using their skills, they outsmart the women warriors, invade the castle, and slay Giulio Cesare while he stretches prostrate in his tub (shades of *Marat/Sade*).

Written and directed by Enzo Peri (believed to the the pseudonym for "art" filmmaker Elio Petri critically acclaimed for *Investigation of a Citizen Above Suspicion* and *The Tenth Victim* with Ursula Andress and her pistol-packing bra), this film remains his only contribution to the Eurowestern genre. The music is by Marcello Giombini; Otello Martelli provides the principle camera work.

The Italian title *(Tre Pistole Contro Cesare)* translates to *Three Gunmen Against Caesar*. Certainly, it's a more accurate descriptive title than the English banner, *Death Walks in Laredo*.

Death's Dealer see *Vengeance Is a Dish Served Cold*

El Dedo en el Gatillo see *Finger on the Trigger*

Deep West see *Heads You Die . . . Tails I Kill You*

Deguejo see *Deguello*

Deguello (1966)

Deguejo Ital. *Director:* Joseph Warren; *Script:* Sergio Garrone/Giuseppe Vari; *Camera:* Silvano Ippoliti; *Music:* Alexander Derevitsky; *Producer:* Gar Film (Italy). *Cast:* Giacomo Rossi Stuart, Dan Vadis, José Torres, Rosy Zichel, Ghia Arlen, Riccardo Garrone, John MacDouglas, Erika Blanc, Daniele Vargas.

Out of his seven entries (see Directors filmography), this is considered the best Joseph Warren (pseudonym for Giuseppe Vari) Spaghetti Western. He is better known for his gangster films *(City in the Jaws of the Racket)*, futuristic action movies *(Urban Warriors)* and outrageous sex romps *(Sister Emanuelle)*. Mostly, this one succeeds because of the fresh plot twists, as cowritten by Warren and popular cult director Sergio Garrone (aka Willy S. Regan).

The Civil War is over and Confederate Colonel Crook (John Douglas) hides a large amount of money inside his house in Danger City. He and his seven accomplices are captured by a marauding bandit named Ramon (Dan Vadis) who had heard rumors of the missing treasure. He tortures the rebels until they give out the secret information, killing everyone afterwards, including a sergeant named David Issac (José Torres).

David's son Norman (Giacomo Rossi Stuart, aka Jack Stuart), aided by his friends, hunts down and destroys Ramon and his gang. Ironically, they know nothing of the money, so after killing the outlaws, they leave the overlooked loot to rot with the corpses in the desert.

Déposez les Colts see *Pistol Packin' Preacher*

El Desafío de Pancho Villa see *Pancho Villa*

Deserter (1970)

The Devil's Backbone; La Spina Dorsale del Diavolo Ital. *Director:* Niska Fulgozzi/Burt Kennedy; *Script:* D'Avack/Byrne/James/Huffaker; *Camera:* Aldo Tonti; *Music:* Piero Piccioni; *Producer:* Dino De Laurentiis/Norm Baer/Ralph Serpe, DeLaurentiis Film/Jadran (Italy/Yugoslavia). *Cast:* Richard Crenna,

Chuck Connors, Bekim Fehmiu, Ricardo Montalban, Fausto Tozzi, Slim Pickens, Woody Strode, John Huston, Mimmo Palmara.

Actually, this is an American-Italian-Yugoslavian production shot in Italy, coproduced by Dino De Laurentiis, featuring a mostly Anglo cast (even in the supporting roles), codirected by Niska Fulgizzi and popular genre filmmaker Burt Kennedy (*War Wagon, Hannie Caulder, Support Your Local Sheriff*, etc.) with camera work by Aldo Tonti.

It's the often-used *Dirty Dozen* theme in a saga about Captain Carter (Bekim Behmiu) and his secret Cavalry unit fighting bad Indians along the Mexican border circa 1880.

Over all, the film is pretty awful due mostly to Clair Huffaker's needlessly confusing and pretentious script, coupled with a terrible acting job from "wooden man" Bekim Fehmiu (who, also in the same year, underwhelmed critics and audiences alike with his cadaverous performance in *Harold Robbins' The Adventurers*). Also, Ricardo Montalban (*Fantasy Island* host extraordinaire) as an Indian scout, Natchai, takes some getting used to. Piero Piccioni provides the bombastic, bordering on ostentatious, music.

Desperado (1972)

Now They Call Him Amen; I Bandoleros della Dodicesima Ora Ital. *Director:* Al Bagrain; *Script:* Alfonso Balcazar; *Camera:* Jaime Deu Casas; *Music:* Willy Brezza; *Producer:* Balcazar De Barcelona (Spain/Italy). *Cast:* Michael Forest, Fred Harrison, Malisa Longo, Paolo Gozlino.

Of course nobody is ever called "Amen" in these movies. It's just a title. It sounds good, right? This time Alfonso Balcazar, hiding behind an odd "Al Bagrain" pseudonym, tells the story of a notorious gunfighter (Michael Forest) who comes to the aid of some terrorized farmers and then falls in love with widowed homesteader, Barbara (Malisa Longo).

Alfonso Balcazar is one of the leading Spanish directors, almost as prolific as Ignacio Iquina (Juan Bosch), Leon Klimovsky and the Romero Marchent brothers, Joaquin and Rafael. Balcazar's "rise to power" as a filmmaker was strongly dependent on his family's control of the theatrical distribution network in Spain, a company aptly called Balcazar de Barcelona, responsible for most of the bookings throughout that country.

For a movie with a gunfighter actually named Amen, see *For a Book of Dollars* (1973).

El Desperado see *Big Ripoff*

Depserado Trail see *Winnetou: The Desperado Trail*

Desperate Men see *Bullet for Sandoval*

Devil Was an Angel see *Colt in the Hand of the Devil* (1967)

The Devil's Backbone see *Deserter*

Di Tressette C'è Ne Uno ... Tutti gli Altri son Nessuno see *Dick Luft in Sacramento*

Dick Luft in Sacramento (1974)

Di Tressette C'è Ne Uno . . . Tutti gli Altri son Nessuno Ital. *Director:* Anthony Ascott; *Script:* Ascott/Simonelli; *Camera:* Emilio Foriscot; *Music:* Alessandro Alessandroni; *Producer:* Mino Loy, Flora Film (Italy). *Cast:* George Hilton, Tony Norton, Chris Huerta, Umberto D'Orsi, Nello Pazzafini, Renato Baldini.

George Hilton is Dick Luft, a hapless wanna-be gunfighter, and Tony Norton is his sidekick, Veleno, in this Western spoof of the "Don Quixote" story. Eventually, Dick Luft becomes notorious, but it's really because Veleno is "pulling the strings" behind the scene.

This is a lesser film from the number one most prolific director of the Spaghetti Western genre, Anthony Ascott (Giuliano Carmineo), with 14 movies to his credit (see Directors filmography for complete listing). He is best known for his *Sartana* and *Santo Spirito (Holy Ghost)* series, both starring Gianni Garko. Plus director Ascott has also made a variety of nongenre films including the classic giallo/thriller *What Are Those Strange Drops of Blood Doing on the Body of Jennifer?* (1972), plus (under the name "Jules Harrison") *Exterminators of the Year 3000* (1983) and *Sterminator* (1984).

Composer Alessandro Alessandroni became well known as the "whistler" on all the early Ennio Morricone soundtracks, including the memorable scores for the Sergio Leone "Dollar" films. If there's a whistler on any Spaghetti Western soundtrack, it's probably Alessandro Alessandroni. He also composed the music for *Legend of the Wolfman* and *Devil's Nightmare*.

Dieci Bianchi Uccisi da un Piccolo Indiano see *Blood River*

10.000 Dollari per un Massacro see *$10,000 Blood Money*

Dig Your Grave, Friend . . . Sabata's Coming (1970)

Dig Your Grave, Friend . . . Sartana's Coming; Stagecoach of the Condemned; Not Sabata or Trinity . . . It's Sartana; First They Pardon Then They Kill; Prima Ti Perdono, Poi Ti Ammazzo Ital.; *Abre Tu Fosa, Amigo . . . Llega Sabata* Sp; *Sabata Revient* Fr; *Rancheros,* Sp. *Director:* John Wood; *Script:* Steve Mac-Cohy/Jackie Kelly; *Camera:* Clinton Taylor; *Music:* Henry Sothe; *Producer:* José Antonio, Ifisa/Devon (Italy/Spain/France). *Cast:* Richard Harrison, Fernando Sancho, Raf Baldassare, Alejandro Ulloa, Erika Blanc, Indio Gonzalez, Luis Induñi.

To avenge his father's death, Steve McGowan (Richard Harrison) teams with a notorious (but likeable) Mexican bandit, Pompero (Fernando Sancho). The targeted killer is land baron Miller (Indio Gonzalez) who meets the threat from the two assailants head-on by hiring the famous gunman Sabata (or Sartana, in some dubbed prints) to eliminate them before they can eliminate him.

The evil Miller is ultimately betrayed by a girlfriend, Helen (Joan Rubin) which leads to his and Sabata's demise. Pompero is superficially wounded in the final gun battle, but his friend Steve emerges unscathed, and with the girl.

Directed by Ignacio Iquino (using the John Wood pseudonym for international prints, and "Juan Bosch" for the Spanish version), this film is also cowritten by Iquino under his "Steve MacCohy" alias. Lensed by Julio Perez de Rozas and Luciano Trasatti under the collective "Clinton Taylor" moniker, the soundtrack is composed by Henry Soteh (actually, Enrique Escobar).

Fernando Sancho made 168 movies from 1941 *(Polizon a Bordo)* until the time of his death in 1990. His last film was *Los Presuntos* (1986).

Dig Your Grave, Friend . . . Sartana's Coming see *Dig Your Grave, Friend . . . Sabata's Coming*

Dinamite Jack see *Dynamite Jack*

Dinamite Jim see *Dynamite Jim*

Dio in Cielo, Arizona in Terra see *God in Heaven . . . Arizona on Earth*

Dio li Crea . . . Io li Ammazzo see *God Made Them . . . I Kill Them*

Dio Non Paga, il Sabato see *God Does Not Pay on Saturday*

Dio Perdona . . . Io No! see *God Forgives, I Don't*

Dio Perdona la Mia Pistola see *God Will Forgive My Pistol*

The Dirty Outlaws see *Big Ripoff*

Dirty Story of the West see *Johnny Hamlet*

Django (1966)

Django Ital. *Director:* Sergio Corbucci; *Script:* Franco Rossetti/Bruno Corbucci/Sergio Corbucci; *Camera:* Enzo Barboni; *Music:* Luis Enrique Bacalov; *Producer:* Manolo Bolognini, BRC/Tecisa (Italy/Spain). *Cast:* Franco Nero, Loredana Nusciak, Eduardo Fajardo, Jimmy Douglas, José Bodaló, Angel Alvarez, Simon Arrag.

Sergio Corbucci made a damn good Western. This one is probably his most remarkable accomplishment. The images of Django (Franco Nero) dragging his apocalyptic coffin through the four-inch-deep mud streets of that godforsaken border town are unforgettable.

Eduardo Fajardo is at his oily best in a portrayal of the sadistic racist villain. Plus, although contrived, the finale in the cemetery (where, despite having had his hands smashed and broken, Django still wins the showdown) is a landmark conclusion.

A good, memorable musical score from Luis Enrique Bacalov *(Price of Power, Bullet for a General,* etc.); strikingly stark, yet alluring, photography by Enzo Barboni, who later directed many of his own films (including the famous *Trinity* series) using the pseudonym E. B. Clucher; extraordinary backup from assistant director Ruggero Deodato, soon to be a filmmaker of harrowing perception *(Cannibal Holocaust, Inferno in Diretta, Camping Del Terrore, Last Cannibal World,* etc.).

Django spawned many wanna-be sequels (see Appendix), but the only one endorsed by Corbucci was *Django Strikes Again* (1988), once again starring Franco Nero in the title role.

Django . . . Adios! see *Death Is Sweet from the Soldier of God*

Django, a Bullet for You (1966)

Django . . . Cacciatore di Taglia Ital. *Director:* Leon Klimovsky; *Script:* Federico De Urrutia/Manuel Sebares; *Camera:* Leopoldo Villaseñor; *Music:* Warren Jellico; *Producer:* Salvador Romero (Spain/Italy). *Cast:* James Philbrook, Aldo Berti, Maria Kost, José Marco, Andres Resino.

Here's one of the early Django "sequels," released within months of the original film's debut. James Philbrook is Django, a vigilante gunfighter, determined to protect the poor farmers in Wagon Valley from an evil land-grabbing town boss (Aldo Berti), working in cahoots with the approaching railroad.

Overall, it's another weak film from Leon Klimovsky with tedious action sequences and limited characterizations. Actress Maria Kost (one of the only good things about the movie) went on to star in *Night of the Sorcerers* (1973) and *Night of the Seagulls* (1975), both directed by Armando De Ossorio.

Django Always Draws Second see *Hero Called Allegria*

Django and Sartana Are Coming . . . It's the End (1970)

Django and Sartana . . . Showdown in the West; Final Conflict . . . Django Against Sartana; Sartana, If Your Left Arm Offends, Cut It Off; Arrivano Django e Sartana . . . È la Fine Ital. *Director:* Dick Spitfire; *Script:* Fidani/ Valenza; *Camera:* Aristide Massaccesi; *Music:* Coriolano Gori; *Producer:* Tarquinia Film (Italy). *Cast:* Hunt Powers, Chet Davis, Gordon Mitchell, Simone Blondell, Krista Nell, Ettore Manni.

It is the genre's favorite hack, Miles Deem (Demofilo Fidani), smiling behind the Dick Spitfire alias (also used again for *Go Away! Trinity Has Arrived in Eldorado*).

Black Burt (Gordon Mitchell) and his gang kidnap Anne, the daughter of a wealthy landowner. The girl's father offers a huge bounty to Django and Sartana (Chet Davis and Hunt Powers) for her safe return. They track the outlaws into Mexico, eventually waging a war and rescuing the girl. At the finale, Django's true motivation is shown as he scurries about collecting the dead bodies for the various rewards offered; Sartana, however, is content with the girl and with (what appears to be) a budding romance.

Even though the plot is Swiss cheese, the film looks great, thanks to the superior camera work of Aristide Massaccesi who later became the controversial director, Joe D'Amato (*Buried Alive, Trap Them and Kill Them*, most of the *Emmanuelle* films with Laura Gemser, plus many more sleaze classics).

Django and Sartana . . . Showdown in the West see *Django and Sartana Are Coming . . . It's the End*

Django . . . Cacciatore di Taglia see *Django, a Bullet for You*

Django Challenges Sartana (1970)

Django Defies Sartana; Django Sfida Sartana Ital. *Director:* William Redford; *Script:* Pasquale Squittieri; *Camera:* Eugenio Bentivoglio; *Music:* Piero Umiliani; *Producer:* Y. V. Bianco, Filmes Cinematografica (Italy). *Cast:* Tony Kendall, Georges Ardisson, Malisa Longo, José Jaspe, José Torres, Rick Boyd.

A scene from *Django* (1966) starring Franco Nero.

Written and directed by critically respected Pasquale *(Third Solution)* Squittieri (using the "William Redford" pseudonym), this is one of his two Spaghetti Westerns (also see *Vengeance Is a Dish Eaten Cold*).

It's a remarkably good, well-photographed example of the genre as two bounty hunters, Django (Tony Kendall) and Sartana (Georges Ardisson), are both on the trail of the same gang of desperadoes. Reminiscent of the uneasy partnership between Malaco and Colonel Mortimer in *For a Few Dollars More*, Django and Sartana initially clash, but then join forces against the outlaws.

Django Defies Sartana see ***Django Challenges Sartana***

Django Does Not Forgive (1967)

Django Non Perdona Ital. *Director:* Julio Buchs (Julio Garcia); *Script:* Ugo Guerra/Julio Buchs; *Camera:* Francisco Sempere; *Music:* Perez A. Olen; *Producer:* Daiano/Atlantida (Italy/Spain). *Cast:* John Clark, Hugo Blanco, Frank Braña, Miguel De La Riva, Gustavo Rojo, Nuria Torray, Manuel Miranda, Luis Induñi, Armando Calvo, Luis Prendes.

This is another "vengeance for a slaughtered family" Spaghetti Western, featuring the popular "Django" character (this time played by John Clark) in a peculiar Canadian setting.

A Royal Mounted Police officer rapes and kills Django's sister; obviously, the notorious bounty hunter swears revenge. But it's a long and winding road that eventually puts Django in the middle of an Indian vs. Army war. During the raging battle, an officer (Frank Braña) admits that he was responsible for the girl's death and asks for forgiveness. Subsequently, he saves the bounty hunter's life by stopping a bullet intended for Django. To say the least, it's all very anticlimactic.

Django: Eine Pistole für 100 Kreuze see Gunman of One Hundred Crosses

Django, If You Want to Live . . . Shoot! see If You Want to Live, Shoot!

Django il Bastardo see Django the Bastard

Django, Kill . . . If You Live, Shoot! (1967)

Se Sei Vivo Spara Ital. *Director:* Giulio Questi; *Script:* Franco Arcalli/Giulio Questi; *Camera:* Franco Delli Colli; *Music:* Ivan Vandor; *Producer:* G.I.A. Cinematografica/Hispamer Film (Italy/Spain). *Cast:* Tomás Milian, Ray Lovelock, Piero Lulli, Milo Quesada, Roberto Camardiel, Frank Braña, Marilu Tolu, Paco Sanz.

Considered by many genre fans as the most unusual of all the Euro-westerns, this movie is directed by eccentric Giulio Questi. He is a mysterious filmmaker (a questionable report in *Screenworld '71* insists that he is actually producer Italo Zingarelli) also responsible for the cult/ sleaze picture *Death Laid an Egg* (1967) and the made for Italian television feature *Non Aprire l'Uomo Nero (Don't Open the Door for the Man in Black)* (1991).

This is the story of Django (Tomás Milian) and his deadly pistol with gold bullets. But it is also the story of a sadistic gay bandit named Zorro (Roberto Camardiel) and his gang of dressed-in-black homosexuals who raid the city and kidnap a teenage boy whom they hold for ransom, while gang-raping him until he kills himself. Plus, it's the story of a store owner who has secretly stolen a shipment of gold dust and when his building catches fire he attempts to save the gold, but (in the intense heat) it melts and drips all over his face, burning and smothering him at the same time.

Many critics called this movie "the most brutally violent Spaghetti Western ever made." Obviously, those critics never saw *Cut Throat Nine*, but nonetheless, it is a shocking (townspeople digging gold bullets out of dead bodies, animals disemboweled before the camera, men roasted on a spit over an open fire) bloody journey. Be so advised.

Ray Lovelock (who plays Evan) also starred in a series of significant nongenre films, including Ruggero Deodato's *Live Like a Man* . . . *Die Like a Cop* (1976) and Jorge Grau's *Living Dead at the Manchester Morgue* (1974).

Django Killer per l'Onore see Outlaw of Red River

Django Kills Softly (1968)

Bill il Taciturno . . . *Django Uccide* Ital. *Director:* Max Hunter; *Script:* Lina Caterini/Marcello Malvestiti; *Camera:* Mario Parapetti; *Music:* Berto Pisano; *Producer:* Alberto Puccini, Avis Film (Italy). *Cast:* George Eastman, Edwin G. Ross, Liana Orfei, Mimmo Maggio, Peter Hellmann, Spartaco Conversi, Rick Boyd.

Producer Max Hunter (pseudonym for Massimo Pupillo) takes over the directing chores this time and he creates a perfect "textbook" example of the genre. Wonderfully creative camerawork, an essential overdose of machismo, and a blood-pumping flamboyant musical soundtrack are the ingredients. Plus there's George Eastman as the mysterious sharp-shooting stranger, Django (more closely resembling an avenging angel than a bounty hunter).

When Linda (Liana Orfei) visits her boyfriend's ranch, she finds him dead, killed by a band of Mexican outlaws. They attempt to rape her, but Django (with his guns blazing) comes to Linda's rescue. A bit later, Django continues his journey to a nearby city. When he attempts to check in at the hotel, he stumbles upon a staggering massacre. Everyone in the hotel has been slaughtered. The local doctor (Edwin G. Ross) blames the violence on the evil town boss, El Santo, and his lunatic brother. The townspeople convince Django to "represent the law" and stand up against the tyrants. But everything becomes a bit complicated when Django discovers that the bad guys are actually Linda's brothers.

After starring in countless peplums, actress Liana Orfei and her sister, Moira, naturally migrated to the booming world of Spaghetti Westerns. Interestingly, they were first discovered as a "knife-throwing" circus act. Musical composer Berto Pisano is best known for his beautiful score to Aristide Massaccesi's *Death Smiles on a Murderer*. Director/producer Max Hunter will always be remembered for putting Mickey Hargitay in red leotards for *Bloody Pit of Horror*.

Django, Last Killer (1967)

L'Ultimo Killer. *Director:* Joseph Warren; *Script:* Augusto Caminito; *Camera:* Angelo Filippini; *Music:* Roberto Pregadio; *Producer:* Otello Cocchi, Jupiter General (Italy). *Cast:* George Eastman, Anthony Ghidra, Dana Ghia, Daniele Vargas, John Hamilton, Mirko Ellis, John MacDouglas, Frank Fargas.

Here's a great looking movie from director (and editor) Giuseppe Vari, using the familiar "Joseph Warren" alias. Unfortunately, the subject matter is a bit worn, yet another variation of the "big trouble with the town boss" theme, coupled with the "revenge for a slaughtered family" motif plus a dash of *Death Rides a Horse.*

A Mexican ranching family is tormented by a land baron named Barrett

(John McDouglas) who is trying to steal their farm through vicious acts of intimidation. When son Ramon (George Eastman) goes to the expansive Barrett estate to complain, he is shot, whipped and beaten. Luckily, he escapes with his life. But soon, he discovers that (while he was being tortured) his parents were killed and the ranch destroyed by Barrett's henchmen.

Meanwhile, in a seemingly unrelated segment, Barrett hires the notorious bounty hunter Django (Anthony Ghidra) to kill an accused outlaw who is determined to testify against him. As Django is preparing for the "hit," a fame-seeking gunman tries to shoot him in the back, but Ramon (still despondent from his tragedy) desultorily saves the bounty hunter's life. Django feels indebted to Ramon, giving him a place to stay while nursing him back to health. Then he teaches the boy "the art of the pistol."

After Django carries out his task of killing the "informer," he and Ramon face each other in a showdown. Ramon shoots Django, and then he rides to town where he also murders sleazy Barrett, while the sheriff stands idly by.

Django Non Perdona see *Django Does Not Forgive*

Django Nudo und die lusternen Mädchen von Porno Hill see *Nude Django*

Django Porte sa Croix see *Johnny Hamlet*

Django Prepare a Coffin see *Get the Coffin Ready*

Django Prépare ton Exécution see *Execution*

Django Rides Again see *Keoma*

Django Sfida Sartana see *Django Challenges Sartana*

Django Shoots First (1966)

He Who Shoots First; Django Spara per Primo Ital. *Director:* Alberto De Martino; *Script:* Sandro Continenza/Massimo Capriccioli/Alberto Fiorenzo Capri/Vincenzo Flamini; *Camera:* Riccardo Pallotini; *Music:* Bruno Nicolai; *Producer:* Edmondo Amati, Fida (Italy). *Cast:* Glenn Saxon, Fernando Sancho, Evelyn Stewart, Erika Blanc, José M. Martin, Lee Burton, Alberto Lupo, Diana Lorys.

Veteran filmmaker Alberto De Martino has made all types of movies from *Operation Kid Brother* (a Bondish spy adventures starring Sean Connery's younger brother, Neil) to *Anti-Christo* (also called *Tempter* (the gross-out devil-possession epic), but he claims to like his Westerns best. Perhaps this one isn't as good as *Charge of the Seventh Cavalry* but it's better than much of the competition.

Django (Glenn Saxon) inherits the "lion's share" of a town and, along with it, an unscrupulous partner, Doc Gordon (Fernando Sancho). Most of the film, however, concerns itself with a search for the man who killed Django's father.

There's lots of action, both gunfights and fistfights, intensified with a very good Bruno Nicolai score. Plus, Erika Blanc and Evelyn Stewart in the same movie: heaven could be less fulfilling.

Django Spara per Primo see *Django Shoots First*

The Django Story see *Reach You Bastard*

Django Strikes Again (1987)

Ritorno di Django Ital. *Director:* Ted Archer; *Script:* Nello Rossati/Franco Reggiani; *Camera:* Sandro Mancori; *Music:* Gianfranco Plenizio; *Producer:* (Italy/Spain/Germany). *Cast:* Franco Nero, Donald Pleasence, Christopher Connelly, William Berger, Lici Lee Lyon.

There are many wanna-be sequels to Sergio Corbucci's original *Django* (see the Django Films Appendix), but this is the only one endorsed by the filmmaker. And it's the only one starring the original Django, Franco Nero.

Director Archer (Nello Rossati) creates an odd tale: Django has been in a monastery for ten years, trying to forget his bloody past. Then he receives word that his daughter has been kidnapped and is being held captive by an evil slaver, Orlowsky (Christopher Connelly). Obviously, Django sheds his monk robe (and apparently his religious philosophy), digs up his legendary Gatling gun (from a grave in the cemetery marked "Django"), and goes to her rescue, avenging countless evils along the way.

The film has a curious alien look about it, probably due to the questionable, unsettling locale. It doesn't look like America, at least not *Northern* America. In fact, it appears to be the Amazon jungle(?).

Director Rossati and composer Plenizio also created the sex farce *The Sensuous Nurse* (1974) with Ursula Andress and Jack Palance. Plus, a strange gorefest called *I'm a Zombie . . . You're a Zombie* (1980). In 1991, Franco Nero rejoined Nello Rossati for a traditional action film called *Top Line,* which included an unexpected climax involving UFOs and grotesque aliens.

Django the Bastard (1969)

Stranger's Gundown; Django il Bastardo Ital. *Director:* Sergio Garrone; *Script:* Sergio Garrone/Antonio De Teffé; *Camera:* Gino Santini; *Music:* Vasco and Mancuso; *Producer:* Pino De Martino, Sepac/Tigielle 33 (Italy/Spain). *Cast:* Anthony Steffen, Lu Kamenke, Paolo Gozlino, Rada Rassimov, Furio Meniconi, Jean Louis, Teodoro Corra, Riccardo Garrone, Carlo Gaddi.

This is the uncredited inspiration for Clint Eastwood's *High Plains Drifter.* It's also Sergio Garrone's very best film. Cowritten with actor Anthony Steffen (under his real name, Antonio De Teffé), director Garrone has designed a remarkable motion picture, ranking as probably one of the all-time top ten Spaghetti Westerns.

Anthony Steffen (also delivering one of his best performances) is the steely-eyed Django, a man (or is he a ghost?) who has come to seek vengeance against a group of former Confederate officers who betrayed and annihilated their regiment for a treasure in gold. Thinking that their secret is safe, especially now that the Civil War is over, these villains are caught by surprise when the "angel of death" visits them. One by one, with supernatural efficiency, Django hunts down the villainous scum. And brutally, he unflinchingly slaughters them. It's violent and horrific, and (as such) it's one of the most extreme examples of this entire Euro film genre.

Movie poster from *Django the Bastard* (1969) starring Anthony Steffen.

The photography (by Gino Santini) is excellent, contrasting the shockingly barbarous action with sensitive soft colors. Sergio Garrone's brilliant use of closeups and dramatic angle shots adds to the overall uneasy atmosphere. The "Vasco and Mancuso" team composes the somber musical score.

Django the Condemned see *Outlaw of Red River*

Django the Honorable Killer see *Outlaw of Red River*

Django's Great Return see *Keoma*

Djurado (1966)

Dyurado; . . . E Djurado Ital. *Director:* Gianni Narzisi; *Script:* Gianni Narzisi/ Will Azzella/Federico De Urrutia; *Camera:* Miguel Mila; *Music:* Gianni Ferrio; *Producer:* Studio T/Cooperativa Astro (Italy/Spain). *Cast:* Montgomery Clark, Scilla Gabel, Mary Jordan, Isarco Ravaioli, Margaret Lee, Luis Induñi, Goyo Lebrero.

An unimpressive Italian-Spanish coproduction that tells the predictable story of a professional gambling gunman named Djurado (Montgomery Clark), nicknamed "Golden Poker" because "he's so unbeatable at cards."

One day, he arrives at a little border town called Silver Mine and proceeds to win half ownership of the saloon, belonging to Barbara (Scilla Gabel). She doesn't mind because Djurado is handsome and (an important "and") he is willing to protect the casino (and the town) from the fierce and sadistic Tucan (Luis Induñi), an evil outlaw who has oppressed the citizens for many years.

Initially, it looks as though Djurado has "bitten off more than he can chew" but soon, with the aid of a traveling federal sheriff named Silvermine, the mission is accomplished. And with Tucan dead, Djurado and Barbara can live happily every after.

Do Not Touch the White Woman (1974)

Touche Pas la Femme Blanche Fr; *Non Toccate la Donna Bianca* Ital. *Director:* Marco Ferreri; *Script:* Marco Ferreri; *Camera:* Étienne Becker; *Music:* Philippe Sarde; *Producer:* Marco Ferreri (Italy). *Cast:* Marcello Mastroianni, Catherine Deneuve, Ugo Tognazzi, Michel Piccoli, Philippe Noiret; Darry-Cowl, Franco Fabrizi.

An esoteric entry from Italy's bad boy of the "art" cinema, Marco Ferreri (who satirizes Italian cannibal films in his *How Tasty Are the White Folks!* and horror in *The Ape Woman* and *Bye Bye Monkey*).

This "Western" takes place in a contemporary urban setting with Marcello Mastroianni as General Custer attacking high-rise developers with a cannon. During the process of the film, the modern backdrop slowly fades away until the characters are indeed in the Old West.

Lots of blood and gore flow in a graphic Indian/Cavalry battle that wipes out the entire cast.

Doc, Hands of Steel see *Man with the Golden Pistol*

Doc, Manos de Plato see *Man with the Golden Pistol*

Un Dólar Recompensa see *Prey of Vultures*

A Dollar a Head see *Navajo Joe*

A Dollar Between the Teeth see *Stranger in Town*

Dollar of Fire (1967)

Un Dollaro di Fuoco Ital. *Director:* Nick Nostro; *Script:* Ignacio Iquino/Astrain Bada; *Camera:* Julian Rosental; *Music:* Henry Escobar; *Producer:* Cineproduzioni/I.F.I.S.A. (Italy/Spain). *Cast:* Michael Riva, Diana Garson, Albert Farley, Indio Gonzales, Jack Rocks, Mario Maranzana, Diana Sorel.

Michael Riva portrays Kelly, the new sheriff of Jerrington; Diana Garson is his beautiful 18-year-old daughter, Liz. The frontier town is a hotbed of corruption and vice, sanctioned by Mayor Baker (Albert Farley) and his cronies. But the citizens of Jerrington want the sheriff to uphold the law and stop the vitiation. When one of his deputies (played by Jack Rocks, obviously a ribald pseudonym) is wounded in Kenton's gambling-saloon whorehouse, Sheriff Kelly closes the place down. The reclusive enigmatic owner, Nora Kenton (Diana Sorel), comes out of hiding. She (joins with the mayor) in a plot against Kelly until she finds out that the sheriff is actually her husband (!) whom she abandoned years before.

Written with tongue-in-cheek gusto by Western director Ignacio Iquino, this Spanish-Italian production is one of two Spaghetti Westerns directed by Nick Nostro; his next effort *(One After Another)* is equally demented. Nostro is best remembered for his James Bond parody *Operation: Counterspy* starring George Ardisson, plus *Spartacus and the Ten Gladiators*, and *Super Argo versus Diabolicus*.

Un Dollaro a Testa see *Navajo Joe*

Un Dollaro di Fuoco see *Dollar of Fire*

Un Dollaro Bucato see *Blood for a Silver Dollar*

Un Dollaro Tra i Denti see *Stranger in Town*

Dollars for a Fast Gun (1968)

One Hundred Thousand Dollars for Lassiter; 100.000 Dollari per Lassiter Ital. *Director:* Joaquin Romero Marchent; *Script:* Sergio Donati; *Camera:* Fulvio Testi; *Music:* Marcello Giombini; *Producer:* Cesar Film (Spain/Italy). *Cast:* Robert Hundar, Peter Martell, Pamela Tudor, Luigi Pistilli, Jesus Puente, Roberto Camardiel, Andrew Ray, Luis Gasper; José Bodaló, Aldo Sambrell.

Confined to a wheelchair, wealthy Adam Martin (José Bodaló) still controls the entire territory. It seems that he owns everything, and what he doesn't own he's trying to buy. Or steal. Heavy taxes have been imposed on the settlers and Martin's henchmen are "very persuasive" in collecting the funds.

Meanwhile, widowed ranch owner Helen Ray (Pamela Tudor) hires a dandy gunfighter named Lassiter (Robert Hundar) to stop the unscrupulous activities of the evil land baron. Lassiter concocts an intricate plot that shakes the very foundation of Martin's fortune, exposing him as a retired double-crossing bank robber. Apparently, his ex-partner Frank Nolan (Antonio Ruiz) had shot him (thus, paralyzing him) when Martin escaped with all the money, money used to originally finance his empire. Lassiter teams with Nolan and Helen's brother (Peter Martell) to defeat the money-grabbing Adam Martin and his outlaw gang.

Prolific costar Aldo Sambrell, featured in many Westerns, made many nongenre films too, including Jackie Chan's *Armour of God 2* (1991).

Domani, Passo a Salutare la Tua Vedova ... Parola di Epidemia see *My Horse, My Gun, Your Widow*

Una Donna Chiamata Apache see *Apache Woman*

Una Donna per Ringo see *Woman for Ringo*

Donne alla Frontiera see *Tall Women*

Don't Turn the Other Cheek (1971)

Long Live Your Death; Viva la Muerte ... Tua Sp. *Director:* Duccio Tessari; *Script:* Dino Maiuri/Massimo de Rita/Günter Eber; *Camera:* José F. Aguayo; *Music:* Gianni Ferrio; *Producer:* Mickey Knox, Hercules/Tritone/Terra (Italy/Spain/West Germany). *Cast:* Franco Nero, Eli Wallach, Lynn Redgrave, Eduardo Fajardo, José Jaspe, Horst Janson, Mirko Ellis, Marilu Tolo, Carla Mancini, Victor Israel, Furio Meniconi, Gisela Hahn.

An entertaining comedy Western from underrated Duccio Tessari (director of the *Ringo* movies) tells the story of a very unlikely partnership between a Russian prince (Franco Nero), a Tuco-ish Mexican bandit (Eli Wallach) and

Movie poster from *Don't Turn the Other Cheek* (1971).

a sexy-air-headed Irish journalist (Lynn Redgrave). Nero and Wallach are after the gold (of course), while Redgrave wants to start a revolution.

Actor Horst Janson had his "15 minutes" when he played lead in the Hammer film *Captain Kronos: Vampire Hunter*. There's a good score and theme form Gianni Ferrio (who also composed *Alive or Preferably Dead* and *Tex and the Lord of the Deep* for Tessari). The whole thing is loosely based on the book *Killer from Yuma* written by Lewis B. Patten.

Don't Wait, Django . . . Shoot! (1969)

Non Aspettare, Django . . . Spara! Ital. *Director:* Edward G. Muller; *Script:* Glenn Vincent Davis; *Camera:* Vitaliano Natalucci; *Music:* Felice Di Stefano; *Producer:* Vincenzo Musolino, Cawall Film (Italy). *Cast:* Sean Todd, Pedro Sanchez, Rada Rassimov, Bill Jackson, Gino Buzzanca, Alfredo Rizzi.

There's a lot of riding and shooting, but it all seems like wasted energy. After traipsing all over the territory, the hero Django (Sean Todd) and his sidekick, Diego (Pedro Sanchez), end up back where they started. It all has to do with yet another variation on the "vengeance for a slaughtered family" theme.

This time, Django is hired by Mary (Rada Rassimov) and her father (Franco Pesce) to avenge the death of Uncle Burke, an old cattle rancher, killed by wealthy land baron Don Alvarez (Bill Jackson) and his henchmen. While Django and Diego are busy tracking down gang members Navarro and Chico, kingpin Don Alvarez raids the ranch, kidnapping Mary and killing her father.

In an odd plot twist, another band of outlaws led by a Mexican named Nico (Alfredo Rizzo) robs and kills Don Alvarez. Nico is about to rape Mary when Django rescues her and eliminates the intruding villain.

The movie has an endearing "make it up as you go" quality, from popular exploitation sleaze-meister Edward G. Muller (pseudonym for Edoardo Mulargia). Rada Rassimov is not the "real life" wife of star Sean Todd (alias Ivan Rassimov). They are sister and brother.

Doomed Fort see *Massacre at Fort Grant*

Doomed Fort see *Fury of the Apaches*

Doomsday see *Drummer of Vengeance*

Doppia Taglia per Minnesota Stinky see *Fistful of Death*

Dos Cruces en Danger Pass see *Two Crosses at Danger Pass*

Dos Mil Dólares por Coyote see *Two Thousand Dollars for Coyote*

Dos Pistolas Gemelas see *Woman for Ringo*

Dove Si Spara di Più see *Fury of Johnny Kid*

Down with Your Hands . . . You Scum! see *Reach You Bastard*

Dream of Zorro see *Grandsons of Zorro*

Drop Them or I'll Shoot see *Specialists*

Drummer della Vendetta see *Drummer of Vengeance*

Drummer of Vengeance (1971)

Day of Judgment; Doomsday; Drummer della Vendetta Ital; *Il Giorno del Giudizio* Ital. *Director:* Robert Paget; *Script:* Robert Paget; *Camera:* Alvaro

Lanzone; *Music:* CAM Recording; *Producer:* Robert Paget, Times Films (England/Italy). *Cast:* Ty Hardin, Craig Hill, Gordon Mitchell, Rossano Brazzi, Ida De Benedetto, Raf Baldassarre; Rosalba Neri, Lee Burton.

Here's a British-Italian coproduction helmed by Italian director Mario Gariazzo using a Robert Paget pseudonym (not to be confused with Italian filmmaker Calvin J. Padget, alias Giorgio Ferroni), starring an impressive collection of genre regulars. Unfortunately, it's not much more than a routine "revenge for a slaughtered family" flick, similar to many others. Ty Hardin is "the stranger," stalking and killing the six men who murdered his wife (Rosalba Neri) and child.

The most unique thing about this film is the production. Usually, British coproductions (i.e., *The Hunting Party, Hannie Caulder, Town Called Hell*) lean toward traditional Hollywood standards, manned with a predominantly Anglo cast and crew. Not so, this time. The story, penned by Paget, is very Euro in scope. And the production crew is mostly Italian, including chief cameraman Alvaro Lanzone. The entire film was shot in Spain and Italy.

The musical score is attributed to "General Music Rome," but it's not an original composition; the soundtrack is actually Ennio Morricone's score to *Hellbenders*, which Times Films apparently bought from CAM Recording, Ennio's publisher.

Duck You Sucker (1971)

Fistful of Dynamite; Giù la Testa Ital. *Director:* Sergio Leone; *Script:* Luciano Vincenzoni/Sergio Donati/Sergio Leone; *Camera:* Giuseppe Ruzzolini; *Music:* Ennio Morricone; *Producer:* Fulvio Morsella, Rafran/San Marco (Italy). *Cast:* James Coburn, Rod Steiger, Maria Monti, Rik Battaglia, Franco Graziosi, Romolo Valli, Domingo Antoine.

This was the least successful of the Sergio Leone films, possibly due to the rather pathetic title, *Duck You Sucker* (it was changed to *Fistful of Dynamite* after the damage had been done). Or maybe the targeted audience didn't care for the politically motivated plot. Or perhaps it suffered from the obvious lack of a strong villain. Or possibly it was James Coburn's irritating (grating, annoying) phony Irish accent.

In reality it's the movie that Leone didn't want to make. Initially, he planned to "oversee" the project; Giancarlo Santi (director of *The Big Showdown*, or *Storm Rider*) was signed to direct this film, but after the shooting began, Coburn and Steiger (feeling compromised and claiming that they had been hired to make a "Leone" film) refused to work. Leone took over the helm, relegating Santi to a "larger-than-normal amount of second unit work."

It is the story of an imported freedom fighter and a Mexican peasant who start out as bandits and end up as heroes during the Mexican Revolution. The film is set in 1913 Mexico, after the collapse of the 35-year Porfirio Diaz dictatorship, the brief assumption of power and resulting assassination of Francisco Madero and the revolt of Pancho Villa against the new dictator, Huerta.

As the title implies, there's an abundance of explosions and "k-a-a-boom" special effects. The FX are engineered by a team, headed by cult filmmaker Anthony Dawson (Antonio Margheriti) who also worked with Leone on the *Dollars* films.

Movie Poster from *Duck You Sucker* (1971).

Due Contro Tutti see *Terrible Sheriff*

Due Croci a Danger Pass see *Two Crosses at Danger Pass*

Le Due Facce del Dollaro see *Two Sides of the Dollar*

Due Figli di Ringo see *Two Sons of Ringo*

I Due Figli di Trinità see *Two Sons of Trinity*

Due Fratelli i un Posto Chiamato Trinità see *Jesse and Lester, Two Brothers in a Place Called Trinity*

Due Mafiosi nel Far West see *Two Gangsters in the Wild West*

Due Once di Piombo see *My Name Is Pecos*

Due Pistole e un Vigliacco see *Two Pistols and a Coward*

Due R-R-Ringos nel Texas see *Two R-R-Ringos from Texas*

Due Sergenti del General Custer see *Two Sergeants of General Custer*

I Due Violenti see *Two Gunmen*

Due Volte Giuda see *Twice a Judas*

Duel at Rio Bravo see *Gunmen of Rio Grande*

Duel at Sundown (1965)

Duel au Crépuscule Fr; *Duell vor Sonneruntergang* Ger. *Director:* Leopoldo Lahola; *Script:* Leopoldo Lahola/Anya Corvin; *Camera:* Janez Kalisnik; *Music:* Zui Borodo; *Producer:* Leopoldo Lahola (France/West Germany). *Cast:* Peter Van Eyck, Carole Gray, Wolfgang Kieling, Mario Girotti, Carl Lange, Walter Barnes.

An early film featuring Terence Hill (when he was still using his real name, Mario Girotti). Terence and Peter Van Eyck are brothers, Larry and Don McGow. Their father (Walter Barnes) is a land-grabbing evil town boss with his eye on the Parker ranch, run by Nancy (Carole Gray) and her father, Punch (Wolfgang Kieling).

Don McGow falls in love with Nancy (adding the ever-popular "Romeo and Juliet" theme to the film) and, eventually, he faces his brother in a showdown, which (despite the title) takes place in the early afternoon.

Duel au Crépuscule see *Duel at Sundown*

Duel in the Eclipse (1967)

Requiem for a Gringo; Requiem per un Gringo Ital. *Director:* Eugenio Martin/ José Luis Merino; *Script:* Michael Martinez Roman/Arrigo Colombo/Giuliana Caravaglia; *Camera:* Mario Pacheco; *Music:* Angelo Francesco Lavagnino; *Producer:* Arrigo Colombo, Hispanea Film (Spain). *Cast:* Lang Jeffries, Femi Benussi, Fernando Sancho, Carlo Gaddi, Ruben Rojo, Aldo Sambrell, Carlo Simoni.

Gringo (Lang Jeffries) is a gunfighter who vows revenge when his brother is tortured and killed by bandits; so he infiltrates the gang. The final gunbattle takes place during a convenient eclipse (thus, the title). A fun film, if you overlook the holes in the plot.

There's an extraordinary good cast, including peplum star Lang Jeffries

(*Revenge of the Gladiators* and *Sword of the Empire*) in his only Spaghetti Western. Plus (absolutely beautiful) Femi Benussi, best known for *The Killer Strikes Again* and *Strip Nude for Your Killer*, adds a puissant luster to this production. There's also an exceptional musical score from grossly unrated Angelo Lavagnino *(Today It's Me, Tomorrow You)* who, incidentally, has a rare acting role in the Italian thriller, *Something's Creeping in the Dark*, directed by Mario Colucci.

Although he made three Westerns and two Zorro pics, codirector José Luis Merino is remembered primarily for his two thrillers, *Scream of the Demon Lover* (1971) and *Return of the Zombies*, or *The Hanging Woman* (1971).

Duell vor Sonneruntergang see *Duel at Sundown*

Duello nel Texas see *Gunfight at Red Sands*

Durango Is Coming, Pay or Die (1972)

Arriva Durango, Paga o Muori Ital. *Director:* Luis Monter; *Script:* Roberto Montero; *Camera:* Alfonso Nieva; *Music:* Coriolano Gori/Lallo Gori; *Producer:* Luis Film/Dauro Film (Italy/Spain). *Cast:* Brad Harris, José Torres, José Rivas Jaspe, Gabriella Giorgelli.

Another obscure Spaghetti Western from director Roberto Montero (this time using his "Luis Monter" alias), best known for his sword-'n'-sorcery *Tharus, Son of Attila* (1961), plus *Wild Nights of Caligula* (1977), and *Eye of the Spider* (1982).

Film Worldbook identifies this movie as "a routine hunt-the-real-killer Western." It's anybody's guess what that means.

Dust in the Sun (1971)

Lust in the Sun; Sole nella Polvere Ital; *Dans la Poussière du Soleil* Fr. *Director:* Richard Balducci; *Script:* Richard Balducci; *Camera:* Tadasu Suzuki; *Music:* Francis Lai; *Producer:* Univers Galaxie (France). *Cast:* Bob Cunningham, Maria Schell, Daniel Beretta, José Calvo, Perla Cristal, Karin Meier.

Little information is available regarding this seldom-seen French production. It remains a curiosity, especially because the music is provided by popular French composer, Francis Lai, renowned for his Claude Lelouch collaborations, especially *Bolero* (1982) and *A Man and a Woman* (1966).

Dynamite Jack (1963)

Dinamite Jack Ital. *Director:* Jean Bastia; *Script:* Jean Manse/Jacques Emmanuel/Bastia; *Camera:* Roger Hubert; *Music:* Jacques De Sagneaux; *Producer:* J.P. Bertrand (France). *Cast:* Fernandel, Eleonore Vargas, Adrienne Corri, Daniel Ivernel, Lucien Raimbourg, Jess Hahn, George Lycan.

Popular French comic Fernandel plays a dual role in this spoof of the Western genre. He plays a tough gunfighter named Dynamite Jack and also a stupid "tenderfoot" Frenchman, Antoine. The jokes are mostly of the slapstick variety, a collection of dated sight gags dealing with twin identities.

Although he starred in over 60 movies since his first film in 1931 (*Le Blanc et le Noir*) until his death in 1971, very few "Fernandel" movies have received

Rik VAN NUTTER
Halina ZALEWSKA
Renato BALDINI
REGIE:
ANTHONY DAWSON
JOE L'IMPLACABLE
DE ONVERBIDDELIJKE

distribution in the United States. His only brush with fame in America was a costarring role alongside Bob Hope in *Paris Holiday* (1957).

Dynamite Jim (1966)

Dinamite Jim Ital. *Director:* Alfonso Balcazar; *Script:* Alfonso Balcazar/José A. De La Loma; *Camera:* Victor Monreal; *Music:* Nico Fidenco; *Producer:* Cinematografias Balcazar/Lux (Spain/Italy). *Cast:* Luis Dávila, Fernando Sancho, Rosalba Neri, Aldo Sambrell, Mary Conte, Charles Sola.

The wonderfully campy theme song is worth the price of admission (or perhaps more correctly, worth the cost of the video tape). Plus, there's the additional bonus of Rosalba Neri as a scantily clad dancehall girl. Who could ask for more?

During the Civil War, a northern spy nicknamed Dynamite Jim (Luis Dávila) tries to sneak a gold shipment from Mexico, through the South, to a Union fortress in Iowa. Along the way he has to deal with outlaws (Aldo Sambrell) and greedy friends (Fernando Sancho). But overall, it's a lighthearted journey.

Dynamite Joe (1966)

Joe l'Implacabile Ital. *Director:* Anthony Dawson; *Script:* Maria Del Carmin Martinez; *Camera:* Manuel Merino; *Music:* Carlo Savina; *Producer:* Seven Film/P.C. Hispamer (Italy/Spain). *Cast:* Rick Van Nutter, Halina Zalewska, Mercedes Caracuel, Renato Baldini, Santiago Rivero, Barta Barry, Aldo Cecconi, Alfonso Rocas.

Rick Van Nutter (alias Clyde Rogers) stars as Dynamite Joe, a special government secret agent. It's a tale of trickery, double-crossing and hidden identities as Dynamite Joe tries to put an end to the inordinate number of stagecoach gold robberies in the west, just after the end of the Civil War. It turns out that the real culprit behind the multiple thefts is Senator Senneth (Santiago Rivero).

Popular cult filmmaker Anthony Dawson (Antonio Margheriti) has directed over 50 feature films, his first being *Assignment Outer Space* in 1960 under the one-time alias Anthony Daisies ("Daisies" is the literal translation of "Margheriti," but he changed it to "Dawson" when he learned of the unflattering connotations).

Besides making many horror films (*Andy Warhol's Frankenstein* and *Dracula, Cannibals in the Streets* and *Castle of Terror* with Sergio Corbucci), Dawson was responsible for five Spaghetti Westerns (see Directors filmography), a variety of peplums (*The Fall of Rome* and *Hercules: Prisoner of Evil*), plus action (*Car Crash*), science fiction (*Treasure Island in Outer Space*), war (*The Last Hunter*), spy (*Lightning Bolt*) and even a mondo film *Go, Go, Go, World!*). *Vengeance* and *Stranger and the Gunfighter* are considered to be his best Westerns.

Dyurado see Djurado

Opposite: Movie poster from Anthony Dawson's *Dynamite Joe* (1966).

E alla Fine lo Chiamavano Jerusalem l'Implacabile see *Calibre .38*

E Continuavano a Fregarsi il Milione di Dollari see *Bad Man's River*

E Cosi Divennero i 3 Superman del West see *Three Supermen of the West*

E Dio Disse a Caino. . . see *And God Said to Cain*

. . .E Divenne il Più Spietato Bandito del Sud see *Man Who Killed Billy the Kid*

. . .E Djurado see *Djurado*

E Intorno a Lui Fu Morte see *Death Knows No Time*

. . .E lo Chiamarono Spirito Santo see *He Was Called Holy Ghost*

. . .E per Tetto un Cielo di Stella see *A Sky Full of Stars for a Roof*

E Poi lo Chiamarono il Magnifico see *Man of the East*

È Tornato Sabata, Hai Chiuso un'Altra Volta see *Return of Sabata*

. . .E Venne il Tempo di Uccidere see *Time and Place for Killing*

E Venne l'Ora della Vendetta see *White Comanche*

E Vennero in Quattro . . . per Uccidere Sartana see *Four Came to Kill Sartana*

Eagle's Wing (1980)

Eagles Wing Brit. *Director:* Anthony Harvey; *Script:* John Briley; *Camera:* Billy Williams; *Music:* Marc Wilkinson; *Producer:* Rank Films (England/Spain). *Cast:* Martin Sheen, Sam Waterston, Harvey Keitel, Stephane Audran, José Carlos Ruiz, Manuel Ojeda, Pedro Damieari.

Written by Oscar winner (for *Gandhi*) John Briley, based on a book by Michael Syson, this British Western is primarily an allegorical tale filled with heavy-handed symbolism. Martin Sheen is Pike, a gringo trapper who battles Comanche chief White Bull (Sam Waterston) over the capture of the legendary "white stallion."

It's a noble attempt from filmmaker Anthony Harvey, director of the award-winning costume drama *A Lion in Winter,* starring Katharine Hepburn and Peter O'Toole.

Actress Stephane Audran was Mrs. Sam Fuller.

Eastman see *Man of the East*

Ehi, Amico . . . C'è Sabata, Hai Chiuso! see *Sabata*

Ehi Amico . . . Sei Morto! see *Hey Amigo! A Toast to Your Death*

Era Sam Walbash . . . Lo Chiamavano "Così Sia" see *His Name Was Sam Walbash, But They Call Him Amen*

Gli Eroi del West see *Heroes of the West*

Un Esercito di Cinque Uomini see *Five Man Army*

Escondido see *Minute to Pray, a Second to Die*

Even Django Has His Price (1971)

Pistol for Django; Anche per Django Hanno un Prezzo Ital. *Director:* Paolo Solvay; *Script:* Mario De Rosa/Luigi Batzella; *Camera:* Giorgio Montagnani; *Music:* Vasili Kojucharov; *Producer:* Diego Alchimede, Constitution (Italy/ Spain). *Cast:* Jeff Cameron, John Desmont, Gengher Gatti, Esmeralda Barros, Edilo Kim, Dominique Badout, William Major.

A great musical score (and a good title) is lost on this hopelessly inferior Spaghetti Western embarrassingly directed by Luigi Batzella (aka Paolo Solvay). "Horrible" is a kind word for this atrocity. It is one of the very worst.

Jeff Cameron, looking more out of place than usual, is Django. He's after the notorious bank-robbing Cortez brothers led by Ramon (Edilo Kim). But a Wells Fargo detective and professional gambler (!?!) named Fulton (William Major) convinces him to "hold off on a showdown" until the two of them discover the whereabouts of the famous Cortez gold mine. In the meantime, one of the brothers turns out to be a "sister," which leads to even more overall, ludicrous confusion.

Director Batzella fared much better with his nongenre films, especially *Devil's Wedding Night* (1973), *Nude Satan* (1974), *The Beast in Heat* (also called *SS Hell Camp*) (1977), and *Desert Tigers* (1977), with Richard Harrison and Gordon Mitchell.

Every Man for Himself see *The Ruthless Four*

Execution (1968)

Django Prépare ton Exécution Fr. *Director:* Domenico Paolella; *Script:* Domenico Paolella/Fernando Franchi; *Camera:* Aldo Scavarda; *Music:* Lallo Gori; *Producer:* Fernando Franchi, Mercedes Film (Italy/France). *Cast:* John Richardson, Mimmo Palmara, Rita Clein, Franco Giornelli, Piero Vida, Nestor Garay, Romano Magnino.

A good, cynical, no-nonsense Spaghetti Western about revenge and retribution. After many years in prison for robbery, Chips (Mimmo Palmara, aka Dick Palmer) is freed and he begins his long hunt for the double-crossing ex-partner John (John Richardson), who ended up with all the gold.

In a surprise ending, after finding his former friend, Chips is killed in a different kind of "double" cross, this time involving John's twin brother, Bill. The two brothers are captured by the law, but manage to buy their freedom with the elusive gold. And "justice" prevails.

Filmmaker Paolella also made the equally misogynistic *Hate for Hate* in 1967. He directed many nongenre films, including *Hercules Against the Bar-*

barians and *Hercules versus the Tyrant of Babylon*, plus *Agent 003: Operation Atlantis, Sisters of Satan, Gardenia,* and *The Prey*. Lead actor, John Richardson, made his mark later with thrillers like Sergio Martino's *Torso* (also called *Bodies Bear Traces of Carnal Violence* in 1973) and Umberto Lenzi's *Eyeball* (1978).

Eye for an Eye (1972)

Taste of the Savage; Occhio per Occhio, Dente per Dente... Ital. *Director:* Albert Marshall; *Script:* Ricardo Cartray/Antonio Shert; *Camera:* J. Xavier Cruz; *Music:* Rueben Fuentes; *Producer:* Produzioni Cinematografica Marte (Italy/Spain/Mexico). *Cast:* Cameron Mitchell, Isela Vega, Helena Rojo, Jorge Luke, Nick Georgiade, Raymando Cafetella, Arthur Hansel.

Spanish filmmaker Alberto Mariscal (aka Albert Marshall) directs this film with an unrelenting vengeance, brimming with brutality and graphic violence. Mexican sex starlet, Isela Vega (best known for her sultry performance in Sam Peckinpah's *Bring Me the Head of Alfredo Garcia*) is effective, but perhaps miscast, as an incestuous mother who becomes obsessed with hate when her husband is killed by a pack of gunmen. She hires a notorious gunfighter named Huck (Cameron Mitchell) to teach her son Judd (Jorge Luke) the "art of the pistol" and then she "controls the boy's new passions" through her warm bed.

Sordid as that may be, the real star of the film is Cameron Mitchell who gives an absolutely over-the-top performance of a bounty hunter with a conscience, deeply regretting that he has turned the boy into a killing machine. In a peculiar way the movie is a loose remake of Mitchell's *Last Gun* (1964), also telling the story of a gunfighter who wants to "stop the lunacy" of senseless showdowns.

Fabulous Trinity see *With Friends, Nothing Is Easy*

Faccia a Faccia see *Face to Face*

Faccia d'Angelo see *Long Days of Vengeance*

Face to Face (1967)

Faccia a Faccia Ital. *Director:* Sergio Sollima; *Script:* Sergio Donati/Sergio Sollima; *Camera:* Raphael Pacheco; *Music:* Ennio Morricone; *Producer:* Alberto Grimaldi, P.E.A. (Italy). *Cast:* Tomás Milian, Gian Maria Volonté, William Berger, Jolanda Modio, Carole André, Nicoletta Machiavelli, José Torres, Ted Carter, Rick Boyd, Frank Braña, Aldo Sambrell.

One of three "Sergio Sollima" Westerns (also see *Big Gundown* and *Run Man, Run*), but the pace is much slower and the film takes on a saga quality, making it quite a deviation from the other two.

In this movie, Gian Maria Volonté ("Indio" in *For a Few Dollars More*) is a former history professor, Brad Fletcher, who goes West for health reasons. He meets (and is enamored with an impetuous outlaw Beauregard Bennet (Tomás Milian), the leader of the notorious gang of bandidos called the Savage Herd. Fletcher and Beauregard team together and become friends. But the friendship causes them to develop into very different beings.

During one philosophical moment, Fletcher says, "In the West, it's most difficult to distinguish the instinct for survival from the quest for power." In that statement lies the basis for Sollima's story. Fletcher becomes fascinated with violence and usurps Beauregard's position as the Herd's leader; Beauregard, fed up with the unnecessary brutality, double-crosses Fletcher and joins with a Pinkerton agent (William Berger) to bring "his friend" to justice.

After directing this movie, Sergio Sollima abandoned the Western genre and became a key filmmaker in the action/exploitation gangster-oriented arena (especially remembered for *The Family* with Charles Bronson, *Blood in the Streets* starring Oliver Reed, and the controversial 1972 horror film, *Devil in the Brain*.

Fall of the Mohicans see *Last of the Mohicans*

Far West Story see *Bandera Bandits*

Fasthand (1972)

Fasthand Is Still My Name; Lo Chiamavano Requiescat Fasthand Ital; *Mano Rapida* Span. *Director:* Frank Bronston; *Script:* Eduardo Brochero/A. Cardone/ Sergio Ciani; *Camera:* Emilio Foriscot; *Music:* Gianni Ferrio; *Producer:* John Wyler (Italy/Spain). *Cast:* Alan Steel, William Berger, Welma Truccol, Paco Sanz, Gill Roland, Celina Bessy, Francisco Braña, Fernando Bilbao.

If "Fasthand" is anybody's name, none of the characters (nor anybody else, for that matter) is aware of it. There's no one with the "Fasthand" moniker. Instead, Macedo (William Berger) is the villain. He was a Confederate officer during the Civil War, and he's still angry at the North for a long list of things, but especially over the death of his brother.

He (and his Rebel gang) terrorize a Cavalry fort, killing everybody except Captain Jeff Madison (Alan Steel, aka producer John Wyler). The outlaws decide to torture him instead. They tie Jeff to a stake, brand him, spit on him (in a very long and disgusting scene), and eventually shoot holes in his hands (certainly destroying his chances of ever being called Fasthand). They leave him to die. But of course, he doesn't.

Jeff is rescued by some friendly Indians, specifically by a beautiful squaw (Celina Bessy), trying her best to impersonate Geneviève Bujold; she's really mastered the posturing of the lips) and he's nursed back to health. Two years pass and the Rebel gang continues to cause trouble, so (feeling strong enough to do the job) Jeff goes after them with a vengeance.

This silliness was written by Eduardo Brochero, Sergio Ciani (the real name of star Alan Steel) and filmmaker Alberto Cardone (who should know better); it was directed by Frank Bronston (alias for Mario Adelchi Bianchi).

Fasthand Is Still My Name see *Fasthand*

Father Jackleg see *Sting of the West*

Fedra West see *I Do Not Forgive . . . I Kill!*

Few Dollars for Django (1966)

Per Pochi Dollari per Django Ital; *Bravo Django*. *Director:* Leon Klimovsky; *Script:* Manuel Sebares/Tito Carpi; *Camera:* Aldo Pennelli; *Music:* Carlo Savina;

Producer: Marino Gerola, Filmar Cinematografica (Italy/Spain). *Cast:* Anthony Steffen, Gloria Osuna, Frank Wolff, Joe Kamel, Alfonso Rojas, Angel Ter, Thomas Moore.

The old "twin" trick is played on bounty hunter Django (Anthony Steffen) in this harmless variation of the "big trouble with the town boss" theme. A bandit named Jim Norton was responsible for a holdup some years before, and Django is on his trail. He arrives in Main City and finds *George* Norton (Frank Wolff), a peaceful man who claims to be Jim's twin brother.

George tells Django that his bandit brother is dead. And Django is willing to believe it because he has taken a liking to George's "niece" Sally (Gloria Osuma). At this piont, the plot takes a big twist toward the mundane (after all, it *is* a Klimovsky film). Enter, evil town boss Logan (Thomas Moore). He and his henchmen are bullying and torturing the poor farmers. Django and George (Jim?) decide to stop him. Together, they wipe out Logan and his gang, but George dies in the process.

Cowriter Tito Carpi went on to pen many of Enzo G. Castellari's better films, including *Sting of the West* (a Spaghetti Western with Jack Palance), plus many nongenre flicks (i.e., *Tuareg Desert Warrior, Day of the Cobra* with Franco Nero and Sybil Danning, *Warriors of the Wasteland*). Filmmaker Leon Klimovsky is best known for directing Paul Naschy in a variety of horror movies. His Westerns, strangely void of "atmosphere" and suspense, are usually rambling and tedious affairs.

Few More Dollars for the MacGregors see *More Dollars for the MacGregors*

Fidarsi è Bene, Sparare è Meglio see *Dead for a Dollar*

Fifteen Scaffolds for the Killer (1968)

Quindici Forche per un Assassino Ital. *Director:* Nunzio Malasomma; *Script:* Mario De Nardo/J. Luis Bayonas; *Camera:* Stelvio Massi; *Music:* Francesco De Masi; *Producer:* Film EOS/Centauro Film (Italy/Spain). *Cast:* Craig Hill, Susy Andersen, Aldo Sambrell, Tomás Blanco, Andrea Bosić, J. Manuel Martin, George Martin, Frank Braña.

Popular cult thriller/action director Stelvio Massi (*Nightmare City, Rebel, Anti-Crime Squad, Six Women for the Killer,* etc.) learned the tricks of his trade as chief cameraman in many Spaghetti Westerns, just like this one.

This Italian-Spanish coproduction tells the story of Billy Mack (Craig Hill) and his friends, unjustly accused of killing Judy Cook and her daughters. When the sheriff tries to arrest them, they flee and take refuge in an abandoned fort.

An intense character drama unfolds as the innocent men are turned into trapped ruthless killers, and they soon begin venting their frustrations on each other. This is one of Craig Hill's better performances, comparable to his role in *I Want Him Dead* (1968). Certainly, it's a long way from his *Whirly Birds* (1954–57) television days.

Fighters from Ave Maria (1970)

Twilight Avengers; Avengers of the Ave Maria; I Vendicatori dell'Ave Maria Ital. *Director:* Al Albert; *Script:* Bito Albertini; *Camera:* Antonio Modica; *Music:*

Piero Umiliani; *Producer:* P.A.C./Caravel Film (Italy/W. Germany). *Cast:* Tony Kendall, Peter Thorris, Alberto Dell'Acqua, Ida Meda, Spartaco Conversi, Albert Farley.

Another film preoccupied with the inappropriate "circus acrobats as heroes" motif (also see *Ace High, Boot Hill,* and *Return of Sabata*). This time, an evil town boss (Albert Farley) appoints himself sheriff of bordertown Goldfield, and he uses his power to oppress and torture the defenseless citizens. A group of acrobats from a traveling circus (led by Tony Kendall) flee to the mountains where they find exiled rebel patriot Serrano (Alberto Dell'Acqua). They ask him and his "underground" revolutionary army for help. The two unlikely factions (acrobats and soldiers) join together to rid the town of the tyrant.

The unintentionally campy Fellini/Rotaish score comes from prolific Piero Umiliani; director Albertini made another Eurowestern (*Return of Shanghai Joe* with Klaus Kinski) and many entertaining Italian exploitation films (i.e., *Zambo* and *The Three Supermen in the Orient*).

Fighting Fists of Shanghai Joe (1973)

My Name Is Shanghai Joe; Il Mio Nome È Shanghai Joe Ital; *Mezzogiorno di Fuoco per an Hao* Ital. *Director:* Mario Caiano; *Script:* Carlo Alfiero/Mario Caiano/T. F. Treccia; *Camera:* Guglielmo Mancori; *Music:* Bruno Nicolai; *Producer:* Renato Angiolini/Roberto Bessi, C.E.A. (Italy). *Cast:* Klaus Kinski, Chen Lee, Robert Hundar, Gordon Mitchell, Carla Romanelli, Carla Mancini, Giacomo Rossi Stuart, George Wang, Rick Boyd, Paco Sanz, Piero Lulli.

Inspired by the success of Terence Young's *Red Sun* and the popular American television series, "Kung Fu" (starring David Carradine), this is another East-meets-West Western (also see *Kung Fu Brothers in the Wild West, Stranger and the Gunfighter,* and Sergio Corbucci's *The White, the Yellow, and the Black,* all released in 1973).

The graphic violence sets this one apart from the others. There's bloodshed and gore-a-plenty, mostly kung fu related. For an example, in the closing sequence, Shanghai Joe (Chen Lee) thrusts his "fighting fist" all the way through the belly of bad guy Stuart.

But the story is predictably standard as Joe is torn between the "nonviolent ideals" taught him in the Chinese Buddhist monastery and the stark lawlessness of the racist American West. There is a sequel called *The Return of Shanghai Joe* (from a different director, Bitto Albertini) again starring Chen Lee, and Klaus Kinski, even though he dies a gruesome death in this one.

Director Mario Caiano (this time not using his familiar "William Hawkins" pseudonym) made many Spaghetti Westerns (see Directors filmography), but he also directed Barbara Steele and Helga Line in the classic horror film *Nightmare Castle,* plus he made many legendary peplums including *Fury of the Titans* (1964), *Ulysses Against Hercules* (1961) and *Erik the Viking* (1965) starring Gordon Mitchell.

Il Figlio di Django see Son of Django

Figlio di Zorro see Son of Zorro

Final Conflict . . . Django Against Sartana see Django and Sartana Are Coming . . . It's the End

Find a Place to Die (1968)

Joe, Find a Place to Die; Joe, Cercati un Posto per Morire Ital. *Director:* Anthony Ascott; *Script:* Hugo Fregonese/Giuliano Carmineo/Leo Benvenuti; *Camera:* Riccardo Pallottini; *Music:* Gianni Ferrio; *Producer:* Atlantis Film (Italy). *Cast:* Jeffrey Hunter, Pascale Petit, Ted Careter, Daniela Giordano, Gianni Pallavicino; Aldo Lastretti, Piero Lulli.

Settlers Lisa (Pascale Petit) and her brother Paul find gold in a deserted mine, but they are attacked by a gang of outlaws (led by Ted Carter, aka Nello Pazzafini). Lisa escapes to a nearby town called Eagle's Nest and finds a down-on-his-luck gunfighter, Joe Collins (Jeffrey Hunter), who is willing to help her.

Joe, with a few friends (including Reverend Riley, an ex-con phony priest played with gusto by Aldo Lastretti), accompanies Lisa to the mine. Her brother is dead and the outlaws have stolen the gold. The vigilante force goes after them. Joe, with a renewed confidence because of his blooming love for Lisa, meets the boss bandido and kills him dead in a showdown.

Finders Killers (1969)

Seven Devils on Horseback; Seven Savage Men; Se t'Incontro t'Ammazzo Ital. *Director:* Gianni Crea; *Script:* Fabio Piccioni; *Camera:* Giovanni Varriano; *Music:* Stelvio Cipriani; *Producer:* Fernando Norbis, Minerva Film (Italy). *Cast:* Donald O'Brien, Gordon Mitchell, Femi Benussi, Mario Brega, Pia Giancaro, Dean Stratford.

This is a remarkably disjoined film, more accurately resembling a collection of vignettes rather than a finished movie. Donald O'Brien plays an unlikely hero named Jack who sets off to avenge the death of his brother. Meanwhile, there's an outlaw gang led by wacko Dexter (Dean Stratford) in cahoots with the town banker, Parker (Mario Brega). They rob a gold shipment while it is escorted between San Antonio and Black Forest, but within a short time, Dexter is captured by some bounty hunters during a poker game in a local saloon.

They take Dexter out of town and shoot him. Then Jack, who has been wandering about aimlessly, suddenly shows up and kills the bounty hunters. As Dexter is dying, he tells Jack about the gold. Finally, Gordon Mitchell (playing a mysterious, bearded man in black) makes an appearance. He does a lot of wonderful posturing. Eventually, he and Jack join together and recover the gold, killing town boss Parker in the process.

Spectacular hand-held camera work from Giovanni Varriano, a tremendous Stelvio Cipriani score, and Femi Benussi (oh! those eyes!) playing a saloon whore named Rosanna are the film's highlights. Donald O'Brien made many Spaghetti Westerns (see Performers filmography) but he will always be remembered for his demented role as *Dr. Butcher M.D.* (Marino Girolami's zombie/cannibal fest initially called *Zombie Holocaust* in 1978).

Finger on the Trigger (1965)

Sentiero dell'Oro Ital; *El Dedo en el Gatillo* Sp. *Director:* Sidney Pink; *Script:* Ramon Crispo/Sidney Pink/Philip Pink; *Camera:* Enrique Bergier; *Music:* José

Sola; *Producer:* Allied Artists (Spain/Italy/U.S.). *Cast:* Rory Calhoun, Aldo Sambrell, James Philbrook, Leo Anchoriz, Todd Martin, Jorge Rigaud, Silvia Solar, Bruce Talbot.

Uprooted American producer, Sidney Pink, took over the directorial chores for this somewhat surreal Spaghetti Western (also see *Christmas Kid* and *The Tall Women*).

At the end of the Civil War, a band of Union soldiers led by Larry Winton (Rory Calhoun) are traveling west, looking for homesteading land. They arrive at Fort Grant in New Mexico, but they find it under control of diehard Southern Confederates who are "waiting for a shipment of golden horseshoes."

Winton and his men journey further to Southernville, a nearby ghost town, where they actually discover golden horseshoes in an abandoned shed. When both Fort Grant and Southernville are attacked by Indians, the Yankees join forces with the Rebels. They melt down the gold and make bullet casings, Then, together, they eliminate the common enemy. Of course, there's also the "required" romantic subplot between a wagon train widow (Silvia Solar) and ruggedly handsome Winton.

American star Rory Calhoun made many Westerns for Hollywood, including one with Marilyn Monroe called *River of No Return.* His most disconcerting project was *Night of the Lepus.* "It's the movie I'd like to forget," he told *Variety* in a 1972 interview, "For Christ's sake, I was fighting giant rabbits."

First They Pardon, Then They Kill see *Dig Your Grave, Friend . . . Sabata's Coming*

Fistful of Death (1971)

Strange Tale of Minnesota Stinky; Ballad of Django; Doppia Taglia per Minnesota Stinky Ital.; *Giù la Testa . . . Hombre* Ital. *Director:* Miles Deem; *Script:* Demofilo Fidani/R. M. Valenza; *Camera:* Aristide Massaccesi; *Music:* Nico Fidenco/Lallo Gori; *Producer:* Demofilo Fidani, Tarquinia (Italy). *Cast:* Hunt Powers, Klaus Kinski, Gordon Mitchell, Jeff Cameron, Dennys Colt, Lucky MacMurray, Pietro Fumelli.

Sort of a cockeyed reconstructing of American history from prolific (and goofy) director Miles Deem (Demofilo Fidani). Jeff Cameron plays Macho Callaghan (the David Jansen U.S.–produced Western, *Macho Callahan,* had been a big hit in Italy a few months earlier, so Deem borrowed the name and to keep from paying royalties, he added a *g*).

Macho Callaghan is the only survivor of an ambush by the "Wild Bunch" (Butch Cassidy's gang). Aided by his friend, Reverend Cotton (Klaus Kinski in a "good guy" role), Macho disguises himself as an outlaw and infiltrates "the Bunch." The Sundance Kid becomes jealous and engineers a clash between the Cassidy Gang and the Iron Head (!) Gang, hoping to discredit the newcomer. But Sundance's plan doesn't work because Callaghan and Cotton are actually Pinkerton agents. Surprise. Surprise.

Fistful of Dollars (1964)

Per un Pugno di Dollari Ital. *Director:* Sergio Leone (Bob Robertson); *Script:* Sergio Leone/Duccio Tessari; *Camera:* Jack Dalmas; *Music:* Ennio Morricone;

Producer: Arrigo Colombo, Jolly/Constanin/Ocean (Italy/West Germany/Spain). *Cast:* Clint Eastwood, Marianne Koch, Gian Maria Volonté, José Calvo, Wolfgang Lukschy, Sieghart Rupp, Daniel Martin.

This is the movie responsible for the popularity of the Spaghetti Western genre. Much has been written about it. And much has been written about director Sergio Leone's impassioned vision. In retrospect, it is worthy of any and all the accolades.

While (perhaps) not as good as the Sergio Leone films to follow, it set a standard, designed a roadmap, for a violently nihilistic cinematic style that dramatically separates Eurowesterns from the Hollywood variety. It borrows the plotline from *Yojimbo* (a Japanese samurai movie) and tells the story of a cynical stranger (Clint Eastwood) who manipulates two rivaling families in San Miguel, as everybody tries to gain control of the town.

The film is an Italian-German-Spanish production cowritten by Leone and Duccio Tessari (later to become a popular Eurowestern filmmaker in his own right with the *Ringo* series and Alain Delon's *Zorro*). Chief cinematographer Jack Dalmas is future thriller director Massimo Dallamano *(What Have You Done to Solange?* and *Secret of Dorian Gray),* aka Max Dillman *(Bandidos).*

Initially, Richard Harrison was approached to play the "man with no name," but, skeptical of Leone's ability (Sergio's preceding film, *The Colossus of Rhodes,* had failed, commercially and critically), he turned down the project. Instead Harrison made a "safe" peplum film, *Giants of Rome,* for Anthony Dawson (Antonio Margheriti).

Eastwood and Leone teamed together again (with the satisfying addition of Lee Van Cleef) for *For a Few Dollars More* (1965) and *The Good, the Bad, and the Ugly* (1966).

Fistful of Dynamite see *Duck You Sucker*

Fistful of Knuckles see *For a Fist in the Eye*

Un Fiume di Dollari see *Hills Run Red*

Five Dollars for Ringo (1968)

Cinque Dollari per Ringo Ital. *Director:* Ignacio Iquino; *Script:* Ignacio F. Iquino; *Camera:* Giuseppe la Torre; *Music:* Enrique Escobar; *Producer:* José Antonio (Italy/Spain). *Cast:* Anthony P. Taber, Frank Wolff, Albert Farley, Maria Pia Conte, Indio Gonzales, Vicky Lagos, Romano Giomini.

Here's yet another attempt to capitalize on the popular "Ringo" films, but writer/director Iquino (this time not using his John Wood pseudonym) is bamboozling the audience. There's not a "Ringo" to be found. Anywhere.

Anthony P. Taber (alias Julio P. Tabernero) is gunfighter Lester Sands, hired to protect a desolate community of hard-working farmers from marauding Mexican outlaws. The subplot, almost a prerequisite, deals with the romantic interlude between Lester and Sara (Vicky Lagos), the daughter of the principal farmer.

Five for Revenge see *Five Giants from Texas*

Five Giants from Texas (1966)

Five for Revenge; I Cinque della Vendetta Ital. *Director:* Aldo Florio; *Script:* Alfonso Balcazar/José Antonio De La Loma/Aldo Florio; *Camera:* Victorio Monreal; *Music:* Franco Salina; *Producer:* Roberto Capitani, Miro/Balcazar Films (Italy/Spain). *Cast:* Guy Madison, Monica Randall, Mariano Vidal Molina, Jose Manuel Martin, Vassili Karamesinis, Antonio Molino Rojo, Giovanni Cianfriglia, Gianni Solaro.

When her husband is brutally murdered and her son kidnapped, Rosaria (Monica Randall) begins working in a saloon. For two years she grieves privately until five men show up (led by Guy Madison) looking for their friend Jim (her dead husband). She tells them what had happened, and they vow revenge. Joining them in their stalk through Mexico, she eventually gets her son back and the bad guys all dance the death ballet.

The overall impact of the film is disturbingly static, caused by wafer thin characterization. Too bad. Director Aldo Florio is capable of better, and four years later would prove his talent with *Dead Men Ride* (1970).

This one was written by a "director's triumvirate" consisting of Alfonso Balcazar (responsible for 11 Eurowesterns, including *Clint the Stranger, Sartana Does Not Forgive* and *Sunscorched*), José Antonio De La Loma *(Blood at Sundown* and *Boldest Job in the West)* and, of course, Aldo Florio. The director of photography is Victorio Monreal, his chief camera operator is Aristide (Joe D'Amato) Massaccesi; the stirring soundtrack comes from Franco Salina.

Five Man Army (1969)

Un Esercito di Cinque Uomini Ital. *Director:* Don Taylor with Italo Zingarelli (and Dario Argento); *Script:* Dario Argento; *Camera:* Enzo Barboni; *Music:* Ennio Morricone/Bruno Nicolai; *Producer:* Italo Zingarelli, MGM (Italy). *Cast:* Peter Graves, Bud Spencer, James Daly, Claudio Gora, Tetsuro Tamba, Piero Lulli, Nino Castelnuovo, Giacomo Rossi Stuart, Daniela Giordano.

Conflicting information and ambiguity clouds the identity of this film's true director. Actor Tamba, in a French television interview, said "American director Don Taylor began the project but returned to the United States before its completion. A team headed by scriptwriter Dario Argento replaced him early on." Aaron Spelling Productions claims that an opportunity arose for Taylor to direct some of their television projects, particularly a film called *Wild Women,* so he returned prematurely to the U.S. However, his agent (Gersh and Company) says that Taylor was the *only* director for the film and that he completed the project.

Whatever the truth, the movie is one of the best examples of the genre. It's a well-written (by Argento), finely photographed (by Enzo Barboni, later to be the *Trinity* director under the pseudonym E. B. Clucher), strongly acted (especially by Bud Spencer who gets to play a character, not a clown) movie. Sort of a *Magnificent Seven*–pull-a-heist film.

A mercenary band of specialists led by the Major (Peter Graves) are hired to rescue a revolutionary (Nino Castelnuovo) and then, with his top secret information regarding a Mexican government train, they steal a $500,000 gold shipment, caper style.

Producer Italo Zingarelli, according to a questionable feature in *Screen-*

world '71, is cult director Giulio Questi (*Django, Kill . . . If You Live, Shoot!* plus the nongenre film *Death Laid an Egg*). The same article claims that he is, in fact, the director of this film. The information is, most likely, erroneous.

Five Thousand Dollars on One Ace (1965)

Pistoleros (Gunmen) from Arizona; 5000 Dollari sull'Asso Ital. *Director:* Alfonso Balcazar; *Script:* Helmut Harun/Alessandro Continenza/José Antonio De La Loma/Alfonso Balcazar; *Camera:* Christian Matras/Roberto Reale; *Music:* Angelo Francesco Lavagnino; *Producer:* Balcazar Producciones/Fida (Spain/Italy). *Cast:* Robert Woods, Fernando Sancho, Helmut Schmidt, Maria Sebalt, Antonio Molino Rojo, Giacomo Rossi Stuart, Paco Sanz, Hans Nielsen, Fernando Rubio.

In an interesting reworking of the previous year's *Gunfighters of Casa Grande* (1965), Robert Woods plays Jeff Clayton, a gunfighting gambler who wins half a ranch in a poker game. While enroute, he's robbed by Mexican bandido Carrancio (Fernando Sancho), so Jeff arrives penniless. His new "house partners," David and sister Helen (played by Antonio M. Rojo and Maria Sebalt) welcome him, secretly hoping that he will help them in their ongoing conflict with the land-grabbing town boss, an attorney named Burke (Helmut Schmidt). An ironic plot twist unites Jeff with the Mexican bandit, Carrancio, and together they wipe out Burke and his henchmen.

The movie is cowritten by a team of scenarists, including filmmaker José Antonio De La Loma (see Scriptwriters filmography) who later directed Lee Van Cleef in *The Killing Machine* (1984) and John Saxon in *Metralleta Stein* (1974), and also wrote *Conquest* for Lucio Fulci in 1983.

The adventures of Jeff and Carrancio continue in *Man from Canyon City*, also called *Viva Carrancio!* (1965), again directed by Alfonso Balcazar, starring Robert Woods and Fernando Sancho once again.

Flaming Frontier (1965)

Old Surehand 1. Teil Ger. *Director:* Alfred Vohrer; *Script:* Eberhard Keindorf/Johanna Sibelius; *Camera:* Karl Löb; *Music:* Martin Böttcher; *Producer:* Horst Wendlandt, Rialto/Jadran Film (Germany/Yugoslavia). *Cast:* Stewart Granger, Pierre Brice, Paddy Fox, Terence Hill, Larry Pennell, Letitia Roman.

This is the last in the series of Stewart Granger "Winnetou" films, preceded by *Among Vultures* (also called *Frontier Hellcat*), 1965, and *Rampage at Apache Wells*, 1966.

When an outlaw known as "The General" (Larry Pennell) kills a friendly Comanche, the community risks another Indian War. Old Surehand (Stewart Granger) contacts his Apache friend, Chief Winnetou (Pierre Brice), to help him calm the townsfolk.

During the process of the film, Granger also takes time to play Cupid, helping unite bashful Toby (a young Terence Hill) with lovely Judith (Letitia Roman). Plus, Granger astonishingly manages to stay within "hearing" distance of his obnoxiuous babbling sidekick, Old Wabble (Paddy Fox), for long and unbearable stretches of time without losing his cool. The man is truly a saint.

And regarding Larry Pennell—didn't he play Dash Riprock on *The Beverly Hillbillies?*

Die Flusspiraten vom Mississippi see *Pirates of the Mississippi*

For a Book of Dollars (1973)

Più Forte Sorelle. Director: Renzo Spaziani; *Script:* Franco Vietri; *Camera:* Mario Parapetti; *Music:* Nando De Luca; *Producer:* John Wyler, New Films (Italy/Spain). *Cast:* Lincoln Tate, Gabriella Farinon, Gill Roland, Gigi Bonos, Clara Colosimo, Franca Maresa, Suzy Monen, Jean-Claude Jabès.

Here's a fun, low-brow comedy directed by Mario Bianchi hiding behind the pseudonym Renzo Spaziani (usually, he uses the Frank Bronston alias). It was produced by his friend, actor Alan Steel (Sergio Ciani, alias John Wyler).

Nuns hire a bounty hunter named Amen (Lincoln Tate) to help them get back their stolen money. The booty was snatched by a surly bunch of badmen known as Catapult's Outlaws (named after their leader, Catapult, of course, played with tongue-in-cheek zeal by Gill Roland, not the Mexican actor). Amen, with the nuns, finds the loot and eliminates the gang. It turns out the nuns were, in reality, disguised female outlaws. So Amen joins them. Everybody is happy.

Some of the humor is decidedly tasteless and relies on fag-bashing for its punchline. For an example, one of the bandits is a big, ugly mountain of man who is gay. Named Tutti Frutti.

For a Dollar in the Teeth see *Stranger in Town*

For a Few Bullets More see *Man Who Killed Billy the Kid*

For a Few Dollars Less (1966)

Per Qualche Dollaro in Meno Ital. *Director:* Mario Mattòli; *Script:* Sergio Corbucci/Bruno Corbucci; *Camera:* Giuseppe Aquari; *Music:* Marcello Giombini; *Producer:* Franco Palaggi, Panda (Italy). *Cast:* Lando Buzzanca, Alberto Giraldi, Raimondo Vianello, Gloria Paul, Lucia Modugno, Angela Luce, Tony Renis, Valeria Ciangottini.

Amazingly, this parody of Sergio Leone's *For a Few Dollars More* was written by filmmakers Sergio and (his brother) Bruno Corbucci. The film remains director Mario Mattòli's only genre outing, which originally led to wild speculation that it was secretly a combined directorial effort from the two Corbucci boys. However, Mattòli is not an "unknown" in the world of Italian exploitation films. He also directed Ugo Tognazzi in *Let's Not Lose Our Heads,* plus he's the man responsible for "giving the world" the only vision of a *nude* Sophia Loren in *Two Nights with Cleopatra.* Inside sources suggest that *For a Few Dollars Less* was, in fact, a combined effort between Mattòli and his friend, Bruno Corbucci.

It's an enjoyable play-by-play lampoon of *For a Few Dollars More,* beginning with the (now famous) elevated long shot of a lone cowboy riding across a mountainous desert, the crack of rifle fire, followed by the rider falling from his horse, dead. Except this time, the unseen gunman keeps shooting and missing the oblivious cowboy.

At the conclusion, Bill (Lando Buzzanca) and Frank (Raimondo Vianello) eliminate the evil Mexican bandit, Blackie (Elio Pandolfi), and his entire gang with hallucinatory drugs, taking the stoned bodies to the sheriff for the ransoms.

For a Few Dollars More (1965)

Per Qualche Dollaro in Più Ital. *Director:* Sergio Leone; *Script:* Luciano Vincenzoni/Sergio Leone/Morsella, Fulvio; *Camera:* Jack Dalmas; *Music:* Ennio Morricone; *Producer:* Alberto Grimaldi, Pea/Gonzales/Constantin (Italy/Spain/West Germany). *Cast:* Clint Eastwood, Lee Van Cleef, Gian Maria Volonté, Luigi Pistilli, Mario Brega, Antonio Molina Rojo, Klaus Kinski, Rosemary Dexter, Peter Lee Lawrence, Tomás Blanco, Aldo Sambrell, Roberto Camardiel, Panos Papadopulos.

Considered by many genre critics as the best example of a Spaghetti Western, this extraordinary two-hour Sergio Leone film (with camerawork by future exploitation director Massimo Dallamano, aka Jack Dalmas, aka Max Dillman) relates the exploits of two cynical (and wildly competitive) bounty hunters (Clint Eastwood and Lee Van Cleef) as they form an uneasy partnership in their quest for the notorious bandit, Indio (Gian Maria Volonté). The Colonel (Van Cleef) has a personal determinant that transcends the huge reward (or even the stolen fortune); he wants to avenge his sister's rape and murder.

This continental coproduction is the second film in director Leone's "Dollars" trilogy, preceded by *Fistful of Dollars*, followed by *The Good, the Bad, and the Ugly*. The explosive soundtrack is provided by wizard Ennio Morricone. It also marks the debut of future Spaghetti star Peter Lee Lawrence in a minor supporting role.

For a Few Extra Dollars see Fort Yuma Gold

For a Fist in the Eye (1965)

Fistful of Knuckles; Por un Pugno nell'Occhio Ital.; *Por un Puñado de Golpes* Ital. *Director:* Michele Lupo; *Script:* Eduardo M. Brochero; *Camera:* Julio Ortas; *Music:* Manuel Parada; *Producer:* Fenix Film/Ramo Film (Italy/Spain). *Cast:* Franco Franchi, Ciccio Ingrassia, Francisco Moran, Monica Randal, Carmen Esbri, Jesus Puente.

Like many other Franco and Ciccio slapstick comedies, this one is also a slapstick parody. Initially *Fistful of Knuckles* was made to satirize *Fistful of Dollars*, but the overabundance of other "Franco and Ciccio" films in the marketplace (they made 23 movies in 1965–66) delayed the release of this production. By the time it was scheduled for theatrical play, Leone's new film, *For a Few Dollars More*, had hit the circuit. So, Fenix Productions changed the title of this one to *For a Fist in the Eye*.

The story is a *Mad* magazine sort of rendering about two strangers (Franco and Ciccio) who arrive in a desert border town to find two "mafia" families fighting for restaurant supremacy.

For One Hundred Thousand Dollars Per Killing (1967)

Vengeance Is Mine; Per 100.000 Dollari t'Ammazzo Ital.; *One Hundred Thousand Dollars Per Killing. Director:* Sidney Lean; *Script:* Sergio Martino/Mino Loy/Luciano Martino; *Camera:* Federico Zanni/Sergio Martino; *Music:* Nora Orlandi; *Producer:* Zenith/Flora Film (Italy). *Cast:* John Garko, Carlo Gaddi, Claudio Camaso, Piero Lulli, Fernando Sancho, Claudie Lange, Bruno Corazzari.

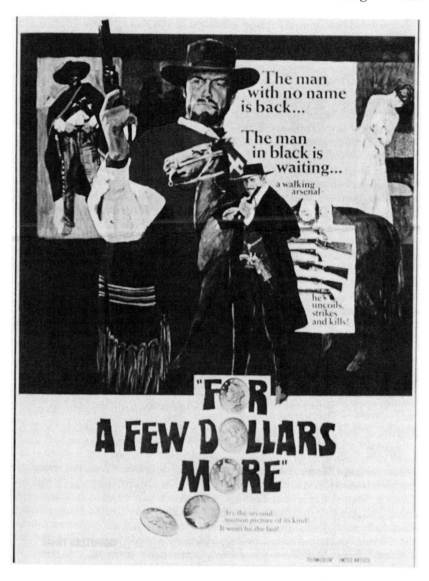

The man with no name is back in Sergio Leone's *For a Few Dollars More* (1965).

An impressive bounty-hunter film, starring John Garko (some prints use a Gary Hudson alias) as a mysterious stranger who sides with a surly sheriff (Claudio Camas) against the rampaging Clement gang (led by Carlos Gaddi).

It's an interesting movie, despite the tired story, thanks mostly to Garko's machismo and his subtle personality nuances. He appears to be "practicing" for his later "Sartana" and "Spirito Santo" roles.

Directed by Giovanni Fago (aka Sidney Lean) with a nihilistic flair, the film isn't as good as his *Magnificent Bandits*. However, it's much better than *To Hell and Back*.

For One Thousand Dollars Per Day (1966)

Renegade Gunfighter; Per Mille Dollari al Giorno Ital. *Director:* Silvio Amadio; *Script:* Silvio Amadio/Tito Carpi/Luciano Gregoretti; *Camera:* Mario Pacheco; *Music:* Gino Peguri; *Producer:* Tirso Film/Petruka Film (Italy/Spain). *Cast:* Dick Palmer, Zachary Hatcher, José Calvo, Ruben Rojo, Mirko Ellis, Manuel Gil, Bruno Scipioni, Annamaria Pierangeli.

Another variation on the standard "vengeance for a slaughtered family" theme. This time a young man named Hud (Zachary Hatcher) sees his parents murdered by the Clark brothers (Jason, Wayne and Lon, played by Ruben Rojo, Mirko Ellis, and Manuel Gil), three men succeeding in their brutal takeover of Sun Valley.

Hud escapes to the mountains where he meets Carranza (José Calvo), a legendary gunfighter, now a paralytic confined to a wheelchair. The old cripple teaches him "the art of the pistol." Eventually, after learning the gunfighting skill, Hud returns to Sun Valley for revenge.

An old friend, Steve (Dick Palmer), is now sheriff. He warns Hud "not to stir up trouble." But, of course, he does anyway. In a ludicrous segment, Hud convinces the Clark brothers to hire him as a bodyguard (a case of the fox guarding the chickens?) for a thousand dollars a day.

Especially noteworthy, Mario Pacheco is the director of photography, but future cult director Aristide Massaccesi (better known as Joe D'Amato) is the talented camera operator (one of his first professional outings).

Supporting actress Annamaria Pierangeli (aka Pier Angeli) committed suicide in 1971, shortly after the release of her feature horror film, *Octaman*.

Forewarned, Half-Killed ... the Word of the Holy Ghost (1971)

Uomo Avvisato Mezzo Ammazzato ... Parola di Spirito Santo Ital. *Director:* Anthony Ascott; *Script:* Tito Carpi/Federico De Urrutia/Giuliano Carmineo. *Camera:* Miguel Fernandez Rodriguez; *Music:* Bruno Nicolai; *Producer:* Lea Film/C.C. Astro (Italy/Spain). *Cast:* John Garko, Paolo Gizlino, Victor Israel, Pilar Velasquez, Jorge Rigaud, Massimo Serato, Piero Lulli.

This is the second *Holy Ghost (Spirito Santo)* movie from prolific director Anthony Ascott (Giuliano Carmineo). Apparently shot back to back or (perhaps) simultaneously with *His Name Was Holy Ghost*, it utilizes the same technical crew and much of the same cast, including John (Gianni) Garko in the title role as the mysterious Angel of Death, the Holy Ghost. He's a sharp-shooting, cape-wearing gunfighter with a dove on his shoulder.

There's lots of action as Holy Ghost (dressed in white) and his partner, the Preacher (Victor Israel), rescue imprisoned farmers from a castle-like fortress run by sadistic commandant General Ruiz (Paolo Gozlino). Then, after reaching safety in a nearby town, they hear about the general's secret gold treasure ensconced in the bowels of the fort. Holy Ghost and Preacher (with the help of some prostitutes) raid the citadel again.

The highlight of the film is a torture sequence involving "bird power." While trying to get information from one of the bad guys, Holy Ghost ties the man, bare-chested, to a table. He spreads a small amount of bird food over the informant's chest. While his dove pecks away at the seeds, Holy Ghost warns, "You'd better talk fast, there's not much food left and he's very hungry."

Another director, Roberto Mauri, unofficially continued the series with Vassili Karis playing John Garko's role (see *He Was Called the Holy Ghost* [1972] and *The Gunman and the Holy Ghost* [1973]).

Forgotten Pistolero (1970)

Gunmen of Ave Maria; Tierra de Gigantes Sp. *Director:* Ferdinando Baldi; *Script:* Federico De Urrutia/Piero Anchisi/Vicenzo Cerami/Ferdinando Baldi; *Camera:* Mario Montuori; *Music:* Roberto Pregadio; *Producer:* Benito Gutierrez, Izaro (Italy/Spain). *Cast:* Leonard Mann, Luciana Paluzzi, Alberto De Mendoza, Pilar Velazquez, Peter Martell, Piero Lulli, José Suarez.

A confusing story, with almost soap opera overtones (i.e., who slept with whom, who is the real father, and who is the half-sister of whom, etc.); however, when the fat is cut away, only a slam-bam revenge story remains.

Brooding Leonard Mann looks great (in his black cape/coat) as the "wronged" gunfighter, Sebastian, searching for his father's killer. Along the way, he falls in love with Anna (beautiful Luciana Paluzzi) who has a few secrets of her own.

Fort Yuma Gold (1966)

For a Few Extra Dollars; Per Pochi Dollari Ancora Ital. *Director:* Calvin J. Padget; *Script:* Augusto Finocchi/Massimilliano Capriccioli; *Camera:* Rafael Pacheco; *Music:* Ennio Morricone/Gianni Ferrio; *Producer:* Edmondo Amati, Fida/Les Productions/Epoca (Italy/France/Spain). *Cast:* Giuliano Gemma, Dan Vadis, Sophie Daumier, Jacques Sernas, Nello Pazzafini, José Calvo, Alfonso Rojas, Jacques Herlin, Angel del Pozo, Andrea Bosić, Antonio Molino Rojo.

Directed by Giorgio Ferroni (using his Calvin J. Padget alias), this Continental coproduction is incredibly involved, perhaps needlessly so. But thanks to good camerawork, fast-paced direction, and another credible performance from Giuliano Gemma, the film is entertaining.

The Civil War is over, but Confederate Major Sanders (Jacques Sernas) refuses to surrender. Union spies discover that he is planning to raid and rob Fort Yuma. The telegraph lines have been severed, so the Army sends two Union messenger soldiers along with a guide, an ex–Rebel named Gary Diamond (Giuliano Gemma), to warn the Fort.

But, one of the soldiers, Lefevre (Angel del Pozo), is actually a traitor in cahoots with Major Sanders. He kills the other messenger and attempts to kill Diamond. However, the wounded Diamond escapes after hiding the "Top Secret" documents in a purse belonging to a dance hall girl named Connie Breastful (Sophie Daumier). His half-dead body is discovered by an old prospector, Golden 44 (José Calvo), who nurses him back to health.

Diamond and Golden 44 find Connie Breastful and they retrieve the papers. Gary Diamond and Connie are captured by a gang of bandidos (working with the evil Major Sanders), but Golden has managed to get away and he delivers the dispatch to Fort Yuma. Diamond and Breastful are tortured for awhile; they escape when (in a preposterous sequence) Diamond catches the outlaws by surprise after pretending to be blind. Eventually, the cavalry arrives. Major Sanders (and his cronies) are exposed as opportunists and arrested. Plus Gary Diamond kills Lefevre in a showdown.

There's a lot going on in this film, but much of it is like riding an exercise bike. It doesn't really go anywhere.

Four Bullets for Joe see *Shots Ring Out!*

Four Came to Kill Sartana (1969)

Sartana, the Invincible Gunman; Beyond the Frontiers of Hate (reissued 1972); *E Vennero in Quattro . . . per Uccidere Sartana* Ital. *Director:* Miles Deem; *Script:* Demofilo Fidani/Luigi Glachin; *Camera:* Franco Villa; *Music:* Italo Fischetti; *Producer:* Gatassia Cinematografica (Italy). *Cast:* Jeff Cameron, Anthony G. Staton, Daniela Giordano, Dennis Colt, Simone Blondell.

Once wasn't enough. Cherished industry hack, Miles Deem (Demofilo Fidani), re-released this standard "let's kill notorious Sartana for a buck" film, three years after its unremarkable debut. For the comeback, the title was changed to *Beyond the Frontiers of Hate* and the directorial credit was altered (at least in promotion and advertising) to yet another alias, Alessandro Santini. Remarkably, most prints of the reissue have no credits at all.

Jeff Cameron sleepwalks through another one as Link, the leader of the "small but mighty" vigilante force against the evil Sartana and his gang.

Over his illustrious years, Demofilo Fidani also used the pseudonyms Dick Spitfire, Sean O'Neal, Dennis Ford, Lucky Dickerson, Slim Alone and (of course) Miles Deem. Plus his screenwriting moniker, Diego Spataro. In all, this "Al Adamson of Italy" is responsible for directing 12 very special, cockeyed Spaghetti Westerns.

Four Candles for Garringo see *My Colt, Not Yours*

Four Dollars for Vengeance (1965)

Quattro Dollari di Vendetta Ital. *Director:* Alfonso Balcazar; *Script:* Bruno Corbucci/Giovanni Grimaldi; *Camera:* Victor Monreal; *Music:* Benedetto Ghiglia; *Producer:* Balcazar of Barcelona/Fida (Spain/Italy). *Cast:* Robert Woods, Ghia Arlen, Angelo Infanti, Antonio Casas, José Manuel Martin, Gerard Tichy, Tómas Torres, Antonio Rojo.

Another "revenge for a slaughtered family" film, similar in style to director Balcazar's *Five Thousand Dollars on One Ace* (made the same year, also with Robert Woods).

This time, Woods is Roy Dexter, a gunman who reluctantly decides to help a stranded settler, Mercedes (Ghia Arlen, aka Dana Ghia), whose parents were killed in an outlaw attack. He and the girl track down (and eliminate) the bandits. Of course, they also fall in love along the way.

The unimaginative screenplay was written by two popular Italian directors, Bruno *(Longest Hunt)* Corbucci and Giovanni *(In a Colt's Shadow)* Grimaldi. The gritty and probing camerawork by Victor Monreal is exceptional, easily the highlight of the film.

Four Gunmen of the Apocalypse (1975)

The Four Horsemen of the Apocalypse; I Quattro dell'Apocalisse Ital. *Director:* Lucio Fulci; *Script:* Lucio Fulci/Ennio De Concini; *Camera:* Sergio Salvati; *Music:* Franco Bixio/Fabio Frizzi/Vince Tempera; *Producer:* Coralta Cinematografica (Italy). *Cast:* Fabio Testi, Tomás Milian, Lynn Frederick, Michael J. Pollard, Harry Baird, Donald O'Brien, Bruno Corazzari.

Director Lucio Fulci is the enormously popular exploitation/horror filmmaker responsible for over 50 movies, including *Zombie* (1979), *The Beyond* (1980), *Gates of Hell* (1980), *House by the Cemetery* (1981), *Demonia* (1989), *Cat in the Brain* (1991), and *Lizard in a Woman's Skin* (1971), plus two other genre entries, *Massacre Time* (1966) and *Silver Saddle* (1978). But, certainly, this is Fulci's most ambitious film.

Besides looking absolutely stunning (with a special acknowledgment to cinematographer Sergio Salvati), this multivariate film is both "heavily symbolic" and immensely entertaining. It's a rarity among rarities, an intelligent revenge flick, complete with one of the most satisfying "vengeance" endings in the Spaghetti Western genre. It also offers one of the very best Fabio Testi performances, plus a remarkably good one from Tomás Milian. Even Michael J. Pollard is okay.

Four prisoners find themselves safely locked away inside a jail when an outlaw gang raids Sand City. Everyone in the town is slaughtered, only the "convicts" in their secret cell are spared. This unusual "cross-section" of society includes a con-man counterfeiter named Preston (Fabio Testi), falsely accused murderess Lisa (Lynn Frederick), Josh the town drunkard (Michael J. Pollard) and a runaway slave, Wilson (Harry Baird). Together, they escape Sand City and begin their trek into the surrounding desert.

Along the way, this ragtag group is joined by a gunfighting loner, Chaco (Tomás Milian), who turns out to be a wildly demented sadist. He manages to overpower the others (in a particularly bizarre segment involving peyote indulgence) and then he tortures them mercilessly, including a very depraved rape. Eventually, Chaco tires of the S&M games and leaves them to die in the desert.

But they don't die. Instead, they free themselves and continue their journey to "nirvana." But along the way, they find horrifying "evidence of Chaco" (i.e., the bloody massacre of a Mormon caravan). When the apocalyptic group reaches a remote outpost in the snowy wilderness of the Rocky Mountains, Lisa surprises Preston by having a baby, but she dies during childbirth. Interpreting it as a "sign from God," Preston reacts by tracking down "the devil" Chaco and he savagely destroys him.

Four Gunmen of Ave Maria see Ace High

Four Gunmen of the Holy Trinity (1971)

I Quattro Pistoleri di Santa Trinità Ital. *Director:* Giorgio Cristallini; *Script:* Giorgio Cristallini; *Camera:* Sandro D'Eva; *Music:* Roberto Pregadio; *Producer:* Buton Film (Italy). *Cast:* Peter Lee Lawrence, Evelyn Stewart, Philippe Hersent, Ralph Baldwin, Valeria Fabrizi, Daniela Giordano.

One of two Spaghetti Westerns from director Giorgio Cristallini (also see

You're Jinxed Friend, You Just Met Sacramento). This film emerges as a rather typical good-guy versus bad-guy horse opera, no better and no worse than many others of the same ilk.

Babyfaced Peter Lee Lawrence is a lawman named Lincoln, secretly disguised as a notorious gunfighter. He helps Sarah (Evelyn Stewart) when her gold mine is taken over by two outlaws. Fortuitously, these are the same two outlaws (Ralph Baldwin and Philippe Hersent) that Lincoln has been trying to catch for an illegal gun-trafficking caper with the Indians.

The Four Horsemen of the Apocalypse see *Four Gunmen of the Apocalypse*

Four Rode Out (1969)

I Quattro sul Sentiero di Sparo Ital. *Director:* John Peyser; *Script:* Don Balluck; *Camera:* Rafael Pacheco; *Music:* Franco Julian; *Producer:* Hercules/U.A. Film (Italy/Spain/U.S.). *Cast:* Pernell Roberts, Leslie Nielsen, Sue Lyon, Julian Mateos, Albert Salmi, Maria Martin.

When falsely accused of robbing a bank and committing murder, a Mexican (Julian Mateos) runs for the border with a lawman (Pernell Roberts) close behind, followed by his girlfriend (Sue Lyon) and a Pinkerton agent (Leslie Nielsen).

This is director John Peyser's only Spaghetti Western. He is an American filmmaker primarily responsible for action exploitation films, including *Centerfold Girls* (1974), *The Young Warriors* (1967), and *Stunt Seven* (1979).

Although Leslie Nielsen eventually became wildly popular as the unlikely lead in many wacky comedies (i.e., *Airplane!*, *Naked Gun*, *Spaceship*, and *Repossessed*), he began his career as a "serious" actor starring in the classic American sci-fi film, *Forbidden Planet* (1956) and he was the "bachelor" in *Tammy and the Bachelor* (1957), a movie recognized as the spearhead for the countless "teen" exploitation films to follow.

Actress Sue Lyon is best known for the title role of a teenage sexpot in Stanley Kubrick's *Lolita* (1962) and, later (in 1972) for the "publicity" wedding and marriage to a convicted murderer serving a 40-year jail term. The following year she filed for divorce, claiming "incompatibility." Big surprise.

I Fratelli di Arizona see *Arizona Kid*

Freddy und das Lied der Prärie see *Sheriff Was a Lady*

Frenchie King (1971)

Legend of Frenchie King; Les Pétroleuses Fr. *Director:* Christian-Jaque; *Script:* Guy Casaril/Daniel Boulanger; *Camera:* Henri Persin; *Music:* Christian Gaubert/Francis Lai; *Producer:* Raymond Erger/Francis Cosne, Francos/Vides/Copercines/Hemdale (France/Italy/Spain/England). *Cast:* Brigitte Bardot, Claudia Cardinale, Michael J. Pollard, Patty Shepard, Micheline Presle, Henri Czarniak, Cris Hverta, Georges Beller, Luis Induñi, Emma Cohen.

In this multi-country coproduction, female "super sex stars," Brigitte Bardot and Claudia Cardinale, take over lead roles usually reserved for "macho males." Bardot is Frenchie King; Cardinale is Maria Sarrazin. But it's still "the good guys" (Brigitte Bardot, dressed in white, and her all-girl gang) versus "the bad guys" (Claudia Cardinale, dressed in black, and her all-guy gang, her brothers actually).

Bardot's second in command, Terry, is Patty Shepard who went on to play the lead in Paul Naschy's *Werewolf vs. the Vampire Woman* (1972), directed by genre filmmaker Leon Klimovsky. She continued making many European films, including Joseph Larraz's *Edge of the Axe* (1989), an interesting *Friday the 13th* ripoff shot in Texas.

French director Christian-Jaque, better known for his adventure/spy films (especially his James Bond parody, *Gentleman from Cocody* with *Fantomas* star Jean Marais) seems uncomfortable in the Western motif. The action in *Frenchie King* is strangely stagnant. Michael J. Pollard, in a totally unnecessary part as the sheriff, provides the lame, slapstick humor.

Friss den Staub von meinen Stiefeln see *Three Bullets for a Long Gun*

Frontier Hellcat see *Among Vultures*

Gli Fumavano le Colt . . . lo Chiamavano Camposanto see *They Call Him Cemetery*

Furia de la Ley see *Billy the Kid*

5000 Dollar für den Kopf von Johnny Ringo see *Who Killed Johnny R.?*

Fuerte Perdido see *Massacre at Fort Grant*

Furia degli Apache see *Fury of the Apaches*

Fury of Johnny Kid (1967)

Ultimate Gunfighter; Dove Si Spara di Più Ital. *Director:* Gianni Puccini; *Script:* Bruno Baretti/Maria Del Carmen Martinez; *Camera:* Mario Montuori; *Music:* Gino Peguri; *Producer:* Francesco Merli (Spain/Italy). *Cast:* Peter Lee Lawrence, Paul Naschy, Cristina Galbo, Peter Martell, Luis Induñi, Piero Lulli, Andres Mejuto, Angel Alvarez.

This film is chiefly significant for being the only Spaghetti Western to feature actor Paul Naschy. Even though his role is of the "guest star" variety (i.e., brief), he looks uncomfortably out of place as a notorious gunfighting cowboy, Blackie, who gives advice to vengeance-seeking Johnny Kid (Peter Lee Lawrence). Otherwise, it's yet another variation of the "revenge for a slaughtered family" theme with Johnny tracking down (and killing) two outlaws (Piero Lulli and Peter Martell) for the annihilation of his parents.

Fury of the Apaches (1966)

El Hombre de la Diligencia Ital; *Furia degli Apache* Ital; *Doomed Fort.* *Director:* Joe Lacy; *Script:* José M. Elorrieta/José Luis Navarro; *Camera:* Alfonso Nieva; *Music:* Fernando Garcia Morcillo; *Producer:* Alesanco/Cesar Films (Spain/Italy). *Cast:* Frank Latimore, Nuria Torray, Georges Gordon, Jesus Puente, Yvonne Bastion, George Martin, Angel Ortiz, Liza Moreno.

Here's a reworking of *Massacre at Fort Grant* (also called *Fuerte Perdido*)

from the same director, José M. Elorrieta (alias Joe Lacy). This time there's a bigger budget, and the added advantage of a coproduction relationship with an Italian film studio, but the end result doesn't eclipse the original modest project.

Indians attack a wagon train, but the settlers are rescued by Major Loman (Frank Latimore) and a cavalry unit from Fort Grant. As in the original film, the main concentration is on the relationships between the survivors as they prepare for the impending Indian attack against the fort.

Fuzzy, halt die Ohren steif! see *Tequila*

Fuzzy the Hero see *Tequila*

Garringo see *Dead Are Countless*

Garter Colt (1067)

Garrettiera Colt Ital. *Director:* Gian Andrea Rocco; *Script:* Pescatori/Rocco/ Mario Maffei; *Camera:* Gino Santini; *Music:* Enzo Fusco; *Producer:* Columbus Cinematografica (Italy/Spain/Germany). *Cast:* Nicoletta Machiavelli, Claudio Camaso Volonté, Marisa Solinas, Walter Barnes, Jasper Zola, Yorgo Voyagis, James Martin.

Mexican revolutionary Benito Juarez (Yorgo Voyagis) is determined to overthrow Emperor Maximilian (Jasper Zola). He enlists the aid of female spy Lulu (Nicoletta Machiavelli) who, in a needlessly confusing plot, wages war against the occupied town of Fort City and, at the same time, against the arms smugglers supplying guns to the fortress.

A ridiculously implausible sequence finds Lulu disguised as a macho cowboy pretending to make a deal with the illegal traffickers while helping her partner, Carlos (Claudio Camaso Volonté) escape. This entire Italian-Spanish-German coproduction is hopelessly inept; laughable; not even worthwhile for voyeuristic reasons. Regardless of the title, there's not a garter to be seen.

Gatling Gun see *Machine Gun Killers*

I Gemelli del Texas see *Twins from Texas*

Un Genio, Due Compari, un Pollo see *Genius*

Genius (1975)

Trinity Is Back Again; Genius, Two Friends, and an Idiot; Nobody Is the Greatest; Un Genio, Due Compari, un Pollo Ital. *Director:* Damiano Damiani; *Script:* Ernesto Gastaldi/Fulvio Morsella/Damiano Damiani; *Camera:* Giuseppe Ruzzolini; *Music:* Ennio Morricone; *Producer:* Fulvio Morsella/Claudio Mancini (France/West Germany/Italy). *Cast:* Terence Hill, Miou Miou, Robert Charlebois, Patrick McGoohan, Klaus Kinski, Raimund Harmstorf, Jean Martin, Rik Battaglia.

After ignoring the genre for almost a decade, filmmaker Damiano Damiani

Opposite: Movie poster from *Fury of the Apaches* (1966).

directed this lighthearted satire in 1975. His first production *(Il Rossetto)* came in 1960; since that time he's made over 30 films, including the highly regarded Spaghetti Western *Bullet for the General,* also called *Quien Sabe?* (1966). However, Damiani is best known for his arty Italian action/dramas, *Confessions of a Police Captain* (1970) and *Goodbye and Amen* (1978).

This one tells the whimsical story of a likable rogue gang, consisting of Joe "the Genius" (Terence Hill), Lilla (Miou Miou), and Paul Lambert (Robert Charlebois). They are petty thieves, generally involved with insignificant robberies (i.e., the silver chalice from the local monastery), until they stumble upon a wrecked Cavalry stagecoach. They repair the wagon and then, disguised as a Union detachment (an officer plus his wife and driver), the three rapscallions try to scam Major Harris (Patrick McGoohan) at Ft. Smith. Instead, they find themselves in the middle of an Indian confrontation.

Some film enthusiasts have erroneously credited Sergio Leone as the "supervisor" for this movie. Apparently, this inaccuracy is based on (and perpetuated by) the "Nobody" aka. In a desperate search for an audience, the producers called it *Nobody ist der grösste (Nobody Is the Greatest)* in Germany and *Trinity e os Seus Companeiros (Trinity and His Friends)* in Portugal. The Italian title, *Un Genio, Due Compari, un Pollo,* translates to *The Genius, Two Friends, and an Idiot.*

Miou Miou is a popular French "sex queen" and the star of many action/exploitation films, including *Robbery of the Sphinx (Vol d'un Sphinx)* and *Tender Dracula.* Costar Patrick McGoohan made his mark by starring in the cult British television series, "The Prisoner," and to a lesser degree, *Danger Man* (also called *Secret Agent*).

Genius, Two Friends, and an Idiot see *Genius*

Gentleman Jo . . . Uccidi see *Gentleman Killer*

Gentleman Killer (1969)

Gentleman Jo . . . Uccidi Ital. *Director:* George Finley; *Script:* J. J. Balcazar/ Giorgio Stegani; *Camera:* Francisco Marin; *Music:* Bruno Nicolai/Ennio Morricone; *Producer:* Corona Film/Dorica (Spain/Italy). *Cast:* Anthony Steffen, Eduardo Fajardo, Silvia Solar, Mariano Vidal Molina, Benito Stefaneli, Angel Lombardo.

As the United States and Mexico argue over territorial rights, the fate of a small Texas border town hangs in the balance. The lack of law enforcement allows a gang of bloodthirsty bandits (led somberly by Eduardo Fajardo) to take over the city. They torture and terrorize the citizens until mysterious Gentleman Jo (Anthony Steffen) rides in to avenge the murder of his brother. Eventually he eliminates the bad guys, and he falls in love with beautiful Jill (Silvia Solar). It's the kind of role that Anthony Steffen was born to play; he doesn't have to say much, he just squints and shoots.

The director, Geoge Finley, is actually Giorgio Stegani, who cowrote the story with another director, J. J. Balcazar *(Man from Oklahoma).* Costar Silvia Solar made other Spaghetti Westerns (see Performers filmography), but she also starred in a perverse Spanish horror film, *Devil Kiss* (1978) where, looking a lot like Elvira, she creates a zombie to avenge her dead husband.

Get Mean (1975)

Get Mean Ital. *Director:* Ferdinando Baldi; *Script:* Ferdinando Baldi; *Camera:* Mario Perino; *Music:* Bixio/Frizzi/Tempera; *Producer:* Tony Anthony (Italy). *Cast:* Tony Anthony, Lloyd Battista, Raf Baldassare, Diana Loris, David Dreyer, Mirta Miller.

Certainly this is one of the most unusual of the Eurowestern entries (similar to *Stranger in Japan*), with mystical and fantasy elements woven into an outrageous story written by star and producer Tony Anthony. In this one, Anthony's "stranger" character (see also *Stranger in Town* and *The Stranger Returns*) is offered $50,000 from a gypsy-witch to safely escort Princess Elizabeth Maria (Diana Loris), heir to the Spanish throne, back to Spain and aid her (and her country) in a battle against the Viking barbarians.

By the time the opening credits have finished rolling, the stranger and the princess have arrived in Spain. He finds himself in the middle of the action, manipulating two warring factions (the Moors and the barbarians) in what turns out to be a displaced *Fistful of Dollars* theme.

Baldi, who also directed Tony Anthony in *Blindman* and the 3-D Western *Comin' at Ya*, made many other Spaghetti Westerns (see Directors filmography). He began his career (like many other Spaghetti filmmakers) in the sword-'n'-sandal movies when he directed *David and Goliath* (1959), *The Daughters of El Cid* (1962) using the alias "Miguel Iglesias," and *Il Figlio di Cleopatra* (1964) using the "Ferdy Baldwyn" moniker. After the "Western boom," Ferdinando Baldi continued working in the Italian exploitation market, usually under the pseudonym Ted Kaplan (i.e., *Warbus, Sicilian Connection, Tenzan*).

Get the Coffin Ready (1968)

Django, Prepare a Coffin; Viva Django; Preparati la Bara Ital. *Director:* Ferdinando Baldi; *Script:* Franco Rossetti/Ferdinando Baldi; *Camera:* Enzo Barboni; *Music:* Gianfranco Reverberi; *Producer:* B.R.C. (Italy). *Cast:* Terence Hill, Horst Frank, George Eastman, José Torres, Pinuccio Ardia, Lee Burton, Andrea Scotti, Spartaco Conversi.

Ferdinando Baldi movies tend to be simple-minded excursions. But they're always very enjoyable, well-made, simple-minded excursions, filled with the type of machismo singular to the Spaghetti Western.

Django (Terence Hill before the *Trinity* series typecast him into an exclusive run of adventure/Western comedies) discovers his wife murdered by a ruffian friend David (Horst Frank) and his outlaw gang. Django becomes a traveling hangman, but secretly saves some of the condemned men (with a suspension device), enlisting them into his private "vengeance" army.

The finale finds the two gangs (Django's "Dirty Dozen" and David's "Wild Bunch") facing each other in a Tucson cemetery where Django digs open a grave, removes his famous machine gun, and eliminates David and everybody else.

The story was scripted by director Baldi and screenwriter/filmmaker Franco Rossetti *(Big Ripoff)*; it's aided by exquisite photography from meticulous Enzo Barboni who later became popular cult filmmaker E. B. Clucher (i.e., *They Call Me Trinity* and *Trinity Is Still My Name* plus many action flicks, including *Crime Busters of Miami* and *Renegade*).

Terence Hill in *Get the Coffin Ready* (1968).

Giarrettiera Colt see *Garter Colt*

I Giorni della Violenza see *Days of Violence*

I Giorni dell'Ira see *Day of Anger*

Giorni di Fuoco see *Winnetou: Last of the Renegades*

Il Giorno dei Lunghi Fucili see *Hunting Party*

Il Giorno del Giudizio see *Drummer of Vengeance*

A Girl Is a Gun (1970)

Une Aventure de Billy le Kid Fr. *Director:* Luc Moullet; *Script:* Luc Moullet; *Camera:* Jean Gonnet/Jean Jacques Flori; *Music:* Patrice Moullet; *Producer:* Luc Moullet (France). *Cast:* Jean-Pierre Léaud, Rachel Keserber, Jean Valmore, Bruno Kresoja, Michel Minaud, Bernard Pinon.

A wacky, offbeat rendering of the "Billy the Kid" legend. Here, Billy is a hapless gunman who falls into one calamitous disaster after another. But, be aware, he is also a vicious gunfighter. After pulling a holdup, Billy (Jean-Pierre Léaud) tracks down and kills a witness. On his way back, he stumbles (yes, actually stumbles) upon a girl, Ann (Rachel Keserber) who has buried herself in the sand, an attempt to commit suicide. It's her way of dealing with the death of her boyfriend (the witness that Billy killed).

The two fall instantly in love and they flee into the wilderness on Billy's donkey. But there's a posse led by Sheriff Holiday (Michel Minaud) plus a tribe of war-hungry Indians on their trail. It all ends happily as the two lovers (wounded, mangled and nearly scalped) limp off together into the sunset.

Giù la Testa see *Duck You Sucker*

Giù la Testa . . . Hombre see *Fistful of Death*

Giù le Mani . . . Carogna! see *Reach You Bastard*

Il Giuaramento di Zorro see *Behind the Mask of Zorro*

Giubbe Rosse see *Red Coat*

Giurò . . . E li Uccise ad Uno ad Uno see *Piluk, the Timid One*

Giustizia del Coyote see *Coyote*

Gli Fumavano le Colt . . . lo Chiamavano Camposanto see *They Call Him Cemetery*

Gli Eroi del West see *Heroes of the West*

Gli Specialisti see *Specialists*

Go Away! Trinity Has Arrived in Eldorado (1972)

Stay Away from Trinity . . . When He Comes to Eldorado; Trinity in Eldorado; Pokerface; Scansati . . . Trinità Arriva ad Eldorado Ital. *Director:* Dick Spitfire; *Script:* Romano Scandariato; *Camera:* Aristide Massaccesi; *Music:* Giancarlo Chiaramello; *Producer:* Massimo Bernardi/Diego Spataro, Organizzatore

Generale (Italy). *Cast:* Stan Cooper, Gordon Mitchell, Lucky McMurry, Craig Hill, Carla Mancini, Daniela Giordano, Paul Crain.

Demofilo Fidani made two movies under the "Dick Spitfire" pseudonym (also see *Django and Sartana Are Coming . . . It's the End*), plus he directed many more under other monikers, including Lucky Dickerson, Dennis Ford, Sean O'Neal, Alessandro Santini, Slim Alone, Diego Spataro and Miles Deem. None of his films are very good. Fidani's biggest problem is that his excesses get the best of him. Sometimes his sight gags are humorous at first, but his timing is so bad that the joke quickly turns from funny to tedious.

In this one, two conmen (Stan Cooper and Gordon Mitchell) wander aimlessly through the West looking for ways of quick buck scamming (their methods range from selling bogus "Elixir of Long Life" bottles to helming crooked poker games). Things get sticky when they confront Mexican General Xavier, a powerful buffoon with a vicious temper.

Go for Broke see All Out

Go Kill and Come Back (1968)

Any Gun Can Play; Blood River Brit.; *Vado . . . l'Ammazzo e Torno* Ital. *Director:* Enzo G. Castellari; *Script:* Romolo Guerrieri/Sauro Scavolini; *Camera:* Giovanni Bergamini; *Music:* Francesco De Masi; *Producer:* Edmondo Amati, Fida Cinematografica (Italy). *Cast:* Edd Byrnes, George Hilton, Gilbert Roland, Kareen O'Hara, Pedro Sanchez, José Torres, Gerard Herter.

Here is Edd Byrnes's second Enzo G. Castellari (Enzo Girolami) Western (also see *Payment in Blood*). This one is decidedly weaker. There's an obvious attempt to capitalize on the three-way dynamics of Sergio Leone's *The Good, the Bad, and the Ugly* including a parody of the final showdown, but the lame plot about missing gold (hidden in the pipes of an organ inside an abandoned church) is too feeble to support it.

The most memorable thing about the film is the "throwaway" opening sequence, showing three men on horseback riding into a desolate town. The first, dressed in full poncho, resembles Clint Eastwood. The second is a Lee Van Cleef clone. And the third looks like Franco Nero's "Django." Within seconds, the three men are cut down, killed, by a bounty hunter (George Hilton). Then the credits start.

Edd Byrnes (like Clint Eastwood, Guy Madison, Craig Hill and Ty Hardin) was a United States television star; in his long-running series "77 Sunset Strip," he played a hipster-cum-private-eye named Kookie). He made one additional Spaghetti Western, *Red Blood, Yellow Gold* (also with George Hilton) for a different director, Nando Cicero, before returning to the States.

This movie is one of five Eurowesterns starring popular Mexican actor Gilbert Roland (see Performers filmography for other titles).

Go Kill Everybody and Come Back Alone see Kill Them All and Come Back Alone

Go with God, Gringo (1966)

Vaya con Dios, Gringo Ital. *Director:* Edward G. Muller; *Script:* Vincenzo Musolini/Edoardo Mulargia; *Camera:* Ugo Brunelli; *Music:* Felice Di Stefano;

Robert Mark aims his gun in *God Does Not Pay on Saturday* (1968).

Producer: Cio Film/International Production SAP (Italy/Spain). *Cast:* Glenn Saxon, Lucretia Love, Ignazio Spalla, Armando Guarnieri, Aldo Berti, Pasquale Simeoli, Spartaco Battisti.

Exploitation sleazemeister Edward G. Muller (alias for Edoardo Mulargia) is best known for his brutal "women in an Amazon prison" films *(Hotel Paradise, Girls in Hell,* and *Escape from Inferno).* He also directed eight Eurowesterns *(Don't Wait Django . . . Shoot!* and *Cjamango* are considered his best). For this one, he uses Ugo Brunelli as chief cameraman and the music is composed by Felice Di Stefano.

An unjustly accused cowboy, Gringo (Glenn Saxon), escapes from prison with a gang of bloodthirsty killers. Eventually, he is sickened by their brutality and turns against them in a climactic showdown which results in his freedom, and a substantial reward.

Costar Lucretia Love went on to star in an Italian thriller, *The Killer Reserved Nine Seats* (1974) with Janet Agren, and the "female/gladiator" peplum, *The Arena* (also called *Naked Warriors)* in 1976 with Pam Grier.

God Does Not Pay on Saturday (1968)

Kill the Wicked; Dio non Paga, il Sabato Ital. *Director:* Amerigo Anton; *Script:* Tanio Boccia/Luke Ashley; *Camera:* Giuseppe Aquinis; *Music:* Angelo Francesco Lavagnino; *Producer:* R.K. Cinematografica (Italy). *Cast:* Robert Mark, Larry Ward, Maria Silva, Daniela Igliozzi, Vivi Gioi, Howard Beniconi, Furio Meniconi.

If there's meaning behind the title *(God Does Not Pay on Saturday)*, it's not revealed anywhere in the film. Instead, the alternative *(Kill the Wicked)* better describes this meandering tale about a bandit, Lam (Larry Ward), saved from the gallows by his loyal gang. Obviously, his near brush with death didn't teach him a lesson because immediately Lam and his men (plus his girlfriend played by Maria Silva) rob a stagecoach and flee to a desolate, almost ghost town village. There they find a retired gunfighter-cum-rancher Wyatt (Robert Mark) and his woman, Mary (Daniela Igliozzi). The bandidos mistake Wyatt and Mary's peaceful existence for weakness, and they proceed to torment them mercilessly until, finally, Wyatt straps on his gun and kills everybody. Incidentally, Wyatt and Mary keep the bandits' stolen money.

The opening credit sequence, drawn by Saverio D'Eugenio, is most effective, as is the rousing Lavagnino score. Director Amerigo Anton (pseudonym for Tanio Boccia) made a total of four Spaghetti Westerns (see Directors filmography). *Saguaro* is considered his most successful.

God Forgives, I Don't (1966)

Blood River; Dio Perdona . . . Io No! Ital. *Director:* Giuseppe Colizzi; *Script:* Giuseppe Colizzi; *Camera:* Alfio Contini; *Music:* Angel Oliver Pina/Bruno Nicolai; *Producer:* Enzo D'Ambrosio, Crono/Pefsa (Italy/Spain). *Cast:* Terence Hill, Bud Spencer, Frank Wolff, Gina Rovere, José Manuel Martin, Luis Barboo, Tito Garcia, Frank Braña.

Not to be confused with Glenn V. Davis's *May God Forgive You . . . But I Won't*, this Italian-Spanish coproduction is the first of three Westerns (followed by 1967's *Ace High* and 1969's *Boot Hill*) directed by Giuseppe Colizzi (who died from a heart attack at age 53 in 1979. This movie remains his best Western because he seems to take the project seriously, creating characters that are multi-dimensional coupled with an intelligent plotline.

Basically, it's the story of a brilliant train robbery and the aftermath, a who's-got-the-gold game played among Cat Stevens (Terence Hill), Earp (Bud Spencer), and Antonio (Frank Wolf). The most awkward thing about this film is the overproduced musical score by Angel Oliver Pina (an unusual alias for Carlo Rustichelli); on the other hand, the best thing about it is that director Colizzi was not yet enamored of circus acrobats and acrobats (the blemish in his latter two films).

Terence Hill plays "Cat Stevens" in all three Colizzi Westerns.

God in Heaven . . . Arizona on Earth (1972)

Arizona on Earth; Dio in Cielo, Arizona in Terra Ital. *Director:* John Wood; *Script:* Juan Bosch/Daniel Ortosolli; *Camera:* Giancarlo Ferrando; *Music:* Bruno Nicolai; *Producer:* Vittorio Galiano, Lea Film/C.C. Astro (Spain/Italy). *Cast:* Peter Lee Lawrence, Roberto Camardiel, Maria Pia Conte, Frank Braña, Luis Induñi, Juan Torres, Indio Gonzales, Carlo Gaddi.

"Pretty boy" Peter Lee Lawrence is a Robin Hood–type bounty hunter named Arizona who rescues an elderly farmer from an outlaw attack. When Arizona asks the old man what had happened, he's told, "Austin Styles is behind it. He owns this whole county, at least he will when he gets done murdering all the small land owners who won't sell out . . . like me."

Thus begins yet another "big trouble with a town boss" Spaghetti Western. And, very soon, the "revenge for a slaughtered family" theme is introduced. While Arizona was away, his father committed suicide (ironically frightening since Lawrence, in real life, killed himself shortly after the completion of this film), leaving one bullet with instructions to "give it back" to Styles—and Arizona does.

God Is My Colt .45 (1972)

La Colt Era il Suo Dio Ital. *Director:* Dean Jones; *Script:* Arpad De Riso; *Camera:* Giorgio Montagnani; *Music:* Vasil Koiucharov; *Producer:* Virginia Cinematografica (Italy). *Cast:* Jeff Cameron, Donald O'Brien, Krista Nell, Esmeralda Barros, Mark Davis, John Turner.

Filmmaker Luigi Batzella, aka "Dean Jones," directed this film. Using a different pseudonym (Arpad De Riso), he also wrote it. He was also the editor, under his better known "Industry" moniker "Paolo Solvay." Even though he borrows large chunks of ideas from his previous films, this one emerges as his best contribution to the genre.

In a story similar to his 1971 *Paid in Blood* (also starring Jeff Cameron), a gang of cattle-hustling crooks, led by Collins (Donald O'Brien) and his mistress Mary (Krista Nell), takes over Langford City. A government agent named James Clinger (John Turner) mysteriously disappears while he's investigating the illegal activities. Sheriff Bill Harris (Mark Davis) realizes he can't control the situation, so he seeks aid from the army. Captain Mike Jackson (Cameron) agrees to "go undercover" and help "clean up" the city. Eventually, he succeeds.

God Made Them ... I Kill Them (1968)

Dio li Crea ... Io li Ammazzo Ital. *Director:* Paolo Bianchi; *Script:* Fernando Di Leo; *Camera:* Sergio D'Offizi; *Music:* Marcello Gigante; *Producer:* P.E.A. (Italy). *Cast:* Dean Reed, Peter Martell, Piero Lulli, Agnes Spaak, Linda Veras, Ivano Staccioli.

Director Paolo Bianchi (aka Bianchini) makes a very tough Spaghetti Western with titles like *I Want Him Dead* and *Hey Amigo! A Toast to Your Death!* His films are balls-to-the-walls violence, with no romantic side steps and not even a suggestion of comic relief, and this one is like the rest.

Written by cult director Fernando *(Slaughter Hotel)* Di Leo, it tells the story of a notorious bounty killer, Compton (Dean Reed). He's been hired by the citizens of a small border town to protect them from a gang of vicious bandits who systematically rob their outgoing gold shipments. Compton suspects that it's an "inside job," and he eventually exposes the town banker as being in cahoots with the bandidos. The plot is certainly wearisome, but Bianchi's no-nonsense direction makes it seem fresh and exciting.

God Was in the West, too, at One Time see *Between God, the Devil and a Winchester*

God Will Forgive My Pistol (1969)

Dio Perdona la Mia Pistola Ital. *Director:* Mario Gariazzo with Leopoldo Savona; *Script:* Mario Gariazzo/Leopoldo Savona; *Camera:* Stelvio Massi; *Music:*

The Good ... Clint Eastwood in *The Good, the Bad, and the Ugly* **(1966).**

Vasco and Mancuso; *Producer:* Ambrosiana Cinematografica (Italy). *Cast:* Wayde Preston, Loredana Nusciak, Dan Vadis, Giuseppe Addobbati, José Torres, Livio Lorenzon, Joe De Santis.

Texas Ranger Johnny Brennan (Wayde Preston) is sent to Oakland City. His initial mission is "to oversee the hanging" of land owner Prescott for the robbery of a post office/bank. Convicted Prescott (José Torres) insists that he has been framed. So, Ranger Brennan investigates.

Sure enough, an evil land baron named Martin (Dan Vadis) is the real culprit. He had concocted the plot to incriminate Prescott so that he could "legally" steal the water-rich property. The film ends with a shootout. Of course, Brennan emerges victorious.

Stelvio Massi's camerawork is on the mark; the double director status is interesting, but not especially remarkable. Savona, who made the excellent *Killer Kid* in 1969 (see Directors filmography for additional titles), went on to direct the controversial "sexual possession" film, *Trio of Lust (Byleth il Demone dell-Incesto)* in 1971, and *La Morte Scende Leggera* in 1972.

The Godless Ones see *Thunder Over El Paso*

God's Gun (1976)

Bullet from God; Pistola di Dio Ital. *Director:* Frank Kramer; *Script:* John Fonseca/Frank Kramer; *Camera:* Sandro Mancori; *Music:* Santa Marie Romitelli; *Producer:* Irwin Yablans, Golan/Globus (Italy/Israel). *Cast:* Lee Van Cleef, Jack Palance, Leif Garrett, Richard Boone, Sybil Danning, Robert Lipton.

Lee Van Cleef plays a dual role, that of a brave priest killed by an evil bandit, Sam Clayton (Jack Palance), and then as the twin brother Louis, a notorious gunfighter. When Father John is gunned down in the streets of Juno City, the Clayton gang takes over the town. A young boy, Johnny (Leif Garrett), journeys across the border into Mexico to get help from the priest's brother, a retired bounty hunter. Strapping on his gun, Louis returns to Juno City with the boy and takes on the entire gang.

The "man with the gunsight eyes" delivers a detached, irritatingly aloof performance, made more unbearable by his distracting appearance (full beard and shoulder-length wig). Frank Kramer (alias Gianfranco Parolini) also directed Lee Van Cleef with much better results in *Sabata*.

Producer Irwin Yablans made wagonloads of money two years later when he produced *Halloween*.

Gold of the Bravados see *Gold of the Heroes*

Gold of the Heroes (1971)

Gold of the Bravados; L'Oro dei Bravados Ital.; *Chapaqua* Ital. *Director:* Don Reynolds; *Script:* Renato Savino; *Camera:* Riccardo Pallottini; *Music:* Luis Enrique Bacalov; *Producer:* Copro/Capitole Film (Italy/France). *Cast:* George Ardisson, Linda Veras, Rik Battaglia, Franco Pesce, Rick Boyd, Bobby Lapointe.

Written and directed by Renato Savino (under the alias Don Reynolds) with camera work by Riccardo Pallottini, this is the story of Doc and Chapaqua (George Ardisson and Bobby Lapointe) and their gold treasure. Inside an abandoned Confederate fortress, they discover $100,000 in gold bars. While taking the ingots to a safe place, they alternate blindfolding each other, thus insuring a lasting, joint partnership.

However, a woman named Maria Shannon (Linda Veras) comes between them. Actually, she is a double-crossing opportunist who first learns Doc's part of the journey and then Chapaqua's, hoodwinking them both. Maria, with an outlaw named Major (Rik Battaglia), finds the gold, but the two friends have followed her. Major is killed in a gun battle; Maria convinces Chapaqua to (once again) betray Doc. The two sneak off with the gold, heading toward Mexico, hoping that Doc doesn't find them. But Doc, having secretly switched fake gold for real gold, is riding in the other direction.

It's an endearing Italian-French coproduction with superb music by Luis Enrique Bacalov (*Bullet for a General, Django, Price of Power*, etc.).

The Good, the Bad, and the Ugly (1966)

The Good, the Bad and the Wicked; Il Buono, il Brutto, il Cattivo Ital. *Director:* Sergio Leone; *Script:* Sergio Leone/Age-Scarpelli/Luciano Vincenzoni; *Camera:* Tonino Delli Colli; *Music:* Ennio Morricone; *Producer:* Alberto Grimaldi, Produzioni Europee (Italy). *Cast:* Clint Eastwood, Lee Van Cleef, Eli Wallach, Aldo Giuffre, Mario Brega, Chelo Alonso, Luigi Pistilli, Rada Rassimov, Enzo Petito, Livio Lorenzon, Al Muloch, Frank Braña.

Remarkable. Conspicuous. Striking. Exceptional. Even those words can't

The Bad ... Lee Van Cleef in *The Good, the Bad, and the Ugly* (1966).

do justice to this significant film. This is the movie that secured Clint Eastwood's immense popularity, and this is the film that elevated Lee Van Cleef to a "headliner" position, later starring in many tailormade roles with salaries to match. But most importantly, this is the motion picture that turned director Sergio Leone into an international success and, at the same time, critically "legitimized" the Spaghetti Westerns.

It's the story of the good (Clint Eastwood), the bad (Lee Van Cleef) and the ugly (Eli Wallach). They are all after a hidden gold treasure buried in a Confederate cemetery. The three-way gunfight at the film's conclusion is a cinema first. And the "Ecstasy for Gold" sequence ranks as an all-time great moment in film history. Plus the Ennio Morricone soundtrack is perfect. United States running time is a stunning 162 minutes, but the Italian print is actually 18 minutes longer. And it includes an important scene showing Angel Eye's (Lee Van Cleef) transition from bounty killer to Union officer.

This film is the third in Sergio Leone's "Dollars" trilogy, preceded by *Fistful of Dollars* and *For a Few Dollars More*. His next film would be *Once Upon a Time in the West*, starring Henry Fonda and Claudia Cardinale, written by Leone, Bernardo Bertolucci, and Dario Argento.

Good Die First see *Beyond the Law*

The Good, the Bad and the Wicked see *The Good, the Bad, and the Ugly*

Goodbye Texas see *Texas, Adios*

The Ugly ... Eli Wallach in *The Good, the Bad, and the Ugly* (1966).

Le Goût de la Violence see *Taste of Violence*

The Grand Duel see *Big Showdown*

Il Grande Duello see *Big Showdown*

Grande Notte di Ringo see *Ringo's Big Night*

Il Grande Silenzio see *Great Silence*

Grandsons of Zorro (1968)

Dream of Zorro; Sogno di Zorro Ital. *Director:* Mariano Laurenti; *Script:* Mariano Laurenti/Luci Tortelli; *Camera:* Mario Vulpiani; *Music:* Ubaldo Continello; *Producer:* Dania Film/Medusa (Italy). *Cast:* Franco Franchi, Ciccio Ingrassia, Gianni Musy, Mario Carotenuto, Vittorio Daverio.

Mariano Laurenti has made a career from directing, basically, two types of movies, "Franco and Ciccio" slapstick comedies (i.e., *Two Magicians of Football, How Faithful Can You Get?*) and Italian sex farces (i.e., *Probation School* and *Night Hospital* with Gloria Guida, *Professor of Sex Education* starring Janet Agren, and a series of film with popular Edwige Fenech, *Tales of Yore* [also called *Tutta Nuda e Tutta Calda*], *Vizio di Famiglia*, and *Bella Antonia Prima Monaca e Poi Dimonia*), plus one motion picture that combined both types called *Satiricosissimo* starring Franco and Ciccio *and* Edwige Fenech.

This one is more of the same Franco and Ciccio silliness as the two miscreants inherit the estate of Don Diego with the stipulation that they must continue the secret escapades of Zorro, aided by trusted confidant Ramirez (Gianni Musy). There is a similar film called *Nephews of Zorro* released the following year.

Grave of the Gunfighter see *Three from Colorado*

Great Silence (1968)

Big Silence; Il Grande Silenzio Ital. *Director:* Sergio Corbucci; *Script:* Sergio Corbucci/Bruno Corbucci/Vittorio Petrilli/Mario Amendola; *Camera:* Silvano Ippoliti; *Music:* Ennio Morricone; *Producer:* Adelphia/Les Films Corona (Italy/France). *Cast:* Jean-Louis Trintignant, Klaus Kinski, Frank Wolff, Luigi Pistilli, Vonetta McGee, Mario Brega, Raf Baldassare.

One of director Corbucci's greatest films, virtually unknown in the United States. With this movie, Corbucci opened the philosophical gate and he began making political statements (sometimes unpopular ones) that reflected his leftist beliefs.

This film presents an uncompromisingly angry view, suggesting that the law protects only the wealthy and powerful. Here the bandits are the "good guys," simple hill people who commit crime in order to survive; the sheriff and his henchmen are sadistic, tyrannical authoritarians who kill and brutalize for fun, because their position allows it. The ending is especially shocking as the hero, Silence (Jean-Louis Trintignant), is slaughtered by the bounty-killer-posse, particularly sadistic arch-enemy Tigero (Klaus Kinski).

It's 1896. There are numerous outlaws and society miscasts who live in the snowy wilderness of the mountains. They have to be especially careful when they go down into Snow Mill for supplies because bounty hunters (led by Tigero), taking advantage of the situation, are waiting in the valley and bushwhack them for pending rewards. A man named Silence (so called because his vocal chords had been cut by the vicious bounty hunters) sides with the "good" outlaws against Tigero and his gang.

There's an innovative script by the director and his brother, Bruno. Plus an excellent score from musical wizard Ennio Morricone. This film is Jean-Louis Trintignant's only contribution to the Spaghetti Western genre; he is best

Movie poster from *Great Silence* (1968).

known for his roles in the award-winning *Man and a Woman* (1966) directed by Claude Lelouch, and *Death Laid an Egg* (1970) from Giulio Questi.

Costar Vonetta McGee went on to appear in Francis Ford Coppola's *The Cotton Club* (1984), plus many exploitive horror-'n'-action pics (i.e., *The Big Bust Out, Blacula, Repo Man, Eiger Sanction*).

Corbucci's next film was *Mercenary*.

Great Treasure Hunt (1967)

Monta in Sella, Figlio Di... Ital. *Director:* Tonino Ricci; *Script:* Tonino Ricci/ Fabio Tallevi; *Camera:* Aldo Giordani; *Music:* Luis Enrique Bacalov; *Producer:* Continental Film (Italy/Spain). *Cast:* Mark Damon, Stan Cooper, Luis Marin, Rosalba Neri, Alfredo Mayo.

A special place is reserved for filmmaker Tonino Ricci in the Spaghetti Western Hall of Fame, in the "all-time worst director" section. However, he doesn't even have the excessive flair of a lovable hack like "Miles Deem."

Ricci is best known for his peculiar fascination with "shark" pictures, specifically for his trilogy: *Shark's Cave* (1978), *Encounters in the Deep* (1979), and *Night of the Sharks* (1987). Besides his "nail the camera down and don't move it" approach, his stories are wildly juvenile. In *Shark's Cave*, he claims that the sea creatures are motivated to savage behavior by extraterrestrial beings, actually mixing UFOs and "the Deep" long before James Cameron's *The Abyss* (1989). Tonino Ricci films are tedious, yet remarkable, excursions.

The only reason to watch this Spaghetti Western is to see beautiful Rosalba Neri. She plays Agnes, a gambling partner of Kansas Lee (Mark Damon). They join with Sam (Alfredo Mayo) and bounty hunter Deam (Stan Cooper) to help a mysterious blind man named Felipe (Luis Marin) steal a gold fortune from the evil bandit El Supremo. At the conclusion, it turns out that Felipe wasn't really blind after all, and he tries (unsuccessfully) to double cross his partners.

Handsome Mark Damon starred in many Spaghetti Westerns including *Ringo and His Golden Pistol* and *Johnny Yuma* (see Performers filmography for complete listing) but he is best known for his role in Roger Corman's *Fall of the House of Usher* plus a variety of classic Italian horror pics (i.e., *Black Sabbath, Devil's Wedding Night, Crypt of the Living Dead*).

Greatest Kidnapping in the West see *Greatest Robbery in the West*

Greatest Robbery in the West (1968)

Greatest Kidnapping in the West; Halleluja for Django; La Più Grande Rapina del West Ital. *Director:* Maurizio Lucidi; *Script:* Augusto Finocchi/Augusto Caminito; *Camera:* Riccardo Pallottini; *Music:* Luis E. Bacalov; *Producer:* Mega Film (Italy). *Cast:* George Hilton, Walter Barnes, Hunt Powers, Sarah Ross, Jeff Cameron, Erika Blanc, Mario Brega, Salvatore Borgese, Enzo Fiermonte, Katia Cristine, Rick Boyd.

Maurizio Lucidi, the director of the *Pecos* movies, with the help of a superb cast and crackshot cameraman Riccardo Pallottini, has made a fun (plus adventurous) film here. The Luis Bacalov musical score is robust and memorable; the opening credit sequence is instantly effective at setting the overall mood.

Middletown is a peaceful and prosperous cattle town, with a *very* wealthy bank. David Faylord (George Hilton in one of his best roles) plots a robbery, aided by the Key Jarrett (Walter Barnes) outlaw gang. Disguising himself as a friar, David rides into town with an enormous wooden statue of St. Abelardo in the back of his wagon. He parks next to the bank window, allowing the bandits to fill the statue with the stolen gold coins. It's a "clean" caper, nobody gets hurt and everybody gets away.

But it's not quite that simple. Seen by neither David nor Jarrett, a third person, a gunman-turned-drunkard-turned-gunman-again named Billy Rum (Hunt Powers), had rerouted the money from the statue into a secret hiding place of his own. Billy Rum hates Jarrett because he killed his brother. So through the "missing loot," Billy convinces David to double-cross Jarrett, thus achieving a certain sense of revenge. The finale brings mixed blessings. Billy had stashed the gold coins in a cellar filled with explosives. During a fierce gun battle there's an explosion, killing Jarrett and blowing the coins sky high. As the end credits roll, it's raining money in Middletown.

Regarding the alternate title, *Halleluja for Django*, it's just another crass example of a production company trying to capitalize on the "Django" name, bearing no relation to the film.

Gringo see *Gunfight at Red Sands*

I Gringo non Perdonano see *Black Eagle of Santa Fe*

Gringos Do Not Forgive see *Black Eagle of Santa Fe*

Gringo's Pitiless Colt see *Ruthless Colt of the Gringo*

Grosstadtprärie see *Prairie in the City*

Gun Shy Piluk see *Piluk, the Timid One*

Gunfight at High Noon (1963)

Three Ruthless Ones; I Tre Spietati Ital. *Director:* Joaquin Romero Marchent; *Script:* Rafael R. Marchent/Joaquin R. Marchent/Jesus Navarro; *Camera:* Rafael Pacheco; *Music:* Riz Ortolani; *Producer:* Centauro Films/P.E.A. (Spain/Italy). *Cast:* Richard Harrison, Fernando Sancho, Robert Hundar, Gloria Osuna, Miguel Palenzuela, Luis Induñi, Gloria Milland, Andrew Scott, Billy Hayden, Raf Baldassare, Evelyn Merrill.

This is one of the first "modern" Spaghetti Westerns, unfortunately marred by a convoluted plotline. However, the camerawork is quite good and director Joaquin R. Marchent has an excellent eye for atmosphere (demonstrated to an extremely violent degree in one of his later films, *Cut-Throats Nine*).

This time there are three brothers: Chet, Brad, and Jeff (Robert Hundar, Billy Hayden, Richard Harrison). Their father had been killed by bandits when they were very young. Years have passed, and now they are grown.

Chet goes off to find the outlaws who murdered his father, while Jeff and Brad stay behind. Jeff eventually becomes sheriff of Silver City. He also falls in love with Louise (Evelyn Merrill). Life is good. But, in a ludicrous plot twist, Jeff discovers that Louise's dad was one of his father's killers.

No sooner than that happens, his brother Chet returns from his "death" hunt with good news. He has killed "all but one" of the evil outlaws. Then things escalate into a desperate struggle between brothers. Jeff can't allow Chet to murder Louise's father. Brad joins Jeff in the confrontation against his vengeance-seeking brother, which results in Chet dying and Louise's father dead.

Richard Harrison, a "bit player" in the United States (i.e., "walkons" in *Kronos, Jeanne Eagels, South Pacific, Master of the World*) went to Italy in 1961 to star in Alberto De Martino's sword-'n'-sandal film, *The Invincible Gladiator*. After that, he made four more peplums, including a pirate movie, *Il Pirata del Diavolo*, and then this film. He followed *Gunfight at High Noon* with *Gunfight at Red Sands*. When his producers, Papi and Colombo, offered a third oater, Richard turned them down. He returned to the "more familiar" historical/peplum genre, starring in *Giants of Rome*—instead of *Fistful of Dollars*.

Gunfight at O Q Corral (1974) (X rated)

Règlements de Femmes O Q Corral Fr; *Arrière-Train Sifflera Trois Fois* Fr (edited version). *Director:* Jean-Marie Pallardy; *Script:* Jean-Marie Pallardy; *Camera:* Jacques Robin; *Music:* Eddie Warner; *Producer:* Europrodis/C.T.C. (France). *Cast:* Alice Arno, Will Van Ammelrooy, Vera Belmont, Jean Claude Stromme, Jacques Isermini, Gilda Arancio.

This French produced novelty is strictly hardcore X-rated fare (a soft version was also released; see alternate title listed above) featuring popular European actress Alice Arno as Lulu. Unlike the American produced X-films of same sex–Western ilk (*A Dirty Western* and *Lipps and McCain*), this one is much better photographed and has an interesting story. There's almost an hour of plot (the film runs an amazing 110 minutes) sandwiched between the sex scenes.

Outlaws Billy the Kid and John Kayket (Jean Claude Stromme and Jean-Marie Pallardy) kidnap a female "troublemaker," Maureen O'Lala (Vera Belmont) during a bank holdup. She manages to turn the amigos against one another, resulting in a final showdown at the O Q Corral.

Gunfight at Red Sands (1963)

Gringo; Duello nel Texas Ital. *Director:* Ricardo Blasco; *Script:* Albert Band/Ricardo Blasco; *Camera:* Jack Dalmas; *Music:* Ennio Morricone; *Producer:* Albert Band, Tecisa/Jolly (Italy/Spain). *Cast:* Richard Harrison, Giacomo Rossi Stuart, Sara Lezana, Mikaela Wood, Daniel Martin, Barta Barri, Aldo Sambrell, Sam Field.

A pre–Leone Spaghetti Western, starring Richard (he's done everything) Harrison, with music by Ennio Morricone (using the Dan Savio pseudonym) and written by Albert Band (who codirected his own Western with Sergio Corbucci the same year, *Massacre at Grand Canyon*). Future sleaze-and-action filmmaker Massimo Dallamano is chief cameraman (behind the Jack Dalmas alias).

The plot is simple, and in actuality, a predecessor of countless similar Spaghetti Western themes spanning the next ten years. Gringo Martinez (Richard Harrison), an adopted son of a Mexican family living in a Mex-hating border town, returns home to find his father robbed and his stepbrother wounded by a band of outlaw racists who had attacked the ranch. Of course, Gringo seeks (and finds) revenge.

The title theme, "A Gringo Like Me," is an unintentional hoot, a campy delight.

Gunfighters Die Harder see *Sartana*

Gunfighters of Casa Grande (1965)

Pistoleros de Casa Grande Sp. *Director:* Roy Rowland; *Script:* Clarke Reynolds/ Bordon Chase; *Camera:* José Aguayo/Manuel Merino; *Music:* Johnny Douglas; *Producer:* Lester Welch, M and M (Spain/U.S.). *Cast:* Alex Nicols, Jorge Mistral, Steve Rowland, Dick Bentley, Mercedes Alonso, Maria Granada, Aldo Sambrell, Diana Lorys.

Here is an early Spanish-U.S. coproduction directed by veteran American filmmaker Roy Rowland (best known for the U.S. 1952 Ray Milland Western, *Bugles in the Afternoon,* and for *Hit the Deck,* a musical comedy with Jane Powell from 1955). He also made the 1964 Eurowestern, *Man Called Gringo.*

This film, based on a book by Bordon Chase, is a simplistic tale of greed and passion as Mexican outlaws led by Rojo (Aldo Sambrell) raid a hacienda, recently won in a poker game by American gunman-now-land-owner Joe Daylight (Alex Nicol) and his partner Traveler (Jorge Mistral).

The best thing about the film is the camera work, provided by Spanish vets José Aguayo and Manuel Merino. The story was (unofficially) reworked as *Five Thousand Dollars on One Ace* the following year.

Gunman Called Nebraska see *Savage Gringo*

Gunman in Town see *Light the Fuse . . . Sartana Is Coming*

Gunman of One Hundred Crosses (1971)

Una Pistola per Cento Croci Ital; *Django: Eine Pistole für 100 Kreuze* Ger. *Director:* Lucky Moore; *Script:* Carlo Croccolo; *Camera:* Franco Villa; *Music:* Marcello Mineri; *Producer:* Kamar/Virgina Cinematagrafica (West Germany/ Italy). *Cast:* Tony Kendall, Marina Mulligan, Dick Palmer, Rai Saunders, Monica Miguel.

While not as good as his other 1971 Spaghetti Western, *Black Killer,* director Lucky Moore (aka Carlo Croccolo) once again "follows the guidelines" and creates another "textbook" example of the genre. However, he does break away from tradition with a remarkably poignant role from a strong female character, Marianne (Marina Mulligan), a beautiful widowed rancher who takes revenge into her own hands when her husband is killed by outlaws. She is aided by a gunfighter, Django (Tony Kendall) who teaches her "the ways of the gun." Dick Palmer plays bad guy Frank Dawson, the evil town boss.

It's an interesting combination of the "revenge for a slaughtered family" theme with the "big trouble with the town boss" motif, plus some "student/ teacher" fun (à la *Death Rides a Horse*). But the movie suffers from slow pacing, mostly caused by long segments of poker playing and barroom brawls.

Gunman Sent by God see *Two Pistols and a Coward*

Gunmen and the Holy Ghost (1973)

Return of the Holy Ghost; Spirito Santo e le 5 Magnifiche Canaglie Ital. *Director:* Roberto Mauri; *Script:* Roberto Mauri; *Camera:* Luigi Ciccarese; *Music:*

Carlo Savina; *Producer:* Victor Produzione (Italy). *Cast:* Vassili Karis, Dick Palmer, Aldo Berti, Craig Hill, Ray O'Connor, Jolanda Modio, José Torres, Gilberto Galimbi, Ken Wood.

This is another film in Roberto Mauri's unofficial "Holy Ghost" sequels. For background details see *He Was Called the Holy Ghost* (1972).

Vassili Karis, once again, plays the title role in a familiar "Magnificent Seven"–inspired story as Holy Ghost and his sidekick Weston (Dick Palmer) recruit an army of sharpshooters to protect a defenseless border town from marauding Mexican bandidos.

It remains the last entry in the series.

Gunmen from Arizona see *Five Thousand Dollars on One Ace*

Gunmen of Ave Maria see *Forgotten Pistolero*

Gunmen of Rio Grande (1964)

Duel at Rio Bravo; Sfida a Rio Bravo Ital; *Jennie Lee Ha una Nuova Pistola* Ital. *Director:* Tullio Demichelli; *Script:* Tullio Demichelli; *Camera:* Aldo Ricci; *Music:* Angelo Francesco Lavagnino; *Producer:* Allied Artists (Italy/Spain/France). *Cast:* Guy Madison, Fernando Sancho, Madeleine Lebeau, Gérard Tichy, Carolyn Davys, Beni Deus, Olivier Hussenot, Massimo Seratto.

When trouble breaks out in a Mexican mining town of Rio Bravo, the French saloon owner, Jennie Lee (Madeleine Lebeau), writes to Marshal Wyatt Earp (Guy Madison) for help. Earp knows that he can't legally work as a lawman in Mexico, so he changes his name to "Laramie" and, posing as a hired gunman, rides to the rescue.

Sure it's illogical, but the direction is swift (Tullio Demichelli is an underrated action filmmaker best known for his thrillers and gangster films) and Madison turns in an another enjoyable performance.

Guns for Dollars see *Heads You Die . . . Tails I Kill You*

Guns for San Sebastian (1967)

Bataille de San Sebastian Fr. *Director:* Henri Verneuil; *Script:* Serge Ganz/Miguel Morayta/Ennio De Concini; *Camera:* Armand Thirard; *Music:* Ennio Morricone; *Producer:* Jacques Bar, Cipra/Peliculas/Filmes (France/Mexico/Italy). *Cast:* Charles Bronson, Anthony Quinn, Jaime Fernandez, Rosa Furman, Sam Jaffe, Silvia Pinal, Anjanette Comer.

Filmed entirely in Mexico, this Italian-French-Mexican coproduction is based on the William B. Faherty book, *A Wall for San Sebastian*, and directed by popular French (although originally from Turkey) filmmaker Henri Verneuil (pseudonym for Achod Malakian). This remains his only Western, but Verneuil made over 30 films starting in 1951 with *La Table aux Crèves*. His long list includes *The Night Caller, The Burglars* with Jean-Paul Belmondo, *The Sicilian Clan,* and *Weekend at Dunkirk.*

This story is a slight variation on the *Magnificent Seven* theme. It could be called *The Magnificent One (with a Cannon).* Anthony Quinn plays Father Leon Alastray, a fake priest who rallies the townspeople of San Sebastian into an effective army against a marauding outlaw, Teclo (Charles Bronson), and his

Indian chief partner Golden Lance (Jaime Fernandez), sort of like Winnetou's evil cousin.

Guns of Nevada see *Joe Dexter*

Guns of Violence see *Ten Thousand Dollars Blood Money*

Hai Sbagliato, Dovete Uccidermi Subito! see *Kill the Poker Player*

Half Breed (1966)

Half Breed Ger. *Director:* Harald Phillipp; *Script:* Fred Denger; *Camera:* Heinz Hölscher; *Music:* Martin Böttcher; *Producer:* Horst Wendlandt, Rialto Film (West Germany/Yugoslavia/Italy). *Cast:* Lex Barker, Pierre Brice, Götz George, Ursula Glass, Walter Barnes, Ralf Wolter.

This is the sixth Lex Barker/Pierre Brice *Winnetou* film, preceded by *Treasure of Silver Lake* (1963), *Winnetou the Warrior* or *Apache Gold* (1963), *Apache's Last Battle* or *Old Shatterhand* (1964), *Winnetou. Last of the Renegades* (1964), and *Winnetou: The Desperado Trail* (1965).

With the blessing of Chief Winnetou (once again played by Pierre Brice), Mac (Walter Barnes) gives ownership of a secret Apache gold mine to his half-breed daughter Apanachi (Ursula Glass) on her twenty-first birthday. But soon evil white opportunists try to "jump the claim" by rallying settlers into a frenzy against the peaceful Indians. Winnetou and his friend, Shatterhand (Lex Barker), eventually calm everybody down, and restore peace to the West—for a while anyway.

The next entry was *Winnetou and Shatterhand in the Valley of Death* (1968). Director Harald Phillipp also made a Stewart Granger/Pierre Brice *Winnetou* film called *Rampage at Apache Wells*.

Halleluja and Sartana Strike Again (1972)

Alleluja & Sartana Are Sons ... Sons of God; Hundred Fists and a Prayer; Alleluja e Sartana Figli di ... Figli di Dio Ital. *Director:* Mario Siciliano; *Script:* Adriano Bolzoni/Kurt Nachmann; *Camera:* Gino Santini; *Music:* Elvio Monti/ Franco Zauli; *Producer:* Lisa Film/Metheus (West Germany/Italy). *Cast:* Robert Widmark, Ron Ely, Uschi Glas, Angelica Ott, Alan Abbott.

Here's another film obviously influenced by the popular *Trinity*esque "buddy" motif, while it also tries to capitalize on the "Sartana" notoriety. And similar to director Mario Siciliano's *Trinity and Sartana Are Coming* of the same year, it emerges only as a one-dimensional action/comedy laced with stupid sight gags smothering an already preposterous story line.

Halleluja and Sartana (Ron Ely and Robert Widmark) are two "on the lam" hapless bandits. Disguised as priests, they arrive in Redemption City to find it under the brutal domination of a vicious outlaw gang. Halleluja and Sartana, in conjunction with the mayor's widow (Uschi Glas, alias Wanda Vismara), reopen the abandoned church and use it as headquarters for a "resistance movement" against the bandidos who raid the city every night.

It sounds much better than it plays.

Costar Uschi Glas went on to star in several Edgar Wallace thrillers, including *The College Girl Murders,* and then later she appeared in Umberto Lenzi's *Seven Orchids for a Murder* (1972).

Halleluja for Django see *Greatest Robbery in the West*

Halleluja to Vera Cruz (1973)

Partirono Preti, Tornarono . . . Curati Ital. *Director:* Newman Rostel; *Script:* Bianco Manini/Ofelia Minardi; *Camera:* Carlo Carlini; *Music:* Luis Enriquez Bacalov; *Producer:* Ferruccio De Martino (Italy). *Cast:* Lionel Stander, Riccardo Salvino, Giampiero Albertini, Jean Louis, Clara Hope, Rick Boyd, Giancarlo Badessi.

Yet another film influenced by the popularity of the *Trinity*esque "buddy" device, but this time it's a most enjoyable excursion seasoned with a few original diversions along the way. The movie is an early directorial debut from proficient cameraman Stelvio Massi (using the "Newman Rostel" moniker); he later became one of Italy's top "action" filmmakers, best known for his *Mark, .44 Specialist* cop series starring Franco Gaspari and John Saxon.

Two rogues posing as priests (seemingly a prevalent Spaghetti Western concept), Sam "the Bishop" and John Dandy (Lionel Stander and Riccardo Salvino) meet a band of Catholic revolutionary outlaws led by General Miguel (Giampiero Albertini) and his niece Adelita (Clara Hope). Miguel likes the idea of having priests in his gang, claiming that it "brings good luck to the cause." But, during his confession, he makes the mistake of mentioning a $500,000 gold shipment being transferred from Texicola to Vera Cruz.

With avaricious thoughts of all that gold, the bogus priests sneak from the camp and race toward Texicola. Enroute they stumble into one predicament after another, including a confrontation with a sadistic land baron ("I hate all priests because they defend the peons who rebel against the rightfully rich!"). Eventually they regroup with the revolutionaries and help them pull off the robbery. But General Miguel is only interested in "guns for the cause." He donates all the gold to the Church, thinking it will make Sam and John happy. Obviously, it doesn't.

The Italian title translates to *They Left as Priests and Returned . . . Curates*.

Hands of a Gunman (1965)

Ocaso de un Pistolero Sp; *Mani di Pistolero* Ital. *Director:* Rafael Romero Marchent; *Script:* Joaquin Romero Marchent; *Camera:* Fausto Zuccoli; *Music:* Angelo Francesco Lavagnino; *Producer:* Fida Films (Italy/Spain). *Cast:* Craig Hill, Gloria Milland, Piero Lulli, Ralph Baldwin, Paco Sanz, Carlos R. Marchent, Jesus Puente, John Bartha.

Directed by Rafael Romero Marchent and written by his filmmaking brother, Joaquin Romero Marchent (alias Joaquin Romero Hernandez), this movie is a gritty variation of the "retired gunfighter" theme.

Craig Hill is Galen Stark, a notorious outlaw who tries to settle down to a peaceful family life with his new bride, Laura (Gloria Milland), in a rural New Mexico community. However, the bounty hunters won't leave him alone.

Handsome, the Ugly, and the Stupid (1967)

Il Bello, il Brutto, e il Cretino Ital. *Director:* Giovanni Grimaldi; *Script:* Giovanni Grimaldi; *Camera:* Aldo Giordani; *Music:* Lallo Gori; *Producer:* Gino Mordini, Claudia/Te. Fi. (Italy). *Cast:* Franco Franchi, Ciccio Ingrassia, Mimmo Palmara, Brigitte Petry, Lotar Guntcher, Ivan Scratuglia, Bruno Scipioni.

"Franco and Ciccio" are a lowbrow Italian comedy team, similar to Abbott and Costello (or Martin and Lewis), only much more prolific. In their heyday, Franco and Ciccio averaged one new movie every month. Most of their films are silly slapstick parodies that capitalize on other popular movies. Case in point, this film, which is an obvious takeoff on *The Good, the Bad, and the Ugly*. The story takes place during the Civil War. Handsome (Mimmo Palmara) is looking for a secret treasure but he's missing an important clue: the name of the cemetery where the gold is buried. In the meantime, Ugly and Mr. Stupid (Franco and Ciccio) know the name of the cemetery but not the name on the grave. Disguised as Northern soldiers they are enroute, but are captured by the Confederates. Next, they're taken to the Rebel prison where Handsome is in charge. The three join a cautious partnership and go after the treasure.

In one particularly funny sequence, Franco and Ciccio have arrived at the cemetery still not knowing the name on the marker, so they are forced to dig up grave after grave while the soundtrack blasts an absurdly macho variation of Morricone's "Ecstasy of Gold."

For other Franco and Ciccio Spaghetti Westerns, see Performers filmography. Director Giovanni Grimaldi also directed the comedy team in a number of nongenre films, including *Brutti di Notte, Don Chisciotte and Sancho Panza*, and *Principe Coronato Cercasi per Ricca Ereditiera*.

A Hanging for Django see *No Room to Die*

Hannie Caulder (1971)

Colt pour Trois Salopards Fr. *Director:* Burt Kennedy; *Script:* Z. X. Jones; *Camera:* Edward Scaife; *Music:* Ken Thorne; *Producer:* Patrick Curtis (England/Spain/France). *Cast:* Raquel Welch, Robert Culp, Ernest Borgnine, Christopher Lee, Jack Elam, Strother Martin, Stephen Boyd.

This is an entertaining British financed Western, filmed in mostly Spain by Burt Kennedy (*Deserter, Welcome to Hard Times, War Wagon*, etc.) with cameraman Edward Scaife, and written by Kennedy (under the alias Z. X. Jones).

Astonishingly, this movie remains one of the very few Spaghetti Westerns with a female featured in a pivotal role. Raquel Welch is Hannie Caulder, a poor rancher's wife, who suddenly finds herself alone, unprotected and obsessed with revenge. She had been viciously gang-raped, her husband slaughtered before her eyes. Her home went up in blazes, and all of her possessions are destroyed. Three psycho brothers, Emmett, Frank, and Rufus (Ernest Borgnine, Jack Elam and Strother Martin), are the maniacs responsible, and just as she vows vengeance, a bounty hunter named Thomas Luther Price (Robert Culp in the best role of his career) appears. He takes her to Bailey, a "specialized" gunsmith (Christopher Lee in an unusual, bearded role), for a "personally fitted weapon," teaches her to shoot it, and escorts her in the execution.

The biggest problem with this film lies in its villains. Their over-the-top, deranged behavior makes them impossible to take seriously. Even when they are doing appalling things, which is most of the time.

British musician Ken Thorne composed the music.

Hasta la Última Gota de Sangre see *Wrath of God*

Movie poster from director Domenico Paolella's *Hate for Hate* (1967) starring Antonio Sabàto and John Ireland.

Hate for Hate (1967)

Odio per Odio Ital. *Director:* Domenico Paolella; *Script:* Bruno Corbucci/Fernando Di Leo/Domenico Paolella; *Camera:* Alejandro Ulloa; *Music:* Willy Brezza; *Producer:* Italo Zingarelli, West Film (Italy). *Cast:* Antonio Sabáto, John Ireland, Piero Vida, Nadia Marconi, Fernando Sancho, Mirko Ellis, Gloria Milland.

Prolific, genre-hopping, exploitation director (and part-time movie critic) Domenico Paolella directed two Spaghetti Westerns, this film and the far better *Execution*. The biggest problem with this movie is "it tries too hard" and, as such, it borders on pretension. Once all the needlessly confusing characterizations and perplexing plot twists are shaven away, the film stands naked as a standard revenge flick. Principally, there was no need to hide the basic storyline behind all the ornate flamboyancy ("a rose is still a rose" etc.). Paolella should have put more time into the fundamentals, and less into the artsy "window dressing." Some of the blame also has to be shared with his prominent cowriters, filmmakers Bruno Corbucci and Fernando Di Leo.

John Ireland is Cooper, a bandit who steps into real trouble when he tries to return some stolen money to a struggling rancher, Michael (Antonio Sabáto). He is caught by the law and tossed in jail. The bandit asks Michael to go and inform his wife of his predicament, and further, to escort her and his young daughter to Mexico. Michael visits Cooper's family, but they refuse to go with him. He leaves without realizing that they were being held captive by Cooper's old partner Moxon (Mirko Ellis). Within a short time, Cooper breaks out of prison and returns to his home, finding it destroyed, his money gone, and his wife and daughter missing.

Presuming that Michael is responsible, Cooper tracks him down and almost kills him. After being convinced of Michael's innocence, they go after the real culprit. The movie takes the long way around the block, but it's still just another variation on the "revenge for a slaughtered family" theme. Or, in this case, "revenge for a kidnapped family."

Hate Is My God see *Hatred of God*

Hate Thy Neighbor (1969)

Odia il Prossimo Tuo Ital. *Director:* Ferdinando Baldi; *Script:* Ferdinando Baldi/Luigi Angelo/Roberto Natale; *Camera:* Enzo Serafin; *Music:* Robbe Poitevin; *Producer:* Enrico C. Detli, Cinecidi (Italy). *Cast:* George Eastman, Clyde Gardner, Nicoletta Machiavelli, Horst Frank, Robert Rice, Paolo Magalotti, Franco Fantasia, Claudio Castellani.

A notorious outlaw Gary Stevens (George Eastman), following instructions from Mexican land baron Chris Malone (Horst Frank), kills renowned bandit Bill Dakota after stealing a map showing the whereabouts of a precious gold mine. Bill's brother, Ken Dakota (Clyde Gardner), accompanied by Duke "the chatterbox undertaker" (Robert Rice) go into Mexico after the scoundrels.

One of the things which sets this film apart from the countless "revenge for a slaughtered family" Spaghetti Westerns is the unique "game" played at Chris Malone's estate. He and his wife spend their leisurely afternoons sipping champagne and watching their slaves participate in barbaric gladiator-type contests, attacking each other with long razorblade claws (years before Freddy visited Elm Street). Eventually, Ken Dakota must face the number one warrior in the "death game."

Costar Franco Fantasia left acting in the 80s for the technical end of the business. He has achieved success as production manager and assistant director on various projects, including Lamberto Bava's *Dinner with a Vampire* (1989).

Hatred of God (1967)

Hate Is My God; L'Odio è il Mio Dio. Director: Claudio Gora; Script: Claudio Gora/Werner Hauff; Camera: Franco Delli Colli; Music: Pippo Franco; Producer: Giano/Prodi Cinematografica (Italy/West Germany). Cast: Tony Kendall, Carlo Giordana, Herbert Fleischmann, Marina Berti, Gunther Philippe, Alberto Pozzilli.

A rather mediocre "revenge for a slaughtered family" movie camouflaged by an exploitive, nihilistic title. Tony Kendall is Carl, a rancher-turned-gunman following the old vengeance trail. In a customary showdown fashion, he despondently exterminates the outlaws who raped and killed his wife (Marina Berti).

Director Claudio Gora is best known as an actor (*Five Man Army, Hellbenders, John the Bastard* and a variety of Italian features).

Have a Good Funeral, My Friend ... Sartana Will Pay (1971)

Stranger's Gold; Buon Funerale, Amigos ... Paga Sartana Ital. Director: Anthony Ascott; Script: Giovanni Simonelli/Roberto Giaviti/Anthony Ascott; Camera: Stelvio Massi; Music: Bruno Nicolai; Producer: Flora Film (Italy). Cast: Gianni Garko, Daniela Giordano, Ivano Staccioli, Helga Line, Luis Hinduñi, Franco Ressel, George Wang, Franco Pesce, Roberto Dell'Acqua, Rick Boyd.

This is a later "Sartana" film, but it still has much of the same flavor as the rest of the popular series. Sartana is "the Angel of Death." His main goal is to kill, not for money or revenge (standard motivation in most Spaghetti Westerns), but rather just because certain people deserve it. He's a bigger-than-life vigilante with a bag of tricks that would make James Bond jealous.

This particular film deals with Sartana's vehemence against the evil town banker (Ivano Staccioli) and his sweet (but swindling) niece Jasmine (Daniela Giordano).

Other titles in the series (with Garko in the lead role): *Sartana* (1968), *I'm Sartana ... Your Angel of Death* or *Sartana the Gravedigger* (1969), *Sartana Kills Them All* (1970), *Light the Fuse ... Sartana's Coming* (1971); George Hilton took over the role for Anthony Ascott's (Giuliano Carmineo's) *I'm Sartana ... Trade Your Guns for a Coffin* (1972).

He Was Called the Holy Ghost (1972)

...And His Name Was Holy Ghost; ...E Lo Chiamarono Spirito Santo Ital. Director: Robert Johnson; Script: Roberto Mauri; Camera: Luigi Ciccarese; Music: Bruno Nicolai; Producer: Victor Produzione (Italy). Cast: Vassili Karis, Dick Palmer, Hunt Powers, Jolanda Modio, Amero Capanna, Carlo Giordana.

Apparently, director Roberto Mauri (alias Robert Johnson) was so enamored of Anthony Ascott's Holy Ghost films, *They Call Him the Holy Ghost* and *Forewarned, Half-Killed ... the Word of the Holy Ghost,* (or at least

Movie poster from *Have a Good Funeral, My Friend . . . Sartana Will Pay* (1971), directed by Anthony Ascott.

George Hilton in *Heads You Die . . . Tails I Kill You* (1971).

enamored of their financial success) that he continued "to carry the ball" for two unofficial sequels. Here is the first entry in his low-rent homage.

Chameleon actor Vassili Karis has etched a career by mimicking popular actors. This time, Karis sports a mustache and wears a white cape; he becomes a poor man's *Holy Ghost*. Interestingly, the budget must not have allowed for the perdurable use of doves. There's barely one around (in the original films, Gianni Garko is constantly accompanied by the white, symbolic birds; he even uses one for a unique torture sequence in *Forewarned, Half-Killed . . . The Word of the Holy Ghost*).

The plot is a simplistic, plodding tale about a crooked sheriff involved in a land-grabbing foreclosure scheme with a wicked banker. He eventually "buys the farm" when the Holy Ghost arrives to help the poor settlers.

Cinematographer Luigi Ciccarese continues to be a sought after exploitation cameraman into the 90s; one of the best examples of his later projects is *After Death: Zombi 4* (1988) with director Claudio Fragasso.

He Who Shoots First see *Django Shoots First*

Heads or Tails (1969)

Testa o Croce Ital. *Director:* Peter E. Stanley; *Script:* Piero Pierotti; *Camera:* Fausto Zuccoli; *Music:* Carlo Savina; *Producer:* Romana/Terra Film (Italy/ Spain). *Cast:* John Ericson, Franco Lantieri, Sheyla Rosin, Edwige Fenech, Teodoro Corra, José Jaspe.

Piero Pierotti (aka Peter E. Stanley), the director of *Hercules Against Rome, Goliath vs. the Living Dead (Golia Contro il Cavaliere Mascherato)* and *Cleopatra, a Queen for Caesar* worked as assistant director for Riccardo Freda (*Maciste in Hell*, 1962) and Mario Bava (*Viking Invasion*, also 1962). He made three Spaghetti Westerns, including a peplum-influenced *Lost Treasure of the Incas* (also called *Samson and the Treasure of the Incas*) and a Zorro entry called *Zorro the Rebel*. This film, *Heads or Tails*, remains his only attempt at telling a "strict" Western tale.

The story is a standard one-dimensional rendering, mostly emphasizing the rambling exploits of bounty hunter Will Hunter (John Ericson) as he searches for a notorious gambling bandido Serpiente (Franco Lantieri).

There is, however, an especially erotic whip-'n'-torture sequence featuring very young Edwige Fenech.

Heads You Die ... Tails I Kill You (1971)

Guns for Dollars; Deep West; They Call Me Hallelujah; Testa t'Ammazzo, Croce Sei Morto ... Mi Chiamano Alleluia! Ital. *Director:* Anthony Ascott; *Script:* Tito Carpi/Anthony Ascott; *Camera:* Stelvio Massi; *Music:* Stelvio Cipriani; *Producer:* Colosseo Artistica (Italy). *Cast:* George Hilton, Charles Southwood, Agata Flori, Roberto Camardiel, Rick Boyd, Paolo Gozlino, Andrea Bosić.

A "wheels-within-wheels" double-cross movie directed by the number one most prolific Spaghetti Western champ, Anthony Ascott (alias Giuliano Carmineo), with 13 films to his credit (see Directors filmography). And this one, partially due to the harmonious participation of the two Stelvios (Massi and Cipriani), is among the best.

Hallelujah (George Hilton) is a gunman hired by a Mexican revolutionary officer, General Ramirez (Roberto Camardiel). His mission is to confiscate a case of jewels escorted by Emperor Maximilian's trusted assistant, Alexi (Charles Southwood).

These valuable gems are intended as payment for a machine gun sold by an unscrupulous arms trafficker named Duke Kranz (Rick Boyd). The exchange is scheduled to take place at a remote monastery (a clever front), but when the jewels turn out to be counterfeit, a bloodbath results.

Beautiful American female spy Anna Lee (Agata Flori), disguised as a nun, falsely accuses Hallelujah of masterminding the massacre. However, in reality, her partner, a Cossack named Fortune (Paolo Gozlino), is the culprit who had switched the gems. Tensions escalate into another frenzied battle, but all ends well. General Ramirez gets the machine gun, Anna Lee arrests arms dealer Duke, and the Cossack divides the real jewels with his new partner, Hallelujah.

Influenced by the European popularity of this film, director Ascott made a (disappointingly average) sequel called *Return of Halleluja*.

Hellbenders (1966)

The Cruel Ones; I Crudeli Ital. *Director:* Sergio Corbucci; *Script:* Albert Band/ Ugo Liberatore; *Camera:* Enzo Barboni; *Music:* Leo Nichols (Ennio Morricone); *Producer:* Albert Band, Alba/Tecisa (Italy/Spain). *Cast:* Joseph Cotten, Norma Benguel, Al Mulock, Aldo Sambrell, Julian Mateos, Angel Aranda, Gino Pernice, Julio Peña, Claudio Gora, Ennio Girolami, Maria Martin, Rafael Vaquero.

After the very successful *Django* and the critically praised *Johnny Oro (Ringo and His Golden Pistol)*, director Corbucci teamed with his old friend producer Albert Band (Alfredo Antonini) who cowrote the script for this film. It's also rumored that Band took a heavy hand in the production and actually acted as codirector on the set.

Veteran actor Joseph Cotten turns in a possessed performance as Jonas, a former Southern officer gone mad (a role very similar to that in *The Tramplers*, which Albert Band directed and also cowrote with Ugo Liberatore in 1965). In this one, Jonas and his men massacre a Union convoy and steal their million dollar shipment, hoping to use it for a Confederate resurrection.

Chief cameraman is the future E. B. Clucher (still Enzo Barboni at this point in his career); the rousing musical score is composed by Ennio Morricone (using the Leo Nichols pseudonym). The assistant director is future cult filmmaker Ruggero Deodato; actor Ennio Girolami is the son of pouplar director Marino Girolami (Frank Martin).

Sergio Corbucci's next film was *Navajo Joe* starring Burt Reynolds.

Hell's Fighters see Big Showdown

Here We Go Again, Eh Providence? (1973)

Ci Ridiamo, Vero Provvidenza? Ital. *Director:* Alberto De Martino; *Script:* Castellano/Pipolo; *Camera:* Alejandro Ulloa; *Music:* Ennio Morricone/Bruno Nicolai; *Producer:* Oceania/Films Corona/Producciones Dia (Italy/France/ Spain). *Cast:* Tomás Milian, Gregg Hunter, Carole André, Rick Boyd, Luciano Catenacci, Angel Ortiz.

This is a sequel to *Sometimes Life Is Hard, Right Providence?*, which also starred Tomás Milian as the "Charlie Chaplin" clone named Providence (complete with tiny mustache, bowler hat and umbrella). It's more of the same kind of fun as the "cultured" bounty hunter Providence (with an arsenal that would make Rambo jealous) rushes to the trial of an old friend, Hurricane Kid (Gregg Hunter). Acting as Hurricane's attorney, Providence succeeds in getting the outlaw convicted, only to rescue him from execution (in a gimmick similar to the Blonde/Tuco arrangement in *The Good, the Bad, and the Ugly*) with plans to turn him in again for a higher bounty. Unfortunately for Providence, the president of the United States announces a general amnesty eliminating the rewards on all "outlaws' heads."

Suddenly, the bounty hunter finds himself jobless, so he decides to take a vacation, and while doing so, saves the life of Countess Pamela de Ortega (Carole André). The story continues to ramble here and there. Providence proposes marriage to the countess, but is rejected. He then joins with the Hurricane Kid again in a search for $500,000, which they almost get ("almost" is the key word).

It's an enjoyable change of pace movie from cult director Alberto De Martino (see Directors filmography), best known for the *Exorcist* ripoff, *L'Anti Cristo*, and the *Omen* carbon copy, *Holocaust 2000*.

Hero Called Allegria (1971)

His Name Was Pot . . . But They Called Him Allegria; Django Always Draws Second; Il Suo Nome Era Pot . . . lo Chiamavano Allegria Ital. *Director:* Dennis Ford/Slim Alone (in England). *Script:* Luigi Glachin/Dino Spataro; *Camera:* Mario Masini (Mancini); *Music:* Nico Fidenco; *Producer:* Elektra Film (Italy). *Cast:* Peter Martell, Gordon Mitchell, Lincoln Tate, Daniela Giordano, Lucky MacMurray.

Yes, once again it's the Western genre's favorite hack, Miles Deem (Demofilo Fidani), hiding behind yet another pseudonym, Dennis Ford. And, interestingly, in England where this film was called *Django Always Draws Second*, the director credit reads "Slim Alone." Besides these new monikers and the more "notorious" Miles Deem alias, Fidani uses Dick Spitfire, Sean O'Neal, Dino (and sometimes, Diego) Spataro, Alessandro Santini and Lucky Dickerson. Forewarned is forearmed.

This film is, arguably, the worst of the Miles Deem Spaghetti Westerns (or perhaps, it's tied with *Reach, You Bastard!* for that dubious distinction). Two brothers, Pot and Ray (Peter Martell and Gordon Mitchell) rob a bank, but things go wrong. They don't get the money and they're almost captured. Have they learned a lesson? No, of course not. With the help of two friends, they try again. This time everything goes okay, but the next day they are robbed by an evil bandit named Lobo (Lincoln Tate). When they attempt to recover the loot, everybody (except Pot) is killed. Miles with a moral. What's next?

Heroes of Fort Worth see *Charge of the Seventh Cavalry*

Heroes of the West (1964)

Gli Eroi del West Ital. *Director:* Steno; *Script:* Sandro Continenza/José Mallorqui/Steno; *Camera:* Tino Santoni; *Music:* Gianni Ferrio/Manuel Parada; *Producer:* Emo Bistolfi, Fenix Film/Cineproduzione (Spain/Italy). *Cast:* Walter Chiari, Raimondo Vianello, Silvia Solar, Benny Deus, Maria Anderson, Tomás Blanco, Miguel Del Castillo, Bruno Scipioni.

This is a "lighthearted" classic Spaghetti Western directed by Steno (pseudonym for Stefano Vanzina), best known for his action-oriented comedies (i.e., *Police Woman* with Edwige Fenech, *My Darling Slave, Flatfoot*, etc.) and various Italian television programs including "The Big Man" starring Bud Spencer as a "Cannon"-like private eye.

Two charismatic rogue bandits, Mike (Walter Chiari) and Colorado (Raimondo Vianello), assume the identity of heirs to a rich gold mine, but they find themselves in the middle of a dangerous feud between two warring families, the Blacks and the Whites. Not too obvious, right?

Hey Amigo! A Toast to Your Death! (1971)

Ehi Amico . . . Sei Morto! Ital. *Director:* Paul Maxwell; *Script:* Renato Savina/Paolo Bianchi; *Camera:* Sergio D'Offizi; *Music:* Carlo Savina; *Producer:*

Movie poster from *Hey Amigo! A Toast to Your Death!* (1971).

P.E.A. (Italy). *Cast:* Wayde Preston, Rik Battaglia, Aldo Berti, Anna Mason, Agnes Spaak, Raf Baldassare.

Tough, balls-to-the-walls director Paolo Bianchini (using his "Paul Maxwell" pseudonym) delivers another nihilistic Spaghetti Western, similar in its misogynistic style to his *God Made Them . . . I Kill Them.*

This time Wayde Preston plays an aging bounty hunter who goes deep into Mexico to capture a notorious bandit. Along the way he is diverted by a tale of "missing gold." Eventually, he finds both the outlaw and the treasure.

Hijo de Jesse James see *Jesse James' Kid*

El Hijo del Pistolero see *Son of a Gunfighter*

Hills Run Red (1966)

River of Dollars; Un Fiume di Dollari Ital *Director:* Lee W. Beaver; *Script:* Mario Pierotti; *Camera:* Toni Secchi; *Music:* Leo Nichols (Ennio Morricone); *Producer:* Manno Donati/Luigi Carpentieri (Italy). *Cast:* Thomas Hunter, Henry Silva, Dan Duryea, Nicoletta Machiavelli, Gianna Serra, Nando Gazzolo.

Two Confederate soldiers, Jerry (Thomas Hunter) and Ken (Nando Gazzolo) find themselves holding a sizable amount of cash intended for the army payroll when the Civil War abruptly comes to an end. Ken steals the money; however, Jerry is blamed and incarcerated. Years later, he's released from prison, bent on revenge. But vengeance is not easy because, in the meantime, Ken Scagall (with the stolen money) has built quite an empire for himself, complete with armed guards led by sadistic Mendez (Henry Silva).

A good Western directed by veteran filmmaker (and former movie critic) Carlo Lizzani (alias Lee W. Beaver), with an exceptional score from Ennio Morricone (using his "Leo Nichols" pseudonym). Competent Toni Secchi (aka Tony Dry) is the chief cameraman.

His Colt, Himself, His Revenge see *They Called Him Trinity*

His Name Was Holy Ghost (1970)

Blazing Guns; Lo Chiamavano Spirito Santo Ital; *They Call Him Holy Ghost.* *Director:* Anthony Ascott; *Script:* Tito Carpi/Federico De Urrutia; *Camera:* Miguel Fernandez Rodriguez; *Music:* Bruno Nicolai; *Producer:* Lea Film/C.C. Astro (Italy/Spain). *Cast:* Gianni Garko, Victor Israel, Poldo Bendanti, Chris Huerta, Pilar Velasquez, Nello Pazzafini.

Here's John (Gianni) Garko in the first of his two "Spirito Santo" films (also see Ascott's *Forewarned, Half-Killed . . . The Word of the Holy Ghost*). He's basically the same character as the one he portrays in the "Sartana" series (this time dressed in white, with the addition of a dove on his shoulder).

It's the familiar Angel-of-Death theme. Garko is the mysterious sharpshooting stranger, Spirito Santo (or the Holy Ghost), the vigilante of the West, rescuing the oppressed people of a border town from cruel Mexican outlaws. However, this time, Holy Ghost has an ulterior motive, too. He is fighting for "law and order" (specifically, trying to reinstate benevolent governor Don Firmino) so that he can take possession of a gold mine that he won in a poker game.

A different director, Roberto Mauri, also made "unofficial" sequels to the series with Vassili Karis in the title role (see *He Was Called the Holy Ghost*, 1972, and *The Gunmen and the Holy Ghost*, also called *Return of the Holy Ghost*, 1973).

His Name Was King (1971)

Lo Chiamavano King Ital. *Director:* Don Reynolds; *Script:* Renato Savino; *Camera:* Guglielmo Mancori; *Music:* Luis Enrique Bacalov; *Producer:* Antonio Lugatelli (Italy). *Cast:* Richard Harrison, Klaus Kinski, Anne Puskin, John Silver, Lorenzo Fineschi, Tom Felleghy, Vassili Karis, John Bartha, Rick Boyd.

Another variation on the "revenge for a slaughtered family" theme as John "King" Marley (Richard Harrison) rides in from the range to find his brother murdered and his sister-in-law, Carol (Anne Puskin), beaten and raped. The brutality was meant as a warning from the vicious Benson gang, wild gun-trafficking outlaws who disliked King's interference in their affairs.

Craving justice, King leaves traumatized Carol with his friend, Sheriff Foster (Klaus Kinski), and then proceeds to rigorously track down the killers. After a brush with Mexican bandidos (in an unrelated segment), he eventually finds the Benson gang and kills them all. But King also discovers that the secret leader of the gunsmugglers is (!) Sheriff Foster. Obviously, John "King" Marley eliminates the lawman, too.

Kinski built a career in the early 1970s by participating in as many films as possible, for as short a time as possible, for the most money possible. His participation in this one clocks in at five minutes. Don Reynolds is the pseudonym for Renato Savino (also see his *Gold of the Heroes*).

His Name Was Pot . . . But They Called Him Allegria see *Hero Called Allegria*

His Name Was Sam Walbash, But They Call Him Amen (1971)

Savage Guns; Era Sam Walbash . . . Lo Chiamavano "Così Sia" Ital. *Director:* Miles Deem; *Script:* Miles Deem; *Camera:* Franco Villa; *Music:* Lallo Gori; *Producer:* Galassia Cinematografica (Italy). *Cast:* Robert Woods, Dean Stratford, Dennis Colt, Simone Blondell, Custer Gail.

Miles Deem (Demofilo Fidani) is the genre's favorite hack, the Italian "Al Adamson" of Westerns. Although Miles made other types of films (like the forgettable *Godfather's Advisor*, which he later re-edited, redubbed and unleashed on the unsuspecting public as a new film, *The Hot Chair*), his main concentration was on the Spaghetti Western. Under various pseudonyms (including Dick Spitfire, Dennis Ford, Sean O'Neal, Alessandro Santini, Slim Alone, Lucky Dickerson, Diego Spatara and, of course, Miles Deem) Fidani is responsible for 12 (11 if *Reach, You Bastard!* is rightfully eliminated) genre oaters.

A sadistic outlaw, Mash Flanigan (Dean Stratford), hears that a saloon owner has issued a warrant for his arrest, and that he's planning to testify in court against the bandit. Outraged, Flanigan and his gang go to the bar. They destroy the place, killing everybody inside. Everybody, except Sam Walbash (Robert Woods) who was having a drink with his (now dead) younger brother.

Movie poster from *Hills Run Red* (1966).

As soon as he recovers from his wounds, Sam goes after Flanigan. The outlaw is informed that "a man is looking for him" so (in a totally out of character sequence) Flanigan changes his name to Donovan and hides in nearby Golden City (amazing considering he slaughtered an entire saloon just days before, there's no logical reason why he would be apprehensive now). But

with the aid of Flanigan's (Donovan's?) new girlfriend Fanny, hero Sam finds the outlaw and kills him in a showdown.
Ridiculous, and entertaining.

His Pistols Smoked . . . They Call Him Cemetery see *They Call Him Cemetery*

Hole in the Forehead (1968)

Un Buco in Fronte Ital. *Director:* Joseph Warren; *Script:* Adriano Bolzoni; *Camera:* Amerigo Gengarelli; *Music:* Roberto Pregadio; *Producer:* Tigielle 33 (Italy/Spain). *Cast:* Robert Hundar, Anthony Ghidra, Rosy Zichell, John Bryan, Giorgio Gargiulo, John MacDouglas, Luigi Marturano.

This Italian/Spanish coproduction directed by Joseph Warren (pseudonym for Giuseppe Vari) tells the story of a cruel and ruthless Mexican bandit named Manguja (Robert Hundar) who is searching for a lost treasure. But he's not alone in the quest.

Bounty hunter John Blood (Anthony Ghidra) is actually the first to find the gold (hidden in the main altar of a church). Then, after donating the fortune to the monastery, he kills Manguja in a showdown and collects the reward.

It's a weak Warren film, especially lacking when compared to his *Deguello* or *Django, Last Killer*. He also directed some exceptional nongenre movies, particularly *War of the Zombies* starring John Drew Barrymore, and *Who Killed the Prosecutor and Why* with Lou Castel.

Die Hölle von Manitoba see *Place Called Glory*

Holy Water Joe (1971)

Acquasanta Joe Ital. *Director:* Mario Gariazzo; *Script:* Franco Poggi/Mario Gariazzo; *Camera:* Franco Villa; *Music:* Marcello Giombini; *Producer:* Cineproduzioni Daunia (Italy). *Cast:* Ty Hardin, Richard Harrison, Lincoln Tate, Silvia Monelli, Lee Banner, Anthony Freeman, Tucci Musumeci.

Jeff Donovan (Ty Hardin) is a notorious outlaw, who (with his gang) has terrorized the entire state. But when he robs the bank in Cutler City, he inadvertently has stolen the savings of famous bounty hunter Acquasanta Joe (Lincoln Tate). It doesn't take long for Acquasanta to find the bandit and demand his money. However, in the meantime, gang member Charlie (Richard Harrison) has absconded with all the loot.

Jeff and Acquasanta Joe form an uneasy partnership (especially complicated because they are both in love with the same woman, Estella, played by Silvia Monelli) and they set out to recover the "stolen" stolen money. However, when the culprit Charlie is caught and hanged by a lawman, all the money is turned over to the authorities.

Depressed, Acquasanta Joe and Jeff Donovan return to their hideout, but things have continued to get worse for them. In their absence, the gang has appointed Butch (Lee Banner) as the new leader. The tense situation escalates into a free-for-all gun battle, and only Acquasanta Joe walks away without a scratch. Jeff is wounded but his injuries "bring the woman out" in Estella as she decides that she really does love him. Everyone else is dead.

Richard Harrison turns in one of his best nonassuming Western roles. Too bad it's only a cameo.

Director Mario Gariazzo continued making films long after the Spaghetti Western faze bit the dust. His productions branched into many different arenas, including sleazy horror with *Sexorcist*, also called *Eerie Midnight Horror Show* (1974), and sexy sci-fi in 1978's *Very Close Encounters of the 4th Kind*, plus serious sci-fi with *Eyes Behind the Stars* (1978). He even dabbled with the "cannibal" motif for his *White Slave* (1984), distributed in some markets as *Cannibal Holocaust 2*.

Hora de Morir see *Hour of Death*

Una Horca para Django see *No Room to Die*

El Hombre de la Diligencia see *Fury of the Apaches*

El Hombre del Río Malo see *Bad Man's River*

Hombre Que Mató Billy el Niño see *Man Who Killed Billy the Kid*

Horseman and the Samurai see *Stranger in Japan*

Hour of Death (1968)

Hora de Morir Sp. *Director:* Paul Marchenti; *Script:* Joaquin L. Hernandez/ Federico De Urrutia/Manuel Sebares/Rafael Romero Marchent; *Camera:* Rafael Pacheco; *Music:* Riz Ortolani; *Producer:* Felix Juran Apario/Manuel Castedo (Spain/Italy). *Cast:* Paul Piaget, Gloria Milland, Robert Hundar, Jesus Puente, Fernando Sancho, Raf Baldassare, Luis Induñi, Pedro Sanz.

For this film, prolific Spanish director Joaquin Romero Marchent uses an alias, Paul Marchenti (perhaps to capitalize on the popularity of the Italian-produced Westerns). However, it's a short on action, long on posturing movie about wagon trains and settlers, Indians and opportunists. The only surprise comes at the finale when the heroine dies, but the journey is slow and tedious. It's difficult to imagine that the same director made the controversial and engrossing *Cut-Throats Nine* (1973).

Humpty Dumpty Gang see *Ben and Charlie*

Hundred Fists and a Prayer see *Halleluja and Sartana Strike Again*

Hunting Party (1971)

Il Giorno dei Lunghi Fucili Ital. *Director:* Don Medford; *Script:* William Norton/Gil Alexander/Lou Morheim; *Camera:* Cecilio Paniagua; *Music:* Riz Ortolani; *Producer:* Lou Morheim (England/Italy/Spain). *Cast:* Oliver Reed, Gene Hackman, Candice Bergen, Simon Oakland, Ronald Howard, Mitchel Ryan.

It opens with the on-screen killing of a cow edited against the awkwardly angry lovemaking of Melissa (Candice Bergen) and Brandt (Gene Hackman). This is, obviously, a message to the audience that the next 108 minutes are going to cover some rugged territory. And they do. Rape, adultery and revenge are the predominant themes in this hard-hitting Italian/British coproduction.

While affluently eccentric husband Brandt (Hackman) is away on a hunting trip with his rich friends (mostly hunting whores on a privately-chartered bordello-equipped train), his schoolteacher wife Melissa (Bergen) is kidnapped by notorious outlaw Frank Caulder (Oliver Reed). He wants her to teach him how to read, but his "noble" intentions soon turn to lust. And, within a short while, love. Mutual, reciprocal love.

When Brandt learns of the abduction, he and his cronies turn the sites of the hunting party towards the outlaw gang. Armed with expensive, telescopic rifles they massacre the bandits in a melodramatic bloodbath finale that results in everyone (yes, everyone) dead or dying.

Good musical score from Riz Ortolani; stark, effective photography by Cecilio Paniagua.

I Am Sartana, Trade Your Guns for a Coffin (1972)

Sartana's Coming, Get Your Coffins Ready; C'è Sartana, Vendi la Pistola e Comprati la Bara Ital; *Sartana's Here . . . Trade Your Pistol for a Coffin; Vendi Pistole per Comprare Cofani* Ital. *Director:* Anthony Ascott; *Script:* Giovanni Simonelli/Anthony Ascott; *Camera:* Stelvio Massi; *Music:* Frank Mason; *Producer:* Flora Film (Italy). *Cast:* George Hilton, Charles Southwood, Franco Fantasia, Peter Carter, Armando Calvo, Erika Blanc, Carlo Giordana, Rick Boyd, Carlo Gaddi, Nello Pazzafini.

Officially, it's the last film in the "Sartana" series, this time without popular John (Gianni) Garko in the lead role. George Hilton takes his place and does an admirable job considering the odds, a new face in an established vehicle.

Sartana joins forces with Sabata (Charles Southwood) to defeat a crooked banker in cahoots with a Mexican bandit. The story is a bit threadbare, camouflaged with many "spy gadgets," indeed more than necessary, converting the entire opus into an extravaganza not unlike an episode of American TV's "Wild Wild West."

I Am Sartana, Your Angel of Death (1969)

Sartana the Gravedigger; Sono Sartana, il Vostro Becchino Ital. *Director:* Anthony Ascott; *Script:* Tito Carpi/Enzo Dell'Aquila; *Camera:* Giovanni Bergamini; *Music:* Vasco & Mancuso; *Producer:* Aldo Addobbati/Paolo Moffa; Ambrosia Cinematografica/Paris Étoile (Italy/France). *Cast:* John Garko, Frank Wolff, Klaus Kinski, Gordon Mitchell, Ettore Manni, Sal Borgese, Renato Baldini, Rick Boyd, José Torres.

This is the second film in the popular "Sartana" collection. The concept was initially created by Frank Kramer (pseudonym for Gianfranco Parolini) in his production *Sartana* (1968), but Anthony Ascott (aka Giuliano Carmino) took over the project and turned it into a "series" that spanned five successful years. Other entries, with John (Gianni) Garko in the lead role, include *Sartana Kills Them All* (1970), *Have a Good Funeral, My Friend . . . Sartana Will Pay* (1971), and *Light the Fuse . . . Sartana's Coming* (1971); George Hilton assumed the title role for *I Am Sartana . . . Trade Your Guns for a Coffin* (1972), also directed by Ascott. Plus there are many "wanna-be" Sartana "sequels," see appendix for complete listing.

Sartana is a bigger-than-life vigilante, "the Angel of Death." His primary motivation is to kill people who deserve to be dead. He's the judge and executioner. No bad guy is safe. In this one, someone posing as Sartana robs the Northwestern Bank, tarnishing the institution's reputation as "the safest bank in the West." The officials, thinking that Sartana "has gone sour," offer a huge reward for his death, which attracts a wide variety of unsavory bounty killers (including a couple played by Gordon Mitchell and Klaus Kinski).

I Came, I Saw, I Shot (1968)

Vado, Vedo e Sparo Ital. *Director:* Enzo G. Castellari; *Script:* Augusto Finocchi/ Enzo G. Castellari; *Camera:* Alejandro Ulloa; *Music:* Carlo Rustichelli/Bruno Nicolai; *Producer:* D.S. Producciones/Aspa (Italy/Spain). *Cast.* Antonio Sabàto, John Saxon Frank Wolff, Agata Flori, Leo Anchóriz, Antonio Vico, Rossella Bergamonti, Hercules Cortes, Tito Garcia.

This is, easily, one of the weakest films directed by Enzo G. Castellari (pseudonym for filmmaker Marino Girolami's son, Enzo Girolami). Unfortunately, it's also John Saxon's only participation in the genre. What a shame.

The story is a tedious comedy about two men, Edwin (Frank Wolff) and Moses (Antonio Sabàto), who steal $300,000 from the Springwood Bank. They are tracked down by a third man, Clay (John Saxon wearing an embarrassingly phony mustache). He claims to be the rightful owner of the money, having won it in a poker game. The three men fight and double-cross each other until some Mexican outlaws get involved and try to snatch the loot. At that point, the three men join together against the common foe.

An Italian-Spanish production with music written by Carlo Rustichelli and conducted by Bruno Nicolai; camera work is from busy Alejandro Ulloa (see Cinematographers filmography).

I Do Not Forgive ... I Kill! (1968)

Ballad of a Bounty Hunter; Phaedra West; Fedra West; Io Non Perdono ... Uccido! Ital. *Director:* Joaquin Romero Marchent; *Script:* Joaquin R. Marchent/ Giovanni Simonelli/Victor Aux; *Camera:* Fulvio Testi; *Music:* Piero Piccioni; *Producer:* Ricardo Sanz/Uni Film (Spain/Italy). *Cast:* James Philbrook, Norma Bengell, Simón Andreu, Luis Induñi, Angel Ortiz, Alfonso Rojas.

Prolific director Joaquin Romero Marchent (with 11 Spaghetti Westerns to his credit) tells the tender-cum-violent story of a bounty hunter (Simon Andreu) who falls in love with Lucy (Norma Bengell) and then is forced to hunt down her outlaw brother (James Philbrook).

I Live for Your Death see Long Ride from Hell

I Protect Myself Against My Enemies see Three Silver Dollars

I Want Him Dead (1968)

Lo Quiero Muerto Sp; *Lo Voglio Morto* Ital. *Director:* Paolo Bianchi; *Script:* Carlos Arabia; *Camera:* Ricardo Andreu; *Music:* Nico Fidenco; *Producer:*

Inducine/Centauro Film (Italy/Spain). *Cast:* Craig Hill, Lea Massari, José Manuel Martin, Andrea Bosić, Licia Calderón, Cristina Businari, Rick Boyd, Andrea Scotti, Frank Braña.

A tough (although historically cockeyed) film from Paolo Bianchi (also Paolo Bianchini), with a rugged Craig Hill performance to match the director's quest for grittiness. Evil arms-trafficking town boss Malleck (Andrea Bosić) has just received information that the Civil War is about to end. If that happens it would foil an important million dollar gun deal, financially destroying his empire. To protect himself, he must put a stop to the "General Lee and General Grant peace conference" conducted at a nearby farm house. So he hires a notorious badman, Jackson Blood (José Manuel Martin), to assassinate one or both of the leaders.

En route, Jackson (with his gang) "takes time out" to rape and kill a beautiful woman named Mercedes (Cristina Businari), the sister of frontier guide Clayton (Craig Hill, in his best role). Clayton is enraged by the atrocity and he vows revenge against the outlaws, without knowing anything about their political agenda. When he gets no assistance from the corrupt sheriff, Clayton decides to track down the culprits by himself. He retaliates against Blood's gang before they can carry out their odious assassination plot. Clayton emerges the ironic but disinterested hero as the closing credits roll.

Excellent soundtrack from Nico Fidenco; good closeup Spaghetti Western camera work by Ricardo Andreu.

If One Is Born a Swine (1972)

One Is Born a Swine; Turn . . . I'll Kill You; Carogne Si Nasce; Volati . . . Ti Ticeide; Winchester Bill. Director: Al Bradly; *Script:* Preston Leonio; *Camera:* Alfonso Nieva/Fausto Rossi; *Music:* Coriolano Gori; *Producer:* Rhodes/Hispamer (Italy/Spain). *Cast:* Richard Wyler, Fernando Sancho, Eleonara Bianchi, Conrado Sanmartin, Ric Burton, Luis Induñi, Spean Convery.

Separated by four years, there are two different films, both directed by Al Bradly (Alfonso Brescia), with very similar titles: *If One Is Born a Swine* and *If One Is Born a Swine . . . Kill Him.* This one, the former, is a wearisome tale redeemed only by a wickedly inspired Fernando Sancho performance. "You killed my father!" a boy cries at villain Sancho. So, he shoots the kid, saying, "You wouldn't've liked being an orphan anyway."

Pepito (Fernando Sancho) and his gang of Mexican bandits are working strong-arm for town boss Ted Shore (Conrado Sanmartin). Following orders, they invade a gold mine and create trouble for the owner, Pops (Spean Convery, aka Spartaco Conversi). A gunfighting stranger named Billy Walsh (Richard Wyler) comes to the rescue and also manages to fall in love with Pops' daughter (Eleonara Bianchi). No surprises here.

More ho-hum entertainment from director Alfonso Bescia, aka Al Bradley, and his lackluster cameraman, Fausto Rossi. The Coriolano Gori score is actually a "greatest hits package" culled from previous entries, but particularly *One Damned Day at Dawn . . . Django Meets Sartana.* This film marks Bradly's last genre outing. He, however, continued his career with a diverse selection of exploitation entries, including *Naked Girl Killed in the Park* (1972), *Battle Force 2000* (1978), *Beast in Space* (1982), and *Iron Warrior* (1985).

Fernando Sancho in *If One Is Born a Swine* (1972).

If One Is Born a Swine . . . Kill Him (1968)

Cry of Death; Lynching; Sei una Carogna, t'Ammazo Ital. *Director:* Al Bradly; *Script:* Aldo Lado; *Camera:* Fausto Rossi; *Music:* Coriolano Gori; *Producer:* Alberto Silvestri, Silpal Film (Italy). *Cast:* Glenn Saxson, Gordon Mitchell, Maria Bardanzellu, Philippe Hersent, Fernando Sancho, Giovanni Pazzafini.

This film was written by horror/adventure filmmaker Aldo Lado *(Night Train Murders)*. And as indicated by the exploitive title, it's a nihilistic tale of greed and power, the cattle breeders versus the farmers.

The cattle cartel have gained control of the local bank and they have initiated an obdurate foreclosure policy against the farmers. Violence becomes a way of life. Many helpless farmers are slaughtered and their ranches are destroyed. Then "Il Mulo" (Glenn Saxson) arrives. He pretends to be a notorious gunman fighting for the farmers, but he's actually a federal sheriff who secretly joins forces with an attorney named Harrison (Philippe Hersent) to foil the banking cattlemen.

Chief cameraman for this project is unimaginative Fausto Rossi. And the familiar story is directed in typical Al Bradly (Alfonso Bescia) one-dimensional fashion.

If You Gotta Shoot Someone . . . Bang! Bang! see *Arizona*

If You Meet Sartana . . . Pray for Your Death see *Sartana*

If You Shoot . . . You Live! (1974)

Si Quieres Vivir . . . Dispara Sp. *Director:* Joe Lacy; *Script:* Manuel Sebares/ José M. Elorrieta; *Camera:* Emilio Foriscot; *Music:* Javier Elorrieta; *Producer:* Trans Overseas Pictures (Spain). *Cast:* James Philbrook, Frank Braña, Alejandro De Enciso, Paula Pattier, José Canalejas, Francisco Nieto.

Director José Maria Elorrieta takes the same story that he cowrote for Sergio Garrone's *If You Want to Live, Shoot!* (1967), and restages it here with James Philbrook in the "Ken Wood" role. The flare is missing, but some of it works, especially the outside shots. Frank Braña turns in a good performance as the wealthy land baron, this time called Marco. It's marginal, at best.

If You Want to Live . . . Shoot! (1967)

Django, If You Want to Live . . . Shoot!; Se Vuoi Vivere, Spara! Ital. *Director:* Willy S. Regan; *Script:* José M. Elorrieta (De Lacy)/Darturo Tejedor/Sergio Garrone; *Camera:* Sandro Mancori; *Music:* Vasco and Mancuso; *Producer:* G.V. Film/Cinegar (Italy/Spain). *Cast:* Sean Todd, Ken Wood, Riccardo Garrone, Isabella Savona, Tom Felleghy, Aldo Cecconi, Peter White.

Wealthy land baron Marlow (Sean Todd, aka Ivan Rassimov) is trying to take over all the farms in the region. He hires a band of Mexican outlaws to terrorize the settlers who won't sell their property to him. Meanwhile, Johnny (Ken Wood) is recovering from a mysterious gunshot wound and is being nursed back to health) by widow Sally McGowan (Isabella Savona) and her son Tommy. When her farm is destroyed by the outlaws, Johnny takes the law into his own hands, thus eliminating Marlow.

Another great-looking movie from Sergio Garrone (using the Willy S. Reagan alias), partially due to the masterful camera work of his usual right hand, Sandro Mancori. Also see *Django the Bastard, Vendetta at Dawn* and *No Graves on Boot Hill* for Garrone's best work.

I'll Kill Him and Return Alone see *Man Who Killed Billy the Kid*

I'll Sell My Skin Dearly (1968)

Vendo Cara la Pelle Ital. *Director:* Ettore Fizarotti; *Script:* Giovanni Simonelli/ Ettore Fizarotti; *Camera:* Stelvio Massi; *Music:* Enrico Ciacci/Marcello Marocchi; *Producer:* Cinemar (Italy). *Cast:* Mike Marshall, Michele Girardon, Valerio Bartoleschi, Dane Savours, Grant Laramy, Spartaco Conversi.

A "text book" example of the genre, uncluttered by any motivation except revenge. Shane (Mike Marshall) is now grown; he returns to the abandoned ranch where his family had been slaughtered by Magdalena (Dane Savours) and his band of vicious killers Shane converts the home into a practice gun range, where he trains constantly until he has mastered the weapon.

Then, the gunfighter ventures out to avenge his family. Shane kills everyone involved, including a bandit who has since become a priest, Father Dominique (Grant Laramy). "If God wants you, let him have you!"

Another film skillfully lensed by cameraman Stelvio Massi, who later became a popular and prolific thriller/action director (see Cinematographers filmography for genre credits); he also directed one Spaghetti Western, *Halleluja to Vera Cruz* (1973), under the pseudonym Newman Rostel.

This film is Ettore Fizarotti's only Western. He also made a Franco and Ciccio comedy called *I'll Try This Evening* with Lola Falana.

In a Colt's Shadow (1965)

All'Ombra di una Colt Ital. *Director:* Giovanni Grimaldi; *Script:* Giovanni Grimaldi/Aldo Barni. *Camera:* Stelvio Massi/Julio Ortas; *Music:* Nico Fidenco/ Willy Brezza; *Producer:* Vincenzo Genesi, Hercules/Hispamer (Italy/Spain). *Cast:* Stephen Forsyte, Conrado Sanmartin, Anne Sherman, Graham Sooty, Helga Line, Andrew Scott, Frank Ressel, Aldo Sambrell, José Calvo.

Here's an interesting variation on the popular "Romeo and Juliet" theme, this time camouflaged behind a loose *Magnificent Seven* motif. Two gunmen, Steve Blane and Duke Buchanan (Stephen Forsyte and José Calvo) are hired for (and successfully complete) a mission protecting a wealthy Mexican village against a marauding bandit gang. During the conflict, Duke is wounded. His injuries keep him from immediately returning to the United States, but his partner Steve is anxious to get back home.

Secretly, he is very happy that his friend can't make the journey because Steve is in love with Duke's daughter. And, even though he's been warned against it ("a bounty hunter's life can't be shared with no woman") and threatened by Duke, Steve plans to marry Susan (Anne Sherman) upon his return to Texas.

Steve and Susan elope to Providence where he tries (unsuccessfully) to give up the life of a gunfighter and settle down. After a series of confrontations with town boss Jackson (Conrado Sanmartin), his old partner Duke shows up, looking for revenge. Instead, the two men join forces to defeat Jackson and his henchmen in a major downtown shootout.

Certainly, the best of Giovanni Grimaldi's three Spaghetti Westerns (also see *Johnny Colt* and the "Franco and Ciccio" farce, *The Handsome, the Ugly, and the Stupid*) aided significantly by the excellent Stelvio Massi photography and a strong musical score from composer Nico Fidenco. It's also fun to see popular cult actress Helga Line in a "haughty" saloon-whore role, even though her part seems forced and is, ultimately, insignificant.

In the Name of the Father (1968)

I Quattro del Pater Noster Ital. *Director:* Ruggero Deodato. *Cast:* Paolo Villaggio.

Very little is known about this obscure Spaghetti Western, apparently the victim of poor distribution and a glut of product in the marketplace (1968 saw more than 75 Eurowestern releases). It's especially disappointing since filmmaker Ruggero Deodato has since become a powerful force in the Italian exploitation film industry, directing such controversial hits as *Live Like a Man . . . Die Like a Cop* (1976), *Cannibal Holocaust* (1977), *House at the Edge of the Park* (1980), and *Camping del Terrore*, also known as *Body Count* (1989).

In the Name of the Father, the Son and the Colt (1972)

Masked Thief; Au Nom du Père, du Fils et du Colt Fr. *Director:* Frank Bronston; *Script:* Arpad De Riso/Mario Gariazzo; *Camera:* Emilio Foriscot; *Music:* Piero Piccioni; *Producer:* John Wyler, New Film (France/Italy). *Cast:* Craig Hill, Nuccia Cardinali, Gill Roland, Agatha Lys, Lorenzo Piani, Frank Braña, Paco Sanz.

Director Mario Bianchi (aka Frank Bronston) makes mediocre films with clever, exploitive titles (i.e., *Winchester Does Not Forgive, Kill the Poker Player* and, obviously, this one). His movies aren't wildly bad (like those of Demofilo Fidani, aka Miles Deem) nor difficult to watch (like Luigi Batzella, aka Paola Solvay), they are simply very average. Standard fare.

In this one, a series of robberies is pulled by a mysterious gang of bandits who use clever disguises to fool their victims. When they hold up a stagecoach dressed as saloon whores, Sheriff Johnston (Craig Hill) investigates.

Incidentally, the costar "Gill Roland" is *not* the popular Mexican star, Gilbert Roland.

In the West There Was a Man Named Invincible see *Man Called Invincible*

In the Wild West see *Sheriff Was a Lady*

Indio Black see *Adios Sabata*

Indio Black: Sai Che Ti Dico . . . Sei un Gran Figlio Di see *Adios Sabata*

Inginocchiati Straniero . . . i Cadaveri non Fanno Ombra see *Stranger That Kneels Beside the Shadow of a Corpse*

L'Invincibile Cavaliere Mascherato see *Terror of the Black Mask*

Io Non Perdono . . . Uccido! see *I Do Not Forgive . . . I Kill!*

L'Ira di Dio 171

L'Ira di Dio see Wrath of God

It Can Be Done ... Amigo (1971)

The Big and the Bad; Si Può Fare ... Amigo Ital. *Director:* Maurizio Lucidi; *Script:* Rafael Azcona; *Camera:* Aldo Tonti; *Music:* Luis Enrique Bacalov; *Producer:* Alfonso Sansone/Enrico Chroscicki, EMI/Terzafilm/Roitfeld/Atlantida (Italy/France/Spain). *Cast:* Bud Spencer, Jack Palance, Renato Cestiè, Dany Saval, Francisco Rabal, Giovanni Pazzafini, Luciano Catenacci, Sal Borgese.

Maurizio Lucidi, the director of *Greatest Robbery in the West* and the *Pecos* series, constructs an enjoyable parody with this film. He recreates the flavor and style of Sergio Leone's *Dollars* trilogy, but substitutes slapstick for violence. Some of it works.

Bud Spencer (well known pseudonym for Carlo Pedersoli) is an unlikely "Casanova" named Coburn who "loves women, everything about 'em." Jack Palance is Sonny Bronston, a gunfighter (with a bark-worse-than-a-bite personality), tracking the Big Man down for seducing his sister, Mary (Dany Saval).

Unlike many other Spencer-tailored roles, this one allows him to be something besides a brutish clown. It's a welcome change, thanks to a good and funny script, best described as a "Tom and Jerry" Western.

Director Lucidi also directed many nongenre films, including *Challenge of the Giants* (Reg Park), *Probability Zero* (Henry Silva), *Sicilian Cross* (Roger Moore), and *Slamout* (Tomás Milian).

Jaguar (1964)

El Llanero Sp. *Director:* Jess Franco; *Script:* Jess Franco; *Camera:* Emilio Foriscot; *Music:* Daniel J. White; *Producer:* Sphinx Films (Spain). *Cast:* José Suarez, Silvia Sorente, Todd Martens, Manuel Zarzo, Georges Rollin, Roberto Camardiel, Beny Deus, Xan Dan Bolas.

Even the uncrowned king of European sex and exploitation films, Jess Franco (with over 150 movies to his credit) made a Spaghetti Western, not counting his continental *Mark of Zorro* (also called *Shadow of Zorro*). Best known for *Succubus, Jack the Ripper, Sadist of Notre Dame* and *Venus in Furs,* Franco directed this "civil war in Venezuela" story in his usual "zoom and pan" style. But, clearly, the filmmaker lacks a basic understanding of American geography, and thus the political ramifications of nationality. He fails to see any difference between North and South America. Inexplicably, his characters, while fighting for Caracas are clearly in the United States.

Regardless, José Suarez is Llanos (sometimes called "Jaguar"), a rebel living in the mountains with his gang of revolutionaries. He falls in love with Marta (Silvia Sorente), the daughter of a land baron who is in cahoots with the evil general (Roberto Camardiel). Eventually she convinces her father to support the "people's war" against the corrupt magistrate.

Jennie Lee Ha una Nuova Pistola see Gunmen of Rio Grande

Jesse and Lester, Two Brothers in a Place Called Trinity (1972)

Two Brothers in Trinity; Due Fratelli i un Posto Chiamato Trinità Ital. *Director:* James London; *Script:* Renzo Genta/Richard Harrison; *Camera:* Antonio

Scene from *It Can Be Done . . . Amigo* (1971).

Modica; *Music:* Carlo Savina; *Producer:* James London/Fernando Piazzo, H.P. International Film (Italy). *Cast:* Richard Harrison, Donald O'Brien, Gino Marturano, Anna Zinneman, George Wong, Rick Boyd.

Actually directed by Richard Harrison (under the James London alias), this is an enjoyable comedy/western telling the story of two brothers with a big inheritance. Jesse (Richard Harrison) is a womanizer who wants to build a whorehouse with the money, but Lester (Donald O'Brien), a gruff Mormon preacher, wants a church. However, their arguing might be unimportant because first they must find the bandits who stole all the loot.

Jesse James' Kid (1966)

Hijo de Jesse James Sp; *One Against All; Solo Contro Tutti* Ital. *Director:* Antonio Del Amo; *Script:* Pino Passalacqua/Antonio Del Amo; *Camera:* Fausto Zuccoli; *Music:* Angelo Lavagnino; *Producer:* Apolo Film/P.E.A. (Spain/Italy). *Cast:* Robert Hundar, Mercedes Alonso, Adrian Hoven, Luis Induñi, Roberto Camardiel, Joe Kamel, Pier Caminnecci, José Jaspe, Raf Baldassare.

Actor-turned-director/producer, Adrian Hoven, made this film under the "Antonio Del Amo" alias instead of his usual Percy G. Parker moniker. He is best known for his highly controversial "witch-hunt and torture" films, *Mark of the Devil* (1969) and *Mark of the Devil 2* (1972). Considering the extraordinary levels of gratuitous violence in his exploitation films (also see *Castle of Bloody Lust, Nature Girl and the Slaver,* and *Revenge of the Yellow God*), this effort is remarkably low-keyed.

It's also silly, and historically distorted. The film opens with Jesse James

Movie poster from *Jaguar* (1964).

(Robert Hundar) attempting to become "a good family man." He has a house with a white picket fence (honest!), plus a wife and two children. When the oldest boy, Billy, is "playing cowboy," Jesse tells him to stop the nonsense and "help hang a picture." The picture is actually one of those "Home Sweet Home" plaques (I know this is hard to believe), but while Jesse James is pounding the

ROBERT HUNDAR

ADRIAN HOVEN • RALPH BALDWYN

EASMANCOLOR
TOTALSCOPE

SEUL ALLEEN
CONTRE TOUS TEGEN ALLEN

LE FILS DE
DE ZOON VAN JESSE JAMES

STELLOR

nail into the wall, Bat Masters (Pier Caminnecci) sneaks into the house and shoots him in the back.

Twenty years pass. Son Billy (also played by Robert Hundar) has changed his name to Billy Smith, and he goes to Cedar City searching for work. There he meets suave, sleepy-eyed Sheriff Alan Davies (Adrian Hoven) who directs him to the Double Horse Ranch. Quickly Billy impresses the beautiful but icy owner, Dorothy (Mercedes Alonso), and he becomes the new foreman replacing Stitch (Roberto Camardiel), who has secretly been stealing horses for a competing ranch owner, none other than Bat Masters. Eventually there's a big gunfight involving the two ranches, followed by a showdown between Billy and Bat. Of course, Billy wins, pumping bullet after bullet into the body of his father's killer. He pulls the trigger 14 times. Without reloading.

Jessy Does Not Forgive . . . He Kills! see *Sunscorched*

Jessy Non Perdona . . , Uccide! see *Sunscorched*

Jim il Primo see *Last Gun*

Joaquin Murieta see *Murieta*

Joe Cercati un Posto per Morire see *Find a Place to Die*

Joe Dakota see *Shoot Joe, and Shoot Again*

Joe Dakota, Spara . . . e Così Sia see *Shoot Joe, and Shoot Again*

Joe Dexter (1965)

Guns of Nevada; La Sfida degli Implacabili Ital. *Director:* Ignacio Iquino; *Script:* Steve McCohy; *Camera:* Giancarlo Ferrando; *Music:* Enrique Escobar; *Producer:* P.E.A. (Spain/Italy). *Cast:* George Martin, Audrey Amber, Katya Loritz, John MacDouglas, Stan Bart, Miguel De La Riva.

Written (under his "Steve McCohy" alias) and directed by Ignacio Iquino (also known as "John Wood" for some of his Westerns), this one stars George Martin (aka Jorge Martin) in the title role.

Joe Dexter, a gunfighting drifter, settles in Iron City where he falls in love with two women. One is feisty Laura (Audrey Amber), who inherited a rich silver mine after the death of her father, and the other is Susan Lee (Katya Loritz), owner of the Crazy Horse Saloon. Eventually, Susan Lee gets jealous and secretly teams with the mine's general manager, Burton (John Mac-Douglas), to steal it from Laura. The deception stops when Joe Dexter kills Burton in a showdown, and chooses (of course) Laura as his main squeeze.

Joe, Find a Place to Die see *Find a Place to Die*

Joe l'Implacabile see *Dynamite Joe*

Joe Navidad see *Christmas Kid*

John il Bastardo see *John the Bastard*

Opposite: Movie poster from *Jesse James' Kid* (1966).

John the Bastard (1967)

John il Bastardo Ital. *Director:* Armando Crispino; *Script:* Romano Scavolini/ Armando Crispino; *Camera:* Sante Achilli; *Music:* Nico Fidenco; *Producer:* Nino Battistrada, Hercules (Italy). *Cast:* John Richardson, Claudio Camaso, Martine Beswick, Claudio Gora, Glauco Onorato, Men Fury, Gordon Mitchell, Nadia Scarpitta, Gia Sandri.

This is an ambitious (if not immoral) project cowritten and directed by Armando Crispino, with unflinching aid from future cult/horror director Romano Scavolini (*Nightmare* and *Spirits of Death*), incorporating the talents of chief cameraman Sante Achilli.

It's a Western retelling of the European myth of Giovanni Giacomo "Casanova," the man who loved countless women and fought many men over "offended honor." This time, John Tenerico (John Richardson) is the amorous seducer, who is also quick (and accurate) with a pistol.

One lusty affair follows another. And then, one night, as John Tenerico escapes the bed of his latest conquest, he runs into his long-lost brother Francisco (Claudio Camaso) who has just married a girl named Antonia (Martine Beswick). Without his brother's knowledge, John makes love to Antonia. Afterwards, she tells him that his father is still alive, very wealthy, and living in Mexico. She further reveals that old Don Diego Tenerico has requested that she and Francisco join him in his opulence, but hadn't called for John because her husband told the wealthy patriarch that "John, the victim of too much frivolity, is dead."

The "hero" immediately leaves for Mexico, but is sidetracked by two beautiful Mormon women who (with their bodies) convince him to protect their caravan against some hooded Ku Klux Klan fanatics. After the battle (which results in the annihilation of the marauding bigots), John resumes his journey to visit his father in Mexico. But the Mormon women feel spurned, and so they send a killer from the allied Danice sect (Gordon Mitchell) to murder him.

John reunites with his father, kills his brother, and (once more) makes love to Antonia. He is a satisfied man; his soul is at peace. But then the Danice avenger arrives and prepares for his affray. He pushes the huge statue of Saint Antonio on top of John, crushing him.

Beautiful Martine Beswick, best known for her Barbara Steele-ish performance as Sister Hyde in Hammer's *Dr. Jekyll and Sister Hyde*, made other Spaghetti Westerns including the excellent *Bullet for a General* (1966). John Richardson is a familiar Italian exploitation actor, the star of Mario Bava's *Black Sunday*, or *Mask of the Devil* (1960), Sergio Martino's *Torso*, also called *Bodies Bear the Traces of Carnal Violence* (1973), and Umberto Lenzi's *Eyeball* (1977).

This film is director Crispino's only Western. He is mostly associated with his sex/horror/farce *Frankenstein all'Italiana* (1975), a controversial Mimsy Farmer film, *Autopsy* (also called *Macchie Solari*) (1974), *The Dead Are Alive* (1972), and *Commandos* (1968), the Lee Van Cleef war movie.

Johnny Colt (1966)

Starblack Ital. *Director:* Giovanni Grimaldi; *Script:* Giovanni Grimaldi; *Camera:* Guglielmo Mancori; *Music:* Benedetto Ghiglia; *Producer:* Ambrosiana Cinematografica (Italy). *Cast:* Robert Woods, Elga Andersen, Franco Lantieri, Jane Tilden, Andea Scotti, Renato Rossini.

Cult actor Robert Woods (best known for the Eurowesterns *My Name Is Pecos* and *Seven Guns for the MacGregors*) stars as Starblack, a Robin Hood–like character who decides to put an end to the tyrannical, oppressing rule of an unscrupulous banker named Curry (Franco Lantieri). He also has a romp in the hay with an attractive girl named Caroline (Elga Andersen).

Written and directed by Giovanni Grimaldi who also made the far-superior *In a Colt's Shadow*, plus the churlish Franco and Ciccio farce, *The Handsome, the Ugly and the Stupid*. Music is by Benedetto Ghiglia *(Stranger in Town* and *Rojo)*, with principle camera work by Guglielmo Mancori.

Johnny Hamlet (1968)

Dirty Story of the West; Quella Sporca Storia del West Ital; *Django Porte sa Croix* Fr. *Director:* Enzo G. Castellari; *Script:* Sergio Corbucci/Enzo G. Castellari; *Camera:* Angelo Flippini; *Music:* De Masi/Alessandroni/Norha; *Producer:* Daniano Film/Leone Film (Italy). *Cast:* Chip Gorman, Gilbert Roland, Gabriella Grimaldi, Enzo Girolami, Horst Frank, Pedro Sanchez, Stefania Careddu.

Based on a story by Sergio Corbucci (which was based on a play by William Shakespeare), *Johnny Hamlet* is a retelling of the Bard's tale, Western style. It's directed by actor-turned-filmmaker Enzo G. Castellari (pseudonym for Enzo Girolami, son of cult director Marino Girolami, aka Frank Martin).

Johnny Hamlet (Chip Gorman, alias for Andrea Giordana) returns from the Civil War to find that his father is dead and his mother is married to Uncle Claude, a despicable man who has taken over the ranch (calling it Rancho El Senor). Suspecting foul play, Johnny investigates, with the aid of his friend and advisor (Gilbert Roland).

Turning the Shakespeare play into a Western is a "cute" idea that might have worked as a Senior High School skit, but it doesn't do well as a full length feature film. Not one of director Castellari's better films, and a dark day for Sergio Corbucci.

Johnny Oro see *Ringo and His Golden Pistol*

Johnny Texas see *Wanted Johnny Texas*

Johnny West il Mancino see *Left Handed Johnny West*

Johnny Yuma (1966)

Johnny Yuma Ital. *Director:* Romolo Guerrieri; *Script:* Romano Scavolini/Giorgio Simonelli/Fernando Di Leo/Romolo Guerrieri; *Camera:* Mario Capriotti; *Music:* Nora Orlandi; *Producer:* Italo Zingarelli, West/Tiger (Italy). *Cast:* Mark Damon, Lawrence Dobkin, Rosalba Neri, Luigi Vanucchi, Fidel Gonzales, Gustavo D'Arpe, Gianni Solaro, Nando Poggi, Dada Galotti.

A team of four men (each later prospered in the Euro exploitation film market) cowrote this Western. They are: Romano Scavolini *(Nightmare* and *Spirit of Death)*, Giorgio Simonelli (many Franco and Ciccio films, including their Westerns, *Two Sons of Ringo, Two Gangsters in the Wild West,* and *Two Sergeants of General Custer)*, Fernando Di Leo *(Slaughter Hotel* with Klaus Kinski and *Gangster Boss)* plus Romolo Guerrieri (director of this film and *Murder House, Final Executor, Sweet Body of Deborah,* and *Young, Violent and Desperate)*.

Filmmaker Enzo Castellari giving directions to Franco Nero on the set of *Keoma* (1975).

Upon its 1967 release in the United States, many critics (including *Variety*'s Byro) called it "the most violent Italian Western ever." But, while it might be conspicuously brutal, it's also very talky and (ultimately) just another variation of the patented Spaghetti Western "revenge theme" as Johnny Yuma (Mark Damon) fights for his inheritance against evil murderess Samantha Felton (Rosalba Neri).

As the plot goes, Samantha had killed her wealthy rancher-husband but then she discovers that his entire fortune is willed to nephew Johnny Yuma. Infuriated, she demands that her lover, Carradine (Lawrence Dobkin), "get rid of the bastard." However, when the two men meet, they become instant friends, mutually respectful of each other's gunfighting ability. Together, they attack Samantha and her gunmen, but she escapes into the desert. Just before the final credits roll, Johnny finds Samantha's sun-baked dead body. And he becomes the undisputed new ranch owner. Neri's dominatrix-laden relationship with Dobkin and Damon is completely opposite of her role in the next Damon/Neri Spaghetti Western, *Great Treasure Hunt* (1967).

Joko, Invoca Dio . . . e Muori see *Vengeance*

Judge Roy Bean (1970)

Trouble in Sacramento; All'Ovest di Sacramento Ital; *La Loi à l'Ouest de Pecos* Fr. *Director:* Richard Owens; *Script:* Jean Girault/Robert Hossein; *Camera:* Henri Persin; *Music:* Pierre Perret; *Producer:* Coisias du Monoe Film (France). *Cast:* Robert Hossein, Silva Monti, Xavier Gelin, Pierre Perret, Anne-Marie Balin.

An obscure French-made Western that preceded the John Huston/Paul Newman Hollywood effort, *Life and Times of Judge Roy Bean* (1972). Continental matinee idol Robert Hossein (popular Euro star of Calvin Jackson Padget's *Battle of El Alamein*, *Warrior's Rest* with Brigitte Bardot, and Claude Lelouch's *Bolero*) plays the infamous self-appointed hanging judge, Roy Bean. He runs Sacramento with an iron fist, bending the law as he pleases, until government agent Burke (Xavier Gelin) comes to town. Silvia Monti is the sexy saloon singer who plays both ends against the middle, and ends up with nothing.

Judgment of Coyote see *Coyote*

Keoma (1975)

Keoma il Vendicatore Ital; *Django Rides Again; Django's Great Return; Violent One. Director:* Enzo G. Castellari; *Script:* Luigi Montefiori; *Camera:* Aiace Parolini; *Music:* Maurizio and Guido De Angelis; *Producer:* Uranos Cine/Ponchielli (Italy/Spain). *Cast:* Franco Nero, Woody Strode, William Berger, Donald O'Brien, Olga Karlatos, Ken Wood.

In various countries this film was released as a Django movie, calling it *Django Rides Again* (France) and *Django's Great Return* (Germany). It was an obviously crass attempt to capitalize on the success of the Django series. But, certainly, an argument can be made supporting the penchant "Django" moniker. The movie stars the original "Django" (Franco Nero) in a very similar role. Plus, it also has a comparable solemn, gothic tone. *Keoma* is more a justifiable "sequel" than laughable dreck like *Django, a Bullet for You; Django, Adios* or *Django and Sartana Are Coming . . . It's the End.*

The first half is great, cryptically mystical, but then (when director Castellari has to begin making sense) it becomes a humdrum "Cain and Abel" story with a subplot about the evil town boss trying to take over everything thrown in. Franco Nero's last Western for 13 years, until *Django Strikes Again* (1988), this film is regarded as the best entry from director Castellari (pseudonym for Enzo Girolami, son of genre director Marino Girolami, alias Frank Martin). It was written by popular actor George Eastman (under his real name, Luigi Montefiori).

Oddly, all Spanish advertising lists Sergio Leone as the "producer." There is no explanation for this (apparently erroneous) credit.

Keoma il Vendicatore see *Keoma*

Kid il Monello del West see *Bad Kids of the West*

Kid Rodelo (1966)

Il Kid Rodelo Ital. *Director:* Richard Carlson; *Script:* Jake Natteford/Eduardo M. Brochero; *Camera:* Manuel Merino; *Music:* Johnny Douglas; *Producer:* Jack

O. Lamont, Paramount (U.S./Spain). *Cast:* Don Murray, Janet Leigh, Broderick Crawford, Richard Carlson, José Nieto, Miguel Del Castilo, José Villa Sante, Julio Peña, Miguel Brendel.

Don Murray is Kid Rodelo in this Spanish-U.S. coproduction, based on a book by Louis L'Amour. The director is Richard Carlson, 50s sci-fi cult actor (best remembered for *It Came from Outer Space, Creature from the Black Lagoon* and Rod Serling's *Doomsday Flight*), but he's also a filmmaker (most notably for *Riders to the Stars* and *Four Guns to the Border*).

Upon being released from prison, the Kid (Don Murray) and his two outlaw partners, Joe (Broderick Crawford) and Link (Richard Carlson) are trying to retrieve the gold they stole before they were incarcerated. But close behind them is Nora (Janet Leigh) and her gang. It all climaxes in a bloody free-for-all.

The music comes from British composer Johnny Douglas; Manuel Merino is the chief cameraman.

Il Kid Rodelo see *Kid Rodelo*

Kid, Terror of the West see *Bad Kids of the West*

Kid Vengeance (1976)

Vengeance; Vendetta Ital. *Director:* Joe Manduke; *Script:* Bud Robbins/Jay Telfer/Ken Globus; *Camera:* David Gurfinkel; *Music:* Francesco De Masi; *Producer:* Frank Johnson/Bob Durkhardt, Globus/Cannon Film (Italy/U.S./Israel). *Cast:* Lee Van Cleef, Jim Brown, Leif Garrett, Glynnis O'Connor, John Marley, David Loden, Matt Clark.

Here's an oddity, a Spaghetti Western produced through an Italian-U.S.-Israeli copartnership and shot in the Middle East rather than Europe. Former pop star Leif Garrett is the kid who (with the aid of a black gunfighter played by Jim Brown) avenges the rape and massacre of his family by tracking down, and killing, the responsible murderous bandit (Lee Van Cleef).

It's a standard variation of the "revenge for a slaughtered family" theme, popular in many Spaghetti Westerns. The only unique factor is the very young age of the avenger. Meanwhile, Lee Van Cleef's participation is miserably insignificant as the seldom-on-screen, one-dimensional villain.

Besides this disappointing film, American filmmaker Joe Manduke directed a drama about racism called *Cornbread, Earl and Me, Omega Syndrome*, plus various episodes of ABC's television series "Dynasty."

Kidnapping see *Twenty Thousand Dollars for Seven*

Kill and Pray see *Let Them Rest*

Kill Django ... Kill First (1971)

Uccidi Django ... Uccidi Primo Ital. *Director:* Willy S. Regan; *Script:* Sergio Garrone; *Camera:* Sandro Mancori; *Music:* Elio Mancuso; *Producer:* Crisanti/Cohen, Junior Film (Italy). *Cast:* Giacomo Rossi Stuart, George Wang, Peter White, Aldo Sambrell, Mirko Ellis, Men Fury, Riccardo Garrone, Krista Neil, Diana Lorys.

Movie poster from *Kill Johnny Ringo* (1966).

Sergio Garrone (using his familiar alias "Willy S. Regan") directed this Django clone in a nontypical whimsical fashion, apparently instructing his lead (the usually very capable) Giacomo Rossi Stuart (aka Jack Start) to treat the role with a nonchalance that borders on slumber.

The emphasis is on bounty hunter Django's determination to stop evil Ramon (George Wang), a Mexican outlaw responsible for numerous robberies throughout the Texas territory. This film is director Garrone's last Spaghetti Western; unfortunately, it is also his weakest.

Kill Johnny Ringo (1966)

Uccidete Johnny Ringo Ital. *Director:* Frank G. Carrol; *Script:* Gianfranco Baldanello; *Camera:* Raffaele Masciocchi; *Music:* Pippo Caruso; *Producer:* Cine Associati (Italy). *Cast:* Brett Halsey, Greta Polyn, Ray Scott, Lee Burton, William Bogart, James Harrison, William Burke.

An amazingly simplistic film from competent filmmaker Gianfranco Baldanello (alias Frank G. Carrol). Except for *Black Jack,* his movies tend to follow the accepted Spaghetti Western formula of "one dimensional characters" in very obvious "black and white" situations.

In this one, a Texas Ranger named Johnny Ringo (Brett Halsey) is dispatched to halt the illegal activities of an elusive counterfeiting ring. He goes to Eagle Pass (the hotbed of the phony money) and, within minutes, is "passed" some bogus $10 bills in a poker game. It doesn't take long for Johnny Ringo to follow the dollar path back to town boss Jackson (James Harrison), and put a stop to the flow. But first, there's a subplot about two young romantics (Lee Burton and Greta Polyn). The film ends with a "mandatory" shootout.

Kill or Be Killed see Kill or Die

Kill or Die (1966)

Kill or Be Killed; Ringo Against Johnny Colt; Uccidi o Muori Ital. *Director:* Amerigo Anton; *Script:* Mario Amendola; *Camera:* Aldo Giordani; *Music:* Carlo Rustichelli; *Producer:* Luigi Rovere, Regafilm (Italy). *Cast:* Robert Mark, Elina De Witt, Fabrizio Moroni, Andrea Bosić, Albert Farley, Men Fury, Gordon Mitchell, Benjamin May.

Here's another attempt to capitalize on the "Ringo" character, introduced to the Spaghetti Western genre through the Duccio Tessari movie, *Pistol for Ringo*, in 1965. This time Ringo (Robert Mark) is a mysterious violin-playing stranger who tries to help the Drumont family, especially pretty Lisa (Elina De Witt), as they fight a grudge battle with the violent and powerful Griffith family.

It's a rather empty attempt by director Tanio Boccia (using the "Amerigo Anton" pseudonym); Carlo Rustichelli provides the ho-hum soundtrack, including the relentless, headache-inspiring, violin solos. Only for the diehard fans.

Kill the Poker Player (1972)

Hai Sbagliato, Dovete Uccidermi Subito! Ital. *Director:* Frank Bronston; *Script:* Mario Bianchi; *Camera:* Rafael Pacheco; *Music:* Carlo Savina; *Producer:* P. E. A./ Hercules Film (Italy/Spain). *Cast:* Robert Woods, Ivano Staccioli, Susan Scott, Frank Braña, Saturno Cerra, Carlo Gaddi, Ernesto Colli.

Veteran director Mario Bianchi (using his "Frank Bronston" moniker) is treading in "tough no-nonsense" territory with this Spaghetti Western, similar in style to his *In the Name of the Father, the Son, and the Colt.*

Robert Woods is a professional gambler called Ace. He's also incredibly fast and accurate with a pistol, a required skill that insures a longer life span to a poker player in the West. His troubles start when he exposes town boss Burton (Frank Braña) as a card cheat. And then everything heats up when he steals Burton's saloon-singer girlfriend, Lilly (Susan Scott).

Director Mario Bianchi continued making movies long after the Spaghetti cycle died, his most popular productions being *Son of Satan* (1981) and *Nightmare in Venice* (1989).

Kill the Wicked see *God Does Not Pay on Saturday*

Kill Them All and Come Back Alone (1967)

Go Kill Everybody and Come Back Alone; Ammazzali Tutti e Torna Solo Ital. *Director:* Enzo G. Castellari; *Script:* Enzo G. Castellari/Joaquin Romero Hernandez; *Camera:* Alejandro Ulloa; *Music:* Francesco De Masi; *Producer:* Edmondo Amati, Fida/Centauro (Italy/Spain). *Cast:* Chuck Connors, Frank Wolff, Franco Citti, Leo Anchóriz, Men Fury, Ken Wood, Alberto Dell'Acqua, Hercules Cortes, John Barta, Antonio Molino Rojo, Alfonso Rojas.

Although the titles are similar and the director is the same, there's no further relationship between this film and *Go Kill and Come Back*. This movie more closely resembles Calvin J. Paget's *Ft. Yuma Gold* (1966).

In this one, Clyde Link (Chuck Connors) is a captured Confederate soldier who schemes with Union prison guard Sergeant Bryant (Frank Wolff) and the commandant, Lynch (Franco Citti), to steal the Army's gold reserve, harbored at that very depot. The heist goes well. After killing everybody who helped (and escaped with him) in the caper, Link goes to join his two real partners (Bryant and Lynch) but they double-cross him. The commandant shoots the Rebel, and thinking he's dead, they bury him. Later that night, he claws his way out of the grave and hunts down the traitorous conspirators.

Chuck Connors starred in a number of Mexican and American Weterns, plus three Euro entries (*Deserter, Pancho Villa,* and this one). There's also a good musical score from underrated Francesco De Masi (Frank Mason).

Killer Adios see Killer Goodbye

Killer Caliber .32 (1967)

Killer Calibro .32 Ital. *Director:* Al Bradly; *Script:* Enzo Gicca; *Camera:* Fulvio Testi (Bob Roberts); *Music:* Robbe Poitevin; *Producer:* Explorer Film (Italy). *Cast:* Peter Lee Lawrence, Agnes Spaak, Sherill Morgan, Cole Kitosch, Max Dean, John Bartha, Andrea Bosich, Giovanni Pazzafini, Mirko Ellis, Silvio Bagolini.

Director Al Bradly creates worlds where people are either good or bad, with no in-between. Also, his films are usually preoccupied with "seemingly" good people being "secretly" bad. Or vice versa. This movie is more of the same, written by his friend (and collaborator for the six *War in Space* science fiction film series) Enzo Gicca. The stagecoach to Carson City is often robbed by, reportedly, the same seven masked men. Bank director Averell (Cole Kitosch) hires an elegantly dressed bounty hunter named Silver (Peter Lee Lawrence) to catch the bandits. Which he does, including the leader, none other than Averell himself.

An unimpressive score from Robbe Poitevin; Fulvio Testi (using the name Bob Roberts) is the director of photography.

Killer Calibro .32 see Killer Caliber .32

Killer Goodbye (1969)

Winchester Justice; Killer, Adios Ital. *Director:* Primo Zeglio; *Script:* Mallorqui Figuerola/Primo Zeglio/Mario Amendola; *Camera:* Julio Ortas; *Music:* Claudio Tallino; *Producer:* Concord/Copercines (Italy/Spain). *Cast:* Peter Lee Lawrence, Marisa Solinas, Eduardo Fajardo, Armando Calvo, Rosalba Neri, Miguel Del Castillo, Nello Pazzafini, Paola Barbara, José Jaspe, Luis Induñi, Luis Barboo, Victor Israel.

A convoluted (but, still interesting) tale of Jess Frain (Peter Lee Lawrence) and his desire to "clean up" Fulton City. Initially, after Jess guns down a notorious bandit, the sheriff (Nello Pazzafini) advises him to leave town. He does, leaving his girlfriend Fannie (Rosalba Neri).

A few years later, when Jess returns, he finds that everything has changed. Now, there are two very powerful men, Bill Bragg and Sam Bradshaw (José Jaspe and Miguel Del Castillo), fighting for control of Fulton City. And, unexpectedly, even his old girlfriend Fannie is strangely distant.

The sheriff offers Jess a deputy position, and the two of them try to re-establish law and order on the streets of the city. There's lots of bloodshed, including the mysterious deaths of Fannie and Sam Ringold. Thinking that Bragg is behind the murders, Jess is outraged.

With vengeance in mind, he visits the town boss. But it turns out that there's yet another mystery man pulling Bragg's strings; the real culprit is a man named Dixon (Eduardo Fajardo). He had been Fannie's secret lover. The deaths were part of an involved layer-upon-layer plan to get rid of Jess and, at the same time, discredit the sheriff, a long-time enemy.

Pretty Marisa Solinas plays the sheriff's daughter, taken captive by Dixon during the film's finale. The cowriter for this film, Mallorqui Figuerola, is actually filmmaker Mario Caiano (see Scriptwriters filmography).

Director Primo Zeglio, using an "Anthony Greepy" pseudonym, made other Spaghetti Westerns including *Relentless Four* and *Two Gunmen*. With Andre De Toth, he also directed Steve Reeves in *Morgan the Pirate* (1961) and is responsible for the flamboyant adaptions of Perry Rhodan's science fiction novels (most notably *Mission Stardust* in 1966).

Killer Kid (1967)

Killer Kid. Director: Leopoldo Savona; *Script:* Leopoldo Savona/Sergio Garrone; *Camera:* Sandro Mancori; *Music:* Berto Pisano; *Producer:* G.V. Film (Italy). *Cast:* Anthony Steffen, Liz Barret, Fernando Sancho, Ken Wood, Nelson Rubien, Virgin Darwell, Adriano Vitale.

It's the best of four Eurowesterns directed by Leopoldo Savona (other titles are *Apocalypse Joe, Pistol Packin' Preacher* and *Rojo*). Plus, it's also one of Anthony Steffen's finest movies, perhaps second only to *Django the Bastard* (see Performers filmography for additional Steffen titles). Busy cameraman Sandro Mancori is the director of photography, on loan from Sergio Garrone who, incidentally, cowrote the screenplay with director Savona and also acted as the film's production manager. Of special interest, the opening animated credit sequence (designed by Rosetti Studios) is particularly eye-catching.

A government agent, Tom Morrison (Anthony Steffen), takes on an espionage mission into war and revolution–torn Mexico using the false cover of an arms-trafficking outlaw called the Killer Kid. After becoming involved with a band of freedom fighters seeing the plight of the Mexican peasants, the Killer Kid begins to doubt his own political convictions, and more importantly, the veracity of his undercover assignment geared at stopping the rebel forces. The situation is further complicated by his growing love and admiration for activist Mercedes (Liz Barret), a revolutionary who ends up sacrificing her life for her ideals. At the conclusion, Morrison rejects his original government mission and he joins the rebels in their attack against the dictator.

Besides Eurowesterns (which gave him the "poor man's Clint Eastwood" label), Anthony Steffen starred in many popular exploitation and horror films, including *The Evil Eye, Crimes of the Black Cat,* and *Escape from Hell.*

Killer's Canyon see *Last Gun*

King of the West see *Big Ripoff*

Kitosch, l'Uomo Che dal Nord see *Kitosch, the Man Who Came from the North*

Kitosch, the Man Who Came from the North (1967)

Man from the North; Kitosch, l'Uomo Che dal Nord Ital. *Director:* Joseph Marvin; *Script:* Joseph Marvin; *Camera:* Fausto Rossi; *Music:* Angelo Francesco

Movie poster from *Kung Fu Brothers in the Wild West* (1973).

Lavagnino; *Producer:* Pacific/Atlantida Films (Italy/Spain). *Cast:* George Hilton, Krista Nell, Piero Lulli, Enrique Ávila, Ricardo Palacios, Gustavo Rojo.

Unconfirmed (but reliable) sources report that José Merino *(Duel in the Eclipse)* is the actual writer/director of this Spanish-Italian production; with camera work by Fausto Rossi, and music from Angelo Lavagnino.

Major Zachary Baker of the Canadian Mounted Police (George Hilton) is given the task of transporting $500,000 in gold bars to Fort Eagles. He hides the gold bars in five coffins, escorted by five "widows." They make the journey through hostile Indian territory only to find that Fort Eagles has been destroyed by a renegade band of outlaws whom they must also fight. It's actually a Euro version of Audie Murphy's *Guns of Fort Petticoat* (1957).

Kung Fu Brothers in the Wild West (1973)

Winchester, Kung Fu and Karate; Kung Fu nel Pazzo West Ital. *Director:* Yeo Ban Yee; *Script:* Tu Lung Li/Carlo Mancori; *Camera:* Raymond Chow/Manuel Ruiz; *Music:* Franco Bracardi; *Producer:* Golden Harvest Film (Italy/Hong Kong). *Cast:* Jason Pai-Pico, William Berger, Po Chih Leo, Donald O'Brien, Sally Leh.

An almost unwatchable "East meets West" motion picture. It has none of the charm of *Stranger and the Gunfighter*, nor the class of *Red Sun*, and not even the violence of *Fighting Fists of Shanghai Joe*. This is a poorly photographed and illogically rendered story of two Chinese brothers separated in Hong Kong, but reunited in America's wild west. Even though they are horribly mistreated by the prejudiced "white folk," Lo and Ping have a solemn mission to protect the community against an evil samurai who has followed them from China.

Kung Fu nel Pazzo West see *Kung Fu Brothers in the Wild West*

Là, Dove non Batte il Sole see *Stranger and the Gunfighter*

Là, Dove Scende il Sole see *Among Vultures*

Land Raiders (1969)

Bruciatelo Vivo Ital; *Last of the Landgrabbers*. *Director:* Nathan Juran; *Script:* Ken Pettus; *Camera:* Wilkie Cooper; *Music:* Bruno Nicolai; *Producer:* Charles H. Schneer (U.S./Spain). *Cast:* Telly Savalas, George Maharis, Arlene Dahl, Janet Landgard, Jocelyn Lane, Peter Dane, George Coulouris.

A United States–Spanish coproduction, directed by American Nathan Juran (best known for his fantasy and horror flicks, including *Seventh Voyage of Sinbad, Deadly Mantis, Boy Who Cried Werewolf,* and *Twenty Million Miles to Earth*), this one tells the story of two brothers (Telly Savalas and George Maharis; absurd for obvious reasons, but even more perplexing because Maharis adopts a Mexican accent and Savalas doesn't).

Telly Savalas is the bigoted, Apache-hating land baron who is trying to eliminate the "savages" from his domain (he is even paying the townsfolk a bounty for Indian scalps). George Maharis is the roving sibling, returning home just in time to stop his brother's immoral assaults. Obviously, the entire opus escalates into a major gun battle.

Lanky Fellow see *Taste for Killing*

Last Gun (1964)

Lonely Gunslinger; Killer's Canyon; Jim il Primo Ital. *Director:* Sergio Bergonzelli; *Script:* Ambrogio Molteni; *Camera:* Amerigo Gengarelli/Romolo Garroni; *Music:* Marcello Gigante; *Producer:* Filmepoca (Italy). *Cast:* Cameron Mitchell, Carl Mohner, Celina Cely, Kitty Carver, Livio Lorenzon, Marty Gordon.

In a familiar theme lifted from many American Westerns, a gunfighter

(Cameron Mitchell) decides to hang up his pistols and call it quits. So he settles down in a small Western town, but when an outlaw (Carl Mohner) begins tormenting the citizens, he straps on his guns for one final shootout.

Considered his best Western by the critics, director Sergio Bergonzelli directs this film with more restraint than he usually shows in his horror and exploitation movies (i.e., *Folds of the Flesh, Nude World, Student Rebel*).

Throughout the 1950s, Cameron Mitchell established himself as a competent "supporting actor" in various Hollywood productions (i.e., *Death of a Salesman, Love Me or Leave Me, Carousel, How to Marry a Millionaire*). In the early 60s, he migrated to Italy where he landed some juicy starring roles, especially in Mario Bava's *Blood and Black Lace* and *Il Duca Nero*. He made many films during this eight-year period (some sources claim upwards of 30, three of which are Spaghetti Westerns) before returning to the United States for a starring role in television's long-running "High Chaparral" series.

Last Gunfight see *Price of Death*

Last of the Badmen see *Time of Vultures*

Last of the Landgrabbers see *Land Raiders*

Last of the Mohicans (1965)

Fall of the Mohicans; L'Ultimo dei Mohicani Ital. *Director:* Matteo Cano; *Script:* Alain Baudry; *Camera:* Carlo Carlini; *Music:* Bruno Canfora; *Producer:* Eguiluz/ Ital Caribe (Italy/Spain/West Germany). *Cast:* Jack Taylor, Paul Müller, Sara Lezana, Dan Martin, José Manuel Martin, Barbara Loy, Luis Induñi, José Marco.

Loosely based on the writings of American novelist James Fenimore Cooper with Luis Induñi playing mountain man Hawkeye (or Strongheart or Leather-stocking, depending on the dubbing) and Dan Martin is his Mohican best friend and sidekick, Luncas (Uga or Chinga in the German and French versions). Jack Taylor is army officer Duncan Heywood, a cohort and liaison, instrumental in exposing the dark forces at work against the peaceful pioneers.

The plot and characterizations are more analogous to Karl May's "Winnetou" tales than to the books of Cooper. The evil Iroquois Indians (led by José Marco, complete with chic mohawk haircut) secretly join forces with the unscrupulous gold hungry commandant of Fort Henry, Colonel Munro (Paul Müller) to drive settlers from the precious land. Duncan, Hawkeye and Luncas put a stop to the plan by rallying the pioneers to self defense.

There's a companion film (also starring Dan Martin as the noble Mohican savage) called *The Last Tomahawk*, directed by Harald Reinl.

Last of the Renegades see *Winnetou: Last of the Renegades*

Last Rebel (1971)

L'Ultimo Pistolero Ital. *Director:* Denys McCoy; *Script:* Warren Kiefer; *Camera:* Carlo Carlini; *Music:* Jon Lord/Tony Ashton; *Producer:* Larry G. Sprangler (Italy/U.S./Spain). *Cast:* Joe Namath, Jack Elam, Woody Strode, Ty Hardin, Victoria George, Renato Romano, Annamaria Chio, Mike Forest.

A scene from *Last of the Mohicans* (1965).

Former New York Jets football star Joe Namath is Burnside Hollis in this Italian-U.S.-Spanish coproduction filmed in Europe by Chief cameraman Carlo Carlini. The music, while typically bombastic and similar in style to other Spaghetti Westerns, is composed and performed by Jon Lord and Tony Ashton, two members of the British heavy metal band "Deep Purple."

The story begins at the close of the Civil War, in Missouri, when Hollis and his Confederate buddy Matt Graves (Jack Elam) rescue a former slave (Woody Strode) from a vigilante lynching. The three join together in a "pool-sharking" scam for $1000 a game, but soon Graves becomes dissatisfied sharing his winnings with a "slave." He betrays Hollis by stealing the cash. The two eventually face each other in a showdown at the film's finale.

Last Ride to Santa Cruz (1969)

Der letzte Ritt nach Santa Cruz Ger. *Director:* Rolf Olsen; *Script:* Otto Pischin/ Herta Hareson/Leo Metzenni; *Camera:* Karl Löb; *Music:* Erwin Halletz; *Producer:* Heinz Pollak (West Germany/France). *Cast:* Edmund Purdom, Mario Adorf, Marianne Koch, Klaus Kinski, Marisa Mell, Edmund Haskins, Thomas Fritson.

Unconfirmed information reveals that (in this instance) "Rolf Olsen" might be a "front" for popular Spaghetti Western filmmaker Giorgio Stegani, who usually makes movies under the name "George Finley" (i.e., *Gentlemen Killer, Adios Gringo, Beyond the Law*). Reportedly, the West German production company was only permitted to hire "native technicians," a rule handed down by the firm's major investor. As the story goes, Stegani used the name of "Olsen" (a German union director) and the rest of the crew (including scriptwriter Fernando Di Leo and cameraman Enzo Serafin) adopted German monikers to guarantee their paycheck.

The film itself is about a crooked lawman (Mario Adorf) who unjustly convicts an innocent man (Edmund Purdom) to federal prison. The man escapes and (obviously) returns for vengeance.

Last Tomahawk (1965)

La Valle delle Ombre Rosse Ital; *Der letzte Mohikaner* Ger. *Director:* Harald Reinl; *Script:* Joachim Bartsch; *Camera:* Ernst Kalinke; *Music:* Peter Thomas; *Producer:* Franz Thierry, Germania/Cineproduzioni/Balcazar (West Germany/Italy/Spain). *Cast:* Anthony Steffen, Karin Dor, Dan Martin, Luis Induñi, Joachim Fuchsberger, Angel Ter, Carl Lange, Stellio Candelli, Marie France.

A companion film to Matteo Cano's *Last of the Mohicans* (also 1965), both starring young Dan Martin as James Fenimore Cooper's lead character Chinga (or Uga, depending on the dubbing). This one is mostly concerned with the romance between "the last of the Mohicans," Chinga (Dan Martin), and his white woman lover Cora Munroe (Karin Dor), while Strongheart (Anthony Steffen under his real name, Antonio De Teffé) tries to keep a lid on settler unrest plus tries to halt the aggression between two warring Indian tribes.

Irrespective of the credited source material, this German-Italian-Spanish production more closely resembles a "Winnetou" plot or a Karl May tale rather than anything written by American James Fenimore Cooper.

Law of Violence (1969)

Legge della Violenza Ital; *Todos o Ninguno* Ital. *Director:* Gianni Crea; *Script:* Alfonso Balcazar/Dean Craig/Gianni Crea; *Camera:* Jaime Deu Dasas; *Music:* Stelvio Cipriani; *Producer:* Balcazar Film (Spain/Italy). *Cast:* George Greenwood, Conrad Steve, Manuel Branchud, Angel Miranda.

An entertaining Spaghetti Western, similar in style to director Crea's *On the Third Day Arrived the Crow.* George Greenwood is a retired bounty hunter, Lester Moore, who has become sheriff in a small border town plagued by nightly attacks from a vicious gang of Mexican outlaws.

Left Handed Johnny West (1965)

Johnny West il Mancino Ital. *Director:* Frank Kramer; *Script:* Gianfranco Parolini/Giovanni Simonelli/Jerez Aloza/Robert De Nesle; *Camera:* Francesco Izzarelli; *Music:* Angelo Francesco Lavagnino; *Producer:* Atlantida Cinematografica/C.E.A. Film (Spain/Italy). *Cast:* Dick Palmer, Mike Anthony, Roger Delaporte, André Bollet, Mara Cruz, Diana Garson, Barta Barry, Roberto Camardiel, Bob Felton.

An early entry from filmmaker Frank Kramer (Gianfranco Parolini) who, just prior to this film, had graduated from the "school of peplums," directing many sword-'n'-sandal movies including *Hercules vs. Sampson* (1961), *The Fury of Hercules* (1962), *The Old Testament* (1962), *Year 79 A.D.* (1963) and *Hercules, Samson and Maciste: The Invincible Three* (1964).

This one finds Dick Palmer (pseudonym for Mimmo Palmara) playing the title role of "Johnny West," a lawman trying to expose the killer of a rich land baron. The primary suspects, Don Trent and Brad McCoy (Roger Delaporte and André Bollet), are two wild gunfighters known as "Brothers Dynamite," but Marshal West is convinced of their innocence, and he proves it.

Legacy of the Incas (1965)

El Último Rey de los Incas Sp; *Das Vermachtnis des Inka* Ger. *Director:* Georg Marischka; *Script:* Georg Marischka/Winfried Groth/Franz Marischka; *Camera:* Siegfried Holt; *Music:* Angelo Francesco Lavagnino; *Producer:* George and Franz Marischka (West Germany/Italy). *Cast:* Guy Madison, Rik Battaglia, Fernando Rey, William Rothlein, Francesco Rabal, Heinz Ehrhardt, Walter Giller.

An oddity of sorts. A "South" American Western set in Peru with a touch of fantasy, starring Guy Madison as Wutuma, the last descendant of the "once proud and noble Incas."

The president of Peru (Fernando Rey) assigns Wutuma the task of "eliminating" a racist renegade Indian tribe (led by over-the-edge Rik Battaglia) in cahoots with a band of revolutionary bandidos. These misfits are trying to re-erect the Inca empire and drive all white people from the land. Wutuma, with the aid of ancient spiritual forces, stops the pending insurrection.

Actor Guy Madison, best known as "Wild Bill Hickok" to a generation of U.S. television fans in the 50s, moved to Italy in the early 1960s when Hollywood roles dried up for him. Guy starred in countless European films throughout the ensuing 20 years, until he retired in 1987. His last film was an Italian/Filipino production directed by Luis Nepomucen called *Stickfighter,* with Gilbert Roland.

The unusual Incas/Aztec motif is also used in *Lost Treasure of the Incas* (1965), *Pyramid of the Sun God* (1965), *Treasure of the Aztecs* (1965), and *Pecos Cleans Up* (1969).

Legend of Frenchie King see *Frenchie King*

Legge della Violenza see *Law of Violence*

Lemonade Joe (1966)

Limonadovy Joe . . . Konska Opera Czech. *Director:* Oldrich Lipsky; *Script:* Jiri Bredecka/Oldrich Lipsky; *Camera:* Vladimir Novotny; *Music:* Jan Rychlik; *Producer:* Jaroslav Jilovec (Czechoslovakia). *Cast:* Karel Fiala, Milos Kopecky, Kveta Fialova, Olga Schoberova, Karel Effa, Waldemar Matuska.

Similar to Popeye's dependency on spinach, here's an Arizona cowboy named Joe (Karel Fiala) who gets his strength from drinking lemonade.

When Joe stops at the Silver City saloon, some bad guys, namely Horace Badman (Milos Kopecky) and his outlaw friends Panjo Kid and Banjo Kid (Karel Effa and Waldemar Matuska) spike his lemonade with whiskey. Joe passes out and soils his white outfit. Provoked, he promptly kills the culprits. But then, to demonstrate the power of his special lemonade elixir, he brings them back to life.

This movie is the only Czechoslovakian contribution to the genre.

Let Them Rest (1967)

Kill and Pray; Requiescant Ital. *Director:* Carlo Lizzani; *Script:* Franco Bucceri/ Adriano Bolzoni/Armando Crispino; *Camera:* Sandro Mancori; *Music:* Riz Ortolani; *Producer:* Castoro Film/Tefi Film (Italy/Germany). *Cast:* Lou Castel, Mark Damon, Pier Paolo Pasolini, Barbara Frey, Rossana Martini, Mirella Maravidi, Carlo Palmucci, Frank Braña, Franco Citti.

This Western is much more surreal, bizarre and sadistic than Carlo Lizzani's previous film, *The Hills Run Red*. As a result, there is speculation that Pier Paolo Pasolini (a kinky filmmaker known for his sleazy and sexy art movies, including *Salò: 120 Days of Sodom, Decameron, Canterbury Tales,* etc.) had more to do with it than merely a costarring role.

Regardless, it's an excellent offbeat psychedelic sort of movie filled with drug overtones, strange showdowns, an eccentrically gay villain (Mark Damon) and loads of S&M with helpless victims being mercilessly tortured and beaten. Sergio Garrone's cameraman-of-choice, Sandro Mancori, is the director of photography; busy Riz Ortolani composed the score.

The Italian title, *Requiescant* (meaning "Let Them Rest") is the name given to the leading character (Lou Castel) because he prays over the dead body of his foes after a showdown. A Spaghetti Western curiosity.

Let's Go and Kill Sartana (1972)

Vamos a Matar Sartana Sp. *Director:* Mario Pinzauti; *Script:* Rafael Marina; *Camera:* Jaime Deu Casas; *Music:* Pat Bodie (José Espieta); *Producer:* Marco Claudio (Italy/Spain). *Cast:* Gordon Mitchell, George Martin, Isarco Ravajoli, Virginia Rodin, Cris Huerta, Monica Taber.

Two men, Clay and Greg (George Martin and Gordon Mitchell), are released from prison. While inside, they were friends. But now, on the outside, they realize that they don't have very much in common. Clay wants to stay away from trouble and work on his family's ranch, but Greg is ready to rob the first stagecoach that comes along. They decide to part their ways.

But in the tradition of much better Spaghetti Westerns, their paths cross again when Greg (as the leader of the new outlaw gang) ironically raids the farmhouse where Clay lives. The two former friends face each other in a showdown, and (obviously) Clay wins.

But what about Sartana? Outside of the mention in the title, he's nowhere to be found.

La Ley del Forasterio see *Man Called Gringo*

Der letzte Mohikaner see *Last Tomahawk*

Der letzte Ritt nach Santa Cruz see *Last Ride to Santa Cruz*

Life Is Tough, Eh Providence? see *Sometimes Life Is Hard, Right Providence?*

Light the Fuse ... Sartana Is Coming (1971)

Gunman in Town; Cloud of Dust ... Cry of Death ... Sartana Is Coming; Una Nuvola di Porvere ... un Grido di Morte, Arriva Sartana Ital. *Director:* An-

192 Limonadovy Joe

thony Ascott; *Script:* Eduardo Brochero/Anthony Ascott/Tito Carpi; *Camera:* Emilio Foriscot/Floriano Trenker; *Music:* Bruno Nicolai; *Producer:* Devon Film/Copercines (Italy/France). *Cast:* John Garko, Susan Scott, Piero Lulli, Bruno Corazzari, Frank Braña, Massimo Serato, José Jaspe.

This is the fifth film in the *Sartana* series, preceded by *Sartana* (directed by Frank Kramer), *I Am Sartana, Your Angel of Death,* or *Sartana the Gravedigger* (Ascott), *Sartana Kills Them All* (Marchent), and *Have a Good Funeral, My Friend . . . Sartana Will Pay* (Ascott).

Sartana is a Western vigilante, a bigger-than-life avenger who kills people solely because they deserve it. Under the proficient direction of filmmaker Anthony Ascott (alias for Giuliano Carmineo) the Sartana character takes on a mystical, perhaps supernatural, quality which adds a new dimension to the action.

In this one, Sartana (John Garko, aka Gianni Garko) breaks into the Sandy Creek Prison because he learns that a convict, the "legendary" gunman (and poker player) Grand Full (Piero Lulli), needs to see him. Grand was imprisoned for killing his partner, a crime he says he didn't do. Sartana believes him and helps the gambler escape.

The two abscond to Mansfield (where the murder had taken place). After many gunfights with bounty hunters plus a vicious confrontation with the town boss (Massimo Serato), Sartana discovers that he was deceived. Not only had Grand Full killed Johnson, but he had also stolen a fortune in gold. Infuriated by the chicanery, Sartana eliminates Grand Full in a showdown finale.

The next film in the series was *I Am Sartana . . . Trade Your Guns for a Coffin,* also directed by Anthony Ascott, but starring George Hilton instead of John Garko.

Limonadovy Joe . . . Konska Opera see *Lemonade Joe*

Little Rita nel Far West see *Rita of the West*

El Llanero see *Jaguar*

Llega Sabata see *Sabata the Killer*

Lo Ammazzo Come un Cane . . . Ma Lui Rideva Ancora see *Death Played the Flute*

Lo Chiamavano California see *California*

Lo Chiamavano Django see *Man Called Django*

Lo Chiamavano King see *His Name Was King*

Lo Chiamavano Mezzogiorno see *Man Called Noon*

Lo Chiamavano Requiescant Fasthand see *Fasthand*

Lo Chiamavano Spirito Santo see *His Name Was Holy Ghost*

Lo Chiamavano Tressette . . . Giocava Sempre colla Morte see *Man Called Invincible*

Lo Chiamavano Trinità see *They Call Me Trinity*

Lo Chiamavano Verità see *They Call Him Veritas*

Lo Credevano uno Stingo di Santo see *Too Much Gold for One Gringo*

Lo Irritarono . . . e Sartana Fece Piazza Pulita see *Sartana Kills Them All*

Lo Quiero Muerto see *I Want Him Dead*

Lo Voglio Morto see *I Want Him Dead*

La Loi à l'Ouest de Pecos see *Judge Roy Bean*

Lola Colt see *Black Tigress*

Lone and Angry Man see *Coffin for the Sheriff*

Lonely Gunslinger see *Last Gun*

Long Cavalcade of Vengeance see *Deadly Trackers*

Long Day of the Massacre (1968)

Il Lungo Giorno del Massacro Ital. *Director:* Albert Cardiff; *Script:* Alberto Cardone; *Camera:* Aldo Greci; *Music:* Michele Lacarenza; *Producer:* Metheus Film (Italy). *Cast:* Peter Martell, Glenn Saxon, Manuel Servano, Liz Barret, Daniela Giordano.

Here's another film that got lost among the avalanche of releases in 1968. Very little is known about this production from competent director Alberto Cardone (alias Albert Cardiff). Apparently, poor distribution against strong competition relegated it to a limited regional run without much success.

This film is not to be confused with a Robert Woods detective movie, *Hypnos: Long Day of the Massacre* (also 1968), directed by genre filmmaker Paolo Bianchi.

Long Days of Hate see *This Man Can't Die*

Long Days of Vengeance (1967)

I Lunghi Giorni della Vendetta Ital; *Faccia d'Angelo* Ital. *Director:* Stan Vance; *Script:* Fernando Di Leo/Augusto Caminito; *Camera:* Francisco Marin; *Music:* Armando Trovajoli; *Producer:* P.C.M./I.F.C. (Italy/Spain). *Cast:* Giuliano Gemma, Francisco Rabal, Gabriella Giorgelli, Conrado Sanmartin, Nieves Navarro, Franco Cobi D'Este, Parajito.

Ted Barnett (Giuliano Gemma) escapes from prison with the intention of proving his innocence and, at the same time, taking revenge against a man named Cobb (Conrado Sanmartin), the double-crossing arms-and-slave-trader initially responsible for his imprisonment.

Stylishly directed by Florestano Vancini (aka Stan Vance), based on a

Movie poster from *Long Days of Vengeance* (1967).

screenplay by popular action/horror director Fernando Di Leo *(Slaughter Hotel* and *Gangsters)*. It's especially memorable for the finale sequence which finds Barnett shot and dying in the street, but (in an unparalleled Ninja fashion) he takes his sheriff's star/badge and flings it at Cobb, fatally wounding him in the throat.

Music is provided by the prolific Armando Trovajoli; Francisco Marin is the chief cameraman.

Long Live the Revolution see *Blood and Guns*

Long Live Your Death see *Don't Turn the Other Cheek*

Long Ride from Hell (1968)

I Live for Your Death; Vivo per la Tua Morte Ital. *Director:* Alex Burkes; *Script:* Steve Reeves/Roberto Natale; *Camera:* Enzo Barboni; *Music:* Carlo Savina; *Producer:* Steve Reeves/Luigi Bazzoni, BRC (Italy). *Cast:* Steve Reeves, Wayde Preston, Lee Burton, Dick Palmer, Ted Carter, Franco Fantasia, Aldo Sambrell, Rosalba Neri, Spartaco Conversi, Mario Maranzana.

Another revenge Western, notable for the participation of Steve "Hercules" Reeves (in his only genre outing). The story is from Gordon Shirreffs' novel *Judas Gun*, with the screenplay adapted by Steve Reeves.

Mike (Steve Reeves), his brother Roy (Franco Fantasia), and ranch foreman Bobcat (Mario Maranzana) go after horse thieves who have stolen the entire herd, but instead they are double-crossed and imprisoned. After his brother dies behind bars, Mike escapes and returns to Yuma City where he enlists the aid of a prostitute (the beautiful and always welcome Rosalba Neri) to help him seek revenge against the evil land baron Mayner (Wayde Preston).

Chief cameraman Enzo Barboni is popular action/exploitation director E. B. Clucher (creator of the *Trinity* series). Filmmaker Alex Burkes, pseudonym for Luigi Bazzoni, made two other Spaghetti Westerns, *Man: His Pride and His Vengeance* with Franco Nero and Klaus Kinski, and *Brothers Blue* starring Jack Palance. He also directed the 1965 horror film, *La Donna del Lago*, or *The Possessed*, written by Giulio Questi, and another in 1972 called *Giornate Nera per l'Ariete*.

The Longest Hunt see *Shoot, Gringo . . . Shoot!*

Lost Treasure of the Aztecs see *Lost Treasure of the Incas*

Lost Treasure of the Incas (1965)

Lost Treasure of the Aztecs; Sansone e il Tesoro degli Incas Ital. *Director:* Piero Pierotti; *Script:* Piero Pierotti/Arpad De Riso; *Camera:* Augusto Tiezzi; *Music:* Angelo Francesco Lavagnino; *Producer:* Der Constantin/Romana/Verleih/Terra (Germany/Italy/France/Spain). *Cast:* Alan Steel, Toni Sailer, Wolfgang Lukschy, Brigitte Heilberg, Mario Petri, Anna Maria Polani, Pierre Cressoy.

Another "Inca" movie, following closely on the footsteps of Guy Madison's successful low-budget Western/fantasy, *Legacy of the Incas* (also 1965). This one starts out like a traditional Spaghetti Western, as crooked town boss Jerry Burton (Mario Petri) kills his arch enemy and puts the blame on somebody else.

A gambler named Samson (Alan Steel) and his gunfighter friend, Alan Fox (Toni Sailer), suspect that Burton is the real killer. After they share their secret with the dead man's daughter, Jenny (Brigitte Heilberg), everything goes berserk. Suddenly, Samson and Alan find themselves in the middle of an

Movie poster from *Lost Treasure of the Incas* (1965).

Indiana Jones–type of adventure, culminating with the discovery of the lost Inca civilization and its fabulous treasure.

The Italian title translates to *Samson and the Treasure of the Incas*. It was released under that title throughout the Continent and Great Britain. Apparently, this was an attempt to attract sword-'n'-sandal fans to a genre Western, by reminding them that Alan Steel is (and was) Samson: he played the peplum hero in *Samson and the Mighty Challenge*.

Love, Bullets and Frenzy see *China 9 Liberty 37*

Lucky Johnny see *Lucky Johnny: Born in America*

Lucky Johnny: Born in America (1973)

Dead Aim; Lucky Johnny Ital. *Director:* José Antonio Balanos; *Script:* José Antonio Balanos/Pedro Miret; *Camera:* Alex Philips; *Music:* Luchi De Jesus; *Producer:* Mirafiori/Regina (Italy/Mexico). *Cast:* Glen Lee, Virgil Frye, James Westerfield, Evaristo Marquez, Sonny Vandeusen.

There's lots of "desert wilderness" stock footage crammed inside this witless (but bloody) Italian/Mexican production, shot in Mexico. Johnny is a notorious gunfighter, raised by an undertaker (an interesting combo). He falls in love with a beautiful woman who happens to have a very jealous outlaw husband. Obvious and predictable.

La Lunga Cavalcata della Vendetta see *Deadly Trackers*

Una Lunga Fila di Croci see *No Room to Die*

I Lunghi Giorni della Vendetta see *Long Days of Vengeance*

I Lunghi Giorni dell'Odio see *This Man Can't Die*

Il Lungo Giorno del Massacro see *Long Day of the Massacre*

Lust in the Sun see *Dust in the Sun*

Lynching see *If One Is Born a Swine . . . Kill Him*

Machine Gun Killers (1968)

Gatling Gun; Damned Hot Day of Fire; Quel Caldo Maledetto Giorno di Fuoco Ital; *Avec Django . . . Ça Va Saigner* Fr. *Director:* Paolo Bianchini; *Script:* Paolo Bianchini/José Luis Merino; *Camera:* Francisco Marin Herrada; *Music:* Piero Piccioni; *Producer:* Fida/Atlantida Film (Italy/Spain). *Cast:* Robert Woods, John Ireland, Evelyn Stewart, Claudie Lange, George Rigaud, Roberto Camardiel, Furio Meniconi, Lewis Jordan, Gerard Herter, Rada Rassimov, Tom Felleghy.

A well-filmed and brilliantly crafted Spaghetti Western directed by no-nonsense balls-to-the-wall Paolo Bianchini (aka Paolo Bianchi, this time not using the familiar Paul Maxwell pseudonym). The entire violent opus is punctuated by astonishingly good editing from genre veteran Vincenzo Tomassi (using the pseudonym "Vincent Thomas," but should not be confused with director Enzo Gicca Palli who also uses the "Vincent Thomas" alias for his directorial credit on *The Price of Death*, also called *The Last Gunfight*, with Klaus Kinski and Gianni Garko, plus a swashbucker with Terence Hill and Bud Spencer called *Blackie the Pirate*).

In this one, Richard Gatlin (Lewis Jordan; no "g" in Gatlin) introduces his new machine gun, capable of firing 300 rounds per minute, to the Union Army ("A small contribution to our cause," he says). But Gatlin is kidnapped by a ruthless Mexican bandido, Tapos (in an over-the-top performance by John Ireland, Spanish accent and all).

The abduction is blamed on Union officer Chris Tanner (Robert Woods) who is immediately scheduled for execution. However, U.S. security agent Pinkerton arranges for Tanner's escape, after getting assurance that he will find the true culprit. And he does.

Director Bianchi also worked with Robert Woods on a contemporary exploitation thriller called *Hypnos: Long Day of Massacre* (1968), a film the actor identifies as his favorite.

El Macho see Macho Killers

Macho Killers (1977)

El Macho Ital. *Director:* Mark Andrew; *Script:* Fabio Pittorru/Mark Andrew; *Camera:* Luciano Trasatti; *Music:* Marcello Romoino; *Producer:* S.B. Productions (Italy). *Cast:* Carlos Monson, George Hilton, Malisa Longo, Susanna Gimenez, Miguel Bosè.

It's a story of double-crossing intrigue, as the sheriff of Abilene (Miguel Bosè) convinces a gunfighting professional gambler, "El Macho" (Carlos Munson), to assume the identity of a "lookalike" outlaw named Buzzard. After a major stagecoach robbery pulled by the Duke (George Hilton) and his gang, the sheriff offers Macho a big reward for infiltrating the gang and snatching back the pilfered loot. With the help of Buzzard's old girlfriend, Kelly (amazingly, she doesn't recognize the imposter), Macho finds the hideout and recovers the stolen gold. But the sheriff betrays everybody. Macho kills the bogus lawman and his crooked posse in a massive town-square gun battle, and then he faces the Duke in a unique "horseback" showdown.

The most significant thing about this movie is its "attitude." Italian art director Marcello Andrei (aka Mark Andrew), best known for his sleazy psychological flick, *Dark Secrets of Deborah* (1974), pushes "machismo" to the limit with lots of posturing and surly glances. George Hilton is especially flamboyant as the vicious (but refined) villain, dressed in a full black cape with white gloves and scarf, drinking champagne in the wilderness hideout.

Los Machos see To Hell and Back

Mad Dog see Mad Dog Morgan

Mad Dog see Manhunt

Mad Dog Morgan (1975)

Mad Dog Brit. *Director:* Philippe Mora; *Script:* Philippe Mora; *Camera:* Mike Molloy; *Music:* Nigel Warren; *Producer:* Jeremy Thomas, Maddog PTY Films (Australia). *Cast:* Dennis Hopper, Jack Thompson, David Gulpilil, Frank Thring, Michael Pate, Wallas Eaton.

Oddly, a striking film based on the exploits of Australia's leading cowboy outlaw, Dan Morgan (also see *Ned Kelly*). The word "oddly" is used to open this entry because the film is directed by Philippe Mora, not known for his quality or expertise (i.e., *The Howling 2: Your Sister Is a Werewolf, Communion, The Return of Captain Invincible: A Legend in Leotards*, and his most infamous film, *The Beast Within*, showing a woman raped by a giant cicada).

Although the setting is not the American West, this Australian production is so similar to the Euro counterparts in theme, characterization, costuming, and style that inclusion in this book seems appropriate. Dennis Hopper's portrayal of Morgan is marvelously psychotic. He's a prospector who, driven by a "desire to eat," becomes a bandit. He gets caught, imprisoned but eventually released. At that point, Morgan takes his "job" seriously as he becomes the "outlaw terror of 1854" in Australia.

Magnificent Bandit see *Viva Cangaceiro*

Magnificent Brutes of the West (1965)

Badmen of the West; I Magnifici Brutos del West Ital. *Director:* Fred Wilson; *Script:* Enzo Girolami/Conchita Pino, *Camera:* José Antonio Rojo; *Music:* Francesco De Masi; *Producer:* Emillano Piedra, Metheus/Interacional/Cineurop (Italy/Spain/France). *Cast:* "I Quattro Brutos," Giacomo Rossi Stuart, Emma Penella, Darry-Cowl, Alfredo Mayo, Julio Peña.

Imagine four Jerry Lewis clones in a slapstick Western free-for-all. Now throw in a romantic subplot between a handsome undercover lawman and a saloon-owner prostitute. Then add the villainous exploits of a power-hungry gang leader who "likes to kill." And, finally, include an agitated tribe of superstitious Indians. The result is this movie.

Directed by veteran Marino Girolami (alias Fred Wilson) and cowritten by his son, Enzo Girolami (the future filmmaker Enzo G. Castellari), this motion picture proves that silly "sight-gag comedies" can (sometimes) be very funny. After watching inane entries like *Once Upon a Time in the Wild, Wild West* or *Patience Has a Limit, We Don't*, it's an easy thing to forget.

This one stars an Italian comedy team, "I Quattro Brutos" (closest English translation would be "The Four Stooges"), consisting of Artie, Lee, Johnny and Pep. They come to Fresno during a fierce gun battle. Thinking that it's a celebration honoring their arrival, they also begin shooting their guns into the air. But, as luck would have it, the Stooges inadvertently kill all the bad guys. Unfortunately, they have eliminated the town undertaker, too. So, they take over "his burying business" which leads to a series of black humor gags (i.e., they have trouble lifting a fat man into his coffin, so they make a crane and try to hoist him in; in another segment, not knowing what to do with formaldehyde, the Stooges make a grand, and disgusting, mess by spreading it all over a corpse).

A nearby Indian tribe gets riled when the Stooges try to bury bodies in the sacred hunting ground. Meanwhile, there's a good-guy gunfighter in buckskin, secretly Marshall Gary Smith (Giacomo Rossi Stuart), who has come to Fresno to stop an aggressive outlaw gang led by Jackson (Darry-Cowl). Smith falls in love with saloon owner, Lucy (Emma Penella), and together with the aid (?) of the Stooges, they eliminate the bandidos and pacify the Indians.

Magnificent Texan (1967)

Il Magnifico Texano Ital. *Director:* Lewis King; *Script:* Robert Keaton/Luigi Capuano; *Camera:* Pablo Ripoll; *Music:* Frank Mason; *Producer:* Ferdinando Feli-

Movie poster from *Magnificent Three* (1963).

cion, Selenia/R.M. Film (Italy/Spain). *Cast:* Glenn Saxson, Benny Deus, Barbara Loy, Luis Induñi, John Barracuda, George Greenwood, Gloria Osuna.

Here's a talky tale of racial tensions (between the Mexicans and the gringos) in a South Texas border town, directed by Luigi Capuano, under the pseudonym Lewis King (see his other genre outing, *Blood Calls to Blood*).

Under the guise of being the new saloon owner, Manny (Glenn Saxson) is secretly a Robin Hood–type of hero, helping the oppressed Mexican peasants who are mistreated by wealthy land baron Thompson (George Greenwood) and his sadistic son (John Barracuda). In yet another variation of the "revenge for a slaughtered family" theme, Manny is actually avenging the death of his parents at the hands of the evil Thompson.

Francesco De Masi (aka Frank Mason) did the rather tiresome score. Actor Glenn Saxson starred in quite a few Spaghetti Westerns, including *Django Shoots First* (see Performers filmography for additional films), but he is best known for the title role in Umberto Lenzi's *Mask of the Kriminal* (1967), based on the popular Italian comic strip.

Magnificent Three (1963)

Three Good Men; I Tre Implacabili Ital. *Director:* Joaquin R. Marchent; *Script:* José Mallorqui; *Camera:* Rafael Pacheco; *Music:* Manuel Parada/Francesco De Masi; *Producer:* Centauro Films/P.E.A. (Spain/Italy). *Cast:* Geoffrey Horne, Robert Hundar, Massimo Carocci, Fernando Sancho, Cristina Gajoni, Paul Piaget, John MacDouglas, Raf Baldassare, Aldo Sambrell.

One of three Spaghetti Westerns filmed by prolific director Joaquin Romero Marchent (aka Joaquin Luis Romero Hernandez) in 1963; the others are *Gunfight at High Noon* with Richard Harrison, and *Shadow of Zorro*. This movie tells the story of three friends (Geoffrey Horne, Robert Hundar, and Paul

Piaget) who band together, uniting the pioneers, when the ranches are threatened by a gang of Mexican bandidos.

Shot in a series of solid earth tones by cinematographer Rafael Pacheco, Marchent manages to capture the grittiness of the West. Although the plot tends to offer nothing new, the style of the film makes it an enjoyable journey.

Magnificent West (1972)

Il Magnifico West Ital. *Director:* Gianni Crea; *Script:* Gianni Crea; *Camera:* Gianni Raffaldi; *Music:* Stelvio Cipriani; *Producer:* Minerva Film (Italy). *Cast:* Vassili Karis, Lorenzo Fineschi, Dario Pino, Italo Gasperini, Enzo Pulcrano, Gordon Mitchell, Sergio Scarchili.

This film wants to be a "sprawling, picturesque tale of the West" but director Gianni Crea's apparent inability to tell a cohesive story (see *Finders Killers*), coupled with a rather unremarkable cast makes the entire endeavor tediously inept. Overall, it's an irritatingly slipshod production, a carelessly constructed tale of a "likable" rogue (Vassili Karis) and his search for missing gold bars, stolen by his former partner, Lefty (Lorenzo Fineschi).

I Magnifici Brutos del West see *Magnificent Brutes of the West*

Magnifico, l'Uomo dell'Est see *Man of the East*

Il Magnifico Texano see *Magnificent Texan*

Il Magnifico West see *Magnificent West*

Le Maledette Pistole di Dallas see *Damned Pistols of Dallas*

Mallory Must Not Die (1971)

My Name Is Mallory . . . M Means Death; Il Mio Nome È Mallory . . . "M" Come Morte Ital. *Director:* Mario Moroni; *Script:* Mario Moroni; *Camera:* Mario Vulpiani; *Music:* Roberto Pregadio; *Producer:* Zalo Film (Italy). *Cast:* Robert Woods, Gabriella Giorgelli, Teodoro Corra, Aldo Berti.

One of the more obscure Robert Woods features, obviously intended as "the first in a series" about a notorious gunfighting bounty hunter named Mallory. He is a man of few words, on the trail of an escaped killer, Stone (Aldo Berti). His trek leads him to the small city of Coppermine where he meets, and falls in love with, Cora (Gabriella Giorgelli). Eventually, Mallory faces Stone in a predictable showdown. With predictable results.

Good camera work by Mario Vulpiani *Night of the Serpent* and *The Big Showdown)* helps the tired story.

Mamma Mia È Arrivato "Così Sia" see *They Still Call Me Amen*

Man: His Pride and His Vengeance (1967)

Pride and Vengeance: L'Uomo, l'Orgoglio, la Vendetta Ital. *Director:* Luigi Bazzoni; *Script:* Luigi Bazzoni/Suso Cecchi D'Amico; *Camera:* Camillo Bazzoni; *Music:* Carlo Rustichelli/Bruno Nicolai; *Producer:* Luigi Rovere, Regal/Fono/

Constantin (Italy/West Germany). *Cast:* Franco Nero, Klaus Kinski, Tina Aumont, Lee Burton, Franco Ressel, Karl Schonboch, Alberto Dell'Acqua.

An odd film. Odd because there is no hero. There's not a "good guy" to be found anywhere. José (Franco Nero) is a Mexican officer, demoted because he allowed a prisoner, Carmen (Tina Aumont), to escape his custody. Later, while attending a reception at the colonel's home, José is surprised to see the woman (disguised as a gypsy exotic dancer); however, instead of exposing her, he induces Carmen to become his lover. This develops into an affair which becomes a stormy but stable relationship.

When she cheats on him with a superior officer, Lt. Garzas (Alberto Dell'Acqua, aka Robert Widmark), José murders his rival. The two flee from the fortress and join a band of smugglers. After a successful robbery (masterminded by José), they double-cross the bandits, killing them and stealing the loot. José decides that they had better leave the country, but when he finds Carmen with yet another man, he finally murders her too and is, in turn, captured by the army.

Klaus Kinski delivers another of his "patented" mini-performances as the scurrilous freelance outlaw Garcia. And Lee Burton (cousin of Italian sex queen Gina Lollobirgida) is the young bandit, Juan. This Italian-German production is directed by Luigi Bazzoni, not using his Alex Burkes alias (see *Long Ride from Hell*) nor his Marc Meyer pseudonym (see *Brothers Blue*). The chief cameraman (with an eye for the unusual) is Luigi's brother, Camillo Bazzoni. The entire thing is based on a European pulp novel called *Carmen,* written by Prosper Mérimée.

Man and a Colt (1967)

L'Uomo e una Colt Ital. *Director:* Tullio Demichelli; *Script:* Nino Stresa/Tullio Demichelli; *Camera:* Oberdan Troiani/Emilio Foriscot; *Music:* Oliver Pina Angel; *Producer:* Allied Artists (Spain/Italy). *Cast:* Robert Hundar, Fernando Sancho, Gloria Milland, Mirko Ellis, Marta Reeves, Jacinto Martin.

Underrated action filmmaker, Tullio Demichelli, delivers another swift-moving, but (unfortunately) lame-brained Spaghetti Western. Robert Hundar is a rogue gunfighter named Dallas who discovers that the town boss (Mirko Ellis) is secretly in cahoots with a notorious Mexican outlaw, Ramon (Fernando Sancho), and that they are planning to rob the Texas Reserve Bank, the central clearinghouse for all ransoms paid to bounty hunters.

Oliver Pina Angel is an alias for musical composer Carlo Rustichelli.

Man Called Amen (1972)

They Called Him Amen; Così Sia Ital. *Director:* Alfio Caltabiano; *Script:* Alfio Caltabiano/Adriano Bolzoni; *Camera:* Riccardo Pallottini; *Music:* Daniele Patucchi; *Producer:* Laser Film (Italy). *Cast:* Luc Merenda, Sydne Rome, Alf Thunder, Tano Cimarosa, Mila Beran, Renato Cestiè.

Some movies shouldn't receive a "rating" as arbitrated by the MPAA. Instead of the standard PG, PG-13, or R, certain films should be given a "skull and crossbones" rating, a direct warning to the consumer that "this motion picture is *poison.*" Deadly, potent, audience-killing poison. If there were such a warning, this movie would definitely be a prime candidate for it.

It's filled with remarkably unfunny sight gags (i.e., a man's glass of beer is stuck-like-crazy-glue to the table because it was set on a wad of chewing gun). Plus, there's an unparalleled collection of tastelessly lecherous sleaze sequences (i.e., "Hand over them panties, I want them for my wife," a Mexican bandit says to a gay robbery victim). But, this film is even worse than most other drek because it is also excruciatingly boring.

Regardless of the misleading title, there's no one called "Amen" anywhere to be found. Horacio (Luc Merenda) is a sharp-shooting, kung fu–fighting rogue who finds his former double-crossing partner in the city of South Forest. The man is now called Reverend Smith (Alf Thunder, aka director Alfio Caltabiano) and he's using his church as a "front" for his illegal activities. Together again, Horacio and Smith, assisted by an old man named Gramps and a child (Towhead), rob the town bank. In the end, the schoolteacher (beautiful Sydne Rome in a cameo) steals all the money.

Popular Italian actress, Sydne Rome (originally from Sandusky, Ohio), is the only breath of fresh air in this production. Unfortunately, her participation is minimal. However (for the voyeurs), she does have a nude bathtub scene which gives this movie the dubious distinction of being one of a limited handful (also see *Apache Woman, Three Musketeers of the West, Black Killer*) that contain female frontal nudity.

Man Called Apocalypse Joe see *Apocalypse Joe*

Man Called Blade (1977)

Mannaja Ital. *Director:* Sergio Martino; *Script:* Sergio Martino/Sauro Scavolini; *Camera:* Federico Zanni; *Music:* Guido and Maurizio De Angelis; *Producer:* Luciano Martino, Devon Film/Medusa (Italy). *Cast:* Maurizio Merli, John Steiner, Donald O'Brien, Sonja Jeannine, Martine Brochard, Rik Battaglia, Philippe Leroy, Ted Carter.

A tremendous revenge flick from cult director Sergio Martino. It's the story of a mountain-man bounty hunter, Blade (Maurizio Merli) who captures a fleeing bandit named Burt Craven (Donald O'Brien) by flinging his deadly hatchet and cutting off the outlaw's hand. Blade takes Craven to nearby Suttonville expecting to receive the $5000 reward, but the town has no sheriff. Instead, he wagers the "bandit's head" in a poker game with Theo Voller (John Steiner), the director of a silver mine owned by town boss McGowan (Philippe Leroy). Blade wins the bet, collects the money, and (since he didn't want to bother with the task of finding "an official" to pay the ransom) lets Craven loose.

Later, when Blade is returning to his home in the mountains, he's ambushed by Voller. After pulling off a double cross (Voller turned against his employer, McGowan, kidnapped his daughter and blamed everything on Blade), the sadistic Theo Voller buries Blade, leaving only his head above ground. Then he stitches Blade's eyelids open for his "eyeballs to be rotted out by the sun."

However, Burt Craven saves Blade and nurses him back to health. Although he is now almost totally blind, Blade is obsessed with revenge. He practices marksmanship with his gun, learning how to shoot accurately from sounds instead of sight. Then he corners Voller and his gang inside the silver mine. Blade has the advantage of the darkness and he makes the most of it. Everybody is killed in a flurry of gunshots. Everybody, that is, except Voller. Blade has saved his hatchet for Voller . . . and he gives it to him.

Sergio Martino, known mostly for his thrillers *Torso* and *Next Victim*, has created a violent (yet, oddly surrealistic) motion picture, very unusual for Western fare. There's a "medieval" quality to the movie, adding a larger-than-life mystique to the production.

This film is actor Maurizio Merli's only Spaghetti Western. Until his untimely death in 1989, he maintained his popularity with many Italian action films, especially cop movies (i.e., Umberto Lenzi's *Violent Protection*, Franco Martinelli's *Special Cop in Action*, plus a number of Stelvio Massi films including *Nightmare City, Rebel, Fearless,* and *Hunted City*). Donald O'Brien made many Westerns (see Performers filmography) but he will always be remembered for his over-the-top performance as *Doctor Butcher, M.D.,* directed by genre filmmaker Marino Girolami. John Steiner is another veteran actor with many great performances spanning over 25 years; his most memorable films are Dario Argento's *Tenebrae*, Mario Bava's *Shock* (also called *Beyond the Door 2*), Anthony M. Dawson's *Ark of the Sun God,* and Ruggero Deodato's *Cut and Run.*

Man Called Django (1971)

Viva! Django; Lo Chiamavano Django Ital; *W Django!* Ital. *Director:* Edward G. Muller; *Script:* Nino Stresa; *Camera:* Marcello Masciocchi; *Music:* Piero Umiliani; *Producer:* Salvatore Crocella, 14 Luglio (Italy). *Cast:* Anthony Steffen, Stelio Candelli, Clauco Ontario, Donato Castellaneta, Esmeralda Barros, Simone Blondell, Chris Avram.

The plot is tiresomely routine, yet another variation on the exhausted vengeance theme. But somehow, crackerjack exploitation director Edward G. Muller (alias for Edoardo Mulargia) makes it all seem fresh and original. He's also aided by a striking, mean-spirited performance from Anthony Steffen, plus Marcello Masciocchi's discordantly gritty photography.

Django (Anthony Steffen) is on the trail of some renegade outlaws who raped and killed "his woman Lara." Enroute, he rescues an accused horse thief named Carranza (Stelio Candelli) from an impromptu hanging, and discovers that the man knows who committed the slaying: three bandits now trafficking in guns to the Mexican revolutionaries. Django goes underground and designs a "sting" against the smugglers, which results in their deaths. Upon his return, Django discovers that there were *four* men responsible for Lara's death; informant Carranza was also involved. The films end with a showdown. And, obviously, Django is victorious.

Of peculiar note, this is the only film that Simone Blondell (Mrs. Miles Deem, aka Demofilo Fidani) made for any other director, besides her husband (see Performers filmography).

Man Called Gringo (1964)

La Ley del Forasterio Ital; *Sie nannten ihn Gringo* Ger. *Director:* Roy Rowland; *Script:* Clarke Reynolds/Helmut Harun; *Camera:* Manuel Merino; *Music:* Piero Piccioni; *Producer:* International Germania/Unidos (West Germany/Spain). *Cast:* Götz George, Sieghardt Rupp, Alexandra Stewart, Helmut Schmidt, Dan Martin, Silvia Solar, Peter Tordy.

Götz George as the marshal in the foreground of a scene from *Man Called Gringo* (1964).

The man called Gringo (Dan Martin) is actually the "missing" bastard son of Dakota cattle rancher and mine owner Sam Martin (Peter Tordy). Neither man is aware of their relationship, and they are fighting on opposite sides.

Sam Martin is left paralyzed after a horse accident. He turns his business over to a corrupt lawyer, Denton (Helmut Schmidt), who secretly hates him because years ago Martin had killed his father. The attorney is determined to rob (and eventually destroy) the old man.

He hires an outlaw, Gringo, to wage a range war and confiscate the mine. And, as part of the perfect "revenge," he orders Gringo (Martin's long lost son) to kill the rancher. All the treachery is stopped in the nick of time by a mysterious stranger (actually the district marshal) named Mace Carson (Götz George).

The film features an early screen performance from popular cult actress Silvia Solar; she plays Kate, Lawyer Denton's prostitute girlfriend. The director Roy Rowland is a veteran Hollywood filmmaker best known for a Ray Milland Western called *Bugles in the Afternoon* and *Hit the Deck*, a 50s musical comedy starring Jane Powell, Debbie Reynolds, Russ Tamblyn, and Vic Damone. Plus he also directed the horror/fantasy classic, *5000 Fingers of Doctor T* (1953), surprisingly written by Dr. Seuss. Rowland also supervised a series of action films (including Sergio Bergonzelli's *Fighting Corsair*) during the same period of time. His cameraman Manuel Merino assisted him again with next year's *Gunfighters of Casa Grande*.

Man Called Invincible (1973)

In the West There Was a Man Named Invincible; They Called Him the Player with the Dead; Lo Chiamavano Tressette . . . Giocava Sempre colla Morte Ital. *Director:* Anthony Ascott; *Script:* Tito Carpi; *Camera:* Stelvio Massi; *Music:* Bruno Nicolai; *Producer:* Mino Loy, Flora Film (Italy). *Cast:* George Hilton, Cris Huerta, Evelyn Stewart, Sal Borgese, Umberto D'Orsi, Rosalba Neri, Carla Mancini, Nello Pazzafini.

Once again, filmmaker Anthony Ascott (Giuliano Carmineo), with 13 genre movies to his credit (see Directors filmography for complete listing), teams with one of his favorite actors, George Hilton, for a breezy Spaghetti Western. This film, with its overtly satirical tone, is a dramatic departure from their previous venture together, *I Am Sartana, Trade Your Guns for a Coffin* (1970).

Quite unusual for an Ascott film, there are many political jabs aimed squarely at the (then) president of the United States, Richard Nixon. These include calling one of the film's inept villains "Tricky Dick" (Sal Borgese).

Hilton turns in another competent performance as a gambling gunfighter named Tressette who has been hired to transport gold from Wagon Bend to Dallas. But he is double-crossed by banker McPherson (Cris Huerta) who has secretly stolen the gold and converted it into dust. Tresette discovers the betrayal just as McPherson and his partner are inside a bakery preparing cakes for export, using gold dust instead of flour. Of course, Tressette quickly stops the banker and the baker from executing their wacky plan, giving new meaning to "having your cake and eating it too."

There remains an unsolved mystery regarding the Bruno Nicolai soundtrack. The same musical tracks (including the vocal theme song) are also used in the Sergio Martino film, *Arizona* (1970). Then the score turned up in Ignacio Iquino's *My Horse, My Gun . . . Your Widow* (1972), before it was used in this movie. What's this all about?

Man Called Joe Clifford see *Apocalypse Joe*

Man Called Noon (1974)

Lo Chiamavano Mezzogiorno Ital. *Director:* Peter Collinson; *Script:* Scott Finch/Peter Collinson; *Camera:* John Cabrera; *Music:* Luis Enrique Bacalov; *Producer:* Euan Lloyd, Frontier LTD/Dania Films (England/Spain/Italy). *Cast:* Richard Crenna, Rosanna Schiaffino, Stephen Boyd, Farley Granger, Patty Shepard, Aldo Sambrell, Charlie Bravo.

Based on a book by Louis L'Amour and filmed with lambent flare by Britain's unappreciated Peter Collinson, it tells the story of Noon (Richard Crenna), a gunslinger suffering from amnesia after he's been struck by a bullet. Aided by an outlaw named Rimes (Stephen Boyd) and a sultry señorita, Fan (Rosanna Schiaffino), Noon struggles to unravel his true identity as he seeks vengeance for his dead wife and child. The remarkable thing about this film is Collinson's direction, particularly his unflinching eye for detail and his exceptional ability to shoot traditional scenes from unique vantage points. He makes a tired tale seem fresh.

Peter Collinson, who died in an automobile accident in 1980 at age 41, was on the "cutting edge" of filmmaking, exploiting many themes long before they "became vogue." His movie *Fright* (1975), with Susan George as a terrified-babysitter-facing-a-psychopathic-madman, preceded John Carpenter's *Halloween* by three years (but the similarities are more amazing than accidental); and *The Penthouse* (1967) starring Suzy Kendall, was the first balls-to-the-wall sadistic horror/torment picture, comparable to the more celebrated *Last House on the Left* (1972), but filmed an ineluctable five years prior. His other films include a brilliant antiwar war movie with David Hemmings, *Long Day's Dying* (1968), an entertaining heist film called *The Italian Job* (1969), plus a vicious search-and-kill flick, *Open Season* (1974), with Peter Fonda, Richard Jaeckel and John Phillip Law as hunters who stalk girls for sport.

Man Called Sledge (1970)

Sledge Ital. *Director:* Vic Morrow with Giorgio Gentili; *Script:* Vic Morrow/Frank Kowalsky; *Camera:* Luigi Kuveiller; *Music:* Gianni Ferrio; *Producer:* Dino De Laurentiis/Harry Bloom (Italy/U.S.). *Cast:* James Garner, Laura Antonelli, Dennis Weaver, Claude Akins, John Marley, Wayde Preston, Ken Clark.

Actor Vic Morrow wrote it and began directing it. But after a major disagreement with producer Dino De Laurentiis, he was replaced by Giorgio Gentili; however, due to a studio contract, total credit is given to Morrow for the project. Perhaps the dual (and dueling) directors account for the disjoined feel and the rambling storyline.

Regardless, it's good to see James Garner in a Spaghetti Western (his only participation in the genre). Here's a gritty story of outlaw Luther Sledge (Garner) and his gang, who steal $300,000 in gold and then fight among themselves for possession, until finally everybody loses.

One of the consistent highlights of this film is the down-and-dirty camera work by Luigi Kuveiller. Plus the appearance of sex goddess Laura Antonelli, who also made Dallamano's *Venus in Furs*, Visconti's *The Innocent*, Fellini's *Satyricon*, and Mario Bava's *Dr. Goldfoot and the Girl Bombs*.

A Man Came to Kill see Man with the Golden Pistol

Man from Canyon City (1965)

Viva Carrancha!; L'Uomo Che Viene da Canyon City Ital. *Director:* Alfonso Balcazar; *Script:* José De La Loma/Adriano Bolzoni; *Camera:* Vicente Rosell; *Music:* Angelo Francesco Lavagnino; *Producer:* Balcazar De Barcelona/Adelphi Cinema. *Cast:* Robert Woods, Fernando Sancho, Luis Dávila, Renato Baldini, Loredana Nusciak, Gérard Tichy, Antonio Molino Rojo, Oscar Carreras, Paco Sanz, José Manuel Martin.

This is a loosely based sequel to Alfonso Balcazar's *Five Thousand Dollars on One Ace*. Apparently shot back to back or perhaps simultaneously, it also stars Robert Woods and Fernando Sancho in the lead roles, playing gambler Jeff Clayton and bandido Carrancio. The film opens with Jeff and Carrancio escaping from a chain gang (fortunately they were chained together), and develops into an unusual character study, concentrating mostly on Sancho's free-spirited persona. Regardless of the title, none of it has anything to do with a place called Canyon City.

Sancho made (an incredible!) 168 films between 1941 *(Polizon a Bordo)* and 1986 *(Los Presuntos),* but he is best remembered for his Spaghetti Westerns, stereotyped as a Mexican bandit leader in a wide sombrero, wearing two bandoleers crisscrossing at his chest. This film gave the fans a chance to see more depth than usual in his traditionally static character. Actor Fernando Sancho died from a prolonged illness in 1990.

Man from Nowhere see *Arizona Colt*

Man from Oklahoma (1965)

Ranch of the Ruthless; Il Ranch degli Spietati Ital. *Director:* Robert M. White; *Script:* Helmut Harun; *Camera:* Giuseppe La Torre; *Music:* Frank Mason (Francesco De Masi); *Producer:* Fida/Neues Film (Italy/Spain/Germany). *Cast:* Rick Horn, José Calvo, Sabine Bethman, John MacDouglas, Tom Felleghi, Leontine May, Karl Otto Alberty, Georg Herzog.

Here's another variation on the "trouble with the town boss" theme, this time directed by Jaime J. Balcazar with Roberto Montero (using the "Robert M. White" pseudonym). The newly appointed sheriff of Wagon Wheel, Thomas Hunter (Rick Horn) is determined to get rid of a marauding outlaw gang. He's convinced that wealthy land baron Jacobs (Tom Felleghi) is the real culprit behind the terrorist activities. He plans to do something about it. And he does. It just takes a while. Seemingly, a very long while.

Man from the North see *Kitosch, the Man Who Came from the North*

Man of the Cursed Valley (1964)

L'Uomo della Valle Maledetta Ital. *Director:* Omar Hopkins; *Script:* Eduardo M. Brochero; *Camera:* Alfredo Fraile/Remo Grisanti; *Music:* Manuel Parada/ Francesco De Masi; *Producer:* Gar Film (Italy/Spain). *Cast:* Ty Hardin, Iran Eory, Peter Larry, Joe Kamel, José Nieto, John Bartha, José Marco.

A rambling tale about white girl Gwen (Iran Eory) who marries an Indian named Torito (Peter Larry) and is disowned by her family. She is kidnapped and held prisoner by another Indian tribe until she manages to escape (with the aid of gunslinger Johnny Walscott, played by Ty Hardin). Gwen tells Johnny about how her father "is unreasonable and indifferent to her love for Torito." So the gunman goes to the patriarch on her behalf.

While Johnny is gone, Gwen's Indian husband arrives and takes her back to his camp. Meanwhile, Johnny convinces her father, Sam Burnett (José Nieto), to accept his daughter's marriage. The two men go to Torito's village and Sam Burnett offers Gwen and Torito a home on his ranch. Initially, the Indian refuses, but when Johnny beats him in a hand-to-hand contest, Torito agrees to go with them.

But then there's more trouble. The tribe of bad Indians (the ones who had kidnapped Gwen originally) attack the ranch, killing Burnett and once more they capture the girl. Johnny and Torito go to her rescue, and obviously everything ends happily.

Humdrum entertainment with a make-it-up-as-you-go feel, directed by

Primo Zeglio (hiding behind the "Omar Hopkins" pseudonym, instead of the more familiar "Anthony Greepy" alias).

Man of the East (1973)

Eastman; E Poi lo Chiamarono il Magnifico Ital; *Magnifico, l'Uomo dell'Est* Ital. *Director:* E. B. Clucher; *Script:* Enzo Barboni; *Camera:* Aldo Giordani; *Music:* Guido De Angelis/Maurizio De Angelis; *Producer:* Alberto Grimaldi, P.E.A./Artistes (Italy/France). *Cast:* Terence Hill, Gregory Walcott, Yanti Sommer, Dominic Barto, Harry Carey, Jr., Dan Sturkie, Sal Borgese, Riccardo Pizzuti.

Many of the *Trinity* stars (Terence Hill, Harry Carey, Jr., Yanti Sommer, Dan Sturkie) join with the *Trinity* writer/director E. B. Clucher (pseudonym of former cameraman Enzo Barboni) for what should have been another fun Western romp.

Instead, this is an overly long (125 minutes), yet impoverished, rambling mess. It's an endurance test. A grueling "one-joke" extended-for-over-two-hours endurance test. And nobody is the winner. Terence Hill not only misunderstands his character, but (seemingly) he doesn't know how to stay within the boundaries of a rigid personality. Where was the director?

Terence Hill plays "the Man of the East," Sir Thomas More, an aristocrat who doesn't understand (but certainly enjoys) the ways of the West. He's constantly the butt of pranks played by an outlaw gang headed by gunslinger Morton Clayton (Riccardo Pizzuti). Eventually Thomas More gets the last laugh. But not from the audience.

Man Who Cried for Revenge (1969)

Il Suo Nome Gridava Vendetta Ital. *Director:* William Hawkins; *Script:* Mario Caiano; *Camera:* Enzo Barboni; *Music:* Robbe Poitevin; *Producer:* United Pictures/Copercines (Italy/Spain). *Cast:* Anthony Steffen, William Berger, Evelyn Stewart, Raf Baldassare, Eleanora Vargas, Robert Hundar.

Mario Caiano (alias William Hawkins) made four Spaghetti Westerns with Anthony Steffen (also see *Coffin for the Sheriff; Ringo, Face of Revenge;* and *Train for Durango*). This one, like *Ringo, Face of Revenge,* is another variation on the "vengeance for a slaughtered family" theme with Steffen playing an avenging vigilante, Drake. He is searching for the three men who raped and killed his wife. However, he finds nothing but trouble. These men are in positions of power and are "protected" by a wealthy land baron, but eventually he eliminates them one by one.

Even though it's not as effective, Steffen's performance is reminiscent of his role in *Django the Bastard.* He is a man of very few words, his brooding face delivers the message. However, director/writer Mario Caiano seems to be confusing "cynical" for "despondent." Often, the vindictive Drake appears melancholy and forlorn, looking more like he craves a good night's sleep rather than retribution for his dead wife.

Man Who Killed Billy the Kid (1967)

For a Few Bullets More; I'll Kill Him and Return Alone; . . .E Divenne il Più Spietato Bandito del Sud Ital; *Hombre Que Mató Billy el Niño* Sp. *Director:*

Movie poster from Man Who Killed Billy the Kid *(1967).*

Julio Buchs; *Script:* Julio Buchs/Federico De Urrutia/Carlo Veo; *Camera:* Miguel Mila; *Music:* Gianni Ferrio; *Producer:* Silvio Battistini, Schulman Film (Italy). *Cast:* Peter Lee Lawrence, Fausto Tozzi, Dianik Zurakowska, Gloria Milland, Antonio Pica, Luis Prendes, Paco Sanz, Tomás Blanco, Luis Induñi.

    The tired story of Pat Garrett (Fausto Tozzi) and Billy the Kid (Peter Lee

Lawrence) is told yet again, but with many altered historical facts including Pat Garrett's inability to shoot his friend in the showdown. Instead, in this Spaghetti Western version, William Bonney (alias Billy the Kid) is gunned down by his arch enemy (and former friend) Mark Liston (Luis Prendes).

Billy the Kid is flaunted as a golden-haired martyr who only kills people in self defense, when no other solution is possible. However, in an unusual glimpse of truth, the film does touch on Billy's rumored unhealthy "love" for his mother (an Oedipal complex usually deleted from most "Billy the Kid" movies). Other than this rather tawdry segment, the action is humdrum and grossly inaccurate.

After the film met initial box office resistance, Anglo distributors tried to spruce it up with the impish title *For a Few Bullets More*.

Man with the Golden Pistol (1966)

A *Man Came to Kill; Doc, Hands of Steel; L'Uomo dalla Pistola d'Oro* Ital; *Doc, Manos de Plato* Sp. *Director:* Alfonso Balcazar; *Script:* Giovanni Simonelli/ Alfonso Balcazar/José Antonio De La Loma; *Camera:* Mario Capriotti; *Music:* Angelo Francesco Lavagnino; *Producer:* Balcazar De Barcelona (Spain/Italy). *Cast:* Carl Möhner, Luis Dávila, Gloria Milland, Fernando Sancho, Umberto Raho, Oscar Pelliceri, Irene Mir.

When he finds the body of murdered Larry Kling, a notorious gunfighter "with a price on his head" (Carl Möhner) assumes the dead man's identity. He wanders into Silvertown looking for work and is quickly hired as a temporary sheriff by the regional marshal, Slater (Luis Dávila). It's their job to protect the town from a band of evil Mexican outlaws, led by the sadistic Reyes (Fernando Sancho).

Soon Slater begins to suspect that Larry isn't who he pretends to be. So, secretly, he wires the county seat for "any information on Larry Kling." Meanwhile, the imposter falls in love with Lily (Gloria Milland), a beautiful saloon-hall entertainer, and he begins making friends with the citizens of Silvertown. It's obvious that Kling wants to "go straight" this time.

Then the Reyes gang attacks the city. A vicious gun battle rages, but the two lawmen emerge victorious. With his mission now completed, Slater is about to leave town when he receives confirmation that Larry Kling is, in fact, a fraud. Instead of confronting him, Slater destroys the evidence, and appoints Larry as the official sheriff of Silvertown.

Interestingly, despite the title, there are no "gold pistols" anywhere. And regarding the alternate title, there's no one named Doc.

Man with the Golden Winchester see *Son of Zorro*

Manhunt (1984)

Mad Dog Ital. *Director:* Larry Ludman; *Script:* Fabrizio De Angelis; *Camera:* Joseph Mercury; *Music:* Francesco De Masi; *Producer:* Fida/Western (Italy). *Cast:* John Ethan Wayne, Henry Silva, Bo Svenson, Ernest Borgnine, Raymund Harmstorf.

Maybe this Italian production does not qualify as a Spaghetti Western since it takes place in a "contemporary" setting, but the theme style, characterization, and music so resemble the genre that inclusion here seems appropriate. Director Fabrizio De Angelis (alias Larry Ludman), best known for his *Thunder Warrior* adventures series, tells the story of a "stranger" (John Ethan Wayne) who buys a couple of horses at a racetrack, but when returning home, he makes the mistake of stopping to water them on some land owned by Ben Robeson (Ernest Borgnine).

Robeson steals the animals and chases the stranger away. Angry but undaunted, the wronged man returns to collect his horses, but Robeson has him arrested by a crooked sheriff (Bo Svenson) and thrown in prison. After a series of ugly encounters with the commandant (Henry Silva), the stranger escapes from jail and, eventually, takes his revenge on Robeson and the sheriff. Interesting in its exploitive naïveté.

Mani di Pistolero see *Hands of a Gunman*

Mannaja see *Man Called Blade*

Mano Rapida see *Fasthand*

Manos Torpes see *Awkward Hands*

El Más Fabuloso Golpe del Far West see *Boldest Job in the West*

Masked Thief see *In the Name of the Father, the Son and the Colt*

Massacre at Fort Grant (1963)

Renegades of Fort Grant; Doomed Fort; Fuerte Perdido Sp. *Director:* J. Douglas; *Script:* José Luis Navarro/José M. Elorrieta; *Camera:* Pablo Ripoll; *Music:* Fernando Garcia Morcillo; *Producer:* José Luis Gamboa, Alescanco Producciones (Spain). *Cast:* Jerry Cobb, Mariano Vidal, Marta May, Aldo Sambrell, Luis Villar, Cris Huerta, Ethel Rojo, Frank Braña.

Proficient Spanish director José M. Elorrieta (alias J. Douglas, aka Joe Lacy) is best known for his medieval adventure pic *Hawk of Castile* and the demonic *Feast of Satan*. He also made three Eurowesterns.

This one opens with a devastating Indian attack on Fort Yellowstone (in the Spanish version; it's Fort Grant in the English print), and closes with an Indian attack on the same fort. The story, however, revolves around newlyweds Captain Jackson (German Cobos, aka Jerry Cobb) and his bride Jane (Marta May), traveling East for their honeymoon when the stagecoach is attacked by warring Apaches. All the surviving passengers take refuge in the nearby "doomed" fort, where Jackson is mistaken for a traitor.

The movie was remade with less than desirable results in 1966 by the same director as *Fury of the Apaches*.

Massacre at Fort Holman (1972)

Reason to Live, a Reason to Die; Una Ragione per Vivere . . . una Ragione per Morire Ital. *Director:* Tonino Valerii; *Script:* Tonino Valerii/Ernesto Gastaldi; *Camera:* Alejandro Ulloa; *Music:* Riz Ortolani; *Producer:* Michael Billingsley

(Italy/France/Spain/West Germany). *Cast:* Telly Savalas, James Coburn, Bud Spencer, José Suarez, Ralph Goodwin, Paco Sanz, Joseph Mitchell, Robert Burton.

A *Dirty Dozen* inspired Civil War film telling the story of Union Colonel Pembroke (James Coburn) with his "special" seven-man squad (hand-picked from the local prison) and their attempt to recapture a fort held by mad Confederate Major Ward (Telly Savalas). After many digressing subplots, including a conflict with a *Deliverance*-type family of psychos, they finally reach the fort where a bloodbath ensues. After the smoke clears (mostly from Pembroke's cracking gatlin guns) the only people left alive are Major Ward, "condemned" Yankee soldier Eli Sampson (Bud Spencer), and Colonel Pembroke.

This continental coproduction (almost everybody had a piece of this one) is a lesser entry from usually proficient Tonino Valerii *(Day of Anger, Price of Power, My Name Is Nobody)*.

Massacre at Grand Canyon (1963)

Red Pastures; I Pascoli Rossi Ital; *Massacro al Grande Canyon* Ital. *Director:* Stanley Corbett; *Script:* Albert Band/Sergio Corbucci; *Camera:* Enzo Barboni; *Music:* Gianni Ferrio; *Producer:* Albert Band, Ultra Film/Prodi (Italy). *Cast:* James Mitchum, Jill Powers, George Ardisson, Giacomo Rossi Stuart, Andrea Giordana, Burt Nelson, Nando Poggi, Milla Sannoner.

One of the early genre Spaghetti Westerns, made a full year before Sergio Leone's *Fistful of Dollars.*

Codirected by Albert Band (Alfredo Antonini) and Sergio Corbucci (under the collective pseudonym Stanley Corbett), this is the story of Wes Evans (James Mitchum, son of veteran actor Robert Mitchum) and his quest for vengeance against the outlaws who killed his father. Suddenly, he finds himself in the middle, between two warring bandit groups (shades of *Fistful?*) over ownership of some Grand Canyon pasture. But eventually, vengeance is his.

An interesting film for historic reasons but, stylistically, it more resembles a Hollywood B-Oater than a gritty Spaghetti Western. The following year Sergio Corbucci directed *Minnesota Clay;* Albert Band wouldn't direct another Western until 1966 with *The Tramplers;* he is best known as founder of the (now defunct) Empire Studios and also for a variety of horror films, including *Face of Fire* (1958), *I Bury the Living* (1959), and *Dracula's Dog* (1978).

Massacre at Marble City (1964)

Conquerors of Arkansas; Alla Conquista dell'Arkansas Ital. *Director:* Franz J. Gottlieb; *Script:* Alex Berg/W. P. Zibaso/Hans Billian; *Camera:* Jan Stallich; *Music:* Heinz Gietz/Francesco De Masi; *Producer:* Ludwig Spitaler (German/Italy/France). *Cast:* Mario Adorf, Brad Harris, Horst Frank, Dorothee Parker, Ralf Wolter, Thomas Alder, Serge Marquand, Marianne Hoppe, Philippe Lemaire.

This is an early project from German filmmaker Franz Gottlieb, director of numerous softcore sex films and several Edgar Wallace thrillers. For the Italo and Anglo marketplace, Gottlieb's name was dropped and replaced with assistant director Alberto Cardone (aka Paul Martin and Albert Cardiff), in an obvious attempt to pass this project off as an "Italian" Western.

It's the story of the Gold Rush and how it affects the rogues of Marble City. Prospectors are forced to contend with Indians and highwaymen in this sprawling, episodic tale. When gold is discovered in Indian territory, chief Burning Arrow (Serge Marquand) refuses to allow "the devil whites" on his land. Meanwhile, bandits (taking advantage of the turbulence) disguise themselves as Indians and attack a wagon train. After the attack, a young rancher, Phil Stone (Brad Harris), finds his father dead. He and his friend Dan McCormick (Horst Frank) vow vengeance.

In a ludicrous segment, they find a footprint at the scene of the crime which they eventually trace to Donovan (Philippe Lemaire), the henchman of evil town boss Matt Ellis (Mario Adorf). Phil, Dan and the sheriff decide to restore law and order to Marble City. They ask for (and get) assistance from Burning Arrow who leads his braves (in typical "Winnetou" fashion) against the bad guys.

This German-Italian-French coproduction is based on a best selling German book, *Die Regulatoren in Arkansas*, by Friedrich Gerstackers.

Music is by Heinz Gietz, with Italian assistance from Francesco De Masi.

Massacre et le Sang see *Big Ripoff*

Massacre Time (1966)

Brute and the Beast; Tempo di Massacro Ital. *Director:* Lucio Fulci; *Script:* Fernando Di Leo; *Camera:* Riccardo Pallottini; *Music:* Lallo Gori; *Producer:* Terry Vanteli, Mega/Colt/LF Produzioni (Italy/Spain/West Germany). *Cast:* Franco Nero, George Hilton, John MacDouglas, Aysanoa Runachagua, Tom Felleghy, Nino Castelnuovo, Lynn Shayne, Tchang Yu, Rina Franchetti.

Here's one of three Eurowesterns directed by Lucio Fulci (also see *Four Gunmen of the Apocalypse* and *The Silver Saddle*). Fulci is the enormously popular exploitation/horror filmmaker responsible for over 50 movies beginning in 1959 with *The Thief (I Ladri)*, including *Zombie, The Beyond, Gates of Hell, House by the Cemetery,* and *Lizard in a Woman's Skin*.

In this one, land baron Scott (John MacDouglas) controls most of the New Mexican territory. However, he's an old man no longer interested in power. Complete governing authority has been given to his sadistic son Jason (Nino Castelnuovo), a madman not afraid to use a bullwhip when the occasion calls for it to keep the citizenry in line.

Meanwhile, Tom (Franco Nero) is panning for gold in a remote area when he receives a mysterious message urging him to return home. Upon arrival, he is amazed at the oppression everywhere. He finds that his half brother Jeff (George Hilton) has become a hopeless drunkard and cannot answer any of his questions, but all around him people are being massacred by young tyrant Jason and his henchmen.

Tom decides to visit patriarch Scott and plead with him to curb his son's aggressions. Instead, Jason keeps Tom from seeing his father, beating him and whipping him unmercifully. Eventually Tom recuperates and, together with a now sober Jeff, they attack the hacienda with a vengeance.

In an ending similar to *Texas, Adios* (another 1966 film, also starring Franco Nero), Tom discovers that he is actually the land baron's "lost" son, and it was the old man who had sent the message to him for help in defeating the too-powerful Jason.

Cowritten by Lucio Fulci and future horror/action filmmaker Fernando Di Leo (i.e., *Slaughter Hotel, Vacation for a Massacre* and *Rulers of the City*).

Massacro al Grande Canyon see *Massacre at Grand Canyon*

Matalo! (1971)

¡*Matalo!* Sp. *Director:* Cesare Canavari; *Script:* Mino Roli/Eduardo Brochero/ Nico Ducci; *Camera:* Julio Ortas Plaza; *Music:* Mario Migliardi; *Producer:* Rofima/Copercines (Italy/Spain). *Cast:* Lou Castel, Corrado Pani, Antonio Salinas, Luis Dávila, Claudia Gravy, Miguel Del Castillo, Annamaria Noe.

A gang of gringos, disguised as Mexicans, rob a stage. During the holdup, one of the bandits, Bart (Corrado Pani) is shot. The three remaining (Theo, Mary, and Philip) dump his body in the river and stash the loot.

Wells Fargo hires bounty hunter Ray Matalo (Lou Castel) to find the outlaws and the stolen gold, which he does. The bandits end up dead in a gunfight; Bart (who was secretly in cahoots with double-crossing Mary) comes out of hiding. He is infuriated over his girlfriend's death, but Matalo guns him down, too.

Good, grandiose soundtrack by Mario Migliardi; chief cameraman is Julio Ortas Plaza. This is a Spaghetti Western with very little dialogue and lots of action from Italian exploitation director Cesare Canavari, also responsible for the Nazi-torture-fest *Gestapo's Last Orgy* (1975) and the very first "Emanuelle" film (before Just Jaekin's better known 1974 Sylvia Kristel entry) called *Io Emanuelle* (1973) staring Erika Blanc. *Matalo!* is his only contribution to the Western genre.

May God Forgive You ... But I Won't (1968)

Chiedi Perdono a Dio ... Non a Me Ital. *Director:* Glenn Vincent Davis; *Script:* Vincenzo Musolino; *Camera:* Mario Mancini; *Music:* Felice Di Stefano; *Producer:* Cio Film/Intercontinental (Italy). *Cast:* Georges Ardisson, Anthony Ghidra, Pete Martell, Cristina Iosani, Pedro Sanchez, Jean Louis, Lilli Lembo.

Not to be confused with *God Forgives, I Don't* (starring Terence Hill and Bud Spencer), this is an effective, no-nonsense flick. It's another "revenge for a slaughtered family" story as Cjamango (Georges Ardisson) hunts down and iniquitously destroys the killers of his brother, father and sister.

Director Glenn Vincent Davis (Vincenzo Musolino) is best known as a genre scriptwriter (see Scriptwriters filmography).

Meet the Sign of the Cross see *Shadow of Sartana ... Shadow of Your Death*

El Mercenario see *Mercenary*

Mercenary (1968)

A Professional Gun; El Mercenario Ital; *Revenge of a Gunfighter. Director:* Sergio Corbucci; *Script:* Luciano Vincenzoni/Sergio Spina/Giorgio Arlorio/ Adriano Bolzoni/Sergio Corbucci; *Camera:* Alejandro Ulloa; *Music:* Ennio Mor-

Movie poster from Sergio Corbucci's *Mercenary* (1968).

ricone; *Producer:* Alberto Grimaldi (Italy/Spain). *Cast:* Franco Nero, Jack Palance, Tony Musante, Giovanna Ralli, Eduardo Fajardo, Julio Peña, Bruno Corazzari, Raf Baldassare, Joe Kamel, Angel Ortiz, Franco Ressel.

    Companion film to the better *Compañeros*. There are some nice touches and a good Ennio Morricone score, but the movie wanders about needlessly. It's also quite heavy handed: Jack Palace as a homosexual gunfighter dressed in white and Mexican rebels made up as angels (!?!).

The year is 1915 and the revolution is hot in Mexico. Colonel Garcia Alfonso (wonderfully sleazy Eduardo Fajardo) is in charge of getting the silver shipments safely to the government seat in Mexico City. He hires a bounty hunter, Serge the Pole (Franco Nero), to escort the shipments, but after a disagreement, the mercenary quits and sells his services to a revolutionary bandit, Paco Ramon (Tony Musante).

As Paco becomes more involved in the "ideals of war" due to the rantings of his libertine girlfriend Columba (Giovanna Ralli), the Pole becomes less interested in helping him; however, they are reunited when Alfonso's new appointee, the sadistic homosexual captain Elam (Jack Palance), begins his personal vendetta against the revolutionaries.

Sergio Corbucci's next film was *Specialist*.

Mezzogiorno di Fuoco per an Hao see *Fighting Fists of Shanghai Joe*

La Mia Colt Ti Cercu . . . Quattro Ceri Ti Attendono see *My Colt, Not Yours*

Mille Dollari sul Nero see *Blood at Sundown* (1969)

Minnesota Clay (1964)

Minnesota Clay Ital. *Director:* Sergio Corbucci; *Script:* Adriano Bolzoni/Sergio Corbucci; *Camera:* José Fernandez Aguayo; *Music:* Piero Piccioni; *Producer:* Danilo Marciani, Ultra/Jaguar/Franco (Italy/Spain/France). *Cast:* Cameron Mitchell, Fernando Sancho, Alberto Cevenini, Georges Rivière, Antonio Casas, Joe Kamel, Diana Martin, Julio Peña, Ethel Rojo.

This is Sergio Corbucci's first Western (not counting the one he codirected with Albert Band in 1963, under the pseudonym Stanley Corbett, *Massacre at Grand Canyon*). Unlike Sergio Leone's first Western (*Fistful of Dollars*, being shot during the same time period) this one follows the "Hollywood formula" and generally produces no surprises, with one exception: the hero dies at the end.

It's the story of a gunfighting sheriff, Minnesota Clay (Cameron Mitchell) who is determined to "clean up" the town, ASAP. His zeal is intensified because he's slowly going blind. The Corbucci staff consisted of scriptwriter Adriano Bolzoni, chief cameraman José Fernandez Aguayo, and musical composer Piero Piccioni. After making this film, Sergio Corbucci (with his brother Bruno) directed a "Franco and Ciccio" comedy called *Figli del Leopardo* and an Italian-French horror production, *The Man Who Laughs* (a remake of the German film with Conrad Veidt from 1922), before returning to the Eurowestern genre in 1966 with *Johnny Oro* (also called *Ringo and His Golden Pistol*).

Minute to Pray, a Second to Die (1967)

Escondido Sp; *Dead or Alive; Minuto per Pregare, un Istante per Morire* Ital. *Director:* Franco Giraldi; *Script:* Ugo Liberatore/Albert Band; *Camera:* Ajace Parolini; *Music:* Carlo Rustichelli; *Producer:* Albert Band, Documento Film (Italy). *Cast:* Robert Ryan, Alex Cord, Arthur Kennedy, Mario Brega, Nicoletta Machiavelli, Spean Covery, Renato Romano, Aldo Sambrell, José M. Martin, Daniel Martin, Enzo Fiermonte, Alberto Dell'Acqua.

A scene from *Minnesota Clay* (1965) with Cameron Mitchell and Diana Martin.

An outlaw who suffers from paralytic seizures, Clay McCord (Alex Cord), attempts to turn himself in, but discovers that Governor Lem Carter (Robert Ryan) has already granted him amnesty. However, there's vengeful sheriff Roy Colby (a tailor-made Arthur Kennedy role) who still holds a grudge and sets out to kill him.

Produced and cowritten by Albert Band (who also directed a few Spaghetti Westerns, *The Tramplers* in 1966, and *Massacre at the Grand Canyon* with Sergio Corbucci in 1963); the film features a memorable (if not overblown) musical score by Carl Rustic (pseudonym for Carlo Rustichelli). The chief cameraman is Ajace Parolin.

Scriptwriter Ugo Liberatore went on to write and direct many offbeat sex/exploitation films (i.e., *Borabora, Sex with the Angels,* and *Bali* with Laura Antonelli).

Minuto per Pregare, un Istante per Morire see *Minute to Pray, a Second to Die*

Il Mio Corpo per un Poker see *Belle Starr Story*

Il Mio Nome È Mallory . . . "M" Come Morte see *Mallory Must Not Die*

Il Mio Nome È Nessuno see *My Name Is Nobody*

Il Mio Nome È Pecos see *My Name Is Pecos*

Il Mio Nome È Scopone e Faccio Sempre Cappotto see *Dallas*

A heavyweight (Mario Brega) in *Minute to Pray, a Second to Die* (1967).

Il Mio Nome È Shanghai Joe see *Fighting Fists of Shanghai Joe*

Miss Dynamite (1972)

Where the Bullets Fly; All the Brothers of the West Support Their Father; Tutti Fratelli nel West . . . per Parte di Padre Ital. *Director:* Sergio Grieco; *Script:* Romano Migliorini/Sergio Grieco; *Camera:* Aldo De Robertis; *Music:* Riz Ortolani; *Producer:* DC7 (Italy/France). *Cast:* Antonio Sabàto, Fernando Sancho, Lionel Stander, Marisa Mell, Peter Carsten, Franco Pesce.

A seldom seen Spaghetti Western from director Grieco, best known for his historical exploitation films, especially *Nights of Lucretia Borgia* with Belinda Lee (1960).

The Moment to Kill (1968)

Il Momente di Uccidere Ital. *Director:* Anthony Ascott; *Script:* Tito Carpi/Franco Scardamaglia/Bruno Leder/Enzo G. Castellari; *Camera:* Stelvio Massi; *Music:* Francesco De Masi; *Producer:* Vico Pavoni, P.C.E./Terra Filmkunst (Italy/ West Germany). *Cast:* George Hilton, Walter Barnes, Horst Frank, Giorgio Sanmartino, Loni von Friedl, Renato Romano, Carlo Alighiero, Rudolf Schündler.

Here's another genre Western lensed by future cult director Stelvio Massi (also see *Fifteen Scaffolds for the Killer, I'll Sell My Skin Dearly* and *Price of Power*).

It's an effective "double-cross" movie, a favorite theme of director Anthony

Ascott (Giuliano Carmineo), involving two notorious gunmen, Lord and Bull (George Hilton and Walter Barnes), and their search for a hidden $500,000 Confederate gold treasure. Their hunt is muddled by a rich and powerful land baron named Forester (Carlo Alighiero) who is also after the prize. Plus there's the mysterious involvement of a paralyzed girl, Regina (Loni von Friedl), who has the only clue: a perplexing book of poetry.

Incidentally, for the German version, the name of Hilton's character was changed from "Lord" to "Django" in the dubbing, and the movie was peddled as *Django . . . Ein Sarg voll Blut (Django . . . It's Time to Kill)*.

Director Ascott is the number one most prolific Spaghetti Western director with 13 films to his credit (see Directors filmography), but he also directed some unusual horror films, including *Rat Man, Exterminators of the Year 2000,* and *What Are Those Strange Drops of Blood Doing on the Body of Jennifer?*

Il Momente di Uccidere see *Moment to Kill*

Monta in Sella, Figlio di . . . see *Great Treasure Hunt*

Montana Trap (1976)

Potato Fritz Ger. *Director:* Peter Schamoni; *Script:* Paul Hengge; *Camera:* Wolf Worth; *Music:* Anton Dvorak/Udo Jurgens; *Producer:* Produktion Filmverlag (West Germany). *Cast:* Hardy Kruger, Stephen Boyd, Anton Diffring, Friedrich Von Ledebur, David Hess, Arthur Brauss, Luis Barboo, Diana Korner.

This is the only Spaghetti Western to star popular cult actor Anton Diffring, best known for his lead roles in *Circus of Horror* (1960), *Fahrenheit 451* (1967) and Hammer's classy remake of *Man in Half Moon Street* called *Man Who Could Cheat Death* (1959), plus countless "German officer" parts including one in *Where Eagles Dare* (1969). It also stars David Hess (from *Last House on the Left*) in his only genre outing.

Unfortunately, this is a rather lame, German-produced comedy/western chronicling the adventures of Potato Fritz (Hardy Kruger) and his buddy Bill Addison (Stephen Boyd). When they find themselves in the middle of an Indian attack, Potato Fritz and Bill take refuge at Fort Benton where they meet disciplinarian Lieutenant Slade (Anton Diffring). It's sort of like *Trinity* meets *Hogan's Heroes.*

More Dollars for the MacGregors (1970)

Few More Dollars for the MacGregors; Ancora Dollari per i MacGregor Ital. *Director:* J. L. Merino (José Luis Merino); *Script:* José Luis Merino/Arrigo Colombo; *Camera:* Emanuele D. Cola; *Music:* Augusto Martelli; *Producer:* Prodimex Film/Hispames (Italy/Spain). *Cast:* Peter Lee Lawrence, George Forsyte, Stan Cooper, Malisa Longo, José Jaspe, Charles Quiney, Luis Marin, Mariano Vidal Molina.

Interestingly, the Spanish version of this film is called *More Dollars for Cjamango (Mas Dólares para Cjamango)*, representing some demented drive to keep the "Cjamango" legend alive, at least in Spain.

A gang of outlaws led by Ross Stewart (Stan Cooper) kills Gladys MacGregor, a bounty hunter's girlfriend. The bounty hunter (George Forsyte) and a mysterious stranger named Blondie (Peter Lee Lawrence) team together to eliminate the bandidos. After the massive (and ultimately successful) battle, the two "partners" face each other in a showdown because the blond stranger is really Robert Macgregor, and he blames his sister Gladys' death on the bounty hunter's negligence.

There is also a subplot about a beautiful Indian witch (Malisa Longo) who befriends and eventually makes love to Blondie. However, the segment has no bearing on the primary story.

Despite the "MacGregor" moniker in the title, this movie has nothing to do with the earlier *Seven Guns for the MacGregors* or *Up the MacGregors*. Furthermore, neither Gladys nor Robert MacGregor ever receive any dollars at all, let alone "more dollars."

La Morte Non Conta i Dollari see *Death at Owell Rock*

La Morte sull'Alta Collina see *Death on High Mountain*

I Morti Non Si Contano (1) see *Cry for Revenge*

I Morti Non Si Contano (2) see *Dead Are Countless*

Muerte de un Presidente see *Price of Power*

Murieta (1963)

Vendetta; Joaquin Murieta Ital. *Director:* George Sherman; *Script:* James O'Hanlon; *Camera:* Miguel F. Mila; *Music:* Antonio Perez Olea; *Production:* Warner Bros. (Spain/U.S.) *Cast:* Jeffrey Hunter, Arthur Kennedy, Diana Lorys, Sara Lezana, Roberto Camardiel, Frank Braña, Pedro Osinaga.

Veteran U.S. filmmaker George Sherman made over 100 movies between 1938 *(Wild Horse Rodeo)* and 1971 *(Big Jake* with John Wayne). Mostly, he functioned as an "in house" director for Republic films (1938–1944) or for Universal Studios (1948–1960); this film remains his only foreign production, financed by Warner Bros. of Spain.

Joaquin Murieta (Jeffrey Hunter) and his wife Rosita (Sara Lezana) immigrate to California in 1849 with dreams of getting rich in the Gold Rush. Instead, one day, Rosita is beaten, raped and murdered by three miners. Murieta goes insane with rage. He and a soldier friend, Captain Lowe (Arthur Kennedy) begin raiding mining camps in search of the murderers. The raids become more intense each time until, finally, they escalate into senseless bloodshed. Murieta is completely demented, and Captain Lowe is forced to kill him.

Mutiny at Fort Sharp (1966)

Per un Dollaro di Gloria Ital. *Director:* Fernando Cerchio; *Script:* Ugo Liberatore/Fernando Cerchio; *Camera:* Emilio Foriscot; *Music:* Carlo Savina; *Producer:* Procusa/C.E.P.C. (Italy/Spain). *Cast:* Broderick Crawford, Elisa Montes, Mario Valdemarin, Umberto Ceriani, Hugo Arden, Julio Peña.

Like many other Spaghetti Western directors, Fernando Cerchio graduated from the "school of peplums." He was responsible for ten sword-'n'-

sandal movies between 1957 and 1963, including *Anthony and Cleopatra* (1963), *Land of the Pharaohs* (1960), and *Queen of the Nile* (1961). His Western output wasn't as prolific; this film and and *Death on High Mountain* (1969) are his lone entries.

In 1864, French troops accidentally cross into Confederate territory in Texas. They are forced to join the Rebels at Fort Sharp who are busily preparing for a massive Indian attack. But soon the French soldiers begin to question the authenticity of the threat. Is it all a delusion of the commandant, Colonel Lennox (Broderick Crawford)?

My Colt Is the Law see Colt Is the Law

My Colt, Not Yours (1972)

Four Candles for Garringo; La Mia Colt Ti Cerca . . . Quattro Ceri Ti Attendono Ital; *Quatre Salopards pour Carringo*. *Director:* Steve McCohy; *Script:* Steve McCohy/Jackie Kelly; *Camera:* Antonio L. Ballesteros; *Music:* Enrique Escobar; *Producer:* Julia De La Fuente (Spain/France/Italy). *Cast:* Robert Woods, Olga Omar, Vidal Molina, Cris Huerta, Maria Martin, Molino Rojo.

There's lots of action when Sheriff Garingo (Robert Woods) butts heads with the owner of the Star Saloon, town boss Jefferson (Cris Huerta), who is running the city with mafia-like control.

Woods gives an amazingly animated performance (even more out-of-control than the one in *Blackjack*), constantly touching or hitting everything and everybody. He has a crazed semblance, as if he might start tearing apart the scenery at any moment, without notice. A very strange sheriff.

This shot-on-a-shoestring Western comes from prolific director Ignacio F. Iquino, this time using his "Steve McCohy" alias. Other known Iquino pseudonyms include John Wood (and the Spanish variation, Juan Bosch), plus Pedro Ramiriz and Juan Xiol Marchel (see Directors filmography). Iquino is best known for his Spaghetti Westerns, but he also dabbled in exploitation (usually under the Bosch alias) and horror, especially with an over-the-top zombie/satanism sex flick, *Sinister Sect*, directed under the name Ignasi P. Ferre Serra.

My Horse, My Gun, Your Widow (1972)

Domani, Passo a Salutare la Tua Vedova . . . Parola di Epidemia Ital. *Director:* John Wood; *Script:* Juan Bosch/Sauro Scavolini; *Camera:* Giorgio Tonti; *Music:* Bruno Nicolai; *Producer:* Lea Film/C.C. Astro (Italy/Spain). *Cast:* Craig Hill, Claudie Lange, Chris Huerta, Luis Induñi, Pedro Sanchez, Carlo Gaddi.

The movie doesn't live up to its exploitive title, instead it's a rather charming tale of camaraderie and deception from director Ignacio Iquino (a.k.a. John Wood).

Craig Hill is Dr. Janos Saxon. In the film's first ten minutes, Doc and his partners break into, and rob, the Crown City security bank. But he is double-crossed by Grasco (Cris Huerta) who, with his own gang, takes the money and leaves him with nothing. Doc Saxon, accompanied by Donovan (Claudie Lange), spends the rest of the movie trying to steal back the stolen money. Eventually he succeeds. But there's an unexpected twist. Donovan has plans of his own, and Doc isn't included.

The soundtrack, interestingly, isn't an original Bruno Nicolai composition. It's the same musical score (including the wonderfully campy "If You Gotta Shoot Someone . . . Bang! Bang!" theme song) originally used for Sergio Martino's *Arizona* (1970).

Coincidentally, the set designer for this film is Michele Massimo Tarantino, long-time associate and cowriter with Sergio Martino (for *Dishonor with Honor*, *Sexy Relations*, *Sex with a Smile*) who also went on to direct many sex scorchers including *The License* with Gloria Guida, *The Policewoman* with Edwige Fenech, and *Women in Fury*, an intense girls-in-the-slammer flick.

My Name Is Mallory . . . M Means Death see *Mallory Must Not Die*

My Name Is Nobody (1973)

Il Mio Nome È Nessuno Ital. *Director:* Tonino Valerii; *Script:* Fulvio Morsella/ Ernesto Gastaldi; *Camera:* Giuseppe Ruzzolini/Armando Nannuzzi; *Music:* Ennio Morricone; *Producer:* Claudio Mancini, Titanus (Italy). *Cast:* Terence Hill, Henry Fonda, Leo Gordon, Geoffrey Lewis, R. G. Armstrong, Piero Lulli.

Exactly how much "hands on" direction came from Sergio Leone, and how much came from Tonino Valerii, has been the subject of frenzied controversy over the years. Some reports claim that Leone directed all the major scenes, but more reliable sources insist that he only did the opening sequence. It's a situation reminiscent of the American *Poltergeist* ballyhoo (was producer Steven Spielberg secretly directing, usurping Tobe Hooper's jurisdiction?).

Some critics irritatingly refer to *My Name Is Nobody* as a "Leone" movie, totally ignoring competent filmmaker Tonino Valerii (whose projects include the highly successful *Day of Anger* and *Price of Power*). Suffice it to say, the opening cedits read "Sergio Leone Presents . . . a Tonino Valerii film; based on an idea by Sergio Leone, directed by Tonino Valerii."

Regardless, this coadventure is a delightful spoof of the Spaghetti Western films (aided by an equally outrageous campy score from Ennio Morricone) telling the story of a cowboy groupie named Nobody (Terence Hill) who worships old-timer Beauregarde (Henry Fonda), a gunfighter with one goal, just to go away (to Europe, preferably) and retire.

In an ironic ending, he gets his wish. And, at the same time, Nobody becomes a "somebody."

My Name Is Pecos (1966)

Il Mio Nome È Pecos Ital; *Due Once di Piombo* Ital. *Director:* Maurice A. Bright; *Script:* Maurizio Lucidi/Adriano Bolzoni; *Camera:* Franco Villa; *Music:* Lallo Gori; *Producer:* Franco Palombi, Italcine (Italy). *Cast:* Robert Woods, Lucia Modugno, Peter Carsten, Chistiana Josani, Peter Kapp, Max Dean, Louis Cassel.

Anglo Robert Woods plays a Mexican named Pecos in this "revenge for a slaughtered family" story. Town boss Joe Kline (Peter Carsten) killed Pecos' parents. So, for the length of the film, the avenger tracks down the sadistic murderer, leaving a trail of bodies (which are collected by an overly enthusiastic gravedigger). There's also an underdeveloped (and seemingly meaningless) subplot about missing money from a bank robbery.

Former editor Maurizio Lucidi keeps the action rough and tough, similar to his nongenre films (i.e., *Street People*, a mafia kill-fest with Roger Moore and Stacy Keach). George Eastman also appears in an uncredited cameo. The sequel, *Pecos Cleans Up* (also starring Woods), goes for laughs and comes up empty-handed, and empty-headed.

My Name Is Shanghai Joe see *Fighting Fists of Shanghai Joe*

Nato per Uccidere see *Born to Kill*

Navajo Joe (1966)

A Dollar a Head; Un Dollaro a Testa Ital. *Director:* Sergio Corbucci; *Script:* Mario Pierotti/Fernando Di Leo; *Camera:* Silvano Ippoliti; *Music:* Leo Nichols; *Producer:* Ermanno Donati/Luigi Carpentieri, Dino De Laurentiis Productions (Italy/Spain). *Cast:* Burt Reynolds, Aldo Sambrell, Nicoleta Machiavelli, Simon Arraga, Fernando Rey, Tanya Lopert, Cris Huerta, Franca Polesello, Peter Cross, Lucia Modugno.

Navajo Joe (Burt Reynolds) is the lone survivor of a massacre inflicted on his Indian tribe. He swears (and gets) revenge in this fun-to-watch adventure. Joe tricks the racist townspeople of Esperanza into paying him one dollar for "every scalp he removes" from the heads of a threatening band of outlaws, led by Marvin Duncan (Aldo Sambrell). It's the same group of killers who destroyed his village and killed his family, so he's getting paid (and sanctioned) to eliminate an enemy that he would have destroyed for free. Thus, the Italian title *Un Dollaro a Testa (A Dollar Per Head)*.

There's a rousing musical score by Ennio Morricone (one of his best) under the curious pseudonym Leo Nichols. Cowritten by Mario Pierotti (based on his book) with future action director Fernando Di Leo, this is Sergio Corbucci's fifth Western, following *Django* and *Hellbenders*, preceding *The Great Silence*.

Nebraska il Pistolero see *Savange Gringo*

Ned Kelly (1970)

Ned Kelly: Outlaw Brit. *Director:* Tony Richardson; *Script:* Tony Richardson/ Ian Jones; *Camera:* Gerry Fisher; *Music:* Shel Silverstein and Waylon Jennings; *Producer:* Neil Hartley, Woodfall (England). *Cast:* Mick Jagger, Allen Bickford, Geoff Gilmour, Serge Lazareff, Clarissa Kaye.

This British-Australian coproduction is included in this book because, even though the motif isn't the American West (similar to the *Magnificent Bandits* and *Savange Pampas* entries), the theme, costuming, and characterization so resembles a Eurowestern that inclusion seems appropriate.

Unfortunately, however, the film is a tedious, tiresome bore. It's a long and talky trek through the Australian backlands following the "misunderstood" outlaw Ned Kelly (Mick Jagger) and his hapless gang of bandidos. Director Tony Richardson (*Tom Jones, The Loved One, Taste of Honey,* etc.) totally misses

Movie poster from *Navajo Joe* (1966).

the point as he frustrates the audience with countless scenes of posturing and bravado, but refuses to deliver on the action.

Of special interest, most of the songs on the fresh soundtrack are sung by American country singer Waylon Jennings, and Mick Jagger sings the title theme, *The Wild Colonial Boy.* However, for a much better bushranger film see *Mad Dog Morgan* with Dennis Hopper.

Ned Kelly: Outlaw see *Ned Kelly*

Nephews of Zorro (1969)

I Nipoti di Zorro Ital. *Director:* Frank Reed; *Script:* Marcello Ciorciolini/Roberto Gianviti; *Camera:* Clemente Santoni; *Music:* Piero Umiliani; *Producer:* Gino Mordini/Claudia/Te. Fi. (Italy). *Cast:* Franco Franchi, Ciccio Ingrassia, Dean Reed, Agata Flori, Pedro Sanchez, Ivano Staccioli.

A sequel (in name only) to "Franco and Ciccio's" *Grandsons of Zorro* (1968). This time, Franco and Ciccio are attracted to California by gold fever. They reach the village of Las Palmas where Zorro is famous for his acts of heroism against the evil garrison captain, Martinez (Pedro Sanchez). When they meet wealthy Don Dieego (Ivano Staccioli) and ask him for a loan, little do they know that he used to be the famous Zorro. His son Raphael (Dean Reed) is secretly Zorro now, and he is in love with the town beauty, Carmencita (Agata Flori).

When Franco and Ciccio see Carmencita, they go wild. Trying to bed the girl, they fib to her, claiming to be Zorro. Captain Martinez overhears the confession and he condemns them to the gallows. The real Zorro rescues the two bozos just as they are about to be hanged, and then (with a crack of his whip) runs them out of town.

Director Marcello Ciorciolini (alias Frank Reed) also directed the Franco and Ciccio Western *Ciccio Forgives . . . I Don't.* Other Spaghetti Weterns starring the Italian comedy team are: *Grandsons of Zorro; Two Gangsters in the West; Two Sergeants of General Custer; Two Sons of Ringo; Two Sons of Trinity; Handsome, the Ugly, and the Stupid; For a Fist in the Eye; Paths of War;* and *Two R-R-Ringos from Texas.*

Nevada Kid see *Showdown for a Badman*

Night of the Serpent (1969)

Notte del Serpente Ital. *Director:* Giulio Petroni; *Script:* Giulio Petroni/Fulvio Gicca; *Camera:* Mario Vulpiani/Silvio Fraschetti; *Music:* Ennio Morricone; *Producer:* Ascot/Cineraid/Madison (Italy). *Cast:* Luke Askew, Luigi Pistilli, Magda Konopka, Chelo Alonso, William Bogart, Franco Balducci, Giancarlo Badessi.

The "Serpent" is a notorious bandit (Luigi Pistilli) who wreaks havoc on Silver City when, after attempting a bank robbery, he and his gang are trapped inside a saloon. The plot synopsis sounds similar to that of *Adios Hombre* (1966), but the film remains a seldom seen, lost-in-the-shuffle Western by popular filmmaker Giulio *(Death Rides a Horse)* Petroni.

Ninguno de los Tres se Llamaba Trinidad see *None of the Three Were Called Trinity*

I Nipoti di Zorro see *Nephews of Zorro*

No Graves on Boot Hill (1968)

Three Crosses of Death; Three Crosses Not to Die; Tre Croci per non Morire Ital. *Director:* Willy S. Regan; *Script:* Sergio Garrone/Luigi Cobianchi; *Camera:*

Sandro Mancori; *Music:* Mancuso & Vasco; *Producer:* G.V. Film (Italy). *Cast:* Craig Hill, Ken Wood, Evelyn Stewart, Peter White, Maria Angela Giordano, Jean Louis.

Watching a Sergio Garrone (alias Willy S. Regan) film is especially enjoyable due to his meticulous pacing and finely crafted camerawork (usually provided by Sandro Mancori), and (while not as good as *Django the Bastard* or *Vendetta at Dawn*) this one is still a treat.

The story is a *Dirty Dozen* clone. A priest (Peter White) recruits the help of three jailed criminals, a casanova rogue named Jerry (Craig Hill), a Mexican petty thief Paco (Jean Louis), and a shady bounty hunter, Reno (Ken Wood). He wants them to save an innocent boy from the gallows by finding the truly guilty culprit. Lots of action, short on story.

For his Westerns, Garrone usually signed the "Willy S. Regan" pseudonym (*Django the Bastard* is the only exception). His horror and exploitation films are signed with his real name (see *Slave of the Monster* and *Hand of the Living Dead*, both starring Klaus Kinski, plus *S. S. Extermination Camp, Girls in Hell* [also called *Hell Behind Bars*], *S. S. Camp 5,* and *Hell Penitentiary*). Sergio Garrone, sadly, retired from filmmaking in 1989 to open a chain of pizza restaurants in Italy.

No Killing Without Dollars see *Death at Owell Rock*

No Room to Die (1969)

Noose for Django; A Hanging for Django; Una Lunga Fila di Croci Ital; *Una Horca para Django* Sp. *Director:* Willy S. Regan; *Script:* Sergio Garrone; *Camera:* Franco Villa/Aristide Massaccesi; *Music:* Vasco and Mancuso; *Producer:* Gabriele Crisanti, Junior Film (Italy). *Cast:* Anthony Steffen, William Berger, Mario Brega, Riccardo Garrone, Nicoletta Machiavelli, Maria Angela Giordano.

The relationship between Sergio Garrone (alias Willy S. Regan) and his chief cameraman, Sandro Mancori, has created many highly enjoyable genre Westerns. Unfortunately, when Garrone shot this film, Mancori was already involved in an over-deadline Gianfranco Parolini project, *Sabata*. And so, (normally competent) Franco Villa was tapped for the primary photography. As it turned out, Garrone, reportedly unhappy with his choice, hired the reputable Aristide Massaccesi (future Joe D'Amato) to act as "chief cameraman" with orders to secretly reshoot many scenes.

The result is a surprisingly enjoyable film about the delicate partnership between two bounty hunters, the stoic Django/Brandon (Anthony Steffen) and bible-thumping preacher Everett Murdoch (William Berger in an inspired role), as they try to stop Fargo (Riccardo Garrone, Sergio's brother) from smuggling Mexican peasants across the border and selling them as slaves.

There's even a surprise ending, in which Brandon discovers that Preacher Murdoch has been in cahoots with Fargo. This information leads to a final and victorious (for Brandon, anyway) showdown.

Nobody Is the Greatest see *Genius*

Non Aspettare, Django ... Spara! see *Don't Wait, Django ... Shoot!*

Non Toccate la Donna Bianca see *Do Not Touch the White Woman*

None of the Three Were Called Trinity (1974)

Ninguno de los Tres se Llamaba Trinidad Sp. *Director:* Pedro L. Ramirez; *Script:* Ignacio Iquino/Jakie Kelly; *Camera:* Antonio Ballesteros; *Music:* Enrique Escobar; *Producer:* Julia de la Fuente (Spain). *Cast:* Danny Martin, Fanny Grey, Margit Kocsis, Cris Huerta, Ricardo Palacios, Tito Garcia, Gustavo Re.

Finally a truthful title! After bogus for-the-bucks ripoffs (i.e., *Ringo: Face of Revenge, Let's Go Kill Sartana,* and festival of *Django* deceptions), director Ignacio Iquino (alias Pedro L. Ramirez) delivers the goods with one of the best, unequivocally most straightforward (plus humorous) titles of all the Spaghetti Westerns.

Regrettably, the story isn't as good. Jim (Danny Martin) is mistaken for a bank robber and he must prove his innocence to a dimwitted sheriff (Cris Huerta) before he can continue the trek after his dishonest cousins (Gustavo Re, Ricardo Palacios, and Tito Garcia) to regain money they stole from him.

Incidentally, lead actor Danny Martin is best known as the noble Indian, Luncas, in *Last Tomahawk* (1965) and *Last of the Mohicans* (1965), loosely based on the writings of James Fenimore Cooper.

Noose for Django see *No Room to Die*

Not Sabata or Trinity ... It's Sartana see *Dig Your Grave, Friend ... Sabata's Coming*

La Notte del Desperado see *Ringo's Big Night*

Notte del Serpente see *Night of the Serpent*

Now They Call Him Amen see *Desperado*

Nude Django (1968)

Django Nudo und die lusternen Mädchen von Porno Hill Ger. *Director:* Ron Elliot; *Script:* Ron Elliot; *Camera:* Andreas Demmer; *Music:* Peter Graf/Walter Baumgartner; *Producer:* A.B.&B./Urania Film (Germany). *Cast:* Peter Graf, Donna West, Steve Allen, Edgar Wertz, Lynn Hall.

Django (Peter Graf) is a bondage freak in this lurid "soft-core" sex Western from Germany. He tantalizes a dance hall girl, Lilly Brown (Donna West), with promises of "sharing his inherited gold mine" if she willingly submits to his sadistic fetishes. But, in the end, she only gets the shaft.

Una Nuvola di Polvere ... un Grido di Morte, Arriva Sartana see *Light the Fuse ... Sartana Is Coming*

Oath of Zorro see *Behind the Mask of Zorro*

Ocaso de un Pistolero see *Hands of a Gunman*

Occhio alla Penna see *Buddy Goes West*

Occhio per Occhio, Dente per Dente . . . see *Eye for an Eye*

Odia il Prossimo Tuo see *Hate Thy Neighbor*

L'Odio è il Mio, Dio see *Hatred of God*

Odio per Odio see *Hate for Hate*

Oggi a Me . . . *Domani a Te* see *Today It's Me, Tomorrow You*

Ognuno per Se see *The Ruthless Four*

Old Shatterhand see *Apache's Last Battle*

Old Surehand 1. Teil see *Flaming Frontier*

Der Ölprinz see *Rampage at Apache Wells*

L'Ombra di Zorro see *Shadow of Zorro*

On the Third Day Arrived the Crow (1972)

Arriva! Il Crow Ital. *Director:* Gianni Crea; *Script:* Mino Roli; *Camera:* Franco Villa/Gianni Raffaldi; *Music:* Nora Orlandi; *Producer:* Maurizio Mannoia (Italy/ Spain). *Cast:* Lincoln Tate, William Berger, Dean Stratford, Florella Mannoia, Lorenzo Fineschi, Richard Melvill, Lars Block.

"And what do you three do for an occupation?" the sheriff asks.

"You might say we're trouble shooters," pretty Sally (Florella Mannoia) replies. "Me and my two brothers help people who are in the right. But sometimes we get into trouble ourselves."

Specifically, Sally and her brothers, Link (Lincoln Tate) and Tornado (Lorenzo Fineschi), are very much like private detectives. And, here, they step into (and out of) one problem after another as they investigate the disappearance of a gold shipment from the Lawson Mining Company. It turns out that the robbery was faked; owner Lawson had pilfered the fortune. When the truth becomes apparent, he hires a notorious gunman named "The Crow" (William Berger) to eliminate the snoopers.

Tornado is killed. Then Link retaliates, shooting both Lawson and "The Crow." Unfortunately for director Gianni Crea, even though the villains have been wiped out and the gold is safely returned, at this point the film has only been running for about an hour. In a remarkably bold move, a new bad guy is introduced! The Crow's brother (also played by William Berger) comes to town looking for revenge. Instead, he "meets his maker" (after much posturing) in a fateful showdown with Link.

Once again, Gianni Crea's direction is disjointed and illogical (also see his other notorious nonmovies, *Finders Killers* and *Magnificent West*), but this time it's masked by the tasty Franco Villa cinematography.

Henry Fonda (left) and Charles Bronson in Sergio Leone's *Once Upon a Time in the West* (1968).

Once Upon a Time in the West (1968)

C'era una Volta il West Ital; *Play Me the Song of Death* Brit. *Director:* Sergio Leone; *Script:* Bernardo Bertolucci/Dario Argento/Sergio Leone; *Camera:* Tonino Delli Colli; *Music:* Ennio Morricone; *Producer:* Fulvio Morsella, Rafran/ Euro International (Italy). *Cast:* Henry Fonda, Claudia Cardinale, Charles Bronson, Jason Robards, Frank Wolff, Gabriele Ferzetti, Paolo Stoppa, Robert Hossein, Jack Elam, Woody Strode, Aldo Sambrell, Fabio Testi, Lionel Stander, Keenan Wynn, Al Mulock, Spartaco Conversi.

Sergio Leone's most ambitious and most acclaimed film, considered by many critics as the greatest of the Spaghetti Westerns, is certainly memorable for its spectacular cast (a virtual who's who) highlighted by Henry Fonda's incongruously villainous role. This is a bigger-than-life, sprawling tale about the advent of the railroad (i.e., the taming of the West) and four unforgettable characters, Frank (Henry Fonda), Jill (Claudia Cardinale), Harmonica (Charles Bronson) and Cheyenne (Jason Robards), each dealing with their personal quests for power.

Written by the diverse (yet oddly harmonious) triumvirate of Sergio Leone (see *Fistful of Dollars, For a Few Dollars More* and *The Good, the Bad, and the Ugly*) with Bernardo Bertolucci (award winning director of *The Last Emperor* and *Last Tango in Paris*) plus Dario Argento (acclaimed horror filmmaker responsible for *Opera, Bird with the Crystal Plumage, Suspiria,* and the *Demon* films), this expansive story begins as Frank (Henry Fonda) viciously slaughters a peaceful pioneering family, Brett McBain (Frank Wolff) and his three children.

Frank is working on orders from the Union Pacific Railroad to "eliminate" any and all obstacles between the oncoming train and the Pacific Ocean. With the death of the McBain family, it's believed that the railroad will have a clear path west, that is, until secret former-prostitute-cum-wife Jill (Claudia Cardinale) arrives from New Orleans, claiming legal ownership of the land. She forms a tenuous relationship with a likable rapscallion, Cheyenne (Jason Robards), and a mysterious stranger, Harmonica (Charles Bronson), against Frank and the railroad.

The "Only at the Point of Death" finale remains one of the all-time great moments in film history (in tandem with "Ecstasy of Gold" in *The Good, the Bad and the Ugly* and the "Hunt in the Cane Field" segment from *The Big Gundown*).

This epic film is an astonishing 168 minutes in length, originally cut to 144 minutes for most of its American theatrical run. The restored, full-length version is currently available on video in the United States (from Paramount Home Video).

Once Upon a Time in the Wild, Wild West (1969)

C'era una Volta questo Pazzo Pazzo West Ital. *Director:* Enzo Matassi; *Script:* Carlo Baltieri; *Camera:* Ugo Brunelli; *Music:* Francesco Santucci; *Producer:* Giuseppe Frontano. *Cast:* Gordon Mitchell, Vincent Scott, Dennis Colt, Malisa Longo, Lucky McMurray, Fiorella Magaloti, Dada Gallotti.

Easily the worst Spaghetti Western ever made. Yes, more dreadful than *any* "Franco and Ciccio" film; more obnoxious than *Patience Has a Limit, We Don't;* more repugnant than *Rita of the West;* more hideous than *Bad Kids of the West;* more tedious than *Cipolla Colt.*

Two constantly quarreling brothers, Joe and Enzo (Dennis Colt and Lucky McMurray) are living in a shack-type barn, sharing the space with cows, a retarded father and an obscenely obese mother. Enough is enough. They decide to move to Carson City, where their cousin Bill (Gordon Mitchell) lives.

Carson City is a town at war with itself. Two bullies, cousin Bill and Blackie (Vincent Scott) are both trying to take over. Clearly, Bill has the advantage because, due to some genetic imbalance in his system, he is indestructible. There are countless sight gags showing "the bad guys" beating on him, but the blows have no effect.

The production (which looks like it was shot on Super 8mm film) is filled with sophomoric (moronic) humor (i.e., looking up dresses, and three prostitutes-sharing-the-same-room jokes). Abysmal.

There is some evidence that director Enzo Matassi may be another alias for Demofilo Fidani (a.k.a. Miles Deem). Say it isn't so . . .

One After Another (1968)

Uno dopo l'Altro Ital; *Day After Tomorrow. Director:* Nick Howard; *Script:* Carlos Rodriguez/Nick Howard/Simon O'Neill; *Camera:* Mario Pacheco De

Usa; *Music:* Fred Bongusto; *Producer:* Nuñez De Balboa, Midega/Atlantica Film (Spain/Italy). *Cast:* Richard Harrison, Pamela Tudor, Paul Stevens, José Bodaló, Jolanda Modio, José Jaspe, José M. Martin, Hugo Blanco, Luis Barboo.

This Italian-Spanish production has little to offer. The characterizations are wafer thin, and the script is a carbon copy of Al Bradly's 1967 entry *Killer Calibre .32.*

The Canyon City bank has been robbed and everyone, except owner Jefferson (Paul Stevens), is killed. A mysterious gunman named Sam (Richard Harrison) arrives in town to discover that his best friend had been murdered in the holdup. Sam is tricked into thinking that an outlaw named Espartero (José Bodaló) was responsible, but the real culprit is the banker Jefferson. Eventually Sam and Espartero team together against Jefferson and his bodyguards.

Filmmaker Nick Howard (pseudonym for Nick Nostro) made an earlier, equally predictable Western (*Dollar of Fire*, 1966). This was his last attempt in the genre. He is more fondly remembered for his *James Bond*–ish spy films (i.e., *Operation: Counterspy*) and his early peplums, especially *Spartacus and the Ten Gladiators* (1964).

Cowriter Simon O'Neill is director Giorgio Simonelli, survivor of numerous "Franco and Ciccio" films, including three of their Spaghetti Westerns.

One Against All see *Jesse James' Kid*

One Against One . . . No Mercy (1968)

One by One; Ad Uno ad Uno . . . Spietatamente Ital. *Director:* Rafael Romero Marchent; *Script:* Eduardo Maria Brochero/Tito Carpi; *Camera:* Emilio Foriscot; *Music:* Vasco and Mancuso; *Producer:* Norborto Solino, 21-Producciones (Spain/Italy). *Cast:* Peter Lee Lawrence, William Bogart, Dianik Zurakowska, Eduardo Fajardo, Alfonso Rojas, Aurora Battista, Sydney Chaplin, Paco Sanz, Cris Huerta, Miguel Del Castillo.

Peter Lee Lawrence, looking more and more like an effeminate Robert Mitchum, is Chico. William Bogart is his double-crossing partner, Grayson, in this proficient but vapid Rafael R. Marchent film. There's lots of deceiving and betraying, but Grayson is the real culprit. He tries to put the blame on town boss Jack Hawkins, even forces him to sign a bogus confession, but in the end Chico unravels the scheme and takes proper revenge.

One by One see *One Against One . . . No Mercy*

One Damned Day at Dawn . . . Django Meets Sartana (1971)

Quel Maledetto Giorno d'Inverno Django e Sartana . . . all'Ultimo Sangue Ital. *Director:* Miles Deem; *Script:* Demofilo Fidani/M. R. Vitelli Valenza; *Camera:* Franco Villa; *Music:* Coriolano Gori; *Producer:* Demofilo Fidani, Tarquinia Film (Italy). *Cast:* Hunt Powers, Fabio Testi, Dean Stratford, Dennis Colt, Lucky McMurray, Simone Blondell.

One of the better Miles Deem (Demofilo Fidani) films (remember, this is a relative statement) benefiting from good performances by Fabio Testi and Hunt Powers, plus creative camera work from Franco Villa, coupled with a rousing Coriolano Gori musical score.

The film opens with a townsman saying: "Welcome to Black City, stranger, welcome to Hell." The stranger replies, "Sounds kinda colorful." (?!?)

The man in black is the new sheriff, Jack Ronson (Fabio Testi), and very quickly he discovers that there's big trouble in Black City. Town boss Bud Wheeler (Dean Stratford) is in cahoots with a vicious Mexican outlaw, Sanchez (Dennis Colt), and Joe "the Worm" Smith (Lucky McMurray). They are using Black City as the headquarters for a very profitable gun trafficking racket. There's also a mysterious gunfighter, bounty hunter Django (Hunt Powers), silently watching all the activities. Eventually Django joins forces with Jack Ronson (secretly, he's Sartana) to eliminate all the bad guys in a 6:00 A.M. showdown. Thus, the title.

Over the years, Demofilo Fidani has employed the pseudonyms Dick Spitfire, Dennis Ford, Slim Alone, Lucky Dickerson, Alessandro Santini, Diego Spataro, Sean O'Neal, and (of course) Miles Deem. This loveable hack is responsible for directing 12 very special, cockeyed Spaghetti Westerns.

One for All see *All Out*

One Hundred Thousand Dollars for Lassiter see *Dollars for a Fast Gun*

One Hundred Thousand Dollars for Ringo (1966)

100.000 Dollari per Ringo Ital. *Director:* Alberto De Martino; *Script:* Giovanni Simonelli/Alberto De Martino/Vincenzo Flamini/Alfonso Balcazar; *Camera:* Eloy Mella/Federico Larraya; *Music:* Bruno Nicolai; *Producer:* Balcazar of Barcelona (Italy/Spain). *Cast:* Richard Harrison, Fernando Sancho, Luis Induñi, Gerard Tichy, Eleonora Bianchi, Lee Burton, Monica Randall.

The story is a familiar tale of a stranger (and secretly a Texas Ranger), Ringo (Richard Harrison), who arrives in a small Texas border town and tries to restore "law and order" between two warring factions, while everybody is in a frenzy over a buried treasure.

A relatively unknown film in the United States, yet this movie remains one of Richard Harrison's biggest international box office hits. It was helmed by Alberto De Martino, the director who made Harrison's very first Italian feature, *The Invincible Gladiator*, and it would also be their final collaboration.

One Hundred Thousand Dollars Per Killing see *For One Hundred Thousand Dollars Per Killing*

One Is Born a Swine see *If One Is Born a Swine*

One More to Hell see *To Hell and Back*

One Silver Dollar see *Blood for a Silver Dollar*

One Thousand Dollars on the Black see *Blood at Sundown* (1969)

Oremus, Alleluia e Così Sia see *They Still Call Me Amen*

L'Oro dei Bravados see *Gold of the Heroes*

Outlaw of Red River (1966)

Django the Honorable Killer (re-release title, 1968); *Django the Condemned; El Proscrito del Río Colorado* Sp; *Django Killer per l'Onore* Ital. *Director:* Maury Dexter; *Script:* Eduardo Brochero; *Camera:* Manuel Merino; *Music:* Manuel Parada; *Producer:* Arturo Margos/Eduardo Manzanos (Spain). *Cast:* George Montgomery, Elisa Montes, José Nieto, Miguel Castillo, Jesus Todesillas, Raf Baldessare, Anna Custodio, Ricardo Valle.

American filmmaker Maury Dexter began his career in 1960 (*High Powered Rifle*) as an "in-house" cheapie director for 20th Century–Fox. After making 15 movies in five years (his most popular features during this period were 1962's *The Day Mars Invaded the Earth* and *The Young Swingers* in 1963), Dexter's contract was canceled, the result of a severe austerity move by the financially troubled company in 1965. At the same time, actor George Montgomery was released from his 20th Century–Fox agreement, too. The two veterans went to Spain and made this Spaghetti Western for an "all Spanish" production company.

Reese O'Brien (George Montgomery) is a "wanted man" in Texas where he's been falsely accused of shooting his wife. Now, Reese is living in Mexico, acting as the right-hand man of powerful and refined General Miguel Camargo (José Nieto). Much of the film resembles an Hispanic soap opera: General Miguel is hesitatingly in love with beautiful and devious Francisca (Elisa Montez); she has a brother, Alfredo (Jesus Tordesillas) who is trying to bed the general's snotty daughter, Marta (Anna Custodio). Marta is always saying things like, "I don't have to take orders from a gringo" to Reese. There's also a subplot with an evil bandido, Espano (Riccardo Valle) who does his very best to look like Fernando Sancho.

After this project, George Montgomery wrote, directed and starred in *Satan's Harvest*, a surprisingly good jungle flick with Tippi Hedren and singer Matt Monro.

Maury Dexter returned to the United States and went to work for Roger Corman at American International, directing some of that company's most bizarre exploitation films, including two female biker movies, *The Mini-Skirt Mob* (1968) and *Hell's Belles* (1970), plus the 60s version of *Reefer Madness* called *Maryjane* (1968), a cult film with ex–pop singer Fabian as a high school art teacher who tries to keep his students from smoking grass.

Padella Calibro .38 see Calibre .38

Paid in Blood (1972)

Quelle Sporche Anime Dannate Ital. *Director:* Paolo Solvay; *Script:* Aldo Seone/Paolo Solvay; *Camera:* Giorgio Montagno; *Music:* Elio Mancuso; *Producer:* Gin Turini (Italy). *Cast:* Jeff Cameron, Donald O'Brien, Alfredo Rizzo, Krista Nell, Edilio Kim, William Mayor.

"Tramps who work in saloons all look alike," says Tom Carter (Jeff Cameron). But Tom soon finds out that Cora (Krista Nell) is different. His brother Jerry was planning to marry her, but after removing all his savings from the Rio Canyon bank, he was murdered and robbed by Ringo Brown (William Mayor). Tom mistakenly thinks that Cora is involved, but she proves her innocence by helping him find the true killer, and, also by exposing the town thug Lee Rastus (Donald O'Brien) who orchestrated the "hit."

There's a subplot about a prospector named Mule and his family. Because of a Lee Rastus land swindle, they are being pushed off their farm. Of course, Tom Carter finds time to protect them, giving this film a combination "standard revenge theme" with an additional "help the farmers against the Evil town boss" motif. Neither is very interesting.

Director Paolo Solvay (alias for Luigi Batzella) made the equally dull *Even Django Has His Price* and (as an actor, of sorts) he played the villain, Colorado Charlie, in the movie of the same name. Under the pseudonym "Dean Jones" he also directed a "loose remake" of this film called *God Is My Colt .45* in 1972.

Pampas Salvaje see Savage Pampas

Pancho Villa (1972)

Challenge of Pancho Villa Brit; *El Desafío de Pancho Villa* Sp. *Director:* Eugenio Martin; *Script:* Julian Halevy/Telly Savalas; *Camera:* Alejandro Ulloa; *Music:* Anton Garcia Abril; *Producer:* Bernard Gordon (Spain/England). *Cast:* Telly Savalas, Clint Walker, Chuck Connors, Anne Francis, Angel Del Pozo, José Maria Prada, Luis Dávila.

Chiefly, this one is remembered for the amazing two-trains-on-the-same-track collision which takes place at the film's conclusion; otherwise it's a rather slow retelling of the bandit-who-would-be-king, the "true" story of Pancho Villa (as interpreted by Telly Savalas with help from scriptwriter Julian Halevy). Together, they present the tale of Pancho Villa (Savalas) and his revolutionary gang who, after feeling betrayed in a bogus arms deal, cross the Mexican/American border and take possession of an Army outpost.

Although responsible for one of the best Spaghetti Westerns (*The Ugly Ones* [also called *Price of a Man*]) and one of the worst (*Bad Man's River*), Eugenio Martin is better known for his string of effective horror films, including *House on the Outskirts* (1980), *Sobrenatural* (1981), and *Horror Express* (1972).

Panhandle Calibre .38 see Calibre .38

Partirono Preti, Tornarono . . . Curati see Halleluja to Vera Cruz

La Parola di un Fuorilegge . . . È Legge! see *Take a Hard Ride*

I Pascoli Rossi see Massacre at Grand Canyon

Passa Sartana . . . È l'Ombra della Tua Morte see *Shadow of Sartana . . . Shadow of Death*

Paths of War (1969)

Sul Sentiero di Guerra Ital. *Director:* Gianni Grimaldi; *Camera:* Aldo Giordani; *Music:* Roberto Pregadio; *Producer:* Claudia/Te. Fi. (Italy). *Cast:* Franco Franchi, Ciccio Ingrassia, Bruno Scipioni, Dick Palmer, Spartaco Conversi.

Don't be fooled by the seemingly "serious" title. This is, in fact, another

"Franco and Ciccio" low-brow comedy Western, the second to be written and directed by Gianni Grimaldi (also see *The Handsome, the Ugly, and the Stupid* from 1967).

Obviously intended as a parody of *Red Badge of Courage*, Franco and Ciccio play two Confederate cooks separated from their unit in this episodic slapstick tale of cowardice during the Civil War. Cinematographer Aldo Giordani (who made his mark lensing the E. B. Clucher *Trinity* films) does remarkably well here, considering the ponderous task.

Patience Has a Limit, We Don't (1974)

La Pazienza Ha un Limite . . . Noi No Ital. *Director:* Armando Morandi; *Script:* Armando De Ossorio/Fabio Carboni; *Camera:* Alessandro Cariello/Miguel R. Mila; *Music:* Leonerbert; *Producer:* Gino Mordini, Clauda Cinematografica (Spain/Italy). *Cast:* Peter Martell, Sal Borgese, Rita Di Lernia, Pepe Ruiz, Ray Nolan, Peter Jacob, Carla Mancini.

This mess of a movie was written by (and unconfirmed sources claim, under the pseudonym Armando Morandi, directed by) Spanish cult filmmaker Armando de Ossorio (known especially for his *Blind Dead* horror series). Regardless, no director with any kind of career aspirations would want to take credit for this atrocity.

The movie makes the Franco and Ciccio entries look like "top drawer," which is no easy task. Here's a lame-brain Spanish/Italian comedy that finds Lt. McDonald (Ray Nolan) still a lieutenant after 20 years of service to the Union cavalry. Why? Because a $20,000 gold shipment was stolen by one of his men during the Indian wars and he is not eligible for a promotion until the treasure is recovered.

The original thief has since died, but his two idiot sons, Bill and Duke (Peter Martell and Sal Borgese) discover the secret map and (impaired by their inability to read) they wander aimlessly through the West in search of the gold. With Lt. McDonald on their rambling trail.

Payment in Blood (1968)

Winchester for Hire; Blake's Marauders (United States video title); *Sette Winchester per un Massacro* Ital. *Director:* E. G. Rowland; *Script:* Tito Carpi/Enzo Girolami; *Camera:* Aldo Pennelli; *Music:* Francesco De Masi; *Producer:* Francesco Orefici (Italy). *Cast:* Edd Byrnes, Guy Madison, Enio Girolami, Louise Barrett, Rick Boyd, Rosella Bergamonti, Pedro Sanchez.

This is a bit complicated: director E. G. Rowland is actually Enzo G. Castellari, pseudonym for Enzo Girolami (son of filmmaker Marino Girolami, alias Frank Martin); Enzo has an actor brother, Enio Girolami, who is one of the stars in this film (as Chamaco). For years, because of the similarity of the names Ennio and Enzo, many genre fans erroneously believed them to be the same person. To make matters more complicated, although his main expertise is directing, Enzo has also tried his hand at acting and scriptwriting (see Performers filmography and Scriptwriters filmography).

The Civil War is over, but Confederate Colonel Blake (Guy Madison) won't let it end. He continues to raid, pillage, and terrorize the Texas countryside. However, the real method behind his madness is a desperate search for General Beauregard's hidden treasure. FBI agent Stuart (Edd Byrnes) goes undercover to stop Blake and his marauders. It's good fun.

Edd Byrnes, hoping to follow in Clint Eastwood's footsteps, went to Italy as an established "American television star." In his long-running "77 Sunset Strip" series, Edd Byrnes played a hipster-cum-detective named "Kookie." He was such a popular teen idol in the late 50s that he even had a Top Ten hit record called "Kookie, Kookie, Lend Me Your Comb" (a duet with Connie Stevens). Unfortunately for Edd, his three Spaghetti Westerns (*Go Kill and Come Back, Red Blood, Yellow Gold,* and this one) didn't revive his slumping career.

La Pazienza Ha un Limite . . . Noi No see *Patience Has a Limit, We Don't*

Pecos Cleans Up (1967)

Pecos È Qui: Prega e Muori Ital. *Director:* Maurizio Lucidi; *Script:* Adriano Bolzoni/Augusto Caminito/Fernando Di Leo/Maurizio Lucidi; *Camera:* Franco Villa; *Music:* Lallo Gori; *Producer:* Franco Palombi, Italcine (Italy). *Cast:* Robert Woods, Luciana Gilli, Erno Crisa, Pedro Sanchez, Umi Raho, Piero Vida, Carlo Gaddi.

All the creative personnel that made *My Name Is Pecos* a success (director, star, photographer, composer) are here again, but this film bears little similarity to the original. Gone is the angry bent-on-revenge Pecos, replaced by a south-of-the-border churl (actually a light-headed Indiana Jones) in a tale about Aztec temples and lost treasure. Too bad.

Pecos È Qui: Prega e Muori see *Pecos Cleans Up*

Per 100.000 Dollari t'Ammazzo see *For $100,000 Per Killing*

Per il Gusto di Uccidere see *Taste for Killing*

Per Mille Dollari al Giorno see *For $1000 a Day*

Per Pochi Dollari per Django see *Few Dollars for Django*

Per Pochi Dollaro Ancora see *Fort Yuma Gold*

Per Qualche Dollaro in Meno see *For a Few Dollars Less*

Per Qualche Dollaro in Più see *For a Few Dollars More*

Per un Dollaro di Gloria see *Mutiny at Fort Sharp*

Per un Pugno di Dollari see *Fistful of Dollars*

Per un Pugno nell'Occhio see *For a Fist in the Eye*

Per una Bara Piena di Dollari see *Showdown for a Badman*

A scene from *Pirates of the Mississippi*, Brad Harris' first Spaghetti Western (1963).

Perché Uccidi Ancora see *Blood at Sundown* (1967)

Les Pétroleuses see *Frenchie King*

Phaedra West see *I Do Not Forgive . . . I Kill!*

Piluk il Timido see *Piluk, the Timid One*

Piluk, the Timid One (1968)

Gun Shy Piluk; Piluk il Timido Ital; *Giurò . . . E li Uccise ad Uno ad Uno* Ital.
Director: Guido Celano; *Script:* Guido Celano; *Camera:* Angelo Baistrocchi;
Music: Carlo Savina; *Producer:* Palinuro Film (Italy). *Cast:* Edmund Purdom,
Peter Holden, Dan Harrison, Micaela Pignatelli, Luis Barboo, Livio Lorenzon.

Another "revenge for a slaughtered family" Western, with a slight twist.
This time the avenger is an elderly man, Piluk (Edmund Purdom) seeking
revenge against the Mason Gang for the death of his only son, Sheriff Albert of
Boise (Peter Holden). Interesting, due to the geriatric variation.

Standard direction from scriptwriter Celano who also made *Black Eagle of
Santa Fe* under the alias William First; cautious camera work by Angelo
Baistrocchi.

Il Piombo e il Carne see *Bullets and the Flesh*

Pirates of the Mississippi (1963)

River Pirates of the Mississippi; Agguato sul Grande Fiume Ital; *Die Flusspiraten vom Mississippi* Ger. *Director:* Jürgen Roland; *Script:* Werner P. Zibaso/ Johannes Kas; *Camera:* Rolf Kastel/Francesco Izzarelli; *Music:* Willy Mattes; *Producer:* Wolfgang Hartwig/Gianni Fuchs, Rapid Film/Produzione Fuchs/ S.N.C. (West Germany/Italy/France). *Cast:* Brad Harris, Horst Frank, Sabine Sinjen, Hansjörg Felmy, Dorothea Parker, Tony Kendall, Jeannette Batti, Paolo Solvay, Dan Vadis.

This is the first Brad Harris genre Western. It tells the story of pioneers and Indians, forgetting their differences and banding together against deadly, cold-blooded pirates who have taken over a river town after stealing a Cherokee land grant in a mail robbery.

Sprawling German-oriented production standards (i.e., a heavy concentration on outdoor scenic shots) by director Jürgen Roland, with assistance from second unit director, Gianfranco Parolini (the future Frank Kramer).

Pistol for a Hundred Coffins (1968)

Una Pistola per Cento Bare. Director: Umberto Lenzi; *Script:* Vittorio Salerno/ Marco Letto/Umberto Lenzi; *Camera:* Alejandro Ulloa; *Music:* Angelo Francesco Lavagnino; *Producer:* Tritone/Copercines (Italy/Spain). *Cast:* Peter Lee Lawrence, John Ireland, Gloria Osuna, Eduardo Fajardo, Victor Israel, Julio Peña, Raf Baldassare, Andrea Scotti, Piero Lulli, Victor Israel.

The Kid (Peter Lee Lawrence) is framed and jailed. When finally released, he attempts to clear his name but he's constantly double-crossed by a former partner, Garff (John Ireland). Most of the film is a barrage of mistaken identities and betrayals.

But oddly, there's a lengthy middle section dealing with lunatics escaping from the local prison. In this unexpected segment, these crazies invade the city with axes and hatchets. And, in horror movie fashion, they slaughter many innocent citizens. Most surprisingly, the leader of this wacko band is Eduardo Fajardo in a *very* out of character role.

Cult filmmaker Umberto Lenzi began his career in 1961 (with *Hell Below Deck*) and, over the years, he has directed more than 60 movies, including another Spaghetti Western called *All Out* (1968). Although Lenzi was schooled as a lawyer, his work experience focused exclusively in the motion picture industry, first as a reviewer, then a scriptwriter, and finally as a director. Although he made all types of films under a collection of monikers (i.e., Humphrey Humbert, Hank Milestone, Bert Lenz), he is best known for creating a peculiar subgenre of Italian exploitation fare called the "Cannibal Movie" with his *Man from Deep River* (1972), plus the highly controversial "sequels" *Eaten Alive by Cannibals* also called *Doomed to Die* (1980) and *Make Them Die Slowly* also called *Cannibal Ferrox* (1981).

Pistol for Django see Even Django Has His Price

Pistol for Ringo (1965)

Una Pistola per Ringo Ital. *Director:* Duccio Tessari; *Script:* Duccio Tessari/Fernando Di Leo; *Camera:* Francisco Marin; *Music:* Ennio Morricone;

Producer: Luciano Ercoli/Alberto Pugliese, P.C.M./Balcazar (Italy/Spain). *Cast:* Montgomery Wood, Fernando Sancho, Nieves Navarro, George Martin, José Manuel Martin, Hally Hammond, Parajito, Antonio Casas, Lorella De Luca, Paco Sanz.

Here is a finely crafted, amoral Spaghetti Western from scriptwriter-cum-director Duccio Tessari telling the story of a feared Mexican outlaw gang and its wounded leader Sancho (Fernando Sancho). After robbing a bank in Quemado, the bandidos take refuge in a hacienda where they torture and kill innocent people until the Sheriff (George Martin) hires a gunfighter named Ringo (Giuliano Gemma, aka Montgomery Wood) to stop the terror. Ringo accepts the job only after Mayor Clyde (Antonio Casas) agrees to the terms of the deal, guaranteeing him 30 percent of the stolen bank money.

This movie was originally inspired by the internationally successful pop record "Ringo" sung (actually, narrated) by Lorne Greene (of American TV's "Bonanza" fame), released worldwide by RCA Victor/BMG in late 1964. The movie spawned a hit sequel, again teaming Tessari and Gemma, called *Return of Ringo*. There were also many unofficial "sequels" quick to capitalize on the "Ringo" name, among them: Sergio Corbucci's *Ringo and His Golden Pistol* (originally filmed under the title *Johnny Oro*), and *Kill or Die* starring Robert Mark as the "famous" Ringo, plus *Ringo and Gringo Against All; Ringo, It's Massacre Time; Ringo, Pray to Your God; Ringo the Lone Rider; Ringo's Big Night; Ringo: Face of Revenge* and, of course, the forgettable "Franco and Ciccio" comedies, *Two R-R-Ringos from Texas* and *Two Sons of Ringo*.

Newcomer Nieves Navarro began using a pseudonym (Susan Scott) shortly after the release of this film. She continues to be a sought-after exploitation star, best known for her performance in Joe D'Amato's *Trap Them and Kill Them*, also called *Emanuelle e Ultimi Cannibali (Emanuelle and the Last Cannibal Tribe)*.

Pistol Packin' Preacher (1972)

Posate le Pistole Reverendo Ital; *Déposez les Colts* Fr. *Director:* Leopoldo Savona; *Script:* Norbert Blake/Leopoldo Savona; *Camera:* Romano Scavolini; *Music:* Coriolano Gori; *Producer:* Agata Film Italy/France). *Cast:* Mark Damon, Veronica Korocia, Floranna Di Bernardo, Richard Melville, Pietro Ceccarelli, Carla Mancini, Allessandro Perrella.

Jeremiah (Richard Melville) and his two daughters Lisa and Linda (Veronica Korocia and Floranna Di Bernardo) are heading West in their covered wagon, flim-flamming their way along. They give a ride to a former Rebel-soldier-now-gunfighter named Slim (Mark Damon), figuring that he'll be good protection for them. Slim, with some quick-cash ideas of his own, convinces Jeremiah to try the "preacher sting." Then, Slim rides ahead to a nearby town where he pretends to be a cripple, waiting for the "healing Padre" to arrive.

Obviously, Jeremiah "heals" Slim. Town boss Garvey (Pietro Ceccarelli) is so impressed that he reopens the abandoned church and appoints the bogus preacher as the new minister. Slim masterminds a promotion scheme that coincides with an eclipse of the sun (how he knew about this freak of nature is anybody's guess). Of course, this makes Padre Jeremiah incredibly popular. A few days later, as a capper, Jeremiah "dies." He's buried, but returns from the dead. It's all part of yet another plot to secure the lion's share of Garvey's fortune. And they do.

There's a rather embarrassing Mark Damon–in-drag sequence. The world would definitely be a better place without it. But there's also an interesting variation on the barroom brawl, as Lisa and Linda use it to their pickpocketing advantage. Plus another unique vignette features Slim successfully shooting a fly off his big toe. Seemingly, there are more pluses than minuses in this Leopoldo Savona comic Western.

Incidentally, cinematographer Romano Scavolini later directed some highly controversial exploitation films, including *Nightmare* (also called *Nightmares in a Damaged Brain*, 1981).

Pistola di Dio see *God's Gun*

Una Pistola per Cento Bare see *Pistol for a Hundred Coffins*

Una Pistola per Cento Croci see *Gunman of One Hundred Crosses*

Una Pistola per Ringo see *Pistol for Ringo*

Las Pistolas no Discuten see *Bullets Don't Argue*

Le Pistole non Discutono see *Bullets Don't Argue*

Il Pistoleri di Arizona see *Arizona Colt*

Pistoleros de Casa Grande see *Gunfighters of Casa Grande*

Pistoleros (Gunmen) from Arizona see *Five Thousand Dollars on One Ace*

Più Forte Sorelle see *For a Book of Dollars*

La Più Grande Rapina del West see *Greatest Robbery in the West*

Place Called Glory (1965)

Place Called Glory City; Die Hölle von Manitoba Ger. *Director:* Ralph Gideon; *Script:* Fernando Lamas/Edward Di Lorenzo; *Camera:* Teresa Alcocer; *Music:* Angel Arteaga; *Producer:* Bruce Balaban/Danilo Sabatini, Midega Film (West Germany/Spain). *Cast:* Lex Barker, Pierre Brice, Gerard Tichy, Angel Del Pozo, Marianne Koch, Jorge Rigaud, Aldo Sambrell.

Significantly, this remains the only Spaghetti Western to employ a female cinematographer, German-based technician Teresa Alcocer. Written by actor Fernando Lamas and directed by Ralph Gideon (pseudonym for British filmmaker Sheldon Reynolds, best remembered as producer/director of the long-running European "Adventuers of Sherlock Holmes" television series starring Ronald Howard, son of Leslie Howard), this Spanish-German production unites Lex Barker and Pierre Brice in their only non–Winnetou project together. Principally, it's a Western version of the old Roman gladiator tale about two "slave friends" who must face each other in the Colosseum.

Bounty hunter Brenner (Lex Barker) meets the "dandy" New Orleans gunslinger Reece (Pierre Brice) on the plains, where they are cautious but courteous to each other. They meet again in Glory City. This time, the two men become instant friends as they are pitted against the town's evil hombres. However, a jealous triangle soon develops over Brenner's former girlfriend, saloon dancer Jade Grande (Marianne Koch), and so, the two gunfighters find themselves facing each other in a showdown at the film's conclusion. Jocund scriptwriting (and a new round of bad guys) allows both Spartan heroes to emerge victorious.

For the "Winnetou" films starring Lex Barker and Pierre Brice see *Apache's Last Battle*, *Winnetou the Warrior* (also called *Apache Gold*), *Half-Breed*, *Winnetou: Last of the Renegades*, and *Winnetou: The Desperado Trail*.

Place Called Glory City see *Place Called Glory*

Play Me the Song of Death see *Once Upon a Time in the West*

Poëlla Calibro 38 see *Calibre .38*

Poker d'As pour Django see *Sheriff Won't Shoot*

Poker d'Assi per Django see *Sheriff Won't Shoot*

Un Poker di Pistola see *Poker with Pistols*

Poker with Pistols (1967)

Un Poker di Pistole. *Director:* Joseph Warren; *Script:* Fernando DI Leo/Augusto Caminito; *Camera:* Angelo Lotti; *Music:* Lallo Gori; *Producer:* Gabriele Silvestri, Italcine (Italy). *Cast:* George Hilton, George Eastman, Annabella Incontera, Dick Palmer, José Torres.

Popular action director Joseph Warren (pseudonym for Giuseppe Vari), best known for *Urban Warriors* and *City in the Jaws of the Racket*, made a series of seven Spaghetti Westerns. This one was cowritten by future exploitation filmmaker Fernando Di Leo (*Slaughter Hotel*) and work-horse script-doctor Augusto Caminito. The combination deft direction and lean plot make this film engaging in its simplicity.

Lucas (George Eastman) loses a lot of money (that he doesn't have) in a poker game. The winner, fellow gambler Ponson (George Hilton), agrees to let him "work off" the debt by "investigating" the clandestine activities of a powerful rancher, Masters (Dick Palmer). Lucas discovers that Masters is kingpin in a counterfeit ring, information which makes the greedy Ponson very hungry.

The movie also marks one of the "early beginnings" for the genre's favorite hack, Miles Deem (Demofilo Fidani). He is the assistant director.

Pokerface see *Go Away! Trinity Has Arrived in Eldorado*

Por un Puñado de Golpes see *For a Fist in the Eye*

Porno-Erotic Western (1978)

Porno Erotico Western Ital; *Western Porno-Érotique* Fr. *Director:* Gerard B. Lennox; *Script:* Walter Fleming; *Camera:* Maurizio Centini; *Music:* Giuliano

Movie poster from *Poker with Pistols* (1967).

Sorgini; *Producer:* Lennox Film (Italy). *Cast:* Ray O'Connor, Karin Well, Tomas Rudy, Lorenz Bien, Rosemarie Lindt, Patrizia Mayer.

An unscrupulous Italian production company, operating behind the bogus name "Lennox Film," took the 1970 Spaghetti Western *Requiem for a Bounty Hunter* and, after adding "hard core" sex scenes, re-released it as a XXX production (removing the name of director Mel "Mark" Welles, replacing it with the spurious "Gerard B. Lennox"). Not only did this destroy the credibility of the initial film, but the sex "inserts" are conspicuously inferior to the quality of the original print, plus there is little attempt to match the "sizes and shapes" of the "bodies in the inserts" to the actual actors and actresses starring in the film. It's an embarrassment.

Porno Erotico Western see *Porno-Erotic Western*

Posate le Pistole Reverendo see *Pistol Packin' Preacher*

Potato Fritz see *Montana Trap*

Prairie in the City (1971)

Grosstadtprärie Ger. *Director:* Claus Tinney; *Script:* Claus Tinney; *Camera:* Peter Reimer; *Music:* Günther Weiss; *Producer:* Claus Tinney (West Germany). *Cast:* Harald Leignitz, Günter Ungeheuer, Emilie Reuer, Hans Nielson, Georg Schlob.

A contemporary fantasy film with Spaghetti Western overtones directed by "experimental" German director, Claus Tinney, whose films usually deal with topical political themes. In this one, two businessmen (Harald Leignitz and Günter Ungeheuer) discover that they are both dating the same woman. Over lunch, they discuss the situation rationally. Unwilling to continue "sharing her charms," the men decide to dress as cowboys and stalk each other in the busy streets of the city. Eventually they face each other in a showdown amidst the rush hour traffic. An ironic ending finds them shooting each other—dead.

The style of the film is very reminiscent of Marco Ferreri's *Do Not Touch the White Woman* (1974).

Pray to Kill and Return Alive see *Shoot the Living . . . Pray for the Dead*

El Precio de un Hombre see *Ugly Ones*

Preda d'Avvoltoi see *Prey of Vultures*

Prega per il Morto e Ammazza il Vivo see *Shoot the Living . . . Pray for the Dead*

Preparati la Bara see *Get the Coffin Ready*

Prey of Vultures (1973)

The Artist Is a Gunfighter; Un Dólar Recompensa Sp; *Preda d'Avvoltoi* Ital. *Director:* Rafael Romero Marchent; *Script:* Rafael R. Marchent/Luis Gaspar; *Camera:* Mario Capriotti; *Music:* Nora Orlandi/Bruno Nicolai; *Producer:* Eduardo Manzanos, Copercines/Devon (Spain/Italy). *Cast:* Peter Lee Lawrence, Orchidea De Santis, Carlos R. Marchent, Andres Mesuto, Eduardo Calvo, Raf Baldassare, Frank Braña, Dada Gallotti.

An older and more mature looking Peter Lee Lawrence plays a "pulp magazine" artist named Kit. Although he's good with a gun (a sharp-shooting marksman, in fact), Kit prefers the quiet, professional life of pencils and paper.

After receiving a big advance from his publisher, he and his father celebrate by taking a stage to Mountain City. Enroute the coach is robbed by masked gunmen; everyone, except Kit, is murdered.

He wanders in the desert until he reaches Mountain City. Having plenty of money (from the magazine), he sets up a new life in the peaceful town. But he is tormented with thoughts of that murderous day when his father was killed. Eventually he meets, and falls in love with, the sheriff's daughter (Orchidea De Santis). Life becomes very complicated when Kit discovers that her father was secretly the leader of the masked gang.

This is one of prolific filmmaker Rafael Romero Marchent's "later" Westerns. The grittiness is missing, replaced by a slicker almost–Hollywood look.

Il Prezzo del Potere see *Price of Power*

The Price of a Man see *Ugly Ones*

Price of Death (1972)

Last Gunfight; Il Venditore di Morte Ital. *Director:* Vincent Thomas; *Script:* Enzo Gicca/Vincent Thomas; *Camera:* Franco Villa; *Music:* Mario Migliardi; *Producer:* Gabriele Silvestri, Mida Cinematog (Italy). *Cast:* John Garko, Klaus Kinski, Alan Collins, Gely Genka, Franco Abbiana, Laura Gianoli, Luciano Lorcas, Luigi Castellato.

Filmmaker Enzo Gicca Palli (using a "Vincent Thomas" alias, not to be confused with popular film editor Vincenzo Tomassi who somtimes uses the "Vincent Thomas" pseudonym as well) creates a new character for John (Gianni) Garko to portray, a suave playboy bounty hunter named Silver (complete with hacienda/mansion and "playmates").

The movie opens with a (seemingly unrelated) vicious bedroom murder of a young woman by an unseen assassin, filmed in nontypical hand-held "horror" fashion. Then after the credits roll comes the first line of dialogue: "We've got high moral standards in Appleby," says the banker to a cowboy inside the town casino. As soon as these words are uttered, three masked bandits raid the place. A bloodbath results. But the bad guys escape.

Although he insists that he was "doing something else" at the time of the robbery, local troublemaker Chester Conway (Klaus Kinski) is arrested on circumstantial evidence. The town judge, realizing that this is a perfect opportunity to "finally put Chester away for good," convicts him in a monkey trial and sentences the black sheep to death.

Chester's attorney (and town drunk), Jeff Plummer (Franco Abbiana), visits his old friend, the notorious now-retired bounty hunter Silver (John Garko). Jeff complains that "the trial was a farce" and, after reminding Silver that he owes him a favor, asks for help in finding the real bandits. Eventually the culprits are exposed and Chester Conway is set free. However (remember the opening scene?), Silver recognizes Chester as the killer of young Carmen Monolo. And, in a showdown, he shoots him — dead.

This film is director Palli's only Spaghetti Western, but he made a swashbuckling pirate movie with Terence Hill and Bud Spencer called *Blackie the Pirate* (1974). He also wrote the screenplay for *Death on High Mountain*.

Price of Power (1969)

Texas Brit; *Il Prezzo del Potere* Ital; *Muerte de un Presidente* Sp. *Director:* Tonino Valerii; *Script:* Massimo Patrizi; *Camera:* Stelvio Massi; *Music:* Luis Enrique Bacalov; *Producer:* Bianco Manini, Patry/Montana (Italy/Spain). *Cast:* Giuliano Gemma, Fernando Rey, Van Johnson, José Suarez, Antonio Casas, Warren Vanders, Manolo Zarzo, Maria Jesus Cuadra, Frank Braña, Rai Saunders, José Calvo, Angel Alvarez, Julio Peña, Francisco Sanz.

An amazing film. A wonderful film. But certainly, as the Spanish title (*La Muerte de un Presidente: The Death of a President*) indicates, it's also a cockeyed film.

Unconcerned with historical facts, director Tonino Valerii retells the "assassination of Kennedy" story in a Western motif. The year is 1890. The Civil War is now over and President Garfield (Van Johnson) goes to Dallas, the "hotbed of ex–Rebel troublemakers," to deliver a "unity" speech.

He is assassinated as his caravan travels down the main street of the city. The sheriff, who is also part of the traitorous conspiracy, concocts evidence to implicate an innocent black man (Warren Vanders). In an astonishingly audacious sequence, the accused assassin is also murdered (à la Oswald/Ruby fashion) while being transported between jails.

Giuliano Gemma is the hero who exposes the perfidious accomplices (led by banker Fernando Rey), foiling their scheme to resurrect the "power and rule" of the South and (at the same time, in a subplot) he also avenges his father's death at the hands of the traitors.

The skillful camera work comes from future action director Stelvio Massi, with music by Luis Enrique Bacalov, comparable to his *Bullet for a General* score.

Just to set the record straight: The real Civil War ended in 1865 and there was a U.S. President Garfield, but he wasn't assassinated in Dallas. He was shot in Washington, D.C. in 1881.

Pride and Vengeance see *Man: His Pride and His Vengeance*

Prima Ti Perdono, Poi Ti Ammazzo see *Dig Your Grave, Friend ...
Sabata's Coming*

Prima Ti Suono e Poi Ti Sparo see *Trinity Plus the Clown and a Guitar*

Los Profesionales de la Muerte see *Red Blood, Yellow Gold*

A Professional Gun see *Mercenary*

Professionals for a Massacre see *Red Blood, Yellow Gold*

Professionisti per un Massacro see *Red Blood, Yellow Gold*

El Proscrito del Río Colorado see *Outlaw of Red River*

Fernando Rey plays the leader of the presidential assassination plot in Tonino Valerii's *Price of Power* (1969).

Pyramid of the Sun God (1965)

Die Pyramide des Sonnengottes Ger. *Director:* Robert Siodmak; *Script:* Ladislas Fodor/R. A. Stemmle/Georg Marischka; *Camera:* Siegfried Hold; *Music:* Erwin Halletz; *Producer:* CCC Ultrascope Farbfilm/Avala/Serene (W. Germany/Italy/France). *Cast:* Lex Barker, Michele Girardon, Gerard Barry, Hans Nielsen, Rik Battaglia, Gustavo Rojo, Teresa Lorca, Ralf Wolter, Kelo Henderson, Alessandro Panaro.

This is Part 2 of director Siodmak's sprawling, epic tale of Dr. Karl Sternau (Lex Barker) and his search for the fabled Aztec treasure, assisted by his partner Graf Alfonso (Gerard Barray) and the beautiful Indian guide Karja (Teresa Lorca). It's faithfully based on a book, *Schlob Rodriganda*, written by Karl May, the popular German pulp writer (see *Treasure of the Aztecs* for Part 1). An edited version, combining elements from Part 1 and Part 2 was released in France under the title *Les Mercenaires du Rio Grande*.

Robert Siodmak made over 50 movies from his directorial debut in 1929 (*Menschen am Sonntag*) until his death in 1973. He is best remembered for his chillingly atmospheric films (i.e., *The Spiral Staircase*, *Phantom Lady*, *Son of Dracula*, *Cobra Woman*, and especially the award-winning *Killers*) shot during his "English" period when he worked in Hollywood (1942–1952).

Die Pyramide des Sonnengottes see *Pyramid of the Sun God*

Quando Satana Impugna la Colt see *Awkward Hands*

Quanto Costa Morire see *Cost of Dying*

Les Quatre Mercénaires d'El Paso see *Bad Man's River*

Quatre Salopards pour Garringo see *My Colt, Not Yours*

I Quattro del Pater Noster see *In the Name of the Father*

I Quattro dell'Apocalisse see *Four Gunmen of the Apocalypse*

I Quattro dell'Ave Maria see *Ace High*

Quattro Dollari di Vendetta see *Four Dollars for Vengeance*

I Quattro Inesorabili see *Relentless Four*

I Quattro Pistoleri di Santa Trinità see *Four Gunmen of the Holy Trinity*

I Quattro sul Sentiero di Spara see *Four Rode Out*

Quei Disperati Che Puzzano di Sudore e di Morte see *Bullet for Sandoval*

Quel Caldo Maledetto Giorno di Fuoco see *Machine Gun Killers*

Quel Maledetto Giorno della Resa dei Conti see *Vendetta at Dawn*

Quel Maledetto Giorno d'Inverno Django e Sartana ... all'Ultimo Sangue see *One Damned Day at Dawn ... Django Meets Sartana*

Quella Sporca Storia del West see *Johnny Hamlet*

Quelle Sporche Anime Dannate see *Paid in Blood*

Quien Grita Venganza see *Cry for Revenge*

Quien Sabe? see *Bullet for the General*

Quindici Forche per un Assassino see *Fifteen Scaffolds for the Killer*

Quinta: Fighting Proud (1969)

Quinta: Non Ammazare Ital. *Director:* Leon Klimovsky; *Script:* Manuel Martinez Remis; *Camera:* Giuseppe La Torre; *Music:* Piero Umiliani; *Producer:* Cines Europa/RM Films (Italy/Spain). *Cast:* Steven Todd, German Cobos, Sarah Ross, Alfonso Rojas, Joe Karmel, José Marco, Roberto Camardiel, Raf Baldassare.

Here is yet another film lost to the glut of product in the 1969–70 marketplace. Little is known about this obscure Spaghetti Western from workhorse director Leon Klimovsky, featuring an interesting cast of predominantly "character" actors. Seemingly, it received limited distribution, and today remains a "lost" film.

Quinta: Non Ammazare see *Quinta: Fighting Proud*

Quintana see *Quintana: Dead or Alive*

Quintana: Dead or Alive (1969)

Quintana Ital. *Director:* Glenn Vincent Davis; *Script:* Glenn Vincent Davis; *Camera:* Vitaliano Natalucci; *Music:* Felice De Stefano; *Producer:* Vincenzo Musolini (Italy/Spain). *Cast:* George Stevenson, Femi Benussi, Pedro Sanchez, John Levery, Marisa Traversi, Celso Faria, Spartaco Conversi.

Scriptwriter-of-choice for filmmakers Edward G. Muller (Edoardo Mulargia) and José A. De La Loma, Glenn Vincent Davis (pseudonym for Vincenzo Musolini) directed two Spaghetti Westerns, *May God Forgive You ... But I Won't* (1968) and this one. Both are highly entertaining action fests.

Quintana (George Stevenson) is a "poor man's Zorro," a people's hero in a poncho. Instead of a mask, a bandana hides his face. He's actually freedom fighter José de Loma (obviously, Davis is making an in-joke, delivering a sly tribute to his director friend) and José is very upset. His friend Manuel (John Levery), falsely arrested for killing three soldiers, has been sentenced to death. "The man's no more violent than a watermelon!" Quintana cries in an unintentionally humorous moment.

The real reason behind the arrest inadvertently involves a woman named Virgina (Femi Benussi). She is beautiful. And she is in love with Manuel. But the evil governor, Don Juan de Leya (John Levery) wants her. He offers to pardon Manuel if Virgina "submits to him." Quintana comes to the rescue in the nick of time. Poor Don Juan.

Una Ragione per Vivere . . . una Ragione per Morire see *Massacre at Fort Holman*

Rainbow see *Shoot, Gringo . . . Shoot!*

Raise Your Hands, Dead Man . . . You're Under Arrest (1971)

Su le Mani, Cadavere! Sei agli Arresti Ital. *Director:* Leon Klimovsky; *Script:* Sergio Bergonzelli/José L. Navarro; *Camera:* Tonino Maccoppi; *Music:* Alessandro Alessadnroni; *Producer:* Luigi Mondello, Sara/Dauro (Italy/Spain). *Cast:* Peter Lee Lawrence, Espartaco Santoni, Franco Agostini, Helga Line, Aurora De Alba, Mary Zan.

A Texas Ranger known as Sando Kid (Peter Lee Lawrence) is dispatched to Springfield. His orders are "to clean up" the territory and put a stop to the tyrannical rule of land baron Mancino (Espartaco Santoni).

Sando Kid, disguised as a perfume salesman (which, incidentally, fits Peter Lee Lawrence better than the macho Texas Ranger image), learns that Springfield Valley will soon be crossed by the railroad and that's why Mancino is trying to take over every possible plot of land. The independent ranchers, who refuse to sell out to the greedy boss, are living in constant fear and danger. Sando and his friend Frank Bamba (Franco Agostini) set a successful trap which results in a huge, climactic gun battle.

Mancino is then killed in a face off with the Ranger, after which Sando Kid (remembering his orders to capture the culprit "alive or dead") handcuffs the dead man. This ending, obviously intended as some kind of symbolic statement, is a perfect example of "how out of touch" director Leon Klimovsky actually is with the genre. His 12 Westerns (an amazing outpour under the circumstances) remain largely unwatchable, endurance tests for the stalwart. It's a genuine mystery, considering the acknowledged proficiency of Klimovsky's horror and mystery films.

Interestingly, the French distributors tried to disguise this film as a "Sartana" sequel, calling it *Ça Va Chauffer, Sartana Revient.*

Ramon il Messicano see *Ramon the Mexican*

Ramon the Mexican (1966)

Ramon il Messicano. Director: Maurizio Pradeaux; *Script:* Maurizio Pradeaux; *Camera:* Oberdan Troiani; *Music:* Felice De Stefano; *Producer:* Magic Films (Italy/Spain). *Cast:* Robert Hundar, Wilma Lindamar, Jean Louis, José Torres, Thomas Clay, Renato Trottolo, Aldo Berti.

Prolific screenwriter Maurizio Pradeaux directs this time. Although he later made numerous exploitation films (especially, *Tormentor* [also called *Death Carries a Cane*] in 1972, and *Death Steps in the Dark* in 1976), this is his only Spaghetti Western effort, a mysogynistic one-dimensional opus.

"Ramon the Mexican" is the villain (Jean Louis), an evil twisted sadist who arrives at the Baxter ranch to avenge his outlaw brother's death. John Baxter is murdered and his sister, Esmeralda (Wilma Lindamar) is kidnapped. When her boyfriend, Slim (Robert Hundar), hears of this, he goes to Ramon and demands a showdown. He ends up seriously wounded.

Esmeralda goes to church and prays for Slim's recovery, promising to become Ramon's lover (!) as a penance. Seemingly, her God was impressed by this "deal" because Slim does recuperate. And so, Esmeralda keeps her vow. Eventually, Ramon decides to marry the girl in a grand ceremony at the town square. But Slim, disguised as the officiating priest, kills Ramon and escapes with Esmeralda. Sort of a demented "Graduate" finale.

Rampage at Apache Wells (1965)

Uccidere a Apache Wells Ital; *Der Ölprinz* Ger. *Director:* Harald Philipp; *Script:* Fred Denger/Harald Philipp; *Camera:* Heinz Holscher; *Music:* Martin Böttcher; *Producer:* Preden Philipson, Atlantis Film (West Germany/Yugoslavia). *Cast:* Stewart Granger, Pierre Brice, Walter Barnes, Harald Leipnitz, Macha Meril, Antje Weisgerber, Mario Girotti, Heinz Erhardt.

Apache chief Winnetou (Pierre Brice) and his white friend Old Surehand (Stewart Granger) try to keep the peace, but outsiders trick the Indians into a battle over the oil fields. It's loosely based on Karl May's *Der Ölprinz* (*The Oil Prince*).

Other titles in this series are *Flaming Frontier* and *Among Vultures*. The original Winnetou series stars Lex Barker (rather than Stewart Granger) playing the lead character (see *Winnetou #1 thru #4* and *Apache's Last Battle*) called Old Shatterhand instead of Old Surehand. As with all the Winnetou films, the chief is always played by Pierre Brice.

Il Ranch degli Spietati see *Man from Oklahoma*

Ranch of the Ruthless see *Man from Oklahoma*

Rancheros see *Dig Your Grave, Friend . . . Sabata's Coming*

Rattler Kid (1968)

L'Uomo Venuto per Uccidere Ital. *Director:* Leon Klimovsky; *Script:* Luigi Mondello; *Camera:* Julio Ortas; *Music:* Francesco De Masi; *Producer:* Super International Pictures, Luigi Mondello (Italy/Spain). *Cast:* Richard Wyler, Brad Harris, William Spolt, Jesus Puente, Femi Benussi, Aurora De Alba, Simon Arraga, William Bogart, Luis Barboo, Luis Induñi, Miguel Del Castillo, Frank Braña.

Although he directed 12 Eurowesterns (giving prolific champ Anthony Ascott some serious competition), Leon Klimovsky is best known for his Spanish horror films with Paul Naschy (*Werewolf versus the Vampire Women, Dr. Jekyll and the Wolfman* and *Vengeance of the Zombies*). His Westerns tend to be rambling, tiresome collections of zoom shots with uninteresting storylines. Unfortunately, this one is as bad as all the rest.

Lt. Tony Garnett (Richard Wyler) is framed for the robbery and death of Captain John David. In a court martial trial, he is sentenced to execution, but a priest helps him escape (they exchange clothes).

Garnett tracks down the real culprits (Frenchie, Martin, an Indian named

Silent Wolf, and the leader Jeff Riff, played by William Spolt). However, all this killing (plus the original offense) has turned him into a notorious outlaw known as the Rattler Kid. He begins to believe "his press" and soon adopts a desperado's lifestyle.

He's hired by some bandidos to kill Sheriff Bill Manors (Brad Harris) while they're pulling a bank heist. He's in town "casing the job" when he bumps into his old grade school teacher (!) who "turns his head around," convincing him to give up lawlessness and fight with the sheriff against the attacking bandits. Incredulous in its naïveté.

Reach You Bastard! (1971)

The Django Story; Down with Your Hands ... You Scum!; Giù le Mani ... Carogna! Ital. *Director:* Lucky Dickerson; *Script:* Lucky Dickerson; *Camera:* Franco Villa; *Music:* Lallo Gori; *Producer:* Tarquina Internazionale (Italy). *Cast:* Hunt Powers, Gordon Mitchell, Dean Stratford, Dennis Colt, Lucky MacMurray, Jerry Ross.

Watch out! It's the genre hack, Miles Deem (alias Demofilo Fidani), hiding behind a "Lucky Dickerson" moniker. This film is critically accepted as being the most endearingly "bad" Spaghetti Western of his questionable career. Without any doubt, it is remarkable for its audacity.

Director Fidani (or Lucky, if you prefer) has taken entire segments from his earlier films, *Django and Sartana Are Coming ... It's the End, One Damned Day at Dawn ... Django Meets Sartana,* and *Stranger That Kneels Beside the Shadow of a Corpse,* re-edited them with a witless wraparound, and created a new movie.

Wild Bill Hickock (Dean Stratford) meets notorious bounty hunter Django (Hunt Powers) in a saloon. Ever since he was a boy, Bill had followed the exploits of the famous gunfighter. Now, here Django sits. They are together at the same table and, apparently, the bounty killer is willing to carry on a conversation. So Bill asks Django to talk about his most exciting adventures.

The audience gets to watch a Miles Deem "Greatest Hits" package. Oh boy. How can we thank you, Miles?

Reason to Live, a Reason to Die see *Massacre at Fort Holman*

Los Rebeldes de Arizona see *Rebels of Arizona*

Rebeldes en Canada see *Canadian Wilderness*

Rebels in Canada see *Canadian Wilderness*

Rebels of Arizona (1969)

Los Rebeldes de Arizona Sp. *Director:* José Maria Zabalza; *Script:* José Maria Zabalza; *Camera:* Leopoldo Villaseñor; *Music:* Ana Satrova; *Producer:* Hesperia Film (Spain). *Cast:* Charles Quiney, Claudia Gravy, Michael Rivers, Luis Induñi, Dianik Zurakowska, José Truchado.

More dumb fun from director José Maria Zabalza (also see *Damned Pistols of Dallas* and *Adios Cjamango*) telling the story of hardy, struggling pioneers in

Movie poster from *Red Blood, Yellow Gold* (1968).

the wilds of Arizona. They spend the entire film defending their homes from pilfering villains. First it's bandidos; then Indians.

Zabalza tends to direct cautiously. He's been criticized for his deliberate pacing, plus a sedulous concentration on unimportant details. His Westerns emerge as inactive action movies. Slow going.

Rebels on the Loose see *Ringo and Gringo Against All*

Red Blood, Yellow Gold (1968)

Professionals for a Massacre; Professionisti per un Massacro Ital; *Sangue Rosse e l'Oro Giallo* Ital; *Los Profesionales de la Muerte* Sp. *Director:* Nando Cicero; *Script:* Nando Cicero/Roberto Gianviti/Enzo Dell'Aquila/Jaime Jesus Balcazar/ José Antonio De La Loma; *Camera:* Francisco Marin; *Music:* Carlos Pes; *Producer:* Oreste Coltellacci, Colt Film/Balcazar (Italy/Spain). *Cast:* George Hilton, Edd Byrnes, George Martin, Milo Quesada, Monica Randall, Gerard Herter, José Bodaló.

This is the third, and final, Spaghetti Western with Edd Byrnes (former U.S. television star of the long-running Warner Bros.' "77 Sunset Strip" series), written by an impressive quartet including popular Spanish director/writer José Antonio De La Loma (responsible for also scripting *Five Giants from Texas, Seven Guns for Timothy, Dynamite Jim* and *Clint the Stranger* during the *same* year).

It's the story of three friends: a defrocked priest and explosives expert known as "Frank the Preacher" (George Hilton), a sharp-shooting bandit called Chattanooga Jim (Edd Byrnes) because of a daring solo bank robbery he pulled in that Tennessee city, and a Mexican horse thief named Fidel Ramirez (George Martin). Unlike the characters in many Eurowesterns, these men are unshakably loyal to one another. Refreshingly, there is never even a hint at a double cross. Instead, it's them against everybody else. In this instance, "everybody else" is (1) El Primero (José Bodaló) and his vicious outlaw gang, (2) the Union Army, (3) the Southern Army, (4) a "suddenly orphaned" Annie (Monica Randall) who inexorably blames them for her parents' death, and, most importantly, (5) a gang of Confederate traitors led by Major Lloyd (Gerard Herter, the German mercenary in *The Big Gundown*) who has stolen a gold shipment and a precious machine gun from the Rebels.

George Hilton's performance is inspired, definitely among his very best. Edd Byrnes comes across as very likable, probably because he seems more confident than he did in his first two Enzo G. Castellari films. George Martin, wearing one of his all-time worst hairpieces, is radically miscast as a Mexican "Dr. Doolittle" who can "talk to horses."

The director of photography is Francisco Marin, but his cameraman is Aristide (Joe D'Amato) Massaccesi. Maybe that's why it looks so good.

Red Coat (1975)

Royal Mounted Police; Giubbe Rosse Ital. *Director:* Joe D'Amato; *Script:* Joe D'Amato/Claudio Bernabei; *Camera:* Aristide Massaccesi; *Music:* Carlo Rustichelli; *Producer:* Coralta Cinematografica (Italy). *Cast:* Fabio Testi, Lionel Stander, Robert Hundar, Renato Cestiè, Guido Mannari, Lynn Frederick.

Although this isn't Aristide Massaccesi's first film, it marks the first time he used the now-famous Joe D'Amato directorial moniker. According to the magazine *ETC*, Massaccesi's first movie was a Klaus Kinski/Ewa Aulin thriller called *Death Smiles on a Murderer* (1973), but there is evidence suggesting that Massaccesi (using an "Oskar Faradine, aka Oscar Santaniello" alias) directed a Spaghetti Western in 1972 called *Bounty Hunter in Trinity*.

Regardless, under the D'Amato pseudonym, Aristide Massaccesi has amassed an unrivaled collection of sleaze and terror flicks, including the controversial *Trap Them and Kill Them* (also called *Emanuelle and the Last Cannibal Tribe [Emanuelle e gli Ultimi Cannibali]*) plus *Caligula: The Untold Story, Buried Alive, Erotic Nights of the Living Dead, Emanuelle in America*, etc.

This film has very little in common with its exploitive brothers and sisters. It's actually a variation of the family-oriented "White Fang" movies, based on the stories of American novelist Jack London. Specifically, inspired by the Charlton Heston film *Call of the Wild* (1972), a huge surprise hit in Italy that spawned many Euro sequels (i.e., *Hellhounds of Alaska* with Doug McClure and Krista Nell, Al Bradly's *Lone Hunter of the Wild North* [also called *White Fang and the Hunter*], *The Great Adventure* with Jack Palance, Harald Reinl's *Cry of the Black Wolves*, and two from Lucio Fulci: *White Fang* and *Return of White Fang* with Franco Nero).

Fabio Testi is a Royal Mounted Policeman who, with his dog (Fang), rescues an orphaned boy (Renato Cestiè) in the wilderness of Canada. They survive an avalanche, a wolf attack, and an assault from four evil outlaws.

Incidentally, the Spanish title for this film is *Colmillo Blanco al Ataque (White Fang Attacks)*.

Red Hot Zorro (1972)

Les Aventures Galantes de Zorro Fr. *Director:* William Russell; *Script:* Henri Dral De Doitselier; *Camera:* William Russell; *Music:* Gilbert Gardot; *Producer:* Pierre Querut (France/Belgium). *Cast:* Jean-Michel Dhermay, Alice Arno, Evelyne Scott, Rose Kiekens, Ghislaine Kay, Evelyne Gatou.

Here's a soft-core sex farce using the Zorro legend as an excuse for countless lusty exploits. Jean-Michel Dhermay is the dashing and amorous Zorro who stands up against the tyrannical California governor (Ghislaine Kay). And lays down against a lot of beautiful women, including French sex star Alice Arno.

Red Pastures see *Massacre at Grand Canyon*

Red Sun (1971)

Sole Rosso Ital; *Soleil Rouge* Fr. *Director:* Terence Young; *Script:* Laird Koenig/ D. B. Petitclere/William Roberts; *Camera:* Henri Alekan; *Music:* Maurice Jarre; *Producer:* Robert Dorfman (Italy/France/Spain). *Cast:* Charles Bronson, Ursula Andress, Toshiro Mifune, Alain Delon, Lee Burton, Capucine, Anthony Dawson, Barta Barry, Luc Merenda, Monica Randall.

An Italian/Spanish/French production directed by competent British action filmmaker, Terence Young (*Dr. No, From Russia with Love, Thunderball, Wait Until Dark*, etc.), is the story of a gunfighter (Charles Bronson), a Samurai warrior (Toshiro Mifune) and a prostitute (Ursula Andress) who join together against a corrupt gambling landowner, Gauche (grossly miscast Alain Delon), to recapture a stolen, valuable Japanese sword.

The music, an interesting blend of Anglo/Japanese themes, is provided by French experimental composer Maurice Jarre who also did the score for two American Westerns, *El Condor* (1970) and *Villa Rides* (1968).

This was the first East-meets-West Western, causing an immediate flurry

Charles Bronson in *Red Sun* (1971).

of Euro imitators, *Fighting Fists of Shanghai Joe, Return of Shanghai Joe, Kung Fu Brothers in the Wild West, Stranger and the Gunfighter* and Sergio Corbucci's *The White, the Yellow, and the Black* (also called *Samurai*).

Règlements de Femmes O Q Corral see *Gunfight at O Q Corral*

Relentless Four (1966)

I Quattro Inesorabili Ital. *Director:* Primo Zeglio; *Script:* Federico De Urrutia/ Manuel Sebaras; *Camera:* Miguel F. Mila; *Music:* Marcello Giombini; *Producer:* Ricardo Sanz (Spain/Italy). *Cast:* Adam West, Robert Hundar, Dina Loy, Luis Induñi, José Jaspe, Raf Baldassare, John Bartha, Cris Huerta, Roberto Camardiel, Paola Barbara, Francisco Sanz.

With his legendary "Batman" television series, Adam West brought a hip self-parody to "the world of superheroes," thus paving the way for Superman and all the imitators. Sadly, he wasn't so fortunate with the Spaghetti Westerns. Even though he tries (and he does try very hard) to rise above the lame story, Adam mostly looks out of of place. And, he also seems to have lots of trouble picking up cues from the Italian-speaking costars, a problem which adds to an already uncomfortable performance. Clearly, director Primo Zeglio (usually known as Anthony Greepy) had trouble working with this "gringo."

Marshall Garrett (Adam West) makes a sizable enemy when he keeps

Movie poster from *Relentless Four* (1966).

bounty hunter Lobo (Robert Hundar) from collecting an ill-gotten reward. Lobo frames the lawman by killing a wealthy land baron and planting incriminating evidence. The conflict becomes a major range war as Garrett, with the aid of girlfriend Lucy (Dina Loy), tries to clear his name.

The cast is a virtual smorgasbord of popular genre "B" actors, almost to the point of distraction.

Renegade Gunfighter see *For One Thousand Dollars per Day*

Renegades of Fort Grant see *Massacre at Fort Grant*

Requiem for a Bounty Hunter (1970)

Requiem per un Bounty Hunter Ital. *Director:* Mark Welles; *Script:* Mark Welles; *Camera:* Maurizio Centini; *Music:* Daniele Patucchi; *Producer:* Universal Cine (Italy). *Cast:* Ray O'Connor, Lawrence Bien, Thomas Rudy, Michael Forest, Steven Tedd, Giovanni Petti, Michele Branca, Anna Bacchi.

Uprooted American filmmaker Mel Welles (costar of *She Beast* with Barbara Steele) is best known for directing Euro horror movies for Roger Corman's production empire, most notably *Island of Dr. Death* also called *Maneaters of Hydra* (1966), and *Lady Frankenstein* (1971). This project, with the directorial credit reading *Mark* rather than *Mel* Welles, is his only Spaghetti Western. It's a shame because he brought a unique "thriller" element to the production, incorporating hand-held photography techniques and eerie camera angles (staples of thriller cinema) into the Western world, which resulted in an overall unsettling effect. Unfortunately, the trite, impoverished Maurizio Centini script is too flimsy for the scope of the project.

A band of outlaws, following orders from land-grabbing town boss Lassiter (Giovanni Petti) attack a farm house, killing Grandpa Barton and raping and or killing the women. When Tom (Ray O'Connor) returns from the range to find the slaughter (in addition to the patriarch, his wife is dead, and daughter Suzy is in shock), he vows vengeance.

While on the trail of the marauders, Tom meets a mysteriously dressed-in-black flute-playing bounter hunter named Sabata (Lawrence Bien, aka Lorenz Bien). For $1,000 Sabata agrees to help Tom in his quest for revenge. The two form a partnership and together they wipe out all the bad guys.

When they return to Tom's farm, daughter Suzy (Anna Bacchi), recognizing the bounty hunter as one of the perpetrators, shoots him off his horse. Then, like a woman possessed, she proceeds to pump rifle rounds (dramatically filmed in slow motion) into various body parts, finally hitting his heart.

In 1978, an unscrupulous production company secured the rights to this film, and, after inserting "hard core" sex scenes, re-released it under the title *Porno Erotic Western.*

Requiem for a Gringo see *Duel in the Eclipse*

Requiem per un Bounty Hunter see *Requiem for a Bounty Hunter*

Requiem per un Gringo see *Duel in the Eclipse*

Requiescant see *Let Them Rest*

La Resa dei Conti see *Big Gundown*

Return of Clint the Stranger (1971)

Ritorno di Clint il Solitario Ital. *Director:* George Martin; *Script:* Giovanni Simonelli/E. Passadore; *Camera:* Jaime Deu Casas; *Music:* Ennio Morricone;

Producer: Doria Film/Balcazar De Barcelona (Italy/Spain). *Cast:* George Martin, Klaus Kinski, Marina Malfatti, Augusto Pesarini, Susanna Atckinson, Daniel Martin, Fernando Sancho.

A particularly significant film, primarily because it is the only Spaghetti Western directed by a genre actor, popular George Martin. He was the star of the first "Clint" film (see *Clint the Stranger* [also called *Clint the Nevada Loner*] and, once again, he resurrects the "Clint Harrison" character, in front of and behind the camera. Stylistically, the film is similar to the first. It's a series of episodic encounters, strongly benefiting from the participation of Klaus Kinski plus an Ennio Morricone soundtrack.

Return of Django see Son of Django

Return of Halleluja (1972)

The West Is Very Close, Amigo; Il West Ti Fa Strello, Amico ... È Arrivato Alleluia Ital. *Director:* Anthony Ascott; *Script:* Giorgio Simonelli/Tito Carpi; *Camera:* Stelvio Massi; *Music:* Stelvio Cipriani; *Producer:* Hermes/Lyre Societe (Italy/W. Germany). *Cast:* George Hilton, Lincoln Tate, Agata Flori, Raymond Bussières, Riccardo Garrone, Michael Hinz, Roberto Camardiel, Nello Pazzafini, Victor Israel, Rado Gozlino, Umberto D'Orsi.

Here's a sequel to the previous year's excellent *Heads You Die ... Tails I Kill You* (1971), also from director Anthony Ascott. But this one is, perhaps, the filmmaker's weakest movie. It fluctuates wildly from broadly drawn humor to silly slapstick to a convoluted heist tale. None of it works.

An Aztec idol is stolen by a band of determined thieves, Halleluja (George Hilton), Archie (Lincoln Tate) and Fleurette (Agata Flori). There's double-crossing and triple-crossing galore, until they finally agree to trust each other.

Return of Ringo (1966)

Ballad of Death Valley (U.S. video title); *Il Ritorno di Ringo* Ital. *Director:* Duccio Tessari; *Script:* Fernando Di Leo/Duccio Tessari; *Camera:* Francisco Marin; *Music:* Ennio Morricone; *Producer:* Alberto Pugliese (Italy/Spain). *Cast:* Giuliano Gemma, Fernando Sancho, Nieves Navarro, Hally Hammond, George Martin, Parajito, Antonio Casas.

This is the only "official" sequel to Duccio Tessari's *Pistol for Ringo*, again starring Giuliano Gemma in the title role. But, in reality, only the name is the same. The character is newly drawn. This time, Ringo is a young soldier returning home from the Civil War (how many times has Gemma seen this device?) to find that his peaceful community has been taken over by a vicious Mexican bandit, Esteban (Fernando Sancho), and his gang. When his family is taken prisoner and his father murdered, Ringo embarks on a courageous (rather than the stereotypical aggressive) vindication. There are many similarities between this film and the mythical tale of Ulysses, especially as demonstrated in Ringo's disguised return to his home. (See William Connolly's comments in Appendix III.)

Many critics found this sequel, cowritten by Fernando Di Leo (future action director of *Mr. Scarface, Violent Breed* and *Slaughter Hotel*) more satisfying than the original; the truth is Duccio Tessari remains one of the top Eurowestern filmmakers, and each of his five Spaghetti Westerns holds a significant rank for originality and technique. His trusted cameraman, Francisco Marin, is the principal photographer; wizard composer Ennio Morricone does the music.

Return of Sabata (1972)

È Tornato Sabata, Hai Chiuso un' Altra Volta Ital. Director: Frank Kramer; Script: Renato Izzo/Frank Kramer; Camera: Sandro Mancori; Music: Marcello Giombini; Producer: Alberto Grimaldi, PEA/Artistes/Artemis (Italy/France/ West Germany). Cast: Lee Van Cleef, Reiner Schöne, Annabella Incontrera, Pedro Sanchez, Mario Brega, Giampiero Albertini, Vasili Karis, Gianni Rizzo.

The "man with the gunsight eyes is back" but it's a disappointingly silly sequel to Sabata, starring Lee Van Cleef in an embarrassing, emasculated role. The beautiful Annabella Incontrera (remains an actress with a cool name but) has little to do in this film. Reiner Schöne is just plain irritating.

Lee Van Cleef is Sabata, formerly a major in the Civil War, now reduced to performing trick sharpshooting in a traveling circus. He accidentally bumps into an old friend, Clyde (Schöne), who owes him $5,000, but obviously he doesn't have it. Instead, the two men concoct a plan to break into and rob the "filthy rich from unfair taxes" Hobsonville bank. However, they soon discover that the money in the evil Irishman McClintock's (Giampiero Albertini) bank is all counterfeit. So, next they turn their attention to the villain's ranch where the real money is stashed.

The Marcello Giombini score is the only glimmer of quality in this otherwise desolate film. A major disappointment from director Gianfranco Parolini (aka Frank Kramer).

Return of Shanghai Joe (1974)

Il Ritorno di Shanghai Joe Ital; Zwei durch Dick und Dunn Ger. Director: Bitto Albertini; Script: Bitto Albertini/Carlo Alberto Alfierio; Camera: Pier Luigi Santi; Music: Maurio Ghiari; Producer: Ennio Onorati/Gerd Scheede, Divina/ CBA (West Germany/Italy). Cast: Klaus Kinski, Chen Lee, Tommy Polgar, Karin Field, Fausto Ulisse, Primiano Muratori, Paul Sholer.

The German title translates to Two (Buddies) Through Thick and Thin, but the stupid-beyond-belief theme song definitely heralds the return of Shanghai Joe: "You've got a flower in your hand/ where a yellow gun used to be/ Oh, oh, Shanghai Joe."

Flim-flam artist Bill Caren (Tommy Polgar) is a "doctor of ailments and elixirs" and he befriends vigilante Shanghai Joe (Chen Lee, or Cheen Lie as some credits read). Together, they go up against the evil stogie-smoking town boss (Klaus Kinski), who gives a surprisingly dignified performance.

But unfortunately, the film is played mostly for laughs. Gone is the graphic violence which established the unique tone for the original film (Fighting Fists of Shanghai Joe), replaced with frenzied bloodless kung fu nonsense. It's almost as wretched as Kung Fu Brothers in the Wild West.

Return of the Holy Ghost see Gunmen and the Holy Ghost

Return of the Holy Spirit see Gunmen and the Holy Ghost

Revenge at El Paso see Ace High

Revenge for Revenge (1968)

Vendetta per Vendetta Ital. *Director:* Ray Calloway; *Script:* Ray Calloway; *Camera:* Giuseppe Aquari; *Music:* Angelo Francesco Lavagnino; *Producer:* 21-Producciones (Italy). *Cast:* John Ireland, John Hamilton, Loredana Nusciak, Lemmy Carson, Giuseppe Lavricella, Conny Caracciolo.

An amazingly nasty, bitter film from director Mario Colucci (alias Ray Calloway). It tells the story of a woman, Clara Bower (Conny Caracciolo), who tells her lover, Chaliko (John Hamilton), where her husband has hidden ten bags of gold. When Major Bower (John Ireland) learns of his wife's indiscretion, he kills her. But it's too late. Chaliko has already stolen the fortune. Eventually, the two men meet in a desert hideout where a gun battle erupts. Both Major Bower and Chaliko are killed. The gold is scattered in the wilderness.

This stark, pungent film remains Mario Colucci's only contribution to the genre.

Revenge of a Gunfighter see **Mercenary**

Reverend Colt (1970)

Reverendo Colt Ital. *Director:* Leon Klimovsky; *Script:* Tito Carpi/Manuel Martinez Remis; *Camera:* Salvatore Caruso; *Music:* Lady Park (Gianni Ferrio); *Producer:* Oceania Produzioni/R.M. Films (Italy/Spain). *Cast:* Guy Madison, Richard Harrison, Thomas Moore, Maria Martin, German Cobos, Pedro Sanchez, Steven Tedd, Perla Cristina, Alfonso Rojas, Mariano Vidal Molina, Cris Huerta.

Leon Klimovsky, best known for his Spanish horror and mystery films (*Dragonfly for Each Corpse, Dracula's Saga, Werewolf versus the Vampire Women*, etc.), made lackluster Westerns with illogical, rambling storylines. Of his 12 entries, this one is his best. But that's not saying much, because unconfirmed information (originating from star Richard Harrison in a "Spaghetti Cinema" interview with William Connolly and Tom Betts) suggests that the actual director for this film is Marino Girolami (alias Frank Martin).

Mysterious Reverend Miller (Guy Madison) comes to Tucson to open a church. The day he arrives, a gang of outlaws led by notorious Meticcio (Pedro Sanchez) robs the bank and escapes with all the cash. For some reason, the townspeople are convinced that Reverend Miller is involved in the holdup (there appears to be no basis for this supposition except that Miller was a former bounty hunter, plus it's also necessary for the advancement of the plot).

Sheriff Donovan (Richard Harrison) saves the preacher from a lynch mob by locking him in jail and then he offers "a deal." The sheriff agrees to release Reverend Miller if he tracks down the bandits and returns the loot.

At that point, Reverend Miller becomes Reverend Colt. Not only does he recover the stolen money and stop the outlaws, but he also finds time to rescue a wagon train, under siege from yet another outlaw gang.

Reverendo Colt see **Reverend Colt**

Revolt in Canada see **Canadian Wilderness**

La Révolte des Indiens Apaches see **Winnetou the Warrior**

Reward for Ringo see *Ringo, It's Massacre Time*

The Reward's Yours, the Man's Mine (1970)

La Taglia È Tua, l'Uomo l'Ammazzo Io Ital. *Director:* Edward G. Muller; *Script:* Ignacio Iquino/Edoardo Mulargia; *Camera:* Antonio Modica; *Music:* Alessandro Alessandroni; *Producer:* Tritone Film (Italy). *Cast:* Robert Woods, Aldo Berti, Mario Brega, Rosalba Neri, Fabrizio Gianni, Maurizio Bonuglia.

Although he's made eight competent Spaghetti Westerns, director and cowriter (with peer filmmaker Ignacio Iquino) Edward G. Muller (pseudonym for Edoardo Mulargia) is better known for his "women in an Amazon prison" movies, *Hotel Paradise* and *Escape from Hell.*

In this film, Muller tells the story of a bounty hunter (Robert Woods) who agrees to capture an outlaw "live" but, unfortunately, he is forced to shoot the wanted man. The ending is highly ironic and satisfying. It's worth the wait.

Reza por Tu Alma . . . Y Muere ou los Bandidos del Fort see *Sabata the Killer*

Ric e Gian all Conquista del West see *Rick and John, Conquerors of the West*

Rick and John, Conquerors of the West (1967)

Rick and John in the Conquest of the West; Ric e Gian all Conquista del West Ital. *Director:* Osvaldo Civirani; *Script:* Osvaldo Civirani/Antonio Ferrau/Tito Carpi; *Camera:* Osvaldo Civirani; *Music:* Piero Umiliani; *Producer:* Denwar Film (Italy). *Cast:* Craig Hill, Riccardo Miniggio, Gianfabio Bosco, Francesco Mulè, Barbara Carroll, Tiberio Murgia, Anna Campori.

Written, photographed and directed by Osvaldo Civirani, there's no one else to blame for this lame comedy about two Union soldiers. During the Civil War, the Northerns decide to buy thousands of horses from a company in the west. The deal is struck, but how will the North get the money to them? By stagecoach (of course), with one distinctive alteration. The payment will be the wagon wheels, solid gold wagon wheels. It's a plan that can't fail. Right? Wrong. After going to such elaborate precautions, amazingly, Captain Stuart (Craig Hill) assigns two utter jackasses to drive the stage. As it turns out, not only are Rick and John idiots, but they're also two-bit con-men who end up selling the wheels (they don't know the true value) to an Indian tribe. At the conclusion, the stage is destroyed. And Stuart, thinking the gold is lost, dishonorably discharges the two morons. Rick and John begin to wander aimlessly, when the angry Indian chief finds them and demands that they take back the bogus, defective wheels. And the morons become rich.

Rick and John in the Conquest of the West see *Rick and John, Conquerors of the West*

Ride and Kill (1964)

Sheriff Brandy; Brandy; Cavalco e Uccidi Ital. *Director:* J. L. Boraw and Mario Caiano; *Script:* José Mallorqui; *Camera:* Aldo Greci/Mario Sbrenna; *Music:* Riz Ortolani; *Producer:* Atlantis Film (Italy/Spain). *Cast:* Alex Nicol, Robert Hundar, Lawrence Palmer, Pauline Baards, John Mac Douglas, Margaret Grayson, Luis Induñi, Antonio Casas, Jorge Ringaud, Natalia Silva.

Movie poster from *Ride and Kill* (1964).

Here's an early Italian/Spanish coproduction directed by J. L. Boraw (alias for José Luis Borau) and written by Spaghetti Western pioneer Mario Caiano (using a "José Mallorqui" moniker). The story is an interesting variation on a standard "gangster film" motif.

A syndicate of powerful citizens (including the mayor, the judge, a banker and a saloon owner) organize a protection racket against the townspeople of Tombstone. When the sheriff tries to stop them, they hire a hitman/gunfighter named Moody (Robert Hundar) who kills him.

With backing from the "mob," the lawman's job is filled by the town drunk, Brandy (Alex Nicol). But, Sheriff Brandy (obviously not realizing that he was appointed as a patsy) is inspired by the badge and by the love of his barmaid girlfriend Eva (Pauline Baards). He stops drinking and is determined to "bring Moody to justice." The two men face each other in an unfair gunfight, but in a scene reminiscent of the U.S. John Ford Western, *The Man Who Shot Liberty Valance* (1962), reformed outlaw Steve Donnelly (Antonio Casas) interrupts the showdown and helps Brandy arrest the killer. Later, Donnelly is shot in the back. And a whole gang of outlaws (plus the syndicate) attack Sheriff Brandy. The townspeople, rallied by Eva, come to Brandy's rescue. Tombstone is saved.

Rimase Uno Solo e Fu la Morte per Tutti see *Brother Outlaw*

Ringo: Face of Revenge (1966)

Ringo Volto della Vendetta Ital. *Director:* Mario Caiano; *Script:* Eduardo Brochero/Mario Caiano; *Camera:* Julio Ortas; *Music:* Francesco De Masi; *Producer:* Emmeci/Estela Film (Italy/Spain). *Cast:* Anthony Steffen, Frank Wolff, Eduardo Fajardo, Armando Calvo, Alejandra Nilo, Alfonso Goda.

Here's yet another attempt to capitalize on the "Ringo" character, or (at

Movie poster from Sergio Corbucci's *Ringo and His Golden Pistol* (1966) starring Mark Damon as Ringo.

best) the Ringo name. Inspired by the internationally successful Lorne Greene record, "Ringo" (RCA/Victor release; 1964) and initially brought to the screen by Duccio Tessari via his film *Pistol for Ringo* starring Giuliano Gemma in the title role, the Ringo moniker was utilized in many Eurowesterns during the mid–60s. For a listing of those films see the Appendix.

This one doesn't even have a character named Ringo. The leads are Tim (Anthony Steffen) and his two friends Tricky (Frank Wolff) and Davy (Eduardo Fajardo in a nontypical, bearded, almost-a-good-guy role) plus a hapless Mexican bandit named Fidel (Armando Calvo). The three (Tim, Davy and Tricky) save Fidel from a tight, bullet-blazing situation. While tending to his wounds, they discover a tattoo of "half-a-map" on his back; the other half is on the back of a friend named Sam, the sheriff of a nearby town (Alfonso Goda). Somehow, when the two maps are put together directions become clear for a treasure consisting of gold. The only survivor at the film's conclusion is Davy who gives the fortune to a poor Mexican village and rides off with Fidel's sister, Emanuela (Alejandra Nilo), Goofy but diversionary.

Mario Caiano (alias William Hawkins) is the director of 11 Eurowesterns, including the lightly fluffy *Train for Durango* and the surprisingly violent *Fighting Fists of Shanghai Joe* (see Directors filmography). He also made numerous exploitation films, including *Blood* (1971), *Nazi Love Camp 27* (1976), plus (under yet another alias, Allan Grunewald) the classic *Nightmare Castle* (1965) with Barbara Steele and Helga Line.

Ringo Against Johnny Colt see *Kill or Die*

Ringo and Gringo Against All (1966)

Rebels on the Loose; Ringo e Gringo Contro Tutti Ital. *Director:* Bruno Corbucci; *Script:* Vittorio Vighi/Ugo Guerra/Scarnicci/Tarabusi; *Camera:* Alessandro D'Eva; *Music:* Gianni Ferrio/Carlo Rustichelli; *Producer:* Panda Films (Italy/Spain). *Cast:* Lando Buzzanca, Raimondo Vianello, Maria Martinez, Monica Randall, Alfonso Rojas, Miguel De Castillo.

With few exceptions, Bruno Corbucci (brother of famed filmmaker, Sergio) has made a career out of directing low-brow comedies (*Messalina, Messalina* and *When Men Carried Clubs and Women Played Ding Dong*) or police action flicks (*Super Cops of Miami* and *Anti-Gangster Squad*) and stooge Westerns (like *Three Musketeers of the West* and this one). It's the story of two idiot Southern soldiers (Lando Buzzanca and Raimondo Vianello) at an isolated fortress. They think the Civil War is still waging, but it's really been over for eight years. The plot becomes hopelessly transparent when the "heroes" meet two outlaw beauties (Maria Martinez and Monica Randall) who urge the dimwits to continue their sabotage activities.

Ringo and His Golden Pistol (1966)

Johnny Oro Ital. *Director:* Sergio Corbucci; *Script:* Adriano Bolzoni/Franco Rossetti; *Camera:* Riccardo Pallottini; *Music:* Carlo Savina; *Producer:* Joseph Fryd, Sanson Film (Italy). *Cast:* Mark Damon, Valeria Fabrizi, Franco De Rosa, Andrea Aureli, John Bartha, Ettore Manni, Ken Wood, Giulia Rubini.

Originally filmed as *Johnny Oro*, it was changed in the dubbing to *Ringo and His Golden Pistol* to capitalize on the success of Duccio Tessari's *Ringo* movies. In this one, Ringo (Mark Damon) is a bounty hunter who suddenly finds himself in over his head when he attempts to arrest outlaw boss Juanito Perez (Franco De Rosa).

Most of Coldstone City is destroyed as he fights the entire gang, single-handedly, until some of the scared townspeople come to his aid. Armed with (a seemingly endless supply of) dynamite, Ringo eliminates all the bad guys and half the town. At the film's conclusion, just before he leaves in search of more adventure, Ringo donates the reward money to the Coldstone City Rebuilding Committee.

Cowritten by prolific screenwriter Franco Rossetti (also director of *Big Ripoff*) and Adriano Bolzoni, with principal photography from Riccardo Pallottini, and a soundtrack composed by Carlo Savina, this film was Sergio Corbucci's second Eurowestern, following *Minnesota Clay* and preceding *Django*.

Mark Damon made many Spaghetti Westerns (see Performers filmography), but he is best known for his role in Roger Corman's *Fall of the House of Usher* plus many Italian thrillers. In the late 1970s, he gave up acting for an industry executive position, becoming the head of PSO films.

Ringo e Gringo Contro Tutti see *Ringo and Gringo Against All*

Ringo el Texano see *Texican*

Ringo from Nebraska see *Savage Gringo*

Ringo il Cavaliere Solitario see *Ringo, the Lone Rider*

Ringo, It's Massacre Time (1970)

Wanted Ringo; Reward for Ringo; Ringo, Tempo di Massacro Ital. *Director:* Mario Pinzauti; *Script:* Mario Pinzauti; *Camera:* Vitaliano Natalucci; *Music:* José Espieta/Felice Di Stefan; *Producer:* Alv Film (Italy). *Cast:* Mickey Hargitay, Omero Gargano, Peter Martell, Lucye Bonerz, Jean Louis, Anna Cerreto.

Virtually, an unknown film stateside, from Mario Pinzauti, the director of the "almost obscure" *Let's Go and Kill Sartana* (1971). It's especially significant due to the "starring status" of popular genre actor Mickey Hargitay. Apparently, this is yet another movie to be lost in the 1969–70 glut.

Ringo, Pray to Your God and Die see *Ballad of a Gunman*

Ringo, Tempo di Massacro see *Ringo, It's Massacre Time*

Ringo, the Lone Rider (1967)

Two Brothers, One Death; Ringo il Cavaliere Solitario Ital. *Director:* Rafael R. Marchent; *Script:* Eduardo Brochero/Mario Caiano; *Camera:* Emmanuele Di Cola; *Music:* Manuel Parada/Francesco De Masi; *Producer:* Ricardo Sanz, Uni Films (Italy/Spain). *Cast:* Peter Martell, Piero Lulli, Dianik Zurakowska, Miguel Del Castillo, Alfonso Rojas, Paolo Hertz, Jesus Puente, Armando Calvo, Antonio Pica, José Jaspe, Frank Braña.

Director Rafael Romero Marchent (brother of filmmaker Joaquin Romero Marchent) makes a good-looking Western, usually short on dialogue, but excelling in action. This one is somewhat a departure. The emphasis is more on tensions and posturing, with a flare toward machismo, actually the subsistence of the Spaghetti Western.

The story is a variation of the *Magnificent Seven* theme, as citizens of Springfield hire Ringo (Peter Martell) to help them eradicate a gang of outlaws, led by Bill Anderson (Piero Lulli). Marchent's deft direction, with cinematographer Di Cola's extreme closeups, give the film an accentuated vehemence.

Ringo Volto della Vendetta see Ringo: Face of Revenge

Ringo's Big Night (1966)

Grande Notte di Ringo; La Notte del Desperado Ital. *Director:* Mario Maffei; *Script:* Mario Mattei; *Camera:* Carlo Bellero/Emilio Foriscot; *Music:* Carlo Rustichelli; *Producer:* Silver Dem (Italy/Spanish). *Cast:* William Berger, Adriana Ambesi, Eduardo Fajardo, Walter Maestosi, Guido De Salvi, Jorge Rigaud, Tom Felleghy, José Bodalo, Armando Calvo, Francisco Moran.

The people of Tombstone are up in arms over a rash of stagecoach robberies, especially the last one. Two hundred thousand dollars has been stolen en route between Silver City and Tombstone. Mayor Joseph Findley (Eduardo Fajardo) and his cronies, saloon owner Jim Bailey, businessman Black Norton and the sheriff, are the real culprits, but Jack Balman (William Berger) has been blamed. Eventually he pierces the clout ("You're wrong about me, I'm respectable!" cries Fajardo in a memorable moment) and exposes them.

At the film's conclusion, federal agent John Crowe (Tom Felleghy) tries to convince Jack to quit the desperado way of life. He says: "The gunmen of today could be the greatest sheriffs of tomorrow." Sounds like the sort of thing that should be on a bumper sticker, doesn't it?

Rita of the West (1967)

Little Rita nel Far West Ital; *Crazy Westerners. Director:* Ferdinando Baldi; *Script:* Franco Rossetti/Ferdinando Baldi; *Camera:* Enzo Barboni; *Music:* Robbe Poitevin; *Producer:* Manolo Bolognini, Cinematografica (Italy). *Cast:* Rita Pavone, Terence Hill, Lucio Dalla, Nina Larker, Kirk Morris, Gordon Mitchell, Fernando Sancho.

This is the embarrassing skeleton in director Ferdinando Baldi's closet. The fact that he is also the cowriter adds further insult to injury.

Little Rita (Rita Pavone) is the princess of the West, everybody loves her. Everybody, except the bad guys. But they know her by reputation and they stay clear. She is the protector of all "God-fearing partners." And she is revered like a goddess. Then one day, Little Rita falls in love with a stranger, Black Star (Terence Hill). However (as amazing as it may seem) he doesn't love her. He's only stringing her along to steal the Indian's sacred gold. But when he attempts the snatch, he's discovered.

Little Rita goes into a serious depression; Black Star is deeply moved by her despair. He tells her that he will "go straight," giving up the criminal life and loving her always (now that's more like it!). Little Rita is happy once more.

She thanks God for "making all that is evil in the world go away." She is so over-joyed that her mortal body can't handle it, and that night she becomes a holy spirit (!?!), disappearing into the vast desert. Unbelievable.

As bad as this movie may be, there are still some unexpected moments of drollery, including a clever Django spoof. Most U.S. prints are minus the song-and-dance segments (they were never translated out of Italian); but, unfortunately, these numbers are the best thing about the film. Overall, it remains a mystery why a genre giant like Fernando Baldi would ever get involved in such an atrocity. And, even more amazing, why he signed his name to it.

Rita Pavone was an Italian pop singer, marketed by RCA in the mid–60s. Her only U.S. Top 40 hit was (ironically) called *Remember Me?* Terence Hill, obviously a glutton for punishment, made an equally pathetic non–Western with Rita called *The Crazy Kids of War*, a German-sympathetic Second World War musical comedy.

Ritorno di Clint il Solitario see *Return of Clint the Stranger*

Ritorno di Django see *Django Strikes Again*

Il Ritorno di Ringo see *Return of Ringo*

Il Ritorno di Shangai Joe see *Return of Shanghai Joe*

River of Dollars see *Hills Run Red*

River Pirates of the Mississippi see *Pirates of the Mississippi*

Road to Fort Alamo (1966)

Arizona Bill; La Strada per Fort Alamo Ital; *Camino de Fuerte Alamo* Sp. *Director:* Mario Bava; *Script:* Vincent Thomas/Charles Price/Jane Brisbane; *Camera:* Claud Raguse/Bud Third; *Music:* Piero Umiliani; *Producer:* Protor/World Entertainment (Italy/France). *Cast:* Ken Clark, Jany Clair, Michel Lemoine, Adreina Paul, Kirk Bert, Antonio Gradoli, Dean Ardow.

It is the best of the three "Mario Bava" Spaghetti Westerns (also see *Roy Colt and Winchester Jack* and *Savage Gringo*), but it pales when compared to his classic horror films, *Black Sunday* (1960) (also called *Demon's Mask*), *Black Sabbath* (1964), *Blood and Black Lace* (1964), or even *Twitch of the Death Nerve* (1972). Bava's expertise is his flamboyant cinematography and stylish art direction, aptly demonstrated in his work for Riccardo Freda's *I Vampiri* (1957) and *Horrible Dr. Hichcock* (1962). His Westerns are surprisingly void of these same touches. They emerge as not necessarily bad films, just average ones. Unfortunately, his purported "lack of interest" in the Spaghetti Western genre seems to show itself on the screen. Even Bava's peplums (*Erik the Viking* and *Hercules in the Haunted World*) are more satisfying.

Arizona Bill (Ken Clark) and his gang, disguised as Union soldiers, rob a bank in Wagon City. When Bill (or Bud in some translations) complains about the killing of an innocent elderly woman, he and his sidekick, Slim (Michel Lemoine), are left to die in the desert. But they are rescued by a federal wagon train bound for Fort Alamo. En route Bill falls in love with Janet (Jany Clair).

His feelings for her convince him to go straight. Eventually, Bill becomes the hero of the expedition, first by protecting them from some nasty outlaws and then by saving everybody during a hostile Indian attack. At the conclusion, Bill returns the stolen money to the authorities and he leaves the wagon train with Janet and his friend Slim.

Rojo (1966)

El Rojo Sp. *Director:* Leo Coleman; *Script:* Roberto Gianviti/José-Maria Seone/ Mario Casacci/Antonio Giambriccio; *Camera:* Aldo Giordani; *Music:* Benedetto Ghiglia; *Producer:* Roberto Amoroso, Ramofilm/Petruka Film (Italy/Spain). *Cast:* Richard Harrison, Peter Carter, Nieves Navarro, Mirko Ellis, Annie Gorassini, José Jaspe, Rita Klein, Andrew Ray, Raf Baldassare, John Bartha, Ray Ressel.

Here's the first Spaghetti Western directed by Leopoldo Savona (alias Leo Coleman). The far superior *Killer Kid* followed a year later.

This one tells the very predictable story of a mysterious stranger named "El Rojo" (Richard Harrison), arcanely avenging a family of pioneers who were slaughtered when they tried to take possession of their valuable gold mine. The murderers, four influential men (including the sheriff played by Peter Carter), are each methodically eliminated by El Rojo.

Why? Why did this Stranger avenge the pioneers? Close up, tight shot of Richard Harrison's face: "The family was my own." Gasp (or was that a yawn?) from the audience.

El Rojo see *Rojo*

The Rope and the Colt see *Cemetery Without Crosses*

Rough Justice see *The Bell*

Roy Colt and Winchester Jack (1970)

Colt e Wincester Jack Ital; *Roy Colt e Winchester Jack* Ital. *Director:* Mario Bava; *Script:* Mario Di Nardo/Roberto Agrin; *Camera:* Antonio Rinaldi; *Music:* Piero Umiliani; *Producer:* P.A.C./Tigielle 33 (Italy). *Cast:* Brett Halsey, Charles Southwood, Marilu Tolo, Teodoro Corra, Lee Burton, Bruno Corazzari, Franco Pesce, Rick Boyd.

This is one of three Eurowesterns directed by the famous horror filmmaker Mario Bava (also see *Road to Fort Alamo* [also called *Arizona Bill*] and *Savage Gringo*]).

Roy and Jack (Brett Halsey and Charles Southwood) are friends. But when Jack forcibly takes over the leadership of their outlaw gang, Roy goes to Carson City and becomes sheriff. Their relationship is immediately strained because they are now on opposite sides of the law; however, the two ultimately join against a common enemy, the sadistic Reverendo (Teodoro Corra), who (with a gang of killers) is slaughtering peaceful Indians and stealing their gold.

Chief cameraman is Antonio Rinaldi; music by prolific Piero Umiliani.

Roy Colt e Winchester Jack see *Roy Colt and Winchester Jack*

Royal Mounted Police see *Red Coat*

Run Man, Run (1967)

Big Gundown 2; Corri, Uomo, Corri. Director: Sergio Sollima; Script: Sergio Sollima/Fabrizio De Angelis; Camera: Guglielmo Mancori; Music: Ennio Morricone/Bruno Nicolai; Producer: Mancori/Chrétien (Italy/France). Cast: Tomás Milian, Donald O'Brien, John Ireland, Rick Boyd, Linda Veras, Chelo Alsono, José Torres, Edward G. Ross, Nello Pazzafini.

A sequel to the previous year's successful film, *Big Gundown.* It reunites director Sollima with Tomás Milian (again as Cuchillo, the misunderstood Mexican knife-throwing bandit). But the film suffers from the absence of the original costar, Lee Van Cleef (or some other strong, in-charge persona), to give a balance to Milian's frenzied, energetic character.

This is the continuing story of Cuchillo's misadventures, perhaps too episodic, against a Mexican Revolution backdrop. It's another search-for-the-lost-gold film, as an uneasy alliance is eventually solidified between Cuchillo and an American opportunist named Cassidy (Donald O'Brien). The gold is ultimately found (inside a printing press) and taken to Mexico. Viva la Revolución!

Ruthless Colt of the Gringo (1967)

Gringo's Pitiless Colt; La Spietata Colt del Gringo Ital. Director: José Luis Madrid; Script: Agustin Navarro; Camera: Marcello Gatti; Music: Francesco De Masi; Producer: Zelyko Kunkera, Danny Film/Filma Films (Italy/Spain). Cast: Jim Reed, Carlo Fabrizi, Martha Dovan, Pat Greenhill, Luis Induñi, Charles Otter, Germana Monteverdi.

Sol Lester (Jim Reed, aka Luigi Giuliano) was sent to prison for killing a mine owner in Paso City. He was innocent. The crime was really committed by evil town boss Holloway (Carlo Fabrizi). When Sol is released from jail, he's only interested in one thing. Revenge.

He goes back to Paso City and discovers that everyone is living in constant fear. Their lives are controlled by Holloway and his merciless gang. Sol (obviously the "Gringo" of the title) decides to "take on" all the bad guys. He's joined by a handful of brave townsmen and Lois (Martha Dovan), the mine owner's exculpating daughter, in a climactic gun battle.

Certainly, while not an original theme, the competent direction and skillful photography make it seem fresh enough. Scriptwriter Agustin Navarro also directed the Spaghetti Western *Shots Ring Out.*

The Ruthless Four (1968)

Sam Cooper's Gold; Every Man for Himself Brit; *Ognuno per Se* Ital. Director: Giorgio Capitani; Script: Fernando Di Leo/Augusto Caminito; Camera: Sergio D'Offizi; Music: Carlo Rustichelli; Producer: P.C.M. (Italy). Cast: Gilbert Roland, Klaus Kinski, George Hilton, Van Heflin, Sarah Ross, Rick Boyd, Sergio Doria, Ivan Scratuglia, Giorgio Groden.

A good cast brings a special chemistry to this film about prospector Sam Cooper (Van Heflin) who strikes gold, but suddenly finds himself with three undesirable partners: his adopted homosexual son Manolo (George Hilton), Mason (Gilbert Roland), and Blond (Klaus Kinski). Unlike much of his work during this period, Kinski's performance is actually for the duration of the film. Or, more correctly, until Mason beats him to death, near the conclusion.

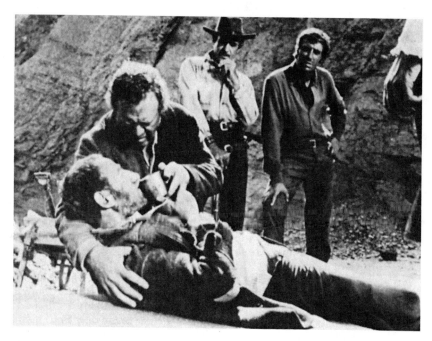

The Ruthless Four (1968) featuring Van Heflin (giving a drink to Sergio Doria) and Gilbert Roland (in hat) and George Hilton.

It's cowritten by future action/horror director Fernando Di Leo (*Slaughter Hotel*, also starring Kinski); the chief cameraman is Sergio D'Offizi.

This movie is one of five Eurowesterns made by popular Mexican star Gilbert Roland. See Performers filmography for complete list.

Sabata (1969)

Ehi, Amico . . . C'è Sabata, Hai Chiuso! Ital. *Director:* Frank Kramer; *Script:* Renato Izzo/Frank Kramer; *Camera:* Sandro Mancori; *Music:* Marcello Giombini; *Producer:* Alberto Grimaldi, PEA/Delphos (Italy). *Cast:* Lee Van Cleef, William Berger, Pedro Sanchez, Franco Ressel, Robert Hundar, Linda Veras, Spean Covery, Ken Wood, Romano Puppo, Gianni Rizzo, Alan Collins.

Advertising for this film coined the phrase: "The man with gunsight eyes." The descriptive proclamation stuck, and became an identifiable affectation for Lee Van Cleef and his squinty-eyed performances (a slogan certainly much better than the ludicrous "Mister Ugly Is Back" utilized by Columbia Pictures for promoting *The Big Gundown*).

This movie is a shoot-first-ask-questions-later killfest, with the humor provided by Sabata's macho quips. It's the story of robbery, blackmail, and greed, as bounty hunter Sabata (Lee Van Cleef) along with his reckless "gun-concealed-inside-a-banjo" partner mows down everybody standing between themselves and a $60,000 ransom. Incidentally, the Italian title translates to *Hey, Friend, There Is Sabata . . . You've Closed.*

Director Frank Kramer (alias Gianfranco Parolini), with talented camera-man Sandro Mancori, made two more films in the series, *Adios Sabata* (an unofficial sequel, originally called *Indio Black* starring Yul Brynner in his only Eurowestern) and *Return of Sabata* with Lee Van Cleef back in the title role. However, Kramer's best genre movie is easily the original *Sartana* with Gianni Garko.

Sabata Is Coming see *Sabata the Killer*

Sabata Revient see *Dig Your Grave, Friend . . . Sabata's Coming*

Sabata the Killer (1970)

Viva Sabata!; Sabata Is Coming; Llega Sabata Ital; *Reza por Tu Alma . . . Y Muere ou los Bandidos del Fort; Arriva Sabata* Sp. *Director:* Tullio Demichelli; *Script:* Nino Stresa/Tullio Demichelli; *Camera:* Aldo Ricci; *Music:* Marcello Giombini; *Producer:* Tritone/Producciones Dia (Italy/Spain). *Cast:* Peter Lee Lawrence, Anthony Steffen, Eduardo Fajardo, Alfredo Mayo, Luis Induñi, Rossana Rovere, Alfonso Rojas, Maria Villa, Cris Huerta.

Peter (Peter Lee Lawrence) tricks his partner in crime, a banker named Garfield (Eduardo Fajardo), by stealing $300,000 and keeping it for himself. Luckily, at the same moment, Sabata and Mangusta (Anthony Steffen and Alfredo Mayo) have just arrived in town driving their brand new Ford motor car. Peter convinces them to escape with him (they don't need much convincing since they were planning to rob the bank anyway) and the three get away.

After a series of misadventures the "heroes" believe that they are safe, but Garfield has organized a group of "professionals" who track down the rogues. The comedy abruptly turns grotesque when Mangusta and Peter are killed, the money is destroyed in a fire, and Sabata barely escapes with his life.

Demichelli directed five Eurowesterns (see Directors filmography) plus many spy and mobster action films, including *077: Intrigue in Lisbon* with Brett Halsey, *My Name Is Sex* starring George Hilton, and *Mean Machine (Rico!)* with Arthur Kennedy. He is, perhaps, best known for *Assignment Terror: Dracula vs. Frankenstein* (1969) with Michael Rennie, Paul Naschy, Craig Hill and Karin Dor.

Sabata 2 see *Adios, Sabata*

Saguaro (1968)

Sapevano Solo Uccidere Ital. *Director:* Amerigo Anton; *Script:* Mario Moroni/ Amerigo Anton; *Camera:* Fausto Rossi; *Music:* Angelo Francesco Lavagnino; *Producer:* Camillo Tanio Boccia (Italy). *Cast:* Kirk Morris, Larry Ward, Alan Steel, Gordon Mitchell, Kim Arden, Ana Castor.

A nihilistic, amoral Western featuring spirited performances from peplum superstars Kirk Morris, Alan Steel and Gordon Mitchell. Produced, cowritten and directed by Tanio Boccia (alias Amerigo Anton), this film is also probably his best.

Demoralized after the Civil War, Confederate soldier Jeff (Kirk Morris) is sluggishly wandering through the West with his friend Enrique. Suddenly, a gang of Mexican bandidos attack them, and Enrique is brutally murdered.

Wanting to avenge his friend's death, Jeff appoints himself as a "territorial lawman." Then, disguised as a Mexican, he robs a bank, using the money to organize his own posse to successfully track down the bandidos.

Sam Cooper's Gold see *The Ruthless Four*

Samurai see *White, the Yellow and the Black*

Sangue Chiama Sangue see *Blood Calls to Blood*

Sangue Rosso e l'Oro Giallo see *Red Blood, Yellow Gold*

Sansone e il Tesoro degli Incas see *Lost Treasure of the Incas*

Sapevano Solo Uccidere see *Saguaro*

Saranda see *Twenty Paces to Death*

Sartana (1968)

If You Meet Sartana . . . Pray for Your Death; Gunfighters Die Harder; Se Incontri Sartana Prega per la Tua Morte. Director: Frank Kramer; Script: Renato Izzo/Gianfranco Parolini; Camera: Sandro Mancori; Music: Piero Piccioni; Producer: Étoile Film/Parnass Film (Italy/West Germany). Cast: John Garko, Klaus Kinski, Fernando Sancho, William Berger, Sydney Chaplin, Gianni Rizzo.

Sartana's first line of dialogue, "I am your pallbearer," sets the stage for all the Sartana films to follow. Sartana is the "Angel of Death." His primary goal is to kill, not for money (although in this particular film he appropriates quite a bit of cash through the death of others) and not for vengeance (the standard motivation in most Spaghetti Westerns), but rather just because certain people deserve it. As portrayed by John (Gianni) Garko, Sartana is a bigger-than-life Western vigilante.

A gold shipment (from a shady deal) is robbed by snuff-sniffing Lasky (William Berger) and his gang, a gang that he mows down with a Gatling gun when they attempt a double-cross. Lasky and his sidekick Morgan (Klaus Kinski, spelled Kinsky in the credits) decide to blackmail the original gold thieves, a seemingly respectable banker and his cronies. The whole plan is manipulated by Sartana, setting his own traps for all the culprits, including the mayor's cunning widow who has hidden the gold in her husband's coffin.

This film is proof positive that Frank Kramer (Gianfranco Parolini) can make a fine movie (it's good to be reminded of this after sitting through his clunkers, *God's Gun* and *Return of Sabata*, not to mention the Smith and Colby atrocity, *We Are Not Angels*).

As the "Sartana" series grew more and more popular, under the filmmaking guidance of Anthony Ascott (Giuliano Carmineo), the character took on a mystical, even supernatural, quality. Other titles in the series (with Garko in the lead role: *I Am Sartana . . . Your Angel of Death (Sartana the Gravedigger)* (1969), *Sartana Kills Them All* (1970), *Light the Fuse . . . Sartana's Coming* (1971), and *Have a Good Funeral . . . Sartana Will Pay* (1971). George Hilton took over the title role for Ascott's continuation, *I Am Sartana, Trade Your Guns for a Coffin* (1972). There were many other films with the "Sartana" tie (see Appendix), but none of them featured the patented character.

A curious side note: Gianni Garko played a wicked villain named "Sartana" in an earlier Alberto Cardone movie, *$1000 on the Black* (1967), which was re-released as *Blood at Sundown* in 1969, and was promoted as a new Sartana film, advertising "You Won't Believe What's Happened to Sartana Now!"

Sartana: Sangue e la Penna see Blood at Sundown (1969)

Sartana and His Shadow of Death see Shadow of Sartana . . . Shadow of Your Death

Sartana Does Not Forgive (1968)

Sonora Sp; *Sartana Non Perdona* Ital. *Director:* Alfonso Balcazar; *Script:* Giorgio Simonelli/Jaime Jesus Balcazar; *Camera:* Jaime Del Casas; *Music:* Francesco De Masi; *Producer:* Balcazar De Barcelona (Spain/Italy). *Cast:* Gilbert Roland, George Martin, Jack Elam, Tony Norton, Hugo Blancho, Gerard Tichy, Diana Lorys, Donatella Turri, Miguel De La Riva, Rosalba Neri, Tomás Torres.

Here's a film that combines the "Sartana" myth with the ever popular "revenge for a slaughtered family" theme. José (Tony Norton) and his wife (Donatella Turri) are murdered by a band of ruthless outlaws, led by Kirchner (Gilbert Roland). José's brother, Sartana (George Martin), seeks revenge.

Interestingly, this deadly serious Spaghetti Western is cowritten by Giorgio Simonelli, the writer/director of many "Franco and Ciccio" slapstick comedies, including *Two Gangsters in the Wild West, Two Sergeants of General Custer,* and *Two Sons of Ringo.*

Sartana, If Your Left Arm Offends, Cut It Off see Django and Sartana Are Coming . . . It's the End

Sartana in the Valley of Death (1970)

Ballad of Death Valley (Euro title); *Sartana in the Valley of the Vultures; Sartana nella Valle degli Avvoltoi* Ital. *Director:* Roberto Mauri; *Script:* Roberto Mauri; *Camera:* Sandro Mancori; *Music:* Augusto Martili; *Producer:* Victor Produzione (Italy). *Cast:* William Berger, Wayde Preston, Aldo Berti, Jolanda Modio, Alan Collins, Pamela Tudor, Carlo Giordana.

This one is written and directed by Roberto Mauri with stately camera work from underrated Sandro Mancori (generally associated with the better productions of Frank Kramer and Sergio Garrone).

Lee Calloway (William Berger) is hired to help the three Douglas brothers break out of prison. In exchange he will receive half of their stolen gold. But once they are safe, the brothers double-cross him. Lee narrowly escapes, wandering in the desert for days until he is rescued by a mysterious woman, Esther (Jolanda Modio), who nurses the miscreant back to health, only to betray him for the price on his head.

Sartana in the Valley of the Vultures see Sartana in the Valley of Death

Sartana Kills Them All (1970)

Lo Irritarono . . . e Sartana Fece Piazza Pulita Ital. *Director:* Rafael Romero Marchent; *Script:* Joaquin Romero Marchent/Santiago Moncada; *Camera:*

Guglielmo Mancori; *Music:* Marcello Giombini; *Producer:* Tarquinia Film (Italy/Spain). *Cast:* John Garko, William Bogart, Maria Silva, Carlos R. Marchent, Luis Induñi, Raf Baldassare, Paco Sanz, Cris Huerta.

Unofficially, this is the third film in the Sartana series. However, aside from John (Gianni) Garko's involvement, none of the other creative personnel are part of this project. A rival Continental film company, Tarquinia, employed competent filmmaker Rafael Romero Marchent to direct this movie and they signed Garko to play the popular Sartana character. But the larger than life charisma is missing. The story remains a cluttered tale of vigilante justice as Sartana attempts to stop a mysterious gang of gun traffickers who are raiding Cavalry forts and stealing weapons.

After this project, elements of the spy/thriller genre were infused into the struggling Sartana motif when Anthony Ascott (Giuliano Carmineo) refurbished the series with *Have a Good Funeral . . . Sartana Will Pay* (1971).

Sartana nella Valle degli Avvoltoi see *Sartana in the Valley of Death*

Sartana Non Perdona see *Sartana Does Not Forgive*

Sartana the Gravedigger see *I Am Sartana, Your Angel of Death*

Sartana, the Invincible Gunman see *Four Came to Kill Sartana*

Sartana's Coming, Get Your Coffins Ready see *I Am Sartana, Trade Your Guns for a Coffin*

Sartana's Here . . . Trade Your Pistol for a Coffin see *I Am Sartana, Trade Your Guns for a Coffin*

Savage Gringo (1966)

Gunman Called Nebraska; Ringo from Nebraska; Nebraska il Pistolero Ital. *Director:* Mario Bava with Antonio Romano; *Script:* Antonio Romano; *Camera:* Guglielmo Mancori; *Music:* Nino Oliviero; *Producer:* P.E.A. (Italy). *Cast:* Ken Clark, Piero Lulli, Yvonne Bastien, Alfonso Rojas, Paco Sanz, Renato Rossini, Angel Ortiz, Frank Braña, Aldo Sambrell, Livio Lorenzon.

Cult director Mario Bava has denounced his Spaghetti Westerns as "work" projects, rather than "labor(s) of love." But, apparently, he recognized the significance of the genre and used it to his advantage. This particular film was intended as a showcase for his young protégé, Antonio Romano (who wrote the script). The actual degree of Bava's directorial involvement has been the subject of much controversy since the release of the film.

A cowboy, Nebraska (Ken Clark), goes to work for a powerful rancher (Alfonso Rojas) who is hated and feared by (seemingly) everybody, including his unfaithful wife (Yvonne Bastien). Nebraska finds himself in the middle of a devious plot, concocted by the wife and her lover, when the town sheriff is mysteriously killed. It's pretty slow going.

Actor Ken Clark starred in two of the three Mario Bava Spaghetti Westerns, this one and *Road to Fort Alamo*.

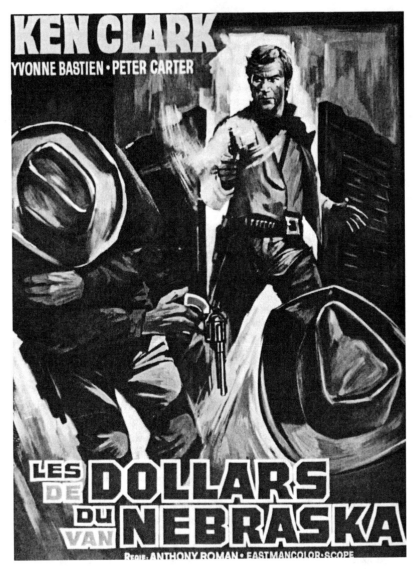

Movie poster from *Savage Gringo* (1966) starring Ken Clark.

Savage Guns (1961)

Tierra Brutal Sp. *Director:* Michael Carreras; *Script:* Jimmy Sangster/José Maesto/Edmund Morris; *Camera:* Alfredo Fraile; *Music:* Anton Garcia Abril; *Producer:* José G. Maesto, Tecisa/Capricorn (Italy/Spain/England). *Cast:* Richard Basehart, Paquita Rico, Don Taylor, Alex Nicol, Fernando Rey, Maria Granada, José Nieto, Victor Israel.

One of the first modern Spaghetti Westerns: *Savage Guns* **(1961) with Pacquita Rico
and Richard Basehart.**

This film is usually regarded (along with Mario Amendola's *Terror of
Oklahoma*) as the first of the "modern" Spaghetti Westerns, made three years
before Sergio Leone directed *Fistful of Dollars* (1964). It's also significant
because, unlike many other early Eurowesterns (i.e., *Massacre at Grand Canyon, Pirates of the Mississippi, Buffalo Bill of the Far West,* and the German *Winnetou* films), this one did not try to duplicate the lush Hollywood vision of grassy
prairies, snow-capped mountains, and wooded frontiers. Instead, this production was one of the first to unravel its story in the parched "deserts of Mexico"
(of course, in reality, the plains of Spain).

The story is a rather simplistic (perhaps racist) tale of a gringo gunfighter

(Richard Basehart) who joins forces with Mike Summers (Don Taylor), a displaced American living in Sonora, Mexico, with his Spanish wife, Maria (Paquita Rico). The three stand strong against an evil Mexican land baron named Sanchez (José Nieto) and his gang of cutthroats. The tensions soon escalate into a war when Sanchez kills Maria's father, Don Hernan (Fernando Rey).

British exploitation meister Michael Carreras, best known for *Maniac* (1963), *Curse of the Mummy's Tomb* (1965), and *Prehistoric Women* (1967), directed the film from a script cowritten by his friend, future Hammer filmmaker Jimmy Sangster (*Horror of Frankenstein, Fear in the Night,* and *Lust for a Vampire*).

American actor Richard Basehart (later became the stoic captain in the "Voyage to the Bottom of the Sea" television series) was chosen as lead because he already had "European acceptance" after starring in two Federico Fellini projects, *La Strada* (1955) and *Il Bidone* (also called *The Swindlers*) (1956).

Savage Guns see His Name Was Sam Walbash, But They Called Him Amen

Savage Pampas (1966)

Pampas Salvaje Sp. *Director:* Hugo Fregonese; *Script:* John Melson; *Camera:* Manuel Berenguer; *Music:* Waldo De Los Rios; *Producer:* Jaime Prades (U.S./Spain/Argentina). *Cast:* Robert Taylor, Ty Hardin, Ron Randell, Rosenda Monteros, Marc Lawrence, Fela Roque, Angel Del Pozo.

Here's a Robert Taylor oddity, reminiscent of his *Westward the Women* (a 1951 American-made Western about mail order brides traveling to California, directed by William Wellman), but clearly based on the 1943 film, *Pampa Barbara* (which was director Hugo Fregonese's first production).

Taylor plays a wagonmaster in charge of delivering a "load of prostitutes" to a distant outpost in the rurals of Argentina. This Spanish-U.S.-Argentinian production was filmed in Spain by chief cameraman Manuel Berenguer and it was cowritten by John Melson and Fregonese.

Hugo Fregonese made two Eurowesterns (if, indeed, this one qualifies). The other is an early Lex Barker "Winnetou" film called *Apache's Last Battle* (*Old Shatterhand*). He is best known for his brief flirtation with Hollywood (1950–54), during which time he directed 11 movies including *Decameron Nights, Untamed Frontier* and *My Six Convicts.* From 1955 through 1966, he was a Euro filmmaker, working in Italy, France, England and Germany. In 1966 he returned to his native Argentina where he continued to make movies (mostly never seen outside South America) until he died in 1987.

Scalps (1987)

Sie kampft wie ein Mann Ger. *Director:* Werner Knox; *Script:* Bruno Mattei/Richard Harrison; *Camera:* Julio Burgos; *Music:* Luigi Ceccarelli; *Producer:* Flora Film (Italy/West Germany). *Cast:* Vassili Karis, Mary Galan, Charlie Bravo, Beny Cardoso, Albert Farley.

This is one of the most graphically violent Spaghetti Westerns (second only to *Cut-Throats Nine*) directed by "Werner Knox," a pseudonym for exploitation sleaze master Bruno Mattei (alias Vincent Dawn). The script was cowritten by popular actor Richard Harrison.

It's a very ugly and mean-spirited film about a Confederate Colonel (Albert Farley) who orders his soldiers to kidnap the Comanche chief's daughter (Mary Galan) for his purpose of bedding her. The resulting massacre is reminiscent of *Soldier Blue*'s finale, following by even greater degrees of excessive (and effective) brutality.

Scansati . . . Trinità Arriva ad Eldorado see *Go Away! Trinity Has Arrived in Eldorado*

Lo Sceriffo Che Non Spara see *Sheriff Won't Shoot*

Lo Sceriffo senza Stella see *Christmas Kid*

Lo Sceriffo di Rock Spring see *Sheriff of Rock Spring*

Uno Sceriffo Tutto d'Oro see *Sheriff with the Gold*

Der Schatz der Azteken see *Treasure of the Aztecs*

Der Schatz im Silbersee see *Treasure of Silver Lake*

Die schwärzen Ädler von Santa Fe see *Black Eagle of Santa Fe*

Schneller Als 1000 Colts see *Thompson 1880*

Se Sparo . . . Ti Uccido see *Shoot to Kill*

Se Incontri Sartana Prega per la Tua Morte see *Sartana*

Se Sei Vivo Spara see *Django, Kill . . . If You Live, Shoot!*

Se T'Incontro T'Ammazzo see *Finders Killers*

Se Vuoi Vivere, Spara! see *If You Want to Live . . . Shoot!*

Secret of Captain O'Hara (1965)

Segreto di Ringo Ital. *Director:* Arturo Ruiz Castillo; *Script:* M. Martinez Remis/José M. Elorrieta/Arturo Ruiz Castillo; *Camera:* Alfonso Nieva; *Music:* M. Moreno Buendia; *Producer:* Rafael Marina (Spain). *Cast:* German Cobos, Marta Padovan, Mariano Vidal Molina, Frank Braña, Charito Tijero, José Canalejas, Tomás Blanco, Jorge Vico.

The film opens with "The army's coming!" as the 5th Cavalry regiment, under the keen leadership of Captain Richard O'Hara (German Cobos), rescues a wagon train under siege from the marauding Navajo Indians. There is only one survivor, Mary McQueen (Marta Padovan), traveling from St. Louis to Fort San Antonio where she plans to marry Major Harvey Brooks. Coincidentally, the 5th Cavalry is part of San Antonio station, so Captain O'Hara offers to escort Mary to the fort.

En route, she discovers that her fiancée and O'Hara are bitter enemies, but none of the soldiers will tell her why. Upon their arrival at the fort, she finds that the biggest difference between the two men seems to be a philosophical one. Her husband-to-be, Major Brooks (Mariano Vidal Molina), hates all Indians, including the peaceful Apaches, and he wants to annihilate them. On the other hand, Captain O'Hara is in favor of honoring the peace treaty, plus he's afraid that the fort's prejudicial climate may influence the Apaches to join forces with the Navajos, leading to a devastating war. It eventually does.

But Captain O'Hara's secret is: he used to be *Colonel* O'Hara. However, after losing a crucial battle during the Civil War due to a faulty command (at least according to testimony from his junior officer, arch enemy Brooks) he was demoted. Captain's O'Hara's real secret (thus the title) is: he has fallen in love with Mary. Obviously, there's going to be trouble.

It's a surprisingly good Cavalry vs. Indians genre Western. Usually, the Euro renderings of this type are an embarrassment, but this one works due to interesting characters and an intricate storyline, plus the extras really look like Indians instead of Spaniards in wigs.

Il Segno di Coyote see *Sign of Coyote*

Il Segno di Zorro see *Sign of Zorro*

Segreto di Ringo see *Secret of Captain O'Hara*

Sei Iettato Amico, Hai Incontrato Sacramento see *You're Jinxed Friend . . . You Just Met Sacramento*

Sei una Carogna, T'Ammazzo see *If One Is Born a Swine . . . Kill Him*

Sella d'Argento see *Silver Saddle*

Seminò la Morte . . . Lo Chiamavano il Castigo di Dio see *Death Is Sweet from the Soldier of God*

Sentence of God see *Thunder Over El Paso*

Sentenza di Morte see *Death Sentence*

I Sentieri dell'Odio see *Bullets and the Flesh*

Sentiero dell'Oro see *Finger on the Trigger*

Sentivano . . . Uno Strano Eccitante Pericoloso Puzzo di Dollari see *And They Smelled the Strange, Exciting, Dangerous Scent of Dollars*

I Senza Dio see *Thunder Over El Paso*

Sette Dollari sul Rosso see *Seven Dollars on the Red*

Sette Donne per i MacGregor see *Up the MacGregors!*

Sette Magnifiche Pistole see *Seven Guns for Timothy*

Sette Monache a Kansas City see *Seven Nuns in Kansas City*

Sette Ore di Fuoco see *Seven Hours of Gunfire*

I Sette Pistolaros del Texas see *Seven Guns from Texas*

Sette Pistole per el Gringo see *Seven Pistols for a Gringo*

Sette Pistole per I MacGregor see *Seven Guns for the MacGregors*

Sette Winchester per un Massacro see *Payment in Blood*

Seven Devils on Horseback see *Finders Killers*

Seven Dollars on the Red (1968)

Seven Dollars to Kill; Sette Dollari sul Rosso Ital. *Director:* Alberto Cordone, *Script:* Amedeo Mollono/Juan Cobos/Melchi Coletti; *Camera:* José F. Aquayo; *Music:* Francesco De Masl; *Producer:* Albert Cardiff (Italy/Spain). *Cast:* Anthony Steffen, Elisa Montes, Fernando Sancho, Loredana Nusciak, Umberto Miali, J. Manuel Martin, Halina Zalenwi.

Begun as a companion film to his *$1000 on the Black* (also called *Blood at Sundown*), director/producer Alberto Cardone (Albert Cardiff) tells yet another revenge tale with a "still angry after all these years" motif. Anthony Steffen is Johnny, a man who catches up with his wife's killer, El Chacal (Fernando Sancho), after 15 years. An especially effective concluding segment begins with a violent gun war in the streets of Desert City and ends with a fistfight (involving meathooks) between Johnny and Chacal. Worth the wait.

Seven Dollars to Kill see *Seven Dollars on the Red*

Seven for Pancho Villa (1966)

Los 7 de Pancho Villa Sp. *Director:* José M. Elorrieta; *Script:* Gonzalo Asensio Rey/Ricardo Vazquez; *Camera:* Alfonso Nieva; *Music:* Felix Sanchez/Manuel Sebares Caso; *Producer:* Lacy Internacional Films (Spain). *Cast:* John Ericson, Nuria Torray, Gustavo Rojo, Mara Cruz, Ricardo Palacios, James Philbrook, Pastor Serrador.

General Pancho Villa (Ricardo Palacios) escapes from his "final battle." Wounded, he is rescued by a band of adoring supporters (regardless of the title, considerably more than seven). They nurse him back to health. Together with a cause-friendly gringo (John Ericson), they resume the revolution.

This is one of four Eurowesterns directed by José M. Elorrieta (better known as Joe Lacy, a pseudonym he used for his medieval adventure, *Hawk of Castile,* and the demonic *Feast of Satan*).

Seven from Texas see *Seven Guns from Texas*

Seven Guns for Seven Bandits see *Colt 45, Five Dollars, and a Bandit*

Seven Guns for the MacGregors (1965)

Sette Pistole per I MacGregor Ital. *Director:* Frank Garfield; *Script:* Vincent Eagle/Fernand Lion/Duccio Tessari; *Camera:* Alejandro Ulloa; *Music:* Ennio

Agata Flori in *Seven Guns for the MacGregors* (1965).

Morricone; *Producer:* Dario Sabatello, Produzione/Jolly/Estela Film (Italy/ Spain). *Cast:* Robert Woods, Fernando Sancho, Agata Flori, Nazzareno Zamperla, Paolo Magalotti, Leo Anchóriz, Perla Cristal, Jorge Rigaud, Manuel Zarzo, Alberto Dell'Acqua, Julio Perez Tabernero, Cris Huerta, Max Dean.
   Scripted by Duccio Tessari (filmmaker of the *Ringo* series), Fernand Lion (pseudonym for Fernando Di Leo, director of many action/gangster films including *The Violent Breed* and *Shoot First . . . Die Later*), and Vincent Eagle (alias for scriptwriter Enzo Dell'Aquila, brother of actor Alberto), this film tells the story of two elderly Scottish patriarchs (MacGregor and Carson) and their children, especially Gregor MacGregor (Robert Woods in his most memorable role) and his fiancée Rosita Carson (Agata Flori). Overall, it's a combined family effort to defeat a band of Mexican outlaws led by evil Miguel (Fernando Sancho). Lots of action.
   The rousing musical score is composed by Ennio Morricone; Alejandro Ulloa acts as chief cameraman. Director Frank Garfield (alias for Franco Giraldi) also made a sequel, *Up the MacGregors!* (1968), with television's David Bailey, regrettably replacing Robert Woods as Gregor.
   A completely unrelated (except by title) *More Dollars for the MacGregors* appeared three years later, starring Peter Lee Lawrence.

Seven Guns for Timothy (1966)

Seven Magnificent Guns; Siete Pistolas para Timothy Sp; *Sette Magnifiche Pistole* Ital. *Director:* Rod Gilbert; *Script:* Alfonso Balcazar/José Antonio De La

Seven Guns for Timothy (1966) starring Sean Flynn (left).

Loma; *Camera:* Victor Monreal; *Music:* Gino Peguri; *Producer:* Balcazar Productions (Spain/Italy). *Cast:* Sean Flynn, Fernando Sancho, Evelyn Stewart, Daniel Martin, Frank Oliveras, Spartaco Conversi, Poldo Bendandi, Tito Garcia.

This one was writen by two different Spaghetti Western directors, José De La Loma (*Blood at Sundown* and *Boldest Job in the West*) and Alfonso Balcazar (*Sartana Does Not Forgive, Clint the Stranger, Sunscorched,* etc.).

A Mexican bandit (Fernando Sancho) and his gang raid a mining development, killing everyone except the foreman (Sean Flynn, son of Errol Flynn) who manages to escape. Then the film develops into a *Magnificent Seven* clone, as the foreman recruits convicts to return with him and face the marauders.

Good title sequence, but everything else is humdrum. Sean Flynn can also be seen in *Woman for Ringo.* Rod Gilbert is a pseudonym for Romolo Guerrieri who also directed the much better *Johnny Yuma* (1966), plus a variety of nongenre exploitation films including *Murder House* and *Young, Violent and Desperate.*

Seven Guns from Texas (1964)

Seven from Texas; Camino del Sur Sp; *I Sette Pistolaros del Texas* Ital. *Director:* Joaquin Romero Marchent; *Script:* Joaquin Romero Marchent; *Camera:* Rafael Pacheco; *Music:* Riz Ortolani; *Producer:* Joaquin R. Marchent, Centauro/P.E.A. (Spain/Italy). *Cast:* Paul Piaget, Robert Hundar, Fernando Sancho, Gloria Milland, Jesus Puente, Paco Sanz, Raf Baldassare, Joe Kamel, Gregory Wu.

Here's an early Spaghetti Western from prolific Spanish director Joaquin

R. Marchent (also known as Joaquin Romero Hernandez) featuring his usual troop of actors, particularly Paul Piaget and Robert Hundar.

Probably because of the international popularity of *The Magnificent Seven*, "7" is considered a "cool" number, and it sounds good in a title. That must be the answer, because if there were really truth in advertising, this movie would be called *Three Guns, a Woman and a Chinese Cook from Texas*.

The three men are Bob Carey (Robert Hundar, pseudonym for Claudio Undari), an insignificant character named Ringo (Jesus Puente) and Clifford (Paul Piaget). The woman is Bob's former girlfriend, now Clifford's wife, Mary (Gloria Milland). And the Chinese cook (Gregory Wu) is just around for lame comic relief.

Mary, unknown to her, has a brain tumor. Husband Clifford is determined to take her to El Paso where she can get medical treatment. He enlists the aid of an old friend just released from prison, Bob Carey, and he also recruits a local half-breed named Ringo. Along with the Chinese cook, the "three men and a woman" embark on the long and dangerous journey.

Unfortunately, this is actually a long and *boring* journey, highlighted by two bandit encounters and one Indian attack. It's difficult to imagine that filmmaker Romero Marchent also directed the similar (but far superior) "trek" film *Cut-Throats Nine*.

Seven Hours of Gunfire (1964)

Adventures in the West; Sette Ore di Fuoco Ital. *Director:* José Hernandez; *Script:* Joaquin Romero Marchent; *Camera:* Rafael Pacheco; *Music:* Angelo Francesco Lavagnino; *Producer:* Centauro Films (Spain/Italy). *Cast:* Rick Van Nutter, Adrian Hoven, Elga Sommerfeld, Gloria Milland, Carlos R. Marchent, Helga Line, Alfonso Rojas, Antonio Molina Rojo, Francisco Sanz, Raf Baldassare, Cris Huerta.

Another 1964 entry from prolific director Joaquin Romero Marchent (alias José Hernandez) with a salient "super-star" approach to the genre. Buffalo Bill (Clyde Rogers, aka Rick Van Nutter), Wild Bill Hickok (Adrian Hoven), and Calamity Jane (Gloria Milland) all meet at a wilderness fort when they try to bring peace between the Indians and the pioneers. Eventually they settle down in Silver City, which becomes the target of a vindictive Apache attack, thus leading to the title, *Seven Hours of Gunfire* (although it seems like considerably less).

The assistant director for this project is Rafael Romero Marchent, the brother of Joaquin, who later became a popular genre and exploitation filmmaker (see Directors filmography).

Seven Magnificent Guns see *Seven Guns for Timothy*

Seven Nuns in Kansas City (1973)

Sette Monache a Kansas City Ital. *Director:* Marcello Zeanile; *Script:* Kidia Puglia/Marcello Cascape; *Camera:* Mario Seronna; *Music:* Gino Peguri; *Producer:* Elido Sorrentino/Pietro Santini (Italy). *Cast:* Lea Gargano, Enzo Maggio, Paul McCray, Tony DeLeo, Pedro Sanchez, Irta D'Angelis, Bruno Boschetti.

Opposite: Movie poster from *Seven Guns from Texas* (1964).

This is an embarrassingly awful film, complete with talking mules. Two prospecting friends, Whiskey and Whiskey Joe (Enzo Maggio and Paul McCray) inadvertently discover gold when they flop into a river after having an accident with their covered wagon. Soon their strike is invaded by poachers, but especially by the nasty Fatty (Pedro Sanchez) and two overtly gay cowboys (Tony DeLeo and Bruno Boschetti).

What does any of this have to do with nuns? Well, eventually all the tired and hungry prospectors try to forcibly take over a convent. But the "good sisters" protect themselves by resorting to violence (throwing food, frying pans, laundry, garbage cans, etc.). It's difficult to find (or imagine) a worse film. On par with *Once Upon a Time in the Wild, Wild West*.

Seven Pistols for a Gringo (1967)

Sette Pistole per el Gringo. Director: Juan Xiol Marchel; *Script:* Roberto Bianchi Montero/I. F. Iquino; *Camera:* Julian P. Rozas; *Music:* Enrique Escobar; *Producer:* Cineproduzioni/I.F.I.S.A. (Italy/Spain). *Cast:* Gérard Landry, Dan Harrison, Fernando Rubio, Marta May, Albert Farley, Patricia Loran.

Cowritten (with Bianchi Montero) and directed by Ignacio Iquino (using an odd Juan Xiol Marchel alias), this Italian-Spanish production is a meandering monstrosity.

Dan (Dan Harrison) is framed for the murder of a card shark. However, the real culprits are the Tennessee brothers, Chuck and Johnny, employed by town boss Torrence (Albert Farley). A traveling dentist named Dr. Clapper (Gérard Landry) allows Dan to hide in his covered wagon, but eventually (it seems like an eternity), they take on the bad guys and, of course, win.

Director Iquino (usually using his John Wood, Steve McCohy, Juan Bosch or Pedro Ramirez pseudonyms) made 12 Spaghetti Westerns. This one is probably his weakest.

Seven Pistols for a Massacre see *Adios Hombre*

Seven Savage Men see *Finders Killers*

Seven Vengeful Women see *Tall Women*

Seven Women for the MacGregors see *Up the MacGregors!*

Sfida a Rio Bravo see *Gunmen of Rio Grande*

La Sfida degli Implacabili see *Joe Dexter*

Sfida dei MacKenna see *Challenge of the MacKennas*

Shadow of Sartana ... Shadow of Your Death (1968)

Meet the Sign of the Cross; Sartana and His Shadow of Death; Passa Sartana ... È l'Ombra della Tua Morte Ital. *Director:* Sean O'Neal; *Script:* Miles Deem; *Camera:* Franco Villa/Aristide Massaccesi; *Music:* Coriolano Gori; *Producer:*

Seven Hours of Gunfire (1964) with (left to right) Clyde Rogers, Adrian Hoven, Raf Baldassare.

Tarquinia Films (Italy). *Cast:* Jeff Cameron, Dennys Colt, Simone Blondell, Frank Fargas, Dino Strano, Miles Deem, Elisabetta Fanti, Luciano Conti.

Sartana (Jeff Cameron) has a problem. Not only have his vigilante activities gained him notoriety, but he also has a price on his head—$10,000 dead or alive. However, the politicians of a Southern Texas border town have "granted him amnesty" if he "eliminates" the marauding Randal Brothers, Benny (Frank Fargas) and Baby Face (Dennys Colt), plus a corrupt sheriff named Nick Logan (Dean Stratford, aka Dino Strano).

It's like a dream come true. Not only is this movie directed by the genre's favorite number one hack Miles Deem (pseudonym for Demofilo Fidani, hiding behind yet another moniker, Sean O'Neal) but the lovable charlatan actually *stars* in it. His performance is brief, but highly animated as the awestruck mayor who says: "Sartana could shoot his way out of hell!" Then, he follows that adulation with the profound: "Sartana is an honorable and fair-dealing man, with a gun, ready to help any poor underdog."

And, just in case somebody in the audience missed the film's message, there's even an epilogue which reads: "In a period when bad men and brute force triumphed in the west, men of honor were feared and respected, and the law enlisted their services against crime. Sartana, more than any other man,

was feared . . . and respected." The world would be a much sadder place
without Demofilo Fidani.

Shadow of Zorro (1963)

Zorro the Avenger; L'Ombra di Zorro Ital; *La Venganza del Zorro* Sp. *Director:*
Joaquin Romero Marchent; *Script:* Joaquin R. Hernandez/Rafael R. Marchent;
Camera: Rafael Pacheco/Enrico Franco; *Music:* Manuel Parada; *Producer:* Centauro Film (Spain/Italy). *Cast:* Frank Latimore, Maria Luz Galicia, Mario Feliciani, Marco Tulli, Robert Hundar, Raf Baldassare, Piero Lulli.

Frank Latimore plays Don José, secretly the masked Mexican freedom
fighter El Zorro ("the fox"), who protects the people of the Southern California
city, San Pueblo, from a gang of Mexican revolutionary bandits led by Chinto
(Raf Baldassare).

It's an early Eurowestern cowritten by brothers Joaquin and Rafael
Romero Marchent. Rafael went on to become a cult film director helming many
Westerns (see Directors filmography) plus a variety of sex dramas (i.e., *Limits
of Love*), thrillers (i.e., *Black Cat in a Dark Room*) and even a "Santo" movie,
Santo vs. Doctor Death (1974).

Shalako (1968)

Director: Edward Dmytryk; *Script:* J. J. Griffith/Hal Hopper/Scott Finch; *Cam-
era:* Ted Moore; *Music:* Robert Farnon; *Producer:* Euan Lloyd (England/
France). *Cast:* Sean Connery, Brigitte Bardot, Stephen Boyd, Woody Strode,
Jack Hawkins, Peter Van Eyck, Honor Blackman, Alexander Knox.

Edward Dmytryk, director of 51 films between 1935 and 1976 including
The Cane Mutiny, The Carpetbaggers and *Walk on the Wild Side,* had nothing
but trouble with this British-French production, based on the Louis L'Amour
book (that "reads" better than it "watches").

Sean Connery is the (miscast) cowboy hero Shalako who rescues Irina
Lazaar (Brigitte Bardot) from some angry Apaches. As it turns out, she is really
a French countess, part of an "aristocratic group of wealthy Europeans" on a
big game hunting trip "gone sour" in New Mexico (photographed in Wales).
Their double-crossing guide, Fulton (Stephen Boyd), had taken the "amateur
adventurers" into restricted Indian territory, robbed them, and left them to die
at the hands of the Apaches.

Shalako takes on the responsibility of protecting them, even though he is
quite obtrusive in demonstrating his dislike for most of the group. Of course,
Brigitte Bardot becomes Connery's main squeeze, and there's a brief semi-nude
scene, but unfortunately sparks never fly.

The two most memorable segments in the film are the realistic hand-to-
hand combat finale between Shalako and Apache Chato (Woody Strode), and
the death of Lady Julia Dagget (Honor Blackman) as she is forced to swallow
a huge diamond necklace (clearly symbolizing her love of material things).

Incidentally, Honor Blackman is best remembered for two different roles,
that of leather-clad Cathy Gale from the cult television series "The Avengers"
in the early 60s, and James Bond's "femme fatale" Pussy Galore of *Goldfinger*
fame. It's interesting to see her and Sean Connery together again here. But
disappointing, too.

Shango (1969)

Shango, la Pistola Infallibile Ital. *Director:* Edward G. Muller; *Script:* Antonio De Teffé/Edoardo Mulargia; *Camera:* Gino Santini; *Music:* Felice Di Stefano; *Producer:* Franco Cuccio/Pino De Martino, P.A.C. (Italy). *Cast:* Anthony Steffen, Eduardo Fajardo, Maurice Poli, Barbara Nelli, Andrea Scotti, Massimo Carrocci, Franco Pesce, Spartaco Conversi, Gabriella Giorgelli.

One of eight Spaghetti Westerns directed by exploitation sleazemeister Edward G. Muller (alias for Edoardo Mulargia), whose nongenre films include *Tropic of Cancer*, plus two cult "women in an Amazon prison" flicks, *Escape from Hell* and *Hotel Paradise*. This one is based on a screenplay cowritten by actor Anthony Steffen (pseudonym for Antonio De Teffé), featuring camera work from Muller's right-hand man, Gino Santini.

The Major (Eduardo Fajardo) and his band of Confederates have joined forces with a gang of outlaws led by Martinez (Maurice Poli). Together, these two groups control and dominate a border town while they are searching for "lost" gold. However, their mission is jeopardized by the arrival of a Texas Ranger, Shango (Anthony Steffen), with news that the war has ended and that the South has lost.

It's a good looking movie (perhaps aided by assistant director Mario Bianchi, aka Frank Bronston), but it's short on logic. Too bad.

Shango, la Pistola Infallibile see *Shango*

Sharp-Shooting Twin Sisters see *Woman for Ringo*

Sheriff Brandy see *Ride and Kill*

Sheriff of Rock Spring (1971)

Lo Sceriffo di Rock Spring Ital. *Director:* Anthony Green; *Script:* Elido Sorrentino/Gianni Luigi; *Camera:* Gianni Raffaldi; *Music:* Gianfranco and Felice Di Stefano; *Producer:* Ras Film (Italy). *Cast:* Richard Harrison, Cosetta Greco, Donald O'Brien, Maria Morgan, Marino Sidri.

A lesser effort from popular Richard Harrison, telling the clichéd story of a former gunfighter who retires to a quiet, peaceful town where he soon becomes the sheriff. Over all, it's a poor man's rendition of *The Last Gun*.

Director Primo Zeglio (using an Anthony Green pseudonym) tries to keep the action moving with a tired subplot about a crooked banker in cahoots with the owner of a saloon/gambling hall, resulting in not one but two barroom brawls. Enough already.

Sheriff Was a Lady (1965)

In the Wild West; Freddy und das Lied der Prärie Ger. *Director:* Söbey Martin; *Script:* Gustav Kampendonk; *Camera:* Siegfried Hold; *Music:* Lotar Olias; *Producer:* Edgar Film (West Germany). *Cast:* Freddy Quinn, Mamie Van Doren, Rik Battaglia, Beba Loncar, Trude Herr, Carlo Croccolo.

Here's an early German example of the prevalent "revenge for a slaughtered family" theme, from director Söbey Martin (pseudonym for Carlo Croccolo, aka Lucky Moore) and his Berlin crew. But, the principal players hail from three different countries. They are German pop singer Freddy Quinn,

American 1950s sex queen Mamie Van Doren, and Italian peplum star Rik Battaglia.

Pretending to be a greenhorn, a young man (Freddy Quinn) hunts for the outlaw gang (led by Rik Battaglia) who killed his parents. He enlists the aid of a beautiful saloon girl (Mamie Van Doren) and together they concoct a bizarre plan that involves her becoming sheriff of a fictional town.

Sheriff with the Gold (1966)

Uno Sceriffo Tutto d'Oro Ital. *Director:* Richard Kean; *Script:* Roberto Gianviti/Enzo Dell'Aquila; *Camera:* Osvaldo Civirani; *Music:* Nora Orlandi/Jan Cristiane; *Producer:* Wonder Film/Fono Roma (Italy/Spain). *Cast:* Louis McJulian, Jacques Berthier, Kathleen Parker, Bob Messenger, Ares Lucky, Ivan Scratuglia.

Directed and photographed by Osvaldo Civirani (using the pseudonym Richard Kean), based on a screenplay cowritten by Enzo Dell'Acquila, alias director Vincent Eagle.

Bandit Arizona Roy (McJulian) is about to be hanged when Federal Sheriff Jeff Randall (Berthier) shows up with papers to interrupt the execution. It seems that Roy has been subpoenaed to be a witness at a trial in another city, so off they go. But it was all part of the sheriff's plan to rescue Arizona Roy and use him in a gold heist. Once the plot is revealed, the pace slows down considerably, tediously so.

Most of Civirani's Westerns are dimwitted. Only *Son of Django* shows any degree of stature. He fared much better with nongenre outings, especially spy movies and peplums (i.e., *Desert Eagle* and *Kindar, Desert Prince*).

Sheriff Won't Shoot (1967)

Lo Sceriffo Che Non Spara Ital; *Poker d'As pour Django; Poker d'Assi per Django* Ital. *Director:* J. Luis Monter; *Script:* Roberto Montero/Franco Verucci; *Camera:* Stelvio Massi; *Music:* Felice Di Stefano; *Producer:* Acaddia/Hispamer/Tigielle 33 (Italy/France/England). *Cast:* Mickey Hargitay, Vincente Cashino, Dan Clark, Manuel Zarzo Nana, Pilar Clemens, Angel Ter, Sancho Garcia.

Fantasy filmmaker Roberto Montero, best known for *Tharus, Son of Attila* (1963), directed four Spaghetti Westerns (see Directors filmography). This was his first, and (as such) it's a rather standard entry, notable mostly for peplum actor Mickey Hargitay's starring role.

A sheriff (Hargitay) is forced into a showdown when he learns that his younger brother (Dan Clark) is involved with an outlaw gang.

Shoot, Django, Shoot see Shoot, Gringo . . . Shoot!

Shoot First . . . Ask Questions Later see White, the Yellow and the Black

Shoot First, Laugh Last see Stranger Returns

Shoot, Gringo . . . Shoot! (1968)

The Longest Hunt; Rainbow; Spara, Gringo, Spara Ital; *Shoot, Django, Shoot; Tire, Django, Tire* Fr. *Director:* Frank B. Corlish; *Script:* Dean Whitcomb; *Camera:* Fausto Zuccoli; *Music:* Richard Ira Silver; *Producer:* Arthur Steloff,

Cemofilm (Italy/France). *Cast:* Brian Kelly, Fabrizio Moroni, Keenan Wynn, Folco Lulli, Erika Blanc, Rik Battaglia, Gigi Bonos, Furio Meniconi, Gianni Pallavicino.

This is a surprisingly taut, efficient Spaghetti Western about a famous gunman Stark (Brian Kelly), hired by wealthy landowner Don Francisco (Folco Lulli) to bring back his son Fidel (Gianni Pallavicino) who has joined up with a group of American bandits led by a former Union officer, "the Major" (Keenan Wynn).

Stark succeeds in his mission, but to his astonishment, he has returned Fidel to the patriarch for a torture session. Don Francisco crucifies the boy on the cross of St. Andrew. As he prepares to kill him, Don Francisco tells his wife (Erika Blanc) that he knows she is unfaithful and that Fidel is not his son. He plans to punish her by killing the "bastard" boy before her eyes. Stark, obviously, does not allow that to happen.

Director Frank B. Corlish is actually Bruno Corbucci (Sergio's younger brother) working under a pseudonym, with cameraman Fausto Zuccoli. The script credited to Dean Whitcomb is, in reality, a Bruno Corbucci–Mario Amendola collaboration. Composer Richard Ira Silver is a pseudonym for Sante Maria Romitelli.

Shoot Joe, and Shoot Again (1972)

Joe Dakota; Joe Dakota, Spara . . . e Così Sia Ital. *Director:* Hal Brady; *Script:* Emilio Miraglia; *Camera:* Silvio Fraschetti; *Music:* Vasco and Mancuso; *Producer:* Neptunia Film (Italy). *Cast:* Richard Harrison, José Torres, Franca Polesello, Indio Gonzales, Rick Boyd, Roberto Maldera.

Hal Brady is a pseudonym for Emilio P. Miraglia (not to be confused with Al Bradly, Alfonso Brescia's alias) and this is an obscure Richard Harrison film about "sex, greed and murder" (according to the Italian advertisement). But mostly, it's about the latter two.

At one point in the film, Joe Dakota (Richard Harrison) is blinded by the outlaw gang when they are torturing him, but miraculously he regains his sight just in time for the gun battle finale. The whole thing has to do with stolen money and a map to its whereabouts, plus a deceitful girl who betrays her man for cash.

Emilio P. Miraglia also directed two classic nongenre films, *The Night Evelyn Came Out of the Grave* (1971) with Erika Blanc, Anthony Steffen and Giacomo Rossi Stuart; plus, *The Red Queen Kills Seven Times* (1972) starring Barbara Bouchet and Sybil Danning.

Shoot the Living . . . Pray for the Dead (1971)

Pray to Kill and Return Alive; Prega per il Morto e Ammazza il Vivo Ital. *Director:* Joseph Warren; *Script:* Marck Salter; *Camera:* Franco Villa; *Music:* Mario Migliardi; *Producer:* Castor Film Production (Italy). *Cast:* Klaus Kinski, Victoria Zinny, Paul Sullivan, Dean Stratford, Ares Lucky, Anthony Rock, Aldo Barberito.

Obviously, this film is Joseph Warren's "epic." Or, at least, that was the intention. Instead, director Warren (Giuseppe Vari), best known for his fast-paced action pics, has created a rather slow character study that offers

Poster from *Shoot, Gringo . . . Shoot!* (1968).

absolutely nothing new to the genre. Primarily, the film deals with a power struggle between Reed (Dean Stratford) and Ken Hogan (Klaus Kinski) for control of a bank-robbing gang. However, Kinski spends so little time "on camera" that the film is mostly a Stratford monologue (that is, until he's shot in the back).

The first two-thirds of the movie takes place in an isolated border way station where the outlaw band is regrouping after a successful $100,000 robbery in Phoenix. Eventually, they begin the journey to Mexico. An "innocent" guide, John Webb (Paul Sullivan) is promised a large share of gold if he can steer them through the dangerous canyons and rugged mountains. Webb accepts the job, but not for the money.

Revenge is the motivating factor. As it turns out, John's real name is "Parker" and he's been following the gang for quite a while. Ken Hogan had killed his parents; John plans to avenge their deaths. By the end of the journey, only John Webb and Ken Hogan remain alive. When John faces the outlaw in a showdown, Hogan screams: "I don't want any Parkers left on this Earth!" Obviously, it's an insurmountable job, but he doesn't have to worry about it for long. A second later, he's dead. The Parkers of the world can sleep tonight.

Shoot to Kill (1963)

Texas Jim; Se Sparo . . . Ti Uccido Ital; *Cuatreros* Sp. *Director:* Ramon Torrado; *Script:* Luis Gasper/Antonio Escribano/Fernando Butragueno; *Camera:* Ricardo Torres; *Music:* Daniele Montoyo; *Producer:* C.C. Atlantida Film (Spain). *Cast:* Edmund Purdom, Frank Latimore, Fernando Sancho, Silvia Solar, Luis Induñi, Santiago Rivero, Laura Granados, Tomás Blanco.

An exasperating love triangle is the central focus of this film. Foreman Tom Jameson (Edmund Purdom) falls in love with the ranch owner's daughter, Mary (Silvia Solar), but so does a nephew (and secretly an outlaw), Lance (Frank Latimore). There's a fierce gun battle inside a burning barn at the film's conclusion. Maybe makes it all worthwhile.

Shotgun (1969)

Vengeance Is My Forgiveness; La Vendetta È il Mio Perdono Ital. *Director:* Roberto Mauri; *Script:* Roberto Mauri; *Camera:* Franco Delli Colli; *Music:* Giancarlo Bizzi; *Producer:* Virginia Cinematografica (Italy). *Cast:* Tab Hunter, Erika Blanc, Piero Lulli, Mimmo Palmara, Daniele Vargas, Renato Romano.

Sheriff Durango (Tab Hunter) has decided to settle down and marry his girlfriend Lucy. But his plans are suddenly thwarted when four masked bandits raid the McClain ranch, murdering Lucy and the entire family. Durango, depressed and morose, climbs "inside a whiskey bottle," to be pulled out by saloon owner Jo Anne (Erika Blanc). After conducting an investigation, he discovers that the killers are respected businessmen, including a banker and a doctor. Eventually, they are brought to justice.

This film is distinguished by having one of the all-time worst honky-tonk saloon songs, "Two Wishes," and Erika Blanc (in an amazing test of dedication and endurance) sings it, not once or twice, but three different times. "Dream a dream all day, singing a song of luck/ Beautiful luck in its luckiest phase/ Let him go/ Let him shoot around/ And what will they do when he will?"

Now, that's a song!

Shots Ring Out! (1965)

Four Bullets for Joe; Si Udirono Quattro Colpi di Fucile Ital. *Director:* Augustin Navarro; *Script:* Mario Guerra/José Mallorqui/Vittorio Vighi; *Camera:* Ricardo

Torres; *Music:* Marcello Gignante; *Producer:* Cineproduzione/Fenix (Italy/ Spain). *Cast:* Paul Piaget, Fred Canow, Liz Poitel, Barbara Nelli, Angela Cavo, Francisco Moran.

A Western whodunnit. A man is mysteriously murdered and his girlfriend (Angela Cavo) accuses town tramp Katie (Liz Poitel). After she is found guilty in a biased trial, Katie tries to escape custody but she is killed. As she's dying, the girl convinces Sheriff Poll (Fred Canow, aka Fernando Casanova) of her innocence.

Her brother, a notorious gunfighter named Frank Dalton (Paul Piaget) arrives in town for the funeral. But very soon, a series of new murders takes place. Members of the jury, witnesses, and even Katie's attorney are all found dead. Naturally, Frank is suspected by the townspeople, but the sheriff digs deeper and discovers the real killer.

This pleasant, change-of-pace film is Augustin Navarro's only directorial contribution to the genre; he is best known as scriptwriter for many Spaghetti Westerns including *The Ruthless Colt of the Gringo* (see Scriptwriters filmography).

Showdown for a Badman (1972)

Nevada Kid; Coffin Full of Dollars; Per una Bara Piena di Dollari Ital. *Director:* Miles Deem; *Script:* Tonino Ricci/Miles Deem; *Camera:* Aristide Massaccesi; *Music:* Coriolano Gori; *Producer:* Massimo Bernardi/Diego Spataro, Elektra Films (Italy). *Cast:* Klaus Kinski, Hunt Powers, Gordon Mitchell, Jeff Cameron, Ray Saunders, Simone Blondell, Dennis Colt.

This is the closest Miles Deem (Demofilo Fidani) ever gets to making a real movie. But most of the credit should go to the star-studded cast and the always masterful camera eye of Aristide Massaccesi (later to become cult director Joe D'Amato).

The story, as written by the genre's two leading hack filmmakers (wretched Tonino Ricci and wondrously wretched Miles Deem), is yet another tedious variation on the "vengeance for a slaughtered family" theme. This time, Nevada (Hunt Powers) and his "no-name" bounty hunter friend (Jeff Cameron) track down sadistic Hagen (Gordon Mitchell). They trick and ultimately destroy Hagen's entire gang, thus avenging the death of Nevada's parents.

Incidentally, Simone Blondell (the star of most every Demofilo Fidani movie) is the filmmaker's beautiful wife.

Si Può Fare ... Amigo see *It Can Be Done ... Amigo*

Si Quieres Vivir ... Dispara see *If You Shoot ... You Live!*

Si Udirono Quattro Colpi di Fucile see *Shots Ring Out!*

Sie kampft wie ein Mann see *Scalps*

Sie nannten ihn Gringo see *Man Called Gringo*

Los 7 de Pancho Villa see *Seven for Pancho Villa*

Siete Pistolas para Timoty see *Seven Guns for Timothy*

Sign of Coyote (1964)

Vengador of California; Il Segno di Coyote Ital. *Director:* Mario Caiano; *Script:* José Mallorqui; *Camera:* Carlo Fiore; *Music:* Francesco De Masi; *Producer:* United Pictures and Films (Italy/Spain). *Cast:* Fernand Canova, Maria Luz Galicia, Mario Feliciani, Piero Lulli, Giulia Rubini, Fernando Sancho, Paola Barbara, Jose Jaspé.

An early film from popular director Mario Caiano, graduate of the peplum school (i.e., *Ulysses Against Hercules* [1961]; *Maciste, Gladiator of Sparta* [1964]; and *Fury of the Titans* [1964]). Basically, it's a variation on the Zorro legend, with guns rather than swords. Coyote (Fernand Canova) is a masked Robin Hood–type character known as the "Vengador of California." He spends most of his time wooing pretty Maria Luz Galicia and making life difficult for the oppressive governor, played by Mario Feliciani.

Joaquin Romero Marchent also directed a "Coyote" film with Abel Salazar called *Coyote* (also called *Judgment of Coyote* (1964).

Sign of Zorro (1964)

Il Segno di Zorro Ital. *Director:* Mario Caiano; *Script:* Guido Malatesta/André Tabet/Arturo Rigal; *Camera:* Adalberto Albertini; *Music:* Gregorio Garcia Segura; *Producer:* United Pictures and Films (Italy/Spain). *Cast:* Sean Flynn, Folco Lulli, Gaby André, Enrique Diosdado, Armando Calvo, Helga Line, Danielle De Metz, Carlo Tamberlani.

This one is among the best of the early "Zorro" films, benefiting from a strong cast plus imaginative direction by cult filmmaker Mario Caiano. It tells the story of a young man, Don Ramon (Sean Flynn), who returns to his home in Mexico to find that his father has been murdered by the self-appointed dictator (Enrique Diosdado). Secretly, wearing a mask and black cape, Ramon adopts the name "Zorro" (the Fox), and he successfully leads a band of revolutionaries against the tyrant.

Sean Flynn is the son of American matinee movie star, Errol Flynn, who played many "adventure hero" roles including *Robin Hood, Captain Blood, General Custer* and *The Sea Hawk,* but never Zorro.

Silent Stranger see *Stranger in Japan*

Silver Saddle (1978)

They Died with Their Boots On; Sella d'Argento Ital. *Director:* Lucio Fulci; *Script:* Ornella Michili/Lucio Fulci; *Camera:* Sergio Salvati; *Music:* Bixio/Frizi/Tempera; *Producer:* Ennio Di Meo/Carlo Barto, Rizzo Film (Italy). *Cast:* Giuliano Gemma, Sven Valsecchi, Ettore Manni, Donald O'Brien, Aldo Sambrell, Cinzia Monreale, Licinia Lentini.

Director Lucio Fulci is the enormously popular exploitation/horror filmmaker responsible for over 50 movies, *Lizard in a Woman's Skin* (1971), *Zombie* (1979), *The Gates of Hell* (1980), *The Beyond* (1980), *House by the Cemetery*

(1981), *Demonia* (1989), *Cat in the Brain* (1991), plus two other Spaghetti Westerns, *Massacre Time* (1966) and *Four Gunmen of the Apocalypse* (1975).

At age ten, Roy kills his first man. He watches as his father is gunned down by Mr. Thomas Barrett's henchman, Luke (Donald O'Brien). In turn, young Roy picks up a shotgun and blasts him. Then he takes Luke's horse (with the famous "Silver Saddle") and rides off into the desert. Over the years his reputation as a gunfighter grows, until he becomes the feared and respected bounty hunter, Roy Blood (Giuliano Gemma).

Inadvertently, when a "job" goes sour, he rescues a child who happens to be related to Thomas Barrett. Roy Blood suddenly finds himself pursued by a would-be kidnapper/outlaw Garincha (Aldo Sambrell) and his gang, the Hyenas of the Rio Grande. Plus, Barrett and his "boys" are after Roy too.

This film has many subplots including an entertaining segment wherein Roy Blood finds and kills a sleazy town boss named Shep. As Roy leaves the saloon, the bartender says: "Shep was a big man around here." Roy pauses for a moment and replies, "Not anymore." Director Fulci handles these scenes with the kind of intense machismo centrally important to the inherent tenacity of the Spaghetti Western. His work is among the genre's best.

A Sky Full of Stars for a Roof (1968)

...E per Tetto un Cielo di Stelle Ital. *Director:* Giulio Petroni; *Script:* Alberto Areal/Francesco Martino; *Camera:* Carlo Carlini; *Music:* Ennio Morricone; *Producer:* Gianni Hecht Lucari, Documento Film (Italy). *Cast:* Giuliano Gemma, Mario Adorf, Magda Konopka, Anthony Dawson, Rick Boyd, Cris Huerta, Julie Menard.

A mystical (although generic) title that could aptly apply to any number of great Western films. Unfortunately, the movie doesn't deserve such a cool title. It's a rambling, confused mess from (usually reliable) Giulio Petroni, director of *Death Rides a Horse*, with music by Italian wizard, Ennio Morricone.

The plot deals with two hapless vagabonds, Tim and Harry (Giuliano Gemma and Mario Adorf) and their misadventures with outlaws, card sharks, a traveling circus, bounty hunters and a phony mermaid. Both stars have made far better films.

Sledge see *Man Called Sledge*

Sogno di Zorro see *Grandsons of Zorro*

Sole nella Polvere see *Dust in the Sun*

Sole Rosso see *Red Sun*

Soleil Rouge see *Red Sun*

Solo Contro Tutti see *Jesse James' Kid*

Sometimes Life Is Hard, Right Providence? (1972)

Life Is Tough, Eh Providence?; *La Vita, a Volte, È Molto Dura, Vero Provvidenza?* Ital. *Director:* Giulio Petroni; *Script:* Dean Craig/Antonio Marino/

Giulio Petroni; *Camera:* Alessandro D'Eva; *Music:* Ennio Morricone; *Producer:* Oceania Internazionali/Undis (Italy/France/West Germany). *Cast:* Tomás Milian, Greg Palmer, Janet Agren, Maurice Poli, Ken Wood, Carla Mancini, Paul Müller.

Competent filmmaker Giulio Petroni, best known for the genre revenge pic *Death Rides a Horse,* has directed a Western/comedy that works, a rarity in the Spaghetti world. But much of the credit also goes to chameleon actor Tomás Milian. He plays a "Charlie Chaplin" clone named Providence (complete with tiny mustache, bowler hat, baggy pants, and umbrella).

Most of the film deals with the relationship between "cultured" bounty hunter Providence and the brute, Hurricane Kid (Gregg Palmer). Using a gimmick similar to the Blonde/Tuco arrangement in *The Good, the Bad, and the Ugly,* Providence catches the Hurricane Kid, delivers the bandit for the reward, and then breaks him out of jail. Off they go to another state, for another bounty. There are the usual (and anticipated) double-crosses between the two partners," but this time there's also an additional scheme brewing. It involves a girlfriend (Janet Agren) who entangles Confederate Colonel Albert James (Maurice Poli) in a plot to steal Providence's cash. They don't succeed.

The film is an enjoyable change of pace, a combination of intelligent humor and funny sight gags, including a humorous sequence when burly Hurricane takes a bath in the lake ("My last bath was three years ago in Nevada"), and then all the fish die from the resulting pollution!

Tomás Milian and Gregg Palmer returned for a sequel called *Here We Go Again, Eh Providence?* (1973), directed by Alberto De Martino.

Son of a Gunfighter (1966)

El Hijo del Pistolero Sp. *Director:* Paul Landres; *Script:* Clarke Reynolds; *Camera:* Manuel Berenguer; *Music:* Frank Barber; *Producer:* Lester Welch/Juan Zurbano (Spain/U.S.). *Cast:* Russ Tamblyn, Kieron Moore, Fernando Rey, James Philbrook, Maria Granada, Julio Perez Tabernero, Aldo Sambrell, Antonio Casas, Barta Barri.

Here is an effective (but short on logic) Spanish-produced "revenge" flick directed by American filmmaker Paul Landres (best known for his dull rock and roll opus, *Go Johnny, Go!* and the insipid *Flipper's Odyssey*). Landres, with cameraman Manuel Berenguer, surprised many audiences with this fun-to-watch shoot-'em-up.

Cult hero Russ Tamblyn (*West Side Story, High School Confidential, Twin Peaks,* and countless motor-psycho films) is Johnny, a vengeance-driven gunfighter chasing an outlaw named Ketchum (James Philbrook), the man who killed his mother. En route, Johnny is wounded, but rescued by a beautiful girl, Pilar (Maria Granada), the daughter of wealthy Don Fortuna (Fernando Rey). Johnny is nursed back to health at the Fortuna hacienda on the Mexican side of the Rio Grande.

Even though Pilar has fallen in love with Johnny, he abandons her to continue the avenging trek. Eventually, Johnny finds Ketchum. And he learns that the outlaw is really his father. Neither man will draw on the other. Instead, they return to the Fortuna estate to help Pilar and her father in a battle against marauding Mexican bandidos, led by Morales (Aldo Sambrell).

The music was composed with a Euro flair by Frank Barber (Franco Barosa).

Son of Django (1967)

Vengeance Is a Colt .45; Return of Django; Il Figlio di Django Ital. *Director:* Osvaldo Civirani; *Script:* Antonio Ferrau/Tito Carpi; *Camera:* Osvaldo Civirani; *Music:* Piero Umiliani; *Producer:* Denwer Films (Italy). *Cast:* Guy Madison, Gabriele Tinti, Ingrid Schoeller, Daniele Vargas, Pedro Sanchez, Andrew Scott, Bob Messenger, Ivan Scratuglia.

This one remains the only accomplished, disciplined Spaghetti Western in Osvaldo Civirani's five-stall stable. It's a good film, highlighted by a particularly enjoyable Gabriele Tinti performance, and an effective soundtrack from prolific Piero Umiliani.

The story (especially the opening sequence) is most reminiscent of *Death Rides a Horse*. On a stormy night, a young boy (Clint) hides under his bed and watches as his father (the famous gunman Django) is killed and his mother is raped and murdered. Years pass, Clint (Gabriele Tinti, aka Mr. Laura Gemser), still hungry for vengeance, goes to Topeka City to murder his father's killer, town boss Clay (Andrew Scott). A traveling preacher/former gunman, Reverend Fleming (Guy Madison) befriends him and tries to divert his reprisal, but eventually the two join together against Clay and his gang. And they are, of course, victorious.

Most of director Civirani's Westerns are lamebrained. This film is the one exception. He fared much better with his nongenre entries, especially his spy movies (*Operation Poker* with Roger Browne; *The Beckett Affair* starring Lang Jeffries), his thrillers (*The Devil with Seven Faces* with Carroll Baker and George Hilton; *Il Pavone Nero* starring Karin Schubert), and his peplums (*Hercules Against the Sons of the Sun* with Giuliano Gemma and Mark Forest; *Kindar the Invincible* starring Mark Forest and stunning Rosalba Neri).

Son of Zorro (1973)

Man with the Golden Winchester; Figlio di Zorro Ital; *L'Uomo dal Winchester* Ital. *Director:* Gianfranco Baldanello; *Script:* Mario De Roso/Guido Zurli/Gianfranco Baldanello; *Camera:* Franco Delli Colli; *Music:* Marcello Gigante; *Producer:* Marcello Simoni/Lorenzo Piani (Italy/Spain). *Cast:* Robert Widmark, Fernando Sancho, Elisa Ramirez, William Berger, George Wang, Franco Fantasia.

Another seldom seen production, initially promoted as *Son of Zorro*, but quickly recalled and re-released as *Man with the Golden Winchester*. It's especially significant for the unusual teaming of Robert Widmark (Alberto Dell'Acqua) and Fernando Sancho in an apparent "buddy motif," similar to the *Trinity* films.

Sonny and Jed see *Bandera Bandits*

Sono Sartana, il Vostro Becchino see *I Am Sartana, Angel of Death*

Sonora see *Sartana Does Not Forgive*

Spaghetti Western see *Cipolla Colt*

Spara, Gringo, Spara see *Shoot, Gringo . . . Shoot!*

Gli Specialisti see *Specialists*

Specialists (1969)

Drop Them or I'll Shoot; Gli Specialisti Ital. *Director:* Sergio Corbucci; *Script:* Sergio Corbucci/Sabattino Ciuffini; *Camera:* Dario Di Palma; *Music:* Angelo Francesco Lavagnino; *Producer:* Adelphia/Marceau/Lichtspielkunst (Italy/France/West Germany). *Cast:* Johnny Hallyday, Sylvie Fennec, Mario Adorf, Françoise Fabian, Gastone Moschin, Serge Marquand, Gino Pernice.

A lightweight entry from genius filmmaker, Sergio Corbucci. Seemingly, he was infatuated with the leftist philosophies of the United States hippies, and this movie was his homage to their lifestyle. But strangely, in retrospect, the film appears to be a social satire, actually ridiculing the liberal viewpoint. Even Sergio Corbucci was unsatisfied with the result, claiming "scriptwriting disagreements" (between himself and cowriter Sabattino Ciuffini) as the muddling factor.

It is the story of a free-thinking, dope-smoking gang of outlaws who revel in their dominance over the "God-fearing" people of Blackstone. At one point they even force the citizens to crawl down main street butt naked, but finally a "stranger" (French pop singer Johnny Hallyday) puts a stop to the mayhem.

After this brief diversionary jaunt, Sergio Corbucci returned to the mainstream (although still proudly left of center) with *Compañeros*.

La Spietata Colt del Gringo see *Ruthless Colt of the Gringo*

La Spina Dorsale del Diavolo see *Deserter*

Spirito Santo e le 5 Magnifiche Canaglie see *Gunmen and the Holy Ghost*

Spur des Falken see *Trail of the Falcon*

Stagecoach of the Condemned see *Dig Your Grave, Friend . . . Sabata's Coming*

Starblack see *Johnny Colt*

Stay Away from Trinity . . . When He Comes to Eldorado see *Go Away! Trinity Has Arrived in Eldorado!*

Sting of the West (1972)

Con Men; Father Jackleg; Te Deum Ital. *Director:* Enzo G. Castellari; *Script:* Giovanni Simonelli/Enzo Girolami/Tito Carpi; *Camera:* Manolo Rojas; *Music:* Guido and Mauruzio De Angelis; *Producer:* Franco Falaggi/Virgilio De Blasi (Italy). *Cast:* Jack Palance, Lionel Stander, Timothy Brent, Eduardo Fajardo, Renzo Palmer, Romana Coluzzi, Carla Mancini, Riccardo Garrone, Maria Vico Villardo.

Scene from *Sting of the West* (1972) with Maria Vico Villardo in the tub.

"Father" Jackleg (Jack Palance), Stinky Manuel (Lionel Stander), and his grandson (Timothy Brent) go to great lengths to find a gullible fool who will buy their worthless gold mine. After getting mixed up with a couple of beautiful con women (Carla Mancini and Maria Vico Villardo), they discover that the mine is actually legitimate. Meanwhile, they are being pursued by a growing number of frenzied people, all of whom were swindled by the rogues in the past.

Obviously influenced by *It's a Mad, Mad, Mad, Mad World* (1963), this is a good-looking (but silly) movie from director Enzo G. Castellari (alas for Enzo Girolami) who made eight Spaghetti Westerns, including one of the all-time best (*Keoma*) and one of the all-time worst (*Cipolla Colt*).

Stop the Slayings see *Blood at Sundown* (1967)

Storm Rider see *Big Showdown*

La Strada per Fort Alamo see *Road to Fort Alamo*

Strange Tale of Minnesota Stinky see *Fistful of Death*

Stranger and the Gunfighter (1973)

Blood Money; Là, Dove non Batte il Sole Ital. *Director:* Anthony Dawson; *Script:* Barth Jules Sussman; *Camera:* Alejandro Ulloa; *Music:* Carlo Savina; *Producer:* Run Run Shaw/Gustave Berne (Italy/Spain/Hong Kong). *Cast:* Lee Van Cleef, Lo Lieh, Karen Yeh, Femi Benussi, Julian Ugarte, Erika Blanc, Goyo Peralta, Al Tung.

The "man with the gunsight eyes" teams up with the star of *Five Fingers of Death* in an action-packed, yet unconventional genre production. Together, Dakota (Lee Van Cleef) and Ho Kiang (Lo Lieh) search for a dead Chinese businessman's fortune. But first they must locate his four mistresses. It seems that the old man had tattooed a series of clues on the butts of his lovers.

Specifically, master thief Dakota secretly arrives in Monterey. That night he sneaks into the town bank and opens a safety deposit vault belonging to a rich Chinese eccentric named Wang. Inside Dakota finds four provocative photographs of different women displaying their naked backsides. As he is pondering the significance of the pictures, old Wang suddenly appears and is accidentally killed in an explosion. Confused and harried, Dakota is arrested before he can escape.

Meanwhile in China, Wang's brother receives a package from America. Inside is a wooden Indian. Uncertain of its significance but fearing the worst, he orders his son Ho Kiang on a fact finding journey to the United States. Once Ho arrives in Monterey, it doesn't take long for him to understand the significance of the photos in his uncle's vault: the old man had tattooed clues to the "whereabouts of his fortune" on the bottoms of his four lovers. Realizing that he needs help, specifically gunfighting help, Ho rescues Dakota from the gallows and enlists his aid in tracking down the women.

There's loads of fun with some beautiful stars (including Femi Benussi, Erika Blanc and Patty Shepard), plus trouble with a demented deacon named Yancy (Julian Ugarte) and his sidekick, Indio the Indian (Goyo Peralta). By the way, the treasure is (of course) inside the wooden Indian back in China.

It's a joint Hong Kong/Italian production directed in Europe by genre favorite Anthony Dawson (Antonio Margheriti), best known for his outrageous horror films, *Andy Warhol's Frankenstein* and *Dracula, Castle of Terror* and *Cannibals in the Streets*.

Stranger in Japan (1969)

Silent Stranger; Horseman and the Samurai; Lo Straniero di Silenzio Ital. *Director:* Vance Lewis; *Script:* Vincenzo Cerami/Giancarlo Ferrando; *Camera:* Mario Capriotti; *Music:* Stelvio Cipriani; *Producer:* Roberto Infascelli/Allen Klein, Primex Italiana/Reverse (Italy/U.S./Japan). *Cast:* Tony Anthony, Lloyd Battista, Kin Omae, Kenji Ohara, Yoshio Nukano, Rita Maura, Raf Baldassare.

This is the third film in Tony Anthony's "Stranger" series, preceded by *Stranger in Town* and *The Stranger Returns*. It was shot immediately after the second film, but due to a disagreement (and lawsuit) between producer Allen Klein and MGM Pictures, the American releasing company, the movie was shelved for almost ten years. In 1977, when the motion picture was finally released domestically, it had been severely re-edited "for a new generation of filmgoer" with most of Anthony's satirical quips scissored out, the action cut, and the humor entirely excised.

The story, similar to *Stranger in Town*, finds the Stranger (Tony Anthony), once again trying to put himself on the receiving end of a large gold shipment. The novelty, however, is that the action is taking place in Japan. It's a bizarre mixture of Spaghetti and Eggrolls, cowboys and samurai. Technically, it's the first East-meets-West genre movie, made two years before *Red Sun*.

The film is also considered one of Anthony's best. In a *Westerns all'Italiana* interview conducted by editor Tom Betts, Tony Anthony said: "Let me tell you something. That's probably the best picture that I made. There was some great stuff in it. . . . I made the mistake of not having the final cut. When it finally went out, mainly in Europe, it was just watered down to nothing."

Stranger in Paso Bravo (1968)

Uno Straniero a Paso Bravo Ital. *Director:* Salvatore Rosso; *Script:* E. M. Brochero/Fernando Morandi/Lucio Battistrada/Federico De Urrutia; *Camera:* Alfonso Nieva/Gino Santini; *Music:* Angelo Francesco Lavagnino; *Producer:* Silver Film/Fenix (Italy/Spain). *Cast:* Anthony Steffen, Eduardo Fajardo, Giulia Rubini, José Jaspe, Pepe Calvo, Antonio Cintado, Adriana Ambesi.

A mysterious drifter named Gary (Anthony Steffen), who doesn't drink and doesn't wear a gun, comes to Paso Bravo. His mission is to avenge the murder of his wife and daughter, killed by the evil land baron (Eduardo Fajardo). He is ridiculed, tortured, and humiliated until he decides to return to his former bounty hunting days. Eventually, the score is settled with his trusty Winchester.

Eduardo Fajardo, who has etched out a substantial career playing slimy, repugnant villains (see his performance in *Django* for the best example), is perversely delightful, as always. Anthony Steffen, once called "the poor man's Clint Eastwood," grimaces and squints well.

Stranger in Sacramento (1964)

Uno Straniero a Sacramento Ital. *Director:* Serge Bergon; *Script:* Sergio Bergonzelli; *Camera:* Al Albert; *Music:* Felice De Stefano; *Producer:* Filmepoca (Italy). *Cast:* Mickey Hargitay, Barbara Frey, Lucky Bennett, Gabriella Giorgelli, Big I. Matthews, Steve Saint-Claire, Aldo Berti.

Another "revenge for a slaughtered family" Western, this time set in California's Sacramento Valley with a cattle rustling theme, based on the Jay Murphy book *I Will Kill You Tomorrow* (certainly, a much better title).

Mike Jordan (Mickey Hargitay) finds his father and brothers dead, plus all their cattle stolen. He vows (and gets) revenge, but it takes quite a while. Early on, Mike discovers that the culprit is land baron Lefty Barnett. However, it's not easy to convince the sheriff. Eventually, his girlfriend Liza (Barbara Frey) tricks the land owner, and Mike shoots him dead.

Former muscleman actor (and Mr. Jayne Mansfield) Mickey Hargitay made a better Spaghetti Western called *Cjamango* with Sean Todd, and a lesser one, *The Sheriff Won't Shoot.* Serge Bergon is a transparent pseudonym for Sergio Bergonzelli; cinematographer Al Albert (Adalberto Albertini) later became a genre director (see Directors filmography) known as Bitto Albertini. Composer Felice De Stefano is also known as Felix De Stephen.

Stranger in Town (1966)

A Dollar Between the Teeth; For a Dollar in the Teeth; Un Dollaro Tra i Denti Ital. *Director:* Vance Lewis; *Script:* Giuseppe Mangione/Warren Garfield; *Camera:* Marcello Masciocchi; *Music:* Benedetto Ghiglia; *Producer:* Carlo Infascelli, Primex/Taka Films (Italy/U.S.). *Cast:* Tony Anthony, Frank Wolff, Gia Sandri,

Raf Baldassare, Jolanda Modio, Aldo Berti, Enrico Capoleoni, Arturo Corso, Antonio Marsina.

Tony Anthony stepped into the shoes vacated by Clint Eastwood, poncho and all, in this film directed by Vance Lewis (alias Luigi Vanzi). It's the first in a series (which also includes *Stranger Returns, Stranger in Japan,* and *Get Mean*), each starring Anthony as a quip-punctuating bounty killer. This time he pits the Cavalry against the Mexican Revolutionaries for a treasure in gold. The competent film editor is Maurizio Lucidi, future director of the *Pecos* movies, plus *Greatest Robbery in the West* and the Sergio Leone parody *It Can Be Done . . . Amigo.*

The Stranger arrives in Cerro Gordo just as revolutionary bandit Anguila and his men have taken over the outpost. They have killed the entire U.S. Cavalry regiment, disguising themselves with the uniforms from the dead army, and they are waiting for a huge gold shipment en route to the Mexican government. Stranger strikes a bargain with Anguila. He will vouch for the legitimacy of the bandits to the incoming paymaster in exchange for a portion of the gold.

Everything goes smoothly, but then Anguila refuses to keep his bargain. Instead, he gives Stranger one dollar for the "endorsement" and tortures him. Eventually, Stranger outwits the bandits and escapes with all the gold, only to face the suspicious U.S. Army Paymaster unit on the outskirts of town.

Stranger Returns (1967)

Shoot First, Laugh Last; Un Uomo, un Cavallo, una Pistola. Director: Vance Lewis; *Script:* Tony Anthony/Bob Ensescalle/Jone Maug; *Camera:* Marcello Masciocchi; *Music:* Stelvio Cipriani; *Producer:* Roberto Infascelli/Allen Klein, Primex Italiana/Juventus/Reverse (Italy/Spain/U.S.). *Cast:* Tony Anthony, Dan Vadis, Marco Gugliemi, Jill Banner, Marina Berti, Raf Baldassare, Luciano Catenacci.

Tony Anthony again plays the lead role in this official sequel to *Stranger in Town*, also directed by Vance Lewis (pseudonym for Luigi Vanzi). Incidentally, the Italian title translates to *A Man, a Horse, a Gun.*

This time the wisecracking, bounty-hunting opportunist tracks down a murderous gang of outlaws, led by En Plein (Dan Vadis), plotting to rob a stagecoach carrying a fortune in gold. As it turns out, the coach isn't carrying gold, it's secretly *made* of gold.

Initially, upon its American release, the movie ran into some censorship problems, especially in the Bible Belt, because Anthony's horse was named "Pussy." Seemingly, these would-be censors forgot about James Bond's girlfriend, Pussy Galore.

The next film in the series is *Stranger in Japan.*

Stranger That Kneels Beside the Shadow of a Corpse (1971)

Inginocchiati Straniero . . . i Cadaveri non Fanno Ombra Ital. *Director:* Miles Deem; *Script:* Demofilo Fidani/R. M. Valenza; *Camera:* Aristide Massaccesi; *Music:* Coriolano Gori; *Producer:* Tarquina Film (Italy). *Cast:* Hunt Powers, Chet Davis, Gordon Mitchell, Dennys Colt, Simone Blondell, Ettore Manni.

Certainly, Miles Deem (Demofilo Fidani) should be congratulated for the most surrealistic title in the Eurowestern genre. (Italo Alfaro runs a noble race with *And They Smelled the Strange, Exciting, Dangerous Scent of Dollars,* but there's really no contest.)

The movie itself is an equally strange, rambling, dreamlike prowl, aided by the potent camera work of Aristide Massaccesi (who later became the controversial sleaze and horror director Joe D'Amato). Blonde (Chet Davis) is chasing bounty hunter Lazar (Hunt Powers), the reason why is never given, but the audience assumes the obvious "price-on-his-head" story.

The two men find themselves in the city of Lamazos where an evil mine owner Barret (Gordon Mitchell) totally controls the townspeople through fear and torture. Barret sends his hit squad to kill Lazar. When they fail he pays the bounty hunter $100,000 to leave town, and he does. Blonde continues to follow him.

Eventually Lazar ends his journey at an isolated shack where an elderly man named Solinas (Ettore Manni) lives. Lazar enslaves the old man, tormenting him mercilessly. Finally, Blonde arrives. He discloses that the old man is his father, and he kills the bounty hunter in a showdown, dividing the $100,000 with his dad.

Sure, none of it makes any sense, but that's all part of Miles Deem's wacky charm.

Stranger's Gold see *Have a Good Funeral, My Friend . . . Sartana Will Pay*

Stranger's Gundown see *Django the Bastard*

Uno Straniero a Paso Bravo see *Stranger in Paso Bravo*

Lo Straniero di Silenzio see *Stranger in Japan*

Uno Straniero a Sacramento see *Stranger in Sacramento*

Su le Mani, Cadavere! Sei agli Arresti see *Raise Your Hands, Dead Man . . . You're Under Arrest*

Sugar Colt (1966)

Sugar Colt Ital. *Director:* Franco Giraldi; *Script:* Giuseppe Mangione/Augusto Finocchi/Sandro Continenza/Fernando Di Leo; *Camera:* Alejandro Ulloa; *Music:* Luis Enrique Bacalov; *Producer:* Franco Cittadini and Stenio Fiorentini, Mega/Eva Film (Italy/Spain). *Cast:* Hunt Powers, James Paker, Soledad Miranda, Julian Rafferty, George Rigaud, Victor Israel, Jeanne Oak.

This Italian-Spanish coproduction is directed by the creator of the *MacGregors* series, Franco Giraldi (alias Frank Garfield). It's cowritten by his friend and associate, filmmaker Fernando Di Leo (best known for directing *Slaughter Hotel* [also called *Cold Blooded Beast*] with Klaus Kinski); once again, Giraldi's cameraman of choice, Alejandro Ulloa, is in charge of the cinematography.

Hunt Powers is Tom Cooper, a famous crack shot government "special agent" known as Sugar Colt. Solving the perplexing mystery of Snake Valley is his number one priority.

During the Civil War, a detachment of 130 Union sharpshooters had disappeared without a trace. Two years later, after the war, the United States government is sent a ransom note. The "kidnappers" are demanding a million dollars in gold or they threaten to slaughter the soldiers. Sugar Colt goes undercover, disguised as a doctor, to the city of Snake Valley where he has reason to believe the solution to the problem lies.

The film is an entertaining break from the norm.

Actress Soledad Miranda was one of cult director Jess Franco's earliest obsessions, starring in his films, *Vampyros Lesbos*, *The Devil Came from Akasawa*, *Death Carries a Suitcase*, and *Eugenie*. She came from a true gypsy background and was killed in a car wreck (much like the character she played in Franco's *Mrs. Hyde*) in 1971.

Sul Sentiero di Guerra see *Paths of War*

Sundance and the Kid see *Alive or Preferably Dead*

Sunscorched (1966)

Jessy Does Not Forgive . . . He Kills! Brit; *Jessy Non Perdona . . . Uccide* Ital. *Director:* Alfonso Balcazar; *Script:* Mark Stevens/Alfonso Balcazar/Irving Dennis/José Antonio De La Loma; *Camera:* Francisco Marin; *Music:* Michel Auzepi/Enzo Silvestri; *Producer:* Balcazar of Balcelona (Spain/Germany). *Cast:* Mark Stevens, Mario Adorf, Marianne Koch, Vivien Dobbs, Oscar Pellicer, Frank Oliveras, Antonio Iranzo.

Four desperate gunmen take over the town of Fraserville. The sheriff, Jess Kinley (Mark Stevens) is hesitant to act against them because they hold a secret to his past. One of the outlaws, Abel Dragna (Mario Adorf), threatens to tell the townspeople that the lawman used to be a kill-crazy member of their gang. The local citizens begin to think that their sheriff is a coward when he doesn't confront the outlaws, but Anna-Lisa (Marianne Koch), who secretly loves Jess, remains loyal.

Eventually, Sheriff Kinley's secret is discovered and his "tin star" is taken away. His wife, Lily (Vivien Dobbs) leaves him. Then the gang attacks the church, killing the minister's son; next they murder Anna-Lisa. Finally the ex-sheriff retaliates, wiping out all the bad guys. This regains him both the townspeople's respect plus his wife's renewed affections.

There's a message in there someplace.

Il Suo Nome Era Pot . . . lo Chiamavano Allegria see *Hero Called Allegria*

Il Suo Nome Gridava Vendetta see *Man Who Cried for Revenge*

Sword of Zorro see *Three Swords of Zorro*

Taglia È Tua, l'Uomo l'Ammazzo Io see *The Reward's Yours, the Man's Mine*

Das Tal der tanzenden Witwen see *Valley of the Dancing Widows*

Take a Hard Ride (1974)

La Parola di un Fuorilegge ... È Legge! Ital. *Director:* Anthony Dawson; *Script:* Eric Bercovici/Jerry Ludwig; *Camera:* Riccardo Pallotini; *Music:* Jerry Goldsmith; *Producer:* Harry Bernsen (Italy/England/Germany). *Cast:* Lee Van Cleef, Jim Brown, Fred Williamson, Catherine Spaak, Jim Kelly, Dana Andrews, Barry Sullivan, Harry Carey, Jr.

Although better than the next Lee Van Cleef/Jim Brown vehicle, *Kid Vengeance*, and much better than the preceding American-made *El Condor*, this movie can't compete with Van Cleef's early Spaghettis. Filmed in the Canary Islands as per Jim Brown's contractual rider, this U.S.-Italian-German coproduction finds Lee Van Cleef playing a ruthless bounty hunter named Kiefer who tries to steal an $86,000 bankroll from Pike (Jim Brown) and Tyree (Fred Williamson), two unsuspecting, hired escorts.

It's directed by Italian cult horror/adventure director, Antonio Margheriti (alias Anthony Dawson) whose *Stranger and the Gunfighter* (also starring Lee Van Cleef) and *Vengeance* (with Richard Harrison) remain his best (and most successful) Westerns. The chief cameraman is Riccardo Pallottini, but much of the crew and almost the entire cast are Americans, many of whom (like Lee Van Cleef, Fred Williamson, Barry Sullivan, and Harry Carey, Jr.) depended on the Italian film market for their income.

Talent for Loving (1969)

Talento por Amor Sp. *Director:* Richard Quine; *Script:* Jack Rose/Richard Condon; *Camera:* Johnny Coquillion; *Music:* Linc Harvey; *Producer:* Dudley Birch Films (England/Spain). *Cast:* Richard Widmark, Cesar Romero, Caroline Munro, Topol, Fran Jeffries, Genieve Page, Judd Hamilton.

Initially this film was deemed "too awful for release." But over the years it has slipped into "television movie packages," finally giving the addicted genre fan an opportunity to see it. Although Richard Widmark starred in many American-made Westerns (i.e., *Alvarez Kelly, The Alamo, Two Rode Together* and *Cheyenne Autumn*), this one remains his only Eurowestern. Joining him is Cesar Romero (destined to be remembered as the original Joker in TV's *Batman*), Broadway's *Fiddler on the Roof* star Topol, plus the incredible Caroline Munro (cult actress of *Star Crash, Maniac, Captain Kronos: Vampire Hunter, Howl of the Devil,* and *Golden Voyage of Sinbad*).

The story is an odd tale (certainly no worse than any Gianni Crea, Paolo Solvay, or Tonino Ricci film) of a notorious and amorous gunfighter, Nevada (Richard Widmark), who goes into Mexico to take possession of a ranch that he inherited. Upon his arrival, he is taken under the wing of land baron Alonso (Cesar Romero) who is suffering from a mystical "sexual" Aztec curse.

The camera work is expertly handled in "Spaghetti Western fashion" by Johnny Coquillon, best known for his cinematography in *Curse of the Crimson Altar* starring Boris Karloff, Christopher Lee, and Barbara Steele.

Director Richard Quine has had an erratic career filled with many "borderline" sleaze classics, including *World of Suzie Wong* (1960), *Strangers When We Meet* (1960), *The Notorious Landlady* (1962), *Paris When It Sizzles* (1964), *Sex and the Single Girl* (1965), *Oh Dad, Poor Dad, Mama's Hung You in the Closet and I'm Feeling So Sad* (1967).

Lee Van Cleef (foreground) in *Take a Hard Ride* (1974).

Talento por Amor see *Talent for Loving*

Tall Women (1966)

Seven Vengeful Women; Donne alla Frontiera Ital. *Director:* Sidney Pink; *Script:* Mino Roli/Jim Heneghan/Mike Ashley; *Camera:* Marcello Gatti; *Music:* Gregorio Garcia Segura/Carlo Savina; *Producer:* Sidney Pink, Danny Film/LM Film/Danubia (Germany/Italy/Spain). *Cast:* Anne Baxter, Maria Perschy, Gustavo Rojo, Rossella Como, Adriana Ambesi, Christa Linder, Luis Prendes, Mara Cruz, Perla Cristal, Maria Mahor.

Some early prints of this film identify the director as Frank Kramer (Gianfranco Parolini). His involvement is questionable. Rather, displaced American film producer, Sidney Pink, is generally believed to be the true director of the movie, and the English language version bears his name.

A wagon train en route to Fort Lafayette is attacked by Apaches, led by the "most feared savage in the West," a warrior named Pope (Luis Prendes). Seven female survivors take refuge in a nearby cave and then, after the immediate danger has passed, they begin the long trek across the Arizona desert. Of course, they have no food, no horses, and no weapons. But, spurred on by Mary Ann (Anne Baxter), they have courage and "the will to survive." Sometimes that's all it takes. Especially in the movies.

Meanwhile, a cavalry unit is dispatched from the fort. Quickly, they also fall prey to the rampaging Indians. Only a scout, Gus McIntosh (Gustavo Rojo), survives the massacre. Eventually he joins with the seven "vengeful women" and they escape by sneaking through a sacred Indian burial ground. However, Pope and his warriors are waiting for them. As the Indian readies his braves for the final attack, Chief White Cloud (Fernando Hilbeck) halts the pending slaughter by granting McIntosh and the women "total freedom" as an "esteem of their courage."

Anne Baxter is best known for her Academy Award–winning performance in *The Razor's Edge* (1950). She also starred in the classic *All About Eve* (1952) plus Alfred Hitchcock's *I Confess* (1953). After completing the filming of *The Tall Women*, she married an Australian sheep herder and retired to his farm outside Sydney.

T'Ammazzo, Raccomandati a Dio see *Dead for a Dollar*

Taste for Killing (1966)

Lanky Fellow; Per il Gusto di Uccidere Ital. *Director:* Tonino Valerii; *Script:* Victor Aux; *Camera:* Stelvio Massi; *Music:* Nico Fidenco; *Producer:* Bianco Manini, Hercules/Montana (Italy/Spain). *Cast:* Craig Hill, George Martin, Peter Carter, Fernando Sancho, Frank Ressel, George Wang, Diana Martin, Graham Sooty, Rada Rassimov, José Marco.

Lanky Fellow (Craig Hill) is the cowboy equivalent to an "ambulance chaser." He's a bounty hunter (of sorts), tagging unofficially behind money transporting convoys. When (and if) the wagons are robbed, he eliminates the bandits, thus recouping the loot, taking it to the bank, and ultimately accepting a generous reward.

This particular story begins to unfold when Lanky returns a large sum of stolen cash to the bank in Omaha. He receives a $10,000 bounty for his trouble. The bank manager, Aarons (Frank Ressel), knows that the shipment "stands a good chance of being robbed again," so he makes a gambling-type-of-deal with Lanky: take the $10,000 reward and "put it on the line" by making it part of the convoy. If the wagon is attacked and the loot stolen, Lanky loses; but, if the shipment gets to the destination safely, the bounty hunter receives *double*. Lanky Fellow takes the bet. Of course, he runs into marauding bandits (led by Fernando Sancho). But obviously, he (and the money) emerge unscathed.

One of Tonino Valerii's lesser films (see *Price of Power, Day of Anger* and *My Name Is Nobody*) but it's still entertaining, partly due to an unusual twist on the bounty hunter theme. It's also significant for (future action director) Stelvio Massi's superb camera work.

Taste of Death see *Cost of Dying*

Taste of the Savage see *Eye for an Eye*

Taste of Vengeance see *Cowards Don't Pray*

Taste of Violence (1961)

Le Goût de la Violence Fr. *Director:* Robert Hossein; *Script:* Robert Hossein/ Louis Martin; *Camera:* Jacques Robin; *Music:* André Hossein; *Producer:* Ralph

Baum, Gaumont Film (France). *Cast:* Robert Hossein, Giovanna Ralli, Mario Adorf, Madeleine Robinson, Hans Neubert, Dany Jacquet.

Released in early 1961, this is one of the first European Westerns. It's mostly the brain child of maverick French actor/director Robert Hossein. He first gained international notoriety in 1956 with a disturbing performance in *Crime and Punishment* (*Crime et Chatiment*), and later wrote, directed, and starred in many of his own films, including another Spaghetti Western called *Cemetery Without Crosses* (1968) and *I Killed Rasputin* (*J'ai Tué Raspoutine*) the following year. He played the lead three times for director Roger Vadim, and starred opposite Brigitte Bardot in 1963's *Warrior Rest*.

Unfortunately, this French production seems to be the victim of poor distribution. Besides the sketchy credit information, little else is known about it.

Te Deum see *Sting of the West*

Il Tempo degli Avvoltoi see *Time of Vultures*

Tempo di Massacro see *Massacre Time*

Ten Thousand Dollars Blood Money (1966)

Guns of Violence; Ten Thousand Dollars for a Massacre; 10.000 Dollari per un Massacro Ital. *Director:* Romolo Guerrieri; *Script:* Franco Fogagnolo/Ernesto Gastaldi/Luciano Martino/Sauro Scavolini; *Camera:* Federico Zanni; *Music:* Nora Orlandi; *Producer:* Luciano Martino, Zenith/Flora (Italy). *Cast:* Gary Hudson, Fidel Gonzales, Loredana Nusciak, Adriana Ambesi, Fernando Sancho, Claudio Camaso.

Yes, that's Gianni Garko behind the Gary Hudson pseudonym. He plays Django in this film, one of the early "unauthorized sequels" to the Sergio Corbucci Eurowestern. (see the appendix for a complete *Django* listing.)

Manuel Cortes (Claudio Camaso) is a Mexican outlaw, fresh from a prison release. Apparently, incarceration taught him nothing because the first thing he does with his new freedom is kidnap the daughter of a wealthy landowner, Mendoza (Fidel Gonzales). The land baron tries to hire Django to kill Manuel and rescue his Dolores (Adriana Ambesi), but the bounty hunter declines, claiming that he only takes on jobs offering $10,000 or more. Later, while playing cards in a local saloon, Django is accosted by Manuel and his gang, so he decides to take Mendoza's offer. There's lots of action and double-crossing, but finally when Django's girlfriend (Loredana Nusciak) is murdered by Mendoza, the bounty hunter "goes for the throat," defeating the outlaw in a showdown.

This film is one of three Spaghetti Westerns from cult director Romolo Guerrieri (also see *Johnny Yuma* and *Seven Guns for Timothy*). It's written by veteran filmmaker Luciano Martino, brother of famed director Sergio Martino; Federico Zanni is the primary cameraman. Nora Orlandi composed the score. Gianni (John) Garko later became the leading star of the popular *Sartana* series.

Ten Thousand Dollars for a Massacre see Ten Thousand Dollars Blood Money

Tepepa . . . Viva la Revolución see *Blood and Guns*

Tequila (1974)

Fuzzy the Hero; Uno, Dos, Tres . . . Dispara Otra Vez Sp; *Tequila* Ital; *Fuzzy, halt die Ohren steif!* Ger. *Director:* Tullio Demichelli; *Script:* Enrique Josa/ Miguel Iglesias/Tullio Demichelli; *Camera:* Memmo Mancori; *Music:* Coriolano Gori; *Producer:* Tritone/Mundial Film (Italy/Spain). *Cast:* Anthony Steffen, Eduardo Fajardo, Roberto Camardiel; Agata Lys, Maria Elena Arpon, Mirko Ellis, John Bartha.

Exploitation director Tullio Demichelli, best known for *Assignment Terror: Dracula vs. Frankenstein* (1969) and *Mean Machine* (also called *Ricco!*) (1978), fluctuates between a violent variation of the "big trouble with the town boss" theme and a less traditional black comedy, with most of the laughs coming from unexpected death scenes (especially during the first 20 minutes) and nihilistic Sabata-like quips.

Anthony Steffen plays it straight. His deadpan machismo is a dramatic counter to the goofy antics of his sidekick, Fuzzy (Roberto Camardiel), but somehow it all works. Eduardo Fajardo, in another tailor-made part of town boss Zenfield, looks both slimy and menacing. Or maybe he's just exasperated. Perhaps a bit weary of doing the same gig unremittingly for umpteen years.

Terrible Day of the Big Gundown see *Vendetta at Dawn*

Terrible Sheriff (1963)

Two Against All; Due Contro Tutti Ital. *Director:* Antonio Momplet; *Script:* José Mallorqui/Mario Guerra/Vittorio Vighi; *Camera:* Ricardo Torres; *Music:* Manuel Parada; *Producer:* Emo Bistolfi, Atlantida Film (Spain/Italy). *Cast:* Walter Chiari, Lici Calderón, Maria Silva, Raimondo Vianello, Antonio Molino Rojo, José Calvo, Fernando Hilbeck, Aroldo Tieri, Emilio Rodriguez.

Simple words can't do justice to this unbelievably atrocious, yet wildly endearing film. It definitely is "one of a kind." But is that good?

While riding across the prairie, Bill and his brother Jonathan (Walter Chiari and Lici Calderón) witness the killing of an evil masked bandit known as "Black Boy." Panicked, they hightail it to Golden City where most of the populace is planning a mass exodus. The townspeople are tired of living under the oppressed rule of Black Boy, so they are moving to a more peaceful place. Bill and Jonathan try to explain that the masked outlaw is dead, but no one listens. The mayor (Antonio Molino Rojo), who wants all the land for himself (it's rich with oil), is pushing for "immediate evacuation."

The two brothers wander off. Hungry, they steal a chicken, not realizing it has been drugged with a "super strength elixir" to win a cock fight. They cook and eat it. The drug turns them into strong and fearless gunfighters. The townspeople are impressed. They instantly appoint Bill and Jonathan as dual sheriffs. But the mayor, hoping to eliminate them permanently, orders the brothers to capture Black Boy (for some reason, everybody thinks he's still alive).

In the meantime, Bill and Jonathan have been hanging out at the town saloon, drinking beer, which is the antidote to the "super strength drug." Once again, they have become cowards. They slink out of town unseen. But soon, the brothers find Black Boy's body floating in the river. They take it and return to Golden City. Obviously, the citizens celebrate, but the mayor is angry. He hides Black Boy's body and, by wearing the mask, the mayor convinces everybody that the outlaw has returned "from the dead to seek revenge." Panic grips the community until Bill and Jonathan fortuitously eat two more drugged chickens and become heroes. Outlandishly eccentric.

Terror of Oklahoma (1961)

La Terrore de Oklahoma Ital. *Director:* Mario Amendola; *Script:* Mario Amendola; *Music:* Manuel Parada; *Producer:* Betauno Film (Italy). *Cast:* Maurizio Arena, Delia Scala, Alberto Bonucci, Livio Lorenzon, Valeria Moriconi, Alberto Sorrentino.

A very early (and seldom seen) genre Western directed by prolific screenwriter Mario Amendola, best known for his joint ventures with filmmaker Bruno Corbucci. There is some speculation that this motion picture never saw distribution beyond the immediate Italian market where it was routinely promoted and quickly forgotten.

Terror of the Black Mask (1963)

L'Invincibile Cavaliere Mascherato Ital; *Terrore di Masque di Indio* Ital. *Director:* Umberto Lenzi; *Script:* Gino De Santis/Guido Malatesta/Umberto Lenzi; *Camera:* Adalberto Albertini; *Music:* Francesco De Masi; *Producer:* P.E.A. (Italy). *Cast:* Pierre Brice, Daniele Vargas, Hélène Chanel, Giselle Arden, Aldo Bufi Landi, Carlo Latimer.

In the early 1960s, filmmaker Umberto Lenzi was busy directing various peplums and peplum derivatives, including his *Sandokan* series (1962 and 1963) plus *The Last Gladiator* (1964), *Revolt of the Titans* (1964), and a very odd timewarp picture, *Zorro versus Maciste* (1963). He also churned out a more traditional version of the Zorro legend called *Terror of the Black Mask* (1964). Although the story takes place in seventeenth century Spain, it is very similar to a standard "California" Zorro tale, significant mostly because of Pierre "Winnetou" Brice's portrayal of the masked super hero.

Pierre Brice is Don Diego, the shy stepson of an evil magistrate. Diego, disguising himself behind a mask and cape, attacks his stepfather's army and rallies the oppressed people to revolution.

Incidentally, this film is included here with reservations since it more closely resembles a "European costume action/drama" than a Spaghetti Western. For Umberto Lenzi's true genre films see *All Out* and *Pistol for a Hundred Coffins* (both 1968). Other non–Western "Zorro" films are listed under the entry for *Zorro, the Navarra Marquis.*

La Terrore de Oklahoma see *Terror of Oklahoma*

Terrore di Masque di Indio see *Terror of the Black Mask*

Testa o Croce see *Heads or Tails*

Testa T'Ammazzo Croce Sei Morto . . . Mi Chiamano Alleluia see *Heads You Die . . . Tails I Kill You*

Franco Nero in *Texas, Adios* (1966).

Tex and the Lord of the Deep (1985)

Tex e il Signore degli Abissi Ital. *Director:* Duccio Tessari; *Script:* Gianfranco Luigi Bonelli; *Camera:* Pietro Morbidelli; *Music:* Gianni Ferrio; *Producer:* Duccio Tessari (Italy). *Cast:* Giuliano Gemma, William Berger, Carlo Mucari, Isabel Russinova, Aldo Sambrell, Flavio Bucci.

Tex Willer (Giuliano Gemma) is investigating a convoy robbery when he discovers that the tribe of Yaqui Indians are planning an all-out Indian War against their enemy, the Aztecs. Their witchdoctor has harbored a fantastic secret weapon, a glowing green rock capable of turning people into instant mummies. The whole thing is loosely based on a popular Italian comic strip.

The idea of mixing fantasy elements with a Western motif is noteworthy, but the finished production seems (unfortunately) stilted. The film suffers mostly from its own laborious attempt to be "hip." A weak entry from both director Duccio Tessari and actor Giuliano Gemma.

Tex e il Signore degli Abissi see *Tex and the Lord of the Deep*

Texas see *Price of Power*

Texas, Addio see *Texas, Adios*

Texas, Adios (1966)

Avenger; Goodbye Texas; Texas, Addio; Adios, Texas Ital. *Director:* Ferdinando Baldi; *Script:* Franco Rossetti/Ferdinando Baldi; *Camera:* Enzo Barboni; *Music:* Anton Abril; *Producer:* Manolo Bolognini, B.R.C./Estela (Italy/Spain). *Cast:* Franco Nero, José Suarez, Hugo Blanco, Alberto Dell'Acqua, Livio Lorenzon, Luigi Pistilli, Cole Kitosch, Antonella Murgia, Elisa Montes, José Guardiola.

Cowritten by Ferdinando Baldi and popular scriptwriter Franco Rossetti (who also directed *Big Ripoff*), with camerawork by the always excellent Enzo Barboni (later to become action director E. B. Clucher), this Continental coproduction delivers the goods.

Franco Nero is Burt, the sheriff of Widow Rock. And the film opens as he relinquishes his badge for a "leave of absence." Burt and his younger brother Jim (Alberto Dell'Acqua, aka Robert Widmark) go off to Mexico to find Cisco Delgado, a sadistic outlaw land baron who had murdered their father when they were very young. During the final confrontation (in a rather ridiculous, but entertaining, soap-opera twist), Cisco reveals a scandalous secret. Apparently, Jim is not really Burt's brother, but rather he is Cisco's son, abandoned many years before. Jim is enraged. He attacks the outlaw, but is mortally wounded. Burt, in turn, kills Cisco. Revenge completed, Burt returns to his sheriff's position in Texas.

A good macho score from Anton Abril adds fire to the brew.

Texas Jim see *Shoot to Kill*

Texas Ranger see *Two Gunmen*

Texican (1966)

Ringo el Texano. *Director:* José L. Espinosa with Lesley Selander; *Script:* John C. Champion/José A. De La Loma; *Camera:* Francisco Marin; *Music:* Nico

Fidenco; *Producer:* John C. Champion/Bruce Balaban, M.C.R./Balcazar (U.S./ Spain). *Cast:* Audie Murphy, Broderick Crawford, Diana Lorys, Luis Induñi, Victor Israel, Antonio Casas, Antonio Peral, Antonio Molino Rojo, Aldo Sambrell.

Here's a United States–Spanish coproduction, shot entirely in Spain by two diverse directors, Euro "artsy" filmmaker José Luis Espinosa (*Two Loves in the Afternoon*) and veteran American B-moviemaker Lesley Selander (with 133 films to his credit including *Brothers in the Saddle, Buckskin Frontier, Range War, The Frontiersman*). This film stars U.S. Western hero Audie Murphy (*Destry, Bullet with No Name, The Unforgiven, Guns of Fort Petticoat*, etc.) in his only Spaghetti entry. He made a career out of playing "good guy" roles, but ran into trouble when some of his business investments went "belly up." Shortly after this film, Audie filed for bankruptcy. He was arrested for attempted homicide in 1969, and died in a private plane crash in 1971. He was 47.

Audie Murphy is Jess Carlin, "The Texican" (a gringo from Texas living in Mexico; Texan + Mexican = Texican, right?). He's a former lawman unjustly accused in a frame-up and now, living south of the border. When he gets news that his brother has been murdered by a town boss arch-enemy named Luke Starr (Broderick Crawford), Jess returns to the United States for revenge (and to, finally, clear his name).

Costar, former Oscar winner (for *All the King's Men*) Broderick Crawford made two other Eurowesterns, *Mutiny at Fort Sharp* (1966) and *Kid Rodelo* (1966), but he is best known for the lead role in the popular television series, "Highway Patrol." He died from a heart attack at age 75 in 1986.

They Believed He Was No Saint *see* ***Too Much Gold for One Gringo***

They Call Him Cemetery (1971)

His Pistols Smoked . . . They Call Him Cemetery; Bullet for a Stranger; Gli Fumavano le Colt . . . lo Chiamavano Camposanto Ital. *Director:* Anthony Ascott; *Script:* E. B. Clucher; *Camera:* Stelvio Massi; *Music:* Bruno Nicolai; *Producer:* Mino Loy, National/Flora Film (Italy/Spain). *Cast:* Gianni Garko, William Berger, Christopher Chittel, Franco Ressel, Nello Pazzafini, John Fordyce.

The technical credits for this film look like a "who's who" of Spaghetti Westerns: directed by Anthony Ascott (Giuliano Carmineo) the number one most prolific director with 13 genre films to his name; written by E. B. Clucher (Enzo Barboni) the legendary cameraman-cum-filmmaker and creator of the enormously popular *Trinity* series; photographed by proficient Stelvio Massi who eventually became a sought-after cult action director; with music by Bruno Nicolai, the former Ennio Morricone student who went on to compose the score for 21 Spaghetti Westerns; plus "Sartana" stars Gianni (John) Garko and William Berger. But, ironically, the film doesn't try to be an "epic." Instead, it's a good example of tough and gritty, exploitive Eurowesterns.

Gianni Garko is the Stranger, a bounty hunter who says very little but is always around when trouble breaks out. He takes a liking to John and George McIntire (Christopher Chittel and John Fordyce), two pacifist ranchers bullied by Duke (William Berger) and his gang of land-grabbing outlaws. The Stranger teaches the two men how to protect their farm (without betraying their beliefs) and eventually he is forced to face Duke in a climactic showdown. It's an enjoyable "little" movie.

They Call Him Holy Ghost see *His Name Was Holy Ghost*

They Call Him Veritas (1972)

Lo Chiamavano Verità Ital. *Director:* Luigi Perelli; *Script:* Oreste Coltellacci; *Camera:* Mario Capriotti; *Music:* Manuel De Sica; *Producer:* R.T.R./Medusa (Italy/Spain). *Cast:* Mark Damon, Pat Nigro, William Bogart, Enzo Fiermonte, Pietro Ceccarelli, Franco Garofalo.

Early in the film Mark Damon says: "They call me Veritas, right? That's because I always tell the truth." Sure, it's a lie. He's a con artist. But he's an educated "I know how to read" con artist and has recently acquired a copy of a book called *How to Make Money in the West*. With his three flim-flamming friends, Veritas wanders aimlessly from one adventure to the next, trying "to make a buck" by applying suggestions from the text.

Eventually, they become involved in a major caper. They successfully steal a load of gold bars from an outlaw gang. Unfortunately, it doesn't take long for them to lose the fortune to a man named William James (William Bogart), who happens to be the notorious author of the instruction book.

Costar Franco Garofalo went on to star in a variety of horror and sleazy exploitation films, including *Night of the Zombies* (1981), *The Other Hell* (1981), and *Secret of the Nuns of Monza* (1980) all for director Vincent Dawn (alias Bruno Mattei).

They Call Me Hallelujah see *Heads You Die ... Tails I Kill You*

They Call Me Trinity (1970)

Lo Chiamavano Trinità Ital. *Director:* E. B. Clucher; *Script:* E. B. Clucher; *Camera:* Aldo Giordani; *Music:* Franco Micalizzi; *Producer:* Italo Zingarelli, West Film (Italy). *Cast:* Terence Hill, Bud Spencer, Farley Granger, Elena Pedemonte, Steffen Zacharias, Dan Sturkie, Gisela Hahn.

Here's the highly successful comedy/Western buddy picture that catapulted the Terence Hill/Bud Spencer "team" to international acclaim, inspired countless (but mostly lame) wanna-be action flicks, and even instigated another Euro studio to make carbon copy films with "Hill and Spencer" lookalikes, Smith and Colby (see *Carambola* and *Carambola's Philosophy*).

This one tells the story of a drifter gunfighter, Trinity (Terence Hill) who goes to Alliance City to visit his brother (the sheriff and a former cattle thief) played by Bud Spencer. Trinity stops drifting long enough to help the sheriff and the underdog Mormon farmers fight against a gang of marauding outlaws, led by evil Major Harriman (Farley Granger). When the battle is over and the city is saved, the townspeople want Trinity to stay and "make a new life for himself." But the Mormon lifestyle, consisting of hard work and sacrifice, doesn't appeal to Trinity; instead, he and his brother, looking for a more adventurous time, join the defeated outlaw gang.

Much of the film's charm is due to deft direction and a good script by former cameraman, Enzo Barboni (alias E. B. Clucher), who also made the popular sequel *Trinity Is Still My Name* (1974). Other Terence Hill sequels, unofficial and sometimes retitled, are *Trinity Is Back Again* (1975), *Trinity Sees Red* (1971) and the contemporary action movie, *Trinity the Renegade* (1976).

Terence Hill played Trinity in *They Call Me Trinity* (1970).

They Called Him Amen see *Man Called Amen*

They Called Him the Player with the Dead see *Man Called Invincible*

They Called Him Trinity (1972)

His Colt, Himself, His Revenge; Allegri Becchini Arriva Trinità Ital; *Arriba Trinity!* Sp. *Director:* Fred Lyon Morris; *Script:* Ferdinando Merighi; *Camera:* Pasqual Panetti/Giorgio Montagnani; *Music:* Marcello Gigante (Gignante); *Producer:* Giulio Giuseppe Nel/John Turner, Nomentana Film (Italy/Spain). *Cast:* Dean Stratford, Gordon Mitchell, Maily Doria, Lucky MacMurray, Gastry Gay, Haim Bogart, Mike Monty.

Fred Lyon Morris is believed to be another pseudonym for Luigi Batzella (aka Paolo Solvay and Dean Jones). Plus, under the "Solvay" name he also worked as editor and, most likely, is the scriptwriter (under the otherwise unknown moniker, Ferdinando Merighi). And, of course, the movie is bad. None of his films are any good, but they tend to be fun in an outrageous sort of way.

Chad Randall (Dean Stratford) is searching for a "man in a black hood" who, along with five other thugs, murdered his sister. He finds and kills each of the accomplices, eventually setting a trap for the leader. It turns out, as in many other Spaghetti Westerns, the secret killer is actually the sheriff. Chad screams at Sheriff Ryan (Lucky MacMurray): "Before I get you hung, I'm gonna beat the shit out of you!" But wait . . . After Chad has pummelled him to a pulp, the real hooded murderer shows up, and it's his brother-in-law, Danny. Talk about a surprise ending. The audience still hasn't recovered.

Incidentally, regardless of the "Trinity" title, there's no one named Trinity in the film.

They Died with Their Boots On see *Silver Saddle*

They Still Call Me Amen (1972)

Mamma Mia È Arrivato "Così Sia" Ital; *Oremus, Alleluia e Così Sia* Ital. *Director:* Alfio Caltabiano; *Script:* Alfio Caltabiano/Alessandro Continenza; *Camera:* Riccardo Pallottini; *Music:* Gianni Ferrio; *Producer:* Laser Film (Italy). *Cast:* Luc Meranda, Sydne Rome, Alf Thunder, Tano Cimarosa, Mila Beran, Renato Cestiè.

Apparently this film was shot back to back, or possibly in tandem, with *A Man Called Amen.* The credits are very similar, with the notable exception of "music." This time, composer Gianni Ferrio replaces Daniele Patucchi.

The movie is (unfortunately) more of the same, singularly unfunny sight gangs and loads of transparent double entendres. Plus, it is tediously boring, an unforgivable quality. Sydne Rome's performance is limited to a cameo at the conclusion, the rest of her involvement relies on "flashbacks" lifted from the first film, as Horacio (Luc Meranda) and his partner, Smith (Alf Thunder, aka director Alfio Caltabiano) are trying to find the swindling schoolteacher who ran off with their stolen money.

Obviously Sydne Rome's nude bath scene from the previous film is included in a "flashback." It's barely the only redeeming moment.

They Were Called Graveyard see *Twice a Judas*

Thirteenth Is a Judas (1971)

Il Tredicesimo È Sempre Giuda Ital. *Director:* Joseph Warren; *Script:* Adriano Bolzoni/Giuseppe Vari; *Camera:* Angelo Lotti; *Music:* Carlo Savina; *Producer:* Castor Film (Italy). *Cast:* Donald O'Brien, Maurice Poli, Dean Stratford, Maily Doria, Fortunato Arena, Giuseppe Bellucci.

Here's another film that suffered from poor distribution, directed and coscripted by Joseph Warren (pseudonym for Giuseppe Vari). Popular character actor Donald O'Brien stars as a crusty lawman-turned–bounty hunter searching for the "Monster of the Prairie," a sadistic outlaw played by squirrelly Dean Stratford.

Warren directed seven Spaghetti Westerns (see Directors filmography), but he is best known for his exceptional nongenre films (i.e., *War of the Zombies* with John Drew Barrymore, *City in the Jaws of the Racket* [also called *Gangsters*], *Urban Warriors*, *Who Killed the Prosecutor and Why*, plus an outrageous sex romp, *Sister Emanuelle*, starring Laura Gemser as a nun!).

Thirty Winchesters for El Diablo (1967)

Trenta Winchester per El Diablo Ital. *Director:* Frank G. Carrol; *Script:* Frank G. Carrol/Al Bradly; *Camera:* Marcel Mascot; *Music:* Ghant; *Producer:* Te.Pu (Italy). *Cast:* Carl Möhner, Topsy Collins, John Heston, Anthony Garof, José Torres, Mila Stanić.

Prolific Spaghetti Western director Gianfranco Baldanello (using his Frank G. Carrol pseudonym) cowrote this script with fellow filmmaker Al Bradly (alias for Alfonso Brescia).

El Diablo is not a place. It's a person. Specifically, it is the Mexican cattle-

Poster advertising *This Man Can't Die* (1968).

thieving, bloodthirsty villain of this film. Cowboy Jeff Benson (Carl Möhner) and his sidekick Jerry (Topsy Collins) go to bordertown, Canyon City, looking for work. Rancher Jim Randall hires them, appointing Jeff as the new foreman in charge of moving cattle crosscountry from one pasture to another. The trick is to do it safely without the herd getting rustled. Jeff concocts a plan that tricks El Diablo (Anthony Garof) and he succeeds.

But an embarrassed El Diablo is a vengeful El Diablo. He recruits all the available gunslingers he can find to "teach Benson a lesson." None of them do, and eventually (after a big gold-train battle) the hero eliminates El Diablo too.

The entire thing is essentially aided by the presence of beautiful Mila Stanić (playing rancher Randall's daughter and Jeff Benson's main squeeze). Without her, it would have been rough going. There is, however, a wonderful "decadently psychedelic" opening title sequence prepared by Biamonte and Grisanti. It's almost worth the price of admission.

This Man Can't Die (1968)

Long Days of Hate; I Lunghi Giorni dell'Odio Ital. *Director:* Gianfranco Baldanello; *Script:* Luigi Emmanuele/Gino Mangini; *Camera:* Claudio Circillo; *Music:* Amedeo Tommasi; *Producer:* Mercurio Films (Italy). *Cast:* Guy Madison, Lucienne Bridou, Rik Battaglia, Rosalba Neri, Robert Widmark, Steve Merrick, Peter Martell.

This is yet one more "revenge for a slaughtered family" movie with Guy Madison as government agent Martin Benson. He becomes the avenger on the trail of Vic Graham (Rik Battaglia), a rich town boss who murdered Martin's parents and raped his mute sister, Jenny (Rosalba Neri). Together with his younger brother, Daniel (Robert Widmark), Martin finds the powerful businessman and kills him in a showdown.

In France, it was promoted as a "Ringo" movie, distributed under the title *Ringo Ne Devrait Pas Mourir* (*Ringo Was Not Born to Die*).

Thompson 1880 (1966)

Thompson 1880 Ital; *Schneller als 1000 Colts* Ger. *Director:* Albert Moore; *Script:* Jesus Balcazar; *Camera:* Victor Monreal; *Music:* Marcello Gigante; *Producer:* Lucy Film/Plaza/Balcazar (Italy/West Germany). *Cast:* George Martin, Gian Sandri, José Bodaló, Gordon Mitchell, José Jaspe, Pedro Sanchez, Dean Stratford, Paul Müller.

Directed by Guido Zurli (under the pseudonym Albert Moore), this one is little more than a poor man's *Django*. Town boss and casino owner, Blackie (José Jaspe) has a firm grip on the city of Desert Spring until a mysterious stranger named Raymond Thompson (George Martin) comes to town. Immediately, there is fiction between the two men. Following orders, Raymond is beaten by Blackie's henchmen (José Bodaló and Pedro Sanchez), and he is left for dead. Fortunately, a pretty town widow decides to help. She rescues Raymond and nurses him back to health. But eventually she is kidnapped and held prisoner inside the brothel portion of Blackie's casino. Raymond straps on (literally) a special "Thompson 1880" machine gun across his chest (it looks more like a camera) and he retaliates, leaving all the bad guys dead in the street.

Guido Zurli went on to direct the nongenre films *The Mad Butcher* (also called *Meat Is Meat* (1972) and *He Kills Quietly* (*Silenzio, Si Uccide*) in 1976.

Those Desperate Men Who Smell of Dirt and Death see *Bullet for Sandoval*

Those Dirty Dogs! (1973)

Campa Carogna . . . la Taglia Cresce Ital; *Los Cuatro de Fort Apache* Sp. *Director:* Giuseppe Rosati; *Script:* Carl Veo/Giuseppe Rosati/Enrique Llovet; *Camera:* Godofredo Pacheco; *Music:* Nico Fidenco; *Producer:* Horse Film/Plata Film (Italy/Spain). *Cast:* John Garko, Stephen Boyd, Howard Ross, Simon Andrew, Harry Baird, Dan Vargas, Helga Line, Lee Burton.

Irish-born American actor, Stephen Boyd (best known as the villain Messala in *Ben-Hur*) plays Chadwell, one of three cavalrymen sent from the East to quell attacks by a band of Mexican revoutionaries in the Texas territory. Korano (John [Gianni] Garko portraying a familiar Sartana-like bounty hunter) joins them for the ensuing, victorious battle.

Director Giuseppe Rosati is rumored to be a pseudonym for scriptwriter Franco Rossetti. John Garko is especially known for his *Sartana* and *Spirito Santo* series. Stephen Boyd, who died of a heart attack while playing golf at age 48, made four additional Eurowestens, *Hannie Caulder*, *Shalako*, *Man Called Noon*, and *Montana Trap*.

Three Amens for Satan see *Vengeance Is a Dish Served Cold*

Three Bullets for a Long Gun (1970)

Friss den Staub von meinen Stiefeln Ger. *Director:* Peter Henkel; *Script:* Beau Brummell; *Camera:* Keith Van Der Wat; *Music:* Kevin Mansfield; *Producer:* Peter Henkel/Beau Brummell (West Germany/South Africa). *Cast:* Beau Brummell, Keith Van Der Wat, Patrick Mynhardt, Tullio Moneta, Don McCorkindale, Gaby Getz, José De Sousa.

Primarily significant due to the odd teaming of production companies (West Germany and South Africa), this film makes good use of the knolls and forests in Africa for a surprisingly authentic-looking American West.

Beau Brummell is a Yankee gunfighter named Major Snap and Keith Van Der Wat is Lucky, a Mexican bandit. The two men becomes partners as they search for a hidden Confederate treasure, but soon Snap and Lucky become enemies. There just isn't enough gold for both.

Three Crosses Not to Die* see *No Graves on Boot Hill

Three Crosses of Death* see *No Graves on Boot Hill

Three Dollars of Lead* see *Damned Pistols of Dallas

Three from Colorado (1967)

Grave of the Gunfighter; Tre del Colorado Ital; *La Tumba del Pistolero* Sp. *Director:* Armando de Ossorio; *Script:* Armando de Ossorio/Julio Soria; *Camera:* Pablo Ripoll; *Music:* Daniel J. White; *Producer:* Plata Films (Spain). *Cast:* George Martin, Luis Dávila, Mercedes Alonso, Silvia Solar, Diana Lorys, Jack Taylor, Juan Cortes, Luis Induñi, Raf Baldassare, Simon Arraga.

Before Armando de Ossorio became the crowned king of Spanish horror filmmakers, most notably for his "Blind Dead" series, *Tombs of the Blind Dead* (1971), *Return of the Evil Dead* (1973), *Horror of the Zombies* (1975) (also called *The Ghost Galleon*), and *Night of the Seagulls* (1976), he toiled on various sex farces, spy films and Westerns (i.e., *Canadian Wilderness* in 1969 and this movie in 1967).

George Martin is a retired bounty hunter who relocates with his wife and her brother in Laramie where they attempt to start a farm. But, as these stories tend to go, there's a greedy town boss who decides to cause trouble. And, eventually, the gunfighter is forced to strap on his pistol.

Three Golden Boys* see *Death Walks in Laredo

Three Good Men* see *Magnificent Three

Three Graves for a Winchester (1966)

Tre Colpi de Winchester per Ringo Ital. *Director:* Erminio Salvi; *Script:* Amborgio Molteni/Erminio Salvi; *Camera:* Mario Parapetti; *Music:* Armando Sciascia; *Producer:* Profilm/Italian Internation (Italy). *Cast:* Gordon Mitchell, Mickey Hargitay, John Heston, Milla Sannoner, Mike Moore, Spean Covery.

A good cast in a relatively unknown film. Regrettably, little information is available regarding plot or production. The filmmaker, Erminio Salvi, later directed the bewildering *Wanted Johnny Texas* (1971) for his own motion picture company, Belloti Films.

Three Musketeers of the West (1972)

Tutti per Uno, Botte per Tutti Ital. *Director:* Bruno Corbucci; *Script:* Bruno Corbucci/Tito Carpi/Leonardo Martino; *Camera:* Rafael Pacheco; *Music:* Carlo

Rustichelli. *Cast:* George Eastman, Timothy Brent, Eduardo Fajardo, Karin Schubert, Cris Huerta, Leo Anchóriz.

With few exceptions, Bruno Corbucci (brother of famed filmmaker, Sergio) has made a career out of directing sleazy action entries (*Cop in Blue Jeans, Super Cops of Miami,* etc.) or low-brow comedies (*When Men Carried Clubs and Women Played Ding Dong, Messalina, Messalina,* etc.) and stooge Westerns like *Ringo and Gringo Against All* and this one.

Timothy Brent (alias for Giancarlo Prete) plays a clodhopper named Darth, Jr. (from Cheese County, no less) who joins up with three Texas Rangers as they escort a clandestine female spy, Dr. Alice (Karin Schubert) into war-torn Mexico. The soundtrack is a very odd combination of Salsa, Trinidad "Steel Drum," Country & Western and 40s Big Band, composed by Carlo Rustichelli (who has a cameo as a hillbilly band leader).

This film also holds a dubious historical significance in the realm of Spaghetti Westerns. It's one of a limited handful (also see *Man Called Amon, Apache Woman,* and *Black Killer*) to show full frontal nudity (Karin Schubert in a bathtub scene). Karin went on to star in a series of Italian hard-core XXX films, most notably *Karin the Desirous Wife* and *Karin and Barbara: Superstars.*

Three Ruthless Ones see *Gunfight at High Noon*

Three Silver Dollars (1968)

I Protect Myself Against My Enemies; Tres Dólares de Plata Sp; . . . *Dai Nemici Mi Guardo Io* Ital. *Director:* Irving Jacobs; *Script:* Mario Amendola/Bruno Corbucci; *Camera:* Aldo Giordani; *Music:* Carlo Rustichelli; *Producer:* Regal/Selenia (Italy). *Cast:* Charles Southwood, Alida Chelli, Julian Mateos, Pietro Cessarelli, Dada Gallotti, Marco Rual, Maria Mizar.

Under the pseudonym Irving Jacobs, scriptwriter Mario Amendola directed this absolutely horrible Spaghetti Western. It is suspected that he was aided by Bruno Corbucci and Tonino Ricci (the trio responsible for the equally terrible *Bad Kids of the West*).

In this one, a dying Confederate officer gives cowboy Alan Burton (Charles Southwood) a silver dollar, telling him that there are two more similar coins with different figures on them (!?!) and that the "three coins together" will reveal the location of a massive treasure. Through the crawl of the film, Alan secures another silver dollar, but the third is held by an evil Mexican bandit named Hondo (Julian Mateos). The finale finds the two men in a showdown. Hondo tries to shoot Alan, but the dollars in Alan's pocket protect him from the blast. But, unfortunately, the bullet has defaced the coins beyond interpre-tation, so the whereabouts of the treasure will always remain a mystery. Amazing.

Three Supermen of the West (1974)

. . . *E Così Divennero i 3 Supermen del West* Ital. *Director:* Italo Martinenghi; *Script:* Italo Martinenghi; *Camera:* Jaime Deus Casas; *Music:* Robert Deramont; *Producer:* Cinesecolo/Transcontinental Films (Italy/Spain). *Cast:* George Martin, Sal Borgese, Frank Braña, Pedro Sanchez, Fernando Sancho, Antonio Casas, Agata Lys, Cris Huerta.

A peculiar motion picture meshing "superhero" antics with the American West. The characters, three reluctant crime-fighting rogues in tights and capes, were initially popularized by director Frank Kramer (Gianfranco Parolini) with his *Three Fantastic Supermen* (1968). They returned to the screen for *Three Supermen in the Jungle* (1969) and *Three Supermen in the Orient* (1971), then again with *Three Supermen at the Olympics* (1972). *Three Supermen in the West* was the final film in the series.

The "time-travel" problem is solved with a quick (but acceptable) "dream" premise, thus from the beginning there is no confusion over "how these superheroes got to the 1890 American West." The plot is similar to the other *Three Supermen* films. Their real goal is an illegal venture (in this case, an impenetrable bank), but quickly the government (this time, represented by federal agents instead of the CIA) recruits them for a more noble project, specifically, thwarting the evil Cucho (Fernando Sancho) and his band of marauding renegades.

As always, Sal Borgese provides the slapstick. George Martin and Frank Braña are his "supermen" partners. But where's Brad Harris?

Three Swords of Zorro (1963)

Sword of Zorro; Le Tre Spade di Zorro Ital. *Director:* Ricardo Blasco; *Script:* Jacques Dumas/Mario Amendola/Luis Lucas/Dan Ribera/Ricardo Blasco; *Camera:* Antonio Borghesi; *Music:* José Pagan/Angel Antonio Ramirez; *Producer:* Rodes Cinematografica/Hispamer (Italy/Spain). *Cast:* Guy Stockwell, Gloria Milland, Mikaela Wood, Antonio Prieto, Franco Fantasia, Rafael Vaquero, Felix Fernandez.

A slight variation from the Zorro legend by director Ricardo Blasco as the "people's hero" teaches his son (Guy Stockwell) and daughter (Gloria Milland) the art of freedom fighting. Basically, it's the good guys against the bad guys in Spanish California of the 1830s.

Filmmaker Blasco also directed *Behind the Mask of Zorro* (1965), but he is best known for his ground-breaking Spaghetti Western, *Gunfight at Red Sands* (1963).

Thunder at the Border see *Winnetou: Thunder at the Border*

Thunder Over El Paso (1972)

The Godless Ones; Sentence of God; I Senza Dio Ital. *Director:* Roberto Montero; *Script:* Maurizio Pradeaux/Arpad De Riso/Tonio Pas; *Camera:* Alfonso Nieva; *Music:* Carlo Savina; *Producer:* Alfonso Nieva, Luis Film/Dauro (Italy/Spain). *Cast:* Antonio Sabàto, Chris Avram, Erika Blanc, Paul Stevens, Pilar Velazquez, José Rivas Jaspe, Ken Wood.

Antonio Sabàto is Minnesota, a dressed-in-black, man-of-few-words bounty hunter, robbed of his latest reward by blood-thirsty Mexican bandit, Corbancho (José Rivas Jaspe). An uneasy alliance is formed between the bounty hunter and a young outlaw named Santo (Chris Avram) with Corbancho's gold-laiden fortress their goal.

Erika Blanc (spelled in the credits as Blank; in other films it can be seen as Blanc) doesn't have much to do, but as always, she's a welcome addition. Even when she's doing nothing.

An Italian-Spanish coproduction with music by Carlo Savina, reminiscent of his *Vengeance* score. The film was cowritten by the director of 1966's *Ramon the Mexican,* Maurizio Pradeaux. Filmmaker Montero would later direct Antonio Sabàto in a variety of action films, including *Eye of the Spider* (1972).

Tierra Brava see *Death Knows No Time*

Tierra Brutal see *Savage Guns*

Tierra de Gigantes see *Forgotten Pistolero*

Time and Place for Killing (1968)

And Then a Time for Killing; ... *E Venne il Tempo di Uccidere. Director:* Vincent Eagle, Script: Fernando Di Leo/Enzo Dell'Aquila; *Camera:* Rino Filippino; *Music:* Francesco De Masi; *Producer:* P.E.A. Film (Italy). *Cast:* Anthony Ghidra, Jean Sobieski, Dick Palmer, Furio Meniconi, Felicità Fanni, Fidel Gonzales.

Knowing that the law forbids it, a determined marshal (Anthony Ghidra) crosses into Mexico as he hunts the bandit who killed his sister. The film is directed with slow, methodical intensity by prolific Spaghetti Western scriptwriter and part-time character actor, Enzo Dell'Aquila (using an alias, Vincent Eagle). The Francesco De Masi score is quite good, but does nothing to hurry along the pacing of the movie.

Time of Vultures (1967)

Last of the Badmen; Il Tempo degli Avvoltoi. Director: Nando Cicero; *Script:* Fulvio Gicca; *Camera:* Fausto Rossi; *Music:* Piero Umiliani; *Producer:* Vico Pavoni, Pacific Cinematograficia (Italy). *Cast:* George Hilton, Frank Wolff, Pamela Tudor, Eduardo Fajardo, Franco Balducci, Femi Benussi, Maria Mareschalchi.

This is one of two Spaghetti Westerns that director Nando Cicero made with George Hilton (the other is *Red Blood, Yellow Gold,* also called *Professionals for a Massacre*).

Cowboy and chief vaquero Kitosch (George Hilton) is a man with woman problems. There are too many vying for his "attentions." Women throw themselves at him, including his employer's wife, Steffi (Pamela Tudor). When he's caught in the act by his boss Don Jaime (Eduardo Fajardo), Kitosch is severely beaten and branded.

Abashed, Kitosch leaves the ranch and joins an outlaw band, led by the Black One (Frank Wolff), a man who enjoys torture and killing. Soon there is a major conflict between the two men because Kitosch prefers more refined villainous behavior. When the Black One insists on attacking the Don Jaime ranch, Kitosch escapes to warn them. He helps the ranchers in the bloody battle, thus winning back his honor. Fun but empty.

Incidentally, George Hilton also played a character named Kitosch in an unrelated production, *Kitosch, the Man Who Came from the North* (1967), directed by Joseph Marvin.

Brett Halsey in *Today It's Me . . . Tomorrow You* (1968).

Tire, Django, Tire see *Shoot, Gringo . . . Shoot!*

To Hell and Back (1968)

One More to Hell; Uno di Più all'Inferno Ital; *Los Machos* Sp. *Director:* Giovanni Fago; *Script:* Ernesto Gastaldi/Giovanni Fago; *Camera:* Antonio Borghesi; *Music:* Gino Peguri; *Producer:* Devon/Flora Film (Italy/Spain). *Cast:* George Hilton, Paul Stevens, Claudie Lange, Gerard Herter, Krista Nell, Carlo Gaddi, Paul Müller, Paolo Gozlino.

A lesser film from Giovanni Fago (this time not using his Sidney Lean pseudonym) adding nothing new to the already tediously tired "revenge for a slaughtered family" motif. George Hilton is the hell-bent avenger, and Gerard Herter is the outlaw who massacred the innocent mother and father. The opening rape and murder sequence is especially effective, but the episodic action quickly becomes routine, and very slow.

Director Fago's best film is *Magnificent Bandits*. This one pales by comparison.

To the Last Drop of Blood see *Bury Them Deep*

Today It's Me . . . Tomorrow You (1968)

Oggi a Me . . . Domani a Te. *Director:* Tonino Cervi; *Script:* Dario Argento/ Tonino Cervi; *Camera:* Sergio D'Offizi; *Music:* Angelo Francesco Lavagnino;

Producer: P.A.C./Splendid (Italy). *Cast:* Brett Halsey, Bud Spencer, William Berger, Wayde Preston, Tatsuya Nakadai, Jeff Cameron, Stanley Gordon.

As a youth, Dario Argento must have been impressed by *The Magnificent Seven.* Two of his three Spaghetti Western screenplays borrow liberally from that story (*Five Man Army* and *Today It's Me* do; *Cemetery Without Crosses* doesn't).

Regardless, this one is a well-written homage, telling the story of a mysterious dressed-in-black stranger named Bill (Brett Halsey, but for some inexplicable reason, billed as Montgomery Ford). He's recruiting eccentric gunmen to help him avenge the outlaw who murdred his wife. Good stirring score by Angelo Lavagnino.

Todos o Ninguno see *Law of Violence*

Too Much Gold for One Gringo (1074)

They Believed He Was No Saint; Lo Credevano uno Stinco di Santo Ital. *Director:* Juan Bosch; *Script:* Juan Bosch/Renato Izzo; *Camera:* Julio Perez De Rosa; *Music:* Marcello Giombini; *Producer:* Alberto De Stefanis, P.E.A./PC Cine (Italy/Spain). *Cast:* Anthony Steffen, Daniel Martin, Fernando Sancho, Tania Alvarado, Robert Hundar, Manuel Guitian.

Prolific Ignacio Iquino is using his Spanish pseudonym, Juan Bosch (usually reserved for his comedies and sex farces), in this tale of double-crossing and chicanery. Fernando Sancho plays Rojas, a blood-thirsty bandit searching for a missing treasure. When the outlaw seizes the statue of a Mexican village's patron saint, he inadvertently stirs the curiosity of a Yankee gunfighter (Anthony Steffen). Yes, in a plot similar to that of *The Greatest Robbery in the West*, the loot was stashed inside the religious icon. Ponderously, the story develops into a struggle between the outlaw gang and the Gringo, when he snatches the gold.

Ignacio Iquino has directed 12 Spaghetti Westerns under various monikers, including "Juan Bosch" and the English translation of the name, "John Wood," plus Steve MacCohy, Juan Xiol Marchel, and Pedro Ramirez. See the Directors filmography for a complete list.

Torrejon City (1961)

Torrejon City Ital. *Director:* Leon Klimovsky; *Script:* R. J. Salvia/Manuel Tamayo/Ramon Barreiro; *Camera:* M. Hernandez Sanjuan; *Music:* Gregorio Garcia Segura; *Producer:* Tyrys Films (Spain). *Cast:* Tony Le Blanc, May Hetherly, Mara Laso, Mari Begona, Antonio Garisa, Venancio Muro.

The kindest thing one can say about this film is, historically, it has some significance. This movie is one of the very first contemporary Eurowesterns. Five were produced in 1961, *Dynamite Jack* (French), *Taste of Violence* (French), *Terror of Oklahoma* (Italian), *Savage Guns* (British/Spanish coproduction), and this one.

But the story, a lame opus about a gringo sheriff (Tony Le Blanc) who brings justice to a boom town in the West, more closely resembles a low grade Hollywood two-reeler than a nihilistic Spaghetti Western.

Touche Pas la Femme Blanche see *Do Not Touch the White Woman*

Town Called Bastard see *Town Called Hell*

Town Called Hell (1971)

Town Called Bastard; Una Ciudad Llamada Bastard Sp. *Director:* Robert Parrish; *Script:* Benjamin Fisz; *Camera:* Manuel Berenguer; *Music:* Waldo De Los Rios; *Producer:* Benjamin Fisz, Benmar/Zurbano (England/Spain). *Cast:* Telly Savalas, Robert Shaw, Stella Stevens, Fernando Rey, Martin Landau, Charlie Bravo, Aldo Sambrell, Cris Huerta.

In a desperate attempt to compete with the influx of Spaghetti Westerns, various British film investors financed some Italian-Spanish productions, in the old "if you can't beat 'em join 'em" show biz tradition. This was one such project.

But instead of just providing the bucks, this particular company (Benmar Films) also demanded a primarily Anglo cast and a decidedly Anglo director, Robert Parrish (best known for his "B" crime movies, *The Mob, Cry Danger, The San Francisco Story* and an underrated science fiction film, *Journey to the Far Side of the Sun*). The result is a Tinseltown version of a genre Western, with all the violence but none of the charm.

Basically, it's the story of a bounty hunter, the Colonel (Martin Landau), and his "ransom motivated" search for a Mexican revolutionary who has since become a priest (Robert Shaw). The less-than-moral priest (complete with a girlfriend and a cynical philosophy) has taken refuge in a city controlled by Mexican bandido, Don Carlos (Telly Savalas). Meanwhile, there's a beautiful and mysterious woman named Alvira (Stella Stevens) who has arrived in town with a coffin, supposedly for the body of the man who killed her husband. That man is Carlos, and since he's not ready to die voluntarily, she joins forces with the Colonel who promises her the body of the bandit as "a bonus" for her sexual favors.

Trail of the Falcon (1968)

Spur des Falken Ger; *Brennende Zelte in den schwarzen Bergen* Ger. *Director:* Gottfried Kölditz; *Script:* Günter Karl; *Camera:* Otto Hanisch; *Music:* Karl-Ernst Sasse; *Producer:* Gottfried Kölditz (East Germany/U.S.S.R.). *Cast:* Gojko Mitic, Hannjo Hasse, Barbara Brylska, Lali Meszchi, Ralf Hoppe, Helmut Schreiber.

Here's an odd production emerging from the Communist bloc nations (namely, East Germany and the Soviet Union) telling the story of "the mistreated" Dakota Indians as they fight against golddiggers, settlers, land speculators, and other "capitalists." It's been criticized as a thinly veiled political allegory. Obviously, that's true. But the film is also an effective, well-shot action flick. Intriguing.

Train for Durango (1967)

Un Treno per Durango. *Director:* William Hawkins; *Script:* Duccio Tessari/Mario Caiano; *Camera:* Enzo Barboni; *Music:* Carlo Rustichelli; *Producer:* Bianco Manini, Selenia/Tecisa (Italy/Spain). *Cast:* Anthony Steffen, Mark Damon, Enrico Maria Salerno, Dominique Boschero, Robert Camardiel, José Bodaló, Manuel Zarzo, Aldo Sambrell.

Gringo (Anthony Steffen, clean-shaven and wearing an eye patch) with his sidekick Luca (Mark Damon) sell everything they have (i.e., horses and guns) for passage on the train from Guantanamo to Durango, Texas (in reality, an impossible journey: originating from a city in Cuba, across the Caribbean, around the Gulf, to Texas!).

Mexican revolutionary bandits attack and rob the train, killing almost everyone and robbing the valuable safe. But only Gringo and Luca can open the safe because they had already stolen the keys prior to the assault. So the "heroes" go off looking for the bandits, hoping to share the loot.

It becomes a surprisingly entangled tale involving a kidnapped American woman, Helen (Dominique Boschero), an elusive gold safe with missing keys, plus three different groups of bad guys (not counting Gringo and Luca). One is led by Brown (Enrico Maria Salerno), an aristocratic insomniac who drives around in a curious luxury car. Another group is headed by a sex-mad bandit named Lobo (Robert Camardiel), and the third, by Heraclio "the Chief" (José Bódalo), a macho gay outlaw.

The Carlo Rustichelli soundtrack is an equally cockeyed mixture, borrowing liberally from the "purely Italian" Fellini/Rota scores coupled with the more traditional Morricone-esque Spaghetti themes. The director is actually Mario Caiano, using his familiar William Hawkins alias.

Tramplers (1965)

Gli Uomini dal Passo Pesante Ital. *Director:* Albert Band; *Script:* Ugo Liberatore/Albert Band; *Camera:* Wolfgang Suschitzky; *Music:* Mario Nascimbene; *Producer:* Joseph Levine, Chrétien Film (Italy). *Cast:* Gordon Scott, Joseph Cotten, Mariel Franklin, James Mitchum, Ilaria Occhini, Franco Nero.

Shades of things to come. Joseph Cotten plays a post–Civil War Southerner who won't let the war end (reminiscent of his next role in Sergio Corbucci's *Hellbenders,* produced by director Band). Confederate General Temple Cordeen (Joseph Cotten) and his followers continue assaults against the settlers and conduct mass "traitor" hangings, until his sons Lon and Hoby (Gordon Scott and Jim Mitchum) turn against him.

Oddly, director Albert Band (Alfredo Antonini) shot this film in Argentina rather than the typically standard Spanish Eurowestern locations. Cowritten by Band and Ugo Liberatore (future director of the controversial horror film, *Venice in Black*) based on a book, *Guns of North Texas,* by Will Cook, with camerawork by veteran Alvaro Mancore, this was the first major break (assistant director) for future cult film director Franco Prosperi, best known for the fantasy-oriented *Throne of Fire* and the gore-fest *The Wild Beasts.*

Interestingly, this movie marks Franco Nero's Spaghetti Western debut, the "featuring" credits read Frank Nero; his real name is Francesco Spartanero. Nero's first important role came a year later when he played Abel in John Huston's *The Bible,* followed immediately by his all-time number one performance as *Django* in Sergio Corbucci's epic film. United States audiences know him best as Sir Lancelot from Joshua Logan's musical *Camelot* (1968) and from the controversy surrounding his illicit affair with costar Vanessa Redgrave. He is the acknowledged father of her out-of-wedlock child.

Tre Colpi de Winchester per Ringo see *Three Graves for a Winchester*

Tre Croci per non Morire see *No Graves on Boot Hill*

Tre del Colorado see *Three from Colorado*

Tre Dollari di Piombo see *Damned Pistols of Dallas*

I Tre Implacabili see *Magnificent Three*

Tre Pistole Contro Cesare see *Death Walks in Laredo*

Tre Ragazzi d'Oro see *Death Walks in Laredo*

Le Tre Spade di Zorro see *Three Swords of Zorro*

I Tre Spietati see *Gunfight at High Noon*

Treasure of Silver Lake (1962–3)

Der Schatz im Silbersee Ger. *Director:* Harald Reinl; *Script:* Harald G. Petersson; *Camera:* Ernest W. Kalinke; *Music:* Martin Böttcher; *Producer:* Horst Wendlandt, Rialto/Jadran Film (West Germany/Yugoslavia). *Cast:* Lex Barker, Herbert Lom, Pierre Brice, Götz George, Karin Dor, Ralf Wolter, Eddi Arent, Marianne Hoppe.

This German production is the first "Winnetou" film, based loosely on the writings of Europe's "Zane Grey," Karl May. The series was wildly successful throughout Europe, but especially in Italy, opening the door for the onslaught of Spaghetti Westerns to follow.

Old Shatterhand (Lex Barker) and his blood brother Indian companion, Winnetou (Pierre Brice) hunt the bandits responsible for a stagecoach attack, the murder of a passenger, and stealing an important map showing the location of an Indian gold treasure.

French actor Pierre Brice starred in many Euro thrillers before he became Winnetou (i.e., *Mill of the Stone Women*, 1961). American Lex Barker was Tarzan from 1948 through 1955 (*Tarzan's Magic Fountain*, *Tarzan and the Slave Girl*, *Tarzan's Peril*, *Tarzan's Savage Fury*, and *Tarzan and the She Devil*) and then he moved to Italy where he starred in Federico Fellini's *La Dolce Vita* (1960) before landing the "Winnetou" series. He died in 1973.

Other "Winnetou" films starring Lex Barker are: *Apache's Last Battle*, *Half Breed*, *Winnetou the Warrior*, also called *Apache Gold*, *Winnetou and Shatterhand in the Valley of Death*, *Winnetou: Last of the Renegades*, and *Winnetou: The Desperado Trail*. Lex Barker and Pierre Brice made a non–Winnetou film in 1966 entitled *Place Called Glory (City)*.

Beginning in 1964, Stewart Granger starred in a similar "Winnetou" series (also featuring Pierre Brice as the Apache Indian chief) that ran in tandem with Barker's films. Those titles are: *Among Vultures (Frontier Hellcat)*, *Rampage at Apache Wells* and *Flaming Frontier*.

In 1967, Rod Cameron made a "Winnetou" film (also with Pierre Brice) called *Winnetou: Thunder at the Border*.

Treasure of the Aztecs (1965)

Der Schatz der Azteken Ger. *Director:* Robert Siodmak; *Script:* Ladislas Fodor/ R. A. Stemmle/Georg Marischka; *Camera:* Siegfried Hold; *Music:* Erwin Halletz; *Producer:* CCC-Ultrascope-Farbfilm/Avala/Serena (West Germany/Italy/ France). *Cast:* Lex Barker, Gerard Barray, Michele Girardon, Rik Battaglia, Teresa Lorca, Fausto Tozzi, Gustavo Rojo, Ralf Wolter, Hans Nielsen.

Part 1 of director Siodmak's grandiose tale featuring Dr. Karl Sternau (Lex Barker) and his search for the legendary Aztec treasure, assisted by his loyal partner Graf Alfonso (Gerard Barray) and the sullenly beautiful Indian guide, Karja (Teresa Lorca). Apparently, Part One and Part Two, *Pyramid of the Sun God*, were shot back to back, or perhaps simultaneously. The crew and cast are identical, with the exception of Fausto Tozzi.

These two films are Robert Siodmak's only contributions to the genre. He was born in the United States when his German parents were visiting on a business trip in 1900. However, he grew up in Dresden, Germany. Siodmak began his long entertainment career as a "title" writer for imported American films. His big break came in 1929 when he codirected his first movie, with Edgar G. Ulmer, called *Menschen am Sonntag*. In 1940, Siodmak fled Hitler's Nazi regime and escaped to the U.S. where he quickly became a sought-after filmmaker, directing many popular atmospheric thrillers (i.e., *Killers, Spiral Staircase, Cobra Woman*, etc.). Homesick, he returned to Germany in 1951 and continued to make films until his death in 1973.

Il Tredicesimo È Sempre Giuda see *Thirteenth Is a Judas*

Un Treno per Durango see *Train for Durango*

Trenta Winchester per El Diablo see *Thirty Winchesters for El Diablo*

Tres Dólares de Plata see *Three Silver Dollars*

Le Trésor des Montagnes Bleues see *Winnetou: Last of the Renegades*

Trinità e Sartana: Figli Di . . . see *Trinity and Sartana Are Coming*

Trinità Voit Rouge see *Trinity Sees Red*

Trinity and Sartana Are Coming (1972)

Trinity and Sartana . . . Those Dirty S.O.B.s; Trinità e Sartana: Figli Di . . . Ital. *Director:* Mario Siciliano; *Script:* Adriano Bolzoni; *Camera:* Gino Santini; *Music:* Carlo Savina; *Producer:* Metheus Film (Italy). *Cast:* Robert Widmark, Harry Baird, Beatrice Pella, Stelio Candelli, Daniela Giordano, Carla Mancini.

Here is an obvious attempt to capitalize on the popularity of the names Trinity and Sartana. This Trinity (Harry Baird) is a black man, with the nickname because he hails from Trinidad. And the loutish Sartana character (Robert Widmark) is 360 degrees away from the "avenging angel" popularized by Gianni Garko in the successful Anthony Ascott series. In this film, these two are bank robbers who change their thieving ways and eventually become heroes. It's a long and tiresome bore.

Director Mario Siciliano made two additional Spaghetti Westerns (see Directors filmography) but he is best remembered for his brutal action/exploitation films, *Seven Red Berets* and *Skin 'Em Alive.*

Trinity and Sartana . . . Those Dirty S.O.B.s see *Trinity and Sartana Are Coming*

Trinity in Eldorado see *Go Away! Trinity Has Arrived in Eldorado*

Trinity Is Back Again see *Genius*

Trinity Is Still My Name (1974)

Continuavano a Chiamarlo Trinità Ital. *Director:* E. B. Clucher; *Script:* E. B. Clucher; *Camera:* Aldo Giordani; *Music:* Guido and Maurizio De Angelis; *Producer:* Italo Zingarelli (Italy). *Cast:* Terence Hill, Bud Spencer, Yanti Sommer, Enzo Tarascio, Harry Carey, Jr., Jessica Dublin.

Trinity (Terence Hill) and his brother Bambino (Bud Spencer) promise to grant their father's dying request. Surprisingly, he wants them to become successful bandits with a price on their heads, so that they'll "amount to somethin'." But they soon discover that being notorious isn't as easy as it seems, especially when they get involved with a gang of arms traffickers supplying weapons out of the back door of a monastery (a gag also used in Anthony Ascott's *Heads You Die . . . Tails I Kill You* three years previously).

This isn't a sequel in the strictest sense, that is, it's not a continuation of the initial *They Call Me Trinity* storyline. Instead, this film offers the same stars (Terence Hill and Bud Spencer, pseudonyms for Mario Girotti and Carlo Pedersoli), with the same names and personalities, playing "similar" roles. It's also directed by the original filmmaker, E. B. Clucher (alias for Enzo Barboni). According to the *Variety* sourcebook 1990, this film remains the top grossing film in Italian cinema history.

Two noteworthy, but unofficial, sequels (both starring Terence Hill) are Mario Camus' politically grim *Trinity Sees Red* and Damiano Damiani's *Trinity Is Back Again* (originally entitled *Genius*). Neither of these films feature Bud Spencer.

Besides Westerns, Hill and Spencer teamed together for many action/adventures movies spanning a 25-year period, including Sergio Corbucci's *Whenever You Find a Friend . . . You Find a Treasure*, Marcello Fondato's *Watch Out! We're Mad*, Italo Zingarelli's *I'm for the Hippopotamus*, and Bruno Corbucci's *Super Cops of Miami.*

Trinity Plus the Clown and a Guitar (1975)

Prima Ti Suono e Poi Ti Sparo Ital. *Director:* François Legrand; *Script:* Oreste Coltellacci/M. Massimo Tarantini; *Camera:* Mario Capriotti; *Music:* Guido and Maurizio De Angelis; *Producer:* Gloria Film/New Delta (Italy/Austria/France). *Cast:* George Hilton, Rinaldo Talamonti, Piero Lulli, Herbert Fux, Pedro Sanchez, Christa Linder.

French filmmaker Franz Autel (using the "François Legrand" pseudonym) directed this movie toward the end of the cycle. Unfortunately the script cowritten by Michele Massimo Tarantini, better known for his Gloria Guida and Edwige Fenech sex farces, offers nothing new. The film's only redeeming value is a spirited performance from George Hilton as the vagabond gunfighter named Trinity.

An acrobat (Rinaldo Talamonti) and a traveling minstrel (Piero Lulli) join him in his wanderings which eventually lead to a border town udner siege by a Mexican outlaw (Pedro Sanchez) and his gang.

The Italian title, *Prima Ti Suono e Poi Ti Sparo*, translates to *First I Play with You . . . Then I Shoot You.*

Trinity Sees Red (1971)

La Collera del Vento Ital; *Trinità Voit Rouge* Fr. *Director:* Mario Camus; *Script:* Manuel Marinero/Miguel Rubio/José Vincent Puente/Mario Camus; *Camera:* Roberto Gerardi; *Music:* Augusto Martelli; *Producer:* Cesareo Gonzalez, Fair Film (Italy/Spain). *Cast:* Terence Hill, Maria Grazia Buccella, Mario Pardo, Maximo Valverde, Fernando Rey, Angel Lombarte, Carlo Alberto.

All the humor is gone and is replaced with an abundance of "leftist philosophical preachings," which tend to be politically naive and culturally inappropriate. However, director Mario Camus has etched out a career by exploiting the "class struggle" of the poor and downtrodden (i.e., *Beehive* in 1981, *Guerrilla* in 1983, *La Casa de Bernaloa Alba* in 1987), especially with his award winning "rural lower class against the wealthy landowners art" film, *Holy Innocents* (1986), thus the caustic anticapitalistic liberal jabs should come as no surprise.

Trinity (Terence Hill) escapes to Mexico when a scam goes sour in Texas. He is a loutish slug of a man with no social conscience. None. Initially he ignores the poverty surrounding him, but then, slowly Trinity begins to develop a compassion for the suffering peasant farmers. Eventually he finds himself in the middle of the Mexican revolution.

Some of the action sequences are well filmed, but Terence Hill looks hopelessly out of place as the galvanized activist. His performance smacks of discordant compunction—sort of like a Spaghetti Billy Jack.

Trouble in Sacramento see *Judge Roy Bean*

Trusting Is Good . . . Shooting Is Better see *Dead for a Dollar*

Tschetan der Indianer Junge see *Chetan, Indian Boy*

La Tumba del Pistolero see *Three from Colorado*

Turn . . . I'll Kill You see *If One Is Born a Swine*

Tutti Fratelli nel West . . . per Parte di Padre see *Miss Dynamite*

Tutti per Uno, Botte per Tutti see *Three Musketeers of the West*

Tutto per Tutto see *All Out*

Twenty Paces to Death (1970)

Saranda; Veinte Pasos para la Muerte Sp. *Director:* Ted Mulligan; *Script:* Ignacio Iquino/Giuseppe Rosati; *Camera:* Luciano Trasatti; *Music:* Enrique Escobar; *Producer:* Admiral International (Italy/Spain). *Cast:* Dean Reed, Albert Farley, Patty Shepard, Luis Induñi, Maria Pia Conte, Tony Chandler.

A convoluted Romeo and Juliet theme, uncomfortably similar to the earlier Spaghetti Western, *Bullet and the Flesh.* Kellaway (Albert Farley) adopts an Indian child, Saranda, the only survivor of an entire tribe massacre. Eleven years pass, Kellaway is now mayor of Silver City and his friend Senator Cedric (Luis Induñi) wants to marry his daughter, Deborah (Patty Shepard). But Saranda (Dean Reed) also loves the girl.

Because of the rivalry between him and the Senator, the Indian is sent away from the ranch. Saranda and Deborah continue to see each other secretly. During one of their rendezvous they overhear an insidious plot against Kellaway involving his girlfriend, Clare (Maria Pia Conte) and an arch enemy named Clegg. This information brings Saranda back "into the fold" resulting in a gun battle that wipes out the two-timing fiancé, plus Clegg and Cedric, paving the way for a Deborah/Saranda marriage.

Not only is the plot incredulous, but the execution is tediously wearisome. This is, compassionately, the only genre outing by Ted Mulligan (pseudonym for Manuel Esteba). There were so many problems with this project, that reportedly it was completed by Ignacio Iquino; American defector to Russia, Dean Read, can also be seen in *Adios Sabata* and *The Winchester Does Not Forgive* plus many nongenre European films, including *Death Knocks Twice* (1978).

Twenty Thousand Dollars for Every Corpse see *Adios Cjamango*

Twenty Thousand Dollars for Seven (1968)

Kidnapping; Ventimila Dollari sul Sette Ital. *Director:* Alberto Cardone; *Script:* Roberto Miali/Gino Santini/Alberto Cardone; *Camera:* Gino Santini; *Music:* Franco Rettaho; *Producer:* J.E. Film (Italy). *Cast:* Brett Halsey, Herman Lang, Aurora Battista, Fernando Sancho, Spartaco Conversi, Antonio Casas, Paco Sanz.

Another casualty of the 1968 product glut, almost a hundred Spaghetti Westerns fought for theater screens during that year. This one didn't fare so well. Outside of credit information, little is known about this "lost" Alberto Cardone (Albert Cardiff) film.

Twice a Judas (1968)

They Were Called Graveyard; Due Volte Giuda Ital. *Director:* Nando Cicero; *Script:* Fernando Cicero/J. J. Balcazar; *Camera:* Francisco Marin/Aristide Massaccesi; *Music:* Carlo Pes; *Producer:* Balcazar Film/P.E.A. (Spain/Italy). *Cast:* Klaus Kinski, Antonio Sabàto, Cristina Galbo, Pepe Calvo, Milo Quesada, Franco Leo.

A needlessly confusing (and dull) story about an unscrupulous land baron named Victor Barrett (Klaus Kinski) who is running illegal Mexican migrant workers across the border to work on land he's stolen from the poor farmers who can't pay their debts. The plot actually centers around a man (Antonio Sabàto) who apparently is the brother of Barrett, but he's not sure because he is suffering from amnesia.

The best thing about this film is the atmospheric camera work by Aristide Massaccesi who (under the pseudonym Joe D'Amato) made countless exploitation movies (*Emanuelle in America, The Grim Reaper, Trap Them and Kill Them*, etc.). Director Nando Cicero made a much better movie, *Red Blood, Yellow Gold*, the previous year. A more effective variation of the "amnesia" theme can be found in Peter Collinson's Spaghetti Western, *A Man Called Noon*.

Twilight Avengers see Fighters from Ave Maria

Twins from Texas (1964)

I Gemelli del Texas Ital. *Director:* Steno; *Script:* Scarnicci and Tarabusi; *Camera:* Manuel Hernandez Sanjuan, *Music:* Gianni Ferrio; *Producer:* Emo Bistolfi, Fenix Films (Italy/Spain). *Cast:* Walter Chiari, Raimondo Vianello, Diana Lorys, Alfonson Rojas, Miguel Del Castillo, Bruno Scipioni.

An early variation on the "two idiot brothers vs. the world" theme, reused by the "Scarnicci and Tarabusi" screenwriting team for their frenzied *Ringo and Gringo Against All* in 1966. This time, under the subdued direction of cautious Steno (alias for Stefano Vanzina) the slapstick gags seem less forced, almost genuine.

Apparently, Steno was so impressed with the on-screen camaraderie between stars Walter Chiari and Raimondo Vianello that he employed them again, in similar roles, for his *Heroes of the West* (also 1964).

Two Against All see Terrible Sheriff

Two Brothers in Trinity see Jesse and Lester, Two Brothers in a Place Called Trinity

Two Brothers, One Death see Ringo, the Lone Rider

Two Crosses at Danger Pass (1968)

Due Croci a Danger Pass Ital; *Dos Cruces en Danger Pass* Sp. *Director:* Rafael R. Marchent. *Script:* Rafael R. Marchent/Joaquim R. Marchent/Eduardo M. Brocher/Enzo Battaglia. *Camera:* Emilio Foriscot; *Music:* Francesco De Masi; *Producer:* United/Copercines (Italy/Spain). *Cast:* Peter Martell, Anthony Freeman, Mara Cruz, Luis Gasper, Armando Calvo, Dianik Zurakowska, Miguel Del Castillo, Jesus Puente, Antonio Pica.

A bounty hunter (Luis Gapser) breaks a bandit (Anthony Freeman) out of jail, killing the deputy in the process. Meanwhile, the bandit's gang retaliates against the sheriff and his family, killing everyone except a young boy who vows revenge. Following a very familiar Eurowestern theme, the boy grows into a notorious gunfighter, the Kid (Peter Martell), and he eventually seeks out and eliminates all the bad guys. Lots of gunplay and nihilistic characterizations make this Italian-Spanish coproduction enjoyable but (ultimately) "same-old, same-old."

Two Faces of the Dollar see *Two Sides of the Dollar*

Two Gangsters in the Wild West (1965)

Two Mafiamen in the Far West; Due Mafiosi nel Far West Ital. *Director:* Giorgio Simonelli; *Script:* Marcello Ciorciolini/Giorgio Simonelli; *Camera:* Juan Julio Baena; *Music:* Giorgio Fabor; *Producer:* Fida Film/Epoca Film (Italy/Spain). *Cast:* Franco Franchi, Ciccio Ingrassia, Fernando Sancho, Aroldo Tieri, Hélène Chanel, Anna Casarès, Aldo Giuffré.

"Franco and Ciccio" is a lowbrow Italian comedy team, similar to Abbott and Costello (or Martin and Lewis). To call them prolific is an understatement; in 1965 and 1966 they made 27 movies. Most of their films are silly slapstick parodies that capitalize on other popular movies or fads (*Ciccio Forgives, I Don't; The Handsome, the Ugly and the Stupid; Two Sons of Trinity*, etc.). This particular motion picture is their first Western, and it's also one of the few with an original plotline.

Rio (an outlaw played by Fernando Sancho) kills two cousins, Franco and Ciccio, over their newly discovered gold mine. The rich land is inherited by two nephews (also named Franco and Ciccio) who are in Sicily, in prison. They escape and flee the country, to Laramie, Texas, where (after many zany adventures with bandits and Indians and dance hall girls) they get the fortune, but decide to share it with the whole town.

Two Gunmen (1964)

Two Violent Men; Texas Ranger; I Due Violenti Ital. *Director:* Anthony Greepy; *Script:* Jesus Navarro/Marc Fondato/Primo Zeglio; *Camera:* Alfredo Fraile; *Music:* Francesco De Masi; *Producer:* Arturo Gonzales, P.E.A. (Spain/Italy). *Cast:* Alan Scott, George Martin, Susy Andersen, Mary Badmayer, Mike Brendell, Andrew Scott, José Jaspe, Silvia Solar, Luis Induñi, Frank Braña, Aldo Sambrell.

Two very familiar themes are the central focus in this early genre outing from Primo Zeglio (alias Anthony Greepy): (1) two former friends find themselves on the opposite sides of the law, à la Billy the Kid/Pat Garrett fashion; and (2) an evil land-grabbing town boss terrorizes the settlers who won't sell out to him.

Alan Scott is Texas Ranger Robert Logan and it's his job to track down and arrest his old friend Cassidy (George Martin), wanted for robbery and murder. After the two men meet, and Cassidy (who claims innocence) is arrested, they are sidetracked by "cries of help" from pretty Mora Sheridan (Silvia Solar). It seems that outlaws led by a bandit named Bates (Mike Brendell), secretly working for emancipated town boss Stella Rattison (Susy Andersen) are trying to drive beautiful Mora from her small ranch. Obviously, the two men bury their immediate differences and help her out. It doesn't take long for Texas Ranger Logan to realize that his friend Cassidy had, indeed, been framed and the real culprit is none other than evil Stella Rattison.

Regardless of the stereotyped plot, later to be incorporated into many more Spaghetti Westerns, this is an entertaining film significant for the inclusion of a female villainess, something seldom found in the misogynistic Spaghetti Westerns (also see Rosalba Neri's performance in *Johnny Yuma* and Nieves

Navarro's cameo in *The Big Gundown*). And, it's good to see cult actress Silvia Solar in an early supporting role.

Two Guns for Two Twins see **Woman for Ringo**

Two Idiots at Fort Alamo see **Two Sergeants of General Custer**

Two Mafiamen in the Far West see **Two Gangsters in the Wild West**

Two Pistols and a Coward (1967)

Gunman Sent by God; Due Pistole e un Vigliacco. *Director:* Calvin J. Padget; *Script:* Augusto Finocchi/Giorgio Ferroni; *Camera:* Sandro Mancori; *Music:* Carlo Rustichelli; *Producer:* G.V. Film (Italy). *Cast:* Anthony Steffen, Richard Wyler, Liz Barret, Ken Wood, Nello Pazzafini, Furio Meniconi, Gia Sandri, Andrea Bosic, Tom Felleghy, Max Dean.

Calvin Jackson Padget (alias for Giorgio Ferroni who sometimes uses the pseudonym Kelvin J. Padget) is one of the top Spaghetti Western filmmakers (see Directors filmography, but *Blood for a Silver Dollar*, *Fort Yuma Gold* and *Wanted* are considered his most accomplished productions; his 1972 horror film, *Night of the Devils* with Gianni Garko, is also worth the watch).

For this one, rather than employing his familiar director of photography, Tony Secchi (alias Tony Dry), Padget borrows cameraman Sandro Mancori from the Sergio Garrone stable (Sandro Mancori is usually photographer-of-choice for Frank Kramer, and was used for the most adept films of Roberto Mauri and Leopoldo Savona). Here, Mancori's visuals are scintillating, but strangely at odds with the rather cumbersome story.

Gary McGuire (Anthony Steffen), is a formidable sharpshooter and, as such, he's the "main event" of a traveling circus. But he is also a coward, hiding behind the safety of the Big Top. One day the people of Texas City ask Gary and the circus men to help stop a band of outlaws camped in the hills.

Separated from the others, Gary arrives at the bandits' hideout in time to see town bully Owl Roy (Richard Wyler) massacre everyone and escape with the stolen loot. The rest of the posse thinks that Gary was responsible for the slaughter, and he becomes an immediate hero, idolized by all but especially by a town kid, Little Tony (Mario Stefanelli).

Owl Roy is not amused by all the undeserved glory heaped upon Gary, and during a circus performance, he challenges (and embarrasses) the coward. In shame, Gary slips out of town; Little Tony follows. Another bandit named Coleman (Nello Pazzafini) captures them both, demanding to know the whereabouts of the stolen money. Terrified, Gary is ready to tell all when Coleman unexpectedly strikes Little Tony. Rage clicks inside of the coward, transforming him into the very essence of machismo. He is beaten and tortured mercilessly, but refuses to speak.

Later Gary and Tony escape, returning to the city where they are confronted by Owl Roy. This time he is defeated in a showdown. Gary retrieves the money just as Coleman's gang raids Texas City. The circus men come to the rescue, helping defeat the outlaws. Once more (but justifiably so) Gary is a hero.

Franco and Ciccio in *Two Sergeants of General Custer* (1965).

The music is provided by Carlo Rustichelli (using the alias Carl Rustic).

Two R-R-Ringos from Texas (1967)

Due R-R-Ringos nel Texas Ital. *Director:* Frank Martin; *Script:* Amedeo Sollazzo/Roberto Gianviti/Enzo Girolami; *Camera:* Mario Fioretti; *Music:* Carlo Savina; *Producer:* Circus Film/Fono Roma (Italy). *Cast:* Franco Franchi, Ciccio Ingrassia, Enio Girolami, Gloria Paul, Livio Lorenzon, Hélène Chanel.

Papa Marino Girolami (father of actor Enio Girolami and director Enzo Castellari) directs a watchable, funny Franco and Ciccio film. Proof positive that such a thing is in the realm of possibilities.

Franco and Ciccio are two "dandies" from Baltimore who inherit a ranch in Texas. When they're not getting into trouble on the farm or fighting a gang of Mexican bandidos, these two goofballs are putting the moves on dance-hall beauty, Gloria Paul. There is a particularly humorous segment involving a goldfish in a glass of beer, reminiscent of the Abbott and Costello "clam chowder" gag.

Two Sergeants of General Custer (1965)

Two Idiots at Fort Alamo; Due Sergenti del General Custer Ital. *Director:* Giorgio Simonelli; *Script:* Marcello Ciorciolini/Giorgio Simonelli; *Camera:* Isidoro Goldberger; *Music:* Angelo Francesco Lavagnino; *Producer:* Fida Film/Balcazar (Italy/Spain). *Cast:* Franco Franchi, Ciccio Ingrassia, Fernando Sancho, Riccardo Garrone, Margaret Lee, Moira Orfei.

Most American audiences are unfamiliar with Franco and Ciccio's brand of humor since only a few of their movies have seen stateside releases (i.e., Buster Keaton's *War Italian Style* and Mario Bava's *Dr. Goldfoot and the Girl Bombs* with Vincent Price). But in Europe, the comedy team is amazingly successful; during their heyday they averaged an unprecedented 10 movies per year. Their first venture into the Spaghetti Western arena was *Two Gangsters in the Wild West* (1965). Six more followed, half of which were directed by Giorgio Simonelli. Is "Combat Pay" in order?

This one tells the story of two Union spies (yes, our boys) who infiltrate the Confederate army but run into trouble with a female undercover agent (Margaret Lee).

Two Sides of the Dollar (1967)

Two Faces of the Dollar; Le Due Facce del Dollaro Ital. *Director:* Roberto Montero; *Script:* Dario Silvestro/Franco Verucci; *Camera:* Stelvio Massi; *Music:* Giosatat with Mario Capuano; *Producer:* Antonio Lugatelli/Francesco Giorgi, Tigielle 33 (France/Italy). *Cast:* Monty Greenwood, Jacques Herlin, Gerard Herter, Mario Maranzana, Andrea Bosić, Gabriella Giorgelli, Tom Felleghy, Andrew Scott, Spartaco Conversi.

Here's a French-Italian coproduction directed by Roberto Montero, best known for *Thunder Over El Paso* (1972), plus various nongenre outings including a fantasy film, *Tharus Son of Attila* (1961), and a sleazy historical movie called *The Wild Nights of Caligula* (1977). It was photographed by future cult filmmaker Stelvio Massi, with music by the Mario Capuano "writing team." For the English language prints, Maurice Poli's name was changed to "Monty Greenwood." And the film was peddled as a "Django" movie in France (*Poker d'As pour Django*) and Germany (*Django . . . Sein Colt Sechs Strophen*).

This is actually (though not really) two movies in one. It's part caper and part "avarice" aftermath. An English professor (shades of *Face to Face*) named Matematica (Maurice Poli) joins with notorious gunman Mad Michael (Jacques Herlin), ex-colonel Blackgrave (Gerard Herter), and prostitute Jane (Gabriella Giorgelli) to rob a gold treasure inside a Union territorial fort.

The first half of the film is involved with the logistics of the caper and the pilfer itself. After that, things turn ugly. The three men begin plotting against each other and Jane is kidnapped by marauding outlaws who learn of the treasure while torturing her. The outlaws, in turn, attack the three tenuous partners. Only Col. Blackgrave and the (severely wounded) professor are alive when the closing credits roll.

Two Sons of Ringo (1966)

Due Figli di Ringo. Director: Giorgio Simonelli; *Script:* Marcello Ciorciolini/Roberto Gianviti/Amedeo Sollazzo; *Camera:* Clemente Santoni; *Music:* Piero Umiliani; *Producer:* Flora Film/Variety Film (Italy). *Cast:* Franco Franchi, Ciccio Ingrassia, Gloria Paul, George Hilton, Pedro Sanchez, Mimmo Palmara, Umberto D'Orsi.

Not to be confused with *Two R-R-Ringos from Texas* released the following year (also starring the lowbrow Italian comedy team of Franco and Ciccio), this one is particularly significant for introducing George Hilton to the Spaghetti

Western genre. Director Giorgio Simonelli had discovered the British stage actor when auditioning parts for his "Franco and Ciccio" James Bond spoof, *Two Gangsters Against Goldginger* (1965), which became Hilton's first feature film. From this inauspicious beginning, George Hilton developed into one of Europe's leading actors, starring in over 60 films, approximately half of which are Westerns.

In this one, Franco and Ciccio "make a living" tricking poor Mexican peasants. They pretend to be celebrities, specifically, notorious sharpshooting bandits. Then one day they meet a real bounty hunter, Joe (George Hilton). He convinces them to join him in a scam: they become the "sons of the legendary Ringo" to collect the dead gunman's fortune.

Upon their arrival in Asta Nueva, they are treated like kings and everything goes perfect until the reading of the will. At that time, they discover that the money (over $100,000) is theirs, but only after they kill Ringo's arch enemy, Indio. Oh, oh, there's trouble brewing.

Two Sons of Trinity (1972)

I Due Figli di Trinità Ital. *Director:* Glenn Eastman; *Script:* Osvaldo Civirani; *Camera:* Walter Civirani; *Music:* Sante Maria Romitelli; *Producer:* International Film (Italy). *Cast:* Franco Franchi, Ciccio Ingrassia, Anny Degli Umberti, Lucretia Love, Franco Ressel, Freddy Hungar.

Perhaps this is the weakest of all the Franco and Ciccio Westerns. Obviously, it arrived late in the cycle and their "shtick" was wearing thin, even for the fans. But director Osvaldo Civirani did nothing to help the dying patient. Civirani (using the odd Glenn Eastman alias) treats the proceedings with a complete disregard for "comedy timing," allowing his cinematographer son, Walter, to nail the camera down and simply push the "on" button.

Even the sluggish pacing of Civirani's clone film, *Rick and John, Conquerors of the West* (1967), was better than this mess. If it weren't for the welcome participation of Lucretia Love the whole thing would have been a bust. No pun intended, maybe.

Two Thousand Dollars for Coyote (1965)

Dos Mil Dólares por Coyote Sp. *Director:* Leon Klimovsky; *Script:* Manuel Sebares/Federico De Urrutia; *Camera:* Pablo Ripoll/Burt Fuchs; *Music:* Fernando Garcia Morcillo; *Producer:* Documento Film/PC Alesandro (Spain). *Cast:* James Philbrook, Nuria Torray, Perla Cristal, Vidal Molina, Julio P. Tabernero, Alfonso Rojas, Rafael Vaquero, Guillermo Mendez.

A half-hearted attempt to continue the "Coyote" legend as originated by Joaquin Romero Marchent with his film *Coyote,* (also called *Judgment of Coyote* (1964). This time James Philbrook plays the notorious gunfighter-turned-freedom-fighter. He's a "poor man's Zorro," fighting against the corrupt governor in Southern California.

The Italian distributor was so underwhelmed with this sequel that they promoted it as a Django film, *Django Cacciatore di Taglie.*

Two Violent Men* see *Two Gunmen

Poster advertising *Ugly Ones* (1966).

Uccidere a Apache Wells see *Rampage at Apache Wells*

Uccidete Johnny Ringo see *Kill Johnny Ringo*

Uccidi Django . . . Uccidi Primo see *Kill Django . . . Kill First*

Uccidi o Muori see *Kill or Die*

Ugly Ones (1966)

Bounty Killer; The Price of a Man; El Precio de un Hombre Sp. *Director:* Eugenio Martin; *Script:* Don Prindle/José Maesso/Eugenio Martin; *Camera:* Enzo Barboni; *Music:* Stelvio Cipriani; *Producer:* Discobolo/Tecisa Film (Spain/ Italy). *Cast:* Tomás Milian, Richard Wyler, Mario Brega, Ella Karin, Hugo Blanco, Luis Barboo, Manolo Zarzo, Frank Braña.

An interesting love triangle is the central focus of this top-notch Spaghetti Western, by far the best of the Eugenio Martin genre efforts (unfortunately he is best known in the U.S. for his clinker, *Bad Man's River*). For this film, he is aided by the keen eye of chief cameraman Enzo Barboni (later to become E. B. Clucher, talented director of the *Trinity* series). And, it's all based on the book *Bounty Killer* by Marvin H. Albert. There's also an excellent musical score from one of Italy's most sought-after composers, Stelvio Cipriani.

A woman, Eden (Ella Karin), has to choose between a professional bounty hunter named Luke Chilson (Richard Wyler) and an outlaw with "inherent" criminal tendencies (Tomás Milian in an especially tormented role). Eden is convinced that outlaw José Gomez Faradin is "deep down" a good man, but soon she discovers that his immoral lifestyle has turned him into a cold-blooded killer. At that point, Eden sides with Luke against her former lover.

Ultimate Gunfighter see *Fury of Johnny Kid*

L'Ultimo dei Mohicani see *Last of the Mohicans*

L'Ultimo Killer see *Django, Last Killer*

L'Último Pistolero see *Last Rebel*

Último Rey de los Incas see *Legacy of the Incas*

Unholy Four see *Chuck Moll*

Uno di Più all'Inferno see *To Hell and Back*

Uno Dopo l'Altro see *One After Another*

Uno, Dos, Tres . . . Dispara Otra Vez see *Tequila*

Unter Geiern see *Among Vultures*

Gli Uomini dal Passo Pesante see *Tramplers*

Uomo Avvisato Mezzo Ammazzato . . . Parola di Spirito Santo see *Fore-warned, Half-Killed . . . the Word of the Holy Ghost*

Un Uomo, un Cavallo, una Pistola see *Stranger Returns*

L'Uomo Che Viene da Canyon City see *Man from Canyon City*

L'Uomo Chiamato Apocalisse Joe see *Apocalypse Joe*

L'Uomo dal Winchester see *Son of Zorro*

L'Uomo dalla Pistola d'Oro see *Man with the Golden Pistol*

L'Uomo della Valle Maledetta see *Man of the Cursed Valley*

L'Uomo e una Colt see *Man and a Colt*

L'Uomo, l'Orgoglio, la Vendetta see *Man: His Pride and His Vengeance*

L'Uomo Venuto per Uccidere see *Rattler Kid*

Up the MacGregors! (1967)

Seven Women for the MacGregors; Sette Donne per i MacGregor Ital. *Director:* Frank Garfield; *Script:* Fernand Lion/Vincent Eagle/Paul Levy; *Camera:* Alejandro Ulloa; *Music:* Ennio Morricone; *Producer:* Dario Sabetello (Italy/Spain). *Cast:* David Bailey, Agata Flori, Alberto Dell'Acqua, Cole Kitosh, Roberto Camardiel, Nick Anderson, Hugo Blanco, George Ringaud, Victor Israel.

Advertising poster for *Up the MacGregors!* (1967).

This sequel to *Seven Guns for the MacGregors* was scripted by two of the original three writers, Fernando Lion (pseudonym for Fernando Di Leo, future director of many gangster/action films including *Violent Breed, Mr. Scarface* and *Slaughter Hotel*) and Vincent Eagle (the alias for Enzo Dell'Aquila).

Gone is Duccio Tessari. And apparently, with him went all creativity and self-respect. The story is a rehash, basically the same plot as the first time around. The MacGregor family and the Carson family join together to capture a band of Mexican outlaws who stole their savings.

In an absolutely absurd attempt to receive a "Family" rating from the International Catholic Office of Motion Pictures (a status that the producers had hoped would guarantee "endorsements" from the pulpit) much of the film's integrity is lost. At one point a character preposterously exclaims: "Son of a she-dog!" instead of the more obvious equivalent.

And, even though they were torrid lovers and eventually got married in the first film, this time Gregor MacGregor (David Bailey unfortunately replacing the far-better Robert Woods) and Rosita Carson (Agata Flori) are "just friends."

The film is an embarrassment for everyone connected to the production, but especially for director Frank Garfield (pseudonym for Franco Giraldi).

Vado ... l'Ammazzo e Torno see *Go Kill and Come Back*

Vado, Vedo e Sparo see *I Came, I Saw, I Shot*

The Valdez Horses see *Chino*

Valdez, il Mezzosangue see *Chino*

La Valle dei Lunghi Coltelli see *Winnetou the Warrior*

La Valle delle Ombre Rosse see *Last Tomahawk*

Valley of the Dancing Widows (1974)

Das Tal der tanzenden Witwen Ger. *Director:* Volker Vogeler; *Script:* Volker Vogeler; *Camera:* Fernando Arribas; *Music:* Carmelo A. Bernaola; *Producer:* Luis Negino, Albatros/Maran (Spain/West Germany). *Cast:* Judith Stephen, Audrey Allen, Hugo Blanco, Harry Baer, Tilo Pruckner, Cris Huerta, George Rigaud.

Here is a Spaghetti Western version of Aristophanes' ancient Greek satire *Lysistrata*, a subject popularized by the international discord over the Vietnam war. Similar to the plot of the original, a group of soldiers (ignoring pleas and complaints from their women) leave a Texas town to fight in the Civil War. Upon their return, they find that the feminists have learned to get along without them. Plus, the women have all agreed to teach their men "a lesson" by participating in a "sex strike."

Interestingly, genre director Bruno Corbucci also made a version of *Lysistrata* during the same period of time, but instead of using a Western motif he placed his characters in "prehistoric time." The film was called *When Men Carried Clubs and Women Played Ding Dong* (1973).

Vamos a Matar, Compañeros! see *Compañeros*

Vamos a Matar Sartana see *Let's Go and Kill Sartana*

Vaya con Dios, Gringo see *Go with God, Gringo*

20.000 Dólares por un Cadaver see *Adios Cjamango*

Veinte Pasos para la Muerte see *Twenty Paces to Death*

Vendetta see *Kid Vengeance*

Vendetta see *Murieta*

Vendetta at Dawn (1971)

Terrible Day of the Big Gundown; Quel Maledetto Giorno della Resa dei Conti Ital. *Director:* Willy S. Regan; *Script:* Luigi Mangini/Sergio Garrone; *Camera:* Guglielmo Mancori/Aristide Massaccesi; *Music:* Francesco De Masi; *Producer:* Felice Zappulla, Pentagona (Italy). *Cast:* George Eastman, Ty Hardin, Lee Burton, Bruno Corazzari, Nello Pazzafini, Costanza Spada, Rick Boyd.

Described by some critics as the "*Last House on the Left*" of Spaghetti Westerns, this film is a constant panorama of contrasts (i.e., intercutting the birth of a baby with the death of the sheriff). It's also a cruel motion picture, telling the story of mindless, psychotic thrill killing.

The "rumor of gold" has brought undesirables to Culver City. The town has become a hotbed of anarchy. Most of the townsfolk have long since moved away, and the sheriff is having a difficult time enforcing law and order. Meanwhile, George Benton (George Eastman) has just returned from medical school in San Francisco. He immediately marries his long-time sweetheart, Lory Baxter (Costanza Spada), and together they move onto brother Jonathan's farm.

Jonathan (Ty Hardin) and his family admit that "things have changed" in Culver City. After being convinced by George, everyone agrees that "for the sake of the children" it would be best "to leave this place and go to San Francisco." They are planning for the move when their home is invaded by some sadistic crazies (led by Rutger Hauer clone, Bruno Corazzari). Doctor George, who happened to be away at a patient's house, returns to find the slaughter. He abandons all restraint as he seeks (and finds) his revenge.

Sergio Garrone (alias for Willy S. Regan) makes a good looking movie, partially due to his continued use of top-notch technical crews. This time he even utilizes filmmaker Mario Bianchi (aka Frank Bronston) as the assistant director. And cinematographer Aristide (Joe D'Amato) Massaccesi continues to substantiate his reputation as one of the best cameramen in the business.

Interestingly, George Eastman later played the "heavy" in many movies directed by Massaccesi, including a renowned horrific performance as a lunatic cannibal in *Grim Reaper* (1980). Also, Eastman (using his real name Luigi Montefiore) directed his own movie for producer Massaccesi in 1990 called *Metamorphosis*.

La Vendetta È il Mio Perdono see *Shotgun*

La Vendetta È un Piatto Che Si Serve Freddo see *Vengeance Is a Dish Served Cold*

Vendetta per Vendetta see *Revenge for Revenge*

Vendi Pistole per Comprare Cofani see *I Am Sartana* . . . *Trade Your Guns for a Coffin*

I Vendicatori dell'Ave Maria see *Fighters from Ave Maria*

Il Venditore di Morte see *Price of Death*

Vendo Cara la Pelle see *I'll Sell My Skin Dearly*

Vengador of California see *Sign of Coyote*

La Venganza del Zorro see *Shadow of Zorro*

Vengeance see *Kid Vengeance*

Vengeance (1968)

Joko, Invoca Dio . . . e Muori. Director: Anthony Dawson; *Script:* Renato Savino/Antonio Margheriti; *Camera:* Riccardo Pallottini; *Music:* Carlo Savina; *Producer:* Renato Savino, Super/Top Film (Italy/West Germany). *Cast:* Richard Harrison, Claudio Camaso, Sheyla Rosin, Lee Burton, Werner Pochath, Paolo Gozlino, Alberto Dell'Acqua, Pedro Sanchez.

Joko (Richard Harrison) finds the drawn-and-quartered body of his friend, Richie (Paolo Gozlino), with ropes still tied to the severed arms, legs and torso. He removes the five pieces of bloodied rope and swears to "return" them to the men who committed the crime. And he does so, with a "vengeance."

Written and directed by popular exploitation filmmaker, Anthony Dawson (Antonio Margheriti), best known for horror/thriller/action movies (i.e., *Cannibals in the Streets, Andy Warhol's Frankenstein, Dawn of the Mummy, The Last Hunter,* etc.) and some Spaghetti Westerns (see Directors filmography), this film has a strange and colorful Gothic flavor. It's one of the most accomplished genre Westerns, mixing an eerie flamboyance with brutal violence. The chief cameraman is (as always) Riccardo Pallottini, Dawson's competent right hand. The lead villain, incarnately evil Mendoza, is played with gusto by Claudio Camaso (actor Gian Maria Volonté's brother).

The Italian title, credited to star Richard Harrison, translates as *Call to Your God . . . and Die.* The film's French distributor promoted it as a "Django" movie, *Avec Django la Mort Est Là (With Django, Death Is Certain).*

Vengeance Is a Colt .45 see *Son of Django*

Vengeance Is a Dish Served Cold (1971)

Vengeance Is a Dish Eaten Cold; Three Amens for Satan; Death's Dealer; Vengeance Trail; La Vendetta È un Piatto Che Si Serve Freddo Ital. *Director:* William Redford; *Script:* William Redford/Monica Feltini; *Camera:* Angelo Lotti; *Music:* Piero Umiliani; *Producer:* Y.V. Bianco, Filme Cinematografica (Italy/Spain). *Cast:* Leonard Mann, Ivan Rassimov, Klaus Kinski, Elizabeth Eversfield, Steffen Zacharias.

This interesting variation on the "revenge for a slaughtered family" theme finds Jeremiah Bridger (Leonard Mann) the lone survivor of an Indian attack against his parents and sister. As a result, he is possessed with a hatred for all "red savages," and he becomes a vicious Indian hunter. During one of his malicious raids, Jeremiah finds a beautiful squaw named Tena (Elizabeth Eversfield). He knows that a female Indian slave is worth top dollar, so he decides to take her to Tucson and sell her. But, en route, they fall in love. Later, in Tucson, the townspeople attack them and threaten to lynch Tena (for all her people's atrocities). The two lovers escape. They hide inside an empty saloon, where they are discovered by a couple of henchmen working for a land baron named Perkins (Ivan Rassimov). One of the brutes, Boone (Steffen Zacharias), shoots Jeremiah and captures Tena, whom he will use as a special gift to his employer. Badly wounded, Jeremiah is rescued by an old traveling dentist. While recuperating, he learns that Indians hadn't killed his family; rather, land-grabbing Perkins had masterminded the raid using "professionals" disguised as Indians. Now, doubly motivated, Jeremiah takes his revenge, eliminating Perkins and rescuing Tena.

Directed by respected Italian filmmaker Pasquale (*Third Solution*) Squittieri, using his William Redford pseudonym, this film remains one of the best examples of the genre. It's a rough, gritty, no-nonsense Spaghetti Western.

And for the Klaus Kinski fans: he continues his "patented" cameo roles, this time as a hatemongering journalist (from Toledo).

Vengeance Is Mine see Bullet for Sandoval

Vengenace Is Mine see For $100,000 Per Killing

Vengeance Is My Forgiveness see Shotgun

Vengeance Trail see Vengeance Is a Dish Served Cold

Ventimila Dollari sul Sette see Twenty Thousand Dollars for Seven

Verflucht dies Amerika see Yankee Dudler

Das Vermachtnis des Inka see Legacy of the Incas

I Vigliacchi Non Pregano see Cowards Don't Pray

Violent One see Keoma

La Vita, a Volte, È Molto Dura, Vero Provvidenza? see Sometimes Life Is Hard, Right Providence?

Viva Cangaceiro (1971)

Magnificent Bandit; O Cangaceiro Port. *Director:* Giovanni Fago; *Script:* Rafael Romero Marchent/José Jerez/Giovanni Fago/Antonio Troisio; *Camera:* Alejandro Ulloa; *Music:* Riz Ortolani; *Producer:* P.C. Dia/Tritone (Spain/Italy). *Cast:* Tomás Milian, Ugo Paplisi, Eduardo Fajardo, Leo Anchóriz, Alfredo Santa Cruz, Jesus Guzman, Claudio Scarchelli.

Perhaps this Italian-Spanish coproduction does not qualify as a "Western" since it doesn't take place in the American West (instead the setting is northeast Brazil, circa 1925), but the theme, costuming, and characterization so resembles a Spaghetti Western that inclusion seems appropriate.

George Hamilton and Jeanne Moreau in *Viva Maria* (1965).

Tomás Milian is outlaw Miguelin, called "the Liberator" by the poor peasant farmers. Their land has been destroyed by the oppressive government, especially by the evil self-serving commandant, Colonel Branco (again, the wonderfully sleazy Eduardo Fajardo). Ugo Paplisi plays Heffen, a Dutch mercenary, hired by "outside trade forces." His job is to kill Miguelin, who has become a real threat to the shady export business, which would be destroyed if the outlaw gains control of the government through a coup d'état.

    The director, Giovanni Fago, made two Eurowesterns under the pseudonym Sidney Lean (*For One Hundred Thousand Dollars Per Killing* and *To Hell and Back*); the chief cameraman for this project was Alejandro Ulloa. Work-horse Riz Ortolani composed the score. And one of the cowriters, Rafael Romero Marchant, is a popular genre filmmaker, responsible for directing ten Spaghetti Westerns (see Directors filmography).

Viva Carrancha! see *Man from Canyon City*

Viva Django see *Get the Coffin Ready*

Viva! Django see *Man Called Django*

Viva la Muerte . . . Tua see *Don't Turn the Other Cheek*

Viva Maria (1965)

Viva Maria Ital and Fr. *Director:* Louis Malle; *Script:* Louis Malle/Jean-Claude Carrière; *Camera:* Henri Decae; *Music:* Georges Delerue; *Producer:* Louis

Malle (France/Italy). *Cast:* Brigitte Bardot, Jeanne Moreau, George Hamilton, Gregor Von Rezzori, Paulette Dubost, Claudio Brook.

French director Louis Malle is a filmmaker of peculiar extremes, ranging from intellectual excursions like *My Dinner with André* (1981) and *The Fire Within* (1963) (also called *A Time to Live, a Time to Die*) to controversial neo-exploitation films, including *Pretty Baby* (1978), a film banned in many countries, dealing with child prostitution, plus *Atlantic City* (1980), an ugly look at the decaying U.S. city, and *Les Amants* (1958) (also called *The Lovers*), a groundbreaking film renounced and condemned for its unabashed nudity.

Louis Malle made very few comedies, which probably accounts for the inconsistent first half of this film. It's the story of two beauties both named Maria, Maria O'Malley (Brigitte Bardot) and Maria 2 (Jeanne Moreau). They are entertainers-cum-revolutionaries in 1910 Mexico.

Initially, the "two Marias" are a song-and-dance act traveling with a circus throughout Central America. During one of their performances, Maria 2's skirt accidentally tears, turning their performance into a successful striptease routine. Of course, they become notorious strippers and people come from miles to see their show. But when the circus visits San Miguel, the women are shocked at the treatment of the people by the powerful dictator, Don Rodriguez (Carlos Lopez). They secretly join forces with freedom fighter Flores (George Hamilton) against the oppressive government.

Shortly after completing this movie, director Malle became "tired of actors, studios, wife and Paris, in that order." He sold his house, divorced his wife and moved to India where he worked on a series of documentaries, *L'Inde Fantôme (Phantom India)* (1967–69) until the Indian government, who objected to his exploitive approach, asked him to leave. Eventually, Louis Malle relocated in America where he met and married actress Candice Bergen.

Viva Sabata! see *Sabata the Killer*

Vivi . . . o Preferibilmente Morti see *Alive or Preferably Dead*

Vivo per la Tua Morte see *Long Ride from Hell*

Voltati . . . Ti Ticcido see *If One Is Born a Swine*

W Django! see *Man Called Django*

Wanted (1968)

Wanted, le Recherche Fr. *Director:* Calvin J. Padget; *Script:* Fernando Di Leo/Augusto Finocchi; *Camera:* Toni Secchi; *Music:* Gianni Ferrio; *Producer:* Gianni Hecht Lucari, Documento (Italy/France). *Cast:* Giuliano Gemma, Teresa Gimpera, Serge Marquand, Daniele Vargas, German Cobos, Gia Sandri, Nello Pazzafini.

In a loose remake of Giuliano Gemma's 1965 *Adios Gringo* (directed by Giorgio Stegani), once again Gemma (this time as framed sheriff Gary Ryan) has to clear his name by "bringing in" the real horse rustler, Lloyd (Serge Marquand).

Except for Calvin J. Padget's affinity for violence, there's not much separating this entry from similar Hollywood efforts. However, Padget (pseudonym for Giorgio Ferroni) does make a good-looking film, due in part to the constant employment of Tony Secchi (alias Tony Dry) as cinematographer. While not as good as *Blood for a Silver Dollar* or *Fort Yuma Gold*, this movie still stands heads-and-shoulders above most of the competition, plus it's always fun to catch German Cobos.

Cowritten by Augusto Finocchi and Fernando Di Leo (future exploitation filmmaker of *Rulers of the City*, *Violent Breed* and *Slaughter Hotel* [*Cold Blooded Beast*] with Klaus Kinski).

Wanted, le Recherche see *Wanted*

Wanted Johnny Texas (1971)

Johnny Texas Ital. *Director:* Erminio Salvi; *Script:* Erminio Slavi; *Camera:* Giovanni Varriano; *Music:* Marcello Gigante; *Producer:* Belloti/Film Kontor Italiana (Italy). *Cast:* James Newman, Fernando Sancho, Monika Brugger, Dante Maggio, Howard Ross, Rosalba Neri.

A remarkably discordant film, perhaps intentionally. Regardless, the movie has an unsettling style that mixes an inordinate amount of gratuitous violence (lots of people sadistically gunned down in cold blood) with bizarre settings and eccentric costuming (especially with the Union Cavalary soldiers wearing blue and red uniforms instead of the traditional "blue and yellow").

Johnny Texas (James Newman, obviously chosen because of his cloned Clint Eastwood appearance) is recruited by the U.S. Army to find a safe passage for a wagon train carrying arms and impatient settlers to the West. Johnny figures his best bet is to "pay off" the local band of desperados helmed by his old friend, a psychotic outlaw named O'Connor (Howard Ross). But when that doesn't work, Colonel Stewart (a *blond* Fernando Sancho) orders Johnny to attack the fortress and detonate a secret stash of dynamite.

The high spot (hot spot?) is sexy Monika Brugger's sensual dance by the campfire. She's a gypsy "saloon girl" named Lucia Cancido who had joined the wagon train in El Paso, but covertly she's a government spy in charge of delivering the important detonator caps to Johnny ("I've traveled 400 miles to get these to you!"). Interestingly, the caps are never used; instead the dynamite is ignited with a simple gunshot.

This film is either one of the best, or one of the worst. But it certainly is not typical. Perhaps, the outlandish excesses stem from the fact that it was shot in Florence (rather than Rome). Or maybe writer/director Erminio Salvi (owner of Belloti Films) is just aesthetically strange. In retrospect, even his "sword-'n'-sandal" movies (i.e. *Vulcan, Son of Jupiter; Seven Adventures of Ali Baba; Treasure of the Petrified Forest*) are a bit off kilter.

Wanted Ringo see *Ringo, It's Massacre Time*

Wanted Sabata (1970)

Wanted Sabata Ital. *Director:* Robert Johnson; *Script:* Roberto Mauri; *Camera:* Mario Mancini; *Music:* Vasili Kojucharov; *Producer:* Three Stars Films (Italy). *Cast:* Brad Harris, Vassili Karis, Enzo Redemonte, Piero Magalotti, Gino Turini.

For many years, it was commonly believed that this "lost" film by Roberto Mauri (alias Robert Johnson) was the "original version" of *Death Is Sweet from the Soldier of God (Django . . . Adios)* (1972). The similarity in credits led to speculation that the two films were actually one and the same. However, because the movies were released by two competing production companies ("3 Stars Films" and "Virginia Cinematografica"), it seems more likely that they are different motion pictures.

Unfortunately, little additional information is available. As of this writing, the film remains elusive.

Watch Out Gringo! Sabata Will Return (1972)

Attento Gringo, È Tornato Sabata Ital. *Director:* Alfonso Balcazar; *Script:* Alfonso Balcazar/José Ramon Larraz/Giovanni Simonelli; *Camera:* Jaime Deus Casas; *Music:* Piero Piccioni; *Producer:* Empire Film/Balcazar (Italy/Spain) *Cast:* George Martin, Victor F. Bioholmy, Fernando Sancho, Rosalba Neri, Daniel Martin, Luciano Rossi, Osvaldo Genazani.

A good cast wasted. Alfonso Balcazar knows how to make a good Western (see Directors filmography), but this time he's far off the mark. He's treading water, trying desperately to tell a story but forgetting to develop the plot. It's a mess of trite characters and unbearable clichés.

Regardless of the title, Sabata never does arrive. Maybe he was never there in the first place. Who knows?

The West Is Very Close, Amigo see *Return of Halleluja*

Il West Ti Fa Stretto, Amico . . . È Arrivato Alleluia see *Return of Halleluja*

Western Kid see *Bad Kids of the West*

Western Porno-Érotique see *Porno Erotic Western*

What Am I Doing in the Middle of the Revolution? (1973)

Che C'Entriamo Noi con la Rivoluzione? Ital. *Director:* Sergio Corbucci; *Script:* Sergio Corbucci; *Camera:* Alejandro Ulloa; *Music:* Ennio Morricone; *Producer:* Fair Film/Midega Film (Italy). *Cast:* Vittorio Gassman, Paolo Villaggio, Eduardo Fajardo, Leo Anchóriz, Rossana Yanni, Riccardo Garrone, Simon Arraga, Victor Israel.

There are many obvious parallels between this film and Sergio Leone's *Duck You Sucker*. Significantly, both films deal with two unlikely "heroes" drawn into the 1910 Mexican Revolution. Plus, *Duck You Sucker* and *What Am I Doing in the Middle of the Revolution?* are among the final contributions to the genre by both Leone and Corbucci. Ironically, the movies remain the least successful endeavors from these two great filmmakers.

In this one, two Italian vagabonds are wandering through Mexico. Don Albino and Guido Guidi (Vittorio Gassman and Paolo Villaggio) see all kinds of suffering and torture as the brutal government is beating the poor peasants into submission. The two men miss their home country. Don and Guido are attempting to raise enough money to return when they are arrested. Suddenly they find themselves in front of a firing squad. Quick thinking saves them; Guido assumes the identity of revolution demagogue, Emiliano Zapata. Eventually he rallies the peons into a bloodlust frenzy against the oppressive government, but he is killed in the process.

This film suffers from a particularly humdrum story line, with aggravating knee-jerk solutions to complicated social problems. Also, director Sergio Corbucci doesn't seem to know whether he's making a serious motion picture or a comedy. Maybe he doesn't care. Certainly that's the overall indication.

When Satan Grips the Colt see *Awkward Hands*

Where the Bullets Fly see *Miss Dynamite*

White Apache (1984)

L'Apache Bianco Ital. *Director:* Vincent Dawn; *Script:* Franco Prosperi; *Camera:* Julio Burgos/Luigi Ciccarese; *Music:* Luigi Ceccarelli; *Producer:* Beatrice Film (Italy/Spain). *Cast:* Sebastian Harrison, Lola Forner, Albert Farley, Charlie Bravo, Cinzia De Ponti.

Sleaze-meister Vincent Dawn (pseudonym for Bruno Mattei) has made some of the more outrageously memorable Italian shock films (*Women's Camp 119, Hell of the Living Dead* [*Night of the Zombies*], *Violence in a Women's Prison, Sexy Night's Report*, etc.). He also directed this competent Western (and a similar film shot back-to-back called *Scalps*, credited to yet another alias, Werner Knox). Written by cult director Franco Prosperi (of *The Wild Beasts* fame), this film stars Sebastian Harrison, the youngest son of actor Richard Harrison.

Supposedly based on a true story, an Irish baby is raised by the Apaches. This baby becomes Shining Sky (Sebastian Harris), adopted son of the chief. Both he and his Indian brother are in love with the same squaw, Rising Star (Lola Forner). In a "jealousy" scrimmage, Shining Sky kills his brother, Black Wolf. Overwhelmed with grief, he leaves the tribe and goes to live "in the land of the White Man." But, because of his background, he makes enemies fast. Especially with the town bully, Redeath (Albert Farley) and his racist buddies.

Shining Sky returns to the Apaches and to his girlfriend, Rising Star (now obviously and surprisingly pregnant with his child). After the birth of the baby, the film turns amazingly ugly. Sadistic Redeath and his gang capture the two lovers and torture them beyond human endurance, including cutting open Rising Star's chest, the insertion of gunpowder, and, finally, setting it off. In a downbeat conclusion, neither Shining Star nor Rising Star survive. Their "legend" lives on through their child.

White Comanche (1967)

E Venne l'Ora della Vendetta Ital; *Comanche Blanco* Sp. *Director:* Gilbert Lee Kay; *Script:* José Briz Mendez/Manuel Rivera; *Camera:* Francisco Fraile; *Music:* Jean Ledrut; *Producer:* Ab Films (Italy/Spain/U.S.). *Cast:* William Shatner, Joseph Cotten, Rossana Yanni, Victor Israel, Perla Cristal, Barta Barry, Luis Prendes, Vidal Molina.

Director José Briz (using the pseudonym Gilbert Lee Kay) tells the story of two feuding halfbreed brothers, Johnny Moon (William Shatner) and Garvin (also William Shatner), complicated by a typical Western love triangle involving a white woman named Kelly (Rossana Yanni) and an Indian squaw, White Fawn (Perla Cristal). Sheriff Logan (Barta Barry) desperately tries to keep peace in Rio Hondo, but eventually tempers flare and evil town boss (Joseph Cotten) leads the citizens into an Indian war.

This film is William Shatner's only contribution to the Spaghetti Western genre. He is, of course, best known for his portrayal of Captain Kirk in the cult "Star Trek" television series.

White, the Yellow, and the Black (1974)

Shoot First . . . Ask Questions Later; Samurai; Il Bianco, il Giallo, il Nero Ital. *Director:* Sergio Corbucci; *Script:* Antonio Troisio/Cello Coscia/Luis Blain/ Sergio Corbucci/Mario Amendola/Rene Assad, *Camera:* Luis Cuadrado; *Music:* Guido and Maurizio De Angelis; *Producer:* Tritone/Mundial/Filmel Film (Italy/ Spain/France). *Cast:* Giuliano Gemma, Tomás Milian, Eli Wallach, Manuel De Blas, Mirta Miller, Victor Israel, Giovanni Petti, Maria Isbert.

Following the marginally successful *Bandera Bandits* (*Sonny and Jed*), Sergio Corbucci's final Spaghetti Western is this rambling humorous adventure caper. Mostly it's the story of on-again/off-again partnerships among three western rogues, characterized in broad racist tones as the White (Giuliano Gemma), the Yellow (Tomás Milian as a Japanese Samurai) and the Black (Eli Wallach). Each of them is looking for a valuable Asian horse, initially intended as a gift from the Emperor of Japan to the president of the United States.

After this film, Sergio Corbucci concentrated on "lighweight" action flicks, particularly Terence Hill/Bud Spencer entries (i.e., *Odds and Evens, Super Fuzz, Whoever Finds a Friend . . . Finds a Treasure*). Sadly, he died from a heart attack at age 62 in December of 1990. During his long career, Corbucci directed over 80 films, but he will be remembered chiefly for his Westerns, especially for the brilliant movies *Django* (1966) and *The Great Silence* (1968).

Who Killed Johnny R.? (1966)

5000 Dollar für den Kopf von Johnny Ringo Ger; *La Balada de Johnny Ringo* Sp. *Director:* José Luis Madrid; *Script:* Ladislaus Fodor/Paul Jarrico; *Camera:* Marcello Gatti; *Music:* Federico Martinez Tudo; *Producer:* Donny Film/Filma Films (Italy/Spain). *Cast:* Lex Barker, Joachim Fushsberger, Marianne Koch, Ralf Wolter, Carlos Otero, Barbara Bold, Sieghardt Rupp.

A relatively obscure film from José Luis Madrid (also see *Ruthless Colt of the Gringo*) starring former Tarzan, Lex Barker, the star of the popular Winnetou series. He plays a gun salesman named Dillon, mistaken for a notorious Arizona outlaw and almost lynched. Marianne Koch is his faithful girlfriend, Jill, who helps prove his innocence.

Director José Luis Madrid is best known for his parody of Mexican/Spanish horror flicks, *Horrible Sexy Vampire* (1970) and his "Jack the Ripper" opus starring Paul Naschy called *Seven Murders for Scotland Yard* (also *Jack the Mangler*) (1972).

Who's Afraid of Zorro (1975)

Ah Si? E Io lo Dico a Zzzzorro! Ital. *Director:* Franco Lo Cascio; *Script:* Augusto Finocchi; *Camera:* Franco Villa; *Music:* Gianfranco Plenizio; *Producer:* Fida Films (Italy/Spain). *Cast:* George Hilton, Lionel Stander, Charo Lopez, Flora Carosello, Rod Licari, Antonio Pica.

Director Franco Lo Cascio is generally believed to be a pseudonym for entertainment publicist and scriptwriter Augusto Finocchi. Here, "Franco" has made a "Cyrano de Bergerac–type" of Western farce, starring George Hilton as a bumbling Zorro (this time dubbing his own voice, allowing the audience to hear his natural British accent).

The legendary freedom fighter is an incompetent bumpkin, fortunately aided by a monk (Lionel Stander) who is the real behind-the-scenes hero. After many diversionary subplots, Zorro (with his deadly shadow) defeats the oppressive governor (Antonio Pica) and spearheads the revolution, freeing the people in Southern California. Hilton and Stander look like they're having fun, but it's only a one-joke vehicle that begins to wear thin after the first half hour.

Why Kill Again? see *Blood at Sundown* (1967)

Winchester Bill see *If One Is Born a Swine*

Il Winchester Che Non Perdona see *Winchester Does Not Forgive*

Winchester Does Not Forgive (1968)

Buckaroo; Il Winchester Che Non Perdona Ital. *Director:* Adelchi Bianchi; *Script:* Antonio Romano/Adelchi Bianchi; *Camera:* Oberdan Troiani; *Music:* Lallo Gori; *Producer:* Magister Film (Italy). *Cast:* Dean Reed, Monika Brugger, Livio Lorenzon, Ugo Sasso, Omero Gargano, Jean Louis.

Directed and cowritten by Adelchi Bianchi (who sometimes uses the other pseudonyms Mari Bianchi or Frank Bronston), it tells the story of two businessmen traveling west to take possession of a silver mine that they purchased. En route one of the men, Lasch (Livio Lorenzon) kills the other. Five years later a mysterious stranger called Buckaroo (Dean Reed) arrives in town under the pretense of taking a foreman job at a horse ranch, but he's secretly planning to avenge the death of his father, Lasch's murdered partner. And he does.

Dean Reed was a popular 1960s American pop singer who defected to Russia but continued a Euro acting career (also see *Twenty Paces to Death* and *Adios, Sabata*). When he died in 1985, his body was ceremoniously buried in Red Square, an honor typically reserved for Russian military heroes.

Winchester for Hire see *Payment in Blood*

Winchester Justice see *Killer Goodbye*

Winchester, Kung Fu, and Karate see *Kung Fu Brothers in the Wild West*

Winnetou: Last of the Renegades (1964)

Last of the Renegades; Winnetou 2 Ger; *Giorni di Fuoco* Ital; *Le Trésor des Montagnes Bleues* Fr. *Director:* Harald Reinl; *Script:* Harald G. Petersson;

Camera: Ernst W. Kalinke; *Music:* Martin Böttcher; *Producer:* Wolfgang Kuhnlenz, Rialto/Jadran/Atlantis (France/Italy/W. Germany/Yugoslavia). *Cast:* Lex Barker, Pierre Brice, Anthony Steel, Mario Girotti (Terence Hill), Horst Frank, Karin Dor, Renato Baldini, Klaus Kinski, Eddie Arent.

Bud Forrester (Anthony Steel) and his gang of outlaws attack and destroy a wagon train, leaving clues that implicate a nearby Indian tribe. Fearing that a new Indian war may erupt at any moment, Old Shatterhand (Lex Barker) and his Indian blood-brother, Chief Winnetou (Pierre Brice), desperately search for proof of the tribe's innocence.

The film features an early costarring appearance by Terence Hill (credited under his real name, Mario Girotti); young Klaus Kinski plays a villainous Indian scout named Luke.

Winnetou: The Desperado Trail (1965)

Desperado Trail; Winnetou 3 Ger. *Director:* Harald Reinl, *Script:* Harald Petersson/Joachim Bartsch; *Camera:* Ernst W. Kalinke; *Music:* Martin Böttcher; *Producer:* Horst Wendlandt, Rialto/Jadran Film (West Germany/Yugoslavia). *Cast:* Lex Barker, Pierre Brice, Rik Battaglia, Renato Baldini, Ralf Wolter, Sophie Hardy, Karin Dor, Veliko Maricic.

Outlaws led by a renegade named Rollins (Rik Battaglia) attempt to destroy the tenuous friendship between the Indians and the white settlers. Apache chief Winnetou (Pierre Brice) and his blood brother Old Shatterhand (Lex Barker) try to keep peace, but instead the "noble savage" is unjustly accused of murder, a deed actually committed by a greedy, land-grubbing speculator (Veliko Maricic).

This is another entry in the German-Yugoslavian–produced series, notable by the surprising death of lead character Winnetou at the film's conclusion. However, somehow, he manages to return for the next sequel.

Winnetou: Thunder at the Border (1967)

Thunder at the Border; Winnetou und sein Freund Old Firehand Ger. *Director:* Alfred Vohrer; *Script:* David De Reske; *Camera:* Karl Löb; *Music:* Martin Böttcher; *Producer:* Horst Wendlandt (Germany/Yugoslavia). *Cast:* Rod Cameron, Pierre Brice, Marie Versini, Todd Armstrong, Harald Leipnitz, Nadia Gray.

For this "Winnetou" outing, Rod Cameron takes over the "Anglo" lead, and the character's name is changed to Old Firehand (it's Old Shatterhand when played by Lex Barker; Old Surehand when portrayed by Stewart Granger).

Apache chief Winnetou (always Pierre Brice) and his braves join forces with fur trapper Old Firehand as they defend a small border town under attack from an outlaw gang.

This film is a particularly significant *Winnetou* effort, because for the first time: 1) the story unravels in the deserted Mexican plains rather than the snowy Rocky Mountains, obviously influenced by the popular style of other Spaghetti Westerns; and 2) the Apache Indians *don't* ride to the rescue at the finale, instead individual heroics shine through.

Winnetou and Shatterhand in the Valley of Death (1968)

Winnetou und Shatterhand im Tal der Toten Ger. *Director:* Harald Reinl; *Script:* Herbert Reinecker; *Camera:* Ernst W. Kalinke; *Music:* Martin Böttcher;

Producer: CCC Filmkunst/Super International (West Germany/Yugoslavia/ Italy). *Cast:* Lex Barker, Pierre Brice, Ralf Wolter, Karin Dor, Eddie Arent, Rik Battaglia, Clarke Reynold.

Generally considered to be the final *Winnetou* film (see the *Treasure of Silver Lake* entry for a capsule introduction to the series), this one deviates slightly from the patented "noble savages against the corrupt white opportunists" theme. Chief Winnetou (Pierre Brice) and his friend Shatterhand (Lex Barker) struggle for survival after they are left for dead in the wilderness.

Winnetou I. Teil see *Winnetou the Warrior*

Winnetou the Warrior (1963)

Apache Gold; Winnetou I. Teil Ger; *La Révolte des Indiens Apaches* Fr; *La Valle dei Lunghi Coltelli* Ital. *Director:* Harald Reinl; *Script:* Harald G. Petersson; *Camera:* Ernst W. Kalinke; *Music:* Martin Böttcher; *Producer:* Horst Wendlandt, Rialto/Jadran Film (France/Italy/W. Germany/Yugoslavia). *Cast:* Lex Barker, Pierre Brice, Mario Adorf, Walter Barnes, Chris Howland, Ralf Wolter, Marie Versini.

This is the second film in the popular German-produced "Winnetou" series. Old Shatterhand (Lex Barker) is an engineer for the Great Western Railway. He becomes concerned when the railroad consultant, an unscrupulous Kiowa Indian named Santer (Mario Adorf), routes the lines into Apache territory, violating a solemn treaty. Further, he learns that Santer's real motive is access to (and theft of) the sacred Apache gold. Old Shatterhand quits the railroad to join the Apaches and their young chief, Winnetou (Pierre Brice) in the righteous battle. Excellent landscape photography by chief cameraman Ernst Kalinke.

In addition to the sequels *Winnetou: Last of the Renegades* and *Winnetou: Desperado Trail,* also see *Treasure of Silver Lake* (the first in the series), *Winnetou and Shatterhand in the Valley of Death,* and *Apache's Last Battle* for other Lex Barker "Winnetou" films. There is also a Lex Barker/Pierre Brice non–Winnetou film entitled *Place Called Glory City.*

For the Stewart Granger entries, see *Rampage at Apache Wells, Flaming Frontier,* and *Among Vultures.* For the Rod Cameron effort, see *Winnetou: Thunder at the Border.*

Winnetou 3 see *Winnetou: The Desperado Trail*

Winnetou 2 see *Winnetou: Last of the Renegades*

Winnetou und sein Freund Old Firehand see *Winnetou: Thunder at the Border*

Winnetou und Shatterhand im Tal der Toten see *Winnetou and Shatterhand in the Valley of Death*

With Friends, Nothing Is Easy (1971)

Fabulous Trinity; Alla Larga Amigos . . . Oggi Ho il Grilletto Facile. Director: Steve MacCohy; *Script:* Ignacio Iquino/Jackie Kelly; *Camera:* Antonio L. Ballesteros; *Music:* Enrique Escobar; *Producer:* New Star/Ifisa (Spain/Italy). *Cast:* Richard Harrison, Fernando Sancho, Cris Huerta, Ricardo Palacios, Tito Garcia, Fanny Grey.

In the previous year, 1970, Richard Harrison and Fernando Sancho starred together in another Ignacio Iquino (alias Steve MacCohy) film. It was a serious vengeance picture called *Dig Your Grave, Friend . . . Sabata's Coming.* This time they take a 360 degree turn and deliver inoffensively humorous performances as Scott (Harrison) and Col. Jimenez (Sancho). The film also includes a couple of good support roles from Cris Huerta and pretty Fanny Grey.

Suave bounty hunter Scott accompanies Nora (Fanny Grey) into Mexico where her three gun-trafficking uncles (genre fat men, Ricardo Palacios, Tito Garcia and Cris Huerta) are imprisoned at St. Augustine penitentiary run by Colonel Jimenez. Scott helps her plan and execute their escape, but his motives are deceitful. Once they return to the United States, he plans to collect the $1,000 bounty on each of their heads. Meanwhile, in typical Spaghetti Western fashion, everybody is trying to bamboozle each other. It becomes needlessly tiresome, but the characters remain charming.

Woman for Ringo (1966)

Two Guns for Two Twins; Sharp-Shooting Twin Sisters; Una Donna per Ringo Ital; *Dos Pistolas Gemelas* Sp. *Director:* Rafael R. Marchent; *Script:* Manuel Sebares/Rafael R. Marchent; *Camera:* Francesco Vitrotti; *Music:* Gregorio Garcia Segura; *Producer:* Benito Perojo, Transmonde/Luxor Film (Italy/Spain). *Cast:* Pili, Mili, Sean Flynn, Jorge Rigaud, Beni Deus, Rogelio Madrid, Renato Baldini, Luis Induñi.

After the tremendous success of Duccio Tessari's *Ringo* films, studios began changing the titles of their new releases to capitalize on the success of that movie. Some films carried the "Ringo" moniker, but they were "Ringoless." Not even a supporting character could be found with the name. A couple of perfect examples are *Ringo, Face of Revenge,* and this film. It was originally prepared as a theatrical vehicle for "Pili and Mili" (an Italian twin sister pop singing duo), but as a result of the last-minute name change, the film was never found by the targeted teen audience and was quickly lost in the "Ringo" avalanche.

Pili and Mili are the stars of their uncle's traveling sharp-shooting show, but times are tough and money is thin, especially because Uncle Carl likes to gamble. In the middle of a poker game, he is fatally wounded. But he died "holding the best hand." So, suddenly, the girls inherit the winning pot, including a deed to a ranch (which becomes their new home).

After lots of "farm humor" (like Mili's awkward attempts at milking a cow), they meet (and eventually fall in love with) their neighbors, Luke (Sean Flynn, Errol's son) and Carl (Jorge Rigaud). Of course, there's also the mandatory "conflict" in the film dealing with the evil town banker and his plot to steal the land.

The best things about this Italian-Spanish coproduction are the spirited song and dance numbers, but (surprisingly) they are kept to a minimum (the first one doesn't take place until the film has unspooled for a half hour). Regardless, competent director Rafael Romero Marchent has managed to create a good looking, enjoyable (but goofy) flick reminiscent of the U.S. "Elvis Presley" fodder.

Wooruzhyon i Ochen Opasen see ***Armed and Dangerous: Times and Heroes of Bret Harte***

Wrath of God (1968)

L'Ira di Dio Ital; *Hasta la Última Gota de Sangre* Sp. *Director:* Alberto Cardone; *Script:* Alberto Cardone/Italo Gasperini/Ugo Guerra; *Camera:* Mario Pacheco; *Music:* Michele Lacerenza; *Producer:* Leone Film/Daiano Fim (Italy/Spain). *Cast:* Brett Halsey, Dana Ghia, Howard Ross, Fernando Sancho, Wayde Preston, Franco Fantasia, Paola Todisco.

A familiar story, but told with ruthless machismo. Mike (Brett Halsey, using a Montgomery Ford pseudonym for Anglo prints) arrives at his ranch to find that his fiancée, Jane, has been murdered and his money (except for seven silver dollars) has been stolen. He vows revenge, but turns down the offer of help from his friend David (Howard Ross), insisting that "it's a personal kind of a hatred."

For the duration of the film he hunts down the killers, leaving a silver dollar on each dead body as a calling card. During the finale, Mike discovers that the real leader of the bandits was his best friend David (similar to the climax of *Death Rides a Horse, His Name Was King*, plus many other Spaghetti Westerns). A showdown results; Mike, of course, is victorious.

This is one of director Cardone's better films, on par with *Blood at Sundown* (also called *$1,000 on the Black*). Brett Halsey plays a similar avenging role in *Today It's Me . . . Tomorrow You.*

Yankee (1967)

Yankee, l'Americano Ital. *Director:* Tinto Brass; *Script:* Alfonso Balcazar/Tinto Brass/Alberto Silvestri; *Camera:* Alfio Contini; *Music:* Nino Rosso; *Producer:* Tigielle/PC Balcazar (Italy/Spain). *Cast:* Philippe Leroy, Adolfo Celi, Mirella Martin, Tomás Torres, Paco Sanz, Victor Israel, Franco De Rosa, Jacques Herlin.

A drifting gunfighter named Yankee (Philippe Leroy) goes into Mexico to help two brothers, Garcia and Rico, defend the city of Pueblo. But when he arrives, Yankee discovers that his potential employers have been murdered by Cobra (Adolfo Celi, doing a remarkable Fernando Sancho imitation) and his gang of renegades. The sheriff is terrified of the bandidos and does nothing to stop them, even though they are "wanted men." The huge bounty offered for their capture and or extermination convinces Yankee to stay. He's a rich man by the film's conclusion.

Philippe Leroy tries. He's got the right attitude and he postures well, but he's one of those men who tends to look goofy in a cowboy hat. Maybe it's because of his Howdy Doody ears. Nonetheless, Tinto Brass has made a very stylish Western with many memorable moments. His unique camera angles, plus his flare for decadently unusual sets, add to the overall impact. He also makes good use of the excellent Nino Rosso musical score.

Filmmaker Tino Brass went on to direct some of Italy's most controversial

Movie poster from *Yankee* (1967).

motion pictures, including *Caligula* (the big-budgeted, X-rated, Penthouse-produced hit), plus the exploitive *Cabaret* ripoff entitled *Salon Kitty* and the erotic sensation, *Key*, with Frank Finlay.

Yankee Dudler (1973)

Verflucht dies Amerika Ger. *Director:* Volker Vogeler; *Script:* Ulf Miehe/ Volker Vogeler; *Camera:* Luis Cuadrado; *Music:* Luis De Pablo; *Producer:* Filmverlag der Autoren (Germany/Spain). *Cast:* Geraldine Chaplin, William Berger, Arthur Brauss, Francisco Algora, Sigi Graue, Kinoto.

Geraldine Chaplin is Kate Elder and William Berger plays her lover, Doc Holliday. But, their participation is largely peripheral. The main crux of the story centers on a family of Bavarian woodcutters, Bastian (Arthur Brauss) and his four brothers, as they try to settle in the lawless West. Somewhat preachy, but the mountainous scenery is worth the view.

The German title, *Verflucht dies Amerika,* translates to *Curse This America.*

Yankee, l'Americano see *Yankee*

You're Jinxed, Friend, You Just Met Sacramento (1970)

Sei Iettato Amico, Hai Incontrato Sacramento Ital. *Director:* Giorgio Cristallini; *Script:* Giorgio Cristallini; *Camera:* Fausto Rossi; *Music:* Franco Micalizzi; *Producer:* Transeuropa/Copercines (Italy/Spain). *Cast:* Ty Hardin, Christian Hay, Jenny Atkins, Giacomo Rossi Stuart, Silvano Tranquilli, Krista Nell, Stan Cooper.

Jack "Sacramento" Thompson (Ty Hardin) is a peaceful cowboy forced into a showdown with town boss Murdock (Giacomo Rossi Stuart) and his gang of ruffians. Fortunately, Sacramento's kids, Jim (Christian Hay) and Maggie (Jenny Atkins), come to his rescue, helping him eliminate a good number of Murdock's men. But vindictive Murdock takes revenge by kidnapping the children, thus forcing a "no-return, fight-to-the-death" confrontation with Sacramento. Obviously, Sacramento wins. And, as the title warns, Murdock is jinxed—dead. "Locked-down camera work" and unimaginative direction spoil the potential fun.

Zorro (1974)

Zorro Ital. *Director:* Duccio Tessari; *Script:* Giorgio Arlorio/Duccio Tessari; *Camera:* Giulio Albonico; *Music:* Guido and Maurizio De Angelis; *Producer:* Mondial Tefi/Labrador (Italy/France). *Cast:* Alain Delon, Stanley Baker, Adriana Asti, Giacomo Rossi Stuart, Ottavia Piccolò, Moustache, Enzo Cerusico.

Miguel Eorrieta is en route to Southern California to become the new governor, but he is murdered by agents sent from the evil Colonel Huerta (Stanley Baker). Miguel's sidekick, Diego (Alain Delon), assumes his identity and becomes the new ruler. Secretly, however, he is fighting to reinstate freedom to the oppressed territory. Diego becomes Zorro, the people's hero, as he leads the citizens in a plot to overturn the military rule.

Fundamentally, Duccio Tessari makes a good film (see Directors filmography). But, there are some particularly embarrassing segments in this venture involving a "talking" doberman named Assassin.

And, there are some movies that are not conducive for a "De Angelis" musical score. This is one of them. The opening theme goes: "Here's to being free/ La La La La La La/ Zorro's back/ Here's to you and me/ Here's to flying high/ La La La Li/ Zorro's back." Do the De Angelis brothers actually get paid for this kind of thing?

Zorro, il Cavaliere della Vendetta see ***Zorro, Rider of Vengeance***

Zorro Marchese di Navarra see ***Zorro, the Navarra Marquis***

Zorro, Rider of Vengeance (1971)

Zorro, il Cavaliere della Vendetta Ital. *Director:* José Luis Merino; *Script:* José Luis Merino; *Camera:* Emanuele D. Cola; *Music:* Francesco De Masi; *Producer:* Hispames Film (Spain/Italy). *Cast:* Charles Quincey, Malisa Longo, Maria Mahor, Arturo Dominici, Ignazio Balsamo.

Zorro (Charles Quincey) is summoned by a mystical spirit known as "The Voice." This deity instructs him to return to Southern California and stop the crimes committed by the Brotherhood of the Scorpion." But Zorro arrives too late. His best friend has been hanged and his new bride (Maria Mihor) kidnapped by a fake Zorro. An interesting mixture of fantasy and action.

Zorro the Avenger see ***Shadow of Zorro***

Zorro, the Navarra Marquis (1969)

Zorro Marchese di Navarra. Director: Jean Monty; *Script:* Piero Pierotti/Francesco Montemurro; *Camera:* Augusto Tiezzi; *Music:* A. F. Lavagnino; *Producer:* Romana Film (Italy/Spain). *Cast:* Nadir Moretti, Maria Luisa Longo, Daniele Vargas, Loris Gizzl, Renato Montalbano, Gisella Arden.

There are many "Zorro" movies that cannot be considered Westerns. They take place in Spain and usually in the seventeenth or eighteenth century. This one is included as an example.

It's a continental coproduction directed by Francesco Montemurro (under the alias Jean Monty). Exiled Spanish king Ferdinand VII (Renato Montalbano) gives a sword and mask to Zorro (Nadir Moretti) and sends him on a dangerous mission of terrorism into the homeland against the occupying French forces. Colonel Brizard (Daniele Vargas) is the sadistic enemy leader who resorts to a lame (and thwarted) kidnapping plot of Zorro's girlfriend, Carmen (Maria Luisa Longo). At the film's conclusion, Ferdinand VII re-enters Spain victoriously, and appoints Zorro to the Marquis of Navarra position for services rendered.

Other similar "Zorro" films include *Zorro in the Court of Spain* (1968) directed by Guido Zurli, starring Giacomo Rossi Stuart, Femi Benussi, Pedro Sanchez, and George Ardisson as the freedom fighter. Plus there's Umberto Lenzi's *Zorro versus Maciste* (1963), Jess Franco's *Shadow of Zorro* (also *Mark of Zorro*) (1965), Piero Pierotti's *Zorro the Rebel* (1966), two more from José Luis Merino called *Zorro the Domineer* (1969) and *Zorro, Knight of Vengeance* (1970), Franco Montemurro's *Zorro and the Court of England* (1973), and two from Luigi Capuano, *Zorro and the Three Musketeers* (1962) and *Zorro the Intrepid* (1981).

Zwei durch Dick und Dunn see ***Return of Shanghai Joe***

II. Personnel

Introduction

These filmographies cover all the personnel mentioned in the credits of "The Films" section of this book. For each individual, all their films in the Spaghetti Western genre are listed. For more information about the film, refer to "The Films" section.

In the Spaghetti Westerns pseudonyms were widely used. Initially, Anglicized names were used to help the performer achieve a wider appeal in the international marketplace. Many actors and actresses have become best known by their alias (i.e., Klaus Kinski rather than Nikolas Nakszynski) and so, they are listed accordingly. Other performers who only flirted with pseudonyms are filed under their true name. Pseudonyms were used at times by directors, composers, etc., as well. All alternate names are cross-referenced. Unfortunately, because of the widespread use of pseudonyms in the Euro film industry, some real identities remain a mystery. Variations in spelling or interchangeable names are indicated with the word *also*. An "alias" is listed as a pseudonym.

Performers

In order to show the relationship between performers and filmmakers, director credits are also shown in parentheses following the film title. Each director is listed according to his "production" name. Check the Directors filmography for corresponding pseudonym information. An asterisk (*) identifies the performer's initial genre endeavor.

Abbiana, Franco: *Price of Death* (Vincent Thomas)
Abbott, Alan: *Hallelujah and Sartana Strike Again* (Mario Siciliano)
Abdulov, Vsevolod: *Armed and Dangerous: Time and Heroes of Bret Harte* (Vladimir Vainstok)
Abril, Victoria: *Comin' at Ya* (Ferdinando Baldi)
Addobbati, Giuseppe *see* **MacDouglas, John**
Adorf, Mario: *Deadlock* (Roland Klick); *Last Ride to Santa Cruz* (Rolf Olsen); *Massacre at Marble City* (Franz J. Gottlieb); *A Sky Full of Stars for a Roof* (Giulio Petroni); *Specialists* (Sergio Corbucci); *Sunscorched* (Alfonso Balcazar); **Taste for Violence* (Robert Hossein); *Winnetou the Warrior* (Harald Reinl)
Agostini, Franco: *Raise Your Hands, Dead Man ... You're Under Arrest* (Leon Klimovsky)
Agren, Janet: *Sometimes Life Is Hard, Right Providence?* (Giulio Petroni)
Agutter, Jenny: *China 9, Liberty 37* (Monte Hellman)
Akins, Claude: *Man Called Sledge* (Morrow/Gentili)
Albert, Charles *see* **Alberty, Karl Otto**
Albertini, Giampiero: *Hallelujah to Vera Cruz* (Newman Rostel); *Return of Sabata* (Frank Kramer)
Alberty, Karl Otto (pseudonym—Charles Albert): *Man from Oklahoma* (Robert M. White)
Alder, Thomas: *Massacre at Marble City* (Franz J. Gottlieb)
Alfonso, José: *Behind the Mask of Zorro* (Ricardo Blasco)
Alighiero, Carlo: *The Moment to Kill* (Anthony Ascott)
Allen, Audrey: *Valley of the Dancing Widows* (Volker Vogeler)
Allen, Steve: *Nude Django* (Ron Elliot)
Aller, Luis: *Charley One-Eye* (Don Chaffey)
Alonso, Chelo: **The Good, the Bad, and the Ugly* (Sergio Leone); *Night of the Serpent* (Giulio Petroni); *Run Man, Run* (Sergio Sollima)
Alonso, Mercedes: *Gunfighters of Casa Grande* (Roy Rowland); *Jesse James' Kid* (Antonio del Amo); *Three from Colorado* (Armando de Ossorio)
Alvarez, Angel: **Damned Pistols of Dallas* (Joseph Trader); *Django* (Sergio Corbucci); *Fury of Johnny Kid* (Gianni Puccini); *Price of Power* (Tonino Valerii)
Amber, Audrey (pseudonym for **Agdriana Ambesi**): *Joe Dexter* (Ignacio Iquino);

Ringo's Big Night (Mario Maffei); *Tall Women* (Sidney Pink); *Stranger in Pasa Bravo* (Salvatore Rosso); *Ten Thousand Dollars Blood Money* (Romolo Guerrieri)
Ambesi, Agdriana *see* **Amber, Audrey**
Amidou: *Buddy Goes West* (Michele Lupo)
Anchóriz, Leo: *Bullet for Sandoval* (Julio Buchs); *Cipolla Colt* (Enzo G. Castellari); *Finger on the Trigger* (Sidney Pink); *I Came, I Saw, I Shot* (Enzo G. Castellari); *Kill Them All and Come Back Alone* (Enzo G. Castellari); *Seven Guns for the MacGregors* (Frank Garfield); *Three Musketeers of the West* (Bruno Corbucci); *Up the MacGregors!* (Frank Garfield); *Viva Cangaceiro* (Giovanni Fago); *What Am I Doing in the Middle of the Revolution?* (Sergio Corbucci)
Andersen, Elga: *Johnny Colt* (Giovanni Grimaldi)
Andersen, Suzy: *Fifteen Scaffolds for the Killer* (Nunzio Malasomma); *Two Gunmen* (Anthony Greepy)
Anderson, Maria: *Heroes of the West* (Steno)
André, Carole: *Face to Face* (Sergio Sollima); *Here We Are Again, Eh Providence?* (Alberto De Martino)
André, Gaby: *Sign of Zorro* (Mar) Catano)
Andreini, Gabriela: *Carambola's Philosophy* (Ferdinando Baldi)
Andress, Ursula: *Red Sun* (Terence Young)
Andreu, Simon (also **Simon Andrew**): *Bad Man's River* (Eugenio Martin); *I Do Not Forgive . . . I Kill!* (Joaquin R. Marchent)
Andrews, Dana: *Take a Hard Ride* (Anthony Dawson)
Anthony, Mike: *Left Handed Johnny West* (Frank Kramer)
Anthony, Robert *see* **Santoni, Espartaco**
Anthony, Tony (pseudonym for **Roger Tony Petitto**): *Blindman* (Ferdinando Baldi); *Comin' at Ya* (Ferdinando Baldi); *Get Mean* (Ferdinando Baldi); *Stranger in Japan* (Vance Lewis); *Stranger in Town* (Vance Lewis); *Stranger Returns* (Vance Lewis)
Antoine, Dominigo: *Duck You Sucker* (Sergio Leone)
Antonelli, Laura: *Man Called Sledge* (Morrow/Gentili)
Arancio, Gilda: *Gunfight at O Q Corral* (J. M. Pallardy)
Aranda, Angel: *And Crows Will Dig Your Grave* (John Wood); *Bullets Don't Argue* (Mike Perkins); *Dallas* (Juan Bosch); *Hellbenders* (Sergio Corbucci)
Arden, Hugo: *Mutiny at Fort Sharp* (Fernando Cerchio)
Arden, Kim: *Saguaro* (Amerigo Anton)
Ardia, Punuccio: *Get the Coffin Ready* (Ferdinando Baldi)
Ardisson, George (also **Georges Ardisson**): *Django Challenges Sartana* (William Redford); *Gold of the Heroes* (Don Reynolds); *Massacre at Grand Canyon* (Stanley Corbett); *May God Forgive You . . . But I Won't* (Glenn V. Davis)
Ardow, Dean: *Road to Fort Alamo* (Mario Bava)
Arena, Fortunato: *Thirteen Is a Judas* (Joseph Warren)
Arlen, Ghia *see* **Ghia, Dana**
Armstrong, R. G.: *My Name Is Nobody* (Tonino Valerii)
Armstrong, Todd: *Winnetou: Thunder at the Border* (Alfred Vohrer)
Arno, Alice: *Gunfight at O Q Corral* (Jean-Marie Pallardy); *Red Hot Zorro* (William Russell)
Arpon, Maria Elena: *Tequila* (Tullio Demichelli)
Arriaga, Simon: *Compañeros* (Sergio Corbucci); *Django* (Sergio Corbucci); *Hellbenders* (Sergio Corbucci); *Man and a Colt* (Tullio Demichelli); *Navajo Joe* (Sergio Corbucci); *Rattler Kid* (Leon Klimovsky); *Three from Colorado* (Armando De Ossorio); *What Am I Doing in the Middle of the Revolution?* (Sergio Corbucci)
Askew, Luke: *Night of the Serpent* (Giulio Petroni)

Atckinson, Susanna: *Return of Clint the Stranger* (George Martin)
Audran, Stephane: *Eagle's Wing* (Anthony Harvey)
Aumont, Tina: *Brothers Blue* (Marc Meyer); *Man: His Pride and His Vengeance* (Luigi Bazzoni)
Aureli, Andrea *see* Ray, Andrew
Ávila, Enrique: *Kitosch, the Man Who Came from the North* (Joseph Marvin)
Avram, Chris: *California* (Michele Lupo); **Man Called Django* (Edward G. Muller); *Thunder Over El Paso* (Roberto Montero)
Baards, Pauline: *Ride and Kill* (J. L. Boraw)
Bacchi, Anna: *Requiem for a Bounty Hunter* (Mark Welles)
Bach, Vivi: *Bullets Don't Agree* (Mike Perkins)
Badessi, Giancarlo: *Halleluja to Vera Cruz* (Newman Rostel); *Night of the Serpent* (Giulio Petroni)
Badmayer, Mary: *Two Gunmen* (Anthony Greepy)
Badout, Dominique: *Even Django Has His Price* (Paolo Solvay)
Baer, Harry: *Valley of the Dancing Widows* (Volker Vogeler)
Bagolini, Silvio: *Killer Caliber .32* (Al Bradly)
Bailey, David: *Up the MacGregors!* (Frank Garfield)
Baird, Harry: **Colt in the Hands of the Devil* (Frank G. Carrol); *Four Gunmen of the Apocalypse* (Lucio Fulci); *Trinity and Sartana Are Coming* (Mario Siciliano)
Baker, Caroll: *Captain Apache* (Alexander Singer)
Baker, Stanley: *Zorro* (Duccio Tessari)
Balbo, Ennio: *Day of Anger* (Tonino Valerii)
Baldassare, Raf (also Raf Baldasar; also Rik Baldassare; sometimes pseudonym — Ralph Baldwin): *All Out* (Umberto Lenzi); *And the Crows Will Dig Your Grave* (John Wood); *Arizona* (Sergio Martino); *Between God, the Devil and a Winchester* (Dario Silvestri); *Blindman* (Ferdinando Baldi); *Canadian Wilderness* (Armando De Ossorio); *Cry for Revenge* (Rafael R. Marchent); *Dead Are Countless [Garringo]* (Rafael R. Marchent); *Dig Your Grave, Friend . . . Sabata's Coming* (John Woods); *Drummer of Vengeance* (Robert Paget); *Four Gunmen of the Holy Trinity* (Giorgio Cristalini); *Get Mean* (Ferdinando Baldi); *Great Silence* (Sergio Corbucci); *Gunfight at High Noon* (Joaquin R. Marchent); *Hands of a Gunman* (Rafael R. Marchent); *Hey Amigo! A Toast to Your Death* (Paul Maxwell); *Hour of Death* (Paul Marchenti); *Jesse James' Kid* (Antonio Del Amo); *Magnificent West* (Gianni Crea); *Man Who Cried for Revenge* (William Hawkins); *Mercenary* (Sergio Corbucci); *Outlaw of Red River* (Maury Dexter); *Pistol for a Hundred Coffins* (Umberto Lenzi); *Prey of Vultures* (Rafael R. Marchent); *Quinta: Fighting Proud* (Leon Klimovsky); *Relentless Four* (Primo Zeglio); *Rojo* (Leo Coleman); *Sartana Kills Them All* (Rafael R. Marchent); *Seven Guns from Texas* (Joaquin R. Marchent); *Seven Hours of Gunfire* (Joaquin R. Marchent); **Shadow of Zorro* (Joaquin R. Marchent); *Stranger in Japan* (Vance Lewis); *Stranger in Town* (Vance Lewis); *Stranger Returns* (Vance Lewis); *Three from Colorado* (Armando De Ossorio)
Baldini, Renato (pseudonym — Ryan Baldwin): **Among Vultures* (Alfred Vohrer); *Dick Luft in Sacramento* (Anthony Ascott); *Dynamite Joe* (Anthony Dawson); *I Am Sartana, Your Angel of Death* (Anthony Ascott); *Man from Canyon City* (Alfonso Balcazar); *Winnetou: Desperado Trail* (Harald Reinl); *Winnetou: Last of the Renegades* (Harald Reinl); *Woman for Ringo* (Rafael R. Marchent)
Balducci, Franco: *Black Tigress* (Siro Marcellini); *Night of the Serpent* (Giulio Petroni)
Baldwin, Ralph *see* Baldassare, Raf

Baldwin, Ryan *see* **Baldini, Renato**
Balestri, Andrea: *Bad Kids of the West* (Tony Good)
Balin, Anne-Marie: *Cemetery Without Crosses* (Robert Hossein); *Judge Roy Bean* (Richard Owens)
Balsam, Martin: *Cipolla Colt* (Enzo G. Castellari)
Banionis, Donatas: *Armed and Dangerous: Time and Heroes of Bret Harte* (Vladimir Vainstok)
Banner, Jill: *Stranger Returns* (Vance Lewis)
Banner, Lee: *Holy Water Joe* (Mario Gariazzo)
Baratto, Luisa *see* **Barrett, Liz**
Barbara, Paolo (pseudonym—**Pauline Bards**): *Killer Goodbye* (Primo Zeglio); *Relentless Four* (Primo Zeglio); *Sign of Coyote* (Mario Caiano)
Barboo, Luis: *Arizona* (Sergio Martino); *Between God, the Devil and a Winchester* (Dario Silvestri); *Cowards Don't Pray* (Marlon Sirko); *Cry for Revenge* (Rafael R. Marchent); *Dead Are Countless* (Rafael R. Marchent); *God Forgives, I Don't* (Giuseppe Colizzi); *Killer, Goodbye* (Primo Zeglio); *Montana Trap* (Peter Schamoni); *One After Another* (Nick Howard); *Piluk, the Timid One* (Guido Celano); *Rattler Kid* (Leon Klimovsky); **The Ugly Ones* (Eugenio Martino)
Bardanzellu, Maria: *If One Is Born a Swine . . . Kill Him* (Al Bradly)
Bardot, Brigitte: *Frenchie King* (Christian-Jaque); *Shalako* (Edward Dmytryk); **Viva Maria* (Louis Malle)
Bards, Pauline *see* **Barbara, Paola**
Barker, Lex: *Apache's Last Battle* (Hugo Fregonese); *Half Breed* (Harald Reinl); *Place Called Glory* (Ralph Gideon); *Pyramid of the Sun God* (Robert Siodmak); *Treasure of the Aztecs* (Robert Siodmak); **Treasure of Silver Lake* (Harald Reinl); *Who Killed Johnny R.?* (Jose Luis Madrid); *Winnetou and Shatterhand in the Valley of Death* (Harald Reinl); *Winnetou the Warrior* (Harald Reinl); *Winnetou: Last of the Renegades* (Harald Reinl); *Winnetou: The Desperado Trail* (Harald Reinl)
Barnes, Walter: *Among Vultures* (Alfred Vohrer); *Another Man, Another Woman* (Claude Lelouch); *Big Gundown* (Sergio Sollima); *Clint the Stranger* (Alfonso Balcazar); *Duel at Sundown* (Leopoldo Lahola); *Garter Colt* (Gian A. Rocco); *Greatest Robbery in the West* (Maurizio Lucidi); *Half Breed* (Alfred Vohrer); *The Moment to Kill* (Anthony Ascott); *Rampage at Apache Wells* (Harald Philipp); **Winnetou the Warrior* (Harald Reinl)
Barracuda, John: *Magnificent Texan* (Lewis King)
Barray, Gerard: *Pyramid of the Sun God* (Robert Siodmak)
Barret, Liz (pseudonym for **Luisa Baratto**): **Killer Kid* (Leopoldo Savona); *Long Day of the Massacre* (Albert Cardiff); *Payment in Blood* (E. G. Rowland); *Two Pistols and a Coward* (Calvin J. Padget)
Barros, Esmeralda: *Even Django Has His Price* (Paolo Solvay); *God Is My Colt .45* (Dean Jones); *Man Called Django* (Edward G. Muller)
Barry, Barta (also **Barta Barri**): *Badman's River* (Eugenio Martin); *Calvary Charge* (Ramon Torrado); *Dead Are Countless* (Rafael R. Marchent); *Dynamite Joe* (Anthony Dawson); **Gunfight at Red Sands* (Ricardo Blasco); *Left Handed Johnny West* (Frank Kramer); *Red Sun* (Terence Young); *Son of a Gunfighter* (Paul Landres); *White Comanche* (Gilbert Lee Kay)
Bart, Stan: *Joe Dexter* (Ignacio Iquino)
Bartha, John: **Hands of a Gunman* (Rafael R. Marchent); *His Name Was King* (Don Reynolds); *Kill Them All and Come Back Alone* (Enzo G. Castellari); *Killer Caliber .32* (Al Bradly); *Man of the Cursed Valley* (Omar Hopkins); *Relentless*

Four (Primo Zeglio); *Ringo and His Golden Pistol* (Sergio Corbucci); *Rojo* (Leo Coleman); *Tequila* (Tullio Demichelli)

Barto, Dominic: *Man of the East* (E. B. Clucher)

Bartoleschi, Valerio: *I'll Sell My Skin Dearly* (Ettore Fizarotti)

Basehart, Richard: *Savage Guns* (Michael Carreras)

Bastien, Yvonne: *Fury of the Apaches* (Joe Lacy); *Savage Gringo* (Bava/Romano)

Battaglia, Riccardo *see* **Battaglia, Rik**

Battaglia, Rik (pseudonym for **Riccardo Battaglia**): **Apache's Last Battle* (Hugo Fregonese); *Black Jack* (Gian Baldanello); *Deadly Trackers* (Amerigo Anton); *Duck You Sucker* (Sergio Leone); *Genius* (Damiano Damiani); *Gold of the Heroes* (Don Reynolds); *Hey Amigo! A Toast to Your Death!* (Paul Maxwell); *Legacy of the Incas* (Georg Marischka); *Man Called Blade* (Sergio Martino); *Pyramid of the Sun God* (Robert Siodmak); *Sheriff Was a Lady* (Sobey Martin); *Shoot, Gringo . . . Shoot!* (Frank B. Corlish); *This Man Can't Die* (Gian Baldanello); *Treasure of the Aztecs* (Robert Siodmak); *Winnetou and Shatterhand in the Valley of Death* (Harald Reinl); *Winnetou: Desperado Trail* (Harald Reinl)

Batti, Jeanette: *Pirates of the Mississippi* (Jürgen Roland)

Battista, Lloyd: *Blindman* (Ferdinando Baldi); *Get Mean* (Ferdinando Baldi); **Stranger in Japan* (Vance Lewis)

Battisti, Spartaco: *Go with God, Gringo* (Edward G. Muller)

Baxter, Anne: *Tall Women* (Sidney Pink)

Begona, Mari: *Torrejon City* (Leon Klimovsky)

Bell, Betsy: *Cost of Dying* (Sergio Merolle)

Beller, Georges: *Frenchie King* (Christian-Jaque)

Belmont, Vera: *Gunfight at O Q Corral* (J. M. Pallardy)

Bendanti, Poldo: *His Name Was Holy Ghost* (Anthony Ascott); *Seven Guns for Timothy* (Rod Gilbert)

Benetti, Luciano: *Colt in Hand of the Devil* (Sergio Bergonzelli)

Benguel, Norma: *Hellbenders* (Sergio Corbucci); *I Do Not Forgive . . . I Kill!* (Joaquin R. Marchent)

Beniconi, Howard: *God Does Not Pay on Saturday* (Amerigo Anton)

Bentley, Dick: *Gunfighters of Casa Grande* (Roy Rowland)

Benussi, Femi (also **Eufemia Benussi**; sometimes pseudonym—**Femi Martin**): *Born to Kill* (Tony Mulligan); **Death Walks in Laredo* (Enzo Peri); *Duel in the Eclipse* (Martino/Merino); *Finders Killers* (Gianni Crea); *Quintana: Dead or Alive* (Glenn V. Davis); *Rattler Kid* (Leon Klimovsky); *Stranger and the Gunfighter* (Anthony Dawson); *Time of Vultures* (Nando Cicero)

Benvenuti, Nino: *Alive or Preferably Dead* (Duccio Tessari)

Beran, Mila: *Man Called Amen* (Alfio Caltabiano)

Berben, Iris: *Compañeros* (Sergio Corbucci)

Beretta, Daniel: *Dust in the Sun* (Ricard Balcuddi)

Bergamonti, Rosella: **I Came, I Saw, I Shot* (Enzo G. Castellari)

Bergen, Candice: *Hunting Party* (Don Medford)

Berger, William: *California* (Michele Lupo); *Cisco* (Sergio Bergonzelli); *Colt in the Hand of the Devil* (Frank G. Carrol); *Django Strikes Again* (Ted Archer); *Face to Face* (Sergio Sollima); *Fasthand* (Frank Bronston); *Keoma* (Enzo G. Castellari); *Kung Fu Brothers in the Wild West* (Yeo Ban Yee); *Man Who Cried for Revenge* (William Hawkins); *No Room to Die* (Willy S. Regan); *On the Third Day Arrived the Crow* (Gianni Crea); **Ringo's Big Night* (Mario Maffei); *Sabata* (Frank Kramer); *Sartana* (Frank Kramer); *Sartana in the Valley of Death* (Roberto Mauri); *Son of Zorro* (Gianfranco Baldanello); *Tex and the Lord of the*

Deep (Duccio Tessari); *They Call Him Cemetery* (Anthony Ascott); *Today It's Me
. . . Tomorrow You* (Tonino Cervi); *Yankee Dudler* (Volker Vogeler)
Bert, Kirk: *Road to Fort Alamo* (Mario Bava)
Berthier, Jack: *Colorado Charlie* (Robert Johnson); *Sheriff with the Gold* (Richard
Kean)
Berti, Aldo (also **Stanley Kent**): *Big Ripoff* (Franco Rossetti); *Blood at Sundown* (José
De La Loma); *Born to Kill* (Tony Mulligan); *Death Played the Flute* (Elio Panac-
cio); *Django, a Bullet for You* (Leon Klimovsky); *Go with God, Gringo* (Edward
G. Muller); *Gunmen and the Holy Ghost* (Roberto Mauri); *Hey Amigo! A Toast
to Your Death!* (Paul Maxwell); *Mallory Must Not Die* (Mario Moroni); *Ramon
the Mexican* (Maurizio Pradeaux); *The Reward's Yours, the Man's Mine* (Edward
G. Muller); *Sartana in the Valley of Death* (Roberto Mauri); **Stranger in Sacra-
mento* (Serge Bergon)
Berti, Marina: *Hatred of God* (Claudio Gora); *Stranger Returns* (Vance Lewis)
Bessy, Celina: *Fasthand* (Frank Bronston)
Beswick, Martine: *Bullet for the General* (Damiano Damiani); *John the Bastard* (Ar-
mando Crispino)
Bethmann, Sabine: *Man from Oklahoma* (Robert M. White)
Betts, Jack *see* **Powers, Hunt**
Bianchi, Eleonara: *If One Is Born a Swine* (Al Bradly); *One Hundred Thousand
Dollars for Ringo* (Alberto De Martino)
Bickford, Allen: *Ned Kelly* (Tony Richardson)
Bien, Lawrence: *Requiem for a Bounty Hunter* (Mark Welles); *Porno Erotic Western*
(Gerard B. Lennox)
Bier, Fred: *Damned Pistols of Dallas* (Joseph Trader)
Bilbao, Fernando: *Apocalypse Joe* (Leopoldo Savona); *Fasthand* (Frank Bronston)
Birks, Ralph: *Dallas* (Juan Bosch)
Blackman, Honor: *Shalako* (Edward Dmytryk)
Blanc, Erika (also **Erika Blank**; pseudonym for **Enrica Bianch Colombatto**; other
pseudonym—**Erica White**): *Blood at Sundown* (Albert Cardiff); **Colorado
Charlie* (Robert Johnson); *Deguello* (Joseph Warren); *Dig Your Grave Friend
. . . Sabata's Coming* (John Wood); *Django Shoots First* (Alberto De Martino);
Greatest Robbery in the West (Maurizio Lucidi); *I Am Sartana, Trade Your Guns
for a Coffin* (Anthony Ascott); *Shoot, Gringo . . . Shoot!* (Frank B. Corlish);
Shotgun (Roberto Mauri); *Stranger and the Gunfighter* (Anthony Dawson);
Thunder Over El Paso (Roberto Montero)
Blanco, Hugo: *Django Does Not Forgive* (Julio Buchs); *One After Another* (Nick
Howard); *Sartana Does Not Forgive* (Alfonso Balcazar); *Texas, Adios* (Ferdi-
nando Baldi); **The Ugly Ones* (Eugenio Martino); *Up the MacGregors!* (Frank
Garfield); *Valley of the Dancing Widows* (Volker Vogeler)
Blanco, Tomás: **Billy the Kid* (Leon Klimovsky); *Charge of the Seventh Cavalry*
(Herbert Martin); *Fifteen Scaffolds for the Killer* (Nunzio Malasomma); *For a
Few Dollars More* (Sergio Leone); *Heroes of the West* (Steno); *Man Who Killed
Billy the Kid* (Julio Buchs); *Secret of Captain O'Hara* (Arturo R. Castillo); *Shoot
to Kill* (Ramon Torrado)
Block, Lars: *On the Third Day Arrived the Crow* (Gianni Crea)
Blondell, Simone: *Anything for a Friend* (Miles Deem); *Django and Sartana Are
Coming . . . It's the End* (Dick Spitfire); *Four Came to Kill Sartana* (Miles
Deem); *His Name Was Sam Walbash, But They Call Him Amen* (Miles Deem);
Man Called Django (Edward G. Muller); *One Damned Day at Dawn . . . Django
Meets Sartana* (Miles Deem); **Shadow of Sartana . . . Shadow of Your Death*

(Sean O'Neal); *Showdown for a Badman* (Miles Deem); *Stranger That Kneels Beside the Shadow for a Corpse* (Miles Deem)

Bodalò, Francisco (also **José Bodalò**): *Compañeros* (Sergio Corbucci); *Dead Are Countless* (Rafael R. Marchent); *Django* (Sergio Corbucci); *Dollars for a Fast Gun* (Joaquin R. Marchent); *One After Another* (Nick Howard); *Red Blood Yellow Gold* (Nando Cicero); **Ringo's Big Night* (Mario Maffei); *Thompson 1880* (Albert Moore); *Train for Durango* (William Hawkins)

Bogart, William: *Carambola* (Ferdinando Baldi); *Death Knows No Time* (Leon Klimovsky); *Death Rides a Horse* (Giulio Petroni); **Kill Johnny Ringo* (Frank G. Carrol); *Night of the Serpent* (Giulio Petroni); *One Against One . . . No Mercy* (Rafael R. Marchent); *Rattler Kid* (Leon Klimovsky); *Sartana Kills Them All* (Rafael R. Marchent); *They Call Him Veritas* (Luigi Perelli)

Bohm, Marquard: *Chetan, Indian Boy* (Mark Bohm); *Deadlock* (Roland Klick)

Boido, Federico *see* **Boyd, Rick**

Bolas, Xan Das *see* **Xan, Das Bolas**

Bollet, André: *Left Handed Johnny West* (Frank Kramer)

Bomez, Lucye: *Cisco* (Sergio Bergonzelli); *Ringo, It's Massacre Time* (Mario Pinzauti)

Bonnin, Bernard: *Arizona Kid* (Luciano Carlos)

Bonos, Gigi: *For a Book of Dollars* (Renzo Spaziani); *Shoot, Gringo . . . Shoot!* (Frank B. Corlish)

Bonuglia, Maurizio: *Brothers Blue* (Marc Meyer); *The Reward's Yours, the Man's Mine* (Edward G. Muller)

Boone, Richard: *God's Gun* (Frank Kramer)

Borgese, Sal: *Adios, Sabata* (Frank Kramer); *Greatest Robbery in the West* (Maurizio Lucidi); **I Am Sartana, Your Angel of Death* (Anthony Ascott); *It Can Be Done Amigo* (Maurizio Lucidi); *Man Called Invincible* (Anthony Ascott); *Man of the East* (E. B. Clucher); *Patience Has a Limit, We Don't* (Armando Morandi); *Three Supermen of the West* (Italo Martinenghi)

Borgnine, Ernest: **Bullet for Sandoval* (Julio Buchs); *Hannie Caulder* (Burt Kennedy); *Manhunt* (Larry Ludman)

Boschero, Dominique: *And the Crows Will Dig Your Grave* (John Wood); *Train for Durango* (William Hawkins)

Bosco, Gianfranco: *Rick and John, Conquerors of the West* (Osvaldo Civirani)

Bosé, Miguel: *Macho Killers* (Mark Andrew)

Bosé, Paolo: *California* (Michele Lupo)

Bosić, Andrea (also **Andrea Bosich**; also **Andrea Bosie**): *Arizona Colt* (Michele Lupo); *Day of Anger* (Tonino Valerii); *Days of Violence* (Al Bradly); *Death Knows No Time* (Leon Klimovsky); *Fifteen Scaffolds for the Killer* (Nunzio Malasomma); *Fort Yuma Gold* (Calvin J. Padget); *Heads You Die . . . Tails I Kill You* (Anthony Ascott); *I Want Him Dead* (Paolo Bianchi); **Kill or Die* (Amerigo Anton); *Killer Caliber .32* (Al Bradly); *Two Pistols and a Coward* (Calvin J. Padget); *Two Sides of the Dollar* (Roberto Montero)

Bosley, Tom: *Bang Bang Kid* (Luciano Lelli)

Bowakow, Deschingis: *Chetan, Indian Boy* (Mark Bohm)

Boyd, Rick (pseudonym for **Federico Boido**): *Ace High* (Giuseppe Colizzi); *Adios, Sabata* (Frank Kramer); *Anything for a Friend* (Miles Deem); *Apache Woman* (George McRoots); **Cjamango* (Edward G. Muller); *Django Challenges Sartana* (William Redford); *Django Kills Softly* (Max Hunter); *Face to Face* (Sergio Sollima); *Fighting Fists of Shanghai Joe* (Mario Caiano); *Gold of the Heroes* (Don Reynolds); *Greatest Robbery in the West* (Maurizio Lucidi); *Halleluja to Vera Cruz* (Newman Rostel); *Have a Good Funeral, My Friend . . . Sartana Will Pay*

(Anthony Ascott); *Heads You Die . . . Tails I Kill You* (Anthony Ascott); *Here We Are Again, Eh Providence?* (Alberto De Martino); *His Name Was King* (Don Reynolds); *I Am Sartana, Your Angel of Death* (Anthony Ascott); *I Want Him Dead* (Paolo Bianchini); *I Am Sartana, Trade Your Gun for a Coffin* (Anthony Ascott); *Jesse and Lester, Two Brothers in a Place Called Trinity* (James London); *Payment in Blood* (E. G. Rowland); *Run Man, Run* (Sergio Sollima); *Ruthless Four* (Giorgio Capitani); *Shoot Joe, and Shoot Again* (Hal Brady); *A Sky Full of Stars for a Roof* (Giulio Petroni); *Vendetta at Dawn* (Willy S. Regan)

Boyd, Stephen: *Hannie Caulder* (Burt Kennedy); *Man Called Noon* (Peter Collinson); *Montana Trap* (Peter Schamoni); **Shalako* (Edward Dmytryk); *Those Dirty Dogs!* (Giuseppe Rosati)

Boyer, Marie Fran: *Apache Woman* (George McRoots)

Bozzuffi, Marcel: *Chino* (John Sturges)

Bradly, Harold: *Days of Violence* (Al Bradly)

Braña, Frank (also **Frank Braz** and **Francisco Braña**): *Adios Gringo* (George Finley); *And the Crows Will Dig Your Grave* (John Wood); *Awkward Hands* (Rafael R. Marchent); *Boldest Job in the West* (José De La Loma); *Cowards Don't Pray* (Marlon Sirko); *Dallas* (Juan Bosch); *Dead Are Countless (Garringo)* (Rafael R. Marchent); *Death on High Mountain* (Fred Ringoold); *Django Does Not Forgive* (Julio Buchs); *Django, Kill . . . If You Live, Shoot!* (Giulio Questi); *Face to Face* (Sergio Sollima); *Fasthand* (Frank Bronston); *Fifteen Scaffolds for the Killer* (Nunzio Malasomma); *God Forgives, I Don't* (Giuseppe Colizzi); *God in Heaven . . . Arizona on Earth* (John Wood); *The Good, the Bad, and the Ugly* (Sergio Leone); *I Want Him Dead* (Paolo Bianchini); *If You Shoot . . . You Live!* (Joe Lacy); *In the Name of the Father, the Son, and the Colt* (Frank Bronston); *Kill the Poker Player* (Frank Bronston); *Let Them Rest* (Carlo Lizzani); *Light the Fuse . . . Sartana Is Coming* (Anthony Ascott); **Massacre at Fort Grant* (J. Douglas); *Murieta* (George Sherman); *Prey of Vultures* (Rafael R. Marchent); *Price of Power* (Tonino Valerii); *Rattler Kid* (Leon Klimovsky); *Ringo, the Lone Rider* (Rafael R. Marchent); *Savage Gringo* (Bava/Romano); *Secret of Captain O'Hara* (Arturo Ruiz Castillo); *Three Supermen of the West* (Italo Martinenghi); *Two Gunmen* (Anthony Greepy); *The Ugly Ones* (Eugenio Martino)

Branchud, Manuel: *Law of Violence* (Gianni Crea)

Branca, Michele: *Requiem for a Bounty Hunter* (Mark Welles)

Branger, Mariela: *Arizona Kid* (Luciano Carlos)

Bravo, Charlie (also **Carlos Bravo**): **Boldest Job in the West* (José A. De La Loma); *Captain Apache* (Alexander Singer); *China 9, Liberty 37* (Monte Hellman); *Man Called Noon* (Peter Collinson); *Scalps* (Werner Knox); *Town Called Hell* (Robert Parrish); *White Apache* (Vincent Dawn)

Brauss, Arthur: *Montana Trap* (Peter Schamoni)

Bray, Lillian: *Animal Called Man* (Roberto Mauri)

Braz, Frank see **Braña, Frank**

Brazzi, Rossano: *Drummer of Vengenace* (Robert Paget)

Brega, Mario: **Buffalo Bill, Hero of the Far West* (John W. Fordson); *Death Rides a Horse* (Guilio Petroni); *Finders Killers* (Gianni Crea); *For a Few Dollars More* (Sergio Leone); *The Good, the Bad, and the Ugly* (Sergio Leone); *Great Silence* (Sergio Corbucci); *Greatest Robbery in the West* (Maurizio Lucidi); *Minute to Pray, a Second to Die* (Franco Giraldi); *No Room to Die* (Willy S. Regan); *Return of Sabata* (Frank Kramer); *The Reward's Yours, the Man's Mine* (Edward G. Muller); *The Ugly Ones* (Eugenio Martin)

Brendel, Miguel: *Kid Rodelo* (Richard Carlson)

Brent, Timothy (pseudonym for **Giancarlo Prete**): *Sting of the West* (Enzo Castellari); *Three Musketeers of the West* (Bruno Corbucci)

Brice, Pierre: *Among Vultures* (Alfred Vohrer); *Apache's Last Battle* (Hugo Fregonese); *Flaming Frontier* (Alfred Vohrer); *Half Breed* (Harald Philipp); *Place Called Glory* (Ralph Gideon); *Rampage at Apache Wells* (Harald Philipp); *Terror of the Black Mask* (Umberto Lenzi); **Treasure of Silver Lake* (Harald Reinl); *Winnetou and Shatterhand in the Valley of Death* (Harald Reinl); *Winnetou the Warrior* (Harald Reinl); *Winnetou: Last of the Renegades* (Harald Reinl); *Winnetou: The Desperado Trail* (Harald Reinl); *Winnetou: Thunder at the Border* (Alfred Vohrer)

Brideu, Lucienne: *Black Jack* (Gianfranco Baldanello); *This Man Can't Die* (Gianfranco Baldanello)

Brochard, Martine: *Man Called Blade* (Sergio Martino)

Bronevoy, Leonis: *Armed and Dangerous: Time and Heroes of Bret Harte* (Vladimir Vainstok)

Bronson, Charles: *Chino* (John Sturges); **Guns for San Sebastian* (Henri Verneuil); *Once Upon a Time in the West* (Sergio Leone); *Red Sun* (Terence Young)

Brook, Claudio: *Viva Maria* (Louis Malle)

Brown, Jim: *Kid Vengeance* (Joe Manduke); *Take a Hard Ride* (Anthony Dawson)

Brugger, Monica: *A Winchester Does Not Forgive* (Adelchi Bianchi)

Brummell, Beau: *Three Bullets for a Long Gun* (Peter Henkel)

Brunell, Juny: *Billy the Kid* (Leon Klimovsky)

Bryan, John: *Hole in the Forehead* (Joseph Warren)

Brylska, Barbara: *Trail of the Falcon* (Gottfried Kölditz)

Brynner, Yul: *Adios, Sabata* (Frank Kramer)

Bucci, Flavio: *Tex and the Lord of the Deep* (Duccio Tessari)

Bujold, Geneviève: *Another Man, Another Woman* (Claude Lelouch)

Burke, William: *Kill Johnny Ringo* (Frank G. Carrol)

Buono, Victor: *Boot Hill* (Giuseppe Colizzi)

Burton, Lee (pseudonym for **Guido Lollobrigida**): *And God Said to Cain* (Anthony Dawson); *Beast* (Mario Costa); *Brothers Blue* (Marc Meyer); *Cemetery Without Crosses* (Robert Hossein); *Django Shoots First* (Alberto De Martino); *Drummer of Vengeance* (Robert Paget); *Get the Coffin Ready* (Ferdinando Baldi); *Kill Johnny Ringo* (Frank G. Carrol); *Long Ride from Hell* (Alex Burkes); *Man: His Pride and His Vengeance* (Luigi Bazzoni); **One Hundred Thousand Dollars for Ringo* (Alberto De Martino); *Red Sun* (Terence Young); *Roy Colt and Winchester Jack* (Mario Bava); *Those Dirty Dogs!* (Giuseppe Rossati); *Vendetta at Dawn* (Willy S. Regan); *Vengeance* (Anthony Dawson)

Burton, Ric: *If One Is Born a Swine* (Al Bradly)

Burton, Robert: *Massacre at Fort Holman* (Tonino Valerii)

Businari, Cristina: *I Want Him Dead* (Paolo Bianchini)

Busner, Joe: *Buddy Goes West* (Michele Lupo)

Butkus, Dick: *Cipolla Colt* (Enzo G. Castellari)

Buzzanca, Gino: *Don't Wait, Django . . . Shoot!* (Edward G. Muller)

Buzzanca, Lando: *For a Few Dollars Less* (Mario Mattòli); *Ringo and Gringo Against All* (Bruno Corbucci)

Byrnes, Edd: *Go Kill and Come Back* (Enzo G. Castellari); **Payment in Blood* (E. G. Rowland); *Red Blood, Yellow Gold* (Nando Cicero)

Caan, James: *Another Man Another Woman* (Claude Lelouch)

Cafetella, Raymondo: *Eye for an Eye* (Albert Marshall)

Caffarel, José: *Bang Bang Kid* (Luciano Lelli)

Calderón, Licia: *I Want Him Dead* (Paolo Bianchini); **Terrible Sheriff* (Antonio Momplet)

Calhoun, Rory: *Finger on the Trigger* (Sidney Pink)

Caltabiano, Alfio (pseudonym—**Al Northon and Alf Thunder**): *Ballad of a Gunman* (Alfio Caltabiano); *California* (Michele Lupo); *Man Called Amen* (Alfio Caltabiano); *They Still Call Me Amen* (Alfio Caltabiano)

Calvo, Armando: *All Out* (Umberto Lenzi); *Coffin for the Sheriff* (William Hawkins); *Django Does Not Forgive* (Julio Buchs); *I Am Sartana, Trade Your Guns for a Coffin* (Anthony Ascott); **Sign of Zorro* (Mario Caiano); *Two Crosses at Danger Pass* (Rafael R. Marchent)

Calvo, José (also **Pepe Calvo**; pseudonym: **Joe Egger**): *Blood at Sundown* (De La Loma/Muller); *Day of Anger* (Tonino Valerii); *Dead Men Ride* (Aldo Florio); *Dust in the Sun* (Richard Balducci); *Fistful of Dollars* (Sergio Leone); *For One Thousand Dollars Per Day* (Silvio Amadio); *Fort Yuma Gold* (Calvin J. Padget); *I Am Sartana . . . Trade Your Guns for a Coffin* (Anthony Ascott); *In a Colt's Shadow* (Gianni Grimaldi); *Killer Goodbye* (Primo Zeglio); *Man from Oklahoma* (Robert M. White); *Prey of Vultures* (Rafael R. Marchent); *Price of Power* (Tonino Valerii); *Ringo, the Lone Rider* (Rafael R. Marchent); *Stranger in Paso Bravo* (Salvatore Rosso); **Terrible Sheriff* (Antonio Momplet); *Twice a Judas* (Nando Cicero)

Camardiel, Roberto: *Adios Gringo* (George Finley); *Adios Hombre* (Mario Caiano); *Arizona* (Sergio Martino); *Arizona Colt* (Michele Lupo); *Between God, the Devil and a Winchester* (Dario Silvestri); *Big Gundown* (Sergio Sollima); *Challenge of the Mackennas* (Leon Klimovsky); *Django, Kill. . . If You Live, Shoot!* (Giulio Questi); *Dollars for a Fast Gun* (Joaquin R. Marchent); *For a Few Dollars More* (Sergio Leone); *God in Heaven . . . Arizona on Earth* (John Wood); *Heads You Die . . . Tails I Kill You* (Anthony Ascott); *It Can Be Done . . . Amigo* (Maurizio Lucidi); **Jaguar* (Jesus Franco); *Jesse James' Kid* (Antonio Del Amo); *Left Handed Johnny West* (Frank Kramer); *Machine Gun Killers* (Paolo Bianchini); *Murieta* (George Sherman); *Price of Power* (Tonino Valerii); *Quinta: Fighting Proud* (Leon Klimovsky); *Relentless Four* (Primo Zeglio); *Return of Halleluja* (Anthony Ascott); *Tequila* (Tullio Demichelli); *Train for Durango* (William Hawkins); *Up the MacGregors!* (Frank Garfield)

Camaso, Claudio (also **Claudio Camaso Volenté**): *For One Hundred Thousand Dollars Per Killing* (Sidney Lean); **Garter Colt* (Gian A. Rocco); *John the Bastard* (Armando Crispino); *Ten Thousand Dollars Blood Money* (Romolo Guerrieri); *Vengeance* (Anthony Dawson)

Cameron, Jeff (pseudonym for **Geoffredo Scarciofolo**): *Bounty Hunter in Trinity* (Oskar Faradine); *Even Django Has His Price* (Paolo Solvay); *Fistful of Death* (Miles Deem); *Four Came to Kill Sartana* (Miles Deem); *God Is My Colt .45* (Dean Jones); **Greatest Robbery in the West* (Maurizio Lucidi); *Paid in Blood* (Paolo Solvay); *Shadow of Sartana. . . Shadow of Your Death* (Sean O'Neal); *Showdown for a Badman* (Miles Deem); *Today It's Me . . . Tomorrow You* (Tonino Cervi)

Cameron, Rod: *Bullets and the Flesh* (Fred Wilson); *Bullets Don't Argue* (Mike Perkins)

Caminnecci, Pier: *Jesse James' Kid* (Antonio Del Amo)

Campori, Anna: *Rick and John, Conquerors of the West* (Osvaldo Civirani)

Canalejas, José: *If You Shoot . . . You Live!* (Joe Lacy); **Secret of Captain O'Hara* (Arturo Ruiz Castillo)

Candelli, Stelio (also **Stello Candelli**): *Apocalypse Joe* (Leopoldo Savona); **Last*

Tomahawk (Harald Reinl); *Man Called Django* (Edward G. Muller); *Trinity and Sartana Are Coming* (Mario Siciliano)

Cannistani, Aldo: *Born to Kill* (Tony Mulligan)

Canova, Fernand *see* **Casanova, Fernando**

Canow, Fred *see* **Casanova, Fernando**

Cantafora, Antonio *see* **Coby, Michael**

Capanna, Amero: *Animal Called Man* (Roberto Mauri); *He Was Called the Holy Ghost* (Robert Johnson)

Capoleoni, Enrico: *Stranger in Town* (Stan Vance)

Capucine: *Red Sun* (Terence Young)

Caracciolo, Conny: *Revenge for Revenge* (Ray Calloway)

Caracuel, Mercedes: *Dynamite Joe* (Anthony Dawson)

Cardinale, Claudia: *Frenchie King* (Christian-Jaque); *Once Upon a Time in the West* (Sergio Leone)

Cardinali, Nuccia: *In the Name of the Father, the Son and the Colt* (Frank Bronston)

Cardosa, Beny: *Scalps* (Werner Knox)

Careddu, Stefania *see* **O'Hara, Kareen**

Carey, Harry, Jr.: *Man of the East* (E. B. Clucher); *Take a Hard Ride* (Anthony Dawson); **Trinity Is Still My Name* (E. B. Clucher)

Carlini, Carlo: *Bad Kids of the West* (Tony Good)

Carlson, Richard: *Kid Rodelo* (Richard Carlson)

Carocci, Massimo: *Magnificent Three* (Joaquin R. Marchent)

Carotenuto, Mario: *Grandsons of Zorro* (Mariano Laurenti)

Carra, Ben: *Dead Men Ride* (Aldo Florio)

Carreras, Oscar: *Man from Canyon City* (Alfonso Balcazar)

Carroll, Barbara: *Rick and John, Conquerors of the West* (Osvaldo Civirani)

Carson, Lemmy: *Revenge for Revenge* (Ray Calloway)

Carson, Stet *see* **Testi, Fabio**

Carsten, Peter *see* **Lulli, Piero**

Carter, Peter *see* **Lulli, Peiro**

Carter, Red *see* **Pazzafini, Nello**

Carter, Ted *see* **Pazzafini, Nello**

Carver, Kitty: *Last Gun* (Sergio Bergonzelli)

Casamonica, Luciano: *Blood and Guns* (Giulio Petroni)

Casanova, Fernando (also **Fred Canow** and **Fernand Canova**): *Shots Ring Out!* (Augustin Navarro); *Sign of Coyote* (Mario Caiano)

Casas, Antonio: *Alive or Preferably Dead* (Duccio Tessari); *Awkward Hands* (Rafael R. Marchent); *Four Dollars for Vengeance* (Alfonso Balcazar); *Minnesota Clay* (Sergio Corbucci); *Pistol for Ringo* (Duccio Tessari); *Price of Power* (Tonino Valerii); *Return of Ringo* (Duccio Tessari); **Ride and Kill* (J. L. Boraw); *Son of a Gunfighter* (Paul Landres); *Texican* (Espinosa/Selander); *Three Supermen in the West* (Italo Martinenghi)

Castellato, Luigi *see* **Castel, Lou**

Cashino, Vincenté: *Sheriff Won't Shoot* (J. Luis Monter)

Cassola, Carla: *Death Rides a Horse* (Giulio Petroni)

Castel, Lou (pseudonym for **Luigi Casellato;** also **Louis Cassel**): *Bullet for the General* (Damiano Damiani); *Let Them Rest* (Carlo Lizzani); *Matalo!* (Cesare Canavari); *My Name Is Pecos* (Maurice A. Bright)

Castellaneta, Donato: *Man Called Django* (Edward G. Muller)

Castellani, Claudio: *Hate Thy Neighbor* (Ferdinando Baldi)

Castelnuovo, Nino: *Five Man Army* (Don Taylor); *Massacre Time* (Lucio Fulci)

Castillo, Miguel: *Outlaw of Red River* (Maury Dexter)

Castor, Anna: *Saguro* (Amerigo Anton)

Catenacci, Luciano: *Eye for an Eye* (Albert Marshall); *Here We Are Again, Eh Providence?* (Alberto De Michelli); *It Can Be Done . . . Amigo* (Maurizio Lucidi)

Cavo, Angela: *Shots Ring Out!* (Augustin Navarro)

Ceccarelli, Pietro: *Pistol Packin' Preacher* (Leopoldo Savona); *They Called Him Cemetery* (Anthony Ascott)

Cecconi, Aldo: **Colt Is the Law* (Al Bradly); *Dynamite Joe* (Anthony Dawson); *If You Want to Live . . . Shoot!* (Sergio Garrone)

Celi, Adolfo: *Death Sentence* (Mario Linfranchi); *Yankee* (Tinto Brass)

Cely, Celina: *Last Gun* (Sergio Bergonzelli)

Ceriani, Umberto: *Mutiny at Fort Sharp* (Fernando Cerchio)

Cerra, Saturno: *Kill the Poker Player* (Frank Bronston)

Cerulli, Fernando: *Apocalypse Joe* (Leopoldo Savona)

Cesti, Renato: *It Can Be Done . . . Amigo* (Maurizio Lucidi); *Red Coat* (Joe D'Amato)

Cesti, Tano: *Man Called Amen* (Alfio Caltabiano), *They Still Call Me Amen* (Alfio Caltabiano)

Cevenini, Alberto: *Minnesota Clay* (Sergio Corbucci)

Chanel, Hélène (pseudonym—Sheril Morgan): *Cjamango* (Edward G. Muller); *Killer Caliber .32* (Al Bradly); *Terror of the Black Mask* (Umberto Lenzi); *Two Gangsters in the Wild West* (Giorgio Simonelli); *Two R-R-Ringos from Texas* (Frank Martin)

Chaplin, Geraldine: *Yankee Dudler* (Volker Vogeler)

Chaplin, Sydney: *Death Knows No Time* (Leon Klimovsky); *Sartana* (Frank Kramer)

Chaquito: *Arizona Kid* (Luciano Carlos)

Charlebois, Robert: *Genius* (Damiano Damiani)

Chavarro, Louis: *Colorado Charlie* (Robert Johnson); *Damned Pistols of Dallas* (Joseph Trader)

Checchi, Andrea: *Bullet for the General* (Damiano Damiani)

Chelli, Alida: *Three Silver Dollars* (Irving Jacobs)

Chentrens, Federico: *Black Jack* (Gianfranco Baldanello)

Chiari, Walter: *Heroes of the West* (Steno); **Terrible Sheriff* (Antonio Momplet); *Twins from Texas* (Steno)

Chimenti, Melissa: *Chino* (John Sturges)

Chio, Anna Maria: *Last Rebel* (Denys McCoy)

Chittel, Christopher: *They Called Him Cemetery* (Anthony Ascott)

Cianfriglia, Giovanni see **Wood, Ken**

Ciangottini, Valeria: *For a Few Dollars Less* (Mario Mattóli)

Ciani, Sergio see **Steel, Alan**

Ciannelli, Eduardo: *Boot Hill* (Giuseppe Colizzi)

Cilli, Zara: *Death Is Sweet from the Soldier of God* (Roberto Mauri)

Cimarosa, Tano: *Death on the High Mountain* (Fred Ringoold); *Man Called Amen* (Alfio Caltabiano); *They Still Call Me Amen* (Alfio Caltabiano)

Cintado, Antonio: *Stranger in Paso Bravo* (Salvatore Rosso)

Citti, Franco: *Kill Them All and Come Back Alone* (Enzo G. Castellari); *Let Them Rest* (Carlo Lizzani)

Clair, Jany: *Road to Fort Alamo* (Mario Bava)

Clark, Anthony (pseudonym for **Angel Del Pozo**): *Big Gundown* (Sergio Sollima); **Colt Is My Law* (Al Bradly); *Face to Face* (Sergio Sollima); *Fort Yuma Gold* (Calvin J. Padget); *Man Called Noon* (Peter Collinson); *Place Called Glory* (Ralph Gideon); *Price of Power* (Tonino Valerii); *Savage Pampas* (Hugo Fregonese); *Today It's Me . . . Tomorrow You* (Tonino Cervi)

Clark, Dan: *Sheriff Won't Shoot* (J. Luis Monter)
Clark, John: *Django Does Not Forgive* (Julio Buchs)
Clark, Ken: *Man Called Sledge* (Vic Morrow); *Road to Fort Alamo* (Mario Bava); *Savage Gringo* (Bava/Romano)
Clark, Matt: *Kid Vengeance* (Joe Manduke)
Clark, Montgomery (also **Dante Posani**): *Djurado* (Gianni Narzisi)
Clarke, Robin: *Death Sentence* (Mario Linfranchi)
Clay, Jim: *Colt Is the Law* (Al Bradly)
Clay, Thomas: *Ramon the Mexican* (Maurizio Pradeaux)
Clein, Rita: *Execution* (Domenico Paolella)
Clemens, Pilar: *Sheriff Won't Shoot* (J. Luis Monter)
Cliff, William: *Colt 45, Five Dollars and Bandit* (Richard Chardon)
Cliver, Al (pseudonym for **Pier Luigi Conti**): *Apache Woman* (George McRoots)
Cobos, German: *Black Tigress* (Siro Marcellini); *Blood Calls to Blood* (Lewis King); **Massacre at Fort Grant* (J. Douglas); *Quinta: Fighting Proud* (Leon Klimovsky); *Reverend Colt* (Leon Klimovsky); *Secret of Captain O'Hara* (Arturo Castillo); *Wanted* (Calvin J. Padget)
Coburn, James: **Duck You Sucker* (Sergio Leone); *Massacre at Fort Holman* (Tonino Valerii)
Cobb, Jerry *see* Cobos, German
Coby, Michael (pseudonym for **Antonio Cantafora**): **And God Said to Cain* (Anthony Dawson); *Black Killer* (Lucky Moore); *Bounty Hunter in Trinity* (Oskar Faradine); *Carambola* (Ferdinando Baldi); *Carambola's Philosophy* (Ferdinando Baldi)
Cohen, Emma: *Cipolla Colt* (Enzo G. Castellari); **Cut-Throats Nine* (Joaquin R. Marchent); *Frenchie King* (Christian-Jaque)
Collete, Pierre: *Cemetery Without Crosses* (Robert Hossein)
Colli, Ernesto: *Kill the Piano Player* (Frank Bronston)
Collins, Alan (pseudonym for **Luciano Pignozzi**): *And God Said to Cain* (Anthony Dawson); **Cowards Don't Pray* (Marlon Sirko); *Dead Men Ride!* (Aldo Florio); *Price of Death* (Vincent Thomas); *Sabata* (Frank Kramer); *Sartana in the Valley of Death* (Roberto Mauri)
Colombaioni, Flavio: *Bad Kids of the West* (Tony Good)
Colosimo, Clara: *For a Book of Dollars* (Renzo Spaziani)
Colt, Dennis (also **Dennys Colt**): *Anything for a Friend* (Miles Deem); *Fistful of Death* (Miles Deem); *Four Came to Kill Sartana* (Miles Deem); *His Name Was Sam Walbash, But They Call Him Amen* (Miles Deem); *Once Upon a Time in Wild Wild West* (Enzo Matassi); *One Damned Day at Dawn* (Miles Deem); *Reach You Bastard!* (Lucky Dickerson); **Shadow of Sartana . . . Shadow of Your Death* (Sean O'Neal); *Showdown for a Badman* (Miles Deem); *Stranger That Kneels Beside the Shadow of a Corpse* (Miles Deem)
Coluzzi, Romana: *Sting of the West* (Enzo G. Castellari)
Comer, Anjanette: *Guns for San Sebastian* (Henri Vernevil)
Como, Rossella: *Tall Women* (Sidney Pink)
Congia, Vittorio: *Ben and Charlie* (Michele Lupo)
Connelly, Christopher: *Django Strikes Again* (Ted Archer)
Connery, Sean: *Shalako* (Edward Dmytryk)
Connors, Chuck: *Deserter* (Fulgozi/Kennedy); *Kill Them All and Come Back Alone* (Enzo G. Castellari); *Pancho Villa* (Eugenio Martin)
Conte, Luciano: *Shadow of Sartana . . . Shadow of Your Death* (Sean O'Neal)
Conte, Maria Pia (pseudonym—**Mary Count**; also **Mary Conte**): *And Crows Will*

Dig Your Grave (John Wood); **Dynamite Jim* (Alfonso Balcazar); *Five Dollars for Ringo* (Ignacio Iquino); *God in Heaven . . . Arizona on Earth* (John Wood)

Conte, Richard: *Death Sentence* (Mario Linfranchi)

Conti, Luciano: *Shadow of Sartana . . . Shadow of Your Death* (Sean O'Neal)

Conversi, Spartaco (also **Spanny Convery;** also **Sean Convery;** also **Spean Covery**): *And They Smelled the Strange, Exciting, Dangerous Scent of Dollars* (Italo Alfaro); *Adios Hombre* (Mario Caiano); *All Out* (Umberto Lenzi); *Bullet for the General* (Damiano Damiani); *Death at Owell Rock* (Riccardo Freda); *Django Kills Softly* (Max Hunter); *Fighters from Ave Maria* (Al Albert); *Get the Coffin Ready* (Ferdinando Baldi); *Great Silence* (Sergio Corbucci); *If One Is Born a Swine* (Al Bradly); *I'll Sell My Skin Dearly* (Ettore Fizarotti); *I Am Sartana . . . Trade Your Guns for a Coffin* (Anthony Ascott); **Left Handed Johnny West* (Frank Kramer); *Long Ride from Hell* (Alex Burks); *Minute to Pray, a Second to Die* (Franco Giraldi); *Once Upon a Time in the West* (Sergio Leone); *Paths of War* (Aldo Grimaldi); *Quintana: Dead or Alive* (Glenn V. Davis); *Sabata* (Frank Kramer); *Seven Dollars on the Red* (Alberto Cardone); *Seven Guns for Timothy* (Rod Gilbert); *Shango* (Edward G. Muller); *Three Graves for a Winchester* (Emimmo Salvi); *Twenty Thousand Dollars for Seven* (Alberto Cardone); *Two Sides of the Dollar* (Roberto Montero)

Convery, Sean *see* **Conversi, Spartaco**

Convery, Spanny *see* **Conversi, Spartaco**

Convery, Spean *see* **Conversi, Spartaco**

Cooper, Stan: *Go Away! Trinity Has Arrived in Eldorado* (Dick Spitfire); **Great Treasure Hunt* (Tonino Ricci); *More Dollars for the MacGregors* (J. L. Merino); *You're Jinxed, Friend, You Just Met Sacramento* (Giorgio Cristallini)

Corazzari, Bruno: *Belle Starr Story* (Nathan Wich); **Cost of Dying* (Sergio Merolle); *Death Rides a Horse* (Giulio Petroni); *Dig Your Grave, Friend . . . Sabata's Coming* (Ignacio Iquina); *For One Hundred Thousand Dollars Per Killing* (Giovanni Fago); *Four Gunmen of the Apocalypse* (Lucio Fulci); *Light the Fuse . . . Sartana Is Coming* (Anthony Ascott); *Man Called Sledge* (Vic Morrow); *Mercenary* (Sergio Corbucci); *Roy Colt and Winchester Jack* (Mario Bava); *Vendetta at Dawn* (Willy S. Regan)

Cord, Alex: *Minute to Pray, a Second to Die* (Franco Giraldi)

Corman, Chip *see* **Giordana, Andrea**

Corra, Teodoro: **Django the Bastard* (Sergio Garrone); *Heads or Tails* (Peter E. Stanley); *Mallory Must Not Die* (Mario Moroni); *Roy Colt and Winchester Jack* (Mario Bava)

Corri, Adrienne: *Dynamite Jack* (Jean Bastia)

Corso, Arturo: *Stranger in Town* (Stan Vance)

Cortes, Hercules: *I Came, I Saw, I Shot* (Enzo G. Castellari); *Kill Them All and Come Back Alone* (Enzo G. Castellari)

Cortes, Juan: *Cavalry Charge* (Ramon Torrado)

Cotten, Joseph: *Hellbenders* (Sergio Corbucci); **Tramplers* (Albert Band); *White Comanche* (Gilbert Lee Kay)

Coulouris, George: *Land Raiders* (Nathan Juran)

Count, Mary *see* **Conte, Maria Pia**

Cowl, Darry: *Magnificent Brutes of the West* (Fred Wilson)

Crain, Paul: *Black Killer* (Lucky Moore); *Go Away! Trinity Has Arrived in Eldorado* (Dick Spitfire)

Crawford, Broderick: *Kid Rodelo* (Richard Carlson); *Mutiny at Fort Sharp* (Fernando Cerchio); *Texican* (Espinosa/Selander)

Crenna, Richard: *Deserter* (Fulgozzi/Kennedy); *Man Called Noon* (Peter Collinson)
Cressoy, Pierre *see* **Cross, Peter**
Crisa, Erno: *Pecos Cleans Up* (Maurizio Lucidi)
Cristal, Perla (also **Perla Cristina**): *Christmas Kid* (Sidney Pink); *Dust in the Sun* (Richard Balducci); *Reverend Colt* (Leon Klimovsky); *Seven Guns for the MacGregors* (Frank Garfield); *Tall Women* (Sidney Pink); **Two Thousand Dollars for Coyote* (Leon Klimovsky); *White Comanche* (Gilbert Lee Kay)
Cristine, Katia: *Greatest Robbery in the West* (Maurizio Lucidi)
Croccolo, Carlo: *Black Killer* (Lucky Moore); **Sheriff Was a Lady* (Sobey Martin)
Cross, Peter (pseudonym for **Pierre Cressoy**): *Adios Gringo* (George Finley); **Blood for a Silver Dollar* (Calvin J. Padget); *Navajo Joe* (Sergio Corbucci)
Cruz, Maria: **Left Handed Johnny West* (Frank Kramer); *Tall Women* (Sidney Pink)
"Cuatro Brutos": *Magnificent Brutes of the West* (Fred Wilson)
Culp, Robert: *Hannie Caulder* (Burt Kennedy)
Cunningham, Bob: *Dust in the Sun* (Richard Balducci)
Curiel, Fernando: *Seven for Pancho Villa* (José M. Elorrieta)
Custodio, Anna: *Outlaw of Red River* (Maury Dexter)
Czarniak, Henri: *Frenchie King* (Christian-Jaque)
Dahl, Arlene: *Land Raiders* (Nathan Juran)
Dalbes, Alberto: **Billy the Kid* (Leon Klimovsky); *Cut-Throats Nine* (Joaquin R. Marchent)
Dalla, Lucio *see* **Dávila, Luis**
Daly, James: *Five Man Army* (Don Taylor)
Damieari, Pedro: *Eagle's Wing* (Anthony Harvey)
Damon, Mark: *All Out* (Umberto Lenzi); *Cry for Revenge* (Rafael R. Marchent); *Death at Owell Rock* (Riccardo Freda); *Great Treasure Hunt* (Tonino Ricci); *Johnny Yuma* (Romolo Guerrieri); *Let Them Rest* (Carlo Lizzani); *Pistol Packin' Preacher* (Leopoldo Savona); **Ringo and His Golden Pistol* (Sergio Corbucci); *They Call Him Veritas* (Luigi Perelli); *Train for Durango* (William Hawkins)
Dane, Peter: *Land Raiders* (Nathan Juran)
D'Anglis, Irta: *Seven Nuns in Kansas City* (Marcello Zeani)
Danning, Sybil: *God's Gun* (Frank Kramer)
D'Arpe, Gustavo: *Johnny Yuma* (Romolo Guerrieri)
Darry-Cowl: *Do Not Touch the White Woman* (Marco Ferreri)
Darwell, Virgin: *Killer Kid* (Leopoldo Savona)
Daumier, Sophie: *Fort Yuma Gold* (Calvin J. Padget)
Davenport, Nigel: *Charley One-Eye* (Don Chaffey)
Daverio, Vittorio: *Grandsons of Zorro* (Mariano Laurenti)
Dávila, Luis (pseudonym — **Luis Dawson** and **Lucio Dalla**): *Death on High Mountain* (Fred Ringoold); *Dynamite Jim* (Alfonso Balcazar); *Man from Canyon City* (Alfonso Balcazar); *Man with the Golden Pistol* (Alfonso Balcazar); *Matalo!* (Cesare Canavari); *Pancho Villa* (Eugenio Martin); *Rita of the West* (Ferdinando Baldi); **Shoot to Kill* (Ramon Torrado); *Three from Colorado* (Armando De Ossorio)
Davis, Chet: *Death Played the Flute* (Elo Panaccio); *Django and Sartana Are Coming . . . It's the End* (Dick Spitfire); *Stranger That Kneels Beside the Shadow of a Corpse* (Miles Deem)
Davis, Mark: *God Is My Colt .45* (Dean Jones)
Davoli, Ivano: *Chrysanthemums for a Bunch of Swine* (Sergio Pastore)
Davys, Carolyn: *Gunmen of Rio Grande* (Tullio Demichelli)
Dawson, Anthony: *Deadlock* (Roland Klick); **Death Rides a Horse* (Giulio Petroni); *Red Sun* (Terence Young); *Sky Full of Stars for a Roof* (Guilio Petroni)

Demichelli); *Heroes of the West (Steno); Magnificent Texan (Lewis King);
    Woman for Ringo (Rafael R. Marchent)
De Witt, Elina: Kill or Die (Amerigo Anton)
Dexter, Rosemarie (also Rosemary Dexter): Big Ripoff (Franco Rossetti); *For a Few
    Dollars More (Sergio Leone)
Dhermay, Jean-Michel: Red Hot Zorro (William Russell)
Diaz, Ricardo: Cut-Throats Nine (Joaquin R. Marchent)
Di Bernardo, Floranna: Pistol Packin' Preacher (Leopoldo Savona)
Diffring, Anton: Montana Trap (Peter Schamoni)
Di Lernia, Rita: Patience Has a Limit, We Don't (Armando Morandi)
Di Mendoza, Alberto (also Alberto De Mendoza): Awkward Hands (Rafael R. Mar-
    chent); Bullet for Sandoval (Julio Buchs); Forgotten Pistolero (Ferdinando Baldi)
Dini, Tiziana: Black Killer (Lucky Moore)
Dobbs, Vivian: Sunscorched (Alfonso Balcazar)
Dobkin, Lawrence: Johnny Yuma (Romolo Guerrieri)
Dolgin, Larry: Black Jack (Gianfranco Baldanello)
Domonici, Arturo see Kent, Arthur
Dor, Karin: Last Tomahawk (Harald Reinl); *Treasure of Silver Lake (Harald Reinl);
    Winnetou and Shatterhand in the Valley of Death (Harald Reinl); Winnetou the
    Warrior (Harald Reinl); Winnetou: Last of the Renegades (Harald Reinl); Win-
    netou: The Desperado Trail (Harald Reinl)
Doria, Luciano: Bury Them Deep (John Byrd)
D'Orsi, Umberto: Death Walks in Laredo (Enzo Peri); Dick Luft in Sacramento (An-
    thony Ascott); Man Called Invincible (Anthony Ascott); Return of Halleluja (An-
    thony Ascott); *Two Sons of Ringo (Giorgio Simonelli)
Dottesio, Attilio: Bounty Hunter in Trinity (Oskar Faradine)
Douglas, Jimmy: Django (Sergio Corbucci)
Dreyer, David: Blindman (Ferdinando Baldi); Get Mean (Ferdinando Baldi)
Dublin, Jessica: Trinity Is Still My Name (E. B. Clucher)
Dubost, Paulette: Viva Maria (Louis Malle)
Duran, Ludwig: Bullets Don't Argue (Mike Perkins)
Duryea, Dan: Hills Run Red (Lee W. Beaver)
Eastman, George (pseudonym for Luigi Montefiori or Luigi Montefiore): Bastard,
    Go and Kill (Gino Mangini); Belle Starr Story (Nathan Wich); Ben and Charlie
    (Michele Lupo); Call of the Wild (Ken Annakin); Chuck Moll (E. B. Clucher);
    Django Kills Softly (Max Hunter); *Django, Last Killer (Joseph Warren); Get the
    Coffin Ready (Ferdinando Baldi); Hate Thy Neighbor (Ferdinando Baldi); Poker
    with Pistols (Joseph Warren); Three Musketeers of the West (Bruno Corbucci);
    Vendetta at Dawn (Willy S. Regan)
Eastwood, Clint: *Fistful of Dollars (Sergio Leone); For a Few Dollars More (Sergio
    Leone); The Good, the Bad, and the Ugly (Sergio Leone)
Easton, Wallas: Mad Dog Morgan (Philippe Mora)
Edwards, Mark: Boldest Job in the West (José De La Loma)
Effa, Karel: Lemonade Joe (Oldrich Lipsky)
Egger, Joe see Calvo, José
Ehrhardt, Heinz: Legacy of the Incas (Georg Marischka)
Ekberg, Anita: Deadly Trackers (Amerigo Anton)
Elam, Jack: Hannie Caulder (Burt Kennedy); Last Rebel (Denys McCoy); *Once
    Upon a Time in the West (Sergio Leone); Sartana Does Not Forgive (Alfonso
    Balcazar)
Ellis, Mirko (also Mirko Elli): Arizona Colt (Michele Lupo); Bad Kids of the West

(Tony Good); *Buffalo Bill, Hero of the Far West* (John W. Fordson); *Canadian Wilderness* (Armando De Ossorio); *Django, Last Killer* (Joseph Warren); *Don't Turn the Other Cheek* (Duccio Tessari); *For One Thousand Dollars Per Day* (Silvio Amadio); *Hate for Hate* (Domenico Paolella); *Kill Django . . . Kill First* (Willy S. Regan); *Killer Caliber .32* (Al Bradly); *Man and a Colt* (Tullio Demichelli); *Rojo* (Leo Coleman); *Tequila* (Tullio Demichelli)

Elm-Rabben, Mascha: *Deadlock* (Roland Klick)

Ely, Ron: *Halleluja and Sartana Strike Again* (Mario Siciliano)

Eory, Iran: *Man of the Cursed Valley* (Omar Hopkins)

Erhardt, Heinz: *Rampage at Apache Wells* (Harald Philipp)

Ericson, John: *Heads or Tails* (Peter E. Stanley); *Seven for Pancho Villa* (José M. Elorrieta)

Esbri, Carmen: *For a Fist in the Eye* (Michele Lupo)

Eversfield, Elizabeth: *Vengeance Is a Dish Served Cold* (William Redford)

Fabian, Françoise: *Specialists* (Sergio Corbucci)

Fabrizi, Carlo: *Ruthless Colt of the Gringo* (José L. Madrid)

Fabrizi, Franco: *Do Not Touch the White Woman* (Marco Ferreri)

Fabrizi, Valeria: *Four Gunmen of Holy Trinity* (Giorgio Cristallini); *Ringo and His Golden Pistol* (Sergio Corbucci)

Fajardo, Eduardo: *Adios Hombre* (Mario Caiano); *All Out* (Umberto Lenzi); *Apocalypse Joe* (Leopoldo Savona); *Bad Man's River* (Eugenio Martin); *Bandara Bandits* (Sergio Corbucci); *Charge of Seventh Cavalry* (Herbert Martin); *Coffin for the Sheriff* (William Hawkins); *Compañeros* (Sergio Corbucci); *Dead Men Ride* (Aldo Florio); *Django* (Sergio Corbucci); *Don't Turn the Other Cheek* (Duccio Tessario); *Gentleman Killer* (George Finley); *Killer Goodbye* (Primo Zeglio); *Magnificent Bandits* (Giovanni Fago); *Mercenary* (Sergio Corbucci); *One Against One . . . No Mercy* (Rafael R. Marchent); *Pistol for a Hundred Coffins* (Umberto Lenzi); *Ringo: Face of Revenge* (Mario Caiano); *Ringo's Big Night* (Mario Maffei); *Sabata the Killer* (Tullio Demichelli); *Shango* (Edward G. Muller); *Sting of the West* (Enzo Castellari); *Stranger in Paso Bravo* (Salvatore Rosso); *Tequila* (Tullio Demichelli); *Three Musketeers of the West* (Bruno Corbucci); *Time of Vultures* (Nando Cicero); *What Am I Doing in the Middle of the Revolution?* (Sergio Corbucci)

Falana, Lola: *Black Tigress* (Siro Marcellini)

Falsi, Antonio: *Brothers Blue* (Marc Meyer)

Fantasia, Franco (pseudonym—Frank Farrel): *Adios Cjamango* (Harry Freeman); *Adios, Sabata* (Frank Kramer); *Blood at Sundown* (Albert Cardiff); *Blood Calls to Blood* (Lewis King); *Canadian Wilderness* (Armando De Ossorio); *Carambola* (Ferdinando Baldi); *Hate Thy Neighbor* (Ferdinando Baldi); *I Am Sartana, Trade Your Guns for a Coffin* (Anthony Ascott); *Long Ride from Hell* (Alex Burkes); *Son of Zorro* (Gianfranco Baldanello); *Three Swords of Zorro* (Ricardo Blasco); *Wrath of God* (Alberto Cardone)

Fanti, Elisabetta: *Shadow of Sartana . . . Shadow of Your Death* (Sean O'Neal)

Fantoni, Sergio: *Bad Man's River* (Eugenio Martin)

Fargas, Frank: *Django, Last Killer* (Joseph Warren); *Shadow of Sartana . . . Shadow of Your Death* (Sean O'Neal)

Faria, Celso: *Brother Outlaw* (Edward G. Muller); *Quintana: Dead or Alive* (Glenn Vincent Davis)

Farinon, Gabriella: *For a Book of Dollars* (Renzo Spaziani)

Farley, Albert (pseudonym for **Alberto Farnese**): *Dollar of Fire* (Nick Nostro); *Fighters from Ave Maria* (Al Albert); *Five Dollars for Ringo* (Ignacio Iquino);

*Kill or Die (Amerigo Anton); Scalps (Werner Knox); Seven Pistols for a Gringo (Juan X. Marchel); Twenty Paces to Death (Ted Mulligan); White Apache (Vincent Dawn)

Farnese, Alberto see **Farley, Albert**

Farrel, Frank see **Fantasia, Franco**

Fehmiu, Bekim: Deserter (Fulgozzi/Kennedy)

Feliciani, Mario: Shadow of Zorro (Joaquin R. Marchent)

Felleghi, Tom (also **Tom Felleghy** and **Tom Felighi**): Big Gundown (Sergio Sollima); Black Tigress (Siro Marcellini); Born to Kill (Tony Mulligan); California (Michele Lupo); *Cisco (Sergio Bergonzelli); Deaf Smith and Johnny Ears (Paolo Cavara); His Name Was King (Don Reynolds); If You Want to Live . . . Shoot! (Willy S. Regan); Machine Gun Killers (Paolo Bianchini); Man from Oklahoma (Robert M. White); Massacre Time (Lucio Fulci); Ringo's Big Night (Mario Maffei); Two Pistols and a Coward (Calvin J. Padget); Two Sides of a Dollar (Roberto Montero)

Felmy, Hansjörg: Pirates of the Mississippi (Jürgen Roland)

Felton, Bob: Left Handed Johnny West (Frank Kramer)

Fenech, Edwige: Heads or Tails (Peter E. Stanley)

Fennell, Sylvie: Specialists (Sergio Corbucci)

Fernandel: Dynamite Jack (Jean Bastia)

Fernandez, Jaime: Guns for San Sebastian (Henri Verneuil)

Ferrara, Pino: Carambola (Ferdinando Baldi)

Ferzetti, Gabriele: Once Upon a Time in the West (Sergio Leone)

Fialova, Kveta: Lemonade Joe (Oldrich Lipsky)

Field, Karin: Return of Shanghai Joe (Bitto Albertini)

Field, Sam: Gunfight at Red Sands (Ricardo Blasco)

Fiermonte, Enzo: Greatest Robbery in the West (Maurizio Lucidi); *Minute to Pray, a Second to Die (Franco Giraldi); They Called Him Veritas (Luigi Perelli)

Fineschi, Lorenzo: His Name Was King (Don Reynolds); Magnificent West (Gianni Crea); On the Third Day Arrived the Crow (Gianni Crea)

Fioraranti, Gilsua: Cjamango (Edward G. Muller)

Fiori, Maurizio: Bad Kids of the West (Tony Good)

Fitzek, Sigurd: Deadlock (Roland Klick)

Fleischmann, Herbert: Hatred of God (Claudio Gora)

Flori, Agata: Heads You Die . . . Tails I Kill You (Anthony Ascott); I Came, I Saw, I Shot (Enzo G. Castellari); Nephews of Zorro (Frank Reed); Return of Halleluja (Anthony Ascott); *Seven Guns for the MacGregors (Frank Garfield); Up the MacGregors! (Frank Garfield)

Flynn, Sean: Seven Guns for Timothy (Rod Gilbert); *Sign of Zorro (Mario Caiano); Woman for Ringo (Rafael R. Marchent)

Fonda, Henry: My Name Is Nobody (Tonino Valerii); *Once Upon a Time in the West (Sergio Leone)

Fontana, Lola: Black Tigress (Siro Marcellini)

Ford, Montgomery see **Halsey, Brett**

Forner, Lola: White Apache (Vincent Dawn)

Forest, Michael: Death Played the Flute (Elo Panaccio); Desperado (Al Bagrain); Last Rebel (Denys McCoy); *Requiem for a Bounty Hunter (Mark Welles)

Forsyte, George: More Dollars for the MacGregors (J. L. Merino)

Forsyte, Stephen: Blood Calls to Blood (Lewis King); *Death at Owell Rock (Riccardo Freda); In a Colt's Shadow (Gianni Grimaldi)

Fox, Herbert see **Fux, Herbert**

Fox, Paddy: *Flaming Frontier* (Alfred Vohrer)

France, Marie: *Last Tomahawk* (Harald Reinl)

Franchetti, Rina: *Massacre Time* (Lucio Fulci)

Franchetti, Sara: *Buddy Goes West* (Michele Lupo)

Franchi, Franco: *Ciccio Forgives, I Don't* (Frank Reed); *For a Fist in the Eye* (Michele Lupo); *Grandsons of Zorro* (Mariano Laurenti); *Handsome, the Ugly, and the Stupid* (Gianni Grimaldi); *Nephews of Zorro* (Frank Reed); *Paths of War* (Aldo Grimaldi); **Two Gangsters in the Wild West* (Giorgio Simonelli); *Two R-R-Ringos from Texas* (Frank Martin); *Two Sergeants of General Custer* (Giorgio Simonelli); *Two Sons of Ringo* (Giorgio Simonelli); *Two Sons of Trinity* (Glenn Eastman)

Francis, Anne: *Pancho Villa* (Eugenio Martin)

Frank, Horst: *Big Showdown* (Giancarlo Santi); *Black Eagle of Santa Fe* (Ernst Hofbauer); *Bullets Don't Argue* (Mike Perkins); *Carambola* (Ferdinando Baldi); *Get the Coffin Ready* (Ferdinando Baldi); *Hate Thy Neighbor* (Ferdinando Baldi); *Johnny Hamlet* (Enzo G. Castellari); *Massacre at Marble City* (Franz J. Gottlieb); *The Moment to Kill* (Anthony Ascott); **Pirates of the Mississippi* (Jürgen Roland); *Winnetou: Last of the Renegades* (Harald Reinl)

Franklin, Mariel: *Tramplers* (Albert Band)

Frederick, Lynn: *Four Gunmen of the Apocalypse* (Lucio Fulci); *Red Coat* (Joe D'Amato)

Freeman, Anthony: **Ballad of a Gunman* (Alfio Caltabiano); *Death Played the Flute* (Elo Panaccio); *Holy Water Joe* (Mario Gariazzo); *Two Crosses at Danger Pass* (Rafael R. Marchent)

Frey, Barbara: *Let Them Rest* (Carlo Lizzani); *Stranger in Sacramento* (Serge Bergon)

Fritson, Thomas: *Last Ride to Santa Cruz* (Rolf Olsen)

Frye, Virgil: *Lucky Johnny: Born in America* (José Antonio Balanos)

Fuchsberger, Joachim (also **Joachim Fushsburger**): *Last Tomahawk* (Harald Reinl); *Who Killed Johnny R.?* (José Luis Madrid)

Furman, Rosa: *Guns of San Sebastian* (Henri Verneuil)

Furstenberg, Ira: *Deaf Smith and Johnny Ears* (Paolo Cavara)

Fury, Men see Meniconi, Furio

Fux, Herbert (also **Herbert Fox**): *Bandara Bandits* (Sergio Corbucci); *Beyond the Law* (Giorgio Stegani); *Trinity Plus the Clown and a Guitar* (François Legrand)

Gabel, Scilla: *Djurado* (Gianni Narzisi); *Bastard, Go and Kill* (Gino Mangini)

Gaddi, Carlo (also **Carlo Gatti** and **Gengher Gatti**): *Beyond the Law* (Giorgio Stegani); *Death Rides Alone* (Joseph Warren); *Django the Bastard* (Sergio Garrone); *Duel in the Eclipse* (Martino/Merino); *Even Django Has His Price* (Paolo Solvay); *For One Hundred Thousand Dollars Per Killing* (Sidney Lean); *God in Heaven . . . Arizona on Earth* (John Wood); *Kill the Poker Player* (Mario Bianchi); *I Am Sartana, Trade Your Guns for a Coffin* (Anthony Ascott); *My Horse, My Gun, Your Widow* (John Wood); **Pecos Cleans Up* (Maurizio Lucidi); *To Hell and Back* (Giovanni Fago)

Gail, Custer: *His Name Was Sam Walbash, But They Call Him Amen* (Miles Deem)

Galan, Mary: *Scalps* (Werner Knox)

Galbo, Cristina: *Fury of Johnny Kid* (Gianni Puccini); *Twice a Judas* (Nando Cicero)

Galiana, Manuel: *Cowards Don't Pray* (Marlon Sirko)

Galimbi, Gilberto: *Animal Called Man* (Roberto Mauri); *Gunmen and the Holy Ghost* (Roberto Mauri)

Galli, Ida see Stewart, Evelyn

Gallotti, Dada (also **Dada Galotti**): *Deadly Trackers* (Amerigo Anton); *Johnny Yuma* (Romolo Guerrieri); *Once Upon a Time in the Wild Wild West* (Enzo Matassi)

Garay, Nestor: *Execution* (Domenico Paolella)

Garcia, Tito: *All Out* (Umberto Lenzi); *God Forgives, I Don't* (Giuseppe Colizzi); *I Came, I Saw, I Shot* (Enzo G. Castellari); *None of the Three Were Called Trinity* (Pedro L. Ramirez); **Seven Guns for Timothy* (Rod Gilbert); *With Friends, Nothing Is Easy* (Steve MacCohy)

Gardner, Clyde: *Hate Thy Neighbor* (Ferdinando Baldi)

Gargano, Lea: *Seven Nuns in Kansas City* (Marcello Zeanile)

Gargano, Omero: *Deadly Trackers* (Amerigo Anton)

Gargiullo, Giorgio: *Death Rides Alone* (Joseph Warren); *Hole in the Forehead* (Joseph Warren)

Garisa, Antonio: *Torrejon City* (Leon Klimovsky)

Garko, Gianni (pseudonym—**Gary Hudson**): *Bad Man's River* (Eugenio Martin); *Blood at Sundown* (Albert Cardiff); *Cowards Don't Pray* (Marlon Sirko); *For One Hundred Thousand Dollars Per Killing* (Sidney Lean); *Forewarned, Half-Killed . . . the Word of the Holy Ghost* (Anthony Ascott); *Have a Good Funeral, My Friend . . . Sartana Will Pay* (Anthony Ascott); *His Name Was Holy Ghost* (Anthony Ascott); *I Am Sartana, Your Angel of Death* (Anthony Ascott); *Light the Fuse . . . Sartana Is Coming* (Anthony Ascott); *Price of Death* (Vincent Thomas); *Sartana* (Frank Kramer); *Sartana Kills Them All* (Rafael R. Marchent); **Ten Thousand Dollars Blood Money* (Romolo Guerrieri); *They Call Him Cemetery* (Anthony Ascott); *Those Dirty Dogs* (Giuseppe Rosati)

Garner, James: *Man Called Sledge* (Morrow/Gentili)

Garof, Anthony: *Thirty Winchesters for El Diablo* (Frank G. Carrol)

Garofalo, Franco: *They Called Him Veritas* (Luigi Perelli)

Garret, Rick *see* **Garrone, Riccardo**

Garrett, Leif: *God's Gun* (Frank Kramer); *Kid Vengeance* (Joe Manduke)

Garrone, Riccardo (pseudonym—**Dick Reagan** and **Rick Garret**): *Bang Bang Kid* (Luciano Lelli); *Deguello* (Joseph Warren); *Django the Bastard* (Sergio Garrone); *If You Want to Live, Shoot!* (Willy S. Regan); *Kill Django . . . Kill First* (Willy S. Regan); *Man Called Sledge* (Vic Morrow); *No Room to Die* (Willy S. Regan); *Return of Halleluja* (Anthony Ascott); *Sting of the West* (Enzo G. Castellari); **Two Sergeants of General Custer* (Giorgio Simonelli); *What Am I Doing in the Middle of the Revolution?* (Sergio Corbucci)

Garson, Diana: *Dollar of Fire* (Nick Nostro); *Left Handed Johnny West* (Frank Kramer)

Gasperini, Italo: *Magnificent West* (Gianni Crea)

Gassman, Vittorio: *What Am I Doing in the Middle of the Revolution?* (Sergio Corbucci)

Gatti, Carlo, or **Gatti, Gengher** *see* **Gaddi, Carlo**

Gattou, Evelyne: *Red Hot Zorro* (William Russell)

Gazzolo, Nando: *Django Shoots First* (Alberto De Martino); *Hills Run Red* (Lee W. Beaver)

Gelin, Xavier: *Judge Roy Bean* (Richard Owens)

Gemma, Giuliano (also **Montgomery Wood**): **Adios Gringo* (George Finley); *Alive or Preferably Dead* (Duccio Tessari); *Arizona Colt* (Michele Lupo); *Ben and Charlie* (Michele Lupo); *Blood for a Silver Dollar* (Calvin J. Padget); *California* (Michele Lupo); *Day of Anger* (Tonino Valerii); *Fort Yuma Gold* (Calvin J. Padget); *Long Days of Vengeance* (Stan Vance); *Pistol for Ringo* (Duccio Tessari); *Price of Power* (Tonino Valerii); *Return of Ringo* (Duccio Tessari); *Silver Saddle* (Lucio Fulci); *Sky Full of Stars for a Roof* (Giulio Petroni); *Tex and*

Lord of the Deep (Duccio Tessari); *Wanted* (Calvin J. Padget); *White, the Yellow and the Black* (Sergio Corbucci)

Genka, Gely: *Price of Death* (Vincent Thomas)

George, Götz: *Among Vultures* (Alfred Vohrer); *Half Breed* (Harald Philipp); *Man Called Gringo* (Roy Rowland); **Treasure of Silver Lake* (Harold Reinl)

George, Susan: *Bandara Bandits* (Sergio Corbucci)

George, Victoria: *Last Rebel* (Denys McCoy)

Georgiade, Dick: *Eye for an Eye* (Albert Marshall)

Getz, Gaby: *Three Bullets for a Long Gun* (Peter Henkel)

Ghia, Dana (pseudonym—Dana Ghia): *Big Ripoff* (Franco Rossetti); *California* (Michele Lupo); *Deguello* (Joseph Warren); *Django, Last Killer* (Joseph Warren); **Four Dollars for Vengeance* (Alfonso Balcazar); *Wrath of God* (Alberto Cardone)

Ghidra, Anthony: **Ballad of a Gunman* (Alfio Caltabiano); *Django, Last Killer* (Joseph Warren); *Hole in the Forehead* (Joseph Warren); *May God Forgive You But I Won't* (Glenn V. Davis), *Time and Place of Killing* (Vincent Eagle)

Giacobini, Franco: *Bandera Bandits* (Sergio Corbucci)

Giancara, Pia: *Finders Killers* (Gianni Crea)

Gianni, Fabrizio: *Reward's Yours, the Man's Mine* (Edward G. Muller)

Gil, Manuel: *For One Thousand Dollars Per Day* (Silvio Amadio)

Giller, Walter: *Legacy of the Incas* (Georg Marischka)

Gilli, Luciana (also **Luciana Gill**; also **Lucy Gilly**): *Coffin for the Sheriff* (William Hawkins); *Colt Is the Law* (Al Bradly); *Death at Owell Rock* (Riccardo Freda); *Pecos Cleans Up* (Maurizio Lucidi)

Gilliam, Reginald: *Christmas Kid* (Sidney Pink)

Gilmour, Geoff: *Ned Kelly* (Tony Richardson)

Gimenez, Susanna: *Macho Killers* (Mark Andrew)

Gimpera, Teresa: *Wanted* (Calvin J. Padget)

Gioi, Viva: *Goes Does Not Pay on Saturday* (Amerigo Anton)

Giomini, Romano: *Five Dollars for Ringo* (Ignacio Iquino)

Giordana, Andrea (pseudonym—**Chip Corman** and **Chip Gorman**): *Big Ripoff* (Franco Rossetti); *Cost of Dying* (Sergio Merolle); *Johnny Hamlet* (Enzo G. Castellari); **Massacre at Grand Canyon* (Stanley Corbett)

Giordana, Daniela: *Challenge of the MacKennas* (Leon Klimovsky); **Find a Place to Die* (Anthony Ascott); *Five Man Army* (Don Taylor); *Four Came to Kill Sartana* (Miles Deem); *Four Gunmen of the Holy Trinity* (Giorgio Cristallini); *Go Away! Trinity Has Arrived in Eldorado* (Dick Spitfire); *Have a Good Funeral, My Friend . . . Sartana Will Pay* (Anthony Ascott); *Hero Called Allegria* (Dennis Ford); *Long Day of the Massacre* (Albert Cardiff); *Trinity and Sartana Are Coming* (Mario Siciliano)

Giordana, Mariangela (also **Maria Angela Giordana**): *No Graves on Boot Hill* (Willy S. Regan); *No Room to Die* (Willy S. Regan)

Giordano, Carlo: *Hatred of God* (Claudio Gora); *He Was Called Holy Ghost* (Robert Johnson); *I Am Sartana, Trade Your Gun for a Coffin* (Anthony Ascott); *Sartana in the Valley of Death* (Roberto Mauri)

Giorgelli, Gabriel: *Beast* (Mario Costa); *Durango Is Coming, Pay or Die* (Luis Monter); *Long Days of Vengeance* (Stan Vance); *Mallory Must Not Die* (Mario Moroni); *Shango* (Edward G. Muller); *Two Sides of the Dollar* (Roberto Montero)

Giornelli, Franco: *Big Ripoff* (Franco Rossetii); *Execution* (Domenico Paolella)

Giraldi, Alberto: *For a Few Dollars Less* (Mario Mattoli)

Girardon, Michele: *I'll Sell My Skin Dearly* (Ettore Fizarotti); *Pyramid of the Sun God* (Robert Siodmak)

Girolami, Enio (pseudonym — Thomas Moore): *Between God, the Devil and a Winchester* (Dario Silvestri); **Black Eagle of Santa Fe* (Ernst Hofbauer); *Bullets and the Flesh* (Fred Wilson); *Death Knows No Time* (Leon Klimovsky); *Few Dollars for Django* (Leon Klimovsky); *Hellbenders* (Sergio Corbucci); *Payment in Blood* (E. G. Rowland); *Reverend Colt* (Leon Klimovsky); *Two R-R-Ringos from Texas* (Frank Martin)

Girolami, Enzo: *Bullets and the Flesh* (Fred Wilson); *Johnny Hamlet* (Enzo G. Castellari)

Giuffré, Aldo:*The Good, the Bad, and the Ugly* (Sergio Leone); *Two Gangsters in the Wild West* (Giorgio Simonelli)

Glas, Uschi (pseudonym for Vismana, Wanda): *Halleluja and Sartana Strike Again* (Mario Siciliano)

Glass, Ursula: *Half Breed* (Harald Philipp)

Goda, Alfonzo: *Ringo: Face of Revenge* (Mario Caiano)

Gonzales, Fidel: *Johnny Yuma* (Romolo Guerrieri)

Gonzales, Indio: *And the Crows Will Dig Your Grave* (John Wood); *Dig Your Grave, Friend . . . Sabata Is Coming* (John Wood); *Dollar of Fire* (Nick Nostro); *Five Dollars for Ringo* (Ignacio Iquino); *God in Heaven . . . Arizona on Earth* (John Wood); *Shoot Joe, and Shoot Again* (Hal Brady)

Goodwin, Ralph: *Massacre at Fort Holman* (Tonino Valerii)

Gora, Claudio: *Five Man Army* (Don Taylor); *Hellbenders* (Sergio Corbucci); *John the Bastard* (Armando Crispino)

Gordon, Georges: *Fury of the Apaches* (Joe Lacy)

Gordon, Leo: *My Name Is Nobody* (Tonino Valerii)

Gordon, Lewis: *Comin' at Ya* (Ferdinando Baldi)

Gordon, Marty: *Last Gun* (Sergio Bergonzelli)

Gorman, Chip *see* Giordana, Andrea

Goritto, Mario *see* Hill, Terence

Gozlino, Paolo (pseudonym — Paul Stevens): *Clint the Stranger* (Alfonso Balcazar); *Desperado* (Al Bagrain); *Django the Bastard* (Sergio Garrone); *Forewarned, Half-Killed . . . the Word of Holy Ghost* (Anthony Ascott); *Heads You Die . . . Tails I Kill You* (Anthony Ascott); *One After Another* (Nick Howard); *Return of Halleluja* (Anthony Ascott); *Thunder Over El Paso* (Roberto Montero); *To Hell and Back* (Giovanni Fago); **Vengeance* (Anthony Dawson)

Gradoli, Antonio (pseudonym — Anthony Gradwell): *Death on High Mountain* (Fred Ringoold); *Road to Fort Alamo* (Mario Bava)

Gradwell, Anthony *see* Gradoli, Antonio

Graf, Peter: *Nude Django* (Ron Elliot)

Granata, Graziella (also Maria Granata and Maria Granada): *Beyond the Law* (Giorgio Stegani); *Big Gundown* (Sergio Sollima); *Gunfighters of Casa Grande* (Roy Rowland); **Savage Guns* (Michael Carreras); *Son of a Gunfighter* (Paul Landres)

Granger, Farley: *Man Called Noon* (Peter Collinson); *They Call Me Trinity* (E. B. Clucher)

Granger, Stewart: **Among Vultures* (Alfred Vohrer); *Flaming Frontier* (Alfred Vohrer); *Rampage at Apache Wells* (Harald Philipp)

Grant, Arthur *see* Lawrence, Peter Lee

Grant, Esther: *Billy the Kid* (Leon Klimovsky)

Graves, Peter: *Five Man Army* (Don Taylor)

Gravy, Claudia: *Matalo!* (Cesare Canavari); *Rebels of Arizona* (José M. Zabalza)

Gray, Carole: *Duel at Sundown* (Leopoldo Lahola)

Grayson, Margaret: *Ride and Kill* (J. L. Boraw)

Graziogsi, Franco: *Deaf Smith and Johnny Ears* (Paolo Cavara); *Duck You Sucker* (Sergio Leone)

Greci, José: *Bury Them Deep* (John Byrd)

Greco, Cosetta: *Sheriff of Rock Spring* (Anthony Green)

Green, Pamela *see* Tudor, Pamela

Green, Peter *see* Lawrence, Peter Lee

Greenwood, George: *Law of Violence* (Gianni Crea); *Magnificent Texan* (Lewis King)

Greenwood, Monty *see* Poli, Maurice

Grey, Fanny: *None of the Three Were Called Trinity* (Pedro L. Ramirez); *With Friends, Nothing Is Easy* (Steve MacCohy)

Grimaldi, Gabriella: *Johnny Hamlet* (Enzo G. Castellari)

Grumberg, Klaus: *Big Showdown* (Giancarlo Santi)

Guarnieri, Armando: *Go with God, Gringo* (Edward G. Muller)

Guglielmi, Marco: *Bandidos* (Max Dillman)

Guitian, Manuel: *Too Much Gold for One Gringo* (Juan Bosch)

Gulpilil, David: *Mad Dog Morgan* (Philippe Mora)

Gunther, Lotar: *Handsome, Ugly, and the Stupid* (Giovanni Grimaldi)

Guzman, Jesus: *Death on High Mountain* (Fred Ringoold)

Guzzanca, Gino: *Don't Wait, Django . . . Shoot* (Edward G. Muller)

Hackman, Gene: *Hunting Party* (Don Medford)

Hahn, Jess (also Gisela Hahn): *Big Showdown* (Giancarlo Santi); *Don't Turn the Other Cheek* (Duccio Tessari); **Dynamite Jack* (Jean Bastia)

Hall, Lynn: *Nude Django* (Ron Elliot)

Hallyday, Johnny: *Specialists* (Sergio Corbucci)

Halsey, Brett (pseudonym—Montgomery Wood and Jerry Wilson): *Cowards Don't Pray* (Marlon Sirko); **Kill Johnny Ringo* (Frank G. Carrol); *Roy Colt and Winchester Jack* (Mario Bava); *Today It's Me . . . Tomorrow You* (Tonino Cervi); *Twenty Thousand Dollars for Seven* (Albert Cardiff); *Wrath of God* (Alberto Cardone)

Hamilton, George: *Viva Maria* (Louis Malle)

Hamilton, John: *Django, Last Killer* (Joseph Warren); *Revenge for Revenge* (Ray Calloway)

Hammond, Hally (pseudonym for Lorella De Luca): *Pistol for Ringo* (Duccio Tessari); *Return of Ringo* (Duccio Tessari)

Hansel, Arthur: *An Eye for an Eye* (Albert Marshall)

Hansen, Joachim: *Black Eagle of Santa Fe* (Ernst Hofbauer)

Hardin, Ty: *Drummer of Vengeance* (Robert Paget); *Holy Water Joe* (Mario Gariazzo); *Last Rebel* (Denys McCoy); **Man of Cursed Valley* (Omar Hopkins); *Savage Pampas* (Hugo Fregonese); *Vendetta at Dawn* (Willy S. Regan); *You're Jinxed Friend, You Just Met Sacramento* (Giorgio Cristallini)

Hargitay, Mickey: *Cjamango* (Edward G. Muller); *Ringo, It's Massacre Time* (Mario Pinauti); *Sheriff Won't Shoot* (J. Luis Monter); **Stranger in Sacramento* (Serge Bergon); *Three Graves for a Winchester* (Emimmo Salvi)

Harmstorf, Raymond: **Genius* (Damiano Damiani); *Manhunt* (Larry Ludman)

Harris, Brad: *Black Eagle of Santa Fe* (Ernst Hofbauer); *Death Is Sweet from the Soldier of God* (Robert Johnson); *Durango Is Coming, Pay or Die* (Luis Monter); *Massacre at Marble City* (Franz J. Gottlieb); **Pirates of the Mississippi* (Jürgen Roland); *Rattler Kid* (Leon Klimovsky); *Wanted Sabata* (Robert Johnson)

Harrison, Dan: **Bullets and the Flesh* (Fred Wilson); *Piluk, the Timid One* (Guido Celano); *Seven Pistols for a Gringo* (Juan X. Marchel)

Harrison, Fred: *Desperado* (Al Bagrain)

Harrison, James: *Kill Johnny Ringo* (Frank G. Carrol)

Harrison, Richard: *Between God, the Devil, and a Winchester* (Dario Silvestri); *Deadly Trackers* (Amerigo Anton); *Dig Your Grave, Friend . . . Sabata's Coming* (John Woods); **Gunfight at High Noon* (Joaquin R. Marchent); *Gunfight at Red Sands* (Richard Blasco); *His Name Was King* (Don Reynolds); *Holy Water Joe* (Mario Gariazzo); *Jesse and Lester, Two Brothers in a Place Called Trinity* (James London); *One After Another* (Nick Howard); *One Hundred Thousand Dollars for Ringo* (Alberto De Martino); *Reverend Colt* (Leon Klimovsky); *Rojo* (Leo Coleman); *Sheriff of Rock Spring* (Anthony Green); *Shoot Joe, and Shoot Again* (Hal Brady); *Vengeance* (Anthony Dawson); *With Friends, Nothing Is Easy* (Steve MacCohy)

Harrison, Sebastian: *White Apache* (Vincent Dawn)

Haskins, Edmund: *Last Ride to Santa Cruz* (Rolf Olsen)

Hasse, Hannjo: *Trail of the Falcon* (Gottfried Költitz)

Hatcher, Zachary: *For One Thousand Dollars Per Day* (Silvio Amadio)

Hawkins, Jack: *Shalako* (Edward Dmytryk)

Hayden, Billy: *Coyote* (Joaquin R. Marchent); **Gunfight at High Noon* (Joaquin R. Marchent)

Hayden, Sterling: *Cipolla Colt* (Enzo G. Castellari)

Haywood, Louis: *Christmas Kid* (Sidney Pink)

Heflin, Van: *Ruthless Four* (Giorgio Capitani)

Heilberg, Brigitte: *Lost Treasure of the Incas* (Piero Pierotti)

Hellman, Peter: *Django Kills Softly* (Max Hunter)

Henderson, Kelo: *Pyramid of the Sun God* (Robert Siodmak)

Hendriks, Jan: *Buffalo Bill, Hero of the Far West* (John W. Fordson)

Henry, Bob: *Colt in Hand of the Devil* (Sergio Bergonzelli)

Herbert, Percy: *Captain Apache* (Alexander Singer)

Herlin, Jacques: *Adios Hombre* (Mario Caiano); *Fort Yuma Gold* (Calvin J. Paget); *Two Sides of the Dollar* (Roberto Montero); *Yankee* (Tinto Brass)

Herr, Trude: *Sheriff Was a Lady* (Söbey Martin)

Hersent, Philippe: *Four Gunmen of Holy Trinity* (Giorgio Cristallini); *If One Is Born a Swine, Kill Him* (Al Bradly)

Herter, Gerard: *Adios, Sabata* (Frank Kramer); **Big Gundown* (Sergio Sollima); *Go Kill and Come Back* (Enzo G. Castellari); *Machine Gun Killers* (Paolo Bianchini); *Red Blood, Yellow Gold* (Nando Cicero); *To Hell and Back* (Giovanni Fago); *Two Sides of the Dollar* (Roberto Montero)

Hertzog, George: *Man from Oklahoma* (Robert M. White)

Hery, Silvette *see* Miou Miou

Heske, Karin: *Dallas* (Juan Bosch)

Hess, David: *Montana Trap* (Peter Schamoni)

Heston, George *see* Stacciolli, Ivano

Heston, John *see* Stacciolli, Ivano

Hetherly, May: *Torrejon City* (Leon Klimovsky)

Hill, Craig: *Adios Hombre* (Mario Caiano); *And Crows Will Dig Your Grave* (John Wood); *Animal Called Man* (Roberto Mauri); *Bury Them Deep* (John Byrd); *Drummer of Vengeance* (Robert Paget); *Fifteen Scaffolds for the Killer* (Nunzio Malasomma); *Go Away! Trinity Has Arrived* (Dick Spitfire); *Gunmen and the Holy Ghost* (Roberto Mauri); **Hands of a Gunman* (Rafael R. Marchent); *I Want Him Dead* (Paolo Bianchi); *In the Name of the Father, the Son, and the Colt* (Frank Bronston); *My Horse, My Gun, Your Widow* (John Wood); *No Graves on*

Boot Hill (Willy S. Regan); *Rick and John, Conquerors of the West* (Osvaldo Civirani); *Taste for Killing* (Tonino Valerii)

Hill, Terence (pseudonym for **Mario Girotti**): *Ace High* (Giuseppe Colizzi); **Among Vultures* (Alfred Vohrer); *Boot Hill* (Giuseppe Colizzi); *Duel at Sundown* (Leopoldo Lahola); *Flaming Frontier* (Alfred Vohrer); *Genius* (Damiano Damiani); *Get the Coffin Ready* (Ferdinando Baldi); *God Forgives, I Don't* (Giuseppe Colizzi); *Man of the East* (E. B. Clucher); *My Name Is Nobody* (Tonino Valerii); *Rampage at Apache Wells* (Harald Philipp); *Rita of the West* (Ferdinando Baldi); *They Call Me Trinity* (E. B. Clucher); *Trinity Is Still My Name* (E. B. Clucher); *Trinity Sees Red* (Mario Camus); *Winnetou: Last of the Renegades* (Harald Reinl)

Hilton, George: *Bullet for Sandoval* (Julio Buchs); *Dead for a Dollar* (Osvaldo Civirani); *Dick Luft in Sacramento* (Anthony Ascott); *Go Kill and Come Back* (Enzo G. Castellari); *Greatest Robbery in the West* (Maurizio Lucidi); *Heads You Die . . . Tails I Kill You* (Anthony Ascott); *I Am Sartana, Trade Your Guns for a Coffin* (Anthony Ascott); *Kitoaah, the Man Who Came from the North* (Joseph Marvin); *Macho Killers* (Mark Andrew); *Man Called Invincible* (Anthony Ascott); *Massacre Time* (Lucio Fulci); *The Moment to Kill* (Anthony Ascott); *Poker with Pistols* (Joseph Warren); *Red Blood, Yellow Gold* (Nando Cicero); *Return of Halleluja* (Anthony Ascott); *Ruthless Four* (Giorgio Capitani); *Time of Vultures* (Nando Cicero); *To Hell and Back* (Giovanni Fago); *Trinity Plus the Clown and a Guitar* (François Legrand); **Two Sons of Ringo* (Giorgio Simonelli); *Who's Afraid of Zorro* (Franco Lo Cascio)

Hinduñi, Luis *see* **Induñi, Luis**

Hinz, Michael: *Return of Halleluja* (Anthony Ascott)

Hirenbach, Karl *see* **Lawrence, Peter Lee**

Holden, Peter: *Piluk, the Timid One* (Guido Celano)

Holden, Scott: *Calibre .38* (Toni Secchi)

Hope, Clara: **Deadly Trackers* (Amerigo Anton); *Death Played the Flute* (Elo Panaccio); *Halleluja to Vera Cruz* (Newman Rostel)

Hoppe, Marriane: *Massacre at Marble City* (Franz J. Gottlieb)

Hoppe, Ralph: *Trail of the Falcon* (Gottfried Kölditz)

Hopper, Dennis: *Mad Dog Morgan* (Philippe Mora)

Horn, Rick: *Man from Oklahoma* (Robert M. White)

Horne, Geoffrey: *Magnificent Three* (Joaquin R. Marchent)

Hossein, Robert: *Cemetery Without Crosses* (Robert Hossein); *Judge Roy Bean* (Richard Owens); *Once Upon a time in the West* (Sergio Leone); **Taste of Violence* (Robert Hossein)

Hoven, Adrian: *Jesse James' Kid* (Antonio Del Amo); *Seven Hours of Gunfire* (Joaquin R. Marchent)

Howard, Ron: *Hunting Party* (Don Medford)

Howland, Chris: *Winnetou the Warrior* (Harald Reinl)

Hoyveld, Tiffany: *Ace High* (Giuseppe Colizzi)

Hudson, Gary *see* **Garko, Gianni**

Huerta, Cris (also **Chris Huertas**, **Chris Huerta**, and **Chris Huertas**): *Alive or Preferably Dead* (Duccio Tessari); *Bandidos* (Max Dillman); *Dick Luft in Sacramento* (Anthony Ascott); *Frenchie King* (Christian-Jaque); *His Name Was Holy Ghost* (Anthony Ascott); *Let's Go and Kill Sartana* (Mario Pinzauti); *Man Called Invincible* (Anthony Ascott); **Massacre at Fort Grant* (J. Douglas); *My Colt, Not Yours* (Steve MacCohy); *My Horse, My Gun, Your Widow* (John Wood); *Navajo Joe* (Sergio Corbucci); *None of the Three Were Called Trinity*

(Pedro L. Ramirez); *One Against One . . . No Mercy* (Rafael R. Marchent); *Relentless Four* (Primo Zeglio); *Reverend Colt* (Leon Klimovsky); *Sabata the Killer* (Tullio Demichelli); *Sartana Kills Them All* (Rafael R. Marchent); *Seven Guns for the MacGregors* (Frank Garfield); *Seven Hours of Gunfire* (Joaquin R. Marchent); *Sky Full of Stars for a Roof* (Giulio Petroni); *Three Musketeers of the West* (Bruno Corbucci); *Three Supermen of the West* (Italo Martinenghi); *Town Called Hell* (Robert Parrish); *Valley of Dancing Widows* (Volker Vogeler); *With Friends, Nothing Is Easy* (Steve MacCohy)

Huetos, Francisco: *Clint the Stranger* (Alfonso Balcazar)

Hundar, Robert (pseudonym for **Claudio Undari;** also **Bob Hunter**): *California* (Michele Lupo); *Cut-Throats Nine* (Joaquin R. Marchent); *Death Rides Alone* (Joseph Warren); *Dollars for a Fast Gun* (Joaquin R. Marchent); *Fighting Fists of Shanghai Joe* (Mario Caiano); *Gunfight at High Noon* (Joaquin R. Marchent); *Hole in the Forehead* (Joseph Warren); *Jesse James' Kid* (Antonio Del Amo); *Magnificent Three* (Joaquin R. Marchent); *Man and a Colt* (Tullio Demichelli); *Man Who Cried for Revenge* (William Hawkins); *Ramon the Mexican* (Maurizio Pradeaux); *Red Coat* (Joe D'Amato); *Relentless Four* (Primo Zeglio); *Return of Sabata* (Frank Kramer); **Ride and Kill* (J. L. Boraw); *Sabata* (Frank Kramer); *Seven Guns from Texas* (Joaquin R. Marchent); *Shadow of Zorro* (Joaquin R. Marchent); *Too Much Gold for One Gringo* (Juan Bosch)

Hunter, Bob *see* **Hundar, Robert**

Hunter, Gregg: *Here We Are Again, Eh Providence?* (Alberto De Martino); *Sometimes Life Is Hard, Right Providence?* (Giulio Petroni)

Hunter, Jeffrey: *Christmas Kid* (Sidney Pink); *Find a Place to Die* (Anthony Ascott); *Murieta* (George Sherman)

Hunter, Tab: *Shotgun* (Robert Mauri)

Hunter, Thomas: *Death Walks in Laredo* (Enzo Peri); *Hills Run Red* (Lee W. Beaver)

Hussenot, Oliver: *Gunmen of Rio Grande* (Tullio Demichelli)

Huster, Francie: *Another Man, Another Woman* (Claude Lelouch)

Huston, John: *Deserter* (Fulgozzi/Kennedy)

Igliozzi, Daniella: *Blood at Sundown* (Albert Cardiff); *God Does Not Pay on Saturday* (Amerigo Anton)

Incontrera, Annabella: **Bullet for Sandoval* (Julio Buchs); *Challenge of the MacKennas* (Leon Klimovsky); *Poker with Pistols* (Joseph Warren); *Return of Sabata* (Frank Kramer)

Induñi, Luis (also **Luis Hinduñi**): *Adios Cjamango* (Harry Freeman); *Awkward Hands* (Rafael R. Marchent); **Billy the Kid* (Leon Klimovsky); *Cowards Don't Pray* (Marlon Sirko); *Cry for Revenge* (Rafael R. Marchent); *Dallas* (Juan Bosch); *Damned Pistols of Dallas* (José M. Zabalza); *Dead Are Countless* (Rafael R. Marchent); *Dig Your Grave . . . Sabata's Coming* (John Wood); *Django Does Not Forgive* (Julio Buchs); *Djurado* (Gianni Narzisi); *Frenchie King* (Christian-Jaque); *Fury of Johnny Kid* (Gianni Puccini); *God in Heaven . . . Arizona on Earth* (John Wood); *Gunfight at High Noon* (Joaquin R. Marchent); *Have a Good Funeral, My Friend . . . Sartana Will Pay* (Anthony Ascott); *Hour of Death* (Paul Marchenti); *I Do Not Forgive . . . I Kill!* (Joaquin R. Marchent); *If One Is Born a Swine* (Al Bradly); *Jesse James' Kid* (Antonio Del Amo); *Killer Goodbye* (Primo Zeglio); *Last of the Mohicans* (Matteo Cano); *Last Tomahawk* (Harald Reinl); *Magnificent Texan* (Lewis King); *Man Who Killed Billy the Kid* (Julio Buchs); *My Horse, My Gun, Your Widow* (John Wood); *One Hundred Thousand for Ringo* (Alberto De Martino); *Rattler Kid* (Leon Klimovsky); *Rebels of Arizona* (José M. Zabalza); *Relentless Four* (Primo Zeglio); *Ride and Kill* (J. L. Boraw); *Ruthless*

Colt of the Gringo (José Luis Madrid); *Sabata the Killer* (Tullio Demichelli); *Sartana Kills Them All* (Rafael R. Marchent); *Shoot to Kill* (Ramon Torrado); *Texican* (Espinosa/Selander); *Three from Colorado* (Armando De Ossorio); *Twenty Paces to Death* (Ted Mulligan); *Two Gunmen* (Anthony Greepy); *Woman for Ringo* (Rafael R. Marchent)

Infanti, Angelo: *Ballad of a Gunman* (Alfio Caltabiano); *Four Dollars for Vengeance* (Alfonso Balcazar)

Ingrassia, Ciccio: *Ciccio Forgives, I Don't* (Frank Reed); *For a Fist in the Eye* (Michele Lupo); *Grandsons of Zorro* (Mariano Laurenti); *Handsome, the Ugly, and the Stupid* (Gianni Grimaldi); *Nephews of Zorro* (Frank Reed); *Paths of War* (Aldo Grimaldi); **Two Gangsters in the Wild West* (Giorgio Simonelli); *Two R-R-Ringos from Texas* (Frank Martin); *Two Sergeants of General Custer* (Giorgio Simonelli); *Two Sons of Ringo* (Giorgio Simonelli); *Two Sons of Trinity* (Glenn Eastman)

Iosani, Cristina: *May God Forgive You . . . But I Won't* (Glenn Vincent Davis)

Iranzo, Antonio: *Sunscorched* (Alfonso Balcazar)

Ireland, Jill: *Chino* (John Sturges)

Ireland, John: *All Out* (Umberto Lenzi); *Blood River* (Gianfranco Baldenello); *Challenge of the MacKennas* (Leon Klimovsky); *Cost of Dying* (Sergio Merolle); *Dead for a Dollar* (Osvaldo Civirani); **Hate for Hate* (Domenico Paolella); *Machine Gun Killers* (Paolo Bianchini); *Pistol for a Hundred Coffins* (Umberto Lenzi); *Revenge for Revenge* (Ray Calloway); *Run Man, Run* (Sergio Sollima)

Isbert, Maria: *White, the Yellow and the Black* (Sergio Corbucci)

Isermini, Jacques: *Gunfight at O Q Corral* (J. M. Pallardy)

Israel, Victor: *Compañeros* (Sergio Corbucci); *Don't Turn the Other Cheek* (Duccio Tessari); *Forewarned, Half-Killed . . . the Word of Holy Ghost* (Anthony Ascott); *Heads You Die . . . Tails I Kill You* (Anthony Ascott); *His Name Was Holy Ghost* (Anthony Ascott); *Killer Goodbye* (Primo Zeglio); *Pistol for a Hundred Coffins* (Umberto Lenzi); *Return of Halleluja* (Anthony Ascott); **Savage Guns* (Michael Carreras); *Sugar Colt* (Franco Giraldi); *Texican* (Les Selander); *Up the MacGregors!* (Frank Garfield); *What Am I Doing in the Middle of the Revolution?* (Sergio Corbucci); *White, the Yellow, and the Black* (Sergio Corbucci); *White Comanche* (Gilbert Lee Kay); *Yankee* (Tinto Brass)

Itanzo, Antonio: *Cut-Throats Nine* (Joaquin R. Marchent)

Ivernel, Daniel: *Dynamite Jack* (Jean Bastia)

Jabès, Jean-Claude: *For a Book of Dollars* (Renzo Spaziani)

Jackson, Bill: *Don't Wait, Django . . . Shoot!* (Edward G. Muller)

Jacob, Peter: *Patience Has a Limit, We Don't* (Armando Morandi)

Jacquet, Dany: *Taste of Violence* (Robert Hossein)

Jaffe, Sam: *Guns for San Sebastian* (Henri Verneul)

Jagger, Mick: *Ned Kelly* (Tony Richardson)

Janson, Horst: *Don't Turn the Other Cheek* (Duccio Tessari)

Jaspe, José (also **José Rivas Jaspe**): *Cowards Don't Pray* (Marlon Sirko); *Django Challenges Sartana* (William Redford); *Don't Turn the Other Cheek* (Duccio Tessari); *Durango Is Coming, Pay or Die* (Luis Monter); *Heads or Tails* (Peter E. Stanley); *Jesse James' Kid* (Antonio Del Amo); *Killer Goodbye* (Primo Zeglio); *Light the Fuse . . . Sartana Is Coming* (Anthony Ascott); *More Dollars for the MacGregors* (J. L. Merino); *One After Another* (Nick Howard); *Relentless Four* (Primo Zeglio); *Ringo, the Lone Rider* (Rafael R. Marchent); *Rojo* (Leo Coleman); **Sign of the Coyote* (Mario Caiano); *Thompson 1880* (Albert Moore); *Thunder Over El Paso* (Roberto Montero); *Two Gunmen* (Anthony Greepy)

Jeannine, Sonja: *Man Called Blade* (Sergio Martino)
Jeffries, Fran: *Talent for Loving* (Richard Quine)
Jeffries, Lang: *Duel in the Eclipse* (Martino/Merino)
Jenkins, Terry: *Bandidos* (Max Dillman)
Johnson, Van: *Price of Power* (Tonino Valerii)
Jordan, Mary: *Djurado* (Gianni Narzisi)
Jordon, Lewis: *Machine Gun Killers* (Paolo Bianchini)
Judica, Antonella: *Blood Calls to Blood* (Lewis King)
Kamel, Joe: *Few Dollars for Django* (Leon Klimovsky); *Jesse James' Kid* (Antonio Del
    Amo); **Man of the Cursed Valley* (Omar Hopkins); *Mercenary* (Sergio Cor-
    bucci); *Minnesota Clay* (Sergio Corbucci); *Quinta: Fighting Proud* (Leon
    Klimovsky); *Seven Guns from Texas* (Joaquin R. Marchent)
Kamenke, Lu: *Django the Bastard* (Sergio Garrone)
Kamma, Sophia: *Brother Outlaw* (Edward G. Muller)
Kapp, Peter: *My Name Is Pecos* (Maurice A. Bright)
Karameinis, Vassili *see* Karis, Vassili
Karin, Ella: *The Ugly Ones* (Eugenio Martin)
Karis, Vassili (pseudonym for Vassili Karameinis): *Animal Called Man* (Roberto
    Mauri); *Death Is Sweet from the Soldier of God* (Robert Johnson); **Five Giants
    from Texas* (Aldo Florio); *Gunmen and the Holy Ghost* (Roberto Mauri); *He Was
    Called Holy Ghost* (Robert Johnson); *His Name Was King* (Don Reynolds);
    Magnificent West (Gianni Crea); *Return of Sabata* (Frank Kramer); *Scalps*
    (Werner Knox); *Wanted Sabata* (Robert Johnson)
Karlatos, Olga: *Keoma* (Enzo G. Castellari)
Kay, Ghislaine: *Red Hot Zorro* (William Russell)
Kaye, Clarissa: *Ned Kelly* (Tony Richardson)
Keitel, Harvey: *Eagle's Wing* (Anthony Harvey)
Kelly, Brian: *Shoot, Gringo . . . Shoot!* (Frank B. Corlish)
Kelly, Jim: *Take a Hard Ride* (Anthony Dawson)
Kendall, Tony (pseudonym for Luciano Stella): *Black Eagle of Santa Fe* (Ernst Hof-
    bauer); *Brother Outlaw* (Edward G. Muller); *Django Challenges Sartana*
    (William Redford); *Fighters from Ave Maria* (Al Albert); *Gunmen of One Hun-
    dred Crosses* (Lucky Moore); *Hatred of God* (Claudio Gora); **Pirates of the
    Mississippi* (Jürgen Roland)
Kennedy, Arthur (pseudonym for Arturo Domonici): *Minute to Pray, a Second to Die*
    (Franco Giraldi); *Murieta* (George Sherman)
Kent, Arthur: *Coffin for the Sheriff* (William Hawkins)
Kent, Stanley *see* Berti, Aldo
Keserber, Rachel: *A Girl Is a Gun* (Luc Moullet)
Kewa, Tara: *Apache Woman* (George McRoots)
Kiekens, Rose: *Red Hot Zorro* (William Russell)
Kieling, Wolfgang: *Duel at Sundown* (Leopoldo Lahola)
Kim, Edilio: *Even Django Has His Price* (Paolo Solvay); *Paid in Blood* (Paolo Solvay)
Kinski, Klaus (pseudonym for Nikolas Nakszynski): *And God Said to Cain* (Anthony
    Dawson); *Beast* (Mario Costa); *Black Killer* (Lucky Moore); *Bullet for the Gen-
    eral* (Damiano Damiani); *Fighting Fists of Shanghai Joe* (Mario Caiano); *Fistful
    of Death* (Miles Deem); *For a Few Dollars More* (Sergio Leone); *Genius* (Dami-
    ano Damiani); *Great Silence* (Sergio Corbucci); *His Name Was King* (Don Rey-
    nolds); *I Am Sartana, Your Angel of Death* (Anthony Ascott); *Last Ride to Santa
    Cruz* (Rolf Olsen); *Man: His Pride and His Vengeance* (Luigi Bazzoni); *Price of
    Death* (Vincent Thomas); *Return of Clint the Stranger* (George Martin); *Return*

of Shanghai Joe (Bitto Albertini); *Ruthless Four* (Giorgio Capitani); *Sartana* (Frank Kramer); *Shoot the Living . . . Pray for the Dead* (Joseph Warren); *Showdown for a Badman* (Miles Deem); *Twice a Judas* (Nando Cicero); *Vengeance Is a Dish Served Cold* (William Redford); **Winnetou: Last of Renegades* (Harald Reinl)

Kitosch, Cole: *Killer Caliber .32* (Al Bradley); *Texas, Adios* (Ferdinando Baldi); *Up the MacGregors!* (Frank Garfield)

Klein, Rita: *Rojo* (Leo Coleman)

Knox, Alexander: *Shalako* (Edward Dmytryk)

Koch, Marianne: *Clint the Stranger* (Alfonso Balcazar); *Fistful of Dollars* (Sergio Leone); **Last Ride to Santa Cruz* (Rolf Olsen); *Man from Oklahoma* (J. J. Balcazar); *Place Called Glory* (Ralph Gideon); *Sunscorched* (Alfonso Balcazar); *Who Killed Johnny R.?* (José Luis Madrid)

Kocsis, Margit: *None of the Three Were Called Trinity* (Pedro L. Ramirez)

Konopka, Magda: *Blindman* (Ferdinando Baldi); *Night of the Serpent* (Giulio Petroni); **Sky Full of Stars for a Roof* (Giulio Petroni)

Kopecky, Milos: *Lemonade Joe* (Oldrich Lipsky)

Körner, Diana: *Montana Trap* (Peter Schamoni)

Korocia, Veronica: *Pistol Packin' Preacher* (Leopoldo Savona)

Kost, Maria: *Django, a Bullet for You* (Leon Klimovsky)

Kresaja, Bruno: *A Girl Is a Gun* (Luc Moullet)

Kruger, Hardy: *Montana Trap* (Peter Schamoni)

Krup, Mara: *For a Few Dollars More* (Sergio Leone)

Krusciarska, Sascia: *Black Jack* (Gianfranco Baldanello)

Lagos, Vicky: *Five Dollars for Ringo* (Ignacio Iquino)

Landau, Martin: *Town Called Hell* (Robert Parrish)

Landers, Peter: *And They Smelled the Strange, Exciting, Dangerous Scent of Dollars* (Italo Alfaro)

Landgard, Janet: *Land Raiders* (Nathan Juran)

Landry, Géraird: *Seven Pistols for a Gringo* (Juan X. Marchel)

Lang, Karl (also **Carl Lange**): *Duel at Sundown* (Leopoldo Lahola); *Last Tomahawk* (Harald Reinl)

Lange, Claudie: *For One Hundred Thousand Dollars Per Killing* (Sidney Lean); *Machine Gun Killers* (Paolo Bianchini); *My Horse, My Gun, Your Widow* (John Wood); *To Hell and Back* (Giovanni Fago)

Lantieri, Franco: *Head or Tails* (Peter E. Stanley); *Johnny Colt* (Giovanni Grimaldi)

Lapointe, Bobby: *Gold of the Heroes* (Don Reynolds)

Laramy, Grant (pseudonym for **Germano Longo**): *Colt Is the Law* (Al Bradley)

Larker, Nina: *Rita of the West* (Ferdinando Baldi)

Larry, Peter (pseudonym for **Piero Lery**): *Man of the Cursed Valley* (Omar Hopkins)

Laso, Mara: *Torrejon City* (Leon Klimovsky)

Lastretti, Aldo (also **Adolfo Lastretti**): *Deaf Smith and Johnny Ears* (Paolo Cavara); *Find a Place to Die* (Anthony Ascott); *I'll Sell My Skin Dearly* (Ettore Fizarotti)

Latimer, Carlo: *Terror of the Black Mask* (Umberto Lenzi)

Latimore, Frank: *Cavalry Charge* (Ramon Torrado); *Fury of the Apaches* (Joe Lacy); **Shadow of Zorro* (Joaquin R. Marchent); *Shoot to Kill* (Ramon Torrado)

Lauricella, Guiseppe: *Revenge for Revenge* (Ray Calloway)

Lavi, Daliah: *Apache's Last Battle* (Hugo Fregonese)

Law, John Phillip: *Death Rides a Horse* (Giulio Petroni)

Lawrence, Charlie *see* **Lorenzon, Livio**

Lawrence, Marc: *Savage Pampas* (Hugo Fregonese)

Lawrence, Peter Lee (pseudonym for **Karl Hirenbach;** also **Arthur Green**): *Awkward*

Hands (Rafael R. Marchent); *Days of Violence* (Al Bradly); *Dead Are Countless* (Rafael R. Marchent); *Death on High Mountain* (Fred Ringoold); **For a Few Dollars More* (Sergio Leone); *Four Gunmen of the Holy Trinity* (Giorgio Cristallini); *Fury of Johnny Kid* (Gianni Puccini); *God in Heaven . . . Arizona on Earth* (John Wood); *Killer Calibre .32* (Al Bradly); *Killer Goodbye* (Primo Zeglio); *Man Who Killed Billy the Kid* (Julio Buchs); *More Dollars for MacGregors* (J. L. Merino); *One Against One . . . No Mercy* (Rafael R. Marchent); *Pistol for a Hundred Coffins* (Umberto Lenzi); *Prey of Vultues* (Rafael R. Marchent); *Raise Your Hands, Dead Man . . . You're Under Arrest* (Leon Klimovsky); *Sabata the Killer* (Tullio Demichelli)

Lazareff, Serge: *Ned Kelly* (Tony Richardson)
Léaud, Jean-Pierre: *A Girl Is a Gun* (Luc Moullet)
Lebeau, Madeleine *Gunmen of Rio Grande* (Tullio Demichelli)
LeBlanc, Tony: *Torrejon City* (Leon Klimovsky)
Lebrero, Goyo: *Djurado* (Gianni Narzisi)
Lee, Chen: *Fighting Fists of Shanghai Joe* (Mario Caiano); *Return of Shanghai Joe* (Bitto Albertini)
Lee, Christopher: *Hannie Caulder* (Burt Kennedy)
Lee, Glen: *Lucky Johnny: Born in America* (José A. Balanos)
Lee, Margaret: *Djurado* (Gianni Narzisi)
Leh, Sally: *Kung Fu Brothers in the Wild West* (Yeo Ban Yee)
Leigh, Janet: *Kid Rodelo* (Richard Carlson)
Leiphnitz, Harald: *Prairie in the City* (Claus Tinney)
Lemaire, Philippe: *Massacre at Marble City* (Franz J. Gottlieb)
Lembo, Lilli: *May God Forgive You . . . But I Won't* (Glenn Vincent Davis)
Lemoine, Michael: *Road to Fort Alamo* (Mario Bava)
Lenci, Giovanni: *Born to Kill* (Tony Mulligan)
Lentini, Licinia: *Silver Saddle* (Lucio Fulci)
Leo, Po Chih: *Kung Fu Brothers in the Wild West* (Yeo Ban Yee)
Leone, Sergio: *Cemetery Without Crosses* (Robert Hossein)
Leroy, Philippe: *Caliber .38* (Toni Secchi); *Man Called Blade* (Sergio Martino); **Yankee* (Tinto Brass)
Lery, Piero *see* **Larry, Peter**
Leverly, John: *Quintana: Dead or Alive* (Glenn Vincent Davis)
Levi, Suzanne: *Death Played the Flute* (Elo Panaccio)
Lewis, Geoffrey: *My Name Is Nobody* (Tonino Valerii)
Lezana, Sara: *Gunfight at Red Sands* (Richard Blasco); *Last of the Mohicans* (Matteo Cano); *Murieta* (George Sherman)
Lieh, Lo: *Stranger and the Gunfighter* (Anthony Dawson)
Lindamar, Wilma: *Ramon the Mexican* (Maurizio Pradeaux)
Linder, Christa: *Day of Anger* (Tonino Valerii); *Tall Women* (Sidney Pink); *Trinity Plus the Clown and a Guitar* (François Legrand)
Lindt, Rosemarie: *Porno Erotic Western* (Gerard B. Lennox)
Line, Helga: *China 9, Liberty 37* (Monte Hellman); *Have a Good Funeral, My Friend . . . Sartana Will Pay* (Anthony Ascott); *In a Colt's Shadow* (Gianni Grimaldi); *Raise Your Hands, Dead Man . . . You're Under Arrest* (Leon Klimovsky); **Seven Hours of Gunfire* (Joaquin R. Marchent); *Sign of Zorro* (Mario Caiano)
Lipton, Robert: *God's Gun* (Frank Kramer)
Lloyd, Barbara *see* **Barbara Loy**
Logan, Joseph: *Chrysanthemums for a Bunch of Swine* (Sergio Pastore)
Lorden, David: *Kid Vengeance* (Joe Manduke)

Lollobrigida, Gina: *Bad Man's River* (Eugenio Martin)
Lollobrigida, Guido *see* **Burton, Lee**
Lom, Herbert: *Treasure of Silver Lake* (Harald Reinl)
Lombardo, Angel: *Gentleman Killer* (George Finley)
Loncar, Beba: *Days of Violence* (Al Bradly)
Longo, Germano *see* **Laramy, Grant**
Longo, Malisa: *California* (Michele Lupo); *Desperado* (Al Bagrain); *Django Challenges Sartana* (William Redford); *Macho Killers* (Mark Andrew); *More Dollars for the MacGregors* (J. L. Merino); **Once Upon a Time in the Wild Wild West* (Enzo Matassi)
Lopert, Tanya: *Navajo Joe* (Sergio Corbucci)
Lopez, Charo: *Dead Men Ride* (Aldo Florio); *Who's Afraid of Zorro?* (Franco Lo Cascio)
Loran, Patricia: *Seven Pistols for a Gringo* (Juan Xiol Marchel)
Lorca, Theresa: *Pyramid of the Sun God* (Robert Siodmak)
Lorcas, Luciano: *Price of Death* (Vincent Thomas)
Lorenzon, Livio (pseudonym — **Charlie Lawrence**): *Ace High* (Giuseppe Colizzi); *Cjamango* (Edward G. Muller); *Colorado Charlie* (Robert Johnson); *Chrysanthemums for a Bunch of Swine* (Sergio Pastore); *Go with God, Gringo* (Edward G. Muller); *God Will Forgive My Pistol* (Gariazzo/Savona); *The Good, the Bad, and the Ugly* (Sergio Leone); *Last Gun* (Sergio Bergonzelli); *Piluk, the Timid One* (Guido Celano); *Savange Gringo* (Bava/Romano); *Terror of Oklahoma* (Mario Amendola); *Texas, Adios* (Ferdinando Baldi); *Two R-R-Ringos from Texas* (Frank Martin); *Winchester Does Not Forgive* (Adelchi Bianchi)
Loritz, Katya: *Joe Dexter* (Ignacio Iquino)
Lorys, Diana (also **Diana Loris**): *Bad Man's River* (Eugenio Martin); *California* (Michele Lupo); *Canadian Wilderness* (Armando De Ossorio); *Cavalry Charge* (Ramon Torrado); *Chino* (John Sturges); *Django Shoots First* (Alberto De Martino); *Get Mean* (Ferdinando Baldi); *Gunfighters of Casa Grande* (Roy Rowland); *Kill, Django . . . Kill First* (Willy S. Regan); **Murieta* (George Sherman); *Sartana Does Not Forgive* (Alfonso Balcazar); *Texican* (Espinosa/Selander); *Three from Colorado* (Armando De Ossorio); *Twins from Texas* (Steno)
Louis, Jean (also **Jean Luis**): *Django the Bastard* (Sergio Garrone); *Halleluja to Vera Cruz* (Newman Rostel); *Man from the East* (E. B. Clucher); *May God Forgive You . . . But I Won't* (Glen V. Davis); *No Graves on Boot Hill* (Willy S. Regan); **Ramon the Mexican* (Maurizio Pradeaux); *Ringo, It's Massacre Time* (Mario Pinzauti); *Winchester Does Not Forgive* (Adelchi Bianchi)
Love, Lucretia: *Blindman* (Ferdinando Baldi); **Colt in Hand of the Devil* (Sergio Bergonzelli); *Go with God, Gringo* (Edward G. Muller); *Two Sons of Trinity* (Glenn Eastman)
Lovelock, Ray: *Django, Kill . . . If You Live, Shoot!* (Giulio Questi)
Loy, Barbara (pseudonym — **Barbara Lloyd**): *Last of the Mohicans* (Matteo Cano); *Magnificent Texan* (Lewis King)
Loy, Dina: *Relentless Four* (Primo Zeglio)
Luce, Angela: *For a Few Dollars Less* (Mario Mattòli)
Lucky, Ares: *Sheriff with the Gold* (Richard Kean); *Shoot the Living . . . Pray for the Dead* (Joseph Warren)
Lukschy, Wolfgang: *Fistful of Dollars* (Sergio Leone); *Lost Treasure of the Incas* (Piero Pierotti)
Lulli, Folco: *Between God, the Devil, and a Winchester* (Dario Silvestri); *Sign of Zorro* (Mario Caiano); *Shoot, Gringo . . . Shoot!* (Frank B. Corlish)

Lulli, Folco: *Sign of Zorro* (Mario Caiano); *Shoot, Gringo . . . Shoot!* (Frank B. Corlish)

Lulli, Piero (pseudonym — **Peter Carter** and **Peter Carsten**): *Adios Hombre* (Mario Caiano); *And God Said to Cain* (Anthony Dawson); *Big Ripoff* (Franco Rosetti); *Boldest Job in the West* (José De La Loma); *Buffalo Bill, Hero of the Far West* (John W. Fordson); *Carambola's Philosophy* (Ferdinando Baldi); *Cjamango* (Edward G. Muller); *Cry for Revenge* (Rafael R. Marchent); *Day of Anger* (Tonino Valerii); *Django, Kill . . . If You Live, Shoot!* (Giulio Questi); *Fighting Fists of Shanghai Joe* (Mario Caiano); *Find a Place to Die* (Anthony Ascott); *Five Man Army* (Don Reynolds); *For One Hundred Thousand Dollars Per Killing* (Sidney Lean); *Forewarned, Half-Killed . . . the Word of Holy Ghost* (Anthony Ascott); *Forgotten Pistolero* (Ferdinando Baldi); *Fury of Johnny Kid* (Gianni Puccini); *God Made Them . . . I Kill Them* (Paolo Bianchi); *Hands of a Gunman* (Rafael R. Marchent); *I Am Sartana, Trade Your Guns for a Coffin* (Anthony Ascott); *Kitosch, the Man Who Came from the North* (Joseph Marvin); *Light the Fuse . . . Sartana Is Coming* (Anthony Ascott); *Miss Dynamite* (Sergio Grieco); *My Name Is Nobody* (Tonino Valerii); *My Name Is Pecos* (Maurice A. Bright); *Pistol for Hundred Coffins* (Umberto Lenzi); *Ringo, the Lone Rider* (Rafael R. Marchent); *Rojo* (Leo Coleman); *Savage Gringo* (Bava/Romano); **Shadow of Zorro* (Joaquin R. Marchent); *Shotgun* (Roberto Mauri); *Sign of the Coyote* (Mario Caiano); *Taste for Killing* (Tonino Valerii); *Trinity Plus the Clown and a Guitar* (François Legrand)

Lupi, Roldano: *Buffalo Bill, Hero of the Far West* (John W. Fordson)

Lupo, Alberto: *Django Shoots First* (Alberto De Martino)

Lycan, George: *Dynamite Jack* (Jean Bastia)

Lyon, Lici Lee: *Django Strikes Again* (Ted Archer)

Lyon, Sue: *Four Rode Out* (John Peyser)

Lys, Agatha: *In the Name of the Father, the Son, and the Colt* (Frank Bronston); *Tequila* (Tullio Demichelli); *Three Supermen of the West* (Italo Martinenghi)

McCarthy, Kevin: *Ace High* (Giuseppe Colizzi)

McCorkindale, Don: *Three Bullets for a Long Gun* (Peter Henkel)

McCren, Paul: *Bounty Hunter in Trinity* (Oskar Faradine)

MacDouglas, John (pseudonym for **Giuseppe Addobbati**): *Blood for a Silver Dollar* (Calvin J. Padget); *Deguello* (Joseph Warren); *Django, Last Killer* (Joseph Warren); *God Will Forgive My Pistol* (Mario Gariazzo); *Hole in the Forehead* (Joseph Warren); *Joe Dexter* (Ignacio Iquino); *Magnificent Three* (Joaquin R. Marchent); *Man from Oklahoma* (Robert M. White); *Massacre Time* (Lucio Fulci); **Ride and Kill* (J. L. Boraw)

McGee, Vonetta: *Great Silence* (Sergio Corbucci)

McGoohan, Patrick: *Genius* (Damiano Damiani)

Machiavelli, Nicoletta: *Face to Face* (Sergio Sollima); *Garter Colt* (Gian A. Rocco); *Hate Thy Neighbor* (Ferdinando Baldi); **Hills Run Red* (Lee W. Beaver); *Minute to Pray . . . a Second to Die* (Franco Giraldi); *Navajo Joe* (Sergio Corbucci); *No Room to Die* (Willy S. Regan)

McJulian, Louis: *Sheriff with the Gold* (Richard Kean)

McKay, Paul: *Seven Nuns in Kansas City* (Marcello Zeani)

McMurry, Lucky (also **Lucky MacMurray**): *Go Away! Trinity Has Arrived in Eldorado* (Dick Spitfire); **Fistful of Death* (Miles Deem); *Hero Called Allegria* (Dennis Ford); *Once Upon a Time in the Wild, Wild West* (Enzo Matassi); *One Damned Day at Dawn . . . Django Meets Sartana* (Miles Deem); *Reach You Bastard!* (Lucky Dickerson); *They Called Him Trinity* (Fred Lyon Morris)

Madison, Guy: *Apache's Last Battle* (Hugo Fregonese); *Bang Bang Kid* (Luciano Lelli); *Five Giants from Texas* (Aldo Florio); *Gunmen of Rio Grande* (Tullio Demichelli); *Legacy of the Incas* (Georg Marischka); *Payment in Blood* (E. G. Rowland); *Reverend Colt* (Leon Klimovsky); *Son of Django* (Osvaldo Civirani); *This Man Can't Die* (Gianfranco Baldanello)

Madrid, Rogelio: *Woman for Ringo* (Rafael R. Marchent)

Magalo, Paolo (also **Paolo Magalotti**): *Animal Called Man* (Roberto Mauri); *Death Is Sweet from the Soldier of God* (Roberto Mauri); *Hate Thy Neighbor* (Ferdinando Baldi)

Magalotti, Fiorella: *Once Upon a Time in the Wild, Wild West* (Enzo Matassi)

Maggio, Enzo: *Seven Nuns in Kansas City* (Marcello Zeani)

Maggio, Mimma: *Brother Outlaw* (Edward G. Muller); *Django Kills Softly* (Max Hunter)

Magnino, Romano: *Execution* (Domenico Paolella)

Maharis, George: *Land Raiders* (Nathan Juran)

Mahor, Maria: *Tall Women* (Sidney Pink)

Major, William: *Even Django Has His Price* (Paolo Solvay)

Malcolm, Robert: *And They Smelled the Strange, Exciting, Dangerous Scent of Dollars* (Italo Alfaro)

Maldera, Roberto: *Shoot Joe, and Shoot Again* (Hal Brady)

Malfatti, Marina: *Return of Clint the Stranger* (George Martin)

Mancini, Carla: *Animal Called Man* (Roberto Mauri); *Anything for a Friend* (Miles Deem); *Bounty Hunter in Trinity* (Oskar Faradine); *Caliber .38* (Toni Secchi); *Don't Turn the Other Cheek* (Duccio Tessari); *Fighting Fists of Shanghai Joe* (Mario Caiano); *Go Away! Trinity Has Arrived in Eldorado* (Dick Spitfire); *Man Called Invincible* (Anthony Ascott); *Patience Has a Limit, We Don't* (Armando Morandi); *Pistol Packin' Preacher* (Leopoldo Savina); *Sometimes Life Is Hard, Right Providence?* (Giulio Petroni); *Sting of the West* (Enzo G. Castellari); *Trinity and Sartana Are Coming* (Mario Siciliano)

Manera, John: *Chrysanthemums for a Bunch of Swine* (Sergio Pastore)

Mann, Leonard: *Chuck Moll* (E. B. Clucher); *Forgotten Pistolero* (Ferdinando Baldi); *Vengeance Is a Dish Served Cold* (William Redford)

Mannari, Guido: *Brothers Blue* (Marc Meyer); *Red Coat* (Joe D'Amato)

Manni, Ettore: *Born to Kill* (Tony Mulligan); *Bury Them Deep* (John Byrd); *Chino* (John Sturges); *Django and Sartana Are Coming . . . It's the End* (Dick Spitfire); *I Am Sartana, Your Angel of Death* (Anthony Ascott); *Ringo and His Golden Pistol* (Sergio Corbucci); *Silver Saddle* (Lucio Fulci); *Stranger Returns* (Vance Lewis); *Stranger That Kneels Beside the Shadow of a Corpse* (Miles Deem); *Twenty Paces to Death* (Tony Mulligan)

Mannoia, Florellia: *On the Third Day Arrived the Crow* (Gianni Crea)

Marandi, Evi: *Damned Pistols of Dallas* (Joseph Trader)

Maranzano, Mario: *Ciccio Forgives, I Don't* (Frank Reed); *Dollar of Fire* (Nick Nostro); *Two Sides of the Dollar* (Roberto Montero)

Maravidi, Mirella: *Let Them Rest* (Carlo Lizzani)

Marchand, Corinne: *Arizona Colt* (Michele Lupo)

Marchent, Carlos: *Cut-Throats Nine* (Joaquin R. Marchent); *Hands of a Gunman* (Rafael R. Marchent); *Prey of Vultures* (Rafael R. Marchent); *Sartana Kills Them All* (Rafael R. Marchent); *Seven Hours of Gunfire* (Joaquin R. Marchent)

Marco, José: *Cry for Revenge* (Rafael R. Marchent); *Django, a Bullet for You* (Leon Klimovsky); *Last of the Mohicans* (Matteo Cano); *Man of Cursed the Valley* (Omar Hopkins); *Quintan: Fighting Proud* (Leon Klimovsky); *Taste for Killing* (Tonino Valerii)

Marconi, Nadia: *Hate for Hate* (Domenico Paolella)
Maresa, Franca: *For a Book of Dollars* (Renzo Spaziani)
Marin, Gloria: *Coyote* (Joaquin R. Marchent)
Martin, Luis *see* **Martin, Luis**
Mark, Robert: *God Does Not Pay on Saturday* (Amerigo Anton); *Kill or Die* (Amerigo Anton)
Marley, John: *Man Called Sledge* (Vic Morrow)
Marquand, Serge: *Black Eagle of Santa Fe* (Ernst Hofbauer); *Cemetery Without Crosses* (Robert Hossein); **Massacre at Marble City* (Franz J. Gottlieb); *Specialist* (Sergio Corbucci); *Wanted* (Calvin J. Padget)
Marquez, Evaristo: *Lucky Johnny: Born in America* (José Antonio Balanos)
Marshall, Mike: *Death Rides Alone* (Joseph Warren); *I'll Sell My Skin Dearly* (Ettore Fizarotti)
Marsina, Antonio: *Stranger in Town* (Vance Lewis)
Martell, Peter: *Black Tigress* (Siro Marcellini); *Chuck Moll* (E. B. Clucher); *Death Rides Alone* (Joseph Warren); *Dollars for a Fast Gun* (Joaquin R. Marchent); *Forgotten Pistolero* (Ferdinando Baldi); **Fury of Johnny Kid* (Gianni Puccini); *God Made Them . . . I Kill Them* (Paolo Bianchi); *Hero Called Allegria* (Dennis Ford); *Long Day of the Massacre* (Albert Cardiff); *May God Forgive You . . . But I Won't* (Glenn V. Davis); *Patience Has a Limit, We Don't* (Armando Morandi); *Ringo, It's Massacre Time* (Mario Pinzauti); *Ringo, the Lone Rider* (Rafael R. Marchent); *This Man Can't Die* (Gianfranco Baldanello); *Two Crosses at Danger Pass* (Rafael R. Marchent)
Martens, Todd: *Jaguar* (Jess Franco)
Martin, Daniel: *Bad Man's River* (Eugenio Martin); *Blood River* (Gianfranco Baldenello); *Dead Men Ride* (Aldo Florio); **Gunfight at Red Sands* (Richard Blasco); *Last of the Mohicans* (Matteo Cano); *Last Tomahawk* (Harald Reinl); *Man Called Gringo* (Roy Rowland); *Minute to Pray, a Second to Die* (Franco Giraldi); *None of the Three Were Called Trinity* (Pedro L. Ramirez); *Return of Clint the Stranger* (George Martin); *Seven Guns for Timothy* (Rod Gilbert); *Too Much Gold for One Gringo* (Juan Bosch); *Watch Out Gringo! Sabata Will Return* (Alfonso Balcazar)
Martin, Diana: *Minnesota Clay* (Sergio Corbucci)
Martin, Femi *see* **Benussi, Femi**
Martin, George (also **Jorge Martin**): **Billy the Kid* (Leon Klimovsky); *Canadian Wilderness* (Armando De Ossorio); *Clint the Stranger* (Alfonso Balcazar); *Fifteen Scaffolds for the Killer* (Nunzio Malasomma); *Joe Dexter* (Ignacio Iquino); *Fury of the Apaches* (José M. Elorrieta); *Last of the Mohicans* (Matteo Cano); *Let's Go and Kill Sartana* (Mario Pinzauti); *Massacre at Fort Grant* (J. Douglas); *Pistol for Ringo* (Duccio Tessari); *Red Blood, Yellow Gold* (Nando Cicero); *Return of Clint the Stranger* (George Martin); *Return of Ringo* (Duccio Tessari); *Sartana Does Not Forgive* (Alfonso Balcazar); *Taste for Killing* (Tonio Valerii); *Thompson 1880* (Albert Moore); *Three from Colorado* (Armando De Ossorio); *Three Supermen of the West* (Italo Martinenghi); *Two Gunmen* (Anthony Greepy); *Watch Out Gringo! Sabata Will Return* (Alfonso Balcazar)
Martin, Jacinto: *Man and a Colt* (Tullio Demichelli)
Martin, James: *Garter Colt* (Gian Andrea Rocco)
Martin, Jean: *Adios Gringo* (George Finley); *Genius* (Damiano Damiani)
Martin, José Manuel: *Arizona* (Sergio Martino); *Arizona Colt* (Michele Lupo); *Badman's River* (Eugenio Martin); *Bastard, Go and Kill* (Gino Mangini); *Bullet for a General* (Damiano Damiani); *Bullet for Sandoval* (Julio Buchs); **Bullets Don't*

Argue (Mike Perkins); *Django Shoots First* (Alberto De Martino); *Fifteen Scaffolds for the Killer* (Nunzio Malasomma); *Five Giants from Texas* (Aldo Florio); *Forgotten Pistolero* (Ferdinando Baldi); *Four Dollars for Vengeance* (Alfonso Balcazar); *God Forgives, I Don't* (Giuseppe Colizzi); *I Want Him Dead* (Paolo Bianchi); *Man from Canyon City* (Alfonso Balcazar); *Minute to Pray, a Second to Die* (Franco Giraldi); *One After Another* (Nick Howard); *Pistol for Ringo* (Duccio Tessari); *Relentless Four* (Primo Zeglio); *Seven Dollars on the Red* (Alberto Cardone)

Martin, Luis (also **Luis Marin**): **Canadian Wilderness* (Armando De Ossorio); *Dead Are Countless* (Rafael R. Marchent); *Great Treasure Hunt* (Tonino Ricci); *More Dollars for the MacGregors* (J. L. Merino)

Martin, Maria (also **Mary Martin** and **Maria Martinez**): *Bandidos* (Max Dillman); *Cry for Revenge* (Rafael R. Marchent); *Four Rode Out* (John Peyser); **Hellbenders* (Sergio Corbucci); *My Colt, Not Yours* (Steve MacCohy); *Reverend Colt* (Leon Klimovsky); *Ringo and Gringo Against All* (Bruno Corbucci)

Martin, Michael *see* **De La Riva, Miguel**

Martin, Strother: *Hannie Caulder* (Burt Kennedy)

Martin, Todd: *Finger on the Trigger* (Sidney Pink); *Jaguar* (Jess Franco)

Martinelli, Elsa: *Belle Starr Story* (Nathan Wich)

Martinez, Maria *see* **Martin, Maria**

Martini, Rossana: *Let Them Rest* (Carlo Lizzani)

Martino, Dan: *Man Called Gringo* (Roy Rowland)

Martinson, Sergei: *Armed and Dangerous: Times and Heroes of Bret Harte* (Vladimir Vainstok)

Marturano, Gino: *Jesse and Lester, Two Brothers in a Place Called Trinity* (James London)

Marturano, Luigi: *Hole in the Forehead* (Joseph Warren)

Mason, Anna (also **Anna Malsson**): *Hey Amigo! A Toast to Your Death!* (Paul Maxwell)

Mason, James: *Bad Man's River* (Eugenio Martin)

Massari, Lea: *I Want Him Dead* (Paolo Bianchi)

Mastroianni, Marcello: *Do Not Touch the White Woman* (Marco Ferreri)

Mateos, Julian: *Four Rode Out* (John Peyser); **Hellbenders* (Sergio Corbucci); *Three Silver Dollars* (Irving Jacobs)

Mathot, Olivier: *Damned Pistols of Dallas* (Joseph Trader)

Mattern, Kitty: *Apache's Last Battle* (Hugo Fregonese)

Matuska, Waldemar: *Lemonade Joe* (Oldrich Lipsky)

Maura, Rita: *Stranger in Japan* (Vance Lewis)

May, Benjamin: *Kill or Die* (Amerigo Anton)

May, Dan: *Ballad of a Gunman* (Alfio Caltabiano)

May, Leontine: *Man from Oklahoma* (Robert M. White)

May, Marta: *Massacre at Fort Grant* (J. Douglas); *Seven Pistols for a Gringo* (Juan X. Marchel)

Mayer, Patriza: *Porno Erotic Western* (Gerard B. Lennox)

Mayo, Alfredo: **Bullets and the Flesh* (Fred Wilson); *Great Treasure Hunt* (Tonino Ricci); *Magnificent Brutes of the West* (Fred Wilson); *Sabata the Killer* (Tullio Demichelli)

Mayor, William: *Paid in Blood* (Paolo Solvay)

Mazza, Marc: *Big Showdown* (Giancarlo Santi)

Meccia, Luigi: *And They Smelled the Strange, Exciting, Dangerous Scent of Dollars* (Italo Alfaro)

Medda, Ida: *Fighters from Ave Maria* (Al Albert)
Meier, Karin: *Dust in the Sun* (Richard Balducci)
Mejuto, Andres: *Fury of Johnny Kid* (Gianni Puccini)
Mell, Marisa: *Ben and Charlie* (Michele Lupo); *Last Ride to Santa Cruz* (Rolf Olsen);
  Miss Dynamite (Sergio Grieco)
Melvill, Richard: *On the Third Day Arrived the Crow* (Gianni Crea); *Pistol Packin'*
  Preacher (Leopoldo Savona)
Menard, Julie: *A Sky Full of Stars for a Roof* (Giulio Petroni)
Meniconi, Furio (pseudonym—**Men Fury**): *Bastard, Go and Kill* (Gino Mangini);
  Deadly Tracker (Amerigo Anton); *Django the Bastard* (Sergio Garrone); *God*
  Does Not Pay on Saturday (Amerigo Anton); *John the Bastard* (Armando
  Crispino); *Kill, Django . . . Kill First* (Willy Regan); **Kill or Die* (Amerigo An-
  ton); *Kill Them All and Return Alone* (Enzo G. Castellari); *Machine Gun Killers*
  (Paolo Bianchini); *Shoot, Gringo . . . Shoot!* (Frank B. Corlish); *Time and Place*
  for Killing (Vincent Eagle); *Two Pistols and a Coward* (Calvin J. Padget)
Mercier, Michèle: *Call of the Wild* (Ken Annakin); *Cemetery Without Crosses*
  (Robert Hossein)
Merenda, Luc: *Man Called Amen* (Alfio Caltabiano); *Red Sun* (Terence Young); *They*
  Still Call Me Amen (Alfio Caltabiano)
Merli, Maurizio: *Man Called Blade* (Sergio Martino)
Merrick, Steve: *This Man Can't Die* (Gianfranco Baldanello)
Merrill, Evelyn: *Gunfight at High Noon* (Joaquin R. Marchent)
Messenger, Bob see **Messina, Robert**
Messina, Robert (pseudonym—**Bob Messenger**): *Damned Pistols of Dallas* (Joseph
  Trader); *Death Is Sweet from the Soldier of God* (Robert Johnson); *Sheriff with*
  the Gold (Richard Kean); *Son of Django* (Osvaldo Civirani)
Mesuto, Andres: *Prey of Vultures* (Rafael R. Marchent)
Meszchi, Lali: *Trail of the Falcon* (Gottfried Kölditz)
Miali, Umberto: *Seven Dollars on the Red* (Alberto Cardone)
Micantoni, Andriano: *Ciccio Forgives, I Don't* (Frank Reed)
Michangeli, Marcella: *And God Said to Cain* (Anthony Dawson)
Mifune, Toshiro: *Red Sun* (Terence Young)
Miguel, Monica: *Gunman of One Hundred Crosses* (Lucky Moore)
Mili: *Woman for Ringo* (Rafael R. Marchent)
Milian, Tomás: *Bandara Bandits* (Sergio Corbucci); *Big Gundown* (Sergio Sollima);
  Blood and Guns (Giulio Petroni); *Compañeros* (Sergio Corbucci); *Death*
  Sentence (Mario Linfranchi); *Django, Kill . . . If You Live, Shoot!* (Giulio
  Questi); *Face to Face* (Sergio Sollima); *Four Gunmen of Apocalypse* (Lucio
  Fulci); *Here We Are Again, Eh Providence?* (Alberto De Martino); *Magnificent*
  Bandits (Giovanni Fago); *Run Man, Run* (Sergio Sollima); *Sometimes Life Is*
  Hard, Right Providence? (Giulio Petroni); **The Ugly Ones* (Eugenio Martin);
  White, the Yellow, and the Black (Sergio Corbucci)
Milland, Gloria: **Gunfight at High Noon* (Joaquin R. Marchent); *Hands of a Gunman*
  (Rafael R. Marchent); *Hate for Hate* (Domenico Paolella); *Hour of Death* (Paul
  Marchenti); *Man and a Colt* (Tullio Demichelli); *Man Who Killed Billy the Kid*
  (Julio Buchs); *Man with the Golden Pistol* (Alfonso Balcazar); *Seven Guns from*
  Texas (Joaquin R. Marchent); *Seven Hours of Gunfire* (Joaquin R. Marchent);
  Three Swords of Zorro (Ricardo Blasco)
Miller, Mirta: *Get Mean* (Ferdinando Baldi); *White, the Yellow and the Black* (Sergio
  Corbucci)
Milo, Sandra: *Bang Bang Kid* (Luciano Lelli)

Minaud, Michael: *A Girl Is a Gun* (Luc Moullet)

Miner, Pat: *Bounty Hunter in Trinity* (Oskar Faradine)

Miniggio, Riccardo: *Rick and John, Conquerors of the West* (Osvaldo Civirani)

Miou Miou (pseudonym for **Sylvette Hery**): *Genius* (Damiano Damiani)

Mir, Irene: *Man with the Golden Pistol* (Sergio Corbucci)

Miranda, Manuel (also **Angel Miranda**): *Bullet for Sandoval* (Julio Buchs); **Django Does Not Forgive* (Julio Buchs); *Law of Violence* (Gianni Crea)

Miranda, Soledad: *Sugar Colt* (Franco Giraldi)

Mistral, Jorge: *Gunfighters of Casa Grande* (Roy Rowland)

Mitchell, Cameron: *Eye for an Eye* (Albert Marshall); *Last Gun* (Sergio Bergonzelli); *Minnesota Clay* (Sergio Corbucci)

Mitchell, Gordon (pseudonym for **Chuck Pendleton**): *Anything for a Friend* (Miles Deem); *Arizona Kid* (Luciano Carlos); *Beyond the Law* (Giorgio Stegani); *Born to Kill* (Tony Mulligan); *Dead for a Dollar* (Osvaldo Civirani); *Django and Sartana Are Coming . . . It's the End* (Dick Spitfire); *Drummer of Vengeance* (Robert Paget); *Fighting Fists of Shanghai Joe* (Mario Caiano); *Finders Killers* (Gianni Crea); *Go Away! Trinity Has Arrived in Eldorado* (Dick Spitfire); *Hero Called Allegria* (Dennis Ford); *I Am Sartana, Your Angel of Death* (Anthony Ascott); *If One Is Born a Swine . . . Kill Him* (Al Bradly); *John the Bastard* (Armando Crispino); *Judgment of God* (Franco Lattanza); *Kill or Die* (Amerigo Anton); *Let's Go and Kill Sartana* (Mario Pinzauti); *Magnificent West* (Gianni Crea); *Once Upon a Time in the Wild, Wild West* (Enzo Matassi); *Reach You Bastard!* (Lucky Dickerson); *Rita of the West* (Ferdinando Baldi); *Saguaro* (Amerigo Anton); *Showdown for a Badman* (Miles Deem); *Stranger That Kneels Beside the Shadow of a Corpse* (Miles Deem); *They Called Him Trinity* (Fred Lyon Morris); *Three Graves for a Winchester* (Erminio Salvi); **Thompson 1880* (Albert Moore)

Mitchell, Joseph: *Massacre at Fort Holman* (Tonino Valerii)

Mitchum, James: *Massacre at Grand Canyon* (Stanley Corbett); *Tramplers* (Albert Band)

Mitic, Gojko: *Trail of the Falcon* (Gottefried Kolditz)

Mizar, Maria: *Cowards Don't Pray* (Marlon Sirko); *Three Silver Dollars* (Irving Jacobs)

Modio, Jolanda: *Face to Face* (Sergio Sollima); *Gunmen and the Holy Ghost* (Roberto Mauri); *He Was Called Holy Ghost* (Robert Johnson); *One After Another* (Nick Howard); *Sartana in the Valley of Death* (Roberto Mauri); **Stranger in Town* (Vance Lewis)

Modugno, Lucia: **For a Few Dollars Less* (Mario Mattòli); *My Name Is Pecos* (Maurice A. Bright); *Navajo Joe* (Sergio Corbucci)

Möhner, Carl: **Last Gun* (Sergio Bergonzelli); *Man with the Golden Pistol* (Alfonso Balcazar); *Thirty Winchesters for El Diablo* (Frank G. Carrol)

Molina, Vidal (also **Mariano Vidal Molina**): *Awkward Hands* (Rafael R. Marchent); *Challenge of the MacKennas* (Leon Klimovsky); *Death Knows No Time* (Leon Klimovsky); *Five Giants from Texas* (Aldo Florio); *Gentleman Killer* (George Findley); *More Dollars for the MacGregors* (J. L. Merino); *My Colt, Not Yours* (Steve MacCohy); *Reverend Colt* (Leon Klimovsky); **Secret of Captain O'Hara* (Arturo Castillo); *Two Thousand Dollars for Coyote* (Leon Klimovsky); *White Comanche* (Gilbert Lee Kay)

Monelli, Silvia: *Holy Water Joe* (Mario Gariazzo)

Monen, Suzy: *For a Book of Dollars* (Renzo Spaziani)

Moneta, Renzo: *Bastard, Go and Kill* (Gino Mangini)

Moneta, Tullio: *Three Bullets for a Long Gun* (Peter Henkel)
Monicini, Furio: *Deadly Tracker* (Amerigo Anton)
Monreale, Cinzia: *Silver Saddle* (Lucio Fulci)
Monroe, Frank *see* **Moroni, Fabrizio**
Monroy, Manuel: *Coyote* (Joaquin R. Marchent)
Monson, Carlos: *Macho Killers* (Mark Andrew)
Montalban, Ricardo: *Deserter* (Fulgozi/Kennedy)
Montefiori, Luigi *see* **Eastman, George**
Monteros, Rosenda: *Savage Pampas* (Hugo Fregonese)
Montes, Elisa (also **Elisa Montez**): *Captain Apache* (Alexander Singer); *Cowards Don't Pray* (Marlon Sirko); *Mutiny at Fort Sharp* (Fernando Cerchio); **Outlaw of Red River* (Maury Dexter); *Seven Dollars on the Red* (Alberto Cardone); *Texas, Adios* (Ferdinando Baldi)
Montgomery, George: *Outlaw of Red River* (Maury Dexter)
Monti, Maria: *Duck You Sucker* (Sergio Leone)
Monti, Silvia: *Judge Roy Bean* (Richard Owens)
Moore, Mike: *Three Graves for a Winchester* (Erminio Salvi)
Moore, Thomas *see* **Girolami, Enio**
Moran, Francisco (pseudonym for **Fabrizio Moroni**): *For a Fist in the Eye* (Michele Lupo); *Ringo's Big Night* (Mario Maffei); *Shoot, Gringo . . . Shoot!* (Frank B. Corlish); *Shots Ring Out!* (Augustin Navarro)
Moreau, Jeanne: *Viva Maria* (Louis Malle)
Morgan, Sherill *see* **Chanel, Hélène**
Moneno, Liza: *Fury of the Apaches* (Joe Lacy)
Moretti, Nadir: *Death Walks in Laredo* (Enzo Peri); *Zorro, the Navarra Marquis* (Jean Monty)
Morgan, Maria: *Sheriff of Rock Spring* (Anthony Green)
Moroni, Fabrizio (pseudonym—**Frank Monroe**): *Kill or Die* (Amerigo Anton); *Shoot, Gringo . . . Shoot!* (Frank B. Corlish)
Morris, Kirk: *Rita of the West* (Ferdinando Baldi); *Saguaro* (Amerigo Anton)
Mucari, Carlo: *Tex and the Lord of the Deep* (Duccio Tessari)
Mule, Francesco: *Rick and John, Conquerors of the West* (Osvaldo Civirani)
Müller, Paul: *Last of the Mohicans* (Matteo Cano); *Sometimes Life Is Hard, Right Providence?* (Giulio Petroni); *Thompson 1880* (Albert Moore); *To Hell and Back* (Giovanni Fago)
Mulligan, Marina: *Black Killer* (Lucky Moore); *Gunman of One Hundred Crosses* (Lucky Moore)
Mulock, Al: *The Good, the Bad, and the Ugly* (Sergio Leone); *Hellbenders* (Sergio Corbucci); *Once Upon a Time in the West* (Sergio Leone)
Munro, Caroline: *Talent for Loving* (Richard Quine)
Muratori, Primiano: *Return of Shanghai Joe* (Bitto Albertini)
Murgia, Antonella: *Cisco* (Sergio Bergonzelli); *Texas Adios* (Ferdinando Baldi)
Murgia, Tiberio: *Rick and John, Conquerors of the West* (Osvaldo Civirani)
Muro, Venancio: *Torrejon City* (Leon Klimovsky)
Murphy, Audie: *Texican* (Espinosa/Selander)
Murray, Don: *Kid Rodelo* (Richard Carlson)
Musante, Tony: *Mercenary* (Sergio Corbucci)
Musumeci, Tucci: *Holy Water Joe* (Mario Gariazzo)
Musy, Gianni: *Grandsons of Zorro* (Mariano Laurenti)
Mynhardt, Patrick: *Three Bullets for a Long Gun* (Peter Henkel)
Nakadai, Tatsuya: *Today It's Me . . . Tomorrow You* (Tonino Cervi)

Nakszynski, Nikolas see **Kinski, Klaus**

Namath, Joe: *Last Rebel* (Denys McCoy)

Nanni, Lea: *Blood Calls to Blood* (Lewis King)

Naschy, Paul: *Fury of Johnny Kid* (Gianni Puccini)

Navarro, Nieves (pseudonym — Susan Scott): *Adios, Sabata* (Frank Kramer); *Big Gundown* (Sergio Sollima); *Kill the Poker Player* (Frank Bronston); *Light the Fuse . . . Sartana Is Coming* (Anthony Ascott); *Long Days of Vengeance* (Stan Vance); **Pistol for Ringo* (Duccio Tessari); *Return of Ringo* (Duccio Tessari); *Rojo* (Leo Coleman)

Nedar, Vladimer: *Belle Starr Story* (Nathan Wich)

Nell, Krista: *Django and Sartana Are Coming . . . It's the End* (Dick Spitfire); *Kill Django . . . Kill First* (Willy S. Regan); *God Is My Colt .45* (Dean Jones); **Kitosch, the Man Who Came from the North* (Joseph Marvin); *Paid in Blood* (Paolo Solvay); *To Hell and Back* (Giovanni Fago); *You're Jinxed, Friend, You Just Met Sacramento* (Giorgio Cristallini)

Nelli, Barbara: *Shango* (Edward G. Muller); *Shoot, Ring Out!* (Augustin Navarro)

Nelson, Burt: *Massacre at Grand Canyon* (Stanley Corbett)

Neri, Rosalba: *And They Smelled the Strange, Exciting, Dangerous Scent of Dollars* (Italo Alfaro); *Arizona* (Sergio Martino); *Arizona Colt* (Michele Lupo); *Blood River* (Gianfranco Baldenello); *Days of Violence* (Al Bradly); *Drummer of Vengeance* (Robert Paget); *Dynamite Jim* (Alfonso Balcazar); *Great Treasure Hunt* (Tonino Ricci); **Johnny Yuma* (Romolo Guerrieri); *Killer Goodbye* (Primo Zeglio); *Long Ride from Hell* (Alex Burkes); *Man Called Invincible* (Anthony Ascott); *The Reward's Yours, the Man's Mine* (Edward G. Muller); *Sartana Does Not Forgive* (Alfonso Balcazar); *This Man Can't Die* (Gianfranco Baldenello); *Wanted Johnny Texas* (Erminio Salvi); *Watch Out Gringo . . . Sabata Is Coming* (Alfonso Balcazar)

Nero, Franco (pseudonym for **Franco Spartanero**): *Cipolla Colt* (Enzo G. Castellari); *Compañeros* (Sergio Corbucci); *Deaf Smith and Johnny Ears* (Paolo Cavara); *Django* (Sergio Corbucci); *Django Strikes Again* (Ted Archer); *Don't Turn the Other Cheek* (Duccio Tessari); *Keoma* (Enzo G. Castellari); *Man: His Pride and His Vengeance* (Luigi Bazzoni); *Massacre Time* (Lucio Fulci); *Mercenary* (Sergio Corbucci); *Texas, Adios* (Ferdinando Baldi); **Tramplers* (Albert Band)

Neubert, Hans: *Taste of Violence* (Robert Hossein)

Newman, James: *Wanted Johnny Texas* (Erminio Salvi)

Newmar, Julie: *Blood River* (Gianfranco Baldenello)

Nicols, Alex: *Gunfighters of Casa Grande* (Roy Rowland); *Ride and Kill* (J. L. Boraw); **Savage Guns* (Michael Carreras)

Nielsen, Hans: **Bullets Don't Argue* (Mike Perkins); *Five Thousand Dollars on One Ace* (Alfonso Balcazar); *Prairie in the City* (Claus Tinney); *Pyramid of the Sun God* (Robert Siodmak); *Treasure of the Aztecs* (Robert Siodmak)

Nielsen, Leslie: *Four Rode Out* (John Peyser)

Nieto, Francisco: *Canadian Wilderness* (Armando De Ossorio); *If You Shoot . . . You Live!* (Joe Lacy)

Nieto, José: *Kid Rodelo* (Richard Carlson); *Man of the Cursed Valley* (Omar Hopkins); *Outlaw of Red River* (Maury Dexter); **Savage Guns* (Michael Carreras)

Nigro, Pat: *They Called Him Veritas* (Luigi Perelli)

Nilo, Alejandro: *Ringo: Face of Revenge* (Mario Caiano)

Noe, Anna Maria: *Matalo!* (Cesare Canavari)

Nolan, Ray: *Patience Has a Limit, We Don't* (Armando Morandi)
Northon, Al *see* **Caltabiano, Alfio**
Norton, Tony: *Dick Luft in Sacramento* (Anthony Ascott); *Sartana Does Not Forgive* (Alfonso Balcazar)
Norvese, Vincenzo: *Bastard, Go and Kill* (Gino Mangini)
Nukano, Yoshio: *Stranger in Japan* (Stan Vance)
Nuscick, Loredana (also **Loredana Nusciak**): *Django* (Sergio Corbucci); *God Will Forgive My Pistol* (Gariazzo/Savona); **Man from Canyon City* (Alfonso Balcazar); *Revenge for Revenge* (Ray Calloway); *Seven Dollars on the Red* (Alberto Cardone); *Ten Thousand Dollars Blood Money* (Romolo Guerrieri)
Oak, Jeanne: *Sugar Colt* (Franco Giraldi)
Oakland, Simon: *Hunting Party* (Don Medford)
Oates, Warren: *China 9, Liberty 37* (Monte Hellman)
O'Brien, Donald (also **Donal O'Brien**): **Finders Killers* (Gianni Crea); *Four Gunmen of the Apocalypse* (Lucio Fulci); *God Is My Colt .45* (Dean Jones); *Jesse and Lester, Two Brothers in a Place Called Trinity* (James London); *Keoma* (Enzo G. Castellari); *Kung Fu Brothers in the Wild West* (Yeo Ban Yee); *Man Called Blade* (Sergio Martino); *Paid in Blood* (Paolo Salvay); *Run Man, Run* (Sergio Sollima); *Sheriff of Rock Spring* (Anthony Green); *Silver Saddle* (Lucio Fulci); *Thirteenth Is a Judas* (Joseph Warren)
O'Brien, Peter: *Big Showdown* (Giancarlo Santi)
Occhini, Ilaria: *Tramplers* (Albert Band)
O'Connor, Glynnis: *Kid Vengeance* (Joe Manduke)
O'Connor, Ray: *Bad Kids of the West* (Tony Good); *Caliber .38* (Tony Secchi); *Gunmen and Holy Ghost* (Roberto Mauri); *Porno Erotic Western* (Gerard B. Lennox); *Requiem for a Bounty Hunter* (Mark Welles)
O'Hara, Kareen (pseudonym for **Stefania Careddu**): *Go Kill and Come Back* (Enzo G. Castellari); *Johnny Hamlet* (Enzo G. Castellari)
Ojeda, Manuel: *Eagle's Wing* (Anthony Harvey)
Oliveras, Frank: *Seven Guns for Timothy* (Rod Gilbert); *Sunscorched* (Alfonso Balcazar)
Olmi, Corrado: *Apache Woman* (George McRoots)
Omae, Kin: *Stranger in Japan* (Stan Vance)
Omar, Olga: *My Colt, Not Yours* (Steve MacCohy)
Ontario, Glauco (also **Clauco Ontario**): *Carambola's Philosophy* (Ferdinando Baldi); *John the Bastard* (Armando Crispino); *Man Called Django* (Edward G. Muller)
Oppedisano, Roque: *Apache Woman* (George McRoots)
Orfei, Liana: *Django Kills Softly* (Max Hunter)
Orfei, Moira: *Two Sergeants of General Custer* (Giorgio Simonelli)
Orsini, Umberto: *Eye for an Eye* (Albert Marshall)
Ortiz, Angel: *Blood and Guns* (Giulio Petroni); **Fury of the Apaches* (Joe Lacy); *Here We Are Again, Eh Providence?* (Alberto De Martino); *I Do Not Forgive . . . I Kill!* (Joaquin R. Marchent); *Mercenary* (Sergio Corbucci); *Savage Gringo* (Bava/ Romano)
Osinaga, Pedro: *Man Called Blade* (Sergio Martino)
Osuna, Gloria: *Few Dollars for Django* (Leon Klimovsky); *Gunfight at High Noon* (Joaquin R. Marchent); *Magnificent Texan* (Lewis King); *Pistol for a Hundred Coffins* (Umberto Lenzi)
Oteroi, Carlos: *Who Killed Johnny R.?* (José Luis Madrid)
Ott, Angelica: *Blood at Sundown* (Albert Cardiff); *Halleluja and Sartana Strike Again* (Mario Siciliano)

Padovan, Marta: *Secret of Captain O'Hara* (Arturo R. Castillo)

Page, Genieve: *Talent for Loving* (Richard Quine)

Pai-Pico, Jason: *Kung Fu Brothers in the Wild West* (Yeo Ban Yee)

Palacios, Ricardo: *Comin' at Ya* (Ferdinando Baldi); *Kitosch, the Man Who Came from the North* (Joseph Marvin); *None of the Three Were Called Trinity* (Pedro L. Ramirez); *With Friends, Nothing Is Easy* (Steve MacCohy)

Palance, Jack (pseudonym for **Vladimir Palanuik**): *Brothers Blue* (Marc Meyer); *Compañeros* (Sergio Corbucci); *God's Gun* (Frank Kramer); *It Can Be Done . . . Amigo* (Maurizio Lucidi); **Mercenary* (Sergio Corbucci); *Sting of the West* (Enzo Castellari)

Palanuik, Vladimir *see* **Palance, Jack**

Palenzuela, Miguel: *Coyote* (Joaquin R. Marchent); *Gunfight at High Noon* (Joaquin R. Marchent)

Pallavicino, Gianni: *Beast* (Mario Costa); *Find a Place to Die* (Anthony Ascott); *Shoot, Gringo . . . Shoot!* (Frank B. Corlish)

Palmara, Mimmo (also **Dick Palmer**): *Black Jack* (Gianfranco Baldanello); *Bullets Don't Argue* (Mike Perkins); *Caliber .38* (Tony Secchi); *Dead for a Dollar* (Osvaldo Civirani); *Deserter* (Fulgozzi/Kennedy); *Execution* (Domenico Paolella); *For One Thousand Dollars Per Day* (Silvio Amadio); *Gunmen and the Holy Ghost* (Roberto Mauri); *Gunmen of One Hundred Crosses* (Lucky Moore); *Handsome, the Ugly, and the Stupid* (Gianni Grimaldi); *He Was Called Holy Ghost* (Robert Johnson); *Left Handed Johnny West* (Frank Kramer); *Long Ride from Hell* (Alex Burkes); *Paths of War* (Aldo Grimaldi); *Poker with Pistols* (Joseph Warren); *Shotgun* (Robert Mauri); *Time and Place of Killing* (Vincent Eagle); *Two Sons of Ringo* (Giorgio Simonelli)

Palmer, Dick *see* **Palmara, Mimmo**

Palmer, Greg: *Here We Are Again, Eh Providence?* (Alberto DeMartino); *Sometimes Life Is Hard, Right Providence?* (Giulio Petroni)

Palmer, Lawrence: *Ride and Kill* (J. L. Boraw)

Palucci, Carlo: *Let Them Rest* (Carlo Lizzani)

Paluzzi, Luciana: *Forgotten Pistolero* (Ferdinando Baldi)

Panaro, Alessandro: *Pyramid of the Sun God* (Robert Siodmak)

Pani, Corrado: *Matalo!* (Cesare Canavari)

Paoletti, Roberto: *Behind the Mask of Zorro* (Umberto Lenzi)

Papadopulos, Panos: *For a Few Dollars More* (Sergio Leone)

Paplisi, Ugo: *Magnificent Bandits* (Giovanni Fago)

Parajito: *Long Days of Vengeance* (Stan Vance); *Pistol for Ringo* (Ducci Tessari); *Return of Ringo* (Duccio Tessari)

Pardo, Monica: *Dead for a Dollar* (Osvaldo Civirani)

Parker, Dorthee (also **Dorothea Parker**): *Massacre at Marble City* (Franz J. Gottlieb); *Pirates of the Mississippi* (Jürgen Roland)

Parker, Kathleen: *Sheriff with the Gold* (Richard Kean)

Parra, Joaquin (also **James Parker**): *All Out* (Umberto Lenzi); *Bullet for the General* (Damiano Damiani); *Sugar Colt* (Franco Giraldi)

Pasolini, Pier Paolo: *Let Them Rest* (Carlo Lizzani)

Pasquetto, Franco: *Death Is Sweet from the Soldier of God* (Robert Johnson)

Pate, Michael: *Mad Dog Morgan* (Philippe Mora)

Pattier, Paula: *If You Shoot . . . You Live!* (Joe Lacy)

Paul, Andreina: *Road to Fort Alamo* (Mario Bava)

Paul, Gloria: *For a Few Dollars Less* (Mario Mattòli)

Pavone, Rita: *Rita of the West* (Ferdinando Baldi)

Pazzafini, Nello (also **Giovanni Pazzafini**) (pseudonym—**Ted Carter**): *Adios Gringo* (George Finley); *Adios Hombre* (Mario Caiano); *Arizona Colt* (Michele Lupo); *Blood for a Silver Dollar* (Calvin J. Paget); *Caliber .38* (Toni Secchi); *Carambola's Philosophy: In the Right Pocket* (Ferdinando Baldi); *Days of Violence* (Al Bradly); *Death at Owell Rock* (Riccardo Freda); *Death on High Mountain* (Fred Ringoold); *Dick Luft in Sacramento* (Anthony Ascott); *Face to Face* (Sergio Sollima); *Find a Place to Die* (Anthony Ascott); *Fort Yuma Gold* (Calvin J. Paget); *His Name Was Holy Ghost* (Anthony Ascott); *I Am Sartana, Trade Your Guns for a Coffin* (Anthony Ascott); *If One Is Born a Swine, Kill Him* (Al Bradly); *It Can Be Done . . . Amigo* (Maurizio Lucidi); *Killer Caliber .32* (Al Bradly); *Killer Goodbye* (Primo Zeglio); *Long Ride from Hell* (Alex Burks); *Man Called Blade* (Sergio Martino); *Man Called Invincible* (Anthony Ascott); *Return of Halleluja* (Anthony Ascott); *Run Man, Run* (Sergio Sollima); *They Call Him Cemetery* (Anthony Ascott); *Two Pistols and a Coward* (Calvin J. Paget); *Vendetta at Dawn* (Willy S. Regan); *Wanted* (Calvin J. Paget)
Peckinpah, Sam: *China 9, Liberty 37* (Monte Hellman)
Pedemonte, Elena: *They Call Me Trinity* (E. B. Clucher)
Pellegrin, Raymond: *Cost of Dying* (Sergio Merolle)
Pelliceri, Oscar: *Man with the Golden Pistol* (Alfonso Balcazar); *Sunscorched* (Alfonso Balcazar)
Peña, Julio: *Alive or Preferably Dead* (Duccio Tessari); *Bullets and the Flesh* (Fred Wilson); *Cowards Don't Pray* (Marlon Sirko); *Hellbenders* (Sergio Corbucci); *Kid Rodelo* (Richard Carlson); *Magnificent Brutes of the West* (Fred Wilson); *Mercenary* (Sergio Corbucci); *Minnesota Clay* (Sergio Corbucci); *Mutiny at Fort Sharp* (Fernando Cerchio); *Pistol for a Hundred Coffins* (Umberto Lenzi); *Price of Power* (Tonino Valerii)
Pendleton, Chuck *see* **Mitchell, Gordon**
Penella, Emma: *Magnificent Brutes of the West* (Fred Wilson)
Pennell, Larry: *Flaming Frontier* (Alfred Vohrer)
Peral, Antonio: *Texican* (Lesley Selander)
Peralta, Goyo: *Stranger and the Gunfighter* (Anthony Dawson)
Perella, Allessandro: *Finders Killers* (Gianni Crea); *Pistol Packin' Preacher* (Leopoldo Savona)
Pernice, Gino: *Hellbenders* (Sergio Corbucci); *Specialist* (Sergio Corbucci)
Perret, Pierre: *Judge Roy Bean* (Richard Owens)
Perschy, Maria: *Tall Women* (Sidney Pink)
Persuad, Joseph: *Adios, Sabata* (Frank Kramer)
Pesarini, Augusto: *Return of Clint the Stranger* (George Martin)
Pesce, Franco: *Blood at Sundown* (De La Loma/Muller); *Gold of the Heroes* (Don Reynolds); *Have a Good Funeral, My Friend . . . Sartana Will Pay* (Anthony Ascott); *Miss Dynamite* (Sergio Grieco); *Roy Colt and Winchester Jack* (Mario Bava); *Shango* (Edward G. Muller)
Peters, Brock: *Ace High* (Giuseppe Colizzi)
Peters, Werner: *Black Eagle of Santa Fe* (Ernst Hofbauer)
Petit, Pascale: *Find a Place to Die* (Anthony Ascott)
Petito, Enzo: *The Good, the Bad, and the Ugly* (Sergio Leone)
Petri, Mario: *Lost Treasure of the Incas* (Piero Pierotti)
Petrucci, Giovanni (pseudonym—**Giovanni Petti**): *Big Ripoff* (Franco Rossetti); *Canadian Wilderness* (Armando De Ossorio); *Cost of Dying* (Sergio Merolle); *Requiem for a Bounty Hunter* (Mark Welles); *White, the Yellow, and the Black* (Sergio Corbucci)

Petry, Brigitte: *Handsome, the Ugly, and the Stupid* (Gianni Grimaldi)
Petti, Giovani *see* **Petrucci, Giovanni**
Philbrook, James: *Django, a Bullet for You* (Leon Klimovsky); *Finger on the Trigger* (Sidney Pink); *I Do Not Forgive . . . I Kill!* (Joaquin R. Marchent); *If You Shoot . . . You Live!* (Joe Lacy); *Seven for Pancho Villa* (José M. Elorrieta); **Son of a Gunfighter* (Paul Landres); *Two Thousand Dollars for Coyote* (Leon Klimovsky)
Philippe, Gunther: *Hatred of God* (Claudio Gora)
Pia, Emilio Delle: *Arizona* (Sergio Martino)
Piaget, Paul: *Charge of the Seventh Cavalry* (Herbert Martin); *Hour of Death* (Paul Marchenti); *Magnificent Three* (Joaquin R. Marchent); *Seven Guns from Texas* (Joaquin R. Marchent); **Shots Ring Out* (Augustin Navarro)
Piani, Lorenzo: *Deadly Trackers* (Amerigo Anton); *In the Name of the Father, the Son, and the Colt* (Frank Bronston)
Picas, Antonio (also **Anthony Pix** and **Antonio Pica):** *Awkward Hands* (Rafael R. Marchent); *Bandidos* (Max Dillman); *Bullet for Sandoval* (Julio Buchs); *Man Who Killed Billy the Kid* (Julio Buchs); *Ringo, the Lone Rider* (Rafael R. Marchent); *Two Crosses at Danger Pass* (Rafael R. Marchent); *Who's Afraid of Zorro?* (Franco Lo Cascio)
Piccoli, Michael: *Do Not Touch the White Woman* (Marco Ferreri)
Pickens, Slim: *Deserter* (Fulgozzi/Kennedy)
Pierangeli, Anna: *For One Thousand Dollars Per Day* (Silvio Amadio)
Pignatelli, Micaela: *Piluk, the Timid One* (Guido Celano)
Pignozzi, Luciano *see* **Collins, Allan**
Pili: *Woman for Ringo* (Rafael R. Marchent)
Pinal, Silva: *Guns for San Sebastian* (Henri Verneuil)
Pino, Dario: *Magnificent West* (Gianni Crea)
Pinon, Bernard: *A Girl Is a Gun* (Luc Moullet)
Pistilli, Luigi: *Bandidos* (Max Dillman); *Death Rides a Horse* (Giulio Petroni); *Dollars for a Fast Gun* (Joaquin R. Marchent); **For a Few Dollars More* (Sergio Leone); *The Good, the Bad, and the Ugly* (Sergio Leone); *Great Silence* (Sergio Corbucci); *Night of the Serpent* (Giulio Petroni); *Texas, Adios* (Ferdinando Baldi)
Pizzuti, Riccardo: *Man of the East* (E. B. Clucher)
Pleasence, Donald: *Django Strikes Again* (Ted Archer)
Pochath, Werner: *Bandara Bandits* (Sergio Corbucci); *Vengeance* (Anthony Dawson)
Poggi, Nando: *Johnny Yuma* (Romolo Guerrieri); **Massacre at Grand Canyon* (Stanley Corbett)
Poitel, Liz: *Shots Ring Out* (Augustin Navarro)
Polesello, Franca: *Navajo Joe* (Sergio Corbucci); *Shoot Joe, and Shoot Again* (Hal Bradey)
Polger, Tommy: *Return of Shanghai Joe* (Bitto Albertini)
Poli, Maurice (pseudonym — **Monty Greenwood**): *Two Sides of the Dollar* (Roberto Montero); *Shango* (Edward G. Muller)
Pollard, Michael J.: *Four Gunmen of Apocalypse* (Lucio Fulci); *Frenchie King* (Christian-Jaque)
Polyn, Greta: *Kill Johnny Ringo* (Frank G. Carrol)
Pondal, Mary Paz: *Apocalypse Joe* (Leopoldo Savona)
Portaluri, Angela: *Anything for a Friend* (Miles Deem)
Posani, Dante *see* **Clark, Montgomery**
Possenti, Marilena: *Chrysanthemums for a Bunch of Swine* (Sergio Pastore)
Powers, Hunt (pseudonym — **Jack Betts):** *Django and Sartana Are Coming . . . It's the End* (Dick Spitfire); *Fistful of Death* (Miles Deem); *Greatest Robbery in the*

West (Maurizio Lucidi); *He Was Called Holy Ghost* (Roberto Mauri); *One Damned Day at Dawn . . . Django Meets Sartana* (Miles Deem); *Reach You Bastard!* (Lucky Dickerson); *Showdown for a Badman* (Miles Deem); *Stranger That Kneels Beside the Shadow of a Corpse* (Miles Deem); *Sugar Colt (Franco Giraldi)

Powers, Jill: *Massacre at Grand Canyon* (Stanley Corbett)

Pozzilli, Alberto: *Hatred of God* (Claudio Gora)

Prada, José Maria: *Pancho Villa* (Eugenio Martin)

Prendes, Luis: *China 9, Liberty 37* (Monte Hellman); *Christmas Kid* (Sidney Pink); *Django Does Not Forgive (Julio Buchs); *Man Who Killed Billy the Kid* (Julio Buchs); *Tall Women* (Sidney Pink); *White Comanche* (Gilbert Lee Kay)

Preston, Wayde: *God Will Forgive My Pistol* (Gariazzo/Savona); *Hey Amigo! A Toast to Your Death!* (Paul Maxwell); *Long Ride from Hell (Alex Burkes); *Man Called Sledge* (Morrow/Gentili); *Sartana in the Valley of Death* (Roberto Mauri); *Today It's Me, Tomorrow You* (Tonino Cervi); *Wrath of God* (Albert Cardone)

Prete, Giancarlo *see* **Brent, Timothy**

Pruckner, Tilo: *Valley of the Dancing Widows* (Volker Vogeler)

Puente, Jesus: *Adios Gringo* (George Finley); *Behind the Mask of Zorro* (Ricardo Blasco); *Damned Pistols of Dallas* (Joseph Trader); *Dollars for a Fast Gun* (Joaquin R. Marchent); *For a Fist in the Eye* (Michele Lupo); *Fury of the Apaches (José M. Elorrieta); *Hands of a Gunman* (Rafael R. Marchent); *Hour of Death* (Paul Marchenti); *Massacre at Fort Grant* (J. Douglas); *Rattler Kid* (Leon Klimovsky); *Ringo, the Lone Rider* (Rafael R. Marchent); *Seven Guns from Texas* (Joaquin R. Marchent); *Two Crosses at Danger Pass* (Rafael R. Marchent)

Pulcrono, Enzo: *Magnificent West* (Gianni Crea)

Puntillo, Salvatore: *And They Smelled the Strange, Exciting, Dangerous Scent of Dollars* (Italo Alfaro)

Puppo, Romano: *Dead Men Ride* (Aldo Florio); *Sabata* (Frank Kramer)

Purdom, Edmund: *Charge of Seventh Cavalry* (Herbert Martin); *Chrysanthemums for a Bunch of Swine* (Sergio Pastore); *Last Ride to Santa Cruz* (Rolf Olsen); *Piluk, the Timid One* (Guido Celano); *Shoot to Kill (Ramon Torrado)

Puskin, Anne: *His Name Was King* (Don Reynolds)

Quesada, Milo: *Django, Kill . . . If You Live, Shoot!* (Giulio Questi); *Red Blood, Yellow Gold* (Nando Cicero); *Twice a Judas* (Nando Cicero)

Quiney, Charles: *Rebels of Arizona* (José M. Zabalza); *More Dollars for the MacGregors* (J. L. Merino)

Quinn, Anthony: *Deaf Smith and Johnny Ears* (Paoo Cavara); *Guns for San Sebastian* (Henri Verneuil)

Quinn, Freddy: *Sheriff Was a Lady* (Sobey Martin)

Quintana, Gene: *Comin' at Ya* (Ferdinando Baldi)

Rabal, Francisco: *It Can Be Done . . . Amigo* (Maurizio Lucidi); *Legacy of the Incas* (Georg Marischka); *Long Days of Vengeance* (Stan Vance)

Raffaelli, Giulaino (pseudonym — **Julian Rafferty**): *And God Said to Cain* (Anthony Dawson); *Sugar Colt* (Franco Giraldi)

Rafferty, Julian *see* **Raffaelli, Giulaino**

Raho, Umberto (also **Umi Raho**): *Pecos Cleans Up* (Maurizio Lucidi); *Man with the Golden Pistol* (Alfonso Balcazar)

Raimbourg, Lucien: *Dynamite Jack* (Jean Bastia)

Ralli, Giovanna: *Mercenary* (Sergio Corbucci); *Taste of Violence (Robert Hossein)

Ramsey, Bill: *Apache's Last Battle* (Hugo Fregonese)

Randall, Bud: *Anything for a Friend* (Miles Deem)

Randall, Monica: *All Out* (Umberto Lenzi); *Five Giants from Texas* (Aldo Florio);

*For a Fist in the Eye (Michele Lupo); One Hundred Thousand Dollars for Ringo (Alberto De Martino); Red Blood, Yellow Gold (Nando Cicero); Red Sun (Terence Young); Ringo and Gringo Against All (Bruno Corbucci)

Rassimov, Ivan (pseudonym for **Ivan Djerrassimovic;** aka **Sean Todd**): Cjamango (Edward G. Muller); Cowards Don't Pray (Marlon Sirko); *Don't Wait, Django . . . Shoot! (Edward G. Muller); If You Want to Live, Shoot! (Willy S. Regan); Vengeance Is a Dish Served Cold (William Redford)

Rassimov, Rada (pseudonym for **Rada Djerassimovic**): Django the Bastard (Sergio Garrone); *Don't Wait, Django . . . Shoot! (Edward G. Muller); The Good, the Bad, and the Ugly (Sergio Leone); Machine Gun Killers (Paolo Bianchini); Taste for Killing (Tonino Valerii)

Ravaioli, Isarco: Djurado (Gianni Narzisi); Let's Go and Kill Sartana (Mario Pinzauti)

Ray, Andrew (pseudonym for **Andea Aureli**): Chuck Moll (E. B. Clucher); Colorado Charlie (Robert Johnson); Dollars for a Fast Gun (Joaquin R. Marchent); Ringo and His Golden Pistol (Sergio Corbucci)

Re, Gustavo: None of the Three Were Called Trinity (Pedro L. Ramirez)

Reagan, Dick see **Garrone, Riccardo**

Reali, Carlo: Buddy Goes West (Michele Lupo)

Redemonte, Enzo: Wanted Sabata (Robert Johnson)

Redgrave, Lynn: Don't Turn the Other Cheek (Duccio Tessari)

Reed, Dean: Adios, Sabata (Frank Kramer); God Made Them . . . I Kill Them (Paolo Bianchi); Nephews of Zorro (Frank Reed); Twenty Paces to Death (Ted Mulligan); *Winchester Does Not Forgive (Adelchi Bianchi)

Reed, Jim: Ruthless Colt of the Gringo (José L. Madrid)

Reed, Oliver: Hunting Party (Don Medford)

Reeves, Marta: Man and a Colt (Tullio Demichelli)

Reeves, Steve: Long Ride from Hell (Alex Burkes)

Renis, Tony: For a Few Dollars Less (Mario Mattòli)

Resino, Andres: Django, a Bullet for You (Leon Klimovsky)

Ressel, Franco (also **Ray Ressel**): Bad Kids of the West (Tony Good); California (Michele Lupo); Day of Anger (Tonino Valerii); Dead for a Dollar (Osvaldo Civirani); Have a Good Funeral, My Friend . . . Sartana Will Pay (Anthony Ascott); In a Colt's Shadow (Gianni Grimaldi); Man: His Pride and Vengeance (Luigi Bazzoni); Mercenary (Sergio Corbucci); *Rojo (Leo Coleman); Sabata (Frank Kramer); Taste for Killing (Tonino Valerii); They Call Him Cemetery (Anthony Ascott); Trinity Is Still My Name (E. B. Clucher); Two Sons of Trinity (Glenn Eastman)

Reuek, Emilie: Prairie in the City (Claus Tinney)

Rey, Fernando: Compañeros (Sergio Corbucci); Legacy of the Incas (Georg Marischka); Navajo Joe (Sergio Corbucci); Price of Power (Tonino Valerii); *Savage Guns (Michael Carreras); Son of a Gunfighter (Paul Landres); Town Called Hell (Robert Parrish); Trinity Sees Red (Mario Camus)

Reynolds, Burt: Navajo Joe (Sergio Corbucci)

Reynolds, Clarke: Winnetou and Shatterhand in the Valley of Death (Harald Reinl)

Ribeiro, Catherine: Buffalo Bill, Hero of the Far West (John W. Fordson)

Rice, Alfred see **Rizzo, Alfredo**

Rice, Robert: Hate Thy Neighbor (Ferdinando Baldi)

Richardson, John: Execution (Domenico Paolella); John the Bastard (Armando Crispino)

Richelmy, Victor: Watch Out, Gringo . . . Sabata Will Return (Alfonso Balcazar)

Rico, Paquintia: *Savage Guns* (Michael Carreras)
Righi, Massimo *see* Dean, Max
Righini, Francesca: *Belle Starr Story* (Nathan Wich)
Rilla, Walter: *Day of Anger* (Tonino Valerii)
Ringaud, George (also George Rigaud and Jorge Rigaud): *Alive or Preferably Dead* (Duccio Tessari); *Coffin for the Sheriff* (William Hawkins); *Finger on the Trigger* (Sidney Pink); *Forewarned, Half-Killed . . . the Word of Holy Ghost* (Anthony Ascott); *Machine Gun Killers* (Paolo Bianchini); *Place Called Glory* (Ralph Gideon); *Ride and Kill* (Boraw/Caiano); *Ringo's Big Night* (Mario Maffei); *Seven Guns for MacGregors* (Frank Garfield); *Sugar Colt* (Franco Giraldi); *Up the MacGregors!* (Frank Garfield); *Valley of the Dancing Widows* (Volker Vogeler); *Woman for Ringo* (Rafael R. Marchent)
Rivelli, Luisa: *Beast* (Mario Costa)
Rivero, Santiago: *Dynamite Joe* (Anthony Dawson); *Shoot to Kill* (Ramon Torrado)
Rivers, Mike: *Adios Cjamango* (Harry Freeman); *Rebels of Arizona* (José M. Zabalza)
Riviere, George: *Minnesota Clay* (Sergio Corbucci)
Riwes, Michael *see* De La Riva, Miguel
Rizzi, Alfredo (pseudonym—Alfred Rice): *Paid in Blood* (Paolo Solvay); *Don't Wait Django . . . Shoot!* (Edward G. Muller)
Rizzo, Gianni: *Adios Sabata!* (Frank Kramer); *Face to Face* (Sergio Sollima); *Return of Sabata* (Frank Kramer); *Run Man, Run* (Sergio Sollima); *Sabata* (Frank Kramer); *Sartana* (Frank Kramer)
Robards, Jason: *Once Upon a Time in the West* (Sergio Leone)
Roberts, Pernell: *Four Rode Out* (John Peyser)
Robinson, Madeleine: *Taste of Violence* (Robert Hossein)
Robsahm, Fred: *Black Killer* (Lucky Moore)
Rocas, Alfonso: *Dynamite Joe* (Anthony Dawson)
Rock, Anthony: *Shoot the Living . . . Pray for the Dead* (Joseph Warren)
Rocks, Jack: *Dollar of Fire* (Nick Nostro)
Rodin, Virginia: *Let's Go and Kill Sartana* (Mario Pinzauti)
Rodriquez, Emilio: *Terrible Sheriff* (Antonio Momplet)
Rogers, Clyde *see* Van Nutter, Rick
Rogers, James: *Brother Outlaw* (Edward G. Muller)
Rojas, Alfonso (also: Gustavo Rojo and Gus Rojas): *Bullet for Sandoval* (Julio Buchs); *Cavalry Charge* (Ramon Torrado); *Christmas Kid* (Sidney Pink); *Dead Are Countless* (Rafael R. Marchent); *Few Dollars for Django* (Leon Klimovsky); *Fort Yuma Gold* (Calvin J. Padget); *Django Does Not Forgive* (Julio Buchs); *I Do Not Forgive . . . I Kill* (Joaquin R. Marchent); *Kill Them All and Return Alone* (Enzo G. Castellari); *Kitosch, the Man Who Came from the North* (Joseph Marvin); *Left Handed Johnny West* (Frank Kramer); *One Against One . . . No Mercy* (Rafael R. Marchent); *Pyramid of the Sun God* (Robert Siodmak); *Quinta: Fighting Proud* (Leon Klimovsky); *Reverend Colt* (Leon Klimovsky); *Ringo and Gringo Against All* (Bruno Corbucci); *Ringo, the Lone Rider* (Rafael R. Marchent); *Sabata the Killer* (Tullio Demichelli); *Savage Gringo* (Bava/Romano); *Seven for Pancho Villa* (José M. Elorrieta); *Seven Hours of Gunfire* (Joaquin R. Marchent); *Tall Women* (Sidney Pink); *Treasure of the Aztecs* (Robert Siodmak); *Twins of Texas* (Steno); *Two Thousand Dollars for Coyote* (Leon Klimovsky)
Rojo, Antonio (also Antonio Molina Rojo and Molina Rojo): *For a Few Dollars More* (Sergio Leone); *Five Giants from Texas* (Aldo Florio); *Four Dollars for Vengeance* (Alfonso Balcazar); *Kill Them All and Return Alone* (Enzo G. Castellari); *Man from Canyon City* (Alfonso Balcazar); *My Colt, Not Yours* (Steve MacCohy); *Seven Hours of Gunfire* (Joaquin R. Marchent); *Texican* (Lesley Selander)

Rojo, Ethel: *Massacre at Fort Grant* (J. Douglas); *Minnesota Clay* (Sergio Corbucci)
Rojo, Helena: *Eye for an Eye* (Albert Marshall)
Rojo, Ruben: *Duel in the Eclipse* (Martino/Merino); *For One Thousand Dollars Per Day* (Silvio Amadio)
Roland, Gilbert (pseudonym for **Luis Antonio Damasco De Alonso**): *Between God, the Devil and a Winchester* (Dario Silvestri); **Go Kill and Come Back* (Enzo G. Castellari); *Johnny Hamlet* (Enzo G. Castellari); *Ruthless Four* (Giorgio Capitani); *Sartana Does Not Forgive* (Alfonso Balcazar)
Roland, Gill: *Fasthand* (Frank Bronston); *For a Book of Dollars* (Renzo Spaziani); *In the Name of the Father, the Son, and the Colt* (Frank Bronston)
Rollin, Georges: *Jaguar* (Jess Franco)
Roman, Letitia: *Flaming Frontier* (Alfred Vohrer)
Romanelli, Carla: *Fighting Fists of Shanghai Joe* (Mario Caiano)
Romano, Renato: *Deaf Smith and Johnny Ears* (Paolo Cavara); *Last Rebel* (Denys McCoy); **Minute to Pray . . . a Second to Die* (Franco Giraldi); *The Moment to Kill* (Anthony Ascott); *Shotgun* (Robert Mauri)
Rome, Sydne: **Alive or Preferably Dead* (Duccio Tessari); *Man Called Amen* (Alfio Caltabiano); *They Still Call Me Amen* (Alfio Caltabiano)
Romero, Cesar: *Talent for Loving* (Richard Quine)
Roque, Fela: *Savage Pampas* (Hugo Fregonese)
Rosato, Lucio: *Days of Violence* (Al Bradly)
Rosin, Sheyla: *Heads or Tails* (Peter E. Stanley); *Vengeance* (Anthony Dawson)
Roso, Antonio: *Five Thousand Dollars on One Ace* (Alfonso Balcazar)
Ross, Edwin G.: *Django Kills Softly* (Max Hunter)
Ross, Howard (pseudonym for **Renato Rossini**): *Johnny Colt* (Giovanni Grimaldi); *Savage Gringo* (Bava/Romano)
Ross, Jerry: *Reach You Bastard!* (Lucky Dickerson)
Ross, Sarah: *Greatest Robbery in the West* (Maurizio Lucidi); *Quinta: Fighting Proud* (Leon Klimovsky); *Ruthless Four* (Giorgio Capitani)
Rossi, Gerardo: *Colt in the Hand of the Devil* (Sergio Bergonzelli)
Rossini, Renato see Ross, Howard
Rothlein, William: *Legacy of the Incas* (Georg Marischka)
Roundtree, Richard: *Charley One-Eye* (Don Chaffey)
Rovere, Gina: *God Forgives, I Don't* (Giuseppe Colizzi)
Rowland, Steve: *Gunfighter of Casa Grande* (Roy Rowland)
Rual, Marco: *Three Silver Dollars* (Irving Jacobs)
Rubini, Giulia: *Adios Hombre* (Mario Caiano); *Ringo and His Golden Pistol* (Sergio Corbucci); *Sign of Coyote* (Mario Caiano)
Rubio, Fernando: *Five Thousand Dollars on One Ace* (Alfonso Balcazar); *Seven Pistols for a Gringo* (Juan Xiol Marchel)
Rudy, Tómas (also **Rudy Thomas**): *Bastard, Go and Kill* (Gino Mangini); *Porno Erotic Western* (Gerard B. Lennox)
Ruiz, José Carlos: *Eagle's Wing* (Anthony Harvey)
Ruiz, Pepé: *Patience Has a Limit, We Don't* (Armando Morandi)
Runachagua, Aysanoa: *Massacre Time* (Lucio Fulci)
Rupp, Sieghardt: **Among Vultures* (Alfred Vohrer); *Blood at Sundown* (Albert Cardiff); *Fistful of Dollars* (Sergio Leone); *Man Called Gringo* (Roy Rowland); *Who Killed Johnny R.?* (José Luis Madrid)
Russell, Tony: *Behind the Mask of Zorro* (Ricardo Blasco)
Russinova, Isabel: *Tex and the Lord of the Deep* (Duccio Tessari)
Ryan, Mitchell: *Hunting Party* (Don Medford)

Ryan, Robert: *Minute to Pray . . . a Second to Die* (Franco Giraldi)
Sabàto, Antonio: *Beyond the Law* (Giorgio Stegani); **Hate for Hate* (Domenico Paolella); *I Came, I Saw, I Shot* (Enzo G. Castellari); *Miss Dynamite* (Sergio Grieco); *Thunder Over El Paso* (Roberto Montero); *Twice a Judas* (Nando Cicero)
Sagrotti, Sergio: *Brother Outlaw* (Edward G. Muller)
Sailer, Toni: *Lost Treasure of the Incas* (Piero Pierotti)
Salazar, Abel: *Coyote* (Joaquin R. Marchent)
Salerno, Enrico M.: *Bandidos* (Max Dillman); *Death Sentence* (Mario Linfranchi); **Death Walks in Laredo* (Enzo Peri); *Train for Durango* (William Hawkins)
Salinas, Antonio: *Matalo!* (Cesare Canavari)
Salmi, Albert: *Four Rode Out* (John Peyser)
Salvino, Riccardo: *Halleluja to Vera Cruz* (Newman Rostel)
Sambrell, Aldo: *Arizona* (Sergio Martino); *Awkward Hands* (Rafael R. Marchent); *Bad Man's River* (Eugenio Martin); *Bullet for the General* (Damiano Damiani); *Charley One-Eye* (Don Chaffey); *Dollars for a Fast Gun* (Joaquin R. Marchent); *Duel in the Eclipse* (Martino/Merino); *Dynamite Jim* (Alfonso Balcazar); *Face to Face* (Sergio Sollima); *Fifteen Scaffolds for the Killer* (Nunzio Malasomma); *Finger on the Trigger* (Sidney Pink); *For a Few Dollars More* (Sergio Leone); *Gunfight at Red Sands* (Richard Blasco); *Gunfighters of Casa Grande* (Roy Rowland); *Hellbenders* (Sergio Corbucci); *In a Colt's Shadow* (Gianni Grimaldi); *Kill Django . . . Kill First* (Willy S. Regan); *Long Ride from Hell* (Alex Burkes); *Man Called Noon* (Peter Collinson); **Magnificent Three* (Joaquin R. Marchent); *Massacre at Fort Grant* (J. Douglas); *Minute to Pray . . . a Second to Die* (Franco Giraldi); *Navajo Joe* (Sergio Corbucci); *Once Upon a Time in the West* (Sergio Leone); *Pistol Packin' Preacher* (Leopoldo Savona); *Place Called Glory* (Ralph Gideon); *Savage Gringo* (Bava/Romano); *Silver Saddle* (Lucio Fulci); *Son of a Gunfighter* (Paul Landres); *Tex and Lord of the Deep* (Duccio Tessari); *Texican* (Espinosa/Selander); *Town Called Hell* (Robert Parrish); *Train for Durango* (William Hawkins); *Two Gunmen* (Anthony Greepy)
Sanchez, Pedro (pseudonym for Ignazio Spalla): *Adios, Sabata* (Frank Kramer); *Blood for a Silver Dollar* (Calvin J. Padget); *Carambola* (Ferdinando Baldi); *Cjamango* (Edward G. Muller); *Death at Owell Rock* (Riccardo Freda); *Death Knows No Time* (Leon Klimovsky); *Don't Wait Django . . . Shoot!* (Edward G. Muller); *Go Kill and Come Back* (Enzo G. Castellari); *Go with God, Gringo* (Edward G. Muller); *Grandsons of Zorro* (Mariano Laurenti); *Johnny Hamlet* (Enzo G. Castellari); *May God Forgive You . . . But I Won't* (Glenn V. Davis); *My Horse, My Gun, Your Widow* (John Wood); *Nephews of Zorro* (Frank Reed); *Payment in Blood* (E. G. Rowland); *Pecos Cleans Up* (Maurizio Lucidi); *Quintana: Dead or Alive* (Glenn V. Davis); *Return of Sabata* (Frank Kramer); *Reverend Colt* (Leon Klimovsky); *Sabata* (Frank Kramer); *Seven Nuns in Kansas City* (Marcello Zeanile); *Son of Django* (Osvaldo Civirani); **Thompson 1880* (Albert Moore); *Three Supermen of the West* (Italo Martinenghi); *Trinity Plus the Clown and a Guitar* (François Legrand); *Two Sons of Ringo* (Giorgio Simonelli); *Vengeance* (Anthony Dawson)
Sancho, Fernando: *All Out* (Umberto Lenzi); *And Crows Will Dig Your Grave* (John Wood); *Arizona Colt* (Michele Lupo); *Big Gundown* (Sergio Sollima); *Blood Calls to Blood* (Lewis King); *Boldest Job in the West* (José De La Loma); *Ciccio Forgives, I Don't* (Frank Reed); *Clint the Stranger* (Alfonso Balcazar); *Dig Your Grave, Friend . . . Sabata's Coming* (John Woods); *Django Shoots First* (Alberto De Martino); *Duel in the Eclipse* (Martino/Merino); *Dynamite Jim* (Alfonso

Balcazar); *Five Thousand Dollars on One Ace* (Alfonso Balcazar); *For One Hundred Thousand Dollars Per Killing* (Sidney Lean); **Gunfight at High Noon* (Joaquin R. Marchent); *Gunmen of Rio Grande* (Tullio Demichelli); *Hate for Hate* (Domenico Paolella); *Hour of Death* (Paul Marchenti); *If One Is Born a Swine* (Al Bradly); *If One Is Born a Swine, Kill Him* (Al Bradly); *Killer Kid* (Leopoldo Savona); *Magnificent Three* (Joaquin R. Marchent); *Magnificent West* (Gianni Crea); *Man and a Colt* (Tullio Demichelli); *Man from Canyon City* (Alfonso Balcazar); *Man with the Golden Pistol* (Alfonso Balcazar); *Minnesota Clay* (Sergio Corbucci); *Miss Dynamite* (Sergio Grieco); *One Hundred Thousand for Ringo* (Alberto De Martino); *Pistol for Ringo* (Duccio Tessari); *Return of Clint the Stranger* (George Martin); *Return of Ringo* (Duccio Tessari); *Rita of the West* (Ferdinando Baldi); *Sartana* (Frank Kramer); *Seven Dollars on the Red* (Alberto Cardone); *Seven Guns for the MacGregors* (Frank Garfield); *Seven Guns for Timothy* (Rod Gilbert); *Seven Guns from Texas* (Joaquin R. Marchent); *Shoot to Kill* (Ramon Torrado); *Sign of the Coyote* (Mario Caiano); *Son of Zorro* (Gianfranco Baldanello); *Taste for Killing* (Tonino Valerii); *Ten Thousand Dollars Blood Money* (Romolo Guerrieri); *Three Supermen of the West* (Italo Martinenghi); *Too Much Gold for One Gringo* (Juan Bosch); *Twenty Paces to Death* (Ted Mulligan); *Twenty Thousand Dollars for Seven* (Albert Cardiff); *Two Gangsters in the Wild West* (Giorgio Simonelli); *Two Sergeants of General Custer* (Giorgio Simonelli); *Wanted Johnny Texas* (Erminio Salvi); *Watch Out Gringo! Sabata Will Return* (Alfonso Balcazar); *With Friends, Nothing Is Easy* (Steve MacCohy); *Wrath of God* (Alberto Cardone)

Sandri, Gia: *Ciccio Forgives, I Don't* (Frank Reed); *John the Bastard* (Armando Crispino); *Stranger in Town* (Vance Lewis); **Thompson 1880* (Albert Moore); *Two Pistols and a Coward* (Calvin J. Padget); *Wanted* (Calvin J. Padget)

Sanmartin, Conrado: *If One Is Born a Swine* (Al Bradly); **In a Colt's Shadow* (Gianni Grimaldi); *Long Days of Vengeance* (Stan Vance); *The Moment to Kill* (Anthony Ascott)

Sannoner, Milla: *Massacre at Grand Canyon* (Stanley Corbett); *Three Graves for a Winchester* (Erminio Salvi)

Sanson, Yvonne: *Day of Anger* (Tonino Valerii)

Sante, José Villa: *Kid Rodelo* (Richard Carlson)

Santoni, Espartaco: *Raise Your Hands, Dead Man . . . You're Under Arrest* (Leon Klimovsky)

Santoveti, Francesco: *Bury Them Deep* (John Byrd)

Sanz, Pedro (also **Paco Sanz;** also **Francisco Sanz):** *Blood and Guns* (Giulio Petroni); *Django, Kill . . . If You Live, Shoot!* (Giulio Questi); *Dollars for a Fast Gun* (Rafael R. Marchent); *Fasthand* (Frank Bronston); *Fighting Fists of Shanghai Joe* (Mario Caiano); **Five Thousand Dollars on One Ace* (Alfonso Balcazar); *Hands of a Gunfighter* (Rafael R. Marchent); *Hour of Death* (Paul Marchenti); *In the Name of the Father, the Son, and the Colt* (Frank Bronston); *Man from Canyon City* (Alfonso Balcazar); *Man Who Killed Billy the Kid* (Julio Buchs); *Massacre at Fort Holman* (Tonino Valerii); *One Against One . . . No Mercy* (Rafael R. Marchent); *One Hundred Thousand for Ringo* (Alberto De Martino); *Pistol for Ringo* (Duccio Tessari); *Price of Power* (Tonino Valerii); *Relentless Four* (Primo Zeglio); *Sartana Kills Them All* (Rafael R. Marchent); *Savage Gringo* (Bava/Roman); *Seven Guns from Texas* (Joaquin R. Marchent); *Seven Hours of Gunfire* (Joaquin R. Marchent); *Twenty Thousand Dollars for Seven* (Albert Cardiff); *Yankee* (Tinto Brass)

Sasso, Uga: *Winchester Does Not Forgive* (Adelchi Bianchi)

Saunders, Rai (also Ray Saunders): *Gunmen of One Hundred Crosses* (Lucky Moore); *Price of Power* (Tonino Valerii); *Showdown for a Badman* (Miles Deem)
Saval, Dany: *It Can Be Done . . . Amigo* (Maurizio Lucidi)
Savalas, Telly: *Bandara Bandits* (Sergio Corbucci); *Land Raiders* (Nathan Juran); *Massacre at Fort Holman* (Tonino Valerii); *Pancho Villa* (Eugenio Martin); *Town Called Hell* (Robert Parrish)
Savona, Isabella: *If You Want to Live. . . Shoot!* (Willy S. Regan)
Savours, Dane: *I'll Sell My Skin Dearly* (Ettore Fizarotti)
Saxon, Glenn (also Glenn Saxson): *Django Shoots First* (Alberto De Martino); *Go with God, Gringo* (Edward G. Muller); *If One Is Born a Swine . . . Kill Him* (Al Bradly); *Long Day of the Massacre* (Albert Cardiff); *Magnificent Texan* (Lewis King)
Saxon, John: *I Came, I Saw, I Shot* (Enzo G. Castellari)
Scaccia, Mario: *Eye for an Eye* (Albert Marshall)
Scarchili, Sergio: *Magnificent West* (Gianni Crea)
Scarciofolo, Geoffredo *see* Cameron, Jeff
Scarpitta, Nadia: *John the Bastard* (Armando Crispino)
Scheider, Helmut: *Chuck Moll* (E. B. Clucher)
Schell, Maria: *Dust in the Sun* (Richard Balducci)
Schiaffino, Rosanna: *Man Called Noon* (Peter Collinson)
Schlöb, Georg: *Prairie in the City* (Claus Tinney)
Schmidt, Helmut: *Five Thousand Dollars on One Ace* (Alfonso Balcazar); *Man Called Gringo* (Roy Rowland)
Schoberova, Olga: *Lemonade Joe* (Oldrich Lipsky)
Schoeller, Ingrid: *Son of Django* (Osvaldo Civirani)
Schone, Reiner: *Return of Sabata* (Frank Kramer)
Schonoboch, Karl: *Man: His Pride and Vengeance* (Luigi Bazzoni)
Schram, Horst: *Chetan, Indian Boy* (Mark Bohm)
Schreiber, Helmut: *Trail of the Falcon* (Gottfried Kölditz)
Schubert, Karin: *Compañeros* (Sergio Corbucci); *Three Musketeers of the West* (Bruno Corbucci)
Schultes, Willy: *Chetan, Indian Boy* (Mark Bohm)
Schundler, Rudolf: *The Moment to Kill* (Anthony Ascott)
Schurer, Erna: *Black Tigress* (Siro Marcellini)
Scipioni, Bruno: *For One Thousand Dollars Per Day* (Silvio Amadio); *Handsome, the Ugly, and the Stupid* (Giovanni Grimaldi); *Heroes of the West* (Steno); *Paths of War* (Aldo Grimaldi); *Twins from Texas* (Steno)
Scott, Andrew *see* Scotti, Andrea
Scott, Alan: *Cavalry Charge* (Ramon Torrado)
Scott, Gordon: *Buffalo Bill, Hero of the Far West* (John W. Fordson); *Tramplers* (Albert Band); *Two Gunmen* (Anthony Greepy)
Scott, Ray: *Kill Johnny Ringo* (Frank G. Carrol)
Scott, Susan *see* Navarro, Nieves
Scott, Vincent: *Once Upon a Time in the Wild, Wild West* (Enzo Matassi)
Scotti, Andrea (pseudonym — Andrew Scott): *Adios, Sabata* (Frank Kramer); *Black Tigress* (Siro Marcellini); *Blood for a Silver Dollar* (Calvin J. Padget); *Get the Coffin Ready* (Ferdinando Baldi); *Gunfight at High Noon* (Joaquin R. Marchent); *I Want Him Dead* (Paolo Bianchi); *In a Colt's Shadow* (Gianni Grimaldi); *Johnny Colt* (Giovanni Grimaldi); *Pistol for One Hundred Coffins* (Umberto Lenzi); *Shango* (Edward G. Muller); *Son of Django* (Osvaldo Civirani); *Two Gunmen* (Anthony Greepy); *Two Sides of the Dollar* (Roberto Montero)

Scratuglia, Ivan (also **Ivan Scrat**): *Sheriff with the Gold* (Richard Kean); *Son of Django* (Osvaldo Civirani)

Sebalt, Maria: *Five Thousand Dollars on One Ace* (Alfonso Balcazar)

Segal, Betty: *Deadlock* (Roland Klick)

Senchina, Ludmilla: *Armed and Dangerous: Time and Heroes of Bret Harte* (Vladimr Vainstok)

Seoane, Naria: *Behind the Mask of Zorro* (Ricardo Blasco)

Serato, Massimo (also **Massimo Seratto**): *Dead Men Ride* (Aldo Florio); *Forewarned, Half-Killed . . . the Word of Holy Ghost* (Anthony Ascott); **Gunmen of Rio Grande* (Tullio Demichelli); *Light the Fuse . . . Sartana Is Coming* (Anthony Ascott)

Sernas, Jacques: *Fort Yuma Gold* (Calvin J. Padget)

Serra, Gianna: *Death Walks in Laredo* (Enzo Peri); *Hills Run Red* (Lee W. Beaver)

Sevilla, Carmen: *Boldest Job in the West* (José De La Loma)

Shatner, William: *White Comanche* (Gilbert Lee Kay)

Shaw, Robert: *Town Called Hell* (Robert Parrish)

Shayne, Lynn: *Massacre Time* (Lucio Fulci)

Sheen, Martin: *Eagle's Wing* (Anthony Harvey)

Shepard, Patty: *Frenchie King* (Christian-Jaque); *Man Called Noon* (Peter Collinson); **Twenty Paces to Death* (Ted Mulligan)

Sherman, Anne: *In a Colt's Shadow* (Gianni Grimaldi)

Shigeta, James: *Death Walks in Laredo* (Enzo Peri)

Sholer, Paul: *Return of Shanghai Joe* (Bitto Albertini)

Sidri, Marino: *Sheriff of Rock Spring* (Anthony Green)

Silva, Henry: *Hills Run Red* (Lee W. Beaver); *Manhunt* (Larry Ludman)

Silva, Natalia: *Ride and Kill* (J. L. Boraw)

Silver, John: *His Name Was King* (Don Reynolds)

Silvia, Maria: *Cavalry Charge* (Ramon Torrado); *God Does Not Pay on Saturday* (Amerigo Anton); *Sartana Kills Them All* (Rafael R. Marchent); **Terrible Sheriff* (Antonio Momplet)

Simeoli, Pasquale: *Go with God, Gringo* (Edward G. Muller)

Simoni, Carlo: *Duel in the Eclipse* (Martino/Merino)

Sinjen, Sabine: *Pirates of the Mississippi* (Jürgen Roland)

Smith, Paul: *Carambola* (Ferdinando Baldi); *Carambola's Philosophy* (Ferdinando Baldi)

Sobieski, Jean: *Time and Place of Killing* (Vincent Eagle)

Sola, Charles: *Dynamite Jim* (Alfonso Balcazar)

Solar, Silvia (also **Sylvia Solar**): *Finger on the Trigger* (Sidney Pink); *Gentleman Killer* (George Findley); *Heroes of the West* (Steno); *Man Called Gringo* (Roy Rowland); **Shoot to Kill* (Ramon Torrado); *Three from Colorado* (Armando De Ossorio); *Two Gunmen* (Anthony Greepy)

Solaro, Gianni: *Johnny Yuma* (Romolo Guerrieri)

Solinas, Marisa: *Blood Calls to Blood* (Lewis King); **Colt in Hand of the Devil* (Sergio Bergonzelli); *Garter Colt* (Gian A. Rocco); *Killer Goodbye* (Primo Zeglio)

Solvay, Paul: *Colorado Charlie* (Robert Johnson); *Pirates of the Mississippi* (Jürgen Roland)

Sommer, Elke: *Among Vultures* (Alfred Vohrer)

Sommer, Yanti: *Man of the East* (E. B. Clucher); *Trinity Is Still My Name* (E. B. Clucher)

Sommerfield, Elga (also **Helga Sommerfield**): *Black Eagle of Santa Fe* (Ernst Hofbauer); *Seven Hours of Gunfire* (Joaquin R. Marchent)

Sooty, Graham: *In a Colt's Shadow* (Giovanni Grimaldi); *Taste for Killing* (Tonino Valerii)

Sorel, Dianna: *Dollar of Fire* (Nick Nostro)

Sorente, Silvia: *Jaguar* (Jess Franco)

Southwood, Charles: *Heads You Die . . . Tails I Kill You* (Anthony Ascott); *I Am Sartana, Trade Your Guns for a Coffin* (Anthony Ascott); **Roy Colt and Winchester Jack* (Mario Bava); *Three Silver Dollars* (Irving Jacobs)

Spaak, Agnes: *Death Knows No Time* (Leon Klimovsky); *Death on High Mountain* (Fred Ringoold); *God Made Them . . . I Kill Them* (Paolo Bianchi); *Hey Amigo! A Toast to Your Death!* (Paul Maxwell); *Killer Caliber .32* (Al Bradly)

Spaak, Catherine: *Take a Hard Ride* (Anthony Dawson)

Spada, Costanza: *Vendetta at Dawn* (Willy S. Regan)

Spalla, Iganzio *see* **Sanchez, Pedro**

Spartanero, Franco *see* **Nero, Franco**

Spencer, Bud (pseudonym for **Carlo Pedersoli**): *Ace High* (Giuseppe Colizzi); *Beyond the Law* (Giorgio Stegani); *Boot Hill* (Giuseppe Colizzi); *Buddy Goes West* (Michele Lupo); *Five Man Army* (Don Taylor); **God Forgives, I Don't* (Giuseppe Colizzi); *It Can Be Done . . . Amigo* (Maurizio Lucidi); *Massacre at Fort Holman* (Tonino Valerii); *They Call Me Trinity* (E. B. Clucher); *Today It's Me . . . Tomorrow You* (Tonino Cervi); *Trinity Is Still My Name* (E. B. Clucher)

Spolt, William: *Rattler Kid* (Leon Klimovsky)

Stacciolli, Ivano (pseudonym — **George Heston** and **John Heston**): *And Crows Will Dig Your Grave* (John Wood); *Cemetery Without Crosses* (Robert Hossein); *Go Kill and Come Back* (Enzo Castellari); *God Makes Them . . . I Kill Them* (Paolo Bianchini); *Have a Good Funeral, My Friend . . . Sartana Will Pay* (Anthony Ascott); *Kill the Poker Player* (Mario Bianchi); *Nephews of Zorro* (Frank Reed); *They Call Him Cemetery* (Anthony Ascott); *Thirty Winchesters for El Diablo* (Frank G. Carrol); *Three Graves for a Winchester* (Erminio Salvi); **Two Sons of Ringo* (Giorgio Simonelli)

Stander, Lionel (also **Red Carter**): *Anything for a Friend* (Miles Deem); *Beyond the Law* (Giorgio Stegani); **Boot Hill* (Giuseppe Colizzi); *Halleluja to Vera Cruz* (Newman Rostel); *Miss Dynamite* (Sergio Grieco); *Once Upon a Time in the West* (Sergio Leone); *Red Coat* (Joe D'Amato); *Sting of the West* (Enzo Castellari); *Who's Afraid of Zorro?* (Franco Lo Cascio)

Stanić, Mila: *Colt in the Hand of the Devil* (Frank G. Carrol); *Thirty Winchesters for El Diablo* (Frank G. Carrol)

Starr, Ringo: *Blindman* (Ferdinando Baldi)

Staton, Anthony G.: *Four Came to Kill Sartana* (Miles Deem)

Steel, Alan (pseudonym for **Sergio Ciani;** aka **John Wyler**): *Fasthand* (Frank Bronston); **Lost Treasure of the Incas* (Piero Pierotti); *Saguaro* (Amerigo Anton)

Steel, Anthony: *Winnetou: Last of the Renegades* (Harald Reinl)

Steele, Patricia: *Charge of the Seventh Cavalry* (Herbert Martin)

Stefaneli, Benito: *Gentleman Killer* (George Finley)

Steffen, Anthony (pseudonym for **Antonio De Teffé**): *Apocalypse Joe* (Leopoldo Savona); *Arizona* (Sergio Martino); *Blood at Sundown* (José De La Loma); *Blood at Sundown* (Albert Cardiff); *Coffin for the Sheriff* (William Hawkins); *Cry for Revenge* (Rafael R. Marchent); *Dallas* (Juan Bosch); *Dead Are Countless* (Rafael R. Marchent); *Django the Bastard* (Sergio Garrone); *Few Dollars for Django* (Leon Klimovsky); *Gentleman Killer* (George Finley); *Killer Kid* (Leopoldo Savona); **Last Tomahawk* (Harald Reinl); *Man Called Django* (Edward G. Muller); *Man Who Cried for Revenge* (William Hawkins); *No Room to Die* (Willy

S. Regan); *Ringo: Face of Revenge* (Mario Caiano); *Sabata the Killer* (Tullio Demichelli); *Seven Dollars on the Red* (Alberto Cardone); *Shango* (Edward G. Muller); *Stranger in Paso Bravo* (Salvatore Rosso); *Tequila* (Tullio Demichelli); *Too Much Gold for a Gringo* (Juan Bosch); *Train for Durango* (William Hawkins); *Two Pistols and a Coward* (Calvin J. Padget)

Steiger, Rod: *Duck You Sucker* (Sergio Leone)

Steiner, John: *Blood and Guns* (Giulio Petroni); *Man Called Blade* (Sergio Martino)

Stella, Luciano *see* **Kendall, Tony**

Stephen, Judith: *Valley of Dancing Widows* (Volker Vogeler)

Steve, Conrad: *Law of Violence* (Gianni Crea)

Stevens, Mark: *Sunscorched* (Alfonso Balcazar)

Stevens, Paul *see* **Gozlino, Paolo**

Stevens, Stella: *Town Called Hell* (Robert Parrish)

Stevenson, George: *Quintana: Dead or Alive* (Glenn V. Davis)

Stevenson, Rob *see* **Dell'Acqua, Alberto**

Stewart, Alexandria: *Man Called Gringo* (Edward G. Muller)

Stewart, Evelyn (pseudonym for **Ida Galli**): *Adios Gringo* (George Finley); *Blood at Sundown* (De La Loma/Muller); **Blood for a Silver Dollar* (Calvin J. Padget); *Chuck Moll* (E. B. Clucher); *Django Shoots First* (Alberto De Martino); *Four Gunmen of the Holy Trinity* (Giorgio Cristallini); *Machine Gun Killers* (Paolo Bianchini); *Man Called Invincible* (Anthony Ascott); *Man Who Cried for Revenge* (William Hawkins); *No Graves on Boot Hill* (Willy S. Regan); *Seven Guns for Timothy* (Ron Gilbert)

Stockwell, Guy: *Three Swords of Zorro* (Ricardo Blasco)

Stoppa, Paolo: *Once Upon a Time in the West* (Sergio Leone)

Strano, Dino *see* **Stratford, Dean**

Stratford, Dean (pseudonym for **Dino Strano**): *Brother Outlaw* (Edward G. Muller); *Chuck Moll* (E. B. Clucher); *Finders Killers* (Gianni Crea); *His Name Was Sam Walbash, But They Call Him Amen* (Miles Deem); *On the Third Day Arrived Crow* (Gianni Crea); *One Damned Day at Dawn . . . Django Meets Sartana* (Miles Deem); *Reach You Bastard!* (Lucky Dickerson); *Shadow of Sartana . . . Shadow of Your Death* (Sean O'Neal); *Shoot the Living . . . Pray for the Dead* (Joseph Warren); *They Called Him Trinity* (Fred Lyon Morris); *Thirteenth Is a Judas* (Joseph Warren); **Thompson 1880* (Albert Moore)

Strode, Woody: *Boot Hill* (Giuseppe Colizzi); *Chuck Moll* (E. B. Clucher); *Deserter* (Fulgozzi/Kennedy); *Keoma* (Enzo G. Castellari); *Last Rebel* (Denys McCoy); **Once Upon a Time in the West* (Sergio Leone); *Shalako* (Edward Dmytryk)

Stromme, Jean Claude: *Gunfight at O Q Corral* (J. M. Pallardy)

Stuart, Giacomo Rossi (also **Jack Stuart**): *Ben and Charlie* (Michele Lupo); *Deguello* (Joseph Warren); *Fighting Fists of Shanghai Joe* (Mario Caiano); *Five Man Army* (Don Taylor); *Five Thousand Dollars on One Ace* (Alfonso Balcazar); *Gunfight at Red Sands* (Richard Blasco); *Kill Django . . . Kill First* (Willy S. Regan); *Magnificent Brutes of the West* (Fred Wilson); **Massacre at Grand Canyon* (Stanley Corbett); *You're Jinxed, Friend, You Just Met Sacramento* (Giorgio Cristallini); *Zorro* (Duccio Tessari)

Stuart, Jack *see* **Stuart, Giacomo R.**

Stubing, Solvi: *Dead Are Countless* (Rafael R. Marchent)

Sturkie, Dan: *They Call Me Trinity* (E. B. Clucher)

Suarez, José: *Forgotten Pistolero* (Ferdinando Baldi); **Jaguar* (Jess Franco); *Price of Power* (Tonino Valerii); *Texas, Adios* (Ferdinando Baldi)

Sullivan, Barry: *Take a Hard Ride* (Anthony Dawson)

Svenson, Bo: *Manhunt* (Larry Ludman)
Taber, Anthony P. (pseudonym for Julio Tabernero): *Five Dollars for Ringo* (Ignacio Iquino); *Seven Guns for the MacGregors* (Frank Garfield); *Son of a Gunfighter* (Paul Landres); *Two Thousand Dollars for Coyote* (Leon Klimovsky)
Taber, Monica: *Let's Go and Kill Sartana* (Mario Pinzauti)
Tabernero, Julio *see* Taber, Anthony P.
Talamonti, Rinaldo: *Trinity Plus the Clown and a Guitar* (François Legrand)
Talbot, Bruce: *Finger on the Trigger* (Sidney Pink)
Tamba, Tetsuro: *Five Man Army* (Don Taylor)
Tamblyn, Russ: *Son of a Gunfighter* (Paul Landres)
Tarascio, Enzo: *Trinity Is Still My Name* (E. B. Clucher)
Tate, Lincoln: *Bastard, Go and Kill* (Gino Mangini); *For a Book of Dollars* (Renzo Spaziani); *Hero Called Allegria* (Dennis Ford); *Holy Water Joe* (Mario Gariazzo); **On the Third Day Arrived Crow* (Gianni Crea); *Return of Halleluja* (Anthony Ascott)
Taylor, Jack: **Billy the Kid* (Leon Klimovsky); *Christmas Kid* (Sidney Pink); *Last of the Mohicans* (Matteo Cano); *Three from Colorado* (Armando De Ossorio)
Taylor, Robert: *Savage Pampas* (Hugo Fregonese)
Tedd, Steven: *Beast* (Mario Costa); *Death Played the Flute* (Elo Panaccio); *Quinta: Fighting Proud* (Leon Klimovsky); *Requiem for a Bounty Hunter* (Mark Welles); *Reverend Colt* (Leon Klimovsky)
Tejada, Manuel: *Cut-Throats Nine* (Joaquin R. Marchent)
Ter, Angel: *Few Dollars for Django* (Leon Klimovsky); *Last Tomahawk* (Harald Reinl); *Sheriff Won't Shoot* (J. Luis Monter)
Testi, Fabio (pseudonym—Stet Carson): *Blood River* (Gianfranco Baldenello); *China 9, Liberty 37* (Monte Hellman); *Dead Men Ride* (Aldo Florio); *Four Gunmen of the Apocalypse* (Lucio Fulci); **Once Upon a Time in the West* (Sergio Leone); *One Damned Day at Dawn . . . Django Meets Sartana* (Miles Deem); *Red Coat* (Joe D'Amato)
Teuber, Monica: *Ballad of a Gunman* (Alfio Caltabiano)
Thinnes, Roy: *Charlie One-Eye* (Don Chaffey)
Thompson, Jack: *Mad Dog Morgan* (Philippe Mora)
Thorris, Peter: *Fighters from Ave Maria* (Al Albert)
Thring, Frank: *Mad Dog Morgan* (Philippe Mora)
Thunder, Alf *see* Caltabiano, Alfio
Tichy, Gerard: *Four Dollars for Vengeance* (Alfonso Balcazar); **Gunmen of Rio Grande* (Tullio Demichelli); *Man from Canyon City* (Alfonso Balcazar); *One Hundred Thousand Dollars for Ringo* (Alberto De Martino); *Place Called Glory* (Ralph Gideon); *Sartana Does Not Forgive* (Alfonso Balcazar)
Tieri, Aroldo: *Terrible Sheriff* (Antonio Momplet)
Tiffin, Pamela: *Deaf Smith and Johnny Ears* (Paolo Cavara)
Tijero, Charito: *Secret of Captain O'Hara* (Arturo Ruiz Castillo)
Tilden, Jane: *Johnny Colt* (Giovanni Grimoldi)
Tinti, Gabriele: *Son of Django* (Osvaldo Civirani)
Todd, Sean *see* Rassimov, Ivan
Todesillas, Jesus: *Outlaw of Red River* (Maury Dexter)
Todisco, Paola: *Wrath of God* (Alberto Cardone)
Tognazzi, Ugo: *Do Not Touch the White Woman* (Marco Ferreri)
Tolu, Marilu (also Marilu Tolo): *Django, Kill . . . If You Live, Shoot!* (Giulio Questi); *Don't Turn the Other Cheek* (Duccio Tessari); **Roy Colt and Winchester Jack* (Mario Bava)

Tondivelli, Gianrico: *China 9, Liberty 37* (Monte Hellman)
Topol: *Talent for Loving* (Richard Quine)
Tordy, Peter: *Man Called Gringo* (Roy Rowland)
Torray, Nuria: *Django Does Not Forgive* (Julio Buchs); **Fury of the Apaches* (José M. Elorrieta); *Seven for Pancho Villa* (José M. Elorrieta); *Two Thousand Dollars for Coyote* (Leon Klimovsky)
Torres, José: *All Out* (Umberto Lenzi); *Blood and Guns* (Giulio Petroni); *Blood at Sundown* (De La Loma/Muller); *Colt in Hands of the Devil* (Frank G. Carrol); *Death Is Sweet from the Soldier of God* (Robert Johnson); *Death Rides a Horse* (Giulio Petroni); **Deguello* (Joseph Warren); *Django Challenges Sartana* (William Redford); *Durango Is Coming, Pay or Die* (Luis Monter); *Face to Face* (Sergio Sollima); *Five Man Army* (Don Taylor); *Get the Coffin Ready* (Ferdinando Baldi); *Go Kill and Come Back* (Enzo Castellari); *God Will Forgive My Pistol* (Gariazzo/Savona); *Gunmen and the Holy Ghost* (Roberto Mauri); *He Was Called the Holy Ghost* (Roberto Mauri); *I Am Sartana, Your Angel of Death* (Anthony Ascott); *Poker with Pistols* (Joseph Warren); *Ramon the Mexican* (Maurizio Pradeaux); *Run Man, Run* (Sergio Sollima); *Shoot Joe, and Shoot Again* (Hal Brady); *Thirty Winchesters for El Diablo* (Frank G. Carrol)
Torres, Juan: *God in Heaven . . . Arizona on Earth* (John Wood)
Torres, Tomás: *Coffin for the Sheriff* (William Hawkins); *Four Dollars for Vengeance* (Alfonso Balcazar); *Sartana Does Not Forgive* (Alfonso Balcazar); *Yankee* (Tinto Brass)
Tozzi, Fausto: *Chino* (John Sturges); *Deserter* (Fulgozzi/Kennedy); *Man Who Killed Billy the Kid* (Julio Buchs); **Treasure of the Aztecs* (Robert Siodmak)
Traversi, Marisa: *Quintana: Dead or Alive* (Glenn Vincent Davis)
Trintignant, Jean-Louis: *Great Silence* (Sergio Corbucci)
Trionfi, Claudio: *Black Killer* (Lucky Moore)
Truccol, Welma: *Fasthand* (Frank Bronston)
Truchado, José: *Adios Cjamango* (Harry Freeman)
Tudor, Pamela (aka **Pamela Green**): *Canadian Wilderness* (Armando De Ossorio); **Death at Owell Rock* (Riccardo Freda); *Dollars for a Fast Gun* (Joaquin R. Marchent); *One After Another* (Nick Howard); *Sartana in the Valley of Death* (Roberto Mauri); *Time of Vultures* (Nando Cicero)
Tulli, Marco: *Shadow of Zorro* (Joaquin R. Marchent)
Tung, Al: *Stranger and the Gunfighter* (Anthony Dawson)
Tuombetta, Piero: *Buddy Goes West* (Michele Lupo)
Turner, John: *God Is My Colt .45* (Dean Jones)
Turri, Donatella: *Sartana Does Not Forgive* (Alfonso Balcazar)
Tyrell, Susan: *Another Man, Another Woman* (Claude Lelouch)
Ulisse, Fausto: *Return of Shanghai Joe* (Bitto Albertini)
Ulloa, Alejandro: *Dig Your Grave, Friend . . . Sabata's Coming* (John Woods)
Umberti, Anny Degli: *Two Sons of Trinity* (Glenn Eastman)
Undari, Claudio *see* **Hundar, Robert**
Ungeheuer, Gunter: *Prairie in the City* (Claus Tinney)
Unger, Freddy: *Black Jack* (Gianfranco Baldanello)
Vadis, Dan: *Deguello* (Joseph Warren); *Fort Yuma Gold* (Calvin J. Padget); *God Will Forgive My Pistol* (Gariazzo/Savona); **Pirates of the Mississippi* (Jürgen Roland); *Stranger Returns* (Vance Lewis)
Valdemarin, Mario: *Mutiny at Fort Sharp* (Fernando Cerchio)
Valle, Ricardo: *Outlaw of Red River* (Maury Dexter)
Valli, Romolo: *Duck You Sucker* (Sergio Leone)

Valmore, Jean: *A Girl Is a Gun* (Luc Moullet)

Van Ammelroy, Will: *Gunfight at O Q Corral* (J. M. Pallardy)

Van Cleef, Lee: *Bad Man's River* (Eugenio Martin); *Beyond the Law* (Giorgio Stegani); *Big Gundown* (Sergio Sollima); *Big Showdown* (Giancarlo Santi); *Captain Apache* (Alexander Singer); *Days of Anger* (Tonino Valerii); *Death Rides a Horse* (Giulio Petroni); **For a Few Dollars More* (Sergio Leone); *God's Gun* (Frank Kramer); *The Good, the Bad, and the Ugly* (Sergio Leone); *Kid Vengeance* (Joe Manduke); *Return of Sabata* (Frank Kramer); *Sabata* (Frank Kramer); *Stranger and the Gunfighter* (Anthony Dawson); *Take a Hard Ride* (Anthony Dawson)

Vanders, Warren: *Price of Power* (Tonino Valerii)

Van Der Wat, Keith: *Three Bullets for a Long Gun* (Peter Henkel)

Vandeusen, Sonny: *Lucky Johnny: Born in America* (José Antonio Balanos)

Van Doren, Mamie: *Arizona Kid* (Luciano Carlos); *Sheriff Was a Lady* (Sobey Martin)

Van Eyck, Peter: *Duel at Sundown* (Leopoldo Lahola); *Shalako* (Edward Dmytryk)

Van Nutter, Rick (also **Clyde Rogers**): *Dynamite Joe* (Anthony Dawson); *Seven Hours of Gunfire* (Joaquin R. Marchent)

Vanny, Rossana: *Bandera Bandits* (Sergio Corbucci)

Van Patten, Vincent: *Chino* (John Sturges)

Vanucchi, Luigi: *Days of Violence* (Al Bradly); *Johnny Yuma* (Romolo Guerrieri)

Vaquero, Rafael: *Hellbenders* (Sergio Corbucci); **Three Swords of Zorro* (Richard Blasco); *Two Thousand Dollars for Coyote* (Leon Klimovsky)

Vargas, Daniel: *Cemetery Without Crosses* (Robert Hossein)

Vargas, Daniele (also **Dan Vargas**): *Deguello* (Joseph Warren); *Django, Last Killer* (Joseph Warren); *Shotgun* (Robert Mauri); *Son of Django* (Osvaldo Civirani); *Stranger Returns* (Vance Lewis); **Terror of the Black Mask* (Umberto Lenzi); *Wanted* (Calvin J. Padget); *Zorro, the Navarra Marquis* (Jean Monty)

Vargas, Eleanora: *Adios Hombre* (Matio Caiano); **Dynamite Jack* (Jean Bastia); *Man Who Cried for Revenge* (William Hawkins)

Vega, Isela: *Eye for an Eye* (Albert Marshall)

Velazquez, Pilar: *Arizona Kid* (Luciano Carlos); **Awkward Hands* (Rafael R. Marchent); *Forewarned, Half-Killed . . . the Word of Holy Ghost* (Anthony Ascott); *Forgotten Pistolero* (Ferdinando Baldi); *His Name Was Holy Ghost* (Anthony Ascott); *Thunder Over El Paso* (Roberto Montero)

Venantini, Venantino: *Apache Woman* (George McRoots); **Bandidos* (Max Dillman)

Veras, Linda: *God Made Them . . . I Kill Them* (Paolo Bianchini); **Gold of the Heroes* (Don Reynolds); *Run Man, Run* (Sergio Sollima); *Sabata* (Frank Kramer)

Verella, Ivan: *Boldest Job in the West* (José De La Loma)

Versini, Marie: *Bullets and the Flesh* (Fred Wilson); **Winnetou the Warrior* (Harald Reinl); *Winnetou: Thunder at the Border* (Alfred Vohrer)

Vianello, Raimondo: *For a Few Dollars Less* (Mario Mattoli); *Heroes of the West* (Steno); *Ringo and Gringo Against All* (Bruno Corbucci); **Terrible Sheriff* (Antonio Momplet); *Twins from Texas* (Steno)

Vico, Antonio: *I Came, I Saw, I Shot* (Enzo G. Castellari)

Vico, Jorge: *Secret of Captain O'Hara* (Arturo Ruiz Castillo)

Vida, Piero: *And They Smelled the Strange, Exciting, Dangerous Scent of Dollars* (Italo Alfaro); *Dead for a Dollar* (Osvaldo Civirani); *Execution* (Domenico Paolella); *Hate for Hate* (Domenico Paolella); *Pecos Cleans Up* (Maurizio Lucidi)

Vidal, Mariano: *Massacre at Fort Grant* (J. Douglas)

Villagio, Paolo: *In the Name of the Father* (Ruggero Deodato); *What Am I Doing in the Middle of the Revolution?* (Sergio Corbucci)

Villar, Luis: *Massacre at Fort Grant* (J. Douglas)
Vingelli, Nino: *Cisco* (Sergio Bergonzelli)
Vismana, Wanda *see* Glas, Uschi
Vitale, Adriano: *Killer Kid* (Leopoldo Savona)
Viterbo, Patricia: *Bullets and the Flesh* (Fred Wilson)
Vogel, Tony: *Captain Apache* (Alexander Singer)
Volenté, Claudio Cama *see* Camaso, Claudio
Volenté, Gian Maria (also John Wells): *Bullet for the General* (Damiano Damiani);
    Face to Face (Sergio Sollima); **Fistful of Dollars* (Sergio Leone); *For a Few
    Dollars More* (Sergio Leone)
Von Borsody, Hans: *Buffalo Bill, Hero of the Far West* (John W. Fordson); Shadow
    of Zorro (Joaquin R. Marchent)
Von Friedol, Loni: *The Moment to Kill* (Anthony Ascott)
Vonledebur, Friebrich: *Montana Trap* (Peter Schamoni)
Voyagis, Yorga: *Garter Colt* (Gian Andrea Rocco)
Walcott, Gregory: *Man of the East* (E. B. Cluchar)
Walker, Clint: *Pancho Villa* (Eugenio Martin)
Wallach, Eli: *Ace High* (Giuseppe Colizzi); *Don't Turn the Other Cheek* (Duccio
    Tessari); **The Good, the Bad, and the Ugly* (Sergio Leone); *White, the Yellow,
    and the Black* (Sergio Corbucci)
Wang, George: *Blood and Guns* (Giulio Petroni); *Cisco* (Sergio Bergonzelli); *Colt in
    Hand of the Devil* (Frank G. Carrol); *Deadly Trackers* (Amerigo Anton); *Fighting
    Fists of Shanghai Joe* (Mario Caiano); *Have a Good Funeral, My Friend . . . Sar-
    tana Will Pay* (Anthony Ascott); *Jesse and Lester, Two Brothers in a Place Called
    Trinity* (James London); *Kill Django . . . Kill First* (Willy S. Regan); *Son of Zorro*
    (Gianfranco Baldanello); **Taste for Killing* (Tonino Valerii)
Ward, Larry: *God Does Not Pay on Saturday* (Amerigo Anton); *Saguaro* (Amerigo
    Anton)
Warren, Jennifer: *Another Man, Another Woman* (Claude Lelouch)
Warren, Sleepy: *Anything for a Friend* (Miles Deem)
Waterston, Sam: *Eagle's Wing* (Anthony Harvey)
Wayne, John Ethan: *Manhunt* (Larry Ludman)
Weaver, Dennis: *Man Called Sledge* (Morrow/Gentili)
Weisgerber, Antje: *Rampage at Apache Wells* (Harald Philipp)
Welch, Raquel: *Hannie Caulder* (Burt Kennedy)
Well, Karin: *Porno Erotic Western* (Gerald B. Lennox)
Welles, Orson: *Blood and Guns* (Giulio Petroni)
Wells, John *see* Volenté, Gian Maria
Wertz, Edgar: *Nude Django* (Ron Elliot)
West, Adam: *Relentless Four* (Primo Zeglio)
West, Donna: *Nude Django* (Ron Elliot)
Westerfield, James: *Lucky Johnny: Born in America* (José Antonio Balanos)
White, Erika *see* Blanc, Erika
White, Peter: **Colt Is the Law* (Al Bradly); *If You Want to Live, Shoot!* (Willy S.
    Regan); *Kill Django . . . Kill First* (Willy S. Regan); *No Graves on Boot Hill*
    (Willy S. Regan)
Whitman, Stuart: *Captain Apache* (Alexander Singer)
Widmark, Richard: *Talent for Loving* (Richard Quine)
Widmark, Robert *see* Dell'Acqua, Alberto
Williamson, Fred: *Take a Hard Ride* (Anthony Dawson)
Wilson, Jerry *see* Halsey, Brett

Wolff, Frank: *Few Dollars for Django* (Leon Klimovsky); **Five Dollars for Ringo* (Ignacio Iquina); *God Forgives, I Don't* (Giuseppe Colizzi); *Great Silence* (Sergio Corbucci); *I Am Sartana, Your Angel of Death* (Anthony Ascott); *I Came, I Saw, I Shot* (Enzo G. Castellari); *Kill Them All and Come Back Alone* (Enzo G. Castellari); *Once Upon a Time in the West* (Sergio Leone); *Ringo: Face of Revenge* (Mario Caiano); *Stranger in Town* (Vance Lewis); *Time of Vultures* (Nando Cicero)

Wolter, Ralf: *Apache's Last Battle* (Hugo Fregonese); *Half Breed* (Harald Philipp); *Massacre at Marble City* (Franz J. Gottlieb); *Pyramid of the Sun God* (Robert Siodmak); *Treasure of Silver Lake* (Harald Reinl); *Who Killed Johnny R.?* (José Luis Madrid); *Winnetou: Desperado Trail* (Harald Reinl); *Winnetou and Shatterhand in the Valley of Death* (Harald Reinl); **Winnetou the Warrior* (Harald Reinl)

Wood, Ken (pseudonym for **Giovanni Cianfriglia**): *Blindman* (Ferdinando Baldi); *Bury Them Deep* (John Byrd); *Challenge of the MacKennas* (Leon Klimovsky); *Five Giants from Texas* (Aldo Florio); *Gunmen and Holy Ghost* (Roberto Mauri); *If You Want to Live, Shoot!* (Willy S. Regan); *Keoma* (Enzo G. Castellari); *Kill Them All and Come Back Alone* (Enzo G. Castellari); *Killer Kid* (Leopoldo Savona); *No Graves on Boot Hill* (Willy S. Regan); **Ringo and His Golden Pistol* (Sergio Corbucci); *Sabata* (Frank Kramer); *Sometimes Life Is Hard, Right Providence?* (Giulio Petroni); *Thunder Over El Paso* (Roberto Montero); *Two Pistols and a Coward* (Calvin J. Padget)

Wood, Mikaela: *Gunfight at Red Sands* (Ricardo Blasco); *Three Swords of Zorro* (Ricardo Blasco)

Wood, Montgomery *see* **Gemma, Giuliano** *and also* **Halsey, Brett**

Woods, Robert (also **Robert Wood**): *Belle Starr Story* (Nathan Wich); *Black Jack* (Gianfranco Baldanello); *Challenge of the MacKennas* (Leon Klimovsky); *Colt in Hands of the Devil* (Frank G. Carrol); **Five Thousand Dollars on One Ace* (Alfonso Balcazar); *Four Dollars for Vengeance* (Alfonso Balcazar); *His Name Was Sam Walbash, But They Call Him Amen* (Miles Deem); *Johnny Colt* (Giovanni Grimaldi); *Kill the Poker Player* (Frank Bronston); *Machine Gun Killers* (Paolo Bianchini); *Mallory Must Not Die* (Mario Moroni); *Man from Canyon City* (Alfonso Balcazar); *My Colt, Not Yours* (Steve MacCohy); *My Name Is Pecos* (Maurice A. Bright); *Pecos Cleans Up* (Maurizio Lucidi); *The Reward's Yours, the Man's Mine* (Edward G. Muller); *Seven Guns for the MacGregors* (Frank Garfield)

Wu, Gregory: *Seven Guns from Texas* (Joaquin R. Marchent)

Wyler, John *see* **Steel, Alan**

Wyler, Richard: *If One Is Born a Swine* (Al Bradly); *Rattler Kid* (Leon Klimovsky); *Two Pistols and a Coward* (Calvin J. Padget); **The Ugly Ones* (Eugenio Martin)

Wynn, Keenan: *Caliber .38* (Toni Secchi); **Once Upon a Time in the West* (Sergio Leone); *Shoot, Gringo . . . Shoot!* (Frank B. Corlish)

Xan Das Bolas: *Clint the Stranger* (Alfonso Balcazar)

Yanni, Rossana: *What Am I Doing in the Middle of the Revolution?* (Sergio Corbucci); *White Comanche* (Gilbert Lee Kay)

Yaraza, Rosita: *Behind the Mask of Zorro* (Ricardo Blasco)

Yeh, Karen: *Stranger and the Gunfighter* (Anthony Dawson)

Yu, Tchang: *Massacre Time* (Lucio Fulci)

Zacharias, Steffen: *Vengeance Is a Dish Served Cold* (William Redford)

Zalenwi, Halina: *Seven Dollars on the Red* (Alberto Cardone)

Zamperla, Nazareno: *Seven Guns for the MacGregors* (Frank Garfield)

Zan, Mary: *Raise Your Hands, Dead Man . . . You're Under Arrest* (Leon Klimovsky)

Zarzo, Manuel (also **Manolo Zarzo**): *Bullets and the Flesh* (Fred Wilson); **Jaguar* (Jess Franco); *Sheriff Won't Shoot* (J. Luis Monter); *Price of Power* (Tonino Valerii); *Train for Durango* (William Hawkins); *The Ugly Ones* (Eugenio Martino)

Zichel, Rosy: *Deguello* (Joseph Warren); *Hole in the Forehead* (Joseph Warren)

Zinneman, Anna: *Jesse and Lester, Two Brothers in a Place Called Trinity* (James London)

Zinny, Victoria: *Shoot the Living . . . Pray for the Dead* (Joseph Warren)

Zola, Jasper: *Garter Colt* (Gian Andrea Rocco)

Zurakowska, Dianik: *Adios Cjamango* (Harry Freeman); *Bang Bang Kid* (Luciano Lelli); *Cry for Revenge* (Rafael R. Marchent); **Man Who Killed Billy the Kid* (Julio Buchs); *One Against One . . . No Mercy* (Rafael R. Marchent); *Rebels of Arizona* (José M. Zabalza); *Ringo, the Lone Rider* (Rafael R. Marchent); *Two Crosses at Danger Pass* (Rafael R. Marchent)

Directors

Albert, Al *see* Albertini, Adalberto

Albertini, Adalberto (sometimes pseudonym—Al Albert; also Bitto Albertini): *Fighters from Ave Maria* (as Albert); *Return of Shanghai Joe*

Alfaro, Italo *see* Regnoli, Piero

Amadio, Silvio: *For One Thousand Dollars Per Day*

Amendola, Mario (sometimes pseudonym—Irving Jacobs): *Bad Kids of the West* (with Tonino Ricci and Bruno Corbucci); *Three Silver Dollars* (as Jacobs) (with Tonino Ricci)

Andrei, Marcello (pseudonym—Mark Andrew): *Macho Killers*

Antel, Franz (pseudonym—François Legrand): *Trinity Plus the Clown and a Guitar*

Anton, Amerigo *see* Boccia, Tanio

Antonini, Alfredo (pseudonym—Albert Band and Stanley Corbett [with Sergio Corbucci]): *Massacre at the Grand Canyon* (as Corbett) (with Sergio Corbucci); *Tramplers*

Archer, Ted *see* Rossati, Nello

Argento, Dario: *Five Man Army* (suspected codirector with Don Taylor); *Today It's Me . . . Tomorrow You* (suspected codirector with Tonino Cervi)

Ascott, Anthony *see* Carmineo, Giuliano

Bagrain, Al *see* Balcazar, Alfonso

Balanos, José Antonio: *Lucky Johnny: Born in America*

Balcazar, Alfonso (sometimes pseudonym—Al Bagrain): *Clint the Stranger; Desperado* (as Bagrain); *Dynamite Jim; Five Thousand Dollars on One Ace; Four Dollars for Vengeance; Man from Canyon City; Man with the Golden Pistol; Sartana Does Not Forgive; Sunscorched; Watch Out Gringo! Sabata Will Return*

Balcazar, J. J. (Jaime) (pseudonym—Robert M. White): *Man from Oklahoma*

Baldanello, Gianfranco (sometimes pseudonym—Frank G. Carrol): *Black Jack; Blood River; Colt in the Hand of the Devil* (as Carrol); *Kill Johnny Ringo* (as Carrol); *Son of Zorro; Thirty Winchesters for El Diablo* (as Carrol); *This Man Can't Die*

Baldi, Ferdinando (nongenre pseudonym—Ted Kaplan): *Blindman; Carambola; Carambola's Philosophy: In the Right Pocket; Comin' at Ya; Forgotten Pistolero; Get Mean; Get the Coffin Ready; Hate Thy Neighbor; Rita of the West; Texas, Adios*

Balducci, Richard: *Dust in the Sun*

Band, Albert *see* Antonini, Alfredo

Barboni, Enzo (pseudonym—E. B. Clucher): *Chuck Moll; Man of the East; They Call Me Trinity; Trinity Is Still My Name*

Batzella, Luigi (pseudonym—Paolo Solvay, Dean Jones, and Fred Lyon Morris): *Even Django Has His Price* (as Solvay); *God Is My Colt .45* (as Jones); *Paid in Blood* (as Solvay); *They Called Him Trinity* (as Morris)

Bava, Mario: *Road to Fort Alamo; Roy Colt and Winchester Jack; Savage Gringo* (with Antonio Romano)

Bazzoni, Luigi (pseudonym — Alex Burkes and Marc Meyer): *Brothers Blue* (as Meyer); *Long Ride from Hell* (as Burkes); *Man: His Pride and His Vengeance*

Beaver, Lee W. *see* Lizzani, Carlo

Bergonzelli, Sergio (sometimes pseudonym — Serge Bergon): *Cisco; Colt in the Hand of the Devil; Last Gun; Stranger in Sacramento* (as Bergon)

Bianchi, Mario (Adelchi) (pseudonym — Frank Bronston; also suspected pseudonym — Renzo Spaziani): *Fasthand; For a Book of Dollars* (as Spaziani); *In the Name of the Father, the Son, and the Colt; Kill the Poker Player; Winchester Does Not Forgive*

Bianchini, Paolo (sometimes pseudonym — Paul Maxwell and Paolo Bianchi): *God Made Them . . . I Kill Them; Hey Amigo! Toast to Your Death!* (as Maxwell); *I Want Him Dead* (as Bianchi); *Machine Gun Killers*

Blasco, Richard: *Behind the Mask of Zorro; Gunfight at Red Sands* (also called *Gringo*); *Three Swords of Zorro*

Boccia, Tanio (pseudonym — Amerigo Anton): *Deadly Trackers; God Does Not Pay on Saturday; Kill or Die; Saguaro*

Böhm, Marquard: *Chetan, Indian Boy*

Borau, José Luis (pseudonym: J. L. Boraw): *Ride and Kill* (with Mario Caiano)

Boraw, J. L. *see* José Luis Borau

Bosch, Juan ("Spanish" pseudonym) *see* Iquino, Ignacio

Bradly, Al *see* Brescia, Alfonso

Brady, Hal *see* Miraglia, Emilio

Brass, Tinto: *Yankee*

Brescia, Alfonso (pseudonym — Al Bradly): *Colt Is the Law; Days of Violence; If One Is Born a Swine; If One Is Born a Swine . . . Kill Him; Killer Caliber .32*

Briz, José (pseudonym — Gilbert L. Kay): *White Comanche*

Bronston, Frank *see* Bianchi, Mario

Buchs, Julio (pseudonym — Julio Garcia): *Bullet for Sandoval; Django Does Not Forgive* (as Garcia); *Man Who Killed Billy the Kid*

Burkes, Alex *see* Bazzoni, Luigi

Byrd, John *see* Moffa, Paola

Caiano, Mario (pseudonym — William Hawkins and Mike Perkins; scriptwriting pseudonym — José Mallorquí): *Adios Hombre; Bullets Don't Argue* (as Perkins); *Coffin for the Sheriff* (as Hawkins); *Fighting Fists of Shanghai Joe; Man Who Cried Revenge* (as Hawkins); *Ride and Kill* (with J. L. Boraw); *Ringo, Face of Revenge; Seven Pistols for a Massacre* (as Hawkins); *Sign of Coyote; Sign of Zorro; Train for Durango* (as Hawkins)

Caltabiano, Alfio: *Ballad of a Gunman; Man Called Amen; They Still Call Me Amen*

Camus, Mario: *Trinity Sees Red*

Canavari, Cesare: *Matalo!*

Cano, Matteo: *Last of the Mohicans*

Capitani, Giorgio: *Ruthless Four*

Capuano, Luigi (pseudonym — Lewis King): *Blood Calls to Blood; Magnificent Texan*

Cardiff, Albert *see* Cardone, Alberto

Cardone, Alberto (pseudonym — Albert Cardiff and Paul Martin): *Blood at Sundown; Long Day of the Massacre; Seven Dollars on the Red; Twenty Thousand Dollars for Seven; Wrath of God*

Carlos, Luciano: *Arizona Kid*

Carlson, Richard: *Kid Rodelo*

Carmineo, Giuliano (pseudonym — Anthony Ascott): *Dick Luft in Sacramento; Find a Place to Die; Forewarned, Half-Killed . . . the Word of the Holy Spirit; Have*

a Good Funeral, My Friend . . . Sartana Will Pay; Heads You Die . . . Tails I Kill
You; His Name Was Holy Ghost; I Am Sartana, Trade Your Guns for a Coffin;
I Am Sartana, Your Angel of Death; Light the Fuse . . . Sartana Is Coming; Man
Called Invincible; The Moment to Kill; Return of Halleluja; They Call Him Cemetery
Carreras, Michael: Savage Guns
Carrol, Frank G. see Baldanello, Gianfranco
Castellari, Enzo G. see Girolami, Enzo
Castillo, Arturo Ruiz: Secret of Captain O'Hara
Cavara, Paolo: Deaf Smith and Johnny Ears
Celano, Guido (pseudonym — William First): Piluk, the Timid One
Cerchio, Fernando (pseudonym — Fred Ringoold): Death on High Mountain (as
    Ringoold); Mutiny at Fort Sharp
Cervi, Tonino: Today It's Me . . . Tomorrow You
Chaffey, Don: Charley One-Eye
Chardon, Richard: Colt 45, Five Dollars, and a Bandit
Chentres, Federico see Girault, Jean
Christian-Jaque: Frenchie King
Cicero, Fernando (aka Nando Cicero): Red Blood, Yellow Gold; Time of Vultures;
    Twice a Judas
Ciorciolini, Marcello (pseudonym — Frank Reed): Ciccio Forgives, I Don't; Nephews
    of Zorro
Civirani, Osvaldo (pseudonym — Glenn Eastman and Richard Kean): Dead for a
    Dollar; Rick and John, Conquerors of the West (as Kean); Sheriff with the Gold
    (as Kean); Son of Django; Two Sons of Trinity (as Eastman)
Clucher, E. B. see Barboni, Enzo
Coleman, Leo see Savona, Leopold
Colizzi, Giuseppi: Ace High; Boot Hill; God Forgives, I Don't
Collinson, Peter: Man Called Noon
Corbucci, Bruno (sometimes pseudonym — Frank B. Corlish): Ringo and Gringo
    Against All; Shoot, Gringo . . . Shoot! (as Corlish); Three Musketeers of the West
Corbucci, Sergio (sometimes pseudonym — Stanley Corbett; joint pseudonym with
    Alfredo Antonini): Bandera Bandits; Compañeros; Django; Great Silence (also
    called Big Silence); Hellbenders; Massacre at the Grand Canyon (as Corbett)
    (with Alfredo Antonini); Mercenary; Minnesota Clay; Navajo Joe; Ringo and His
    Golden Pistol; Specialist; What Am I Doing in the Middle of the Revolution?;
    White, the Yellow and the Black
Corlish, Frank B. see Corbucci, Bruno
Costa, Mario (sometimes pseudonym — John W. Fordson): Beast; Buffalo Bill, Hero
    of Far West (as Fordson)
Crea, Gianni: Finders Killers; Law of Violence; Magnificent West; On the Third Day
    Arrived the Crow
Crispino, Armando: John the Bastard
Cristallini, Giorgio: Four Gunmen of the Holy Trinity; You're Jinxed, Friend, You Just
    Met Sacramento
Croccolo, Carlo (pseudonym — Lucky Moore and Sobey Martin): Black Killer (as
    Moore); Gunmen of One Hundred Crosses (as Moore); Sheriff Was a Lady (as
    Martin)
Dallamano, Massimo (pseudonym — Max Dillman): Bandidos
D'Amato, Joe see Massaccesi, Aristide
Damiani, Damiano: Bullet for the General; Genius
Davis, Glenn V. see Musolino, Vincenzo

Dawn, Vincent *see* Mattei, Bruno
Dawson, Anthony *see* Margheriti, Antonio
De Angelis, Fabrizio (pseudonym—Larry Ludman): *Manhunt*
Deem, Miles *see* Fidani, Demofilo
De La Loma, José: *Blood at Sundown* (with Eduardo Mulargia); *Boldest Job in the West*
Del Amo, Antonio *see* Hoven, Adrian
Dell'Aquila, Enzo (pseudonym—Vincent Eagle): *Time and Place for Killing*
De Martino, Alberto (sometimes pseudonym—Herbert Martin): *Charge of the Seventh Cavalry* (as **Martin**); *Django Shoots First; Here We Go Again, Eh Providence?; One Hundred Thousand Dollars for Ringo*
Demichelli, Tullio: *Gunmen of the Rio Grande; Man and a Colt; Sabata the Killer; Tequila*
Deodato, Ruggero: *In the Name of the Father*
De Ossorio, Armando (plus suspected alias—Armando Morandi): *Canadian Wilderness; Patience Has a Limit, We Don't* (as **Morandi**); *Three from Colorado*
Dexter, Maury: *Outlaw of Red River*
Dickerson, Lucky *see* Fidani, Demofilo
Dillman, Max *see* Dallamano, Massimo
Dmytryk, Edward: *Shalako*
Douglas, J. *see* José Maria Elorrieta
Eagle, Vincent *see* Dell'Aquila, Enzo
Eastman, Glenn *see* Civirani, Osvaldo
Elliot, Ron: *Nude Django*
Elorrieta, José M. (pseudonym—Joe Lacy and J. Douglas): *Fury of the Apaches; If You Shoot . . . You Live!* (as **Lacy**); *Massacre at Fort Grant* (as **Douglas**); *Seven for Pancho Villa*
Espinosa, José L.: *Texican* (with Lesley Selander)
Esteba, Manuel (pseudonym—Ted Mulligan): *Twenty Paces to Death*
Fago, Giovanni (pseudonym—Sidney Lean): *For One Hundred Thousand Dollars Per Killing; To Hell and Back; Viva Cangaceiro*
Faradine, Oskar *see* Massaccesi, Aristide
Ferreri, Marco: *Do Not Touch the White Woman*
Ferroni, Giorgio (pseudonym—Calvin Jackson Padget): *Blood for a Silver Dollar; Fort Yuma Gold; Two Pistols and a Coward; Wanted*
Fidani, Demofilo (pseudonym—Miles Deem; additional pseudonyms—Slim Alone, Lucky Dickerson, Dennis Ford, Sean O'Neal, Dick Spitfire, Alessandro Santini, Diego Spataro): *Anything for a Friend* (as **Deem**); *Django and Sartana Are Coming . . . It's the End* (as **Spitfire**); *Fistful of Death* (as **Deem**); *Four Came to Kill Sartana* (as **Deem**) (reissued title: *Beyond the Frontiers of Hate*—as **Santini**) *; Go Away! Trinity Has Arrived in Eldorado* (as **Spitfire**); *Hero Called Allegria* (as **Ford**); *His Name Was Sam Walbash, But They Call Him Amen* (as **Deem**); *One Damned Day at Dawn . . . Django Meets Sartana* (as **Deem**); *Reach You Bastard!* (as **Dickerson**); *Shadow of Sartana . . . Shadow of Your Death* (as **O'Neal**); *Showdown for a Bad Man* (as **Deem**); *Stranger That Kneels Beside the Shadow of a Corpse* (as **Deem**)
Finley, George *see* Stengani, Georgio
First, William *see* Celano, Guido
Fizarotti, Ettore: *I'll Sell My Skin Dearly*
Florio, Aldo: *Dead Men Ride; Five Giants from Texas*
Ford, Dennis *see* Fidani, Demofilo

Fordson, John *see* Costa, Mario
Franco, Jess: *Jaguar*
Freda, Riccardo (pseudonym—George Lincoln): *Death at Owell Rock*
Freeman, Harry *see* Zabalza, Jose Maria
Fregonese, Hugo: *Apache's Last Battle; Savage Pampas*
Fulci, Lucio: *Four Gunmen of the Apocalypse; Massacre Time; Silver Saddle*
Fulgozi, Niska: *Deserter* (with Burt Kennedy)
Garcia, Julio *see* Buchs, Julio
Garfield, Frank *see* Giraldi, Franco
Gariazzo, Mario (sometimes pseudonym—Robert Paget): *Drummer of Vengeance*
    (as **Paget**); *God Will Forgive My Pistol* (with Savona); *Holy Water Joe*
Garrone, Sergio (pseudonym—Willy S. Regan): *Django the Bastard; If You Want to*
    Live . . . Shoot!; Kill Django . . . Kill First; No Graves on Boot Hill; No Room to
    Die; Vendetta at Dawn
Gentili, Giorgio: *Man Called Sledge* (with Vic Morrow)
Gideon, Ralph *see* Reynolds, Sheldon
Giraldi, Franco (pseudonym—Frank Garfield): *Minute to Pray . . . a Second to Die;*
    Seven Guns for the MacGregors; Sugar Colt; Up the MacGregors!
Girault, Jean (pseudonym—Richard Owens and Federico Chentres [in Italy]):
    Judge Roy Bean
Girolami, Enzo (pseudonym—Enzo G. Castellari and E. G. Rowland): *Cipolla Colt;*
    Go Kill and Come Back; I Came, I Saw, I Shot; Johnny Hamlet; Keoma; Kill Them
    All and Come Back Alone; Payment in Blood (as **Rowland**); *Sting of the West*
Girolami, Marino (pseudonym—Frank Martin and Fred Wilson): *Between God, the*
    Devil and a Winchester (erroneously credited as **Dario Silvestri**); *Bullets and the*
    Flesh (as **Wilson**); *Magnificent Brutes of the West; Two R-R-Ringos from Texas*
    (as **Martin**)
Good, Tony *see* Ricci, Tonino
Gora, Claudio: *Hatred of God*
Gotlieb, Franz J.: *Massacre at Marble City*
Green, Anthony *see* Zeglio, Primo
Greepy, Anthony *see* Zeglio, Primo
Grieco, Sergio: *Miss Dynamite* (also called *Where Bullets Fly*)
Grimaldi, Aldo: *Paths of War*
Grimaldi, Giovanni (also **Gianni Grimaldi**): *Handsome, the Ugly and the Stupid; In*
    a Colt's Shadow; Johnny Colt
Guerrieri, Romolo: *Johnny Yuma; Seven Guns for Timothy; Ten Thousand Dollars*
    Blood Money
Harrison, Richard (pseudonym—James London): *Jesse and Lester, Two Brothers in*
    a Place Called Trinity
Harvey, Anthony: *Eagle's Wing*
Hawkins, William *see* Caiano, Mario
Hellman, Monty: *China 9, Liberty 37*
Henkel, Peter: *Three Bullets for a Long Gun*
Hofbauer, Ernst: *Black Eagle of Santa Fe*
Hopkins, Omar *see* Zeglio, Primo
Hossein, Robert (sometimes pseudonym—Steffen Tinelli): *Cemetery Without*
    Crosses (as **Tinelli**); *Taste of Violence*
Hoven, Adrian (pseudonym—Antonio Del Amo): *Jesse James' Kid*
Howard, Nick *see* Nostro, Nick
Hunter, Max *see* Pupillo, Massimo

Iquino, Ignacio (sometimes pseudonym — John Wood; additional pseudonyms — Steven MacCohy and Juan Xiol Marchel, plus "Spanish production" pseudonyms — Juan Bosch and Pedro Ramirez): *And the Crows Will Dig Your Grave* (as Wood); *Dallas* (as Bosch); *Dig Your Grave, Friend . . . Sabata's Coming* (as Wood); *Five Dollars for Ringo; God in Heaven, Arizona on Earth* (as Wood); *Joe Dexter; My Colt, Not Yours* (as MacCohy); *My Horse, My Gun, Your Widow* (as Wood); *None of the Three Were Called Trinity* (as Ramirez); *Seven Pistols for a Gringo* (as Marchel); *Too Much Gold for One Gringo* (as Bosch); *With Friends, Nothing Is Easy* (as MacCohy)

Jacobs, Irving *see* Amedola, Mario

Johnson, Robert *see* Mauri, Roberto

Jones, Dean *see* Batzella, Luigi

Juran, Nathan: *Land Raiders*

Kay, Gilbert L. *see* Briz, José

Kean, Richard *see* Civirani, Osvaldo

Kennedy, Burt: *Deserter* (with Niska Fulgozi)*; Hannie Caulder*

King, Lewis *see* Capuano, Luigi

Klick, Roland: *Deadlock*

Klimovsky, Leon: *Billy the Kid; Challenge of the Mackennas; Death Knows No Time; Django, a Bullet for You; Few Dollars for Django; Quinta: Fighting Proud; Raise Your Hands, Dead Man . . . You're Under Arrest; Rattler Kid; Reverend Colt; Torrejon City; Two Thousand Dollars for Coyote*

Knox, Werner *see* Mattei, Bruno

Kölditz, Gottfried: *Trail of the Falcon*

Kramer, Frank *see* Parolini, Gianfranco

Lacy, Joe *see* Elorrieta, José M.

Lahola, Leopoldo: *Duel at Sundown*

Landres, Paul: *Son of a Gunfighter*

Lanfranchi, Mario: *Death Sentence*

Laurenti, Mariano: *Grandsons of Zorro*

Lean, Sidney *see* Fago, Giovanni

Legrand, François *see* Antel, Franz

Lelli, Luciano *see* Praeger, Stanley

Lelouch, Claude: *Another Man, Another Woman*

Lennox, Gerard B.: *Porno Erotic Western*

Lenzi, Umberto: *All Out; Pistol for a Hundred Coffins; Terror of the Black Mask*

Leone, Sergio (initial pseudonym — Bob Robertson): *Duck You Sucker; Fistful of Dollars* (as Robertson); *For a Few Dollars More; The Good, the Bad, and the Ugly; My Name Is Nobody* (with Tonino Valerii); *Once Upon a Time in the West*

Lewis, Vance *see* Vanzi, Luigi

Lincoln, George *see* Freda, Riccardo

Lipsky, Oldrich: *Lemonade Joe*

Lizzani, Carlo (sometimes pseudonym — Lee W. Beaver): *Hills Run Red* (as Beaver); *Let Them Rest*

Lo Cascio, Franco: *Who's Afraid of Zorro?*

Lucidi, Maurizio (sometimes pseudonym — Maurice Bright): *Greatest Robbery in the West; It Can Be Done . . . Amigo; My Name Is Pecos* (as Bright); *Pecos Cleans Up*

Ludman, Larry *see* De Angelis, Fabrizio

Lupo, Michele: *Arizona Colt; Ben and Charlie; Buddy Goes West; California; For a Fist in the Eye*

MacCohy, Steve *see* Iquino, Ignacio
McCoy, Denys: *Last Rebel*
McRoots, George *see* Marcuzzo, Giorgio
Madrid, José Luis: *Ruthless Colt of the Gringo; Who Killed Johnny R.?*
Maffi, Mario: *Ringo's Big Night*
Malasomma, Nunzio: *Fifteen Scaffolds for the Killer*
Malle, Louis: *Viva Maria*
Manduke, Joe: *Kid Vengeance*
Mangini, Gino: *Bastard, Go and Kill*
Marcellini, Siro: *Black Tigress*
Marchel, Juan Xiol *see* Iquino, Ignacio
Marchent, Joaquin Romero (sometimes pseudonym—Paul Marchenti): *Coyote* (also called *Judgment of Coyote); Cut-Throats Nine; Dollars for a Fast Gun; Gunfight at High Noon; Hour of Death* (as **Marchenti**); *I Do Not Forgive . . . I Kill; Magnificent Three; Seven Guns from Texas; Seven Hours of Gunfire; Shadow of Zorro*
Marchent, Rafael Romero: *Awkward Hands; Cry for Revenge; Dead Are Countless; Hands of a Gunman; One Against One . . . No Mercy; Prey of Vultures; Ringo, the Lone Rider; Sartana Kills Them All; Two Crosses at Danger Pass; Woman for Ringo*
Marcuzzo, Giorgio (pseudonym—George McRoots): *Apache Woman*
Margheriti, Antonio (pseudonym—Anthony Dawson): *And God Said to Cain; Dynamite Joe; Stranger and the Gunfighter; Take a Hard Ride; Vengeance*
Maron, Anthony *see* Romano, Antonio
Mariscal, Alberto (pseudonym—Albert Marshall): *Eye for an Eye*
Marischka, Georg: *Legacy of the Incas*
Martin, Eugenio: *Bad Man's River; Duel in the Eclipse* (with José L. Merino); *Pancho Villa; The Ugly Ones*
Martin, Frank *see* Girolami, Marino
Martin, George: *Return of Clint the Stranger*
Martin, Herbert *see* De Martino, Alberto
Martin, Paul *see* Cardone, Alberto
Martin, Sobey *see* Croccolo, Carlo
Martinenghi, Italo: *Three Supermen of the West*
Martino, Sergio: *Arizona; Man Called Blade*
Marvin, Joseph *see* Merino, José
Massaccesi, Aristide (pseudonym—Joe D'Amato; suspected alias—Oskar Faradine): *Bounty Hunter in Trinity* (as **Faradine**); *Red Coat*
Massi, Stelvio (pseudonym—Newman Rostel): *Halleluja to Vera Cruz*
Matassi, Enzo: *Once Upon a Time in the Wild, Wild West*
Mattei, Bruno (pseudonym—Vincent Dawn and Werner Knox): *Scalps* (as **Knox**); *White Apache* (as **Dawn**)
Mattòli, Mario: *For a Few Dollars Less*
Mauri, Roberto (sometimes pseudonym—Robert Johnson): *Animal Called Man; Colorado Charlie* (as **Johnson**); *Death Is Sweet from the Soldier of God* (as **Johnson**); *Gunmen and the Holy Ghost; He Was Called the Holy Ghost; Sartana in the Valley of Death; Shotgun; Wanted Sabata* (as **Johnson**)
Maxwell, Paul *see* Bianchini, Paolo
Medford, Don: *Hunting Party*
Merino, José (plus suspected alias—Joseph Marvin): *Duel in the Eclipse* (with Eugenio Martin) (aka *Requiem for a Gringo); Kitosch, Man Who Came from North* (as **Marvin**); *More Dollars for the MacGregors; Zorro, Rider of Vengeance*
Merolle, Sergio: *Cost of Dying*

Meyer, Marc *see* Bazzoni, Luigi
Miraglia, Emilio (pseudonym—Hal Brady): *Shoot Joe, and Shoot Again*
Moffa, Paolo (pseudonym—John Byrd): *Bury Them Deep*
Mollica, Antonio (pseudonym—Tony Mulligan): *Born to Kill*
Momplet, Antonio: *Terrible Sheriff*
Montemurro, Francesco (pseudonym—Jean Monty): *Zorro, the Navarra Marquis*
Monter, Luis *see* Montero, Roberto
Montero, Roberto (sometimes pseudonym—Luis Monter and Robert M. White
    [with J. J. Blacazar]): *Durango Is Coming, Pay or Die* (as **Montero**); *Man from
    Oklahoma* (as **White**); *Sheriff Won't Shoot* (as **Montero**); *Thunder Over El Paso*;
    Two Sides of the Dollar
Monty, Jean *see* Montemurro, Francesco
Moore, Lucky *see* Croccolo, Carlo
Mora, Philippe: *Mad Dog Morgan*
Morandi, Armando *see* De Ossorio, Armando
Moroni, Marlo: *Mallory Must Die*
Morris, Fred Lyon *see* Batzella, Luigi
Morrow, Vic: *Man Called Sledge* (with Giorgio Gentili)
Moullet, Luc: *A Girl Is a Gun*
Mulargia, Edoardo (pseudonym—Edward Muller): *Blood at Sundown* (with José A.
    De La Loma); *Brother Outlaw; Cjamango; Don't Wait, Django . . . Shoot!; Go with
    God, Gringo; Man Called Django; Reward's Yours, the Man's Mine; Shango*
Muller, Edward *see* Mulargia, Edoardo
Mulligan, Ted *see* Esteba, Manuel
Mulligan, Tony *see* Mollica, Antonio
Musolini, Vincenzo (pseudonym—Glenn V. Davis): *May God Forgive You . . . But
    I Won't; Quintana: Dead or Alive*
Narzisi, Gianni: *Djurado*
Navarro, Augustin: *Shots Ring Out!*
Nostro, Nick (sometimes pseudonym—Nick Howard): *Dollar of Fire; One After
    Another* (as **Howard**)
Olsen, Rolf: *Last Ride to Santa Cruz*
O'Neil, Sean *see* Giovanni Simonelli
Owens, Richard *see* Chentres, Federico
Padget, Calvin Jackson *see* Ferroni, Giorgio
Paget, Robert *see* Gariazzo, Mario
Pallardy, Jean-Marie: *Gunfight at O Q Corral*
Palli, Enzo Gicca (pseudonym—Vincent Thomas): *Price of Death*
Panaccio, Elio: *Death Played the Flute*
Paolella, Domenico: *Execution; Hate for Hate*
Parolini, Gianfranco (pseudonym—Frank Kramer): *Adios, Sabata* (also called *Indio
    Black*); *God's Gun; Left Handed Johnny West; Return of Sabata; Sabata; Sartana*
Parrish, Robert: *Town Called Hell*
Pastore, Sergio: *Chrysanthemums for a Bunch of Swine*
Perelli, Luigi: *They Call Him Veritas*
Peri, Enzo (suspected pseudonym for **Elio Petri**): *Death Walks in Laredo*
Perkins, Mike *see* Caiano, Mario
Petri, Elio *see* Peri, Enzo
Petroni, Guilio: *Blood and Guns; Death Rides a Horse; Night of the Serpent; Sky Full
    of Stars for a Roof; Sometimes Life Is Hard, Right Providence?*
Peyser, John: *Four Rode Out*

Phillip, Harald: *Half Breed; Rampage at Apache Wells*
Pierotti, Piero (sometimes pseudonym — Stanley, Peter E.): *Heads or Tails* (as Stanley); *Lost Treasure of the Incas*
Pink, Sidney: *Christmas Kid; Finger on the Trigger; Tall Women*
Pinzauti, Mario: *Let's Go and Kill Sartana; Ringo, It's Massacre Time*
Pradeaux, Maurizio: *Ramon the Mexican*
Praeger, Stanley (pseudonym — Luciano Lelli): *Bang Bang Kid*
Puccini, Gianni: *Fury of Johnny Kid*
Pupillo, Massimo (pseudonym — Max Hunter): *Django Kills Softly*
Questi, Giulio: *Django, Kill . . . If You Live, Shoot!*
Quine, Richard: *Talent for Loving*
Ramirez, Pedro *see* Iquino, Ignacio
Regan, Willy S. *see* Garrone, Sergio
Redford, William *see* Squittieri, Pasquale
Reed, Frank *see* Ciorciolini, Marcello
Regnoli, Piero (pseudonym — Italo Alfaro): *And They Smelled the Strange, Exciting, Dangerous Scent of Dollars*
Reinl, Harald: *Half Breed; Last Tomahawk; Treasure of Silver Lake; Winnetou: Last of the Renegades; Winnetou: The Desperado Trail; Winnetou and Shatterhand in the Valley of Death; Winnetou the Warrior*
Reynolds, Don *see* Savino, Renato
Reynolds, Sheldon (pseudonym — Ralph Gideon): *Place Called Glory*
Richardson, Tony: *Ned Kelly*
Ricci, Tonino (sometimes pseudonym — Tony Good): *Bad Kids of the West* (as Good) (with Mario Amendola and Bruno Corbucci); *Great Treasure Hunt; Three Silver Dollars* (with Mario Amendola)
Ringoold, Fred *see* Cherchio, Fernando
Rocco, Gian Andrea: *Garter Colt*
Roland, Jürgen: *Pirates of the Mississippi*
Romano, Antonio (pseudonym — Anthony Maron): *Savage Gringo* (with Mario Bava)
Rosati, Giusseppe (Giuss): *Those Dirty Dogs*
Rossati, Nello (pseudonym — Ted Archer): *Django Strikes Again*
Rossetti, Franco: *Big Ripoff*
Rosso, Salvatore: *Stranger in Paso Bravo*
Rostel, Newman *see* Massi, Stelvio
Rowland, E. G. *see* Girolami, Enzo
Rowland, Roy: *Gunfighters of Casa Grande; Man Called Gringo*
Russell, William: *Red Hot Zorro*
Salvi, Erminio: *Three Graves for a Winchester; Wanted Johnny Texas*
Santi, Giancarlo: *Big Showdown*
Santini, Alessandro *see* Fidani, Demofilo
Savino, Renato (pseudonym — Don Reynolds): *Gold of the Heroes; His Name Was King*
Savona, Leopoldo (pseudonym — Leo Coleman): *Apocalypse Joe; God Will Forgive My Pistol* (with Mario Gariazzo); *Killer Kid; Pistol Packin' Preacher; Rojo*
Schamoni, Peter: *Montana Trap*
Secchi, Toni: *Caliber .38*
Selander, Lesley: *Texican* (with José L. Espinosa)
Sherman, George: *Murieta*
Siciliano, Mario (sometimes pseudonym — Marlon Sirko; nongenre pseudonym — Roy Garrett): *Cowards Don't Pray* (as Sirko); *Halleluja and Sartana Strike Again; Trinity and Sartana Are Coming*

Simonelli, Giorgio (sometimes pseudonym—Sean O'Neil): *Two Gangsters in the Wild West* (as O'Neil); *Two Sergeants of General Custer; Two Sons of Ringo*
Singer, Alexander: *Captain Apache*
Siodmak, Robert: *Pyramid of the Sun God; Treasure of the Aztecs*
Sirko, Marlon *see* Siciliano, Mario
Sollima, Sergio: *Big Gundown; Face to Face; Run Man, Run*
Solvay, Paolo *see* Batzella, Luigi
Spaziani, Renzo *see* Bianchi, Mario
Spitfire, Dick *see* Fidani, Demofilo
Squittieri, Pasquale (sometimes pseudonym—William Redford): *Django Challenges Sartana; Vengeance Is a Dish Served Cold* (as **Redford**)
Stanley, Peter E. *see* Pierotti, Piero
Stegani, Giorgio (pseudonym—George Finley): *Adios Gringo* (as **Finley**); *Beyond the Law; Gentleman Killer* (as **Finley**)
Steno *see* Vanzina, Stefano
Sturges, John: *Chino*
Tessari, Duccio: *Alive or Preferably Dead; Don't Turn the Other Cheek; Pistol for Ringo; Return of Ringo; Tex and the Lord of the Deep; Zorro*
Thomas, Vincent *see* Palli, Enzo Gicca
Tinelli, Steffen *see* Hossein, Robert
Tinney, Claus: *Prairie in the City*
Torrado, Ramon: *Cavalry Charge; Shoot to Kill*
Trader, Joseph *see* Zabalza, José
Vainstok, Vladimir: *Armed and Dangerous: Time and Heroes of Bret Harte*
Valerii, Tonino: *Day of Anger; Massacre at Fort Holman; My Name Is Nobody; Price of Power; Taste for Killing*
Vance, Stan *see* Vancini, Florestano
Vancini, Florestano (pseudonym—Stan Vance): *Long Days of Vengeance*
Vanzi, Luigi (pseudonym—Vance Lewis): *Stranger in Japan; Stranger in Town; Stranger Returns*
Vanzina, Stefano (pseudonym—Steno): *Heroes of the West; Twins of Texas*
Vari, Giuseppe (pseudonym—Joseph Warren): *Death Rides Alone; Deguello; Django, Last Killer; Hole in the Forehead; Poker with Pistols; Shoot the Living . . . Pray for the Dead; Thirteenth Is a Judas*
Verneuil, Henri: *Guns for San Sebastian*
Vogeler, Volker: *Valley of the Dancing Widows; Yankee Dudler*
Vohrer, Alfred: *Among Vultures; Flaming Frontier; Winnetou: Thunder at the Border*
Warren, Joseph *see* Vari, Giuseppe
Welles, Mark (Mel): *Requiem for a Bounty Hunter*
Wertmüller, Lina (pseudonym—Nathan Wich): *Belle Starr Story*
Wich, Nathan *see* Wertmüller, Lina
White, Robert M. *see* Montero, Roberto
Wood, John *see* Iquino, Ignacio
Yee, Yeo Ban: *Kung Fu Brothers in the Wild West*
Young, Terence: *Red Sun*
Zabalza, José (pseudonym—Harry Freeman and Joseph Trader): *Adios Cjamango* (as **Freeman**); *Damned Pistols of Dallas* (as **Trader**); *Rebels of Arizona*
Zeanile, Marcello: *Seven Nuns in Kansas City*
Zeglio, Primo (sometimes pseudonym—Anthony Greepy, Anthony Green, and Omar Hopkins): *Killer Goodbye; Man of the Cursed Valley* (as **Hopkins**); *Relentless Four; Sheriff of Rock Spring* (as **Green**); *Two Gunmen* (as **Greepy**)
Zurli, Guido (sometimes pseudonym—Albert Moore): *Thompson 1880*

Music Composers

Abril, Anton: *Awkward Hands; Pancho Villa; Savage Guns; Texas, Adios*
Alessandroni, Alessandro: *Dick Luft in Sacramento; Raise Your Hands, Dead Man
. . . You're Under Arrest; The Reward's Yours, The Man's Mine*
Alonso, Odon: *Coyote*
Angel, Oliver Piña: *Man and a Colt*
Angel, Paegan Ramirez: *Behind the Mask of Zorro*
Angelo, Gioacchino: *Damned Pistols of Dallas; Colorado Charlie*
Arteaga, Angel: *Place Called Glory*
Ashton, Tony: *Last Rebel*
Auzepi, Michael: *Sunscorched*
Bacalov, Luis Enrique: *Big Showdown; Bullet for a General; Death on High Mountain; Django; Gold of the Heroes; Great Treasure Hunt; Greatest Robbery in the West; Halleluja to Vera Cruz; His Name Was King; In the Name of the Father; It Can Be Done . . . Amigo; Man Called Noon; Price of Power; Sugar Colt*
Barber, Frank: *Son of a Gunfighter*
Bardotti, Sergio: *Big Showdown*
Baumgartner, Walter: *Nude Django*
Bernaola, Carmelo: *Cut-Throats Nine; Valley of the Dancing Widows*
Bixio, Franco (with Fabio Frizzi and Vince Tempera): *Carambola; Carambola's Philosophy; Four Gunmen of the Apocalypse; Get Mean; Silver Saddle*
Bizzi, Giancarlo: *Shotgun*
Bodie, Pat *see* Espieta, José
Borodo, Zui: *Duel at Sundown*
Bötcher, Martin: *Among Vultures; Apache's Last Battle; Flaming Frontier; Half Breed; Rampage at Apache Wells; Treasure of Silver Lake; Winnetou: Last of the Renegades; Winnetou: The Desperado Trail; Winnetou: Thunder at the Border; Winnetou and Shatterhand in the Valley of Death; Winnetou the Warrior*
Bracardi, Franco: *Desperado; Kung Fu Brothers in the Wild West*
Brezza, Willy: *Hate for Hate*
Buendia, Morena M.: *Secret of Captain O'Hara*
Cameron, John: *Charley One-Eye*
Can: *Deadlock*
Canfora, Bruno: *Last of the Mohicans*
Capuano, Mario: *Two Sides of the Dollar*
Caruso, Pippo: *Kill Johnny Ringo*
Caso, Sebares Manuel: *Seven for Pancho Villa*
Ceccabrelli, Luigi: *Scalps; White Apache*
Chiaramello, Giancarlo: *Go Away! Trinity Has Arrived in El Dorado*
Christian, Jan *see* Orlandi, Nora
Ciaman, Delores: *Captain Apache*
Cipriani, Stelvio: *Beast; Blindman; Boldest Job in the West; Finders Killers; Heads*

You Die . . . Tails I Kill You; Law of Violence; Magnificent West; Return of Halleluja; Stranger in Japan; Stranger Returns; The Ugly Ones

Continiello, Ubaldo: *Black Tigress; Grandsons of Zorro*

Critine, Jan: *Sheriff with the Gold*

De Angelis, Guido and Maurizio: *Chino; Cipolla Colt; Keoma; Man Called Blade; Man of the East; Sting of the West; Trinity Is Still My Name; Trinity Plus the Clown and a Guitar; White, the Yellow and the Black; Zorro*

De Jesus, Luchi: *Lucky Johnny: Born in America*

De Lerue, Georges: *Viva Maria*

De Los Rios, Waldo: *Bad Man's River; Savage Pampas; Town Called Hell*

De Luca, Nando: *For a Book of Dollars*

De Masi, Francesco (sometimes pseudonym—**Frank Mason**): *Adios Hombre; Arizona Colt; Blood Calls to Blood; Challenge of the Mackennas; Coffin for the Sheriff; Cost of Dying; Fifteen Scaffolds for a Killer; For a Fist in the Eye; Go Kill and Come Back; Kill Them All and Come Back Alone; I Am Sartana, Trade Your Pistol for a Coffin; Johnny Hamlet; Kid Vengeanoo; Magnificent Brutes of the West; Magnificent Texan; Magnificent Three, Man of the Cursed Valley; Man from Oklahoma; Man with the Golden Winchester; Massacre at Marble City; The Moment to Kill; Payment in Blood; Rattler Kid; Ringo, Face of Vengeance; Ringo, the Lone Rider; Ruthless Colt of the Gringo; Sartana Does Not Forgive; Seven Dollars on the Red; Sign of the Coyote; Terror of the Black Mask; Time and Place for Killing; Two Crosses at Danger Pass; Two Gunmen; Vendetta at Dawn; Zorro, Rider of Vengeance*

De Pablo, Luis: *Yankee Dudler*

Deramont, Robert: *Three Supermen of the West*

Derevitsky, Alexander: *Deguello*

DeSagneaux, Jacques: *Dynamite Jack*

De Sica, Manuel: *They Called Him Veritas*

De Stefano, Felice (sometimes: Gianfranco and Felice De Stefano): *Blood at Sundown; Born to Kill; Brother Outlaw; Cjamango; Don't Wait, Django . . . Shoot!; Go with God, Gringo; May God Forgive You . . . But I Won't; Quintana; Ramon the Mexican; Ringo, It's Massacre Time; Shango, Sheriff of Rock Spring, Sheriff Won't Shoot; Stranger in Sacramento*

De Usa, Mario Pacheco: *One After Another*

Donoaggio, Pino: *China 9, Liberty 37*

Douglas, Johnny: *Gunfighters of Casa Grande; Kid Rodelo*

Durov, Lev: *Armed and Dangerous: Time and Heroes of Bret Harte*

Dvorak, Anton: *Montano Trap*

Elorrieta, Javier: *If You Shoot . . . You Live!*

Escobar, Enrique (also **Henry Escobar**; pseudonym—**Henry Sothe**): *Dig Your Grave, Friend . . . Sabata's Coming; Five Dollars for Ringo; Joe Dexter; My Colt, Not Yours; None of the Three Were Called Trinity; Seven Pistols for a Gringo; Twenty Paces to Death; With Friends, Nothing Is Easy*

Espieta, José (pseudonym—**Pat Bodie**): *Let's Go and Kill Sartana*

Esposite, Carlo: *Deadly Trackers*

Fabor, Giorgio: *Two Gangsters in the Wild West*

Farnon, Robert: *Shalako*

Ferrio, Gianni: *Alive or Preferably Dead; Ben and Charlie; Big Ripoff; Blood for Silver Dollar; Bullet for Sandoval; California; Charge of the Seventh Cavalry; Death Sentence; Djurado; Don't Turn the Other Cheek; Fasthand Is Still My Name; Find a Place to Die; Fort Yuma Gold; Heroes of the West; Man Called Sledge; Man Who*

Killed Billy the Kid; Massacre at the Grand Canyon; Reverend Colt; Ringo and Gringo Against All; Tex and the Lord of the Deep; They Still Call Me Amen; Twins from Texas; Wanted

Fidenco, Nico: *Bang Bang Kid; Bury Them Deep; Dynamite Jim; Hero Called Allegria; I Want Him Dead; In a Colt's Shadow; John the Bastard; Taste for Killing; Texican; Those Dirty Dogs; To Hell and Back*

Fischetti, Italo: *Four Came to Kill Sartana*

Franco, Pippo: *Hatred of God*

Frizzi, Fabio *see* **Bixio, Franco**

Fuentes, Ruben: *Eye to Eye*

Fusco, Enzo: *Garter Colt*

Gardot, Eilbert: *Red Hot Zorro*

Ghant: *Thirty Winchesters for El Diablo*

Ghiari, Maurio: *Return of Shanghai Joe*

Ghiglia, Benedetto: *Adios Gringo; Four Dollars for Vengeance; Johnny Colt; Rojo; Stranger in Town*

Gignante, Marcello: *God Made Them . . . I Kill Them; Last Gun; Ringo, It's Massacre Time; Shots Ring Out; Son of Zorro; They Called Him Trinity; Thompson 1880; Wanted Johnny Texas*

Giombini, Marcello: *All Out; Ballad of a Gunman; Dallas; Dead Are Countless; Death Walks in Laredo; Dollars for a Fast Gun; For a Few Dollars Less; Holy Water Joe; Relentless Four; Return of Sabata; Sabata; Sabata the Killer; Sartana Kills Them All; Too Much Gold for One Gringo*

Giosafat: *Two Sides of the Dollar*

Goldsmith, Jerry: *Take a Hard Ride*

Gomes, Carlos Castellanos: *Colt Is the Law*

Gori, Cariolano: *Django and Sartana Are Coming . . . It's the End; Durango Is Coming, Pay or Die; If One Is Born a Swine; One Damned Day at Dawn . . . Django Meets Sartana; Pecos Cleans Up; Pistol Packin' Preacher; Shadow of Sartana . . . Shadow of Your Death; Stranger That Kneels Beside the Shadow of a Corpse*

Gori, Lallo: *Anything for a Friend; Blackjack; Death Rides Alone; Durango Is Coming, Pay or Die; Execution; Fistful of Death; Handsome, the Ugly and the Stupid; His Name Was Sam Walbash, But They Call Him Amen; If You Want to Live . . . Shoot!; Massacre Time; My Name Is Pecos; One Against One . . . No Mercy; Pecos Cleans Up; Poker with Pistols; Showdown for a Bad Man; Reach You Bastard!; Tequila; Winchester Does Not Forgive*

Graf, Peter: *Nude Django*

Halletz, Erwin: *Last Ride to Santa Cruz; Pyramid of the Sun God; Treasure of the Aztecs*

Harvey, Linc: *Talent for Loving*

Hossein, André: *Cemetery Without Crosses; Taste of Violence*

Jarre, Maurice: *El Condor* (U.S. production); *Red Sun; Villa Rides* (U.S. production)

Jellico, Warren: *Django, a Bullet for You*

Jennings, Waylon: *Ned Kelly*

Julian, Franco: *Four Rode Out*

Jurgens, Udo: *Montana Trap*

Kojucharov, Vasil: *Bounty Hunter in Trinity; Death Is Sweet from the Soldier of God; Even Django Has His Price; God Is My Colt .45; Wanted Sabata*

Lacarenza, Michele: *Blood at Sundown; Long Day of the Massacre; Twenty Thousand Dollars for Seven; Wrath of God*

Lai, Francis: *Another Man, Another Woman; Dust in the Sun; Frenchie King*

Lavagnino, Angelo (also **Angelo Francesco Lavagnino**): *Dead for a Dollar; Duel in the Eclipse; Five Thousand Dollars on One Ace; God Does Not Pay on Saturday; Gunmen of Rio Grande; Hands of a Gunman; Jesse James' Kid; Kitosch, Man Who Came from the North; Left Handed Johnny West; Legacy of the Incas; Lost Treasure of the Incas; Man from Canyon City; Man with the Golden Pistol; Pistol for One Hundred Coffins; Revenge for Revenge; Saguaro; Seven Hours of Gunfire; Specialist; Stranger at Paso Bravo; Today It's Me . . . Tomorrow You; Tramplers; Two Sergeants of General Custer; Zorro, the Navarra Marquis*

Ledrut, Jean: *White Comanche*

Leonerbert: *Patience Has a Limit, We Don't*

Macchi, Egisto: *Bandidos*

Maglione, Budy: *Apache Woman*

Mancuso, Elio *see* **Vasco and Mancuso**

Mansfield, Kevin: *Three Bullets for a Long Gun*

Marchetti, Gianni: *Adios Cjamango*

Marocchi, Marcello: *I'll Sell My Skin Dearly*

Martelli, Augusto: *Few More Dollars for the MacGregors; Sartana in the Valley of Death; Trinity Sees Red*

Mason, Frank *see* **De Masi, Francesco**

Mattes, Willy: *Pirates of the Mississippi*

Micalizzi, Franco: *Caliber .38; They Call Me Trinity; You're Jinxed, Friend, You Just Met Sacramento*

Migliardi, Mario: *Matalo!; Price of Death; Shoot the Living . . . Pray for the Dead*

Mineri, Marcello: *Gunmen of One Hundred Crosses*

Monti, Elvio: *Halleluja and Sartana Strike Again*

Montoyo, Daniele: *Shoot to Kill*

Morcillo, Fernando Garcia: *Christmas Kid; Fury of the Apaches; Massacre at Fort Grant; Two Thousand Dollars for Coyote*

Morricone, Ennio (plus pseudonyms — **Leo Nichols** and **Dan Savio**): *Bandera Bandits; Big Gundown; Blood and Guns; Buddy Goes West; Bullets Don't Argue; Compañeros; Death Rides a Horse; *Drummer of Vengeance; Duck You Sucker; Face to Face; Fistful of Dollars; Five Man Army; For a Few Dollars More; Fort Yuma Gold; Genius; The Good, the Bad, and the Ugly; Great Silence; Gunfight at Red Sands; Guns for San Sebastian; *Hellbenders; Here We Go Again, Eh Providence?; Hills Run Red; Mercenary; My Name Is Nobody; Night of the Serpent; Once Upon a Time in the West; Navajo Joe; Pistol for Ringo; Return of Clint the Stranger; Return of Ringo; Run Man, Run; Seven Guns for the MacGregors; Sky Full of Stars for a Roof; Sometimes Life Is Hard, Right Providence?; Up the MacGregors; What Am I Doing in the Middle of the Revolution?* (*Drummer of Vengeance and The Hellbenders have the same score.)

Moullet, Patrice: *A Girl Is a Gun*

Nascimbene, Mario: *Tramplers*

Nichols, Leo *see* **Morricone, Ennio**

Nicolai, Bruno: *Adios, Sabata; And the Crows Will Dig Your Grave; Apocalypse Joe; *Arizona; Cisco; Days of Violence; Dead Men Ride; Django Shoots First; Fighting Fists of Shanghai Joe; Forewarned, Half-Killed . . . the Word of the Holy Ghost; Gentleman Killer; God Forgives, I Don't; God in Heaven . . . Arizona on Earth; Have a Good Funeral, My Friend . . . Sartana Will Pay; He Was Called the Holy Ghost; His Name Was Holy Ghost; Land Raiders; Light the Fuse . . . Sartana Is Coming; *Man Called Invincible; *My Horse, My Gun, Your Widow; One Hundred Thousand Dollars for Ringo; Prey of Vultures; Run Man, Run; They Called*

Him Cemetery (**Arizona, Man Called Invincible,* and *My Horse, My Gun, Your Widow* all have the same soundtrack.)

Nieto, Pepé: *Captain Apache*

Olea, Perez Antonio: *Django Does Not Forgive*

Olias, Lotar: *Sheriff Was a Lady*

Oliviero, Nino: *Savage Gringo*

Orlandi, Nora (sometimes pseudonym — **Jan Christian**): *Clint the Stranger; Death at Owell Rock; For One Hundred Thousand Dollars Per Killing; Johnny Yuma; On the Third Day Arrived the Crow; Sheriff with the Gold; Ten Thousand Dollars Blood Money*

Ortolani, Riz: *Apache's Last Battle; Beyond the Law; Chuck Moll; Cry for Vengeance; Day of Anger; Gunfight at High Noon; Hour of Death; Hunting Party; Let Them Rest; Massacre at Fort Holman; Miss Dynamite; Night of the Serpent; Ride and Kill; Seven Gunmen from Texas; Viva Cangaceiro*

Parada, Manuel: *Cowards Don't Pray; For a Fist in the Eye; Magnificent Three; Man of the Cursed Valley; Outlaw of Red River; Shadow of Zorro; Shoot to Kill; Shots Ring Out; Terrible Sheriff*

Patucchi, Daniele: *Black Killer; Deaf Smith and Johnny Ears; Death Played the Flute; Man Called Amen; Requiem for a Bounty Hunter*

Peguri, Gino: *For One Thousand Dollars Per Day; Fury of Johnny Kid; Seven Guns for Timothy; Seven Nuns in Kansas City; To Hell and Back*

Perret, Pierre: *Judge Roy Bean*

Pes, Carlo: *Red Blood, Yellow Gold; Twice a Judas*

Piccioni, Piero: *Colt in the Hands of the Devil; Deserter; I Do Not Forgive . . . I Kill; In the Name of the Father, the Son, and the Colt; Judgment of God; Machine Gun Killers; Man Called Gringo; Minnesota Clay; Sartana; Watch Out Gringo! Sabata Will Return*

Pisano, Berto: *Django Kills Softly; Killer Kid*

Plenizio, Gianfranco: *Django Strikes Again; Who's Afraid of Zorro?*

Poitevin, Robbe: *Hate Your Neighbor; Killer Caliber .32; Man Who Cried Revenge; Rita of the West*

Pregadio, Roberto: *Ciccio Forgives, I Don't; Django, Last Killer; Forgotten Pistolero; Four Gunmen of the Holy Trinity; Hole in the Forehead; Mallory Must Not Die; Paths of War*

Raven, Peer: *Chetan, Indian Boy*

Renis, Tony: *Brothers Blue*

Rettano, Franco: *Twenty Thousand Dollars for Seven*

Reverberi, Gianfranco: *Colt in the Hand of the Devil; Get the Coffin Ready*

Romitelli, Sante Maria (pseudonym — **Richard Ira Silver**): *God's Gun; Shoot, Gringo . . . Shoot!; Two Sons of Trinity*

Romoino, Marcello: *Macho Killer*

Rosenthal, Julian: *Dollar of Fire*

Rosso, Nino: *Yankee*

Rustic, Carl *see* **Rustichelli, Carlo**

Rustichelli, Carlo (sometimes pseudonym — **Carl Rustic**): *Ace High; Bastard, Go and Kill; Boot Hill; Buffalo Bill, Hero of the Far West; Charge of the Seventh Cavalry; God Forgives . . . I Don't; I Came, I Saw, I Shot; Kill or Die; Man: His Pride and Vengeance; Man and a Colt; Minute to Pray, a Second to Die; Red Coat; Ringo's Big Night; Ruthless Four; Three Silver Dollars; Three Musketeers of the West; Train for Durango; Two Gunmen and a Coward*

Rychlik, Jan: *Lemonade Joe*

Salina, Franco: *Five Giants from Texas*

Sanchez, Felix: *Seven for Pancho Villa*
Santucci, Francesco: *Once Upon a Time in the Wild, Wild West*
Sarde, Philquippe: *Do Not Touch the White Woman*
Sasse, Karl-Ernst: *Trail of the Falcon*
Satrova, Ana: *Adios Cjamango; Rebels of Arizona*
Savina, Carlo: *And God Said to Cain; Animal Called Man; Between God, the Devil and a Winchester; Bullets and the Flesh; Canadian Wilderness; Colt Is the Law; Comin' at Ya; Death Knows No Time; Django, the Honorable Killer; Dynamite Joe; Few Dollars for Django; Gunmen and the Holy Ghost; Heads or Tails; Hey Amigo, a Toast to Your Death!; Jesse and Lester, Two Brothers in a Place Called Trinity; Long Ride from Hell; Mutiny at Fort Sharp; Piluk, the Timid One; Ringo and His Golden Pistol; Stranger and the Gunfighter; Tall Women; Thirteenth and a Judas; Three from Colorado; Thunder Over El Paso; Trinity and Sartana Are Coming; Two R-R-Ringos from Texas; Vengeance*
Savo, Dan *see* **Morricone, Ennio**
Sciascia, Armando: *Three Graves for a Winchester*
Segura, Gregario Garcia: *Sign of Zorro; Tall Woman; Torrejon City; Woman for Ringo*
Silver, Ira Richard *see* **Romitelli, Sante Maria**
Silverstein, Shel: *Ned Kelly*
Silvestri, Enzo: *Sunscorched*
Sorgini, Giuliano: *Porno Erotic Western*
Sothe, Henry *see* **Escobar, Enrique**
Tallino, Claudio: *Killer Goodbye*
Tempera, Vince *see* **Bixio, Franco**
Thomas, Peter: *Last Tomahawk*
Thorne, Ken: *Hannie Caulder*
Tommasi, Amedeo: *This Man Can't Die*
Troviajol, Armando: *Long Days of Vengeance*
Tudo, Martinez Federico: *Who Killed Johnny R.?*
Umali, Restie: *Arizona Kid*
Umiliani, Piero: *Blood River; Chrysanthemums for a Bunch of Swine; Django Challenges Sartana; Fighters from Ave Maria; Man Called Django; Nephews of Zorro; Quinta: Fighting Proud; Rick and John, Conquerors of the West; Road to Fort Alamo; Roy Colt and Winchester Jack; Son of Django; Time of Vultures; Two Sons of Ringo; Vengeance Is a Dish Served Cold*
Vandor, Ivan: *Django Kill . . . If You Live, Shoot!*
Vasco and Mancuso: *Django the Bastard; God Will Forgive My Pistol; I Am Sartana, Your Angel of Death; If You Want to Live . . . Shoot!; Kill Django . . . Kill First (Mancuso solo); No Graves on Boot Hill; No Room to Die; One Against One . . . No Mercy; Paid in Blood (Mancuso solo); Shoot Joe, and Shoot Again; Three Crosses of Death*
Warner, Nigel: *Mad Dog Morgan*
White, Daniel: *Billy the Kid; Cavalry Charge; Jaguar; Three from Colorado*
Wilden, Gert: *Black Eagle of Santa Fe*
Wilkinson, Marc: *Eagle's Wing*
Zambrini, Bruno: *And They Smelled the Strange, Exciting, Dangerous Scent of Dollars*

Scriptwriters

Note: Sometimes it is considered standard procedure for a motion picture director to arbitrarily take cowriting credit of his own production, regardless of any scripting involvement. Because of this practice, it is impossible to judge the actual *screenwriting participation* of some directors listed in this appendix.

Addessi, Giovanni: *And God Said to Cain*
Age-Scarpelli: *The Good, the Bad, and the Ugly*
Agrin, Roberto: *Roy Colt and Winchester Jack*
Albertini, Bito: *Fighters from Ave Maria; Return of Shanghai Joe*
Alcocer, Santos: *Twins from Texas*
Alexander, Gil: *Hunting Party*
Alfiero, Carlo: *Fighting Fists of Shanghai Joe; Return of Shanghai Joe*
Aloza, Jerez: *Left Handed Johnny West*
Amadio, Silvio: *For One Thousand Dollars Per Day*
Amendola, Mario (sometimes pseudonym—Irving Jacobs): *Bad Kids of the West; Bandera Bandits; Behind the Mask of Zorro; Calibre .38; Days of Violence; Great Silence; Hate for Hate; Kill or Die; Killer Goodbye; Shoot, Gringo . . . Shoot!; Three Silver Dollars; Three Swords of Zorro; White, the Yellow and the Black*
Amoroso, Roberto: *Bad Kids of the West; Rojo*
Anchisi, Piero: *Forgotten Pistolero*
Andrei, Marcello (pseudonym—Mark Andrew): *Macho Killer*
Andrew, Mark *see* **Andrei, Marcello**
Angelo, Luigi: *Black Tigress; Hate Thy Neighbor*
Anthony, Tony *see* **Pettito, Tony**
Anton, Amerigo *see* **Boccio, Tanio**
Antonelli, Lamberto: *Black Tigress*
Antonini, Alfredo (pseudonym—Albert Band): *Gunfight at Red Sands; Hellbenders; Massacre at Grand Canyon; Minute to Pray, a Second to Die; Tramplers*
Arabia, Carlos: *I Want Him Dead*
Arcalli, Franco: *Django, Kill . . . If You Live, Shoot!*
Areal, Alberto: *Sky Full of Stars for a Roof*
Argento, Dario: *Cemetery Without Crosses; Five Man Army; Once Upon a Time in the West; Today It's Me, Tomorrow You*
Arlorio, Giorgio: *Mercenary; Zorro*
Ascott, Anthony *see* **Carmineo, Giuliano**
Ashley, Luke: *God Does Not Pay on Saturday*
Ashley, Mike: *Tall Women*
Assed, Rene: *White, the Yellow and the Black*

Aux, Victor: *I Do Not Forgive . . . I Kill; Taste for Killing*
Azcona, Maurizio: *It Can Be Done . . . Amigo*
Azzella, Will: *Djurado*
Badda, Astrain: *Dollar of Fire*
Balanos, José Antonio: *Lucky Johnny: Born in America*
Balcazar, Alfonso: *Clint the Stranger; Desperado; Dynamite Jim; Five Giants from Texas; Five Thousand Dollars on One Ace; Law of Violence; Man from Oklahoma; Man with the Golden Pistol; One Hundred Thousand Dollars for Ringo; Pistol for Ringo; Red Blood, Yellow Gold; Seven Guns for Timothy; Sunscorched; Watch Out Gringo! Sabata Will Return; Yankee*
Balcazar, Jaimi Jesus: *Gentleman Killer; Red Blood, Yellow Gold; Sartana Does Not Forgive; Thompson 1880; Time of Vultures; Twice a Judas*
Baldanello, Gianfranco (sometimes pseudonym — **Frank G. Carrol**): *Colt in the Hand of the Devil; Kill Johnny Ringo; Son of Zorro* (as **Carrol**); *Thirty Winchesters for El Diablo* (as **Carrol**)
Baldi, Ferdinando (sometimes pseudonym — **Miguel Iglesias**): *Carambola; Carambola's Philosophy; Forgotten Pistolero; Get Mean; Get the Coffin Ready, Hate Thy Neighbor; Rita of the West; Tequila* (as **Iglesias**); *Texas, Adios*
Balducci, Richard: *Dust in the Sun*
Balluck, Don: *Four Rode Out*
Baltieri, Carlo: *Once Upon a Time in the Wild, Wild West*
Band, Albert *see* **Antonini, Alfred**
Barboni, Enzo (sometimes pseudonym — **E. B. Clucher**): *Man of the East; They Call Him Cemetery; They Call Me Trinity; Trinity Is Still My Name*
Baretti, Bruno: *Fury of Johnny Kid*
Barni, Aldo: *In a Colt's Shadow; Man and a Colt*
Barreiro, Ramon: *Torrejon City*
Bartsch, Joachim: *Last Tomahawk; Winnetou: The Desperado Trail*
Bastia, Jean: *Dynamite Jack*
Battaglia, Enzo: *Two Crosses at Danger Pass*
Battista, Lloyd: *Comin' at Ya*
Battistrada, Lucio: *Stranger in Paso Bravo*
Batzella, Luigi (pseudonym — **Paolo Solvay**): *Even Django Has His Price; Paid in Blood*
Baudry, Alain: *Last of the Mohicans*
Bayonas, Luis Jose: *Bang Bang Kid; Fifteen Scaffolds for the Killer*
Benvenuti, Leo: *Find a Place to Die*
Bercovici, Eric: *Take a Hard Ride*
Berg, Alex: *Massacre at Marble City; Winnetou and Shatterhand in Death Valley*
Bergonzelli, Sergio (sometimes pseudonym — **Serge Bergon**): *Cisco; Colt in the Hand of the Devil; Raise Your Hands, Dead Man . . . You're Under Arrest; Stranger in Sacramento* (as **Bergon**)
Bernabei, Claudio: *Red Coat*
Bertolucci, Bernardo: *Once Upon a Time in the West*
Bianchi, Adelchi: *Winchester Does Not Forgive*
Bianchi, Maria: *Black Tigress; Kill the Poker Player*
Bianchini, Paolo (also **Paolo Bianchi**): *Hey Amigo! A Toast to Your Death!; Machine Gun Killers*
Billian, Hans: *Massacre at Marble City*
Blain, Luis: *White, the Yellow and the Black*
Blake, Norbert: *Pistol Packin' Preacher*

Blasco, Ricardo: *Gunfight at Red Sands; Three Swords of Zorro*
Boccacci, Antonio: *Days of Violence*
Boccia, Tanio (pseudonym — Amerigo Anton): *Deadly Trackers; God Does Not Pay on Saturday; Saguaro*
Bohm, Mark: *Chetan, Indian Boy*
Bologna, Carmine: *Death Walks in Laredo*
Bolzoni, Adriano: *Bandera Bandits; Halleluja and Sartana Strike; Hole in the Forehead; Let Them Rest; Man Called Amen; Man from Canyon City; Mercenary; Minnesota Clay; My Name Is Pecos; Pecos Cleans Up; Ringo and His Golden Pistol; Thirteenth Is a Judas; Trinity and Sartana Are Coming; Trinity and Sartana Coming*
Bonelli, Gianfranco Luigi: *Tex and the Lord of the Deep*
Bosch, Juan *see* **Iquino, Ignacio**
Boulanger, Daniel: *Frenchie King*
Bradly, Al *see* **Brescia, Alfonso**
Brass, Tinto: *Yankee*
Bredecka, Jira: *Lemonade Joe*
Brescia, Alfonso (pseudonym — Al Bradly): *Colt in the Hand of the Devil; Colt Is the Law; Thirty Winchesters for El Diablo*
Briley, John: *Eagle's Wing*
Brisbane, Jane: *Road to Fort Alamo*
Brochero, M. Eduardo: *All Out; Adios Hombre; Apocalypse Joe; Charge of the Seventh Cavalry; Cowards Don't Pray; Dead Men Ride; Death on High Mountain; Fasthand; For a Fist in the Eye; Kid Rodelo; Light the Fuse . . . Sartana Is Coming; Man of the Cursed Valley; Matalo!; One Against One . . . No Mercy; Outlaw of Red River; Ringo: Face of Revenge; Ringo, the Lone Rider; Stranger in Paso Bravo; Two Crosses at Danger Pass*
Brocks, Lino: *Arizona Kid*
Brummell, Beau: *Three Bullets for a Long Gun*
Bucceri, Franco: *California; Let Them Rest*
Buchs, Julio: *Django Does Not Forgive; Man Who Killed Billy the Kid*
Butragueno, Ferdnando: *Shoot to Kill*
Buzzi, Gian Luigi: *Days of Violence*
Caiano, Mario (also **José Mallorqui**): *Man Who Cried for Revenge; Ringo the Lone Rider*
Calabrese, Franco: *Beast*
Calloway, Ray: *Revenge for Revenge*
Caltabiano, Alfio: *Ballad of a Gunfighter; Man Called Amen; They Still Call Me Amen*
Caminito, Augusto: *Brothers Blue; Death Rides Alone; Django, Last Killer; Greatest Robbery in the West; Long Days of Vengeance; Pecos Cleans Up; Poker with Pistols; Ruthless Four*
Camus, Mario: *Trinity Sees Red*
Capri, Fiorenzo: *Django Shoots First*
Capriccioli, Massimiano: *Django Shoots First; Fort Yuma Gold; Wanted*
Capuano, Luigi: *Magnificent Texan*
Caravaglia, Giuliana: *Duel in the Eclipse*
Carboni, Fabio: *Patience Has a Limit, We Don't*
Cardone, Alberto: *Fasthand; Long Day of the Massacre; Twenty Thousand Dollars for Seven; Wrath of God*
Carmineo, Giuliano (pseudonym — Anthony Ascott): *Dick Luft in Sacramento; Find a Place to Die; Forewarned, Half-Killed . . . Word of Holy Ghost; Have a Good*

*Funeral, My Friend . . . Sartana Will Pay; Heads You Die . . . Tails I Kill You;
I Am Sartana, Trade Your Guns for a Coffin; Light the Fuse . . . Sartana Is
Coming*

Carpi, Tito: *Between God, the Devil, and a Winchester; Dead for a Dollar; Few
Dollars for Django; For One Thousand Dollars Per Day; Forewarned, Half-Killed
. . . Word of Holy Ghost; Go Kill Them All and Come Back; Go Kill and Come
Back Alone; Heads You Die . . . Tails I Kill You; His Name Was Holy Ghost; I
Am Sartana, Your Angel of Death; I Am Sartana, Trade Your Guns for a Coffin;
Johnny Hamlet; Light the Fuse . . . Sartana Is Coming; Man Called Invincible;
The Moment to Kill; One Against One . . . No Mercy; Payment in Blood; Return
of Halleluja; Reverend Colt; Rick and John, Conquerors of the West; Son of
Django; Sting of the West; Three Musketeers of the West*

Carrière, Jean-Claude: *Viva Maria*

Carrol, Frank G. *see* **Baldanello, Gianfranco**

Cartray, Ricardo: *Eye for an Eye*

Casacci, Mario: *Rojo*

Casaril, Guy: *Franchie King*

Cascape, Marcello: *Seven Nuns in Kansas City*

Castellano and Pipolo: *Here We Are Again, Eh Providence?*

Castillo, Arturo Ruiz: *Secret of Captain O'Hara*

Caterini, Lina: *Django Kills Softly*

Cavara, Paolo: *Deaf Smith and Johnny Ears*

Celano, Guido: *Piluk, the Timid One*

Cerami, Vicenzo: *Forgotten Pistolero; Stranger in Japan*

Cerchio, Fernando: *Mutiny at Fort Sharp*

Cervi, Tonino: *Today It's Me . . . Tomorrow You*

Chaffey, Don: *Charley One-Eye*

Champion, John C.: *Texican*

Chase, Bordon: *Gunfighters of Casa Grande*

Chianetta, Oscar: *Cowards Don't Pray*

Chiro, Alessandro: *Brother Outlaw*

Ciani, Sergio: *Fasthand*

Cicero, Nando: *Twice a Judas*

Ciogna, Bino: *Ace High*

Ciorciolini, Marcello: *Ciccio Forgives, I Don't; Two Gangsters in the Wild West; Two
Sergeants of General Custer; Two Sons of Ringo; Nephews of Zorro*

Ciuffini, Osvaldo: *Specialist*

Civirani, Osvaldo: *Dead for a Dollar; Rick and John, Conquerors of the West; Two
Sons of Trinity*

Clucher, E. B. *see* **Barboni, Enzo**

Cobianchi, Luigi: *No Graves on Boot Hill*

Cobos, Juan: *Bandidos; Seven Dollars on the Red*

Coletti, Melchi: *Seven Dollars on the Red*

Colizzi, Giuseppe: *Ace High; God Forgives, I Don't*

Collinson, Peter: *Man Called Noon*

Coltellacci, Oreste: *They Call Him Veritas; Trinity Plus the Clown and a Guitar*

Columbo, Arrigo (also **Enrico Columbo**): *Duel in the Eclipse; More Dollars for the
MacGregors*

Condon, Richard: *Talent for Loving*

Continenza, Alessandro: *Five Thousand Dollars on One Ace*

Continenza, Sandro (also **Alessandro Continenza**): *Django Shoots First; Five Thou-*

sand Dollars on One Ace; Fort Yuma Gold; Heroes of the West; Sugar Colt; They Still Call Me Amen; Twins of the West

Corbucci, Bruno: *Bad Kids of the West; Django; For a Few Dollars Less; Four Dollars for Vengeance; Great Silence; Hate for Hate; Three Musketeers of the West; Three Silver Dollars*

Corbucci, Sergio: *Django; Compañeros; For a Few Dollars Less; Johnny Hamlet; Massacre at the Grand Canyon; Mercenary; Minnesota Clay; Specialist; What Am I Doing in the Middle of the Revolution?; White, the Yellow and the Black*

Corvin, Anya: *Duel at Sundown*

Coscia, Cello: *White, the Yellow and the Black*

Costa, Mario: *Beast*

Craig, Dean see **Pierotti, Mario**

Crea, Gianni: *Law of Violence; Magnificent West*

Crispino, Armando: *John the Bastard; Let Them Rest*

Crispo, Ramon: *Finger on the Trigger*

Cristallini, Giorgio: *Four Gunmen of the Holy Trinity; You're Jinxed, Friend, You Just Met Sacramento*

Croccolo, Carlo: *Gunman of One Hundred Crosses*

Cusso, Miguel: *Death Knows No Time*

Damiani, Damiano: *Genius*

De Angelis, Fabrizio: *Manhunt; Run Man, Run*

De Castillo, Angel: *Billy the Kid*

De Concini, Ennio: *China 9, Liberty 37; Four Gunmen of the Apocalypse; Guns for San Sebastian*

De Doitselier, Henri: *Red Hot Zorro*

De La Loma, José A.: *Clint the Stranger; Dynamite Jim; Five Giants from Texas; Five Thousand Dollars on One Ace; Man from Canyon City; Man with the Golden Pistol; Red Blood, Yellow Gold; Seven Guns for Timothy; Sunscorched; Texican*

Del Amo, Antonio see **Hoven, Adrian**

Dell'Aquila, Enzo (sometimes pseudonym — **Vincent Eagle**): *Bury Them Deep; I Am Sartana, Your Angel of Death; Red Blood, Yellow Gold; Seven Guns for the MacGregors* (as **Eagle**); *Sheriff with the Gold; Time and Place for Killing* (as **Eagle**); *Up the MacGregors* (as **Eagle**)

De Martino, Alberto: *Django Shoots First; One Thousand Dollars for Ringo*

Demichelli, Tullio: *Gunmen of Rio Grande; Man and a Colt; Sabata the Killer; Tequila*

De Nardo, Mario (also **Mario Di Nardo**): *Fifteen Scaffolds for the Killer; Roy Colt and Winchester Jack*

De Nesle, Robert: *Left Handed Johnny West*

Denger, Fred: *Half Breed; Rampage at Apache Wells*

De Ossorio, Armando: *Canadian Wilderness; Patience Has a Limit, We Don't; Three from Colorado*

De Reske, David: *Winnetou: Thunder at the Border*

De Riso, Arpad: *Dead Are Countless; God Is My Colt .45; In the Name of the Father, Son and the Colt; Lost Treasure of the Aztecs; Magnificent Texan; Man with Golden Winchester; Thunder Over El Paso*

De Rita, Massimo: *Chino; Compañeros; Don't Turn the Other Cheek*

De Rosa, Mario: *Even Django Has His Price; Son of Zorro*

De Sailly, Claude: *Cemetery Without Crosses; Taste of Violence*

De Santis, Gino: *Bullets and the Flesh; Terror of the Black Mask*

DeTeffe, Antonio (acting pseudonym — **Anthony Steffen**): *Django the Bastard; Shango*

De Urrutia, Federico: *Bullet for Sandoval; Django, a Bullet for You; Djurado; Forewarned, Half-Killed* . . . *Word of Holy Ghost; Forgotten Pistolero; His Name Was Holy Ghost; Hour of Death; Man Who Killed Billy the Kid; Relentless Four; Seven for Texas; Shoot to Kill; Stranger in Paso Bravo; Two Gunmen; Thunder Over El Paso; Two Thousand Dollars for Coyote*

Di Geronimo, Bruno: *Dead Men Ride*

Di Leo, Fernando (sometimes pseudonym — Fernand Lion): *Beyond the Law; Death Rides Alone; God Made Them* . . . *I Kill Them; Hate for Hate; Johnny Yuma; Long Days of Vengeance; Massacre Time; Navajo Joe; Pecos Strikes Again; Pistol for Ringo; Poker with Pistols; Return of Ringo; Ruthless Four; Seven Guns for the MacGregors* (as Lion); *Sugar Colt; Time and Place for Killing; Up the MacGregors!* (as Lion); *Wanted*

Di Lorenzo, Edward: *Place Called Glory*

Donati, Sergio: *Ben and Charlie; Big Gundown; Buddy Goes West; Cipolla Colt; Dollars for a Fast Gun; Duck You Sucker; Face to Face; Navajo Joe*

Ducci, Nico: *Carambola; Carambola's Philosophy; Matalo!*

Dumas, Jacques: *Three Swords of Zorro*

Eagle, Vincent *see* **Dell'Aquila, Enzo**

Ebber, Günter: *Don't Turn the Other Cheek*

Ebert, Fritz: *Compañeros*

Elliot, Ron: *Nude Django*

Elorrieta, José Maria (pseudonym — Joe Lacy): *Fury of the Apaches; Secret of Sergeant O'Hara; If You Shoot* . . . *You Live!; If You Want to Live* . . . *Shoot!; Massacre at Fort Grant; Secret of Captain O'Hara*

Emanuelle, Luigi: *Damned Pistols of Dallas; This Man Can't Die*

Emmanuel, Jacques: *Dynamite Jack*

Ensescalle, Bob: *Stranger Returns*

Escribano, Antonio: *Shoot to Kill*

Essex, Harry: *Deaf Smith and Johnny Ears*

Fago, Giovanni: *To Hell and Back; Viva Cangaceiro*

Feltini, Monica: *Vengeance Is a Dish Served Cold*

Ferrando, Giancarlo: *Stranger in Japan*

Ferrau, Antonio: *Rick and John, Conquerors of the West; Son of Django*

Ferreri, Marco: *Do Not Touch the White Woman*

Ferroni, Giorgio: *Two Pistols and a Coward*

Fidani, Demofilo (scriptwriting pseudonyms — Dino Spataro; Diego Spataro; Miles Deem; Lucky Dickerson): *Anything for a Friend; Django and Sartana Are Coming* . . . *It's the End; Fistful of Death; Four Came to Kill Sartana; Hero Called Allegria; His Name Was Sam Walbash, But They Call Him Amen; One Damned Day at Dawn* . . . *Django Meets Sartana; Reach You Bastard; Shadow of Sartana* . . . *Shadow of Your Death; Showdown for a Badman; Stranger That Kneels Beside the Shadow of a Corpse*

Figuerola, José Mallo (also **Mallorqui Figuerola**): *Death on High Mountain; Killer Goodbye*

Finch, Scott: *Man Called Noon; Shalako*

Finn, Pavel: *Armed and Dangerous: Time and Heroes of Bret Harte*

Finocchi, Augusto: *Black Jack; Colt in Hand of the Devil; Deaf Smith and Johnny Ears; Fort Yuma Gold; Go Kill and Come Back; Greatest Robbery in the West; I Came, I Saw, I Shot; Sugar Colt; Two Pistols and a Coward; Wanted; Who's Afraid of Zorro?*

Fiory, Odoardo: *Death Knows No Time*

Fisz, Benjamin: *Town Called Hell*
Fizarotti, Ettore: *I'll Sell My Skin Dearly*
Flamini, Vincenzo: *Django Shoots First; One Hundred Thousand Dollars for Ringo*
Fleming, Walter: *Porno Erotic Western*
Florio, Aldo: *Dead Men Ride; Five Giants from Texas*
Fodor, Ladislas: *Apache's Last Battle; Pyramid of the Sun God; Treasure of the Aztecs; Who Killed Johnny R.?*
Fogagnolo, Franco: *Ten Thousand Dollars Blood Money*
Fondato, Marcello: *Jesse James' Kid; Magnificent Three; Relentless Four; Two Gunmen*
Fonseca, John: *God's Gun*
Foster, Frank: *Bullets Don't Argue*
Franchi, Fernando: *Execution*
Franciosa, Massimo: *Calibre .38*
Franco, Jess: *Jaguar*
Freda, Riccardo: *Death at Owell Rock*
Fregonese, Hugo: *Find a Place to Die*
Fulci, Lucio: *Four Gunmen of the Apocalypse; Silver Saddle*
Ganz, Serge: *Guns for San Sebastian*
Garfield, Warren: *Stranger in Town*
Gariazzo, Mario: *God Will Forgive My Pistol; Holy Water Joe; In the Name of the Father, the Son and the Colt*
Garrone, Sergio: *Bastard, Go and Kill; Deguello; If You Want to Live . . . Shoot!; Kill Django . . . Kill First; Killer Kid; No Graves on Boot Hill; No Room to Die; Vendetta at Dawn*
Gasper, Luis: *Prey of Vultures; Shoot to Kill*
Gasperini, Italo: *Wrath of God*
Gastaldi, Ernesto: *Arizona; Arizona Colt; Big Showdown; Blood at Sundown; Cowards Don't Pray; Day of Anger; Genius; For One Hundred Thousand Dollars Per Killing; It Can Be Done . . . Amigo; Light the Fuse . . . Sartana Is Coming; Massacre at Fort Holman; My Name Is Nobody; Prey of Vultures; Ten Thousand Dollars Blood Money; To Hell and Back*
Genta, Renzo: *Jesse and Lester, Two Brothers in a Place Called Trinity*
Giambattista, Mussetto: *Bandidos*
Giambriccio, Antonio: *Rojo*
Gianviti, Roberto: *And the Crows Will Dig Your Grave; Dallas; Have a Good Funeral, My Friend . . . Sartana Will Pay; Nephews of Zorro; Red Blood, Yellow Gold; Rojo; Sheriff with the Gold; Two R-R-Ringos from Texas; Two Sons of Ringo*
Gicca, Enzo (also Fulvio Gicca, Enzo Gicca Palli; additional pseudonym—Vincent Thomas): *Killer Caliber .32; Night of the Serpent; Price of Death; Road to Fort Alamo; Thompson 1880; Time of Vultures*
Girault, Jean: *Judge Roy Bean*
Girolami, Enzo (director pseudonym—Enzo G. Castellari): *I Came, I Saw, I Shot; Johnny Hamlet; Kill Them All and Come Back Alone; Magnificent Brutes of the West; The Moment to Kill; Payment in Blood; Sting of the West; Two R-R-Ringos from Texas*
Girolami, Marino: *Between God, the Devil, and a Winchester; Bullets and the Flesh*
Glachin, Luigi: *Four Came to Kill Sartana; Hero Called Allegria*
Globus, Ken: *Kid Vengeance*
Gora, Claudio: *Hatred of God*
Gregoretti, Luciano: *Dead for a Dollar; For One Thousand Dollars Per Day*
Grieco, Sergio: *Miss Dynamite*

Griffith, J. J.: *Shalako*
Grimaldi, Giovanni: *Four Dollars for Vengeance; Handsome, the Ugly, and the Stupid; In a Colt's Shadow; Johnny Colt; Paths of War*
Groth, Winfried: *Legacy of the Incas*
Guerra, Mario: *Durango Is Coming, Pay or Die; Ringo and Gringo Against All; Shots Ring Out!; Terrible Sheriff*
Guerra, Ugo: *Django Does Not Forgive; Ringo and Gringo Against All; Wrath of God*
Guerrieri, Romolo: *Go Kill and Come Back; Johnny Yuma*
Halevy, Julian: *Pancho Villa*
Harrison, Richard: *Jesse and Lester, Two Brothers in a Place Called Trinity; Scalps*
Harum, Helmut: *Clint the Stranger; Five Thousand Dollars on One Ace; Man Called Gringo; Man from Oklahoma*
Harvey, Jerry: *China 9, Liberty 37*
Hauff, Werner: *Hatred of God*
Henaghan, James: *Christmas Kid; Tall Women*
Hengge, Paul: *Montana Trap*
Hopper, Hal: *Shalako*
Hossein, Robert: *Cemetery Without Crosses; Judge Roy Bean; Taste of Violence*
Hoven, Adrian (pseudonym—**Antonio Del Amo**): *Jesse James' Kid*
Huffaker, Clair: *Chino*
Iglesias, Miguel see **Baldi, Ferdinando**
Iquino, Ignacio (sometimes pseudonyms—**Steve MacCohy, Juan Bosch**, and **John Wood**): *And the Crows Will Dig Your Grave* (as **Wood**); *Dallas* (as **MacCohy**); *Dig Your Grave, Friend . . . Sabata's Coming* (as **MacCohy**); *Dollar on Fire; Five Dollars for Ringo; God in Heaven . . . Arizona on Earth* (as **Bosch**); *Joe Dexter* (as **MacCohy**); *My Colt, Not Yours* (as **MacCohy**); *My Horse, My Gun, Your Widow* (as **Wood**); *None of the Three Were Called Trinity; The Reward's Yours, The Man's Mine; Seven Pistols for a Gringo; Too Much Gold for One Gringo* (as **Bosch**); *Twenty Paces to Death; With Friends, Nothing Is Easy*
Izzo, Renato: *Adios, Sabata; Return of Sabata; Sabata; Sartana; Too Much Gold for One Gringo*
Jacobs, Irving see **Amendola, Mario**
Jarrico, Paul: *Who Killed Johnny R.?*
Jeres, José: *Adios Gringo; Viva Cangaceiro*
Johnson, Robert see **Mauri, Roberto**
Jones, Ian: *Ned Kelly*
Jones, Z. X. (pseudonym for **Burt Kennedy** and **Edward Scaife**): *Hannie Caulder*
Josa, Enrique: *Tequila*
Kampendonk, Gustav: *Sheriff Was a Lady*
Karl, Günter: *Trail of the Falcon*
Kas, Johannes: *Pirates of the Mississippi*
Keaton, Robert: *Magnificent Texan*
Keindorff, Eberhard: *Among Vultures; Flaming Frontier*
Kelly, Jackie: *Dig Your Grave, Friend . . . Sabata's Coming; My Colt, Not Yours; None of the Three Were Called Trinity; With Friends, Nothing Is Easy*
Kiefer, Warren: *Beyond the Law; Last Rebel*
Klick, Roland: *Deadlock*
Klimovsky, Leon: *Death Knows No Time*
Koenig, Laird: *Red Sun*
Kowalsky, Frank: *Man Called Sledge*

Lacy, Joe *see* Elorietta, José M.
Lado, Aldo: *If One Is Born a Swine . . . Kill Him*
Lahola, Leopoldo: *Duel at Sundown*
Lamas, Fernando: *Place Called Glory*
Lanfranchi, Mario: *Death Sentence*
Larraz, José Ramon: *Watch Out Gringo! Sabata Will Return*
Laurani, Salvatore: *Bullet for a General*
Laurenti, Mariano: *Grandsons of Zorro*
Leader, Bruno: *The Moment to Kill*
LeLouch, Claude: *Another Man, Another Woman*
Lenzi, Umberto: *Pistol for One Hundred Coffins; Terror of the Black Mask*
Leonard, Keith: *Charley One-Eye*
Leone, Sergio: *Duck You Sucker!; Fistful of Dollars; For a Few Dollars More; The Good, the Bad, and the Ugly; Once Upon a Time in the West*
Leoni, Roberto: *California*
Leonio, Preston: *If One Is Born a Swine*
Leto, Marco (also Marco Letto): *Cry for Revenge; Pistol for One Hundred Coffins*
Levy, Paul: *Up the MacGregors!*
Lewis, Jack: *Black Eagle of Santa Fe*
Li, Ban Yee: *Kung Fu Brothers in the Wild West*
Liberatore, Ugo: *Hellbenders; Minute to Pray, a Second to Die; Mutiny at Fort Sharp; Tramplers; Train for Durango*
Lipsky, Oldrich: *Lemonade Joe*
Llovet, Enrique: *Those Dirty Dogs!*
Lombardo, Paolo: *Cisco; Days of Violence*
Loy, Mino: *For One Hundred Thousand Dollars Per Killing*
Lucas, Luis: *Three Swords of Zorro*
Luciano, Carlos: *Arizona Kid*
Lucidi, Maurizio: *My Name Is Nobody; Pecos Cleans Up*
Ludwig, Jerry: *Take a Hard Ride*
Luigi, Gianni: *Sheriff of Rock Spring*
MacCohy, Steve (pseudonym for Ignacio Iquino): *Dallas; Dig Your Grave, Friend . . . Sabata's Coming; Joe Dexter; My Colt, Not Yours*
Maesto, José: *Savage Guns; The Ugly Ones*
Maffei, Mario: *Garter Colt; Ringo's Big Night*
Maiuri, Dino: *Chino; Compañeros; Don't Turn the Other Cheek*
Malatesta, Guido: *Coffin for the Sheriff; Sheriff Won't Shoot; Sign of Zorro; Terror of the Black Mask*
Malle, Louis: *Viva Maria*
Mallorqui, José (screenwriting pseudonym for Mario Caiano): *Bullet for Sandoval; Death on a Mountain Top; Heroes of the West; Killer Goodbye; Magnificent Three; Ride and Kill; Ringo: Face of Revenge; Ringo, the Lone Rider; Shots Ring Out!; Sign of Coyote; Terrible Sheriff; Train for Durango; Twins of the West*
Malvestiti, Marcello: *Django Kills Softly*
Mancori, Carlo: *Kung Fu Brothers in the Wild West*
Manera, John: *Chrysanthemums for a Bunch of Swine*
Mangini, Gino: *This Man Can't Die; Vendetta at Dawn*
Mangione, Giuseppe: *Stranger in Town; Sugar Colt*
Manini, Bianco: *Halleluja to Vera Cruz*
Manse, Jean: *Dynamite Jack*
Manzanos, Eduardo: *Charge of the Seventh Cavalry*

Marchent, Joaquin Romero (sometimes pseudonym—**Joaquin Romero Hernandez**): *Awkward Hands; Coyote; Cut-Throats Nine; Dead Are Countless; Gunfight at High Noon; Hands of a Gunman; Hour of Death; I Do Not Forgive . . . I Kill!; Kill Them All and Come Back Alone; Sartana Kills Them All; Seven Guns from Texas; Seven Hours of Gunfire; Shadow of Zorro; Two Crosses at Danger Pass*

Marchent, Rafael Romero: *Cry for Revenge; Gunfight at High Noon; Prey of Vultures; Shadow of Zorro; Two Crosses at Danger Pass; Viva Cangaceiro; Woman for Ringo*

Margheriti, Antonio: *And God Said to Cain; Vengeance*

Marina, Craig: *Death Played the Flute; Let's Go and Kill Sartana*

Marinero, Manuel: *Trinity Sees Red*

Marino, Antonio: *Sometimes Life Is Hard, Right Providence?*

Marischka, Franz: *Legacy of the Incas*

Marischka, Georg: *Legacy of the Incas; Pyramid of the Sun God; Treasure of the Aztecs*

Martın, Eugenio: *Ugly Ones*

Martin, Louis: *Taste of Violence*

Martinenghi, Italo: *Three Supermen of the West*

Martinez, Maria Del Carmin: *Dynamite Joe; Fury of Johnny Kid*

Martino, Francesco: *Sky Full of Stars for a Roof*

Martino, Leonardo: *Three Musketeers of the West*

Martino, Luciano: *Buffalo Bill, Hero of the Far West; For One Hundred Thousand Dolars Per Killing; Ten Thousand Dollars Blood Money*

Martino, Sergio: *For One Hundred Thousand Dollars Per Killing; Man Called Blade*

Maruizzo, Giorgio: *Apache Woman*

Marvin, Joseph *see* **Merino, José Luis**

Masini, Luigi: *Death at Owell Rock*

Massacesi, Aristide (also see **Romano Scandariato**): *Bounty Hunter in Trinity; Red Coat*

Mattei, Bruno: *Scalps*

Maug, Jone: *Stranger Returns*

Mauri, Roberto (sometimes pseudonym—**Robert Johnson**): *Animal Called Man* (as **Johnson**); *Death Is Sweet from the Soldier of God; Gunmen and the Holy Ghost; He Was Called the Holy Ghost; Sartana in the Valley of Death; Shotgun; Wanted Sabata* (as **Johnson**)

Mellone, Amedeo: *Seven Dollars on the Red*

Melson, John: *Savage Pampas*

Mendez, José Briz: *White Comanche*

Merighi, Ferdinando: *They Called Him Trinity*

Merino, José Luis (sometimes pseudonym—**Joseph Marvin**): *Kitosch, Man Who Came from North* (as **Marvin**); *Machine Gun Killers; More Dollars for the MacGregors; Zorro, Rider of Vengeance*

Miali, Roberto: *Twenty Thousand Dollars for Seven*

Michili, Ornella: *Silver Saddle*

Miehe, Ulf: *Yankee Dudler*

Migliorini, Romano: *Bandidos; Miss Dynamite*

Minardi, Ofelia: *Halleluja to Vera Cruz*

Miraglia, Emilio: *Shoot Joe, and Shoot Again*

Miret, Pedro: *Lucky Johnny: Born in America*

Moffa, Paolo: *Bury Them Deep*

Molteni, Ambrogio: *Last Gun; Three Graves for a Winchester*
Mondello, Luigi: *Rattler Kid*
Monicada, Santiago: *Awkward Hands; Cut-Throats Nine; Sartana Kills Them All*
Montefiori, Luigi (acting pseudonym — **George Eastman**): *Ben and Charlie; Keoma*
Montemurro, Francesco: *Zorro, the Navarra Marquis*
Montero, Roberto (also **Roberto Bianchi Montero**): *Death Is Sweet from the Soldier of God; Durango Is Coming, Pay or Die; Seven Pistols for a Gringo; Sheriff Won't Shoot*
Mora, Philippe: *Mad Dog Morgan*
Morandi, Fernando: *Big Gundown; Stranger in Paso Bravo*
Morayta, Miguel: *Guns for San Sebastian*
Moreno, David: *Coffin for the Sheriff*
Morheim, Lou: *Hunting Party*
Moroni, Mario: *Mallory Must Not Die; Saguro*
Morris, Edmund: *Savage Guns*
Morrow, Vic: *Man Called Sledge*
Morsella, Fulvio: *For a Few Dollars More; Genius; My Name Is Nobody*
Moullet, Luc: *A Girl Is a Gun*
Mulargia, Eduardo: *Brother Outlaw; Go with God, Gringo; The Reward's Yours, the Man's Mine; Shango*
Mulligan, Tony: *Born to Kill*
Musolino, Vincenzo (director pseudonym — **Glenn Vincent Davis**): *Blood at Sundown; Cjamango; Don't Wait, Django . . . Shoot!; Go with God, Gringo; May God Forgive You . . . But I Won't; Quintana*
Nando, Federico: *Forewarned, Half-Killed . . . Word of Holy Ghost*
Narzisi, Gianni: *Djurado*
Natale, Roberto: *Hate Thy Neighbor; Long Ride from Hell*
Natteford, Jake: *Kid Rodelo*
Navarro, José (also **Jesus Navarro**): *Challenge of the Mackennas; Coyote; Fury of the Apaches; Gunfight at High Noon; Massacre at Fort Grant; Raise Your Hands, Dead Man . . . You're Under Arrest; Ruthless Colt of the Gringo; Two Gunmen*
Norton, William: *Hunting Party*
Nostro, Nick (director pseudonym — **Nick Howard**): *One After Another*
O'Hanlon, James: *Murieta*
O'Neill, Simon: *One After Another*
Ortosolli, Daniel: *God in Heaven . . . Arizona on Earth*
Paget, Robert: *Drummer of Vengeance*
Pallardy, Jean-Marie: *Gunfight at O Q Corral*
Palli, Vincenzo G. (also **Enzo Gicca Palli**; pseudonym — **Vincent Thomas**): *Death on High Mountain; Price of Death*
Panaccio, Elo: *Death Played the Flute*
Paolella, Domenico: *Execution; Hate for Hate*
Parolini, Gianfranco (director pseudonym — **Frank Kramer**): *Adios, Sabata; God's Gun; Left Handed Johnny West; Return of Sabata; Sabata; Sartana*
Pas, Tonio: *Thunder Over El Paso*
Passadore, E.: *Return of Clint the Stranger*
Pastore, Sergio: *Chrysanthemums for a Bunch of Swine*
Patrizi, Massimo: *Price of Power*
Pazziloro, Fulvio: *Blood Calls to Blood*
Peri, Enzo: *Death Walks in Laredo*
Pescatori, Pino: *Garter Colt; Jesse James' Kid*

Peterson, Harald G.: *Treasure of Silver Lake; Winnetou: Last of the Renegades; Winnetou: The Desperado Trail; Winnetou the Warrior*
Petitclere, D. B.: *Red Sun*
Petrilli, Vittorio: *Great Silence*
Petroni, Giulio: *Night of the Serpent; Sometimes Life Is Hard, Right Providence?*
Pettito, Tony (actor pseudonym — Tony Anthony): *Blindman; Comin' at Ya; Stranger Returns*
Pettus, Ken: *Land Raiders*
Philipp, Harald: *Rampage at Apache Wells*
Piccioni, Fabio: *Finders Keepers*
Pierotti, Mario (pseudonym — Dean Craig): *Death Walks in Laredo; Hills Run Red; Law of Violence; Navajo Joe; Sometimes Life Is Hard, Right Providence?*
Pierotti, Piero (sometimes pseudonym — Paul Stanley): *Heads or Tails; Lost Treasure of the Incas; Zorro, the Navarra Marquis*
Pink, Philip: *Finger on the Trigger*
Pink, Sidney: *Finger on the Trigger*
Pino, Conchita: *Magnificent Brutes of the West*
Pinzauti, Mario: *Ringo, It's Massacre Time*
Pipolo *see* Castellano and Pipolo
Pirro, Ugo: *Navajo Joe*
Pittorru, Fabio: *Macho Killers*
Poggi, Franco: *Holy Water Joe*
Pradeaux, Maurizio: *Thunder Over El Paso; Ramon the Mexican*
Price, Charles: *Road to Fort Alamo*
Prindele, Don: *The Ugly Ones*
Proietti, Biagio: *Cost of Dying*
Prosperi, Franco: *White Apache*
Puente, José Vincent: *Trinity Sees Red*
Puglia, Kidia: *Seven Nuns in Kansas City*
Questi, Giulio: *Django, Kill . . . If You Live, Shoot!*
Quintana, Gene: *Comin' at Ya*
Raccioppi, Antonio: *Apache Woman*
Redford, William *see* Squittieri, Pasquale
Reed, James: *Coffin for the Sheriff*
Reeves, Steve: *Long Ride from Hell*
Reggiani, Franco: *Django Strikes Again*
Regnoli, Piero: *And They Smelled the Strange, Exciting, Dangerous Scent of Dollars*
Reinecker, Herbert: *Winnetou and Shatterhand in the Valley of Death*
Remis, Manuel Martinez: *Quinta: Fighting Proud; Reverend Colt; Secret of Captain O'Hara*
Rey, Gonzalo Asensio: *Seven for Pancho Villa*
Reynolds, Clarke: *Gunfighters of Casa Grande; Man Called Gringo; Son of a Gunfighter*
Ribera, Dan: *Three Swords of Zorro*
Ricci, Tonino: *Great Treasure Hunt; Shadow of a Badman*
Richardson, Tony: *Ned Kelly*
Rigal, Arturo: *Sign of Zorro*
Rivera, Manuel: *White Comanche*
Rivero, Rodrigo: *Christmas Kid*
Robbins, Bud: *Kid Vengeance*
Roberts, William: *Red Sun*
Rocco, Gian Andrea: *Garter Colt*

Rodriguez, Carlos: *One After Another*
Roli, Mino: *Carambola; Carambola's Philosophy; Matalo!; On the Third Day Arrived the Crow; Tall Women*
Roman, Michael Martinez: *Duel in the Eclipse; Man and a Colt*
Romano, Antonio: *Savage Gringo; Winchester Does Not Forgive*
Rosati, Giuseppe: *Those Dirty Dogs!; Twenty Paces to Death*
Rose, Jack: *Talent for Loving*
Rossati, Nello: *Django Strikes Again*
Rossetti, Franco: *Chuck Moll; Django; Get the Coffin Ready; Ringo and His Golden Pistol; Rita of the West; Texas, Adios*
Rubio, Miguel: *Trinity Sees Red*
Salerno, Vittorio: *Blood at Sundown; Cry for Revenge; Dead Are Countless; Fasthand; Pistol for a Hundred Coffins*
Salter, Marck: *Shoot the Living . . . Pray for the Dead*
Salvi, Erminio: *Wanted Johnny Texas; Three Graves for a Winchester*
Salvia, R. J.: *Torrejon City*
Sangster, Jimmy: *Savage Guns*
Santini, Gino: *Twenty Thousand Dollars for Seven*
Saul, Oscar: *Deaf Smith and Johnny Ears*
Savalas, Telly: *Pancho Villa*
Savino, Renato: *Gold of the Heroes; Hey Amigo! A Toast to Your Death!; His Name Was King; Vengeance*
Savona, Leopoldo: *God Will Forgive My Pistol; Killer Kid; Pistol Packin' Preacher*
Scandariato, Romano (unconfirmed pseudonym for **Aristite Massaccesi**): *Go Away! Trinity Has Arrived in Eldorado*
Scardamaglia, Franco: *Go Kill and Return Alone; Man Killed Billy the Kid; The Moment to Kill*
Scarnicci: *Ringo and Gringo Against All*
Scarpelli, Furio: *The Good, the Bad, and the Ugly*
Scavolini, Romano: *John the Bastard; Johnny Yuma*
Scavolini, Sauro: *Go Kill and Come Back; Man Called Blade; My Horse, My Gun, Your Widow; Ten Thousand Dollars Blood Money*
Sebares, Manuel: *Django, a Bullet for You; Few Dollars for Django; If You Shoot . . . You Live; Moment to Kill; Relentless Four; Seven for Pancho Villa; Seven for Texas; Shoot to Kill; Twenty Thousand Dollars for Seven; Two Gunmen; Two Thousand Dollars for Coyote; Woman for Ringo*
Secchi, Toni: *Calibre .38*
Seone, Aldo: *Paid in Blood; Rojo*
Shert, Antonio: *Eye for an Eye*
Sibelius, Johanna: *Among Vultures; Flaming Frontier*
Silvestri, Alberto: *Yankee*
Silvestro, Dario: *Two Sides of the Dollar*
Simonelli, Giovanni: *Dick Luft in Sacramento; Go Kill and Come Back; Gunmen of Rio Grande; Have a Good Funeral, My Friend . . . Sartana Will Pay; I Am Sartana, Trade Your Guns for a Coffin; I Do Not Forgive . . . I Kill!; I'll Sell My Skin Dearly; Johnny Yuma; Left Handed Johnny West; Man with Golden Pistol; One Hundred Thousand Dollars for Ringo; Return of Clint the Stranger; Return of Halleluja; Sartana Does Not Forgive; Seven Guns for Timothy; Sting of the West; Stranger and Gunfighter; Two Gangsters in the Wild West; Two Sergeants of General Custer; Watch Out Gringo! Sabata Will Return; Winnetou and Shatterhand in the Valley of Death*

Sirens, Bob: *Billy the Kid*
Sirko, Marlon: *Cowards Don't Pray*
Solinas, Franco: *Big Gundown; Blood and Guns; Bullet for the General; Mercenary*
Sollazzo, Amedeo: *Ciccio Forgives, I Don't; Two R-R-Ringos from Texas; Two Sons of Ringo*
Sollima, Sergio: *Face to Face; Run Man, Run*
Solvay, Paolo *see* Batzella, Luigi
Soria, Julio: *Three from Colorado*
Sorrentino, Elido: *Sheriff of Rock Spring*
Sperling, Milton: *Captain Apache*
Spina, Sergio: *Mercenary*
Squittieri, Pasquale (sometimes pseudonym — **William Redford**): *Django Challenges Sartana; Vengeance Is a Dish Served Cold* (as **Redford**)
Stanley, Paul *see* Pierotti, Piero
Steffen, Anthony *see* De Teffe, Antonio
Stegani, Giorgio: *Blood at Sundown; Blood for a Silver Dollar; Gentleman Killer*
Stemmle, R. A.: *Pyramid of the Sun God; Treasure of the Aztecs*
Steno *see* Vanzina, Stefano
Stevens, Mark: *Sunscorched*
Stresa, Nino: *All Out; Buffalo Bill, Hero of the Far West; Colorado Charlie; Man and a Colt; Man Called Django; Sabata the Killer*
Sussman, Barth Jules: *Stranger and the Gunfighter*
Tabet, André: *Sign of Zorro*
Tallevi, Fabio: *Great Treasure Hunt*
Tamayo, Manuel: *Torrejon City*
Tarabusi: *Ringo and Gringo Against All*
Tarantini, M. Massimo: *Arizona; Trinity Plus the Clown and a Guitar*
Tejedor, Darturo: *If You Want to Live, Shoot!*
Telfer, Jay: *Kid Vengeance*
Tessari, Duccio: *Fistful of Dollars; Seven Guns for the MacGregors; Train for Durango; Pistol for Ringo; Return of Ringo; Seven Guns for the MacGregors; Train for Durango; Zorro*
Thomas, Vincent *see* Gicca, Enzo
Tinney, Claus: *Prairie in the City*
Torrado, Ramon: *Cavalry Charge*
Tortelli, Luci: *Grandsons of Zorro*
Treccia, T. F.: *Fighting Fists of Shanghai Joe*
Troisio, Antonio: *Viva Cangaceiro; White, the Yellow and the Black*
Turner, Ramon C.: *Colt Is the Law*
Valenza, R. M. (also **M. R. Vitelli Valenza**): *Django and Sartana Are Coming . . . It's the End; Fistful of Death; One Damned Day at Dawn . . . Django Meets Sartana; Stranger That Kneels Beside Shadow of a Corpse*
Valerii, Tonino: *Day of Anger; Massacre at Fort Holman*
Vanzina, Stefano (pseudonym — **Steno**): *Heroes of the West; Twins of Texas*
Vari, Giuseppe: *Deguello; Thirteenth Is a Judas*
Vazquez, Ricardo: *Seven for Pancho Villa*
Veo, Carlo: *Man Who Killed Billy the Kid; Those Dirty Dogs!*
Venturelli, Douglas: *China 9, Liberty 37*
Verucci, Franco: *Sheriff Won't Shoot; Two Sides of the Dollar*
Vietri, Franco: *For a Book of Dollars*
Vighi, Vittorio: *Ringo and Gringo Against All; Shots Ring Out!; Terrible Sheriff*

Villerot, Michele: *Adios Gringo*
Vincenzoni, Luciano: *Cipolla Colt; Death Rides a Horse; Duck You Sucker!; For a Few Dollars More; The Good, the Bad, and the Ugly; Mercenary; Navajo Joe*
Vitelli, Mila: *Anything for a Friend*
Vladimirov, Vladimar: *Armed and Dangerous: Time and Heroes of Bret Harte*
Vogeler, Volker: *Valley of Dancing Widows; Yankee Dudler*
Von Theumer, Ernst: *Ballad of a Gunfighter*
Welles, Mark (also Mel Welles): *Requiem for a Bounty Hunter*
Whitcomb, Dean: *Shoot, Gringo . . . Shoot!*
White, Peter: *Colt Is the Law*
Whitman, Stuart E.: *Captain Apache*
Wich, Nathan: *Belle Starr Story*
Yordan, Philip: *Bad Man's River; Captain Apache*
Zibaso, Werner P.: *Massacre at Marble City; Pirates of the Mississippi*
Zabalza, José Maria: *Adios Cjamango; Rebels of Arizona*
Zeglio, Primo: *Killer Goodbye; Two Gunmen*
Zurli, Guido: *Son of Zorro*

Cinematographers

Note: The First and Second Unit cameramen are not included in this filmography.

Achilli, Sante: *John the Bastard*
Aguayo, José F. (also **José Aquayo**): *Don't Turn the Other Cheek; Gunfighters of Casa Grande; Minnesota Clay; Seven Dollars on the Red*
Alhort, Al *see* **Albertini, Adalberto**
Albertini, Adalberto (sometimes pseudonym – **Al Albert**): *Sign of Zorro; Stranger in Sacramento* (as **Albert**); *Terror of the Black Mask*
Albonico, Giulio: *Zorro*
Alcocer, Teresa: *Place Called Glory*
Andreu, Ricardo: *I Want Him Dead*
Angelo, Luigi: *Black Killer*
Aquari, Giuseppe (also **Giuseppe Aquinis**): *For a Few Dollars Less; God Does Not Pay on Saturday* (as **Aquinis**); *Revenge for Revenge*
Arribas, Fernando: *Comin' at Ya; Valley of the Dancing Widows*
Atfronti, Edmondo: *Damned Pistols of Dallas*
Baena, Juan Julio: *Two Gangsters in the Wild West*
Baistrocchi, Angelo: *Piluk, the Timid One*
Ballesteros, Antonio: *My Colt, Not Yours; None of the Three Were Called Trinity; With Friends, Nothing Is Easy*
Ballhaus, Michael: *Chetan, Indian Boy*
Barboni, Enzo: *Django; Five Man Army; Get the Coffin Ready; Hellbenders; Long Ride from Hell; Man Who Cried for Revenge; Massacre at Grand Canyon; Rita of the West; Texas, Adios; Train for Durango; The Ugly Ones*
Bazzoni, Camillo: *Man: His Pride and His Revenge*
Becker, Étienne: *Do Not Touch the White Woman*
Bentiviglio, Eugenio: *Django Challenges Sartana*
Berenguer, Manuel: *Savage Pampas; Son of a Gunfighter; Town Called Hell*
Bergamini, Giovanni: *Go Kill and Come Back; I Am Sartana, Your Angel of Death*
Bergier, Enrique: *Finger on the Trigger*
Borghesi, Antonio: *Three Swords of Zorro; To Hell and Back*
Brunelli, Ugo: *Go with God, Gringo; Once Upon a Time in the Wild Wild West*
Burgos, Julio: *Scalps; White Apache*
Burmann, Hans: *Blood at Sundown; Boldest Job in the West*
Cabrera, John: *Captain Apache; Man Called Noon*
Caltabiano, Alfio: *They Still Call Me Amen*
Capriotti, Mario: *Johnny Yuma; Man with the Golden Pistol; Prey of Vultures; Stranger in Japan; They Call Him Veritas; Trinity Plus the Clown and a Guitar*

Carlini, Carlo: *Big Gundown; Death Rides a Horse; Halleluja to Vera Cruz; Last of the Mohicans; Last Rebel; Sky Full of Stars for a Roof*

Caruso, Salvatore: *Reverend Colt*

Centini, Maurizio: *Porno Erotic Western; Requiem for a Bounty Hunter*

Chaffey, Don: *Charley One-Eye*

Chow, Raymond: *Kung Fu Brothers in the Wild West*

Ciccarese, Luigi: *Animal Called Man; Gunmen and the Holy Ghost; He Was Called the Holy Ghost; White Apache*

Civirani, Osvaldo: *Dead for a Dollar; Rick and John, Conquerors of the West; Sheriff with the Gold; Son of Django*

Civirani, Walter: *Two Sons of Trinity*

Continenza, Alessandro: *They Still Call Me Amen*

Contini, Alfio: *God Forgives, I Don't; Yankee*

Cooper, Wilkie: *Land Raiders*

Coquillion, Johnny: *Talent for Loving*

Cortez, Stanley: *Another Man, Another Woman*

Cruz, J. Xavier: *Eye for an Eye*

Cuadrado, Luis: *Bandera Bandits; Cut-Throats Nine; White, the Yellow and the Black; Yankee Dudler*

Dallamano, Massimo (pseudonym—**Jack Dalmas** and **Max Dillman**): *Buffalo Bill, the Hero of the Far West; Fistful of Dollars; For a Few Dollars More; Gunfight at Red Sands*

Dalmas, Jack *see* **Dallamo, Massimo**

Decae, Henri: *Viva Maria*

Del Casas, Jaime: *Sartana Does Not Forgive*

Delli-Colli, Franco: *Cry for Revenge; Django Kill . . . If You Live, Shoot!; Hatred of God; Shotgun; Son of Zorro*

Delli-Colli, Tonino: *Deaf Smith and Johnny Ears; The Good, the Bad, and the Ugly; Once Upon a Time in the West*

Demmer, Andreas: *Nude Django*

De Robertis, Aldo: *Miss Dynamite*

Deu Casa, Jaime (also **Jamie Deu Dasas;** also **Jaime Del Casas**): *Death Played the Flute; Desperado; Law of Violence; Let's Go and Kill Sartana; Return of Clint the Stranger; Sartana Does Not Forgive; Three Supermen in the West; Watch Out Gringo! Sabata Will Return*

Deva, Alessandro (also **Alessandro D'Eva**): *Belle Starr Story; Ciccio Forgives, I Don't; Four Gunmen of Holy Trinity; Ringo and Gringo Against All; Sometimes Life Is Hard, Right Providence?*

Di Cola, Emanuele (also **Emanuele D'Cola;** also **Emanuele D. Cola**): *More Dollars for the MacGregors; Ringo, the Lone Rider; Zorro, Rider of Vengeance*

Di Giacomo, Franco: *Buddy Goes West*

Dilman, Max *see* **Dallamano, Massimo**

Di Palma, Dario: *Specialist*

D'Offizi, Sergio: *God Made Them . . . I Kill; Hey Amigo! A Toast to Your Death!; Ruthless Four; Today It's Me . . . Tomorrow You*

Dry, Tony *see* **Secchi, Antonio**

Ferrando, Giancarlo: *And the Crows Will Dig Your Grave; Dallas; God in Heaven . . . Arizona on Earth; Joe Dexter*

Filippini, Angelo (also **Angelo Flippini**): *Big Ripoff; Django, Last Killer; Johnny Hamlet; Time and Place of Killing*

Fioretti, Mario: *Black Jack; Bullets and the Flesh; Two R-R-Ringos from Texas*

Fisher, Gerry: *Ned Kelly*

Flori, Jean Jacques: *A Girl Is a Gun*

Foriscot, Emilio (also **Farlscot** and **Fariscot**): *Bandidos; Dead Men Ride; Death Knows No Time; Dick Luft in Sacramento; Fasthand; If You Shoot . . . You Live!; In the Name of the Father, Son and the Colt; Jaguar; Light the Fuse . . . Sartana Is Coming; Man and a Colt; Mutiny at Fort Sharp; One Against One . . . No Mercy; Ringo's Big Night; Two Crosses at Danger Pass*

Fraile, Alfredo: *Man of the Cursed Valley; Savage Guns; Two Gunmen; White Comanche*

Fraschetti, Silvio: *Bad Kids of the West; Night of the Serpent; Shoot Joe, and Shoot Again*

Frattari, Benito: *Cost of Dying*

Fuchs, Burt: *Two Thousand Dollars for Coyote*

Fusi, Alberto: *Between God, the Devil, and a Winchester*

Garroni, Romolo: *Deadly Trackers; Last Gun*

Gatti, Marcello: *Ruthless Colt of the Gringo; Tall Women; Who Killed Johnny R.?*

Gengarelli, Amerigo: *Death Rides Alone; Hole in the Forehead; Last Gun*

Gerardi, Roberto: *Trinity Sees Red*

Giordani, Aldo: *Great Treasure Hunt; Handsome, the Ugly, and the Stupid; Kill or Die; Man of the East; Paths of War; Rojo; They Call Me Trinity; Three Silver Dollars; Trinity Is Still My Name*

Goldberger, Isidoro: *Two Sergeants of General Custer*

Gonnet, Jean: *A Girl Is a Gun*

Greci, Aldo: *Cisco; Colt in the Hand of the Devil; Long Day of the Massacre; Ride and Kill*

Grisanti, Remo: *Man of the Cursed Valley*

Gurfinkel, David: *Kid Vengeance*

Hanisch, Otto: *Trail of the Falcon*

Höld, Siegfried (also **Siegfried Hölt**): *Apache's Last Battle; Legacy of the Incas; Pyramid of the Sun God; Sheriff Was a Lady; Treasure of the Aztecs*

Hölscher, Heinz: *Half Breed; Rampage at Apache Wells*

Herrada, Francisco M. *see* **Marin, Francisco**

Hubert, Roger: *Dynamite Jack*

Ippoliti, Silvano: *Deguello; Great Silence; Navajo Joe*

Izzarelli, Francesco: *Left Handed Johnny West; Pirates of the Mississippi*

Jura, Hans: *Black Eagle of Santa Fe*

Kalinke, Ernst: *Last Tomahawk; Treasure of Silver Lake; Winnetou: Desperado Trail; Winnetous: Last of the Renegades; Winnetou and Shatterhand in Death Valley; Winnetou the Warrior*

Kalisnik, Janez: *Duel at Sundown*

Kastel, Rolf: *Pirates of the Mississippi*

Kuveiller, Luigi: *Man Called Sledge*

Lanzone, Alvaro: *Drummer of Vengeance*

LaTorre, Giuseppe: *Black Tigress; Five Dollars for Ringo; Man from Oklahoma; Quinta: Fighting Proud*

Le François, Jacques *see* **Lelouch, Claude**

Lelouch, Claude (pseudonym—**Jacques Le François**): *Another Man, Another Woman*

Löb, Karl: *Among Vultures; Flaming Frontier; Last Ride to Santa Cruz; Winnetou: Thunder at the Border*

Lotti, Angelo: *Poker with Pistols; Thirteenth Is a Judas; Vengeance Is a Dish Served Cold*

Macasoli, Antonio: *Bang Bang Kid*

Maccoppi, Tonino: *Raise Your Hands, Dead Man . . . You're Under Arrest*

Mancini, Mario (also **Mario Masini**): *Death Is Sweet from the Soldier of God; Hero Called Allegria; May God Forgive You . . . But I Won't; Wanted Sabata*

Mancori, Guglielmo (also **Memmo Mancori**): *Arizona Colt; Ballad of a Gunman; Fighting Fists of Shanghai Joe; His Name Was King; Johnny Colt; Run Man, Run; Sartana Kills Them All; Savage Gringo; Tequila; Vendetta at Dawn*

Mancori, Sandro: *Adios, Sabata; And They Smelled the Strange, Exciting, Dangerous Scent of Dollars; Django Strikes Again; God's Gun; If You Want to Live, Shoot; Kill Django . . . Kill First; Killer Kid; Let Them Rest; No Graves on Boot Hill; Return of Sabata; Sabata; Sartana; Sartana in the Valley of Death; Two Pistols and a Coward*

Marin, Francisco (sometimes pseudonym — **Francisco M. Herrada**): *Blood and Guns; Gentleman Killer; Long Days of Vengeance; Machine Gun Killers* (as **Herrada**); *Pistol for Ringo; Red Blood, Yellow Gold; Return of Ringo; Sunscorched; Texican; Twice a Judas*

Martelli, Otello: *Death Walks in Laredo*

Martino, Sergio: *Adios Hombre; For One Hundred Thousand Dollars Per Killing*

Masciocchi, Marcello (also **Masiocchi**; aka **Marcel Mascot**): *Ace High; Boot Hill; Colt in the Hand of the Devil; Man Called Django; Stranger in Town; Stranger Returns; Thirty Winchesters for El Diablo*

Masciocchi, Raffaele: *Kill Johnny Ringo*

Massaccesi, Aristide (director pseudonym — **Joe D'Amato**): *Bastard, Go and Kill; Ben and Charlie; Bounty Hunter in Trinity; Bury Them Deep; Django and Sartana Are Coming . . . It's the End; Fistful of Death; For One Thousand Dollars a Day; Go Away! Trinity Has Arrived in Eldorado; No Room to Die; Red Coat; Shadow of Sartana . . . Shadow of Your Death; Showdown for a Badman; Stranger That Kneels Beside the Shadow of a Corpse; Twice a Judas; Vendetta at Dawn*

Massi, Stelvio: *Fifteen Scaffolds for Killer; God Will Forgive My Pistol; Have a Good Funeral, My Friend . . . Sartana Will Pay; Heads You Die . . . Tails I Kill You; I Am Sartana, Trade Your Guns for a Coffin; I'll Sell My Skin Dearly; In a Colt's Shadow; Man Called Invincible; The Moment to Kill; Price of Power; Return of Halleluja; Sheriff Won't Shoot; Taste for Killing; They Call Him Cemetery; Two Sides of the Dollar*

Matras, Christian: *Five Thousand Dollars on One Ace*

Mella, Eloy: *Charge of the Seventh Cavalry; Colt Is the Law; One Hundred Thousand Dollars for Ringo*

Mercury, Joseph: *Man Hunt*

Merino, Manuel: *Dynamite Joe; Gunfighters of Casa Grande; Kid Rodelo; Man Called Gringo; Outlaw of Red River*

Midei, Marcello: *Colorado Charlie*

Mila, Miguel: *Arizona; Awkward Hands; Djurado; Man Who Killed Billy the Kid; Murieta; Patience Has a Limit, We Don't; Relentless Four*

Modica, Antonio: *Brother Outlaw; Fighters from Ave Maria; Jesse and Lester, Two Brothers in a Place Called Trinity; The Reward's Yours, the Man's Mine*

Molloy, Mike: *Mad Dog Morgan*

Monreal, Victor: *Clint the Stranger; Dynamite Jim; Five Giants from Texas; Four Dollars for Vengeance; Seven Guns for Timothy; Thompson 1880*

Montagnani, Giorgio (also **Giorgio Montagno**): *Even Django Has His Price; God Is My Colt .45; Paid in Blood; They Called Him Trinity*

Montuori, Mario: *Chuck Moll; Forgotten Pistolero; Fury of Johnny Kid*

Moore, Ted: *Shalako*
Morabito, Claudio: *Anything for a Friend*
Morbidelli, Pietro: *Tex and the Lord of the Deep*
Muñoz, Francisco: *Challenge of the Mackennas*
Nannuzzi, Armando: *Chino; My Name Is Nobody*
Natalucci, Vitaliano: *Cjamango; Don't Wait, Django . . . Shoot!; Quintana; Ringo, It's Massacre Time*
Nieva, Alfonso: *Durango Is Coming, Pay or Die; Fury of the Apaches; Secret of Captain O'Hara; Seven for Pancho Villa; Stranger in Paso Bravo; Thunder Over El Paso*
Novotny, Vladimir: *Lemonade Joe*
Ortas, Julio (also **Julio Octas;** sometimes pseudonym — **Julio Plaza**): *Adios Hombre; Behind the Mask of Zorro; Bullets Don't Argue; Coffin for the Sheriff; Death on High Mountain; For a Fist in the Eye; In a Colt's Shadow; Killer Goodbye; Matalo!; Rattler Kid; Ringo: Faces of Revenge*
Pacheco, Mario: *Duel in the Eclipse; For One Thousand Dollars Per Day; Wrath of God*
Pacheco, Rafael (also **Godofredo Pacheco**): *Coyote; Face to Face; Fort Yuma Gold; Four Rode Out; Gunfight at High Noon; Hour of Death; Kill the Poker Player; Magnificent Three; Seven Guns from Texas; Seven Hours of Gunfire; Shadow of Zorro; Those Dirty Dogs!; Three Musketeers of the West*
Pallottini, Riccardo: *And God Said to Cain; Blindman; Django Shoots First; Find a Place to Die; Gold of the Heroes; Greatest Robbery in the West; Man Called Amen; Massacre Time; Ringo and His Golden Pistol; Take a Hard Ride; They Still Call Me Amen; Vengeance*
Panetti, Pasqual: *They Called Him Trinity*
Paniagua, Cecilio: *Hunting Party*
Parapetti, Mario: *Django Kills Softly; For a Book of Dollars; Three Graves for a Winchester*
Parolini, Ajace (also **Aiace Parolini**): *Carambola; Carambola's Philosophy; Keoma; Minute to Pray, a Second to Die*
Pennelli, Aldo: *Few Dollars for Django; Payment in Blood*
Perez De Rosa, Julio: *Too Much Gold for One Gringo*
Perino, Mario: *Get Mean*
Persin, Henri: *Cemetery Without Crosses; Frenchie King; Judge Roy Bean*
Philips, Alex: *Lucky Johnny: Born in America*
Plaza, Julio *see* **Ortas, Julio**
Pogany, Gabor: *Death at Owell Rock*
Raffaldi, Gianni: *Magnificent West*
Raguse, Claud: *Road to Fort Alamo*
Reale, Roberto: *Five Thousand Dollars on One Ace*
Regis, Giorgio: *Calibre .38*
Reimer, Peter: *Prairie in the City*
Ricci, Aldo: *Dead Are Countless; Gunmen of Rio Grande; Sabata the Killer*
Rinaldi, Antonio: *Roy Colt and Winchester Jack*
Ripoll, Pablo: *Between God, the Devil, and a Winchester; Canadian Wilderness; Magnificent Texan; Massacre at Fort Grant; Three from Colorado; Two Thousand Dollars for Coyote*
Roberts, Bob *see* **Testi, Fulvio**
Robin, Jacques: *Gunfight at O Q Corral; Taste of Violence*
Rodriguez, Miguel F.: *Forewarned, Forearmed . . . the Word of Holy Ghost; His Name Was Holy Ghost*
Rojas, Manuel (also **Manolo Rojas**): *Alive or Preferably Dead; Sting of the West*

Rojo, José Antonio: *Magnificent Brutes of the West*
Rosell, Vicente: *Man from Canyon City*
Rosenthal, Julian: *Dollar of Fire*
Rossi, Fausto (also Fausto Ross): *Days of Violence; If One Is Born a Swine; Kitosch, Man Who Came from the North; Saguaro; Time of Vultures; You're Jinxed, Friend, You Just Met Sacramento*
Rotunno, Giuseppe: *China 9, Liberty 37*
Rozas, Julian P.: *Seven Pistols for a Gringo*
Rubini, Sergio: *Apache Woman*
Ruiz, Manuel: *Kung Fu Brothers in the Wild West*
Russell, William: *Red Hot Zorro*
Ruzzolini, Giuseppe: *Duck You Sucker!; Genius; My Name Is Nobody*
Ryzhov, Konstantin: *Armed and Dangerous: Time and Life of Bret Harte*
Salvati, Sergio: *Four Gunmen of the Apocalypse; Silver Saddle*
Sanches, Francisco: *Challenge of the Mackennas*
Sanjuan, Manuel H.: *Billy the Kid; Christmas Kid; Torrejon City; Twins from Texas*
Santi, Pier Luigi: *Return of Shanghai Joe*
Santini, Gino (also Tino Santini): *Blood at Sundown; Cowards Don't Pray; Django the Bastard; Garter Colt; Halleluja and Sartana Strike Again; Shango; Stranger in Paso Bravo; Trinity and Sartana Are Coming; Twenty Thousand Dollars for Seven*
Santoni, Clemente: *Nephews of Zorro; Two Sons of Ringo*
Santoni, Dino (also Tino Santoni): *Blood Calls to Blood; Chrysanthemums for a Bunch of Swine; Heroes of the West*
Saodalan, Felipe: *Arizona Kid*
Scaife, Edward: *Hannie Caulder*
Scavarda, Aldo: *Execution*
Scavolini, Romano: *Pistol Packin' Preacher*
Secchi, Antonio (aka Tony Dry): *Blood for a Silver Dollar; Bullet for the General; Death Sentence; Hills Run Red; Wanted*
Sempere, Francisco: *Adios Gringo; Bullet for Sandoval; Django Does Not Forgive*
Serafin, Enzo: *Beyond the Law; Day of Anger; Hate Thy Neighbor*
Seronna, Mario: *Seven Nuns in Kansas City*
Sorrentino, Elido: *Sheriff of Rock Spring*
Stallich, Jan: *Massacre at Marble City*
Storaro, Vittorio: *Brothers Blue*
Suschitzky, Wolfgang: *Tramplers*
Suzuki, Tadasu: *Dust in the Sun*
Taylor, Clinton: *Dig Your Grave, Friend . . . Sabata Is Coming*
Testi, Fulvio (aka Bob Roberts): *Dollars for a Fast Gun; I Do Not Forgive . . . I Kill; Killer Caliber .32*
Thirard, Armand: *Guns for San Sebastian*
Third, Bud: *Road to Fort Alamo*
Tiezzi, Augusto: *Lost Treasure of the Incas; Zorro, the Navarra Marquis*
Tonti, Aldo: *Deserter; It Can Be Done . . . Amigo*
Tonti, Giorgio: *My Horse, My Gun, Your Widow*
Torres, Ricardo: *Cavalry Charge; Shoot to Kill*
Trasatti, Luciano: *And God Said to Cain; Beast; Macho Killers; Twenty Paces to Death*
Trenker, Floriano: *Light the Fuse . . . Sartana Is Coming*
Troiani, Oberdan: *Born to Kill; Man and a Colt; Ramon the Mexican; Winchester Does Not Forgive*

Ulloa, Alejandro: *All Out; Bad Man's River; California; Cipolla Colt; Compañeros; Hate for Hate; Here We Are Again, Right Providence?; I Came, I Saw, I Shot; Kill Them All and Come Back Alone; Massacre at Fort Holman; Mercenary; Pancho Villa; Pistol for One Hundred Coffins; Seven Guns for the MacGregors!; Stranger and the Gunfighter; Sugar Colt; Up the MacGregors; Viva Cangaceiro; What Am I Doing in the Middle of the Revolution?*

Van Acherman, Robert: *Deadlock*

Van Der Wat, Keith: *Three Bullets for a Long Gun*

Varriano, Giovanni: *Finders Killers; Wanted Johnny Texas*

Villa, Franco: *Apocalypse Joe; Black Killer; Bury Them Deep; Four Came to Kill Sartana; Gunmen of One Hundred Crosses; His Name Was Sam Walbash, But They Call Him Amen; Holy Water Joe; My Name Is Pecos; No Room to Die; On the Third Day Arrived the Crow; One Damned Day at Dawn . . . Sartana Meets Django; Pecos Cleans Up; Price of Death; Reach You Bastard!; Shadow of Sartana . . . Shadow of Your Death; Shoot the Living . . . Pray for the Dead; Who's Afraid of Zorro?*

Villaseñor, Leopoldo: *Adios Cjamango; Django, a Bullet for You, Rebels of Arizona*

Vitrotti, Francesco: *Woman for Ringo*

Vulpiani, Mario: *Big Showdown; Grandsons of Zorro; Mallory Must Not Die; Night of the Serpent*

Williams, Billy: *Eagle's Wing*

Worth, Wolf: *Montana Trap*

Zanni, Federico: *For One Hundred Thousand Dollars Per Killing; Man Called Blade; Ten Thousand Dollars Blood Money*

Zuccoli, Fausto: *Hands of a Gunman; Heads or Tails; Jesse James' Kid; Shoot, Gringo . . . Shoot!*

III. Appendices

The Django Films

In early 1966, Sergio Corbucci introduced «Django» to the fans of Spaghetti Westerns. Quickly, the character's popularity grew and many production companies capitalized on the notoriety. Sometimes Django was a bounty hunter, sometimes an avenging angel, and sometimes a buffoon, but swiftly he eclipsed the fame of "The Man with No Name," Ringo, and Minnesota Clay. Django is the most popular international Spaghetti Western hero. Here is a listing of the «Django» films:

Year	Title	Director	Featuring
1966	Django	Sergio Corbucci	Franco Nero
1966	Django Shoots First	Alberto De Martino	Glenn Saxon
1966	Django a Bullet for You	Leon Klimovsky	James Philbrook
1966	Outlaw of Red River (alternate title: Django Honorable Killer)	Maury Dexter	George Montgomery
1966	$10,000 Blood Money	Romolo Guerrieri	Gianni Garko
1967	Django Kill . . . If You Live, Shoot!	Giulio Questi	Tomás Milian
1967	Django Does Not Forgive	Julio Buchs	John Clark
1967	Son of Django	Osvaldo Civirani	Guy Madison
1967	Django, Last Killer	Giuseppe Vari	George Eastman
1967	Two Sides of the Dollar (French title: Poker with Django [Poker d'As pour Django])	Roberto Montero	Monty Greenwood
1968	Few Dollars for Django	Leon Klimovsky	Anthony Steffen
1968	Django Kills Softly	Massimo Pupillo	George Eastman
1968	Get the Coffin Ready (alternate title: Django, Prepare a Coffin)	Ferdinando Baldi	Terence Hill
1968	Execution (European title: Django Prepare for Execution [Django Pré-pare ton Exécution])	Domenico Paolella	John Richardson
1968	Machine Gun Killers (European title: With Django, It's Blood	Paolo Bianchini	Robert Woods

Year	Title	Director	Featuring
	[Avec Django, Ça Va Saigner])		
1968	Johnny Hamlet (European title: Django's Crossroads [Django Porte sa Croix])	Enzo Girolami	Chip Gorman
1968	Nude Django	Ron Elliot	Peter Graf
1968	Shoot, Gringo . . . Shoot! (European title: Tire, Django, Tire)	Bruno Corbucci	Brian Kelly
1969	Don't Wait, Django . . . Shoot!	Edoardo Mulargia	Sean Todd
1969	Django the Bastard	Sergio Garrone	Anthony Steffen
1970	Django and Sartana Are Coming . . . It's the End	Demofilo Fidani	Hunt Powers
1970	Django Challenges Sartana	Pasquale Squittieri	Tony Kendall
1971	One Damned Day at Dawn . . . Django Meets Sartana	Demofilo Fidani	Hunt Powers
1971	Man Called Django	Edoardo Mulargia	Anthony Steffen
1971	Even Django Has His Price	Paolo Solvay	Jeff Cameron
1971	Kill Django . . . Kill First	Sergio Garrone	Giacomo R. Stuart
1971	Hero Called Allegria (British title: Django Always Draws Second)	Demofilo Fidani	Peter Martell
1971	If You Want to Live . . . Shoot! (alternate title: Django, If You Want to Live, Shoot!)	Sergio Garrone	Sean Todd
1972	Death Is Sweet from the Soldier of God (alternate title: Django . . . Adios!)	Roberto Mauri	Brad Harris
1973	Reach You Bastard! (alternate title: The Django Story)	Demofilo Fidani	Hunt Powers
1975	Keoma (French title: Django Rides Again) (German title: Django's Great Return)	Enzo Girolami	Franco Nero
1987	Django Strikes Again	Nello Rossati	Franco Nero

The Sartana Films

«Sartana» was born in 1968 with Gianfranco Parolini's film *Sartana* (alternate title: *If You Meet Sartana . . . Pray for Your Death*) starring Gianni Garko. Subsequently, Giuliano Carmineo continued the concept through numerous "official" sequels. Because of the continuing popularity of the films, many other production companies capitalized on the character's notoriety. Here is a listing of the «Sartana» films:

Year	Title	Director	Featuring
1968	*Sartana*	Gianfranco Parolini	Gianni Garko
1968	*Santana Does Not Forgive* (re-release; originally *Sonora*)	Alfonso Balcazar	George Martin
1968	*Shadow of Sartana . . . Shadow of Your Death*	Demofilo Fidani	Jeff Cameron
1969	*Blood at Sundown* (alternate title: *Sartana's Blood at Sundown*) (re-release; originally *One Thousand Dollars on the Black*)	Alberto Cardone	Gianni Garko
1969	*I Am Sartana . . . Your Angel of Death* (alternate title: *Sartana the Gravedigger*)	Giuliano Carmineo	Gianni Garko
1969	*Four Came to Kill Sartana*	Demofilo Fidani	Jeff Cameron
1970	*Sartana Kills Them All*	Rafael R. Marchent	Gianni Garko
1970	*Django Challenges Sartana*	Pasquale Squittieri	Georges Ardisson
1970	*Django and Sartana Are Coming . . . It's the End*	Demofilo Fidani	Chet Davis
1970	*Sartana in the Valley of Death*	Roberto Mauri	William Berger
1971	*Light the Fuse . . . Sartana Is Coming*	Giuliano Carmineo	Gianni Garko
1971	*Have a Good Funeral,*	Giuliano Carmineo	Gianni Garko

Year	Title	Director	Featuring
1971	*My Friend . . . Sartana Will Pay* *Raise Your Hands, Dead Man . . . You're Under Arrest* (French title: *Ça Va Chauffer, Sartana Revient*)	Leon Klimovsky	Peter Lee Lawrence
1971	*Gunmen of One Hundred Crosses* (European title: *Sartana, Gunman for 100 Crossings* [*Sartana, Eine Pistole für 100 Kreuze*])	Carlo Croccolo	Tony Kendall
1972	*I Am Sartana . . . Trade Your Guns for a Coffin*	Giuliano Carmineo	George Hilton
1972	*Halleluja and Sartana Strike Again* (alternate title: *Halleluja and Sartana Are Sons . . . Sons of God*)	Mario Siciliano	Robert Widmark
1972	*Trinity and Sartana Are Coming* (alternate title: *Trinity and Sartana . . . Those Dirty S.O.B.s*)	Mario Siciliano	Robert Widmark
1972	*Let's Go and Kill Sartana*	Mario Pinzauti	George Martin

Anglo Counterparts

The following "American-made" films were obvious in their attempt to duplicate the style of the Spaghetti Westerns, especially the machismo, cinematography, and stylish music. These few choice films are included in this book because they are truly more "Euro" than "Anglo" in their attitude and point of view.

Title and Year	Director	Featuring
Barquero (1970)	Gordon Douglas	Lee Van Cleef Warren Oates Forrest Tucker Kerwin Mathews Mariette Hartley Marie Gomez
Blue (1968) United States/England coproduction	Silvio Narizzano	Terence Stamp Karl Malden Ricardo Montalban Joanna Pettet
Cannon for Cordoba (1970)	Paul Wendkos	George Peppard Giovanna Ralli Peter Duel Don Gordon Nico Minardos
Catlow (1971)	Sam Wanamaker	Yul Brynner Richard Crenna Leonard Nimoy Jo Ann Pflug Jeff Corey
Charro! (1969)	Charles M. Warren	Elvis Presley Victor French Ina Balin Lynn Kellogg
Chato's Land (1972)	Michael Winner	Charles Bronson Jack Palance Richard Basehart James Whitmore Simon Oakland Victor French

Title and Year	Director	Featuring
Custer of the West (1967)	Robert Siodmak	Robert Shaw Jeffrey Hunter Ty Hardin Robert Ryan Marc Lawrence Lawrence Tierney
Doc (1968)	Frank Perry	Stacey Keach Harris Yulin Faye Dunaway Denver J. Collins
El Condor (1970)	John Guillermin	Lee Van Cleef Jim Brown Patrick O'Neal Marianna Hill Iron Eyes Cody
El Topo (1971) (Mexican production)	Alexandro Jodorowsky	Alexander Jodorowsky Brontis Jodorowsky Mara Lorenzio David Silva Paula Romo Hector Martinez
Glory Guys (1965)	Arnold Laven	Tom Tryon Harve Presnell Senta Berger James Caan Andrew Duggan Slim Pickens Wayne Rogers
Hang 'Em High (1968)	Ted Post	Clint Eastwood Inger Stevens Ed Begley Pat Hingle Ben Johnson Bruce Dern Dennis Hopper
High Plains Drifter (1973)	Clint Eastwood	Clint Eastwood Verna Bloom Marianna Hill Mitchell Ryan
Lawman (1971)	Michael Winner	Burt Lancaster Robert Ryan Lee J. Cobb Sheree North Robert Duvall Albert Salmi
Macho Callahan (1970)	Bernard Kowalski	David Janssen Lee J. Cobb

Title and Year	Director	Featuring
Man Called Gannon (1969)	James Goldstone	Jean Seberg David Carradine Tony Franciosa Michael Sarrazin Judi West John Anderson David Sheiner
Professionals (1966)	Richard Brooks	Burt Lancaster Lee Marvin Robert Ryan Jack Palance Claudia Cardinale Woody Strode Ralph Bellamy
Scalphunters (1968)	Sydney Pollack	Burt Lancaster Telly Savalas Shelley Winters Ossie Davis Armando Silvestre Dabney Coleman
Scavengers (1971)	Frost/Cresse	Jonathan Bliss Maria Lease Michael Divoka Roda Spain John Riazzi Wes Bishop Bruce Kemp
Skin Game (1971)	Paul Bogart	James Garner Louis Gossett, Jr. Brenda Sykes Edward Asner
Soldier Blue (1970)	Ralph Nelson	Candice Bergen Peter Strauss Donald Pleasence Jorge Rivero
Two Mules for Sister Sara (1970)	Don Siegel	Clint Eastwood Shirley MacLaine Manolo Fabregas Alberto Morin Armando Silvestre
Valdez Is Coming (1971)	Edwin Sherin	Burt Lancaster Susan Clark Jon Cypher Barton Heyman Richard Jordan
Villa Rides! (1968)	Buzz Kulik	Yul Brynner Robert Mitchum

Title and Year	Director	Featuring
		Grazia Buccella
		Charles Bronson
		Herbert Lom
Wild Bunch (1969)	Sam Peckinpah	William Holden
		Ernest Borgnine
		Robert Ryan
		Ben Johnson
		Warren Oates
		Edmond O'Brien
		Strother Martin
		L. Q. Jones
		Emilio Fernandez
Will Penny (1968)	Tom Gries	Charlton Heston
		Joan Hackett
		Donald Pleasence
		Lee Majors
		Bruce Dern
		Ben Johnson
		Slim Pickens

Top Ten and
Top Twenty Lists

William Connolly*

Top Ten lists are always problematic. Should one really list only ten individual works? Or should one attempt to suggest a "variety on a subject" by listing the best of ten different types? And should one consider the influence of the works as well? I'll try to incorporate all these aspects and see what results.

1. *The Sergio Leone Westerns.* It is impossible to leave *A Fistful of Dollars* off the list. It wasn't the first Western directed by an Italian to be shot in Spain, nor is it the best, but it was the most influential. *For a Few Dollars More* is a better film, but was less influential. *The Good, the Bad, and the Ugly* is also essential, as is *Once Upon a Time in the West,* the latter if for no other reason than it was the film which gained the genre some mainstream respectability. However, *Duck, You Sucker* is my favorite because it is the most "emotionally involving" of all the Westerns credited to Leone, even if it is also the most uneven.

2. *Django.* Director Sergio Corbucci had made a Western before Sergio Leone, but Leone's worldwide success and his innovative style relegated Corbucci to the position of "the other Sergio." The fact that Corbucci would often include allusions to Leone's films in his own didn't stop the critical comparisons. However with *Django,* his third Western, Corbucci succeeded in reworking plot and visual ideas, mostly from *For a Few Dollars More,* with some striking innovations of his own. The result, a worldwide success—except for the United Kingdom (where it was banned as "too violent") and the United States (where it wasn't released, probably because it didn't have an American star)—which became as influential as the Leone Westerns. More influential, if you consider that Leone's films were becoming too expensive to duplicate.

3. *¿Quien Sabe?* (or, *Bullet for the General*). Director Damiano Damiani only did two Westerns, but in collaboration with screenwriters Salvatore Laurani and Franco Solinas, his first genre entry successfully introduced the important themes of revolution to the Spaghetti Western. While the film is action-packed humorous entertainment, the theme is treated seriously, and upon its release, sparked heated debate in the European intellectual circles. The film also inspired the even more popular Sergio Corbucci "revolution" films, *The Mercenary* and *Compañeros,* which eventually led to Sergio Leone's *Duck, You Sucker,* a commentary on them all. The film has been released in the United States as *Bullet for the General;* it's been edited but doesn't suffer too much from the trimming.

*Editor of *Spaghetti Cinema.*

473

4. *Great Silence.* Another Corbucci Western that was banned in the U.K. for violence and was unreleased in the United States. Inverting the successful "bounty-killer/hero" formula popularized by *For a Few Dollars More,* Corbucci made a singular film that is an obvious social commentary. In addition to that, it is also a thrilling action film spiced with the director's penchant for mutilation and sensuality.

5. *The Ugly Ones* (or, *The Bounty Killer*). Released in the United States as *The Ugly Ones,* this is the best Western made with the Spanish participants as the principal partners in the coproduction. Spanish director Eugenio Martin stages the drama well, but more importantly, this is Cuban actor Tomás Milian's first genre endeavor. Starring opposite English-born actor Richard Wyler, Milian completely dominates this film with a convincing and multidimensial portrayal of a notorious Mexican criminal who is harbored by the good townspeople he grew up among. *The Ugly Ones* also boasts the most interesting female character ever to appear in a Spaghetti, and the part is well played by Ella Karin.

6. *Django, Kill . . . If You Live, Shoot!* While Tomás Milian's character in this film is never actually called Django (at least in the English dubbed version) the title seems appropriate as a nod to the baroque atmosphere and style which Sergio Corbucci's film brought to the Spaghetti Western. In collaboration with frequent Bernardo Bertolucci–cowriter Franco Arcalli, director Giulio Questi has fashioned the most unusual, the most violent, and the most sensual Western that Italian censors of the 1960s would allow. Frequently described as "Sadian," this is actually an "art" film that succeeds in entertaining a non-art audience.

7. *The Return of Ringo.* Partnered with actor Giuliano Gemma, the first Italian star of Spaghetti Westerns, director Duccio Tessari produced a series of highly entertaining action comedies. This is the sequel to the popular *Pistol for Ringo.* Though it is very different, it still has plenty of laughs and odd characters. Inspired by the mythical tale of Ulysses, *The Return of Ringo* tells of a Union officer disguising himself as an unwashed drifter to see if his wife has been faithful while he was away fighting the Civil War. In addition to thrilling action scenes, this film boasts effective romantic scenes as well. Released as *Ballad of Death Valley* on home video in the United States.

8. *Blindman.* After the surprising worldwide success of his first two "Stranger" films, actor-producer Tony Anthony seemed to have realized that his odd sense of humor (which remains singular many years after) deserves much of the "success credit." There's also his unique reuse of the Leone clichés. With Blindman, Anthony, in collaboration with director Ferdinando Baldi, decided to really push the boundaries of the Spaghetti Western. The result was another international success, and one of the most unusual films ever made.

9. *My Name Is Nobody.* This probably should be included among the Sergio Leone Westerns, but Tonino Valerii gets the actual director's credit. Partly a reaction to the hugely successful Terence Hill–Bud Spencer Western comedies, and partly a summation of the cinematic treatment of the Western myth, *My Name Is Nobody* is able to be kneeslappingly funny at one moment, and truly touching in the next.

10. *Heads You Die . . . Tails I Kill You* (or, *They Call Me Hallelujah* and *Guns for Dollars*). Towards the end of the Spaghetti Western cycle, a lot of the films got goofy, especially after the international success of *They Call Me Trinity.* Obviously, audiences didn't want to take these movies seriously anymore. This is one of the goofiest, and it still succeeds in being "laugh-out-loud" funny. Elements from the Revolutionary Westerns, the Super Hero Gunslinger films, and even the James

Bond thrillers get mixed together to create a stew filled with mischievous mayhem and massacre.

Four Experts' Twenty Favorite Spaghetti Westerns

(*in alphabetical order*)

Craig Ledbetter

Big Gundown
Compañeros
Death Rides a Horse
Django
Django, Kill . . . If You Live, Shoot!
Django the Bastard
Duck You Sucker
Face to Face
Fistful of Dollars
For a Few Dollars More

Four Gunmen of the Apocalypse
The Good, the Bad, and the Ugly
Great Silence
Hellbenders
Keoma
Massacre Time
Matalo!
No Room to Die
Once Upon a Time in the West
Price of Power

Tom Betts

Bandidos
Big Gundown
Day of Anger
Death Rides a Horse
Dead Men Ride
Django
Fistful of Dollars
For a Few Dollars More
Forgotten Pistolero
The Good, the Bad, and the Ugly

Great Silence
I Want Him Dead
Keoma
Light the Fuse . . . Sartana's Coming
Man Called Blade
My Name Is Nobody
Once Upon a Time in the West
Red Sun
Silver Saddle
Ten Thousand Dollars Blood Money

Dave Todarello*

Bandidos
Big Gundown
Blood for a Silver Dollar

Bullet for the General
Cemetery Without Crosses
Cut-Throats Nine

*Editor of Naked Screaming Terror; cofounder of Kronos Productions.

Death Rides a Horse
Django
Django, Kill . . . If You Live, Shoot!
Fistful of Dollars
For a Few Dollars More
The Good, the Bad, and the Ugly
Great Silence

Keoma
Man Called Blade
Massacre Time
The Moment to Kill
Ruthless Four
Sartana
Stranger in Town

Thomas Weisser

Big Gundown
Black Killer
Death Rides a Horse
Django
Django the Bastard
For a Few Dollars More
Four Gunmen of the Apocalypse
The Good, the Bad, and the Ugly
I Want Him Dead
I Am Sartana, Your Angel of Death

Johnny Yuma
Killer Kid
Macho Killers
Man Called Blade
Price of Power
Red Blood, Yellow Gold
Scalps
Vendetta at Dawn
Vengeance Is a Dish Served Cold
Wanted Johnny Texas

The Worst
Spaghetti Westerns

Not all European Westerns are great. As with any other film genre, there are many movies directed by hacks, written by monkeys, and filmed on a shoestring. This is a list of the ten worst Spaghetti Westerns; for further information regarding these atrocities, check the text portion of this book (The film regarded as the all-time worst is number one.)

1. *Once Upon a Time in the Wild, Wild West*
2. *Patience Has a Limit, We Don't*
3. *Cipolla Colt* (alternate title: *Spaghetti Western*)
4. *Seven Nuns in Kansas City*
5. *Bad Kids of the West*
6. *Man Called Amen*
7. *Even Django Has His Price*
8. *Kung Fu Brothers in the Wild West*
9. *Rita of the West*
10. *Rick and John, Conquerors of the West*

And be wary of any film directed by **Demofilo Fidani** (pseudonym — **Miles Deem;** additional pseudonyms include **Slim Alone, Lucky Dickerson, Dennis Ford, Sean O'Neal, Dick Spitfire, Alessandro Santini,** and **Diego Spataro**). Forewarned is forearmed.

Select Bibliography

*Especially meritorious sources
are indicated with an asterisk*

Annuario del Cinema Italiano, sezione 1, anno 1978–1979.

Badekerl, Klaus. *Western und Italowestern*, Filmkritik Publications, Berlin, 1969.

Baudry, Pierre. *Cahiers du Cinéma*, "Western à l'Italienne," 1967.

*Betts, Tom. *Westerns* . . . *All'Italiana*, periodical volumes 1–30, PO Box 25042, Anaheim, CA 92825

Biner, Tony. *Celluloid Nightmare*, periodical #2, 7605 Santa Monica Blvd., #641, West Hollywood, CA 90046.

Boussinot, Roger. *L'Encyclopédie du Cinéma*, two vols. (A–H and I–Z), Bordas Publications, Paris, 1980.

Catalogo Bolaffi del Cinema Italiano (Encyclopedia of Italian Films), Bianco e Nero Books (Centro Sperimentale di Cinematografica), Volume I: 1956–1965; Volume II: 1966–1975; Volume III: 1975–1976; Volume IV: 1976–1977; Volume V: 1977–1978.

Cinématographe: La Revue de l'Actualité Cinématographique, monthly periodical, Paris, 1972–1978.

Cinepresse, "Revue Professionnelle de Corporation Cinématographique," yearly periodical 1977, 1978, 1979, 1980.

*Connolly, William. *Spaghetti Cinema*, periodical volumes 1–42, 6635 DeLongpre #4, Hollywood, CA 90028.

De Luca. *History of the Italian Western (C'era una Volta il Western Italiano)*, Istituto Bibliografico, Roma, 1987.

Durgnat, Raymond. *Films and Filming*, "The Good, the Bad and the Ugly," November 1968.

Fornari, Oreste De. *Sergio Leone*, Colosseum Books, Milan, 1977.

*Frayling, Christopher. *Spaghetti Westerns: Cowboys and Europeans from Karl May to Sergio Leone*, Routledge & Kegan Paul Books, London/Boston, 1981.

Hardy, Phil. *Encyclopedia of Western Movies*, National Video Books, 100 Lafayette Drive, Syosset, NY 11791, 1990.

Johnson, Joseph. *3 AM*, periodical volumes 1–3, 608 West 1st Street, Oil City, PA 16301.

*Ledbetter, Craig. *E.T.C. (European Trash Cinema)*, volumes 1–6, PO Box 5367, Kingwood, TX 77325.

*Lhassa, Gian, and Lequeux, Michel. *Dictionary of Italian Westerns (Dictionnaire du Western Italien)*, Grand Angle Books, Brussels, 1983.

Lloyd, Ann, and Fuller, Graham. *Who's Who of the Cinema*, Portland House, New York, 1987.

*Lucas, Tim. *Video Watchdog*, periodical volumes 1–6, PO Box 5283, Cincinnati, Ohio 45205-0283.

Maltin, Leonard. *TV Movies*, Signet Books, New York, 1992.

Martin, Mich, and Porter, Marsha. *Video Movie Guide*, Ballantine Books, New York, 1992.

Morton, Jim. *Incredibly Strange Films*, Re/Search Books, San Francisco, 1986.

*Petit, Alain. *Twenty Years of European Westerns (20 Ans de Westerns Européen)*, Editions de la Méduse, Paris, 1990.

Produzione Italiana, Production manual for Italian Cinema (La Produzione Italiana), Associazione Nazionale, Roma (1973–1976).

Screen-World, bi-monthly periodical; "Italian Westerns: The Western Is Still Alive," New York, 1971.

Singer, Michael. *Film Directors: A Complete Guide*, Lone Eagle Books, Beverly Hills, CA, 1990.

*Stag, Laurence, and Williams, Tony. *Italian Westerns: The Opera of Violence*, Lorrimer Books, 1975.

Uniespania Yearbooks (Spanish Cinema Release Manuals), 1965–1970.

Unifrance Yearbooks (French Cinema Release Manuals), "Catalogue des films annuel," 1964–1971.

Unitalia Yearbooks (Italian Cinema Release Manuals), Associazione nazionale industrie cinematografiche ed affini, Roma, 1961–1977.

Weldon, Michael. *Psychotronic Encyclopedia of Film*, Ballantine Books, New York, 1983.

Variety Yearbooks; collection of reviews and articles from *Variety* newspaper, 1965–1976.

Index